Summary of FORTRAN 77 Statements

STATEMENT	DESCRIPTION (Page in Text)	EXAMPLE OF USAGE
ENTRY	Specifies entry point in a subprogram (536)	ENTRY POLY (X)
EQUIVALENCE	Establishes sharing of memory locations by different variables in same program unit (532)	EQUIVALENCE (X, Y), (ALPHA, Z, T(3))
EXTERNAL	Specifies externally defined subprograms that may be used as arguments (411)	EXTERNAL F, QUAD
FORMAT	Defines a list of descriptors (90)	20 FORMAT (1X, 'ROOTS ARE', 2F8.3)
FUNCTION	Heading for a function subprogram (345)	FUNCTION AVE(X, N)
GO TO	Unconditionally transfers control to a specified statement (135)	GO TO 100
IMPLICIT	Used to establish a naming convention (524)	IMPLICIT REAL (L, N-Z), INTEGER (A-K)
INQUIRE	Determines properties of a file or of its connection to a unit number (497)	INQUIRE (EXIST = FLAG, NAME = FNAME)
INTEGER	Specifies integer type (62)	INTEGER X, CLASS, TABLE(10,20)
INTRINSIC	Specifies intrinsic functions that may be used as arguments (412)	INTRINSIC SIN, DSQRT
LOGICAL	Specifies logical type (215)	LOGICAL P, Q, TABLE(4,6)
Logical IF	Executes or bypasses a statement, depending on the truth or falsity of a logical expression (102)	IF (DISC .GT. 0) DISC = SQRT(DISC)
OPEN	Opens a file (119, 493)	OPEN(UNIT = 12, FILE = FNAME, STATUS = 'OLD')
PARAMETER	Defines parameters (262)	PARAMETER (LIM = 100, RATE = 1.5)
PAUSE	Interrupts program execution, program may be restarted (524)	PAUSE PAUSE 'PROGRAM PAUSE'
PRINT	Output statement (76, 174)	PRINT *, 'X = ', X PRINT * PRINT '(1X, 3I7)', M, N, M + N
PROGRAM	Program heading (80)	PROGRAM WAGES
READ	Input statement (77, 189, 197, 499)	READ *, ALPHA, BETA READ '(I5, F7.2)', NUM, Z READ (12, *, END = 20) HOURS, RATE
REAL	Specifies real type (62)	REAL NUM, GAMMA, MAT(10,10)
RETURN	Returns control from subprogram to calling program unit (346, 538)	RETURN RETURN 2
REWIND	Position file at initial point (502)	REWIND 12
SAVE	Save values of local variables in a subprogram for later references (353)	SAVE X, Y, NUM SAVE
Statement function	Function defined within a program unit by a single statement (342)	F(X,Y) = X**2 + Y**2
STOP	Terminates execution (81)	STOP STOP 'PROGRAM HALTS'
SUBROUTINE	Heading for subroutine subprogram (375)	SUBROUTINE CONVER (U, V, RHO, PHI)

WHILE	First statement of a WHILE loop; not in standard FORTRAN 77 (131)	WHILE X > 0 DO
		   PRINT *, X
		   X = X − .1
		END WHILE

WRITE	Output statement (194, 502)	WRITE (*, *) A, B, C WRITE (12, '(1X, 3I6)') N1, N2, N3

FORTRAN 77
for Engineers
and Scientists

LARRY NYHOFF

SANFORD LEESTMA

Department of Mathematics and Computer Science
Calvin College, Grand Rapids, Michigan

FORTRAN 77

for Engineers and Scientists

SECOND EDITION

Macmillan Publishing Company
NEW YORK

Collier Macmillan Publishers
LONDON

Macmillan Publishing Company
866 Third Avenue, New York, New York 10022

Collier Macmillan Canada, Inc.

Library of Congress Cataloging-in-Publication Data

Nyhoff, Larry R.
  FORTRAN 77 for engineers and scientists.

  Includes index.
  1. FORTRAN (Compute program language) I. Leestma,
Sanford. II. Title.   III. Title: FORTRAN seventy-
seven.
QA76.73.F25N9   1988   005.13′3   87-18516
ISBN 0-02-388631-5

Printing: 5 6 7 8   Year: 9 0 1 2 3 4 5 6 7

PREFACE

FORTRAN, now more than thirty years old, is a language that is used throughout the world to write programs for solving problems in science and engineering. Since its creation in the late 1950s, it has undergone a number of modifications that have made it a very powerful yet easy-to-use language. These modifications, however, led to a proliferation of different dialects of FORTRAN, which hindered program portability. Since some uniformity was desirable, the American National Standards Institute (ANSI) published the first FORTRAN standard in 1966. In the years following, extensions to this standard version of FORTRAN were developed, some of which came into common use. It became apparent that many of these features should be incorporated into a new standard. This updated ANSI FORTRAN standard (ANSI X3.9-1978), popularly known as FORTRAN 77, is the basis for this text.

FORTRAN is one of the most widely used programming languages for solving problems in science and engineering. This text emphasizes these applications in the examples and exercises. It contains more than 60 complete examples and over 250 exercises, both written and programming exercises, chosen from areas that are relevant to science and engineering students.

Although this book gives a complete presentation of FORTRAN 77, it is more than just a programming manual. It reflects our view that the main reason for learning a programming language is to use the computer to solve problems. The basic steps in program development are discussed and illustrated in the text: (1) problem analysis and specification, (2) algorithm development, (3) program coding, (4) program execution and testing, and (5) program maintenance. We also feel that an intelligent user of the computer must have some elementary understanding of the manner in which a computer operates, how it stores information, how it processes data, and what some of its capabilities and limitations are. For this reason the text also contains a brief sketch of the history of computers and a simple description of a computer system, including techniques for representing data and machine instructions in binary form.

The text also emphasizes the importance of good structure and style in programs. In addition to describing these concepts in general, it contains a large number of complete examples. Each of these consists of a description of the algorithm using pseudocode and/or flowcharts together with a program and sample run. These are intended to demonstrate good algorithm design and programming style. At the end of each chapter a Programming Pointers section summarizes the main points regarding structure and style as well as language features presented and some problems that beginning programmers may experience.

Like the first edition, this text is intended for a first course in computing and assumes no previous experience with computers. It provides a comprehensive description of FORTRAN 77, and most of the material presented can be covered in a one-semester course. Each chapter progresses from the simpler features to the more complex ones; the more difficult material thus appears in the last sections of the chapters. More advanced and/or esoteric features are described in starred sections near the end of each chapter or in Chapter 13 and may be omitted without loss of continuity.

New to the Second Edition

Since publication of the first edition, we have received a number of constructive comments and suggestions for improvements from instructors and students and we have incorporated many of these into the second edition. The significant changes in the new edition include the following:

- More examples and exercises drawn from a variety of engineering areas are included.
- The discussion of data representation and of other basic concepts of computer systems has been expanded.
- The presentation of formatted input/output has been simplified. The nonnumeric data types, logical and character, are discussed in a separate chapter.
- Special Variations and Extensions sections at chapter ends and an appendix describe the variations and extensions provided in other versions of FORTRAN, including Microsoft FORTRAN and IBM Professional FORTRAN.

Supplementary Materials

The supplementary materials have also been revised and expanded and are available from the publisher:

- An instructor's manual containing lecture notes, sample test questions, and transparency masters.
- Solutions manual.
- Data disks containing all the sample programs and data files used in the text. (Standard FORTRAN 77, Microsoft FORTRAN, and IBM Professional FORTRAN versions are available.)
- A test bank and test generation software for microcomputers.

Acknowledgments

We express our sincere appreciation to all those who were involved in the preparation of this text. We especially thank David Johnstone and Ron Harris and other Macmillan personnel who initiated this project and guided it to completion. The contribution of a number of engineering examples and exercises by Larry Genalo of Iowa State University and the work of Vic Norman and Jeff Nyhoff in the preparation of some of the supplementary materials are also much appreciated. We also wish to thank the following reviewers whose comments and suggestions have been very valuable: Susan M. Simons, Memphis State University; Robert D. Slonneger, West Virginia University; Thomas A. Lackey, Lawrence Institute of Technology; Paul Sand, University of New Hampshire; Asghar Bhatti, University of Iowa; and Val Tareski, North Dakota State University. And as always, our families have provided much needed encouragement and understanding; without their support and love we would not have been able to write this text. We thank you, Shar, Jeff, Dawn, Jim, Julie, Joan, Marge, Michelle, Sandy, and Michael. And above all, we give thanks to God for allowing us to see the completion of our work.

L. N.
S. L.

CONTENTS

1

Introduction and History

I wish these calculations had been executed by steam.

CHARLES BABBAGE

For, contrary to the unreasoned opinion of the ignorant, the choice of a system of numeration is a mere matter of convention.

BLAISE PASCAL

The modern electronic computer is one of the most important products of the twentieth century. It is an essential tool in many areas including business, industry, government, science, and education; indeed, it has touched nearly every aspect of our lives. The impact of this twentieth-century information revolution brought about by the development of high-speed computing systems has been nearly as widespread as the impact of the nineteenth-century industrial revolution. This chapter gives a summary of the history of computer systems and briefly describes their components.

1.1 History of Computing Systems

There are two important concepts in the history of computation: the **mechanization of arithmetic** and the concept of a **stored program** for the automatic control of computations. We shall focus our attention on some of the devices that have implemented these concepts.

A variety of computational devices were used in ancient civilizations. One of the earliest, which might be considered a forerunner of the modern computer, is the **abacus** (Figure 1.1), which has movable beads strung on rods to count and make computations. Although its exact origin is unknown, the abacus was used by the Chinese perhaps three to four thousand years ago and is still used today.

1

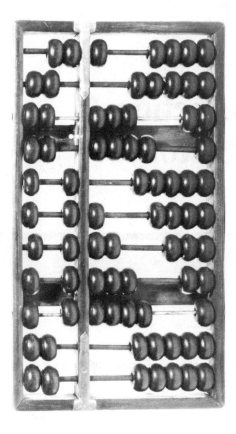

Figure 1.1   Abacus.

The ancient British stone monument **Stonehenge** (Figure 1.2a), located in southern England, was built between 1900 and 1600 B.C. and evidently was an astronomical calculator used to predict the changes of the seasons. Five hundred years ago, the Inca Indians of South America used a system of knotted cords called **quipus** (Figure 1.2b) to count and record divisions of land among the various tribal groups. In Western Europe, **Napier's bones** (Figure 1.2c) and tables of **logarithms** were designed by the Scottish mathematician John Napier (1550–1617) to simplify calculations. These led to the subsequent invention of the **slide rule** (Figure 1.2d).

In 1642, the young French mathematician **Blaise Pascal** (1623–1662) invented one of the first mechanical adding machines (Figure 1.3). This device used a system of gears and wheels similar to that used in odometers and other modern counting devices. **Pascal's adder** could both add and subtract and was invented to calculate taxes. Pascal's announcement of his invention reveals the labor-saving motivation for its development:

> Dear reader, this notice will serve to inform you that I submit to the public a small machine of my invention, by means of which you alone may, without any effort, perform all the operations of arithmetic, and may be relieved of the work which has often times fatigued your spirit, when you have worked with the counters or with the pen. As for simplicity of movement of the operations, I have so devised it that, although the operations of arithmetic are in a way opposed the one to the other—as addition to subtraction, and

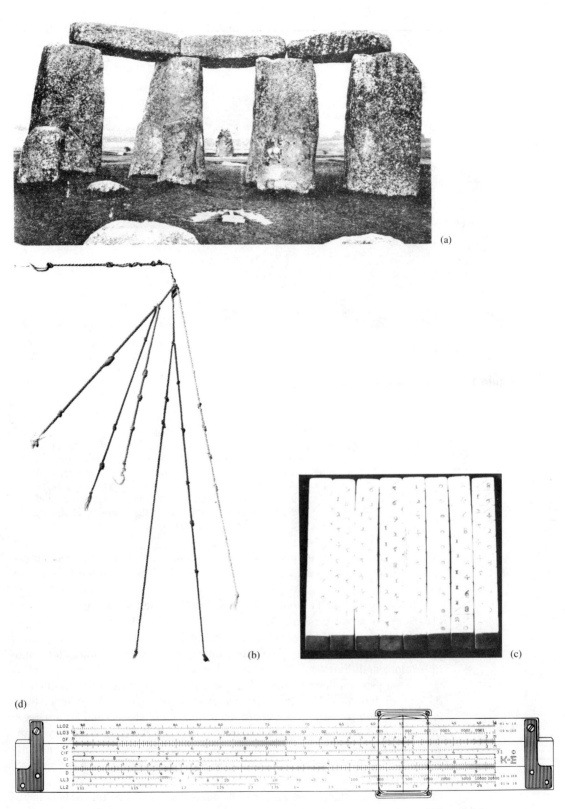

Figure 1.2 (a) Stonehenge. (b) Quipus. (Courtesy of the American Museum of Natural History. (c) Napier's bones. (Courtesy of the Smithsonian Institution. (d) Slide rule.

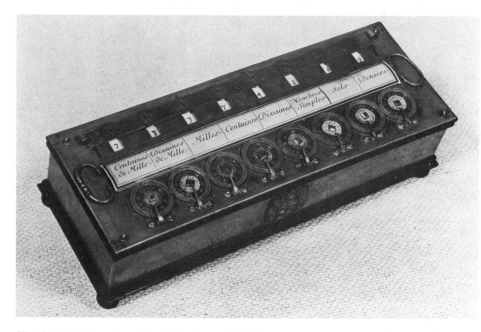

Figure 1.3 Pascal's adder. (Courtesy of IBM.)

> multiplication to division—nevertheless they are all performed on this machine by a single movement. The facility of this movement of operation is very evident since it is just as easy to move one thousand or ten thousand dials, all at one time, if one desires to make a single dial move, although all accomplish the movement perfectly. The most ignorant find as many advantages as the most experienced. The instrument makes up for ignorance and for lack of practice, and even without any effort of the operator, it makes possible shortcuts by itself, whenever the numbers are set down.

Although Pascal built more than fifty of his adding machines, his commercial venture failed because the devices could not be built with sufficient precision for practical use.

In the 1670s, the German mathematician **Gottfried Wilhelm von Leibniz** (1646–1716) produced a machine that was similar in design to Pascal's, but somewhat more reliable and accurate (Figure 1.4). Leibniz's calculator could perform all four of the basic arithmetic operations: addition, subtraction, multiplication, and division.

A number of other mechanical calculators followed that further refined the designs of Pascal and Leibniz. By the end of the nineteenth century, these calculators had become important tools in science, business, and commerce.

As noted earlier, the second idea to emerge in the history of computing was the concept of a stored program to control the calculations. One early example of an automatically controlled device is the weaving loom (Figure 1.5) invented by the Frenchman **Joseph Marie Jacquard** (1752–1834). This automatic loom, introduced at a Paris exhibition in 1801, used metal cards punched with holes to position threads for the weaving process. A collection of these cards made up a program that directed the loom. Within a decade, 11,000 of

Figure 1.4 Liebniz's calculator. (Courtesy of IBM.)

these machines were in use in French textile plants, resulting in what may have been the first incidence of unemployment caused by automation. Unemployed workers rioted and destroyed several of the new looms and cards. Jacquard wrote: ''The iron was sold for iron, the wood for wood, and I its inventor delivered up to public ignominy.'' The **Jacquard loom** is still used today,

Figure 1.5 Jacquard loom. (Courtesy of IBM.)

although modern versions are controlled by magnetic tape rather than punched cards.

These two concepts, mechanized calculation and stored program control, were combined by the English mathematician **Charles Babbage** (1792–1871), who began work in 1822 on a machine that he called the **Difference Engine** (Figure 1.6a). This machine was designed to evaluate polynomials for the preparation of mathematical tables. Babbage continued his work until 1833 with support from the British government, which was interested in possible military applications of the Difference Engine. But Babbage later abandoned this project, because the metal-working technology of that time was not sufficiently advanced to manufacture the required precision gears and linkages. Babbage was not discouraged, however, but designed a more sophisticated machine that he called his **Analytical Engine** (Figure 1.6b). This machine had several special-purpose components that were intended to work together. The "mill" was supposed to carry out the arithmetic computations; the "store" was the machine's memory for storing data and intermediate results; and other components were designed for the input and output of information and for the transfer of information between components. The operation of this machine was to be fully automatic, controlled by punched cards, an idea based on Jacquard's earlier work. In fact, Babbage himself said, "The analogy of the Analytical Engine with this well-known process is nearly perfect." **Ada Augusta,** Lord George Byron's daughter and the Countess of Lovelace, understood how the device was to work and supported Babbage. Considered by some to be the first programmer, Lady Lovelace described the similarity of Jacquard's and Babbage's inventions: "The Analytical Engine weaves algebraic patterns just as the Jacquard loom weaves flowers and leaves." Although Babbage's machine was not built during his lifetime, it is nevertheless part of the history of computing because many of the concepts of its design are used in modern computers.

A related development in the United States was the census bureau's use of punched-card systems to help compile the 1890 census (Figure 1.7). These systems, designed by **Herman Hollerith,** a young mathematician employed by the bureau, used electrical sensors to interpret the information stored on the punched cards. In 1896, Hollerith left the census bureau and formed his own tabulating company, which in 1924 became the International Business Machines Corporation (IBM).

The development of computing devices continued at a rapid pace in the United States. Some of the pioneers in this effort were Howard Aiken, John Atanasoff, J. P. Eckert, J. W. Mauchly, and John von Neumann. Repeating much of the work of Babbage, Aiken designed a system consisting of several mechanical calculators working together. This work, which was supported by IBM, led to the invention in 1944 of the electromechanical **Mark I** computer (Figure 1.8). This machine is the best-known computer built before 1945 and may be regarded as the first realization of Babbage's Analytical Engine.

The first fully electronic computer was developed by **John Atanasoff** at Iowa State University. With the help of his assistant, **Clifford Berry,** he built a prototype in 1935, and in 1942, the first working model was completed (Figure 1.9a). The best known of the early electronic computers was the **ENIAC** (Electronic Numerical Integrator and Computer), constructed in 1946

(a)

(b)

Figure 1.6 (a) Babbage's Difference Engine. (b) Babbage's Analytical Engine. (Courtesy of IBM.)

by J. P. Eckert and J. W. Mauchly at the Moore School of Electrical Engineering of the University of Pennsylvania (Figure 1.9b). This extremely large machine contained over 18,000 vacuum tubes and 1500 relays and nearly filled a room 20 feet by 40 feet in size. It could multiply numbers approximately 1000 times faster than the Mark I could, though it was quite limited in its applications and was used primarily by the Army Ordnance Department to calculate firing tables and trajectories for various types of shells. Eckert and Mauchly later left the University of Pennsylvania to form the Eckert–Mauchly Computer Corporation, which built the **UNIVAC** (Universal Automatic Computer), the first commercially available computer designed for both scientific and business applications. The first UNIVAC was sold to the census bureau in 1951.

The instructions, or program, that controlled the ENIAC's operation were entered into the machine by rewiring some parts of the computer's circuits. This complicated process was very time-consuming, sometimes taking several people several days, and during this time, the computer was idle. In other early computers, the instructions were stored outside the machine on punched cards or some other medium and were transferred into the machine one at a time for interpretation and execution. A new scheme, developed by Princeton mathematician John von Neumann and others, used internally stored commands. The advantages of this stored program concept are that internally stored instructions can be processed more rapidly and, more importantly, that they can be modified by the computer itself while computations are taking place. The stored program concept makes possible the general-purpose computers so commonplace today.

The actual physical components used in constructing a computer system are its **hardware.** Several generations of computers can be identified by the type of hardware used. The ENIAC and UNIVAC are examples of **first-generation** computers, which are characterized by their extensive use of vacuum tubes. Advances in electronics brought changes in computing systems, and in 1958, IBM introduced the first of the **second-generation** computers, the IBM 7090. These computers were built between 1959 and 1965 and used transistors in place of vacuum tubes. Consequently, these computers were smaller and less expensive, required less power, generated far less heat, and were more reliable than their predecessors. The **third-generation** computers that followed used integrated circuits and introduced new techniques for better system utilization, such as multiprogramming and time-sharing. The IBM System/360 introduced in 1964 is commonly accepted as the first of this generation of computers. Computers of the 1980s, commonly called **fourth-generation** computers, use very large-scale integrated circuits (VLSI) on silicon chips and other microelectronic advances to shrink their size and cost still more while enlarging their capability. A typical memory chip is equivalent to many thousands of transistors, is smaller than a baby's fingernail, weighs a small fraction of an ounce, requires only a trickle of power, and costs but a few dollars. Such miniaturization has made possible the development of the personal computers so popular today (Figure 1.10).

The stored program concept was a significant improvement over manual programming methods, but early computers were still difficult to use because of the complex coding schemes required for the representation of programs and data. Consequently, in addition to improved hardware, computer manufacturers

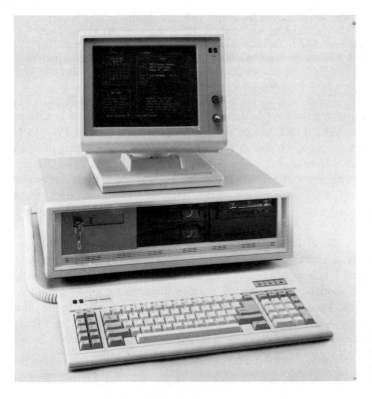

Figure 1.10 A modern personal computer. (Courtesy of OnSite Business Systems, a Division of Dale Computer Corporation.)

began to develop collections of programs known as **system software,** which make computers easier to use. One of the more important advances in this area was the development of **high-level languages,** which allow users to write programs in a language similar to natural language. A program written in a high-level language is known as a **source program.** For most high-level languages, the instructions that make up a source program must be translated into **machine language,** that is, the language used directly by a particular computer in all its calculations and processing. This machine language program is called an **object program.** The programs that translate source programs into object programs are called **compilers.** Another part of the system software, the **operating system,** controls the translation of the source program, allocates storage for the program and data, and carries out many other supervisory functions. In particular, it acts as an interface between the user and the machine. The operating system interprets commands given by the user and then directs the appropriate system software and hardware to carry them out.

One of the first high-level languages to gain widespread acceptance was **FORTRAN (FOR**mula **TRAN**slation). It was developed for the IBM 704 computer by **John Backus** and a team of thirteen other programmers at IBM over a three-year period (1954–1957). The group's first report on the completed language included the following comments:

> The programmer attended a one-day course on FORTRAN and spent some more time referring to the manual. He then programmed the job in four hours, using 47 FORTRAN statements. These were compiled by the 704 in six minutes, producing about 1000 instructions. He ran the program and found

the output incorrect. He studied the output and was able to localize his error in a FORTRAN statement he had written. He rewrote the offending statement, recompiled, and found that the resulting program was correct. He estimated that it might have taken three days to code the job by hand, plus an unknown time to debug it, and that no appreciable increase in speed of execution would have been achieved thereby.

As computer hardware improved, the FORTRAN language also was refined and extended. By 1962 it had undergone its fourth revision, and in 1977 there appeared the fifth revision, known as FORTRAN 77. A large number of other high-level languages have also developed—ALGOL, BASIC, COBOL, Pascal, PL/I, and Ada, to name but a few. There has been a considerable effort to standardize several of these languages so that programs written in one of these higher-level languages are "portable"; that is, they can be processed on several different machines with little or no alteration.

In summary, the history of computation and computational aids began several thousands of years ago, and in some cases, the theory underlying such devices developed much more rapidly than did the technical skills required to produce working models. Although the modern electronic computer with its mechanized calculation and automatic program control has its roots in the mid-nineteenth-century work of Charles Babbage, the electronic computer is a fairly recent development. The rapid changes that have marked its progression since its inception in 1945 can be expected to continue into the future.

1.2   Computing Systems

In our discussion of the history of computing, we noted that Babbage designed his Analytical Engine as a system of several separate components, each with its own particular function. This general scheme was incorporated in many later computers and is, in fact, a common feature of most modern computers. In this section we briefly describe the major components of a modern computing system.

The heart of any computing system is its **central processing unit,** or **CPU.** The CPU controls the operation of the entire system, performs the arithmetic and logic operations, and stores and retrieves instructions and data. The instructions and data are stored in a high-speed **memory unit,** and the **control unit** fetches these instructions from memory, decodes them, and directs the system to execute the operations indicated by the instructions. Those operations that are arithmetical or logical in nature are carried out using special registers and circuits of the **arithmetic-logic unit (ALU)** of the CPU.

The memory unit is called the **internal** or **main** or **primary memory** of the computer system. In older machines this memory usually consisted of magnetic cores, whereas newer machines use semiconductors (although memory is still sometimes referred to as **core memory**). Information stored in these devices can be retrieved rapidly, but because they are rather expensive, most computing systems also contain components that serve as **external** or **auxiliary** or **secondary memory.** Common forms of this type of memory are magnetic disks and magnetic tapes. These **peripheral devices** provide relatively inex-

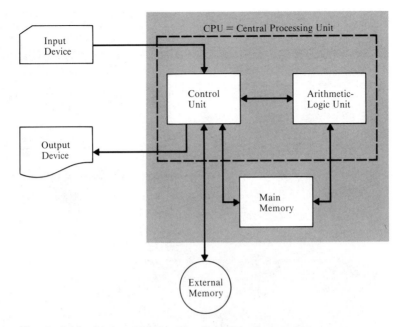

Figure 1.11   Major components of a computing system.

pensive storage for large collections of information, but the rate of transfer of information to and from them is considerably slower than that for internal memory.

Other peripherals are used to transmit instructions, data, and computed results between the user and the CPU. These are the **input/output devices** and may take a variety of forms such as card readers, remote terminals, paper tape readers, optical scanners, voice input devices, and high-speed printers. Their function is to convert information from an external form understandable to the user to a form that can be processed by the computer system, and vice versa.

The diagram in Figure 1.11 shows the relationship among these components in a computer system, and Figure 1.12 shows these components as they appear in a modern computer system.

1.3   Internal Representation

The devices that comprise the memory unit of a computer are two-state devices. If one of the states is interpreted as 0 and the other as 1, then it is natural to use a **binary scheme,** using only the two binary digits (**bits**) 0 and 1 for representation within a computer. These two-state devices are organized into groups called **bytes,** each of which contains a fixed number of these devices, usually eight, and thus can store a fixed number of bits. Memory is commonly measured in bytes; for example, a 512K memory usually refers to a memory that consists of $2^9 \times 2^{10} = 2^{19} = 524,288$ bytes ($1K = 2^{10} = 1,024$), or, equivalently, $2^{22} = 4,194,304$ bits.

A larger grouping of bits and bytes is into **words.** Word sizes vary with computers, but common sizes are 16 bits ($= 2$ bytes) and 32 bits ($= 4$ bytes).

Figure 1.12   A typical minicomputer system. (Courtesy of Prime Computer Corporation.)

Each word is identified by an **address** and can be directly accessed using this address. This makes it possible to store information in a specific memory word and then retrieve it later. To understand how this is done, we must first examine the binary number system.

The number system that we are accustomed to using is a decimal or **base-10** number system, which uses the digits 0, 1, 2, 3, 4, 5, 6, 7, 8, and 9. The significance of these digits in a numeral depends on the positions that they occupy in that numeral. For example, in the numeral

$$485$$

the digit 4 is interpreted as

$$4 \text{ hundreds}$$

and the digit 8 as

$$8 \text{ tens}$$

and the digit 5 as

$$5 \text{ ones}$$

Thus, the numeral 485 represents the number four-hundred eighty-five and can be written in **expanded form** as

$$(4 \times 100) + (8 \times 10) + (5 \times 1)$$

or

$$(4 \times 10^2) + (8 \times 10^1) + (5 \times 10^0)$$

The digits that appear in the various positions of a decimal (base-10) numeral thus represent coefficients of powers of 10.

Similar positional number systems can be devised using numbers other than 10 as a base. The **binary** number system uses 2 as the base and has only two digits, 0 and 1. As in a decimal system, the significance of the bits in a binary numeral is determined by their positions in that numeral. For example, the binary numeral

$$101$$

can be written in expanded form (using decimal notation) as

$$(1 \times 2^2) + (0 \times 2^1) + (1 \times 2^0)$$

that is, the binary numeral 101 has the decimal value

$$4 + 0 + 1 = 5$$

Similarly, the binary numeral 111010 has the decimal value

$$(1 \times 2^5) + (1 \times 2^4) + (1 \times 2^3) + (0 \times 2^2) + (1 \times 2^1) + (0 \times 2^0)$$

$$= 32 + 16 + 8 + 2$$

$$= 58$$

When necessary, to avoid confusion about which base is being used, it is customary to write the base as a subscript for nondecimal numerals. Using this convention, we could indicate that 5 and 58 have the binary representations just given by writing

$$5 = 101_2$$

and

$$58 = 111010_2$$

Two other nondecimal numeration systems are important in the consideration of computer systems: **octal** and **hexadecimal.** The octal system is a base-8 system and uses the eight digits 0, 1, 2, 3, 4, 5, 6, and 7. In an octal numeral such as

$$1703_8$$

the digits represent coefficients of powers of 8; this numeral is, therefore, an abbreviation for the expanded form

$$(1 \times 8^3) + (7 \times 8^2) + (0 \times 8^1) + (3 \times 8^0)$$

and thus has the decimal value

$$512 + 448 + 0 + 3 = 963$$

A hexadecimal system uses a base of 16 and the digits 0, 1, 2, 3, 4, 5, 6, 7, 8, 9, A (10), B (11), C (12), D (13), E (14), and F (15). The hexadecimal numeral

$$5E4_{16}$$

has the expanded form

$$(5 \times 16^2) + (14 \times 16^1) + (4 \times 16^0)$$

which has the decimal value

$$1280 + 224 + 4 = 1508$$

Table 1.1 displays the decimal, binary, octal, and hexadecimal representations for the first 31 nonnegative integers.

When an integer value such as 5 or 58 must be stored in the computer's memory, the binary representation of that value is typically stored in one memory word. To illustrate, consider a computer whose word size is sixteen, and suppose that the integer value 58 is to be stored. A memory word is selected, and a sequence of sixteen bits formed from the binary representation 111010

Table 1.1

Decimal	Binary	Octal	Hexadecimal
0	0	0	0
1	1	1	1
2	10	2	2
3	11	3	3
4	100	4	4
5	101	5	5
6	110	6	6
7	111	7	7
8	1000	10	8
9	1001	11	9
10	1010	12	A
11	1011	13	B
12	1100	14	C
13	1101	15	D
14	1110	16	E
15	1111	17	F
16	10000	20	10
17	10001	21	11
18	10010	22	12
19	10011	23	13
20	10100	24	14
21	10101	25	15
22	10110	26	16
23	10111	27	17
24	11000	30	18
25	11001	31	19
26	11010	32	1A
27	11011	33	1B
28	11100	34	1C
29	11101	35	1D
30	11110	36	1E
31	11111	37	1F

of 58 is stored there:

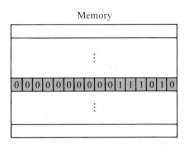

Negative integers must also be stored in a binary form in which the sign of the integer is part of the representation. There are several ways this can be done, but one of the most common is the **two's complement** representation. In this scheme, positive integers are represented in binary form as just described, with the leftmost bit set to 0 to indicate that the value is positive. The representation of a negative integer $-n$ is obtained by first finding the binary representation of n, complementing it, that is, changing each 0 to 1 and each 1 to 0, and then adding 1 to the result. For example, the two's complement representation of -58 using a string of sixteen bits is obtained as follows:

1. Represent 58 by a 16-bit binary numeral:

$$0000000000111010$$

2. Complement this bit string:

$$1111111111000101$$

3. Add 1:

$$1111111111000110$$

Note that the leftmost bit in this two's complement representation of a negative integer will always be 1, indicating that the number is negative.

The fixed word size limits the range of the integers that can be stored internally. For example, the largest positive integer that can be stored in a 16-bit word is

$$0111111111111111_2 = 2^{15} - 1 = 32767$$

and the smallest negative integer is

$$1000000000000000_2 = -2^{15} = -32768$$

The range of integers that can be represented using a 32-bit word is

$$10000000000000000000000000000000_2 = -2^{31} = -2147483648$$

through

$$01111111111111111111111111111111_2 = 2^{31} - 1 = 2147483647$$

An attempt to store an integer outside the allowed range will result in the loss of some of the bits of its binary representation, a phenomenon known as **overflow.** This limitation may be partially overcome by using more than one word to store an integer. Although this technique enlarges the range of integers that can be stored exactly, it does not resolve the problem of overflow; the range of representable integers is still finite.

Numbers that contain decimal points are called **real numbers** or **floating point numbers.** In the decimal representation of such numbers, each digit is the coefficient of some power of 10. Digits to the left of the decimal point are coefficients of nonnegative powers of 10, and those to the right are coefficients of negative powers of 10. For example, the decimal numeral 56.317 can be written in expanded form as

$$(5 \times 10^1) + (6 \times 10^0) + (3 \times 10^{-1}) + (1 \times 10^{-2}) + (7 \times 10^{-3})$$

or, equivalently, as

$$(5 \times 10) + (6 \times 1) + \left(3 \times \frac{1}{10}\right) + \left(1 \times \frac{1}{100}\right) + \left(7 \times \frac{1}{1000}\right)$$

Digits in the binary representation of a real number are coefficients of powers of two. Those to the left of the **binary point** are coefficients of nonnegative powers of two, and those to the right are coefficients of negative powers of two. For example, the expanded form of 110.101 is

$$(1 \times 2^2) + (1 \times 2^1) + (0 \times 2^0) + (1 \times 2^{-1}) + (0 \times 2^{-2}) + (1 \times 2^{-3})$$

and thus has the decimal value

$$4 + 2 + 0 + \frac{1}{2} + 0 + \frac{1}{8} = 6.625$$

There is some variation in the schemes used for storing real numbers in computer memory, but one common method is the following. The binary representation

$$110.101_2$$

of the real number 6.625 can be written equivalently as

$$0.110101_2 \times 2^3$$

Typically, one part of a memory word (or words) is used to store a fixed number of bits of the **mantissa** or **fractional part** 0.110101_2, and another part to store the **exponent** $3 = 11_2$. For example, if the leftmost eleven bits in a 16-bit word are used for the mantissa and the remaining five bits for the exponent, 6.625 could be stored as

0	1	1	0	1	0	1	0	0	0	0	0	0	0	1	1

mantissa   exponent

where the first bit in each part is reserved for the sign.

Because the binary representation of the exponent may require more than the available number of bits, we see that the overflow problem discussed in connection with integer representation may also occur in storing a real number. Also, there obviously are some real numbers whose mantissas have more than the allotted number of bits; consequently, some of these bits will be lost in storing such numbers. In fact, most real numbers do not have finite binary representations and thus cannot be stored exactly in any computer. For example, the binary representation of the real number 0.7 is

$$0.10110011001100110\ldots._2$$

where the block 0110 is repeated indefinitely. If only the first eleven bits are stored and all remaining bits are truncated, then the stored representation of 0.7 is

$$0.10110011100_2$$

which has the decimal value 0.69921875. If the binary representation is rounded to eleven bits, then the stored representation for 0.7 is

$$0.10110011101_2$$

which has the decimal value 0.700195312. In either case, the stored value is not exactly 0.7. This error, called **roundoff error** (in both cases), can be reduced, but not eliminated, by using a larger number of bits to store the binary representation of real numbers.

Computers store and process not only numeric data but also boolean or logical data (false or true), character data, and other types of nonnumeric information. Storing logical values is easy; false can be encoded as 0, true as 1, and these bits stored. The schemes used for the internal representation of character data are based on the assignment of a numeric code to each of the characters in the character set. Several standard coding schemes have been developed, such as **ASCII** (American Standard Code for Information Interchange) and **EBCDIC** (Extended Binary Coded Decimal Interchange Code). Table 1.2 shows these codes for capital letters. A complete table of ASCII and EBCDIC codes for all characters is given in Appendix A.

Characters are represented internally using these binary codes. A byte consisting of eight bits can thus store the binary representation of one character, and a 16-bit word consisting of two bytes can store two characters. For example, the character string HI can be stored in a single 16-bit word with the code for H in the left byte and the code for I in the right byte; with ASCII code, the result would be as follows:

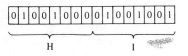

Memory words of size 32 (bits) are usually divided into four bytes and thus can store four characters. Character strings of a length greater than the number of bytes in a word are usually stored in two or more consecutive memory words.

We have now seen how various types of data can be stored in a computer's memory. Program instructions for processing data must also be stored in memory. As an example, suppose three values $8 = 1000_2$, $24 = 11000_2$, and $58 = 111010_2$ have been stored in memory locations with addresses 4, 5, and

Table 1.2   Character codes.

| | ASCII | | EBCDIC | |
Character	Decimal	Binary	Decimal	Binary
A	65	01000001	193	11000001
B	66	01000010	194	11000010
C	67	01000011	195	11000011
D	68	01000100	196	11000100
E	69	01000101	197	11000101
F	70	01000110	198	11000110
G	71	01000111	199	11000111
H	72	01001000	200	11001000
I	73	01001001	201	11001001
J	74	01001010	209	11010001
K	75	01001011	210	11010010
L	76	01001100	211	11010011
M	77	01001101	212	11010100
N	78	01001110	213	11010101
O	79	01001111	214	11010110
P	80	01010000	215	11010111
Q	81	01010001	216	11011000
R	82	01010010	217	11011001
S	83	01010011	226	11100010
T	84	01010100	227	11100011
U	85	01010101	228	11100100
V	86	01010110	229	11100101
W	87	01010111	230	11100110
X	88	01011000	231	11100111
Y	89	01011001	232	11101000
Z	90	01011010	233	11101001

6, and we want to multiply the first two values, add the third, and store the result in memory word 7.

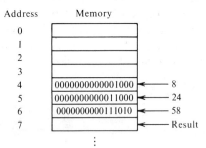

To perform this computation, the following instructions must be executed:

1. Fetch the contents of memory word 4 and load it into the accumulator register of the ALU.
2. Fetch the contents of memory word 5 and compute the product of this value and the value in the accumulator.
3. Fetch the contents of memory word 6 and add this value to the value in the accumulator.
4. Store the contents of the accumulator in memory word 7.

In order to store these instructions in computer memory, they must be represented in binary form. The addresses of the data values present no problem, as they can easily be converted to binary addresses:

$$4 = 100_2$$
$$5 = 101_2$$
$$6 = 110_2$$
$$7 = 111_2$$

The operations load, multiply, add, store, and other basic machine instructions are represented by numeric codes, called **opcodes;** for example,

$$LOAD = 16 = 10000_2$$
$$STORE = 17 = 10001_2$$
$$ADD = 35 = 100011_2$$
$$MULTIPLY = 36 = 100100_2$$

Using part of a word to store the opcode and another part for the address of the **operand,** we could represent our sequence of instructions in **machine language** as

1. 0001000000000100
2. 0010010000000101
3. 0010001100000110
4. 0001000100000111

opcode   operand

These instructions can then be stored in four (consecutive) memory words. When the program is executed, the control unit will fetch each of these instructions, decode it to determine the operation and the address of the operand, fetch the operand, and then perform the required operation, using the ALU if necessary.

Programs for early computers had to be written in such machine language. Later it became possible to write programs in **assembly language,** which uses mnemonics (names) in place of numeric opcodes and variable names in place of numeric addresses. For example, the preceding sequence of instructions might be written in assembly language as

1. LOAD A
2. MULT B
3. ADD C
4. STORE X

An **assembler,** part of the system software, translates such assembly language instructions into machine language.

Today, most programs are written in a high-level language such as FORTRAN, and a **compiler** translates each statement in this program into a sequence of basic machine (or assembly) language instructions.

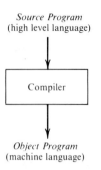

Source Program
(high level language)

Compiler

Object Program
(machine language)

For example, for the preceding problem, the programmer could write the FORTRAN statement

$$X = A * B + C$$

which instructs the computer to multiply the values of A and B, add the value of C, and assign the value to X. The compiler would then translate this statement into the sequence of four machine (or assembly) language instructions considered earlier.

As the preceding diagram indicates, a compiler translates the entire source program into an equivalent object program consisting of machine language instructions. After this translation is complete, this object program is executed by the computer. Some languages are processed using an **interpreter** rather than a compiler. An interpreter also examines a source program statement by statement. However, after each statement is translated, the resulting machine language instructions are immediately executed, before the next statement is examined; no object program is actually produced. Still another approach is to compile the source program into a simple machine-independent language called **intermediate code.** The resulting program might be either interpreted or compiled. In any case, the original source program in a high-level language must be translated into strings of 0s and 1s that represent machine instructions.

Exercises

1. Describe the importance of each of the following persons to the history of computing:

    (a) Charles Babbage   **(b)** Blaise Pascal
    (c) John von Neumann   **(d)** Herman Hollerith
    (e) Joseph Jacquard   **(f)** Gottfried Wilhelm von Leibniz

2. Describe the importance of each of the following devices to the history of computing:

    (a) ENIAC   **(b)** Analytical Engine
    (c) Jacquard loom   **(d)** UNIVAC
    (e) Mark I

3. Distinguish the four different generations of computers.

4. Briefly define each of the following terms:

(a) stored program concept   (b) FORTRAN
(c) Pascal   (d) CPU
(e) ALU   (f) peripheral devices
(g) bit   (h) byte
(i) word   (j) overflow
(k) roundoff error   (l) ASCII
(m) EBCDIC   (n) source program
(o) object program   (p) compiler
(q) assembler   (r) assembly language
(s) machine language

5. Convert each of the following unsigned binary numerals to base 10:

(a) 1001   (b) 110010
(c) 1000000   (d) 111111111111111 (fifteen 1's)
(e) 1.1   (f) 1010.10101

6. Convert each of the following octal numerals into base 10:

(a) 123   (b) 2705   (c) 10000
(d) 77777   (e) 7.2   (f) 123.45

7. Convert each of the following hexadecimal numerals to base 10:

(a) 12   (b) 1AB   (c) ABC
(d) FFF   (e) 8.C   (f) AB.CD

8. Conversion from octal representation (see Exercise 6) to binary representation is easy, as we need only replace each octal digit with its three-bit binary equivalent. For example, to convert 617_8 to binary, replace 6 with 110, 1 with 001, and 7 with 111 to obtain 110001111_2. Convert each of the octal numerals in Exercise 6 to binary numerals.

9. Imitating the conversion scheme in Exercise 8, convert each of the hexadecimal numerals in Exercise 7 to binary numerals.

10. To convert a binary numeral to octal, place the digits in groups of three, starting from the binary point, or from the right end if there is no binary point, and replace each group with the corresponding octal digit. For example, $10101111_2 = 010\ 101\ 111_2 = 257_8$. Convert each of the binary numerals in Exercise 5 to octal numerals.

11. Imitating the conversion scheme in Exercise 10, convert each of the binary numerals in Exercise 5 to hexadecimal numerals.

12. One method for finding the **base-b** representation of a whole number given in base-10 notation is to divide the number repeatedly by b until a quotient of zero results. The successive remainders are the digits from right to left of the base-b representation. For example, the binary representation of 26 is 11010_2, as the following computation shows:

```
         0 R 1
      2)1 R 1
      2)3 R 0
      2)6 R 1
     2)13 R 0
     2)26
```

Convert each of the following base-10 numerals to (i) binary, (ii) octal, (iii) hexadecimal:

(a) 27   **(b)** 99   **(c)** 314   **(d)** 5280

13. To convert a decimal fraction to its base-b equivalent, repeatedly multiply the fractional part of the number by b. The integer parts are the digits from left to right of the base-b representation. For example, the decimal numeral 0.6875 corresponds to the binary numeral 0.1011_2, as the following computation shows:

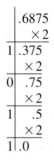

Convert the following base-10 numerals to (i) binary , (ii) octal, (iii) hexadecimal:

(a) 0.5   **(b)** 0.25   **(c)** 0.625
(d) 16.0625   **(e)** 8.828125

14. Even though the base-10 representation of a fraction may terminate, its representation in some other base need not terminate. For example, the following computation shows that the binary representation of 0.7 is $(0.1011001100110011001100110 \ldots)_2$, where the block of bits 0110 is repeated indefinitely. This representation is commonly written as $0.10\overline{110}_2$.

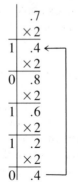

Convert the following base-10 numerals to (i) binary, (ii) octal, (iii) hexadecimal:

(a) 0.3　　(b) 0.6　　(c) 0.05　　(d) $0.\overline{3} = 0.33333 \cdots = \frac{1}{3}$

15. Find the decimal value of each of the following 16-bit integers, assuming a two's complement representation:

(a) 0000000001000000　　(b) 1111111111111110
(c) 1111111110111111　　(d) 0000000011111111
(e) 1111111100000000　　(f) 1000000000000001

16. Find the 16-bit two's complement representation for each of the following integers:

(a) 255　　　　　(b) 1K
(c) -255　　　　(d) -256
(e) -34567_8　　(f) $-3ABC_{16}$

17. Assuming two's complement representation, what range of integers can be represented in 8-bit words?

18. Assuming an 11-bit mantissa and a 5-bit exponent, as described in the text, and assuming that two's complement representation is used for each, indicate how each of the following real numbers would be stored in a 16-bit word if extra bits in the mantissa are (i) truncated or (ii) rounded:

(a) 0.375　　　　(b) 37.375
(c) 0.03125　　　(d) 63.84375
(e) 0.1　　　　　(f) 0.01

19. Using the tables for ASCII and EBCDIC in Appendix A, indicate how each of the following character strings would be stored in 2-byte words using (i) ASCII and (ii) EBCDIC:

(a) TO　　　　(b) FOUR　　　(c) AMOUNT
(d) ETC.　　　(e) J. DOE　　　(f) A#*4$-$C

20. Using the instruction mnemonics and opcodes given in the text, write a sequence of (a) assembly language and (b) machine language instructions equivalent to the FORTRAN statement

$$X = (A + B) * C$$

For the machine language instructions, assume that the values of A, B, and C are stored in memory words 15, 16, and 17, respectively, and the value of X is to be stored in memory word 23.

21. Repeat Exercise 20 for the FORTRAN statement

$$X = (A + B) * (C + D)$$

assuming that the value of D is stored in memory word 18.

2

Program Development

People always get what they ask for; the only trouble is that they never know, until they get it, what it actually is that they have asked for.

ALDOUS HUXLEY

The main reason that people learn programming languages is to use the computer as a problem-solving tool. At least four steps can be identified in the computer-aided problem-solving process:

1. Problem analysis and specification.
2. Algorithm development.
3. Program coding.
4. Program execution and testing.

In this chapter we describe and illustrate each of these steps. In the last section, we discuss one additional step that is particularly important in the **life cycle** of programs developed in real-world applications:

5. Program maintenance.

2.1 Problem Analysis and Specification

The first step in the problem-solving process is to review the problem carefully in order to determine its **input**—what information is given and which items are important in solving the problem—and its **output**—what information must be produced to solve the problem. For a problem that appears as an exercise in a programming text its input and output are the two major parts of the problem's **specification** and are usually not too difficult to identify. In a real-world problem encountered by a professional programmer, the problem's specification often includes other items, as described in Section 2.6, and it may require considerable effort to formulate a complete specification. In this section we consider three problems and illustrate what is involved in their analyses.

PROBLEM 1: Radioactive Decay.   John Doe is a nuclear physicist at Dispatch University and is conducting research with the radioactive element polonium. The half-life of polonium is 140 days; that is, the amount of polonium that remains after 140 days is one half of the original amount. John would like to know how much polonium will remain after running his experiment for 180 days if 10 milligrams are present initially.

Identifying the input and output of this problem is easy:

Input	Output
Initial amount: 10 mg Half-life: 140 days Time period: 180 days	Amount remaining

The other given items of information—the physicist's name, the name of the university, the name of the particular radioactive element—are not relevant (at least not to this problem) and can be ignored.

Determining the residual amount of polonium can be easily done by hand, or still more easily by using a calculator, and does not warrant the development of a computer program for its solution. A program written to solve this particular problem would probably be used just once; because if the experiment runs longer, or if there is a different initial amount, or if a radioactive element with a different half-life is used, we have a new problem requiring the development of a new program. This is obviously a waste of effort since it is clear that each such problem is a special case of the more general problem of finding the residual amount of a radioactive element at any time, given any initial amount and the half-life for that element. Thus a program that solves the general problem can be used in a variety of situations and is consequently more useful than is one designed for solving only the original special problem.

One important aspect of problem analysis, therefore, is **generalization.** The effort involved in later phases of the problem-solving process demands that the program eventually developed be sufficiently flexible, that it solve not only the given specific problem but also any related problem of the same kind with little, if any, modification required. In this example, therefore, the specification of the problem could better be formulated in general terms:

Input	Output
Initial amount Half-life Time period	Amount remaining

PROBLEM 2: Pollution Indices.   The level of air pollution in the city of Dogpatch is measured by a pollution index. Readings are made at 12:00 P.M. at three locations: the Abner Coal Plant, downtown at the corner of Daisy

Avenue and 5th Street, and at a randomly selected location in a residential area. The average of these three readings is the pollution index, and a value of 50 or greater for this index indicates a hazardous condition, whereas values less than 50 indicate a safe condition. Because this calculation must be done daily, the Dogpatch Environmental Statistician would like a program that calculates the pollution index and then determines the appropriate condition, safe or hazardous.

The relevant given information consists of three pollution readings and the cutoff value used to distinguish between safe and hazardous conditions. A solution to the problem consists of the pollution index and a message indicating the condition. Generalizing so that any cutoff value, not just 50, can be used, we could specify the problem as follows:

Input	Output
Three pollution readings	Pollution index = the average of the pollution readings
Cutoff value to distinguish between safe and hazardous conditions	Condition—safe or hazardous

PROBLEM 3: Summation. When the famous mathematician Carl Friedrich Gauss was a young student, his teacher instructed him to add the first 100 positive integers, 1, 2, 3, . . . , 100. (Perhaps this was a form of punishment comparable to "writing lines" today.) What is the value of this sum,

$$1 + 2 + 3 + \cdots 100 = ?$$

Here the problem analysis is straightforward. Generalizing to find the sum

$$1 + 2 + 3 + \cdots + LAST$$

for any positive integer LAST, we can specify the problem by

Input	Output
LAST	Value of $1 + 2 + \cdots + LAST$

2.2 Algorithm Development

Once a problem has been specified, a procedure to produce the required output from the given input must be designed. Because the computer is a machine possessing no inherent problem-solving capabilities, this procedure must be formulated as a detailed sequence of simple steps. Such as procedure is called an **algorithm.**

The steps that comprise an algorithm must be organized in a logical and clear manner so that the program that implements this algorithm is similarly well structured. **Structured algorithms and programs** are designed using three basic methods of control:

1. Sequential: Steps are performed in a strictly sequential manner, each step being executed exactly once.

2. Selection: One of a number of alternative actions is selected and executed.

3. Repetition: One or more steps is performed repeatedly.

These three structures appear to be very simple, but in fact they are sufficiently powerful that any algorithm can be constructed using them.

Programs to implement algorithms must be written in a language that can be understood by the computer. It is natural, therefore, to describe algorithms in a language that resembles the language used to write computer programs, that is, in a "pseudoprogramming language," or as it is more commonly called, **pseudocode.**

Unlike high-level programming languages such as FORTRAN, there is no set of rules that defines precisely what is and what is not pseudocode. It varies from one programmer to another. Pseudocode is a mixture of natural language and symbols, terms, and other features commonly used in one or more high-level languages. Typically one finds the following features in the various pseudocodes that appear in textbooks.

1. The usual computer symbols are used for arithmetic operations: + for addition, − for subtraction, ∗ for multiplication, / for division, and ∗∗ for exponentiation.
2. Symbolic names (variables) are used to represent the quantities being processed by the algorithm.
3. Some provision is made for including comments. This is often done by enclosing each comment line between special symbols such as asterisks (*).
4. Certain key words that are common in high-level languages may be used: for example, *Read* or *Enter* to indicate input operations, and *Display, Print,* or *Write* for output operations.
5. Indentation is used to indicate certain key blocks of instructions.

The details of an algorithm or part of an algorithm can also be displayed graphically using a **flowchart.** A flowchart is a diagram that uses the standard symbols shown in Figure 2.1. Each step of the algorithm is displayed within the appropriate symbol, and the order in which these steps are to be carried out is indicated by connecting them with arrows called **flow lines.**

The structure of an algorithm can also be displayed in a **structure diagram** that shows the various tasks that must be performed and their relation to one another. These diagrams are especially useful in describing algorithms for more complex problems and will be described in more detail in Section 2.6. In this section we restrict our attention to the three simple examples introduced in the preceding section. Using these examples, we illustrate the three basic control structures—sequential, selection, and repetition—and how to present algorithms using both pseudocode and flowcharts.

PROBLEM 1: Radioactive Decay—Sequential Structure.   As we noted in the preceding section, the input for this problem consists of the initial amount of some radioactive element, its half-life, and a time period; the output to be

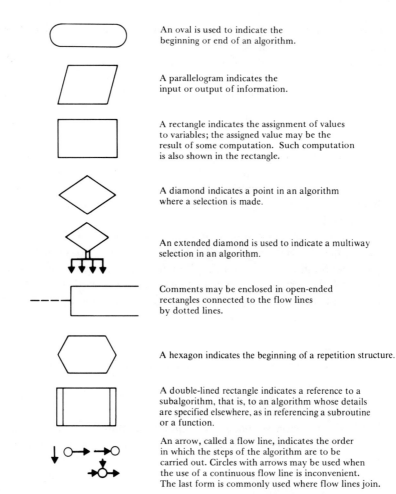

An oval is used to indicate the beginning or end of an algorithm.

A parallelogram indicates the input or output of information.

A rectangle indicates the assignment of values to variables; the assigned value may be the result of some computation. Such computation is also shown in the rectangle.

A diamond indicates a point in an algorithm where a selection is made.

An extended diamond is used to indicate a multiway selection in an algorithm.

Comments may be enclosed in open-ended rectangles connected to the flow lines by dotted lines.

A hexagon indicates the beginning of a repetition structure.

A double-lined rectangle indicates a reference to a subalgorithm, that is, to an algorithm whose details are specified elsewhere, as in referencing a subroutine or a function.

An arrow, called a flow line, indicates the order in which the steps of the algorithm are to be carried out. Circles with arrows may be used when the use of a continuous flow line is inconvenient. The last form is commonly used where flow lines join.

Figure 2.1

produced is the amount of the substance that remains at the end of the specified time period.

The first step in an algorithm for solving this problem is to obtain the values for the input items—initial amount, half-life, and time period. Next we must determine how to use this information to calculate the amount remaining after the given time period. Since the half-life of polonium is 140 days, we see that after 140 days, or one half-life,

$$10 \times .5$$

milligrams remain. At the end of 280 days or two half-lives, the amount of polonium remaining is one half of this amount,

$$(10 \times .5) \times .5$$

which can also be written

$$10 \times (.5)^2$$

Similarly, the amount of polonium at the end of 420 days or three half-lives is

$$10 \times (.5)^3$$

The general formula for the amount of the substance remaining is

$$\text{Amount remaining} = \text{initial amount} \times (.5)^{\text{time/half-life}}$$

Thus, the second step in our algorithm is to perform this calculation for the data entered in Step 1. Finally, the value of the amount remaining must be displayed.

This rather lengthy description of the algorithm can be summarized in pseudocode as follows:

ALGORITHM FOR RADIOACTIVE DECAY PROBLEM

* This algorithm calculates the amount RESID of a radioactive *
* substance that remains after a specified TIME for a given initial *
* amount INIT and a given half-life HFLIFE. *

1. Enter INIT, HFLIFE, and TIME.
2. Calculate

$$\text{RESID} = \text{INIT} * (.5) ** (\text{TIME} / \text{HFLIFE})$$

3. Display RESID.

A flowchart representation of this algorithm might be as follows:

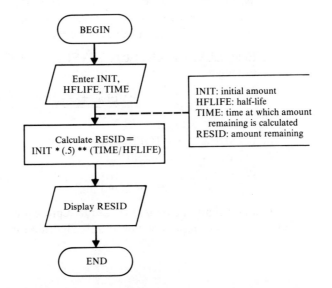

In this example, the steps of the algorithm must be performed in sequence, from beginning to end, with each step being performed exactly once. For other problems, however, the solution may require that some of the steps be performed in some situations and bypassed in others. This is illustrated by our second example.

PROBLEM 2: Pollution Index—Selection Structure. Recall that for this problem, the input consists of three pollution readings and a cutoff value that distinguishes between safe and hazardous conditions. The output to be produced consists of the pollution index, which is the average of the three readings, and a message indicating the appropriate condition.

Once again, the first step in an algorithm to solve this problem is to obtain values for the input items—the three pollution readings and the cutoff value. The next step is to calculate the pollution index by averaging the three readings. Now, one of two possible actions must be selected. Either a message indicating a safe condition must be displayed or a message indicating a hazardous condition must be displayed. The appropriate action is selected by comparing the pollution index with the cutoff value. In the pseudocode description of this algorithm that follows, this selection is indicated by

If INDEX < CUTOFF then
    Display 'Safe condition'
Else
    Display 'Hazardous condition'

ALGORITHM FOR POLLUTION INDEX PROBLEM

```
*  This algorithm reads three pollution levels, LEVEL1, LEVEL2,    *
*  and LEVEL3, and a CUTOFF value. It then calculates the          *
*  pollution INDEX. If the value of INDEX is less than CUTOFF, a   *
*  message indicating a safe condition is displayed; otherwise, a  *
*  message indicating a hazardous condition is displayed.          *
```

1. Enter LEVEL1, LEVEL2, LEVEL3, and CUTOFF.
2. Calculate

$$INDEX = \frac{LEVEL1 + LEVEL2 + LEVEL3}{3}$$

3. If INDEX < CUTOFF then
    Display 'Safe condition'
   Else
    Display 'Hazardous condition'

In a flowchart, a diamond is used to represent a selection (see Figure 2.1). Thus, a flowchart representation of this algorithm might be as follows:

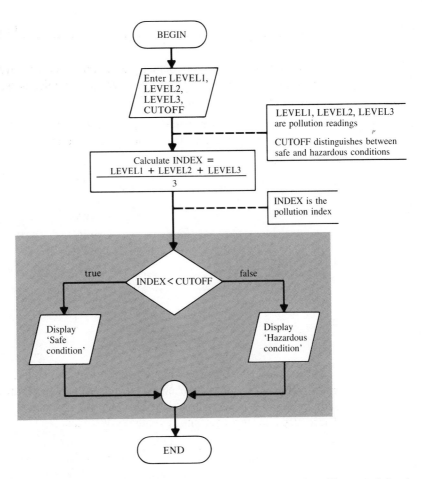

In addition to the sequential processing and selection illustrated in the preceding two examples, the solution of other problems may require that a step or a collection of steps be repeated. This is illustrated in our third example.

PROBLEM 3: Summation—Repetition Structure. The input for this problem consists simply of some positive integer LAST, and the output is the value of the sum $1 + 2 + \cdots + LAST$. To solve this problem in a ''brute force'' manner (and not using the clever technique discovered by Gauss), we might begin as follows:

$$
\begin{array}{r}
0 \\
+1 \\
\hline
1 \\
+2 \\
\hline
3 \\
+3 \\
\hline
6 \\
+4 \\
\hline
10 \\
+5 \\
\hline
15 \\
\cdot \\
\cdot \\
\cdot
\end{array}
$$

(Although we might not actually write down the first two lines but rather, only ''think'' them, they are included here for completeness.) We see that the procedure involves two quantities:

1. A counter that is incremented by 1 at each step.
2. The sum of the integers from 1 up to that counter.

$$
\begin{array}{r}
0 \;-\; \text{sum} \\
+1 \;-\; \text{counter} \\
\hline
1 \;-\; \text{sum} \\
+2 \;-\; \text{counter} \\
\hline
3 \;-\; \text{sum} \\
+3 \;-\; \text{counter} \\
\hline
6 \;-\; \text{sum} \\
+4 \;-\; \text{counter} \\
\hline
10 \;-\; \text{sum}
\end{array}
$$

.
.
.

The procedure begins with 1 as the value of the counter and with 0 as the initial value of the sum. At each stage, the value of the counter is added to the sum, producing a new sum, and the value of the counter is increased by 1. These steps are repeated until eventually we reach

.
.
.

$$
\begin{array}{r}
+\text{LAST} \;-\; \text{counter} \\
\hline
???? \;-\; \text{sum} \\
\text{LAST}+1 \;-\; \text{counter} \quad \text{Stop!}
\end{array}
$$

When the value of the counter exceeds LAST, the value of the sum is the desired answer, and the computation stops.

In the following pseudocode description of this algorithm, the repetition is indicated by

> While COUNT $\leq$ LAST do the following:
>   a. Add COUNT to SUM.
>   b. Increment COUNT by 1.

This specifies that statements a and b are to be repeated as long as the condition COUNT $\leq$ LAST remains true. Thus, when the value of COUNT exceeds LAST, this repetition is terminated, and the remaining statements of the algorithm are performed.

ALGORITHM FOR SUMMATION PROBLEM

```
*   This algorithm calculates the value of the sum 1 + 2 + · · ·      *
*    + LAST. It uses the variable COUNT as a counter and the           *
*   variable SUM for the sum 1 + 2 + · · · + COUNT.                    *
```

1. Enter value for LAST.
2. Set COUNT to 1.
3. Set SUM to 0.
4. While COUNT $\leq$ LAST do the following:
   a. Add COUNT to SUM.
   b. Increment COUNT by 1.
5. Display SUM.

In a flowchart, repetition is commonly indicated by placing a hexagon containing the information that controls the repetition at the beginning of the steps to be repeated and an arrow from the last of these statements back to the

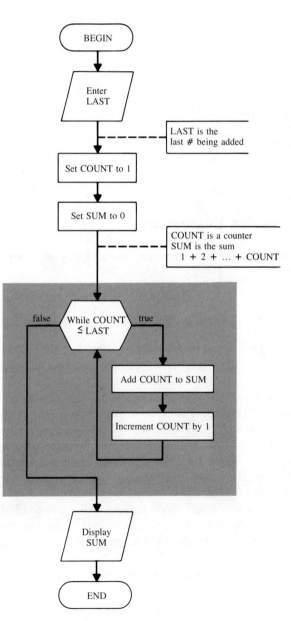

Figure 2.2

hexagon. For example, in the flowchart in Figure 2.2, which represents the algorithm for the summation problem, repetition is indicated by

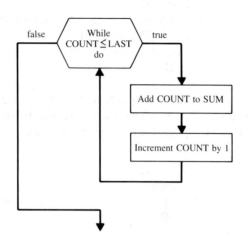

The three control structures in these examples, **sequential, selection,** and **repetition,** are used throughout this text in designing algorithms to solve problems. The implementation of each of them in a FORTRAN program is considered in detail in later chapters.

2.3 Example: Series Evaluation

The cosine of an angle X measured in radians may be computed using the infinite series

$$\cos(X) = 1 - \frac{X^2}{2!} + \frac{X^4}{4!} - \cdots + (-1)^N \frac{X^{2N}}{(2N)!} + \cdots$$

$$= \sum_{N=0}^{\infty} \frac{(-1)^N X^{2N}}{(2N)!}$$

We wish to design an algorithm to calculate the approximate value of $\cos(X)$ for a user-supplied value of X using this series.

The input for this problem will consist of the angle in degrees whose cosine is to be calculated. The user will also input two values NMAX and EPSIL that will be used to determine how many terms of the series are to be used in computing the approximation. The evaluation of the series is to terminate when the number of terms that have been included exceeds NMAX or when the value of the next term is less some small positive real number EPSIL in absolute value. The output is to be the approximation obtained by summing these terms; if the number of terms exceeds NMAX, an appropriate message should also be displayed.

An algorithm for computing this approximate value of the cosine function is

ALGORITHM FOR APPROXIMATING THE COSINE FUNCTION

```
* This algorithm calculates the approximate value of cos(X)      *
* using its infinte series. NMAX is the maximum number           *
* of terms of the series to be used. EPSIL is the desired        *
* accuracy. TERM is a term in the series; FACT is used to        *
* compute TERM; and SUM is the sum of the first N terms.         *
```

1. Enter NMAX and EPSIL.
2. Enter X in degrees.
3. Multiply X by $\pi/180$ to convert it to radians.
4. Initialize SUM to 0, N to 1, TERM to 1, and FACT to 1.
5. While $|\text{TERM}| \geq$ EPSIL and N $\leq$ NMAX, do the following:
   a. Add TERM to SUM.
   b. Set FACT equal to $(2N - 1) \cdot (2N)$.
   c. Replace TERM by

$$\frac{(-\text{TERM}) \times X^2}{\text{FACT}}$$

   d. Increment N by 1.
6. Display SUM and N.
7. If N > NMAX, then display an appropriate message indicating that the desired precision may not have been achieved.

A flowchart representation of this algorithm is shown in Figure 2.3.

2.4 Program Coding

The third step in using the computer to solve a problem is to express the algorithm in a programming language. In the second step, the algorithm may be described in a natural language or pseudocode, but the program that implements that algorithm must be written in the vocabulary of a programming language and must conform to the **syntax,** or grammatical rules, of that language. The major portion of this text is concerned with the vocabulary and syntax of the programming language FORTRAN. In this section we introduce some elementary features of this language and give an example of a simple FORTRAN program. These features are discussed in detail in subsequent chapters.

In the three examples in the preceding section, we used names to identify various quantities. These names are called **variables.** In the first example, the variables INIT, HFLIFE, and TIME represented the initial amount of a radioactive substance, its half-life, and time, respectively. The output in this example was the amount of the substance remaining after the specified time and was represented by the variable RESID. In the second example, the variables LEVEL1, LEVEL2, LEVEL3, CUTOFF, and INDEX were used, and in the third example, our variables were LAST, COUNT, and SUM.

In FORTRAN, variable names must begin with a letter, which may be followed by up to five letters or digits. For example, INIT, HFLIFE, TIME,

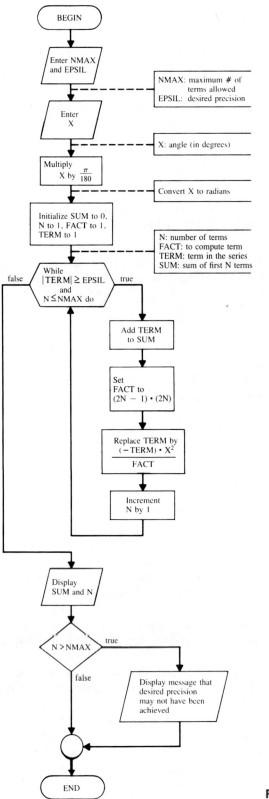

Figure 2.3

RESID, LEVEL1, LEVEL2, LEVEL3, CUTOFF, INDEX, LAST, COUNT, and SUM are valid FORTRAN variable names, and each name suggests what the variable represents. *Meaningful variable names should always be used because they make the program easier to read and understand.*

In the examples we have been considering, two types of numbers are used. The values of LAST, COUNT, and SUM in the third example and perhaps also the value of LEVEL1, LEVEL2, LEVEL3, and CUTOFF in the second example are integers, whereas the values of INIT, HFLIFE, TIME, and RESID in the first example and INDEX in the second are real; that is, they may have fractional parts. FORTRAN distinguishes between these two types of numeric data, and the types of values that each variable may have must be declared. This may be done by placing statements of the form

INTEGER *list1*
REAL *list2*

at the beginning of the program, where *list1* is a list of the variable names of integer type and *list2* is a list of variable names of real type. Thus, the types of the FORTRAN variables in the first example can be declared by

```
REAL INIT, HFLIFE, TIME, RESID
```

those in the second example by

```
INTEGER LEVEL1, LEVEL2, LEVEL3, CUTOFF
REAL INDEX
```

and those in the third example by

```
INTEGER LAST, COUNT, SUM
```

Addition and subtraction are denoted in FORTRAN by the usual + and − symbols. Multiplication is denoted by * and division by /. Exponentiation is denoted by **. The operation of assigning a value to a variable is denoted by = in FORTRAN programs. For example, the assignment statement

```
RESID = INIT * (.5) ** (TIME / HFLIFE)
```

assigns the value of the expression

```
INIT * (.5) ** (TIME / HFLIFE)
```

to the variable RESID.

In the pseudocode description of an algorithm in the preceding section, the words *Read* and *Enter* are used for input operations and *Display*, *Print*, and *Write* for output operations. In a flowchart, a parallelogram is used to indicate the input or output of information. The FORTRAN statement used for input is the READ statement. A simple form of this statement is

```
READ *, list
```

where *list* is a list of variables for which values are to be read.[1] For example, the statement

```
READ *, INIT, HFLIFE, TIME
```

reads values for the variables INIT. HFLIFE, and TIME from some input device.

A simple output statement in FORTRAN is the PRINT statement of the form

PRINT *, *list*

where *list* is a list of items to be displayed. For example, the statement

```
PRINT *, 'AMOUNT REMAINING = ', RESID
```

displays the label

```
AMOUNT REMAINING =
```

followed by the value of the variable RESID.

Comment lines can also be incorporated into FORTRAN programs. Any line that is completely blank or that contains the letter C or an asterisk (*) in the first position of the line is a comment line.

Figure 2.4 shows a FORTRAN program for the algorithm to solve the radioactive decay problem considered earlier in this chapter; also shown is a sample run of the program. The program begins with the PROGRAM statement

```
PROGRAM DECAY
```

which marks the beginning of the program and associates the name DECAY with it.

The first step in the algorithm is an input instruction to enter values for the variables INIT, HFLIFE, and TIME:

1. Enter INIT, HFLIFE, and TIME.

This is translated into two statements in the program:

```
PRINT *, 'ENTER INITIAL AMOUNT, HALF-LIFE, AND TIME'
READ *, INIT, HFLIFE, TIME
```

The PRINT statement is used to prompt the user that the values are to be entered. The READ statement actually assigns the three values entered by the user to the three variables INIT, HFLIFE, and TIME. Thus, in the sample run

---

[1] Some versions of FORTRAN may use other forms of the input/output statements. Consult the reference manuals for the system you are using.

shown, when the user enters

```
10, 140, 700
```

the value 10 is assigned to INIT, 140 to HFLIFE, and 700 to TIME.
The next step in the algorithm

2. Calculate RESID = INIT * (.5) ** (TIME / HFLIFE).

easily translates into the FORTRAN assignment statement

```
RESID = INIT * (.5) ** (TIME / HFLIFE)
```

The output instruction

3. Display RESID.

is translated into the FORTRAN statement

```
PRINT *, 'AMOUNT REMAINING = ', RESID
```

The end of the program is indicated by the FORTRAN statement

```
END
```

This statement terminates execution of the program.

```
      PROGRAM DECAY
***********************************************
* This program calculates the amount of a     *
* radioactive substance that remains after    *
* a specified time, given an initial amount    *
* and its half-life.  Variables used are:      *
*     INIT    :  initial amount of substance *
*     HFLIFE  :  half-life of substance        *
*     TIME    :  time at which the amount      *
*                remaining is calculated       *
*     RESID   :  the amount remaining          *
***********************************************

      REAL INIT, HFLIFE, TIME, RESID

      PRINT *, 'ENTER INITIAL AMOUNT, HALF-LIFE, AND TIME'
      READ *, INIT, HFLIFE, TIME
      RESID = INIT * .5 ** (TIME / HFLIFE)
      PRINT *, 'AMOUNT REMAINING = ', RESID
      END
```

Figure 2.4

Figure 2.4 (continued)

```
Sample run:
==========


        ENTER INITIAL AMOUNT, HALF-LIFE, AND TIME
        10, 140, 700
        AMOUNT REMAINING =      0.312500
```

2.5   Program Execution and Testing

The fourth step in using the computer to solve a problem is to execute and test
the program. The procedure for submitting a program to a computer varies
from one system to another; the details regarding your particular system can
be obtained from your instructor, computer center personnel, or user manuals
supplied by the manufacturer.

Access to the computer system must first be obtained. In the case of a
personal computer, this may require turning the machine on and inserting the
appropriate diskette in the disk drive. For a larger system, some **login** procedure
may be required to establish contact between a remote terminal and the computer. The details of this procedure vary from one computer system to another,
but some general principles are the same for all systems. Usually the first step
is to enter some identification information, which the system checks to ensure
that the person attempting to login is an authorized user. This identification can
also be used for accounting purposes. For example, on a PRIME 9950 computer
running the PRIMOS operating system (revision 20.0.3c), a typical login procedure is as follows:

```
        LOGIN S12345
        Password?
        Project id? CPSC141C

        S12345 (user 76) logged in Friday, 18 Dec 87 08:32:40.
        Welcome to PRIMOS Version 20.0.3C
        Last login Thursday, 17 Dec 87 14:35:20


        ==========================================================
            Disk space in use:          50 records
             Resources used:         27.35 dollars
         Resources allocated:       100.00 dollars
            Percentage used:         27.35 %

        ==========================================================
        Ok,
```

The identification information entered by the user typically includes a user name
or number (S12345), a password (usually not displayed for security reasons),
and perhaps a project identification (CPSC141C). After the user has entered
the required information, the system verifies that the person logging in is an
authorized user, displays some login information and messages, and displays
a prompt (OK,) indicating that it is ready to accept commands from the user.

Once access has been gained, the program must be entered, often using an **editor** provided as part of the system's software. For example, to enter a program like that in Figure 2.4, the user might access an editor for entering FORTRAN programs and then enter the program as follows:

```
Ok, EDFOR
INPUT
&        PROGRAM DECAY
& *********************************************
& * This program calculates the amount of a   *
& * radioactive substance that remains after  *
& * a specified time, given an initial amount  *
& * and its half-life.  Variables used are:   *
& *      INIT    :  initial amount of substance *
& *      HFLIFE  :  half-life of substance     *
& *      TIME    :  time at which the amount    *
& *                 remaining is calculated    *
& *      RESID   :  the amount remaining        *
& *********************************************
&
&        REAL INIT, HFLIFE, TIME, RESID
&
&        PRINT *, 'ENTER INITIAL AMOUNT, HALF-LIFE, AND TIME'
&        READ *, INIT, HFLIFE, TIME
&        RESID = INIT * .5 ** (TIME / HFLIFE)
&        PRINT *, 'AMOUNT REMAINING =, RESID
&        END
&
EDIT
$ FILE SAMPLE.F77
```

In this example, the user gives the command EDFOR to access the editor used for creating FORTRAN programs. A message (INPUT) and a prompt (&) are issued by the computer to indicate that the user is to begin entering the program statements. After the program is entered, a command (FILE) is given by the user to file the program under a specified name (SAMPLE.F77).

Positions within a line are called **columns** and are numbered 1, 2, 3, ... 80. All FORTRAN statements must be positioned in columns 7 through 72. If a statement requires a **statement label,** this label must appear in columns 1 through 5. Statement labels must be integers in the range 1 through 99999.

Occasionally it may not be possible to write a complete FORTRAN statement using only columns 7 through 72 of a line. In this case, the statement may be continued onto another line or lines (up to a maximum of 19), provided that a **continuation indicator** appears in column 6 of the line(s) on which the statement is continued. This continuation indicator may be any alphabetic or numeric character other than a zero or a space. A zero or a space in column 6 indicates the first line of a statement.

Lines that contain only blanks or that have the letter C or an asterisk (∗) in column 1 represent **comment lines.** Comments are not executed but, rather, appear only in the listing of the program. Comments themselves may not be continued from one line onto another by using a continuation indicator in column 6; instead, all comments must begin with a C or ∗ in column 1.

Once the program has been entered, it is compiled and executed by giving appropriate system commands; for example,

```
Ok, FTN77 SAMPLE.F77 -LGO
[FTN77 VER 199]
        NO ERRORS [<.MAIN.   >FTN77-VER 199]

        PROGRAM ENTERED
        ENTER INITIAL AMOUNT, HALF-LIFE, AND TIME
        10, 140, 700
        AMOUNT REMAINING =       0.312500
```

Here the user gave the command FTN77, instructing the operating system to compile the program that had previously been saved on disk under the name SAMPLE.F77. Because no errors were detected during compilation, execution of the resulting object program was initiated (because the compiler "load-and-go" option LGO was appended to the command). The program displayed a message prompting the user for three input values, and after these values were entered, the desired output values were calculated and displayed.

Because the program has been successfully executed and the desired output produced, the user might now obtain a final clean listing of the program and then **logout** from the system.

```
Ok, SLIST SAMPLE.F77
        PROGRAM DECAY
        ***********************************************
        * This program calculates the amount of a     *
        * radioactive substance that remains after    *
        * a specified time, given an initial amount   *
        * and its half-life.  Variables used are:     *
        *     INIT   :  initial amount of substance *
        *     HFLIFE :  half-life of substance        *
        *     TIME   :  time at which the amount       *
        *               remaining is calculated       *
        *     RESID  :  the amount remaining           *
        ***********************************************

        REAL INIT, HFLIFE, TIME, RESID

        PRINT *, 'ENTER INITIAL AMOUNT, HALF-LIFE, AND TIME'
        READ *, INIT, HFLIFE, TIME
        RESID = INIT * .5 ** (TIME / HFLIFE)
        PRINT *, 'AMOUNT REMAINING = ', RESID
        END
OK, LOGOUT

S12345 (user 76) logged out Friday, 18 Dec 87 08:51:16.
Time used: 00h 18m connect, 00m 13s CPU, 00m 03s I/O.
```

In this example, the program was entered, compiled, and executed without error. Usually, however, the beginning programmer will make some errors in designing the program or in attempting to enter and execute it. Errors may be detected at various stages of program processing and may cause the processing to be terminated ("aborted"). For example, an incorrect system command will be detected early in the processing and will usually prevent compilation and execution of the program. Errors in the program's syntax, such as incorrect punctuation or misspelled key words, will be detected during compilation. (In some systems, syntax errors may be detected while the program is being entered.) Such errors are called **syntax errors** or **compile-time errors** and will usually make it impossible to complete the compilation and execution of the program. For example, if the output statement that displays the residual amount of radioactive substance were mistakenly entered as

```
PRINT *, 'AMOUNT REMAINING =, RESID
```

without a quotation mark after the equals sign, an attempt to compile and execute the program might result in a message like the following, signaling a "fatal" error:

```
Ok, FTN77 SAMPLE.F77 -LGO
[FTN77 VER 199]
    0018              PRINT *, 'AMOUNT REMAINING =, RESID
*** Unterminated or empty character constant
    1 ERRORS [<.MAIN.   >FTN77-VER 199]
    0019              END
*** Compilation failed
```

Less severe errors may generate "warning" messages, but the compilation will be continued, and execution of the resulting object program attempted.

Other errors, such as an attempt to divide by zero in an arithmetic expression, may not be detected until execution of the program has begun. Such errors are called **run-time errors.** The error messages displayed by your particular system can be found in the user manuals supplied by the manufacturer. In any case, the errors must be corrected by replacing the erroneous statements with correct ones, and the modified program must be recompiled and then reexecuted.

Errors that are detected by the computer system are relatively easy to identify and correct. There are, however, other errors that are more subtle and difficult to identify. These are **logical errors** that arise in the design of the algorithm or in the coding of the program that implements the algorithm. For example, if the statement

```
RESID = INIT * (.5) ** (TIME / HFLIFE)
```

in the program of Figure 2.3 were mistakenly entered as

```
RESID = INIT * (.5) * (TIME / HFLIFE)
```

with the exponentiation symbol (**) replaced by the symbol for multiplication (*), the program would still be syntactically correct. No error would occur during the compilation or execution of the program. But the results produced by the program would be incorrect because an incorrect formula would have been used to calculate the residual amount of the substance. Thus, if the values 10, 140, and 700 were entered for the variables INIT, HFLIFE, and TIME, respectively, the output produced by the program would be

```
AMOUNT REMAINING = 25.000000
```

instead of the correct output

```
AMOUNT REMAINING = 0.312500
```

as shown in the sample run in Figure 2.4.

Because it may not be obvious whether the results produced by a program are correct, *it is important that the user run a program several times with input data for which the correct results are known in advance.* For the preceding example, it is easy to calculate by hand the correct answer for values such as 100, 5, and 10 for INIT, HFLIFE, and TIME, respectively, in order to check the output produced by the program. This process of **program validation** is extremely important because *a program cannot be considered to be correct until it has been validated with several sets of test data.* The test data should be carefully selected so that each part of the program is checked.

In this example, we illustrated the **interactive mode** of processing in which the user enters data values 10, 140, and 700 from the terminal during program execution, and the output produced by the program is also displayed at the terminal. Another common mode of operation is **batch processing.** In this processing mode, a file containing the program, the data, and certain **command lines** must be prepared by the user. This file is then submitted to the system, and execution proceeds without any user interaction. In a batch mode of operation, the file for the preceding example might be as follows:

```
$JOB IDENT = S12345    PROJECT ID = CPSC141C
       PROGRAM DECAY
*********************************************
* This program calculates the amount of a    *
* radioactive substance that remains after   *
* a specified time, given an initial amount  *
* and its half-life.  Variables used are:    *
*      INIT   :  initial amount of substance *
*      HFLIFE :  half-life of substance       *
*      TIME   :  time at which the amount      *
*               remaining is calculated       *
*      RESID  :  the amount remaining          *
*********************************************

       REAL INIT, HFLIFE, TIME, RESID

       READ *, INIT, HFLIFE, TIME
       RESID = INIT * .5 ** (TIME / HFLIFE)
       PRINT *, 'AMOUNT REMAINING = ', RESID
       END
$DATA
10, 140, 700
$ENDJOB
```

(Note that the PRINT statement preceding the READ statement has been omitted, as the user will not be entering values during program execution.)

For some systems, programs, data, and control lines may be entered using punched cards. These cards are prepared using a **keypunch,** which has a typewriterlike keyboard and which codes the information entered from the keyboard by punching holes in a card. The information from these cards is then entered into a computer via a card reader, and the results are returned to the user via an output device such as a line printer.

2.6 Software Engineering

Programming and problem solving is an art in that it requires a good deal of imagination, ingenuity, and creativity. But it is also a science in that certain techniques and methodologies are commonly used. The term **software engineering** has come to be applied to the study and use of these techniques.

As we noted in the introduction to this chapter, the **life cycle** of software, that is, programs, consists of five basic phases:

1. Problem analysis and specification.
2. Algorithm development.
3. Program coding.
4. Program execution and testing.
5. Program maintenance.

In the preceding sections we have described the first four phases and illustrated them with some examples. It must be emphasized, however, that these examples were deliberately kept simple so the main ideas could be emphasized without getting lost in a maze of details. In real-world applications and in later problems in this text, these phases may be considerably more complex. In this section we reexamine each of these phases and describe some of the additional questions and complications that face professional programmers, and some of the software engineering techniques used in dealing with them.

PROBLEM ANALYSIS AND SPECIFICATION. Like the exercises and problems in most programming texts, the examples we have considered thus far were quite simple and, we hope, clearly stated. Analysis of these problems to identify the input and output was, therefore, quite easy. This is not the case, however, in most real-world problems. These problems are often stated vaguely and imprecisely, because the person posing the problem does not fully understand it. For example, the president of a land development company might request a programmer to "use the computer to estimate costs for constructing Celestial Condominiums."

In these situations, there are many questions that must be answered in order to complete the problem's specifications. Some of these answers are required to describe more completely the problem's input and output. What information is available regarding the construction project? How is the program to access this data? Has the information been validated, or must the program provide error checking? In what format should the output be displayed? Must reports be generated for company executives, zoning boards, environmental agencies, and/or other government agencies?

Other questions deal more directly with the required processing. Are employees paid on an hourly or a salaried basis, or are there some of each? What premium, if any, is paid for overtime? What items must be withheld—for federal, state, and city income taxes, retirement plans, insurance, and the like—

and how are they to be computed? What materials are required? What equipment will be needed?

Many other questions must be answered before the specification of the problem is complete and before the design of the algorithms and programs can begin. Will the users of the program be technically sophisticated, or must the program be made very user friendly to accommodate novice users? How often will the program be used? What are the response time requirements? What is the expected life of the program; that is, how long will it be used, and what changes can be expected in the future? What hardware and software are available?

Although this list is by no means exhaustive, it does indicate the wide range of information that must be obtained in analyzing and specifying the problem. In some situations this is done by a **systems analyst,** and in others it is part of the programmer's responsibility.

Algorithm Design.   The solution of a complex problem may require so many steps in the final algorithm that they cannot all be anticipated at the outset. To attack such problems, a **top-down** approach is commonly used. We begin by identifying the major tasks to be performed to solve the problem and arranging them in the order in which they are to be carried out. These tasks and their relation to one another can be displayed in a one-level **structure diagram.** for example, a first structure diagram for the problem might have the form

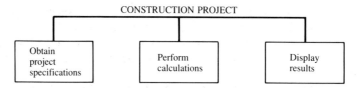

Usually one or more of these first-level tasks is still quite complex and must be divided into subtasks. For example, in the construction problem, some of the input data pertains to personnel requirements. Other data items refer to material requirements, and still others to equipment needs. Consequently, the task "Obtain input data" can be subdivided into three subtasks:

1. Obtain personnel requirements.
2. Obtain equipment requirements.
3. Obtain materials requirements.

Similarly, the task "Perform calculations" may be split into three subtasks:

1. Calculate personnel cost.
2. Calculate equipment cost.
3. Calculate cost of materials.

In a structure diagram, these subtasks are placed on a second level below the corresponding main task, as pictured in Figure 2.5. These subtasks may require further division into still smaller subtasks, resulting in additional levels, as illustrated in Figure 2.6. This **successive refinement** continues until each subtask is sufficiently simple that design of an algorithm for that subtask is straightforward.

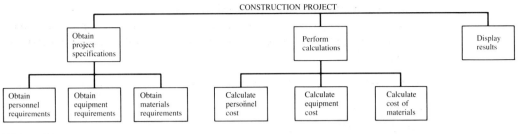

Figure 2.5

This **divide-and-conquer** approach can thus be used to divide a complex problem into a number of simpler subproblems. This allows the programmer to design and test an algorithm and a corresponding program **module** for each subproblem independently of the others. For very large projects, a team approach might be used in which the low-level subtasks are assigned to different programmers. The individual program modules developed by them are eventually combined into one complete program that solves the original problem.

Program Coding.   The first decision that must be made in translating an algorithm into a program is what programming language to use. This obviously depends on the languages available to the programmer, but other factors also influence the decision. There may be characteristics of the problem that make one language more appropriate than another. For example, if the problem involves scientific computations requiring extended precision and/or complex arithmetic, FORTRAN may be the most suitable language. Problems that involve a large amount of file input/output and report generation can perhaps best be handled in COBOL. Applications in artificial intelligence that require making logical inferences might best be written in PROLOG.

Regardless of which language is used, there are certain programming principles that have been developed to assist in designing programs that can be easily read and understood. The first principle is that each program should

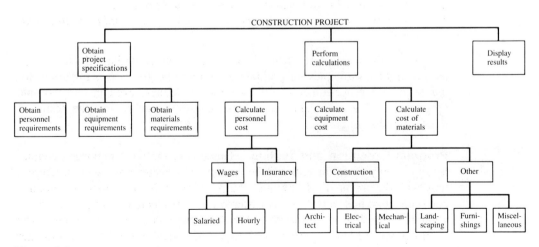

Figure 2.6

contain **documentation,** that is, information that explains what the program does, how it works, what variables it uses, any special algorithms it implements, and so on. There are two simple guidelines that are especially useful in this regard:

1. *Each variable name should suggest the quantity it represents.*

For example, the statement

    DIST = RATE * TIME

means more than does

    X7 = R * ZEKE

2. *The program should include comments that make it easier to understand.*

This may include comments at the beginning of the program that identify the author of the program, indicate the date it was written, and briefly describe the variables and the purpose of the program. In addition, comments should be used throughout the program to explain the purpose of the main sections of the program. Such comments should be few and brief. Too many or too detailed comments clutter the program, making it more difficult to read.

A second principle is that the program should be readable, and its physical appearance should reflect its structure. Three simple guidelines that are useful in this regard are the following:

1. *Spaces between items in a FORTRAN statement should be used as needed to improve its readability.* For example, the statement

    SUM = SUM + COUNT

is more readable and pleasing to the eye than is either

    SUM=SUM+COUNT

or

    SUM   =SUM+   COUNT

2. *Blank comment lines should be used to separate program sections.*
3. *Statements making up a block should be indented to emphasize this relationship.*

As we discuss features of the FORTRAN language in the following chapters, additional principles for program design will be given. It is important for the beginning programmer to follow these guidelines, even in early simple programs, so that good habits are established and carried on into the design of more complex programs.

Program Execution and Testing.   Obviously, the most important characteristic of any program is that it be *correct*. No matter how well structured, how well documented, or how nice the program looks, if it does not produce correct results, it is worthless. As we have seen, the fact that a program executes without producing any error messages is no guarantee that it is correct. The results produced may be erroneous because of logical errors that the computer system cannot detect. It is the responsibility of the programmer to test each program in order to ensure that it is correct. (See Section 4.10 for more about program testing.)

Program Maintenance. The life cycle of a program written by a student programmer normally ends with the fourth phase; that is, once the program has been written, executed, and tested, the assignment is complete. Programs in real-world applications, however, will likely be used for a number of years and will probably require some modification as time passes. Especially in large programs developed for complex projects, there will usually be obscure bugs that do not become apparent until after the program has been placed in use. Correction of these flaws is obviously one aspect of program maintenance. It may also be necessary or desirable to modify the program in order to improve its performance, add new features, and so on. Other modifications may be required owing to changes in the computer hardware and/or the system software such as the operating system. External factors may also force program modification; for example, changes in the tax laws may require revision of part of a payroll program.

Software maintenance is, in fact, a major component of the life cycle of a program and may account for as much as 80 percent of its total cost. This fact, combined with the fact that most program maintenance is done by someone not involved in the original design, makes it mandatory that the programmer do his or her utmost to design a program that is readable, documented, and well structured so that it is easy to understand and modify.

Exercises

1. Consider the following algorithm:

    1. Initialize X to 0, Y to 5, and Z to 25.
    2. While X ≤ 3 do the following:
        a. Set Y = Z − Y, A = X + 1, and then increment X by 1.
        b. If A > 2 then
            Set Z = Z − 5, A = A², and then set B = Z − Y.
    3. Display A, B, X, Y, and Z.

Complete the following **trace table** for this algorithm which displays the labels of the statements in the order in which they are executed and the values of the variables at each stage:

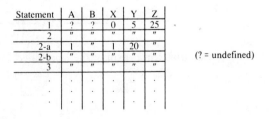

Statement	A	B	X	Y	Z
1	?	?	0	5	25
2	"	"	"	"	"
2-a	1	"	1	20	"
2-b	"	"	"	"	"
3	"	"	"	"	"
.	.	.	.	.	.
.	.	.	.	.	.
.	.	.	.	.	.

(? = undefined)

2. Construct a trace table similar to that in Exercise 1 for the following algorithm:

1. Enter A.
2. While A ≤ 0.3 do the following:
    a. Increment A by 0.1.
    b. If X ≠ 0.3 then do the following:
        i. Set S and X to 0, T to 1.
        ii. While T ≤ 6 do the following:
            (a) Add T to X and then increment T by 2.
    c. Else do the following:
        i. Set T to 0, X to 1, and S = 3 * S.
        ii. While T ≤ 5 do the following:
            (a) Increment T by 1 and then set X = X * T.
    d. Display A, S, and X.

3. Construct a trace table similar to that in Exercise 3 for the algorithm given in Figure 2.7, assuming the following data values are entered for b, h, and k:

(a) b = 3, h = 6, k = 1.
(b) b = 4, h = 3, k = 2.
(c) b = 5, h = 2, k = 0.
(d) b = 2, h = 6, k = 2.

For each of the problems described in Exercises 4 through 17, identify the information that must be produced to solve the problem and the given information that will be useful in obtaining the solution. Then design an algorithm to solve the problem.

4. Calculate and display the radius, circumference, and area of a circle with a given diameter.

5. Three resistors are arranged in parallel in the following circuit:

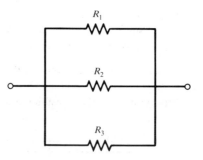

Calculate and display the combined resistance

$$\frac{1}{\dfrac{1}{R_1} + \dfrac{1}{R_2} + \dfrac{1}{R_3}}$$

for given values of R_1, R_2, and R_3.

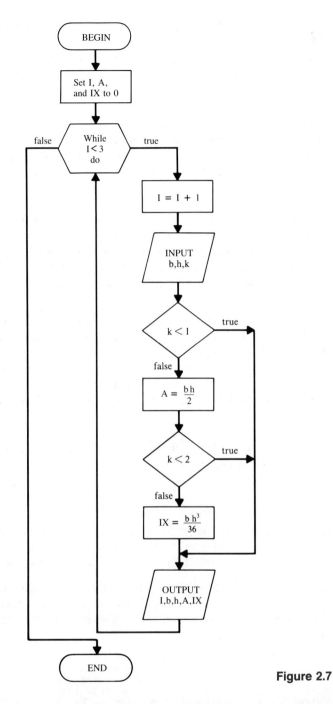

Figure 2.7

6. The boiling point of water is 212° on the Fahrenheit scale and 100° on the Celsius scale. The freezing point of water is 32° on the Fahrenheit scale and 0° on the Celsius scale. Assuming a linear relationship $(F = a \cdot C + b)$ between these two temperature scales, convert a temperature of C degrees on the Celsius scale to the corresponding Fahrenheit temperature, and display both temperatures.

7. Calculate and display the largest and the smallest of three given voltage readings.

8. Calculate and display the largest number, the smallest number, and the range (largest number − smallest number) for any given set of numbers.

9. A certain city classifies a pollution index of less than 35 as pleasant, 35 through 60 as unpleasant, and above 60 as hazardous. The city's pollution control officer desires a program that will accept several values of the pollution index and produce the appropriate classification for each.

10. Suppose that a professor gave a quiz to his class and compiled a list of scores ranging from 50 through 100. He intends to use only three grades: A if the score is 90 or above, B if it is below 90 but above or equal to 75, and C if it is below 75. He would like a program to assign the appropriate letter grades to the numeric scores.

11. A car manufacturer wants to determine average noise levels for the ten different models of cars the company produces. Each can be purchased with one of five different engines. Design an algorithm to enter the noise levels (in decibels) that were recorded for each possible model and engine configuration, and to calculate the average noise level for each model as well as the average noise level over all models and engines.

12. **(a)** Develop an algorithm like that in Section 2.3 to approximate the value of e^x using the infinite series

$$e^x = \sum_{n=0}^{\infty} \frac{x^n}{n!}$$

(b) Construct a trace table for your algorithm, and trace the values of n, x^n, $n!$, each term $x^n/n!$, and the value of the sum of all terms up through the current one for $n = 0, 1, \ldots, 10$, and $x = 0.8$.

13. The "divide and average" algorithm for approximating the square root of any positive number A is as follows: For any initial approximation X that is positive, find a new approximation by calculating the average of X and A/X, that is,

$$\frac{X + A/X}{2}$$

Repeat this procedure with X replaced by this new approximation, stopping when X and A/X differ in absolute value by some specified error allowance, such as .00001.

14. The quadratic equation $Ax^2 + Bx + C = 0$ has no real roots if the discriminant $B^2 - 4AC$ is negative; it has one real root, $-B/2A$, if the discriminant is zero; and it has two real roots given by the quadratic formula

$$\frac{-B \pm \sqrt{B^2 - 4AC}}{2A}$$

if the discriminant is positive. A program is to be developed to solve several different quadratic equations or to indicate that there are no real roots.

15. Dispatch Die-Casting currently produces 200 castings per month and realizes a profit of $300 per casting. The company now spends $2000 per month on research and development and has a fixed operating cost of $20,000 per month that does not depend on the amount of production. If the company doubles the amount spent on research and development, it is estimated that production will increase by 20 percent. The company president would like to know, beginning with the company's current status and successively doubling the amount spent on research and development, at what point the net profit will begin to decline.

16. Consider a cylindrical reservoir with radius = 30.0 feet and height 40.0 feet that is filled and emptied by a 12-inch diameter pipe. The pipe has a 1000.0-foot-long run and discharges at an elevation 20.0 feet lower than the bottom of the reservoir. The pipe has been tested and has a roughness factor of 0.0130.

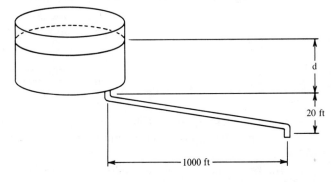

Several formulas have been developed experimentally to determine the velocity of flow of fluids through such pipes. One of these, the *Manning formula,* is

$$V = \frac{1.486}{N} R^{2/3} S^{1/2}$$

where

V = velocity in feet per second

N = roughness coefficient

R = hydraulic radius = $\dfrac{\text{cross-sectional area}}{\text{wetted perimeter}}$

S = slope of the energy gradient $\left(= \dfrac{d + 20}{1000} \text{ for this problem} \right)$

The rate of fluid flow is equal to the cross-sectional area of the pipe multiplied by the velocity.

Design an algorithm to enter the reservoir's height, roughness coefficient, hydraulic radius, and pipe radius and then estimate the time required to empty the reservoir. Do this by assuming a constant flow rate for 5-minute segments.

17. A 100.0-lb sign is hung from the end of a horizontal pole of negligible mass. The pole is attached to the building by a pin and is supported by a cable, as shown below. The pole and cable are each 6.0 feet long.

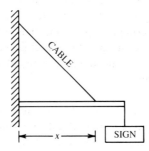

Design an algorithm to find the appropriate place (indicated by x in the diagram) to attach the cable to the pole so that the tension in the cable will be minimized. The equation governing static equilibrium tells us that

$$\text{Tension} = \frac{100 \cdot 6 \cdot 6}{x\sqrt{36 - x^2}}$$

Calculate the tension for x starting at 1.0 and incrementing it by 0.1 until the approximate minimum value is located.

18. Enter and execute the following FORTRAN program on your computer system:

```
      PROGRAM ARITH
****************************************************
* John  Doe          CPSC 141C          Dec. 18, 1987 *
*                  ASSIGNMENT #1                      *
* Program to add two numbers X and Y giving SUM      *
****************************************************

      REAL X, Y, SUM

      X = 3.14
      Y = 2.057
      SUM = X + Y
      PRINT *, 'SUM OF', X, ' AND', Y, ' IS', SUM
      END
```

19. For the program in Exercise 18, make the following changes and execute the modified program:

   (a) Change 3.14 to 17.2375 in the statement that assigns a value to X.

   (b) Change the variable names X and Y to ALPHA and BETA throughout.

   (c) Insert the comment

```
*** Calculate the sum
```

   before the statement SUM = X + Y.

   (d) Insert the following comment and statement before the PRINT statement:

```
*** Now calculate the difference
    DIFF = ALPHA - BETA
```

   change the REAL statement to

```
REAL ALPHA, BETA, SUM, DIFF
```

   and add the following statement after the PRINT statement:

```
PRINT*, 'DIFF. OF', ALPHA, BETA, ' IS', DIFF
```

   Also modify the comments in lines 2 and 3 appropriately.

20. Using the program in Figure 2.4 as a guide, write a FORTRAN program for the circle problem in Exercise 4.

21. Using the program in Figure 2.4 as a guide, write a FORTRAN program for the resistance problem in Exercise 5.

22. Using the program in Figure 2.4 as a guide, write a FORTRAN program for the temperature conversion problem in Exercise 6.

3

Basic FORTRAN

Kindly enter them in your note-book. And, in order to refer to them conveniently, let's call them A, B, and Z.

The tortoise in LEWIS CARROLL'S
What the Tortoise Said to Achilles

In language, clarity is everything.

CONFUCIUS

The programming language FORTRAN, developed in the 1950s, was one of the first high-level languages. Since its introduction it has undergone several revisions, so that today there are a number of different versions of FORTRAN in use. In an attempt to minimize the differences among these versions, the American National Standards Institute (ANSI) has established standards for the FORTRAN language. The most recent ANSI FORTRAN standard is contained in the document ANSI X3.9-1978 and is commonly referred to as **FORTRAN 77.** It is this standard FORTRAN 77 that is considered in this text. However, a number of variations of and extensions to the standard have become quite popular. Some of these features are summarized in the Variations and Extensions sections at the chapter ends and in Appendix E.

3.1 From Algorithms to Programs

An algorithm for solving a problem is a sequence of steps that must be performed based on the information given in the problem's specification. Thus, a computer program that implements such an algorithm must accept and store the given information, perform the sequence of steps required to solve the problem (which may also require calculating and storing some intermediate

58

results), and finally, display the results. This general structure is reflected in the organization of a FORTRAN program.

The format of a simple FORTRAN program is

PROGRAM statement
Opening documentation
Variable declarations
Program statements
END

A program statement like that in the example of the preceding chapter,

```
PROGRAM DECAY
```

marks the beginning of the program and associates a name (DECAY) with it. This name, like all variable names and other identifiers, must begin with a letter and may be followed by up to five letters or digits.

The opening documentation in a program is a sequence of comments that describe the purpose of the program, the variables it uses, and other relevant information such as the date the program was written and the name of the programmer. These comment lines are either blank or begin with a C or an asterisk (*) in the first position of the line.

The variable declaration part of a program consists of type statements that specify the names and types of all variables used in the program. These type statements are followed by the program statements that actually implement the steps of the algorithm. Finally, an END statement is used to mark the end of the program and to halt execution.

As we have noted, comment lines are blank or contain a C or an asterisk in column 1. All FORTRAN statements must appear in columns 7 through 72 of a line; characters that appear in columns 73 and beyond are ignored. If it is necessary to continue a statement from one line to the next, a character other than a zero or a space must be placed in column 6 to indicate that this line is a continuation of the preceding line. If a statement requires a statement label, then this label must appear in columns 1 through 5. The following diagram summarizes these rules:

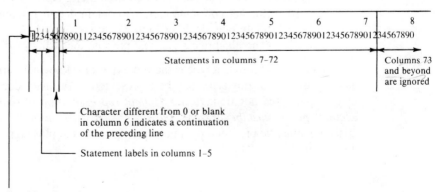

3.2 Data Types

Computer programs, regardless of the language in which they are written, are designed to manipulate data. Thus, we begin our discussion of the FORTRAN language by considering the data types that can be processed in a FORTRAN program.

FORTRAN provides six data types:

1. Integer
2. Real
3. Double precision
4. Complex
5. Character
6. Logical

The first four are numeric types and are used to process different kinds of numbers. The character type is used to process data consisting of strings of characters. The logical type is used to process logical data; such data may have either .TRUE. or .FALSE. as its value. In this chapter we restrict our attention mainly to integer and real types; logical and character types are considered in Chapter 6, and double precision and complex types in Chapter 10.

Constants. Constants are quantities whose values do not change during program execution. They may be of numeric, character, or logical type.

An **integer constant** is a string of digits that *does not include commas or a decimal point; negative integer constants must be preceded by a negative sign, but a plus sign is optional for nonnegative integers.* Thus

$$
\begin{array}{r}
0 \\
137 \\
-2516 \\
+17745
\end{array}
$$

are valid integer constants, whereas the following are invalid for the reasons indicated:

$$
\begin{array}{l}
5,280 \text{ (Commas are not allowed in numeric constants.)} \\
16.0 \text{ (Integer constants may not contain decimal points.)} \\
--5 \text{ (Only one algebraic sign is allowed.)} \\
7- \text{ (The algebraic sign must precede the string of digits.)}
\end{array}
$$

Another numeric data type is the **real** type, also known as **single precision** data. Constants of this type may be represented as ordinary decimal numbers or in exponential notation. *In the decimal representation of real constants, a decimal point must be present, but no commas are allowed.* Negative real constants must be preceded by a negative sign, but the plus sign is optional for nonnegative reals. Thus

$$
\begin{array}{r}
1.234 \\
-.01536 \\
+56473.
\end{array}
$$

are valid real constants, whereas the following are invalid for the reasons indicated:

12,345 (Commas are not allowed in numeric constants.)
63 (Real constants must contain a decimal point.)

The scientific representation of a real constant consists of an integer or decimal number, representing the mantissa or fractional part, followed by an exponent written as the letter E *with an integer constant following.* For example, the real constant 337.456 may also be written as

3.37456E2

which means 3.37456×10^2, or it may be written in a variety of other forms, such as

.337456E3
337.456E0
33745.6E–2
337456E–3

Character constants, also called **strings,** are sequences of symbols chosen from the FORTRAN character set. The ANSI standard character set for FORTRAN is given in the following table:

Character	Meaning
blank	blank or space
0, . . . , 9	digits
A, . . . , Z	uppercase letters
$	dollar sign
'	apostrophe (single quote)
(	left parenthesis
)	right parenthesis
*	asterisk
+	plus sign
−	minus sign
/	slash
,	comma
.	period
:	colon
=	equals sign

Many versions of FORTRAN also include lowercase letters and other special symbols in their character sets. The sequence of characters that comprise a character constant *must be enclosed within apostrophes* (single quotes), and the number of such characters is the **length** of the constant. For example,

'PDQ123-A'

is a character constant of length 8;

'JOHN Q. DOE'

is a character constant of length 11, because blanks are characters and are thus included in the character count. *If an apostrophe is to be one of the characters of a constant, it must be entered as a pair of apostrophes;*

```
'DON''T'
```

is thus a character constant consisting of the five characters D, O, N, ', and T.

Variables. In mathematics, a symbolic name is often used to refer to a quantity. For example, the formula

$$A = l \cdot w$$

is used to calculate the area (denoted by A) of a rectangle with a given length (denoted by l) and a given width (denoted by w). These symbolic names, A, l, and w, are called **variables.** If specific values are assigned to l and w, this formula can be used to calculate the value of A, which then represents the area of a particular rectangle.

Variables were also used in Chapter 2 in the discussion of algorithms and programs. When a variable is used in a FORTRAN program, the compiler associates it with a particular memory location. The value of a variable at any time is the value stored in the associated memory location at that time.

The names of variables used in FORTRAN programs must consist of one to six letters or digits, the first of which must be a letter. Thus

```
MASS
RATE
VELOC
AB1
```

are valid FORTRAN variable names, but the following are invalid for the reasons indicated:

```
TOOLONG          (Names must consist of at most six characters.)
R2-D2            (Only letters and digits are allowed in variable names.)
6FEET            (Names must begin with a letter.)
```

The type of a FORTRAN variable must be one of the six data types given previously, and the type of each variable determines the type of value that may be assigned to that variable. It is therefore necessary to declare the type of each variable in a FORTRAN program. This can be done by using **type statements.** *These type statements must appear at the beginning of the program before all executable statements* (which are discussed in the following sections).

The type statements used for real variables and integer variables are of the form

> **REAL** *list*
> **INTEGER** *list*

where *list* is a list of variable names, separated by commas, whose types are being declared real or integer, respectively. Thus, the statements

```
REAL MASS, VELOC
INTEGER COUNT, FACTOR, SUM
```

declare MASS and VELOC to be of real type, and COUNT, FACTOR, and SUM to be of integer type.

For any variable whose type is not *explicitly* specified in a type statement, FORTRAN will *implicitly* assign it a type according to its **naming convention:** All variables whose names begin with I, J, K, L, M, or N are integer variables, whereas all those whose names begin with any other letter are real variables. (This naming convention may be modified using the IMPLICIT statement described in Chapter 13.)

It is important that variables of a given type be used in a manner that is appropriate to that data type, since otherwise the program may fail to execute correctly. *It is therefore important to declare explicitly the type of each variable used in a program.* This practice encourages one to think carefully about each of these variables, what each represents, what types of values it will have, what operations will be performed with it, and so on.

Exercises

1. Which of the following are legal FORTRAN variable names?

   (a) XRAY   (b) X-RAY   (c) PRESSURE
   (d) R2D2   (e) 3M   (f) CARB14
   (g) PS.175   (h) X   (i) 4
   (j) N/4   (k) M$ (l) ZZZZZZ
   (m) ANGLE   (n) AGNLE   (o) ANGEL
   (p) X AXIS   (q) A+   (r) Z0000Z

2. Classify each of the following as an integer constant, a real constant, or neither:

   (a) 12   (b) 12.   (c) '12'
   (d) 8 + 4   (e) -3.7   (f) 3.7-
   (g) 1,024   (h) +1   (i) $3.98
   (j) 0.357E4   (k) 24E0   (l) E3
   (m) FIVE   (n) 3E.5   (o) .000001
   (p) 1.2 * 10

3. Which of the following are legal character constants?

   (a) 'X'   (b) RATE'
   (c) '$1.98'   (d) '3.14159'
   (e) 'OHM''S LAW'   (f) 'ISN''T'
   (g) 'CONSTANT'   (h) 'A''B''C'
   (i) 'RESULTANT FORCE:'   (j) 'NEWTON'S'
   (k) '12 + 34'   (l) '''S LAW'

4. Write type statements to declare

  (a) TEMP, PRESS, and VOLUME to be of real type.
  (b) ZETA to be of integer type.
  (c) MU to be of real type.
  (d) TIME and DIST to be of integer type.

5. Assuming the standard FORTRAN naming convention, classify each of the following as an integer variable, a real variable, or neither:

(a) GAUSS	**(b)** FORTRAN	**(c)** H
(d) I	**(e)** LIST	**(f)** TABLE
(g) D3	**(h)** 3D	**(i)** DISTANCE
(j) DISTNCE	**(k)** H20	**(l)** CHAR
(m) LOGIC	**(n)** DIGIT	**(o)** TWO
(p) DOUBLE		

3.3 Arithmetic Operations and Functions

In the preceding section we considered variables and constants of various types. These variables and constants can be processed by using operations and functions appropriate to their types. In this section we discuss the arithmetic operations and functions that are used with numeric data.

In FORTRAN, **addition** and **subtraction** are denoted by the usual plus ($+$) and minus ($-$) signs. **Multiplication** is denoted by an asterisk ($*$). This symbol must be used to denote every multiplication; thus, to multiply N by 2, we must use 2 $*$ N or N $*$ 2, not 2N. **Division** is denoted by a slash (/), and **exponentiation** is denoted by a pair of asterisks ($**$). For example, the quantity $B^2 - 4AC$ would be written as

    B ** 2 - 4 * A * C

in a FORTRAN program.

An expression containing these operations will be evaluated in accordance with the following **priority rules:**

1. *All exponentiations are performed first; consecutive exponentiations are performed from right to left.*
2. *All multiplications and divisions are performed next, in the order in which they appear from left to right.*
3. *The additions and subtractions are performed last, in the order in which they appear from left to right.*

The following examples illustrate this order of evaluation:

    2 ** 3 ** 2 = 2 ** 9 = 512
    10 - 8 - 2 = 2 - 2 = 0
    10 / 5 * 2 = 2 * 2 = 4
    2 + 4 / 2 = 2 + 2 = 4
    2 + 4 ** 2 / 2 = 2 + 16 / 2 = 2 + 8 = 10

The standard order of evaluation can be modified by using parentheses to enclose subexpressions with an expression. These subexpressions are first evaluated in the standard manner, and the results are then combined to evaluate the complete expression. If the parentheses are "nested," that is, if one set of parentheses is contained within another, the computations in the innermost parentheses are performed first.

For example, consider the expression

$$(5 * (11 - 5) ** 2) * 4 + 9$$

The subexpression $11 - 5$ is evaluated first, producing

$$(5 * 6 ** 2) * 4 + 9$$

Next, the subexpression $5 * 6 ** 2$ is evaluated in the standard order, giving

$$180 * 4 + 9$$

Now the multiplication is performed, giving

$$720 + 9$$

and the addition produces the final result

$$729$$

Expressions containing two or more operations must be written carefully to ensure that they are evaluated in the order intended. Even though parentheses may not be required, they should be used freely to clarify the intended order of evaluation and to write complicated expressions in terms of simpler subexpressions. However, parentheses must balance; that is, they must occur in pairs, as an unpaired parenthesis will result in an error.

The symbols $+$ and $-$ can also be used as **unary operators;** for example, $+X$ and $-(A + B)$ are allowed. But unary operators must be used carefully, because FORTRAN *does not allow two operators to follow in succession.* (Note that $**$ is interpreted as a single operator rather than two operators in succession.) For example, the expression $N * -2$ is not allowed; rather, it must be written $N * (-2)$. The unary operations have the same low priority as the corresponding binary operations.

When two constants or variables of the same type are combined using one of the four basic arithmetic operations $(+, -, *, /)$, the result has the same type as the operands. For example, the sum of the integers 3 and 4 is the integer 7, whereas the sum of the real numbers 3.0 and 4.0 is the real number 7.0. This distinction may seem unimportant until one considers the division operation. Division of the real constant 9.0 by the real constant 4.0,

$$9.0 / 4.0$$

produces the real quotient 2.25, whereas dividing the integer 9 by the integer 4,

$$9 \ / \ 4$$

produces the integer quotient 2, which is equal to the integer part of the real quotient 2.25. Similarly, if N has the value 2 and X has the value 2.0, the real division

$$1.0 \ / \ X$$

yields .5, whereas the integer division

$$1 \ / \ N$$

yields 0.

It is also possible to combine an integer quantity with a real quantity using these arithmetic operations. Expressions involving different types of numeric operands are **mixed-mode** expressions. When an integer quantity is combined with a real one, the integer quantity is automatically converted to its real equivalent, and the result is of real type. The following examples illustrate the evaluation of some mixed-mode expressions; note that type conversion does not take place until necessary.

```
1. / 4 → 1. / 4. → .25
3. + 8 / 5 → 3. + 1 → 3. + 1. → 4.
3 + 8. / 5 → 3 + 8. / 5. → 3 + 1.6 → 3. + 1.6 → 4.6
```

These last two examples illustrate why *mixed-mode expressions should ordinarily be avoided.* The two expressions 3. + 8 / 5 and 3 + 8. / 5 seem to be algebraically equal but are in fact unequal because of the differences in real and integer arithmetic.

These differences also affect the manner in which exponentiations are performed. If the exponent is an integer quantity, exponentiation is carried out using repeated multiplication. The following examples illustrate:

```
2 ** 3 → 2 * 2 * 2 → 8
(−4.0) ** 2 → (−4.0) * (−4.0) → 16.0
1.5 ** 2 → 1.5 * 1.5 → 2.25
```

If, however, the exponent is a real quantity, exponentiation is performed using logarithms. For example,

$$2.0 \ ** \ 3.0$$

is evaluated as

$$e3.0 \ * \ \ln(2.0)$$

which will not be exactly 8.0 because of roundoff errors that arise in storing real numbers and because the exponentiation and logarithm functions produce only approximate values. Another consequence of this method of performing exponentiation is that a negative quantity raised to a real power is undefined, because the logarithms of negative values are not defined. Consequently, $(-4.0) ** 2.0$ will be undefined, even though $(-4.0) ** 2$ is evaluated as $(-4.0) * (-4.0) = 16.0$. These examples illustrate why *a real exponent should never be used in place of an integer exponent.*

There are, however, computations in which real exponents are appropriate. For example, in mathematics, $7^{1/2}$ denotes $\sqrt{7}$, the square root of 7. In FOR-TRAN this operation of extracting roots can be implemented using exponentiation with real exponents. Thus, to compute the square root of 7, we could write $7 ** .5$, $7 ** (1. / 2.)$ or even $7 ** (1. / 2)$. (Note, however, that $7 ** (1 / 2)$ yields $7 ** 0 = 1$.) In general, the Nth root of X can be computed by using

$$X ** (1.0 / N)$$

for any positive-valued X.

Because many computations involve the square root of a real quantity, FORTRAN provides a special **function** to implement this operation. This function is denoted by SQRT and is used by writing

SQRT(*argument*)

where *argument* is a *real-valued* constant, variable, or expression. For example, to calculate the square root of 7, we would write

SQRT(7.0)

but not SQRT(7). If $B ** 2 - 4.0 * A * C$ is a nonnegative real-valued expression, its square root can be calculated by writing

SQRT(B ** 2 - 4.0 * A * C)

TABLE 3.1 Some FORTRAN Functions

Function	Description	Type of Argument(s)*	Type of Value
ABS(x)	Absolute value of x	Integer or real	Same as argument
COS(x)	Cosine of x radians	Real	Real
EXP(x)	Exponential function e^x	Real	Real
INT(x)	Integer part of x	Real	Integer
LOG(x)	Natural logarithm of x	Real	Real
MAX($x_1, \ldots, x_n$)	Maximum of $x_1, \ldots, x_n$	Integer or real	Same as arguments
MIN($x_1 \ldots, x_n$)	Minimum of $x_1, \ldots, x_n$	Integer or real	Same as arguments
MOD(x, y)	x (mod y); $x - \text{INT}(x / y) * y$	Integer or real	Same as arguments
NINT(x)	x rounded to nearest integer	Real	Integer
REAL(x)	Conversion of x to real type	Integer	Real
SIN(x)	Sine of x radians	Real	Real
SQRT(x)	Square root of x	Real	Real

*In several cases, the arguments (and values) may be of double precision or complex types. See Table 9.1.

If the value of the expression B ** 2 − 4.0 * A * C is negative, an error will result because the square root of a negative number is not defined.

There are several other functions provided in FORTRAN; some of the more commonly used functions are listed in Table 3.1. To use any of these functions, we simply give the function followed by the argument(s) enclosed within parentheses. In each case, the argument(s) must be of the type specified for that function in the table.

Exercises

1. Find the value of each of the following expressions.

    (a) 9 − 5 − 3
    (b) 2 ** 3 + 3 / 5
    (c) 2.0 / 4
    (d) 2 + 3 ** 2
    (e) (2 + 3) ** 2
    (f) 3 ** 2 ** 3
    (g) (3 ** 2) ** 3
    (h) 3 ** (2 ** 3)
    (i) (3 ** 2 ** 3)
    (j) 25 ** 1 / 2
    (k) −3.0 ** 2
    (l) 12.0 / 2.0 * 3.0
    (m) ((2 + 3) ** 2) / (8 − (2 + 1))
    (n) ((2 + 3) ** 2) / (8 − 2 + 1)
    (o) (2 + 3 ** 2) / (8 − 2 + 1)
    (p) (2. + 3 ** 2) / (8 − 2 + 1)
    (q) SQRT(6.0 + 3.0)

2. Given that TWO = 2.0, TRI = 3.0, FOUR = 4.0, IJK = 8, INK = 5, find the value for each of the following.

    (a) TWO + TRI * TRI
    (b) INK / 3
    (c) (TRI + TWO / FOUR) ** 2
    (d) IJK / INK * 5.1
    (e) FOUR ** 2 / TWO ** 2
    (f) INK ** 2 / TWO ** 2
    (g) SQRT(TWO + TRI + FOUR)

3. Write FORTRAN expressions equivalent to the following:

    (a) $10 + 5B − 4AC$
    (b) Three times the difference $4 − N$ divided by twice the quantity $M^2 + N^2$
    (c) The square root of $A + 3B^2$
    (d) The cube root of X (calculated as X to the one-third power)
    (e) $A^2 + B^2 − 2AB \cos T$

(f) The natural logarithm of the absolute value of

$$\frac{X - Y}{X + Y}$$

3.4 The Assignment Statement

The **assignment statement** is used to assign values to variables and has the form

variable = expression

where *expression* may be a constant, another variable to which a value has previously been assigned, or a formula to be evaluated. For example, suppose that XCOORD and YCOORD are real variables and NUMBER and TERM are integer variables, as declared by the following statements:

```
REAL XCOORD, YCOORD
INTEGER NUMBER, TERM
```

These declarations associate memory locations with these variables. This might be pictured as follows, where the question marks indicate that these variables are initially undefined:

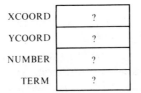

Now consider the following assignment statements:

```
XCOORD = 5.23
YCOORD = SQRT(25.0)
NUMBER = 17
TERM = NUMBER / 3 + 2
XCOORD = 2.0 * XCOORD
```

The first assignment statement assigns the real constant 5.23 to the real variable XCOORD, and the second assigns the real constant 5.0 to the real variable YCOORD. The next assignment statement assigns the integer constant 17 to the integer variable NUMBER; the variable TERM is still undefined.

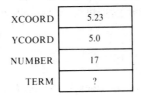

This means that until the contents of these memory locations are changed, these values are substituted for the variable names in any subsequent expression containing these variables. Thus, in the fourth assignment statement, the value 17 is substituted for the variable NUMBER, the expression NUMBER / 3 + 2 is evaluated, yielding 7, and this value is then assigned to the integer variable TERM; the value of NUMBER is unchanged.

XCOORD	5.23
YCOORD	5.0
NUMBER	17
TERM	7

In the last assignment statement, the variable XCOORD appears on both sides of the assignment operator (=). In this case, the current value 5.23 for XCOORD is used in evaluating the expression 2.0 * XCOORD, yielding the value 10.46; this value is then assigned to XCOORD. The old value 5.23 is lost because it has been replaced with the new value 10.46.

XCOORD	10.46
YCOORD	5.0
NUMBER	17
TERM	7

Because there are different types of numeric variables and constants, it is possible to have not only mixed-mode arithmetic, as described in the preceding section, but also mixed-mode assignment. This occurs when the variable to be assigned a value is of different type than the value being assigned.

If a real expression is assigned to an integer variable, the fractional part of the expression value is truncated, and the integer part is assigned to the variable. For example, if the real variable X has the value 5.75, and I, KAPPA, and MU are integer variables, the statements

```
I = 3.14159
KAPPA = X / 2.0
MU = 1. / X
```

assign the integer constants 3, 2, and 0 to the variables I, KAPPA, and MU, respectively.

In the case of an assignment of an integer-valued expression to a real variable, the value is converted to a real constant and then assigned to the variable. Thus, if the integer variable N has the value 9, and ALPHA and BETA are real variables, the statements

```
ALPHA = 3
BETA = (N + 3) / 5
```

assign the real constant 3.0 to ALPHA and the real constant 2.0 to BETA.

In every assignment statement, the variable to be assigned a value must appear on the left side of the assignment operator (=), and a legal expression must appear on the right. For example, if we assume the declarations

```
INTEGER M, N
REAL X
```

then the following are not valid FORTRAN statements for the reasons indicated.

Statement	Error
5 = N	Variable must be on the left of the equal sign.
X + 3.5 = 4.26	Numeric expressions may not appear to the left of the equal sign.
N = 'FIVE'	Character constant may not be assigned to a numeric variable.
N = '2' + '3'	'2' + '3' is not a legal expression.
M = N = 1	N = 1 is not a legal expression.

It is important to remember that *the assignment statement is not a statement of algebraic equality; rather, it is a* replacement *statement*. Some beginning programmers forget this and write the assignment statement

```
A = B
```

when the statement

```
B = A
```

is intended. These two statements produce very different results; the first assigns the value of B to A, leaving B unchanged;

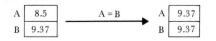

the second assigns the value of A to B, leaving A unchanged.

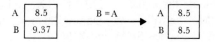

To illustrate further the replacement function of an assignment statement, suppose that DELTA and RHO are integer variables with values 357 and 59, respectively. The following statements interchange the values of DELTA and

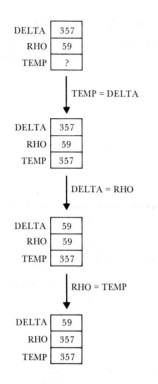

Figure 3.1

RHO, using the auxiliary integer variable TEMP:

```
INTEGER DELTA, RHO, TEMP
       .
       .
       .
TEMP = DELTA
DELTA = RHO
RHO = TEMP
```

Figure 3.1 shows the replacement of values produced by each of the three assignment statements.

As another example, consider the statement

```
SUM = SUM + X
```

Such a statement, in which the same variable appears on both sides of the assignment operator, often confuses beginning programmers. Execution of this statement causes the values of SUM and X to be substituted for these variables to evaluate the expression SUM + X, and the resulting value is then assigned to SUM. The following diagram illustrates this statement for the case in which the real variables SUM and X have the values 132.5 and 8.4, respectively:

SUM	132.5	SUM = SUM + X	SUM	140.9
X	8.4	⟶	X	8.4

Note that the old value of the variable SUM is lost because it was replaced with a new value.

Another statement in which the same variable appears on both sides of the assignment operator is

```
COUNT = COUNT + 1
```

This statement implements the operation "increment COUNT by 1." When it is executed, the current value of COUNT is substituted for this variable to evaluate the expression COUNT + 1, and this new value is then assigned to COUNT. For example, if COUNT has the value 3, the value of COUNT + 1 is 3 + 1 = 4, which is then assigned as the new value for COUNT:

Note once again that the old value of the variable has been lost because it was replaced with a new value.

In a FORTRAN program, variables are undefined until their values have been explicitly specified by an assignment statement or by one of the other statements discussed later. The results of attempting to use undefined variables are unpredictable and depend on the particular FORTRAN compiler being used.

Exercises

1. Assuming the declarations

   ```
   INTEGER N
   REAL PI, ALPHA
   ```

   determine which of the following are valid FORTRAN assignment statements. If they are not valid, explain why they are not.

   (a) `PI = 3.141592`   (b) `3 = N`
   (c) `N     = N+    1`   (d) `N+1 = N`
   (e) `ALPHA = 1`   (f) `ALPHA = '1'`
   (g) `ALPHA = ALPHA`

2. Given that TWO = 2.0 TRI = 3.0, FOUR = 4.0, NUM = 8, and MIX = 5 and that the following declarations have been made

   ```
   REAL TWO, TRI, FOUR, X
   INTEGER NUM, MIX, J
   ```

   find the value assigned to the given variable for each of the following, or indicate why the statement is not valid.

   (a) `X = (TWO + TRI) ** TRI`
   (b) `X = (TRI + TWO / FOUR) ** 2`
   (c) `X = NUM / MIX + 5.1`
   (d) `J = NUM / MIX + 5.1`

(e) X = MIX ** 2 / NUM ** 2
(f) J = MIX ** 2 / NUM ** 2
(g) NUM = NUM + 2
(h) X = SQRT(TRI ** 2 + FOUR ** 2)
(i) NUM = ABS(TRI - 4.5)
(j) J = MAX(INT(FOUR / 3), MIX)

3. Write a FORTRAN assignment statement for each of the following that calculates the given expression and assigns the result to the specified variable:

(a) RATE times TIME to DIST

(b) $\sqrt{A^2 + B^2}$ to C

(c) $\dfrac{1}{\dfrac{1}{R1} + \dfrac{1}{R2} + \dfrac{1}{R3}}$ to RESIST

(d) P times $(1 + R)^N$ to VALUE

(e) Area of triangle (one-half base times height) of base B and height H to AREA

(f) 5/9 of the difference F − 32 to C (conversion of Fahrenheit to Celsius)

(g) $\dfrac{2V^2 \sin A \cos A}{G}$ to RANGE

4. For each of the following, give values for the integer variables I, J, and K and the real variable X for which the two expressions are not equal:

(a) I * (J / K) and I * J / K
(b) X * I / J and X * (I / J)
(c) (I + J) / K and I / K + J / K

3.5 List-Directed Input/Output

In the preceding section, we considered the assignment statement which enables us to calculate the values of expressions and store the results of these computations by assigning them to variables. An assignment statement does not, however, display these results on some output device, nor does it allow the user to enter new values during execution. For example, if a projectile is launched from an initial height of HGHT0 with an initial vertical velocity of VELOC0 and a vertical acceleration of ACCEL, then the equations

```
HGHT = 0.5 * ACCEL * TIME ** 2 + VELOC0 * TIME + HGHT0
```

and

```
VELOC = ACCEL * TIME + VELOC0
```

give the height (HGHT) and the vertical velocity (VELOC) at any TIME after launch. The program in Figure 3.2 assigns the value −9.807 (m/sec²) to ACCEL, 150.0 (m) to HGHT0, 100.0 (m/sec) to VELOC0, and 5.0 (sec) to TIME and then computes the corresponding values of HGHT and VELOC.

```
      PROGRAM PROJEC
***********************************************************************
* This program calculates the velocity and height of a projectile    *
* given its initial height, initial velocity, and constant           *
* acceleration.  Variables used are:                                 *
*      HGHTO   :  initial height                                      *
*      HGHT    :  height at any time                                  *
*      VELOCO  :  initial vertical velocity                           *
*      VELOC   :  vertical velocity at any time                       *
*      ACCEL   :  vertical acceleration                               *
*      TIME    :  time elapsed since projectile was launched          *
***********************************************************************

      REAL HGHTO, HGHT, VELOCO, VELOC, ACCEL, TIME

      ACCEL = -9.807
      HGHTO = 150.0
      VELOCO = 100.0
      TIME = 5.0
      HGHT = 0.5 * ACCEL * TIME ** 2  +  VELOCO * TIME  +  HGHTO
      VELOC = ACCEL * TIME + VELOCO
      END
```

Figure 3.2

The values of HGHT and VELOC are calculated as desired, but they are only stored internally and are not displayed to the user. Moreover, if the same calculation is to be done for the same acceleration but with values 100.0 for HGHT0, 90.0 for VELOC0 and 4.3 for TIME, then several statements must be modified, as shown in Figure 3.3, and the program executed again.

```
      PROGRAM PROJEC
***********************************************************************
* This program calculates the velocity and height of a projectile    *
* given its initial height, initial velocity, and constant           *
* acceleration.  Variables used are:                                 *
*      HGHTO   :  initial height                                      *
*      HGHT    :  height at any time                                  *
*      VELOCO  :  initial vertical velocity                           *
*      VELOC   :  vertical velocity at any time                       *
*      ACCEL   :  vertical acceleration                               *
*      TIME    :  time elapsed since projectile was launched          *
***********************************************************************

      REAL HGHTO, HGHT, VELOCO, VELOC, ACCEL, TIME

      ACCEL = -9.807
      HGHTO = 100.0
      VELOCO = 90.0
      TIME = 4.3
      HGHT = 0.5 * ACCEL * TIME ** 2  +  VELOCO * TIME  +  HGHTO
      VELOC = ACCEL * TIME + VELOCO
      END
```

Figure 3.3

The output statement that we consider in this section provides a method for easily displaying information. We also consider an input statement to provide a convenient method to assign values from an external source during execution of the program.

FORTRAN provides two types of input/output statements. In the first type, the programmer must explicitly specify the format in which the data is presented for input or, in the case of output, the precise format in which it is to be displayed. In the second type of input/output, certain predetermined standard formats that match the types of items in the input/output list are automatically provided by the compiler. It is this second type, known as **list-directed input/output,** that is considered in this section.

List-Directed Output.   The simplest form of the list-directed output statement is

> PRINT *, *output-list*

where *output-list* is a single expression or a list of expressions separated by commas. Each of these expressions is a constant, a variable, or a formula. For example, to display some of the relevant information from the preceding example, we might add two PRINT statements, as shown in Figure 3.4. Execution of the program will produce output similar to that shown. Note that each PRINT statement produces a new line of output. The exact format and spacing used in displaying these values are compiler dependent; for example, in some systems, real values might be displayed in scientific notation, and the number of spaces in an output line might be different from that shown.

```
      PROGRAM PROJEC
***********************************************************************
* This program calculates the velocity and height of a projectile   *
* given its initial height, initial velocity, and constant           *
* acceleration.  Variables used are:                                 *
*      HGHTO   :  initial height                                     *
*      HGHT    :  height at any time                                 *
*      VELOCO  :  initial vertical velocity                          *
*      VELOC   :  vertical velocity at any time                      *
*      ACCEL   :  vertical acceleration                              *
*      TIME    :  time elapsed since projectile was launched         *
***********************************************************************

      REAL HGHTO, HGHT, VELOCO, VELOC, ACCEL, TIME

      ACCEL = -9.807
      HGHTO = 100.0
      VELOCO = 90.0
      TIME = 4.3
      HGHT = 0.5 * ACCEL * TIME ** 2  +  VELOCO * TIME  +  HGHTO
      VELOC = ACCEL * TIME + VELOCO
      PRINT *, 'AT TIME ', TIME, ' THE VERTICAL VELOCITY IS ', VELOC
      PRINT *, 'AND THE HEIGHT IS ', HGHT
      END
```

Figure 3.4

Figure 3.4 (continued)

Sample run:
====== ===

```
AT TIME       4.30000    VERTICAL VELOCITY IS      47.8299
AND THE HEIGHT IS        396.334
```

In some situations, one or more blank lines in the output improve readability. A blank line is displayed by a PRINT statement of the form

PRINT *

in which the output list is empty. Note that the comma that normally follows the asterisk is also omitted. Execution of each statement of this form causes a single blank line to be displayed.

List-Directed Input. The simplest form of the list-directed input statement is

READ *, *input-list*

where *input-list* consists of a single variable or a list of variables separated by commas. Execution of this READ statement causes the transfer of values from some external source (terminal, card reader, file) and the assignment of these values to the variables in the input list. For example, the statement

READ *, HGHT0, VELOC0, TIME

assigns values to the variables HGHT0, VELOC0, and TIME. Therefore, this single READ statement replaces the three assignment statements used to assign values to these variables in the preceding examples. The modified program is shown in Figure 3.5.

```
      PROGRAM PROJEC
****************************************************************
* This program calculates the velocity and height of a projectile  *
* given its initial height, initial velocity, and constant         *
* acceleration.  Variables used are:                               *
*     HGHT0   :  initial height                                    *
*     HGHT    :  height at any time                                *
*     VELOC0  :  initial vertical velocity                         *
*     VELOC   :  vertical velocity at any time                     *
*     ACCEL   :  vertical acceleration                             *
*     TIME    :  time elapsed since projectile was launched        *
****************************************************************

      REAL HGHT0, HGHT, VELOC0, VELOC, ACCEL, TIME

      ACCEL = -9.807
      READ *, HGHT0, VELOC0, TIME
      HGHT = 0.5 * ACCEL * TIME ** 2  +  VELOC0 * TIME  +  HGHT0
      VELOC = ACCEL * TIME + VELOC0
      PRINT *, 'AT TIME ', TIME, ' THE VERTICAL VELOCITY IS ', VELOC
      PRINT *, 'AND THE HEIGHT IS ', HGHT
      END
```

Figure 3.5

The values assigned to the variables in the input list may be prepared in advance and saved on punched cards or in a file and read from these sources during program execution. This is the typical procedure followed in a batch mode of operation. In an interactive mode the values may be entered by the user during program execution. In both modes, all columns of the input line may be used, and the following rules apply:

1. A new line of data is processed each time a READ statement is executed.
2. If there are fewer entries in a line of input data than there are variables in the input list, successive lines of input data are processed until values for all variables in the input list have been obtained.
3. If there are more entries in a line of input data than there are variables in the input list, the first data values are used, and all remaining values are ignored.
4. The entries in each line of input data must be constants and of the same type as the variables to which they are assigned. (However, an integer value may be assigned to a real variable, with automatic conversion taking place.)
5. Consecutive entries in a line of input data must be separated by a comma or by one or more spaces.

For example, to assign the values 100.0, 90.0, and 4.3 to the variables HGHT0, VELOC0, and TIME, respectively, in the statement

```
READ *, HGHTO, VELOCO, TIME
```

the following line of input data could be used:

```
100.0, 90.0, 4.3
```

Spaces could be used as separators in place of the commas,

```
100.0 90.0 4.3
```

or more than one line of data could be used:

```
100.0 90.0
4.3
```

In a batch mode of operation, these lines of input data, together with the program and certain command lines, are placed in a file (or on punched cards) prepared by the user. When a READ statement is encountered, the values from these data lines are retrieved automatically and assigned to the variables in the input list.

In an interactive mode of operation, the values assigned to variables in an input list are entered during program execution. In this case, when a READ statement is encountered, program execution is suspended while the user enters values for all variables in the input list. Program execution then automatically resumes. Because execution is interrupted by a READ statement and because the correct number and types of values must be entered before execution can resume, *it is good practice to provide some message to prompt the user when it is necessary to enter data values*. This is accomplished by preceding each READ statement with a PRINT statement that displays the appropriate prompts. The program in Figure 3.6 illustrates this by prompting the user when values for HGHT0, VELOC0, and TIME are to be entered; it is a modification of the program in Figure 3.5.

```
      PROGRAM PROJEC
*****************************************************************************
* This program calculates the velocity and height of a projectile    *
* given its initial height, initial velocity, and constant           *
* acceleration.  Variables used are:                                 *
*     HGHT0    :  initial height                                     *
*     HGHT     :  height at any time                                 *
*     VELOC0   :  initial vertical velocity                          *
*     VELOC    :  vertical velocity at any time                      *
*     ACCEL    :  vertical acceleration                              *
*     TIME     :  time elapsed since projectile was launched         *
*****************************************************************************
      REAL HGHT0, HGHT, VELOC0, VELOC, ACCEL, TIME

      ACCEL = -9.807
      PRINT *, 'ENTER THE INITIAL HEIGHT AND VELOCITY:'
      READ *, HGHT0, VELOC0
      PRINT *, 'ENTER TIME AT WHICH TO CALCULATE HEIGHT AND VELOCITY:'
      READ *, TIME
      HGHT = 0.5 * ACCEL * TIME ** 2  +  VELOC0 * TIME  +  HGHT0
      VELOC = ACCEL * TIME + VELOC0
      PRINT *, 'AT TIME ', TIME, ' THE VERTICAL VELOCITY IS ', VELOC
      PRINT *, 'AND THE HEIGHT IS ', HGHT
      END
```

Sample runs:
====== ====

```
ENTER THE INITIAL HEIGHT AND VELOCITY:
100.0 90.0
ENTER TIME AT WHICH TO CALCULATE HEIGHT AND VELOCITY:
4.3
AT TIME        4.30000      THE VERTICAL VELOCITY IS       47.8299
AND THE HEIGHT IS       396.334


ENTER THE INITIAL HEIGHT AND VELOCITY:
150.0 100.0
ENTER TIME AT WHICH TO CALCULATE HEIGHT AND VELOCITY:
5.0
AT TIME        5.00000      THE VERTICAL VELOCITY IS       50.9650
AND THE HEIGHT IS       527.412
```

Figure 3.6

Figure 3.6 (continued)

```
ENTER THE INITIAL HEIGHT AND VELOCITY:
150.0 100.0
ENTER TIME AT WHICH TO CALCULATE HEIGHT AND VELOCITY:
0
AT TIME      0.000000E+00 THE VERTICAL VELOCITY IS      100.000
AND THE HEIGHT IS      150.000


ENTER THE INITIAL HEIGHT AND VELOCITY:
150.0 100.0
ENTER TIME AT WHICH TO CALCULATE HEIGHT AND VELOCITY:
21.79
AT TIME       21.7900    THE VERTICAL VELOCITY IS      -113.695
AND THE HEIGHT IS     0.798088
```

3.6 Program Composition: The PROGRAM, STOP, and END Statements

In Section 3.1 we noted that a simple FORTRAN program has the format

> PROGRAM statement
> Opening documentation
> Variable declarations
> Program statements
> END

The **PROGRAM statement** has the form

> PROGRAM *name*

where *name* is a legal FORTRAN name; that is, it consists of up to six letters or digits, the first of which must be a letter. This name must be distinct from all other names used in the program. It should be chosen to indicate the purpose of the program. Thus, the first statement in the program of Figure 3.6 to calculate the height and velocity of a projectile is

```
PROGRAM PROJEC
```

The PROGRAM statement is optional, but if it is used, it must appear as the first statement in the program.

Following the PROGRAM statement there should be **opening documentation** that explains the purpose of the program, clarifies the choice of variable names, and provides other pertinent information about the program. This documentation consists of comment lines, which are blank lines or lines having the letter C or an asterisk (*) in the first position of the line. Comment lines are not considered to be program statements and may be placed anywhere in the program. Such comment lines can be used to clarify the purpose and structure of key parts of the program. Program documentation is invaluable when revisions and modifications are made in the future, especially when they are made by persons other than the original programmer.

The **variable declaration part** of a program must appear next. This part consists of type statements whose purpose is to specify the type of each of the variables used in the program. For example, the statement

```
REAL HGHT0, HGHT, VELOC0, VELOC, ACCEL, TIME
```

specifies that HGHT0, HGHT, VELOC0, VELOC, ACCEL, and TIME are real variables.

Type statements and the PROGRAM statement are called **nonexecutable statements** because they provide information that is used during compilation of the program, but they do not cause any specific action to be performed during execution. These nonexecutable statements are followed by **executable statements** such as the assignment statement and input/output statements that specify the actions to be performed during the execution of the program. *The last statement of every program must be the* **END statement.** This statement indicates to the compiler the end of the program unit; it also halts execution of the program and thus is an executable statement.

In more complex programs, it may be necessary to stop execution before the END statement is reached. In such cases, execution can be terminated with a **STOP statement.**[1] This statement has the form

    STOP

or

    STOP *constant*

where *constant* is an integer constant with five or fewer digits or is a character constant. Usually the constant is displayed when execution is terminated by a STOP statement of the second form, but the precise form of the termination message depends on the compiler. (The PAUSE statement described in Chapter 13 may be used to interrupt rather than terminate execution and has a form similar to that of the STOP statement.) Although a program may have any number of STOP (or PAUSE) statements, it may have only one END statement, and it must be the last statement of the program.

There are many FORTRAN statements that we have not yet discussed. The placement of these statements in a FORTRAN program will be described as they are considered in the following chapters. (Also, Appendix C contains a diagram displaying the composition of a FORTRAN program.)

---

[1] In some versions of FORTRAN, a STOP statement is required to terminate execution of a program. In these versions, the END statement is not an executable statement and only serves to mark the physical end of the program.

3.7 Example: Acidity of a Diluted Mixture

In this chapter we have introduced several FORTRAN statements, operations, and functions and have considered how they are used in a FORTRAN program. In this section we present an example illustrating each of the steps of the problem-solving process. The FORTRAN program that results uses only the statements we have considered thus far.

Suppose that the manufacturing process for castings at a certain plant includes cooling each casting in a water bath, followed by cleaning it by immersion in an acid bath. When the casting is transferred from the water bath to the acid bath, a certain amount of water accompanies it, thereby diluting the acid. When the casting is removed from the acid bath, the same amount of this diluted mixture is also removed; thus the volume of the liquid in the acid bath remains constant, but the acidity decreases each time a casting is immersed. We wish to design a program to determine the acidity of the liquid in the acid bath after a given number of castings are immersed and to determine when the acidity falls below some lower limit at which the mixture becomes too diluted to clean the castings.

The input to the program consists of the volume of the acid bath, the amount of water that is mixed with the acid when a casting is transferred from the water bath, the number of castings immersed, and the lower limit on the acidity. The output must include a measure of the acidity after the specified number of castings have been immersed and the number of castings that may be immersed before the acidity falls below the specified lower limit.

To solve this problem, we observe that if A is the original amount of acid and W is the amount of water that is mixed in at each stage, the proportion of acid in the mixture when the first casting is immersed is

$$\frac{A}{A + W}$$

When this casting is removed from the acid bath, the amount of acid in the diluted mixture is

$$\left(\frac{A}{A + W} \right) \cdot A$$

This means that when the second casting is immersed, the proportion of acid in the mixture becomes

$$\frac{\left(\dfrac{A}{A + W} \right) \cdot A}{A + W}$$

which can be written equivalently as

$$\left(\frac{A}{A + W} \right)^{2}$$

In general, the proportion of acid in the diluted mixture after n castings have been immersed is given by

$$\left(\frac{A}{A + W}\right)^n$$

This provides the formula needed to solve the first part of the problem.

For the second part, if L denotes the lower limit on acidity, we must determine the least value of n for which

$$\left(\frac{A}{A + W}\right)^n < L$$

Taking logarithms, we find that this inequality is equivalent to

$$n > \frac{\log L}{\log A - \log(A + W)}$$

and the desired value of n is thus the least integer greater than the expression on the right side.

Selecting names for the quantities involved that are somewhat self-explanatory, we arrive at the following algorithm to solve this problem:

ALGORITHM FOR ACID DILUTION PROBLEM

* This algorithm determines the acidity of a diluted mixture in an   *
* acid bath after a given number of castings are immersed in it and   *
* also determines how often the mixture can be used before its   *
* acidity falls below some lower limit. ACID represents the amount   *
* of acid in the mixture, WATER is the amount of water added   *
* with each immersion, and CONCEN is the proportion of acid in   *
* the mixture. The number of castings is NCASTS, and LIMIT   *
* is the lower limit on acidity.   *

1. Enter ACID, WATER, and NCASTS.
2. Calculate CONCEN = (ACID/(ACID + WATER)) ** NCASTS.
3. Display CONCEN.
4. Enter LIMIT.
5. Calculate NCASTS =
        1 + log(LIMIT)/(log(ACID) − log(ACID + WATER)).
6. Display NCASTS.

Figure 3.7 displays this algorithm in flowchart form.

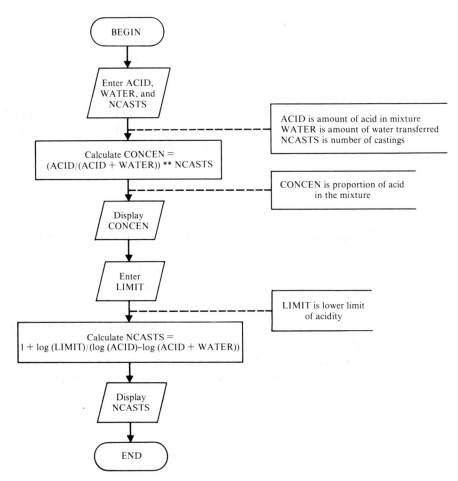

Figure 3.7

The program in Figure 3.8 implements this algorithm. Note the inclusion of the variable directory in the opening documentation of the program to explain what each variable represents. Several sample runs using test data to verify that the program is correct are also shown.

```
      PROGRAM DILUTE
******************************************************************************
* Program to determine the acidity of a diluted mixture in an acid    *
* bath after a given number of castings are immersed in it, and to    *
* determine how often the mixture can be used before its acidity falls *
* below some specified lower limit.  Variables used are:              *
*     ACID    :  Amount of acid in the mixture                        *
*     WATER   :  Amount of water added with each casting immersion    *
*     CONCEN  :  Proportion of acid in the mixture                    *
*     NCASTS  :  Number of castings                                   *
*     LIMIT   :  Lower limit on acidity                               *
******************************************************************************
```

Figure 3.8

Figure 3.8 (continued)

```
        INTEGER NCASTS
        REAL ACID, WATER, CONCEN, LIMIT

        PRINT *, 'ENTER ORIGINAL AMOUNT OF ACID, AMOUNT OF WATER ADDED'
        PRINT *, 'AND THE NUMBER OF CASTINGS'
        READ *, ACID, WATER, NCASTS
        CONCEN = (ACID / (ACID + WATER)) ** NCASTS
        PRINT *, 'THE PROPORTION OF ACID IN THE MIXTURE AFTER'
        PRINT *, NCASTS, ' IMMERSIONS IS ', CONCEN
        PRINT *, 'NOW ENTER THE LOWER LIMIT ON THE ACIDITY'
        READ *, LIMIT
        NCASTS = 1 + LOG(LIMIT) / (LOG(ACID) - LOG(ACID + WATER))
        PRINT *, NCASTS, ' CASTINGS CAN BE IMMERSED BEFORE THE ACIDITY'
        PRINT *, 'FALLS BELOW THIS LIMIT'
        END
```

Test run #1:
===========


```
ENTER ORIGINAL AMOUNT OF ACID, AMOUNT OF WATER ADDED
AND THE NUMBER OF CASTINGS
100, 100, 1
THE PROPORTION OF ACID IN THE MIXTURE AFTER
        1 IMMERSIONS IS      0.500000
NOW ENTER THE LOWER LIMIT ON THE ACIDITY
.9
        1 CASTINGS CAN BE IMMERSED BEFORE THE ACIDITY
FALLS BELOW THIS LIMIT
```


Test run #2:
===========


```
ENTER ORIGINAL AMOUNT OF ACID, AMOUNT OF WATER ADDED
AND THE NUMBER OF CASTINGS
100, 100, 2
THE PROPORTION OF ACID IN THE MIXTURE AFTER
        2 IMMERSIONS IS      0.250000
NOW ENTER THE LOWER LIMIT ON THE ACIDITY
.1
        4 CASTINGS CAN BE IMMERSED BEFORE THE ACIDITY
FALLS BELOW THIS LIMIT
```


Test run #3:
===========


```
ENTER ORIGINAL AMOUNT OF ACID, AMOUNT OF WATER ADDED
AND THE NUMBER OF CASTINGS
90, 10, 2
THE PROPORTION OF ACID IN THE MIXTURE AFTER
        2 IMMERSIONS IS      0.810000
NOW ENTER THE LOWER LIMIT ON THE ACIDITY
.7
        4 CASTINGS CAN BE IMMERSED BEFORE THE ACIDITY
FALLS BELOW THIS LIMIT
```

Figure 3.8 (continued)

```
Test run #4:
============


ENTER ORIGINAL AMOUNT OF ACID, AMOUNT OF WATER ADDED
AND THE NUMBER OF CASTINGS
400, .05, 190
THE PROPORTION OF ACID IN THE MIXTURE AFTER
        190 IMMERSIONS IS       0.976513
NOW ENTER THE LOWER LIMIT ON THE ACIDITY
.75
        2308 CASTINGS CAN BE IMMERSED BEFORE THE ACIDITY
FALLS BELOW THIS LIMIT
```

Exercises

1. Write a program to read the lengths of the two legs of a right triangle and to calculate and print the area of the triangle (one-half the product of the legs) and the length of the hypotenuse (square root of the sum of the squares of the legs).

2. The Pythagorean theorem states that the sum of the squares of the sides of a right triangle is equal to the square of the hypotenuse. Thus, for a right triangle with sides 3 and 4, the length of the hypotenuse is 5. Similarly, a right triangle with sides 5 and 12 has a hypotenuse of 13, and a right triangle with sides 8 and 15 has a hypotenuse of 17. Triples such as 3, 4, 5, or 5, 12, 13, or 8, 15, 17, which represent the two sides and the hypotenuse of a right triangle, are called *Pythagorean triples*. There are infinitely many such triples, and they all can be generated by the formulas

$$\text{side1} = m^2 - n^2$$

$$\text{side2} = 2mn$$

$$\text{hypotenuse} = m^2 + n^2$$

where m and n are positive integers and $m > n$. Write a program that reads values for m and n and then calculates the Pythagorean triple that is generated by these formulas.

3. Write a program to read values for the three sides a, b, and c of a triangle and then calculate its perimeter and its area. These should be printed together with the values of a, b, and c using appropriate labels. (For the area, you might use Hero's formula for the area of a triangle:

$$\text{area} = \sqrt{s(s - a)(s - b)(s - c)}$$

where s is one-half the perimeter.)

4. The current in an alternating current circuit that contains resistance, capacitance, and inductance in series is given by

$$I = \frac{E}{\sqrt{R^2 + (2\pi fL - 1/2\pi fC)^2}}$$

where I = current (amperes), E = voltage (volts), R = resistance (ohms), L = inductance (henrys), C = capacitance (farads), and f = frequency (hertz). Write a program that reads values for the voltage, resistance, inductance, capacitance, and frequency and then calculates and displays the current.

5. The minimum velocity V_0 with which a space ship to the moon must be launched from the earth to escape the earth's gravitational field is called the *escape velocity* and can be calculated by

$$V_0^2 = 2gE - \frac{200E^2}{81(D + M + E)} + \frac{2gE^2}{81(D + M)}$$

where E is the radius of the earth, M is the radius of the moon, D is the distance between the earth and moon, and g is the acceleration due to gravity on earth. If there is no attraction of the space ship by the moon or any other celestial body, the escape velocity is given by

$$V_0^2 = 2gE$$

Write a program that reads values for D, E, and M (e.g., D = 240000, E = 4000, and M = 1000), calculates the escape velocity using each of these two formulas, and then displays each and the difference between them.

6. The speed in miles per hour of a satellite moving in a circular orbit about a celestial body is given approximately by

$$\text{speed} = \sqrt{\frac{C}{D}}$$

where C is a constant depending on the celestial body and D is the distance from the center of the celestial body to the satellite (in miles). Write a program that reads the value of the constant C for a celestial body and a value for D and that then displays the speed of the satellite. Run the program with the following values: (earth) C = 1.2E12; (moon) C = 1.5E10; (Mars) C = 1.3E11.

7. One set of *polar coordinates* of a point in a plane is given by (r, θ), where r is the length of the ray from the origin to the point and θ is the measure of an angle from the positive x axis to this ray.

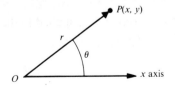

Write a program that reads polar coordinates for a point and calculates and displays its rectangular coordinates (x, y) obtained by using the formulas

$$x = r \cos \theta$$

$$y = r \sin \theta$$

8. The equation of the curve formed by a hanging cable weighing w pounds per foot of length can be described by

$$y = a \cosh \frac{x}{a}$$

where $a = H/w$ with H representing the horizontal tension pulling on the cable at its low point and cosh is the hyperbolic cosine function defined by

$$\cosh u = \frac{e^u + e^{-u}}{2}$$

Write a program that reads values of w, H, and x and calculates and displays the corresponding value of y.

9. Write a program to convert a measurement given in feet to the equivalent number of (a) yards, (b) feet, (c) inches, (d) centimeters, and (e) meters. (1 foot = 12 inches, 1 yard = 3 feet, 1 inch = 2.54 centimeters, 1 meter = 100 centimeters.) Read the number of feet, and print the number of yards, number of feet, number of inches, number of centimeters, and number of meters, with appropriate labels.

10. The formula for the volume of an oblate spheroid, such as the earth, is

$$V = \frac{4}{3} \pi a^2 b$$

where a and b are the half-lengths of the major and minor axes, respectively. Write a program that reads values for a and b and then calculates and displays the volume. Use your program to find the volume of the earth for which the values of a and b are 3963 miles and 3950 miles, respectively.

11. In order for a shaft with an allowable shear strength of S lbs/in^2 to transmit a torque of T in-lbs, it must have a diameter of at least D inches, where D is given by

$$D = \sqrt[3]{\frac{16T}{S}}$$

If P horsepower is applied to the shaft at a rotational speed of N rpm, the torque is given by

$$T = 63000 \frac{P}{N}$$

Write a program that reads values for P, N, and S and calculates the torque developed and the required diameter to transmit that torque. Run your program with the following inputs:

P (hp)	N (rpm)	S (psi)
20	1500	5000
20	50	5000
270	40	6500

12. The period of a pendulum is given by the formula

$$P = 2\pi \sqrt{\frac{L}{g}\left(1 + \frac{1}{4}\sin^2\left(\frac{\alpha}{2}\right)\right)}$$

where

$g = 980$ cm/sec^2

L = pendulum length

α = angle of displacement

Write a program to read values for L and α and calculate the period of a pendulum having this length and angle of displacement. Run your program with the following inputs:

L (cm)	α (degrees)
120	15
90	20
60	5
74.6	10
83.6	12

13. A containing tank is to be constructed that will hold 500 cubic meters of oil when filled. The shape of the tank is to be that of a cylinder (including a base) surmounted by a cone, whose height is equal to its radius. The material and labor costs to construct the cylindrical portion of the tank are $300 per square meter, and the costs for the conical top are $400 per square meter. Write a program that calculates the heights of the cylinder and the cone for a given radius that is input and that also calculates the total cost to construct the tank. Starting with a radius of 4.0 meters and incrementing it by various (small) step sizes, run your program several times to determine the dimensions of the tank that will result in the least cost.

14. Write a program to read the thickness, density, and outside radius of a hollow ball and to calculate its volume and the mass. Starting with a value of 0.2 cm, run your program several times to find the largest wall thickness of a copper ball (density = .0089 kg/cm^3) with an

outside radius of 50.0 cm that will float in water. (For the ball to float, its volume must be at least 1000 times its mass.)

15. The declining balance formula for calculating depreciation is

$$V_N = V_0(1 - R)^N$$

where

V_N = the value after N years

V_0 = the initial value

R = the rate of depreciation

N = the number of years

Write a program to read values for V_0, R, and N and to calculate the depreciated value. Run the program several times to find the depreciated value of a new machine just purchased by Dispatch Die-Casting for $50,000 at the end of each year of its useful life. Assume that the rate of depreciation is 12 percent and that the usual life of the machine is five years.

16. The castings produced at Dispatch Die-Casting must be shipped in special containers that are available in four sizes—huge, large, medium, and small—which can hold 50, 20, 5, and 1 casting, respectively. Write a program that reads the number of castings to be shipped and displays the number of containers needed to send the shipment most efficiently. The output for input value 598 should be similar to the following:

```
CONTAINER    NUMBER
HUGE           11
LARGE          2
MEDIUM         1
SMALL          3
```

Run the program for 3, 18, 48, and 10598 castings.

17. The length of the line segment joining two points $P_1(x_1, y_1)$ and $P_2(x_2, y_2)$ is given by

$$\sqrt{(x_2 - x_1)^2 + (y_2 - y_1)^2}$$

and the midpoint of the segment has the coordinates

$$\left(\frac{x_1 + x_2}{2}, \frac{y_1 + y_2}{2}\right)$$

The slope of the line through P_1 and P_2 is given by

$$\frac{y_2 - y_1}{x_2 - x_1}$$

(provided $x_1 \neq x_2$), and the slope-intercept equation of this line is

$$y = mx + b$$

where m is the slope and b is the y intercept; b can be calculated by

$$b = y_1 - mx_1$$

The perpendicular bisector of the line segment joining P_1 and P_2 is the line through the midpoint of this segment having slope $-1/m$ (provided $m \neq 0$). Write a program that reads the coordinates of two points, P_1 and P_2, with distinct x coordinates and distinct y coordinates and calculates and displays the length of the segment P_1P_2, the midpoint of the segment, the slope of the line through P_1 and P_2, its y intercept, its slope-intercept equation, and the equation of the perpendicular bisector of P_1P_2.

18. Write a program that will read a student's number as well as his or her old grade point average (GPA) and old number of course credits (for example, 34179, 3.25, 19) and then print these with appropriate labels. Then read the course credit and grade for each of four courses; for example, C1 = 1.0, G1 = 3.7, C2 = 0.5, G2 = 4.0, and so on. Calculate

old number of honor points =

(old # of course credits) $*$ (old GPA)

new number of honor points = C1 $*$ G1 $+ \cdots +$ C4 $*$ G4

total # of new course credits = C1 + C2 + C3 + C4

$$\text{current GPA} = \frac{\text{# of new honor points}}{\text{# of new course credits}}$$

Print the current GPA with an appropriate label. Then calculate cumulative GPA =

$$\frac{(\text{# of old honor points}) + (\text{# of new honor points})}{(\text{# of old course credits}) + (\text{# of new course credits})}$$

and print this with a label.

Programming Pointers

In this section we consider some aspects of program design and suggest guidelines for good programming style. We also point out some errors that may occur in writing FORTRAN programs.

Program Design

1. *Programs cannot be considered correct until they have been validated using test data.* Test all programs with data for which the results are known or can be checked by hand calculations.

2. *Programs should be readable and understandable.*

- *Use meaningful variable names that suggest what each variable represents.* For example,

    ```
    DIST = RATE * TIME
    ```

    is more meaningful than

    ```
    D = R * T
    ```

    or

    ```
    Z7 = ALPHA * X
    ```

    Also, avoid "cute" identifiers, as in

    ```
    HOWFAR = GOGO * SQUEAL
    ```

- *Do not use "magic numbers."* To illustrate, suppose that the statements

    ```
    CHANGE = (.1758 - .1257) * POPUL
    POPUL = POPUL + CHANGE
    ```

    appear at one point in a program and the statements

    ```
    POPINC = .1758 * POPUL
    POPDEC = .1257 * POPUL
    ```

    appear later. In these statements, the constants .1758 and .1257 magically appear, without explanation. If they must be changed, it will be necessary for someone to search through the program to determine what they represent and which are the appropriate ones to change, and to locate all the places where they appear. To make the program more understandable and to minimize the number of statements that must be changed when other values are required, it is better to associate these constants with names, as in

    ```
    * Set birth rate and death rate
        BIRTH = .1758
        DEATH = .1257
    ```

    or

    ```
    PRINT *, 'ENTER BIRTH RATE AND DEATH RATE'
    READ *, BIRTH, DEATH
    ```

    (or in DATA statements or PARAMETER statements as described later) and then use these names in place of the magic numbers:

    ```
    CHANGE = (BIRTH - DEATH) * POPUL
    POPUL = POPUL + CHANGE
                 .
                 .
    POPINC = BIRTH * POPUL
    POPDEC = DEATH * POPUL
    ```

- *Use comments to describe the purpose of a program, the meaning of variables, and the purpose of key program segments.* However, don't clutter the program with needless comments; for example, the comment

```
* ADD 1 TO COUNT
      COUNT = COUNT + 1
```

is not helpful in explaining the statement that follows it and so should be omitted.

● *Label all output produced by a program.* For example,

```
PRINT *, 'RATE = ', RATE, ' TIME = ', TIME
```

produces more informative output than does

```
PRINT *, RATE, TIME
```

3. *Programs should be efficient.* For example, duplicate computations as in

```
ROOT1 = (−B + SQRT(B * B − 4 * A * C)) / (2 * A)
ROOT2 = (−B − SQRT(B * B − 4 * A * C)) / (2 * A)
```

should be avoided. It is not efficient to calculate the value of B * B − 4 * A * C or its square root twice; instead calculate it once, assign it to a variable, and then use this variable in these calculations.

4. *Programs should be general and flexible.* They should solve a class of problems rather than one specific problem. It should be relatively easy to modify a program to solve a related problem without changing much of the program. Avoiding the use of magic numbers, as described in Programming Pointer 2, is important in this regard.

Potential Problems

1. *Do not confuse* I *or* l *(lower case "ell") and* 1 *or* 0 *(zero) and* O *(the letter "oh").* For example, the statement

```
STOP
```

produces an error, because the numeral 0 is used in place of the letter O. Many programmers distinguish between these in handwritten programs by writing the numeral 0 as Ø.

2. *When preparing a FORTRAN program, do not let any statement extend past column 72.* Most FORTRAN compilers will ignore any characters beyond column 72, which can easily lead to errors caused by incomplete statements. For example, if one uses

```
PRINT * 'FOR THE X−VALUE ', X, ' THE CORRESPONDING Y−VALUE IS ', Y
```

in a program where the last character (Y) is in column 73, an error message such as the following may result:

```
PRINT *, 'FOR THE X−VALUE ', X, ' THE CORRESPONDING Y−VALUE IS ',
*** Input/output list is incomplete
```

3. *String constants must be enclosed within single quotes.* If either the beginning or ending quote is missing, an error results. An apostrophe is represented in a string constant as a pair of apostrophes, for example,

```
'ISN''T'.
```

4. *String constants should not be broken at the end of a line.* All character positions through column 72 of a line are read, and unintended blanks may be produced in a string constant. For example, the statement

```
   PRINT *, 'ENTER THE VALUES ON SEPARATE LINES. SEPARATE
 + THEM BY COMMAS.'
```

produces the output

```
ENTER THE VALUES ON SEPARATE LINES. SEPARATE          THEM BY COMMAS.
```

5. *All multiplications must be indicated by* $*$. For example, $2 * N$ is valid, but 2N is not.

6. *Division of integers produces an integer.* For example, 1 / 2 has the value 0.

7. *Parentheses within expressions must be paired.* For each left parenthesis there must be a matching right parenthesis.

8. *All variables are initially undefined.* Although some compilers may initialize variables to specific values (e.g., 0 for numeric variables), it should be assumed that all variables are initially undefined. For example, the statement $Y = X + 1$ usually produces a "garbage" value for Y if X has not previously been assigned a value.

9. *A value assigned to a variable must be of a type that is appropriate to the type of the variable.* Thus entering the value 2.7 for an integer variable NUMBER in the statement

```
   READ *, NUMBER
```

may generate an error message such as

```
   INPUT/OUTPUT ERROR.    2.7
                           ↑
```

However, an integer value read for a real variable is automatically converted to real type.

10. *The types of all variables should be declared in type statements.* Any variable whose type is not explicitly specified will have its type determined by the FORTRAN naming convention. Thus, if the variable NUMBER has not been declared to be of real type, the function reference SQRT(NUMBER) causes an error since SQRT requires a real argument and NUMBER is of integer type according to the naming convention. If A, B, and C are real variables but NUMBER has not

been declared real, the statement

        NUMBER = −B + SQRT(B ** 2 − 4 * A * C)

calculates the real value of the expression on the right side correctly, but then assigns only the integer part to NUMBER.

11. *A comma must precede the input/output list in input/output statements of the form*

READ *, *input-list*
PRINT *, *output-list*

Program Style

In the examples in this text, we adopt certain stylistic guidelines for FORTRAN programs, and you should write your programs in a similar style. The following standards are used (others are described in the Programming Pointers of subsequent chapters).

1. When a statement is continued from one line to another, indent the continuation line(s).

2. Document each program with comment lines at the beginning of the program to explain the purpose of the program and what the variables represent. You should also include in this documentation your name, date, course number, assignment number, and so on.

3. Break up long expressions into simpler subexpressions.

4. Insert a blank comment line between the opening documentation and the specification statements at the beginning of the program and between these statements and the rest of the program.

5. To improve readability, insert a blank space between the items in a FORTRAN statement such as before and after assignment operators and arithmetic operators.

Variations and Extensions

Variations and extensions of the features described in this chapter are provided in many versions of FORTRAN (see Appendix F for details). Some of these are

- The number of continuation lines may be different from the 19 lines specified in standard FORTRAN.

- Some upper limit may be imposed on the length of a character string.

- Free form source code may be allowed.

- Modified forms of the type statements may be allowed or required. For example, INTEGER∗2 and INTEGER∗4 are common type specifiers used to specify short integers $(-2^{15}, \ldots, 2^{15} - 1)$ and long integers $(-2^{31}, \ldots, 2^{31} - 1)$, respectively.

- It may be possible to initialize variables in type statements.

- Longer variable names may be allowed.

- Other characters (blanks, dollar signs) may be allowed in variable names.

- Lower case letters may be allowed.

- Modified forms of the input/output statements may be allowed or required. Common alternatives to PRINT ∗, *list* and READ ∗, *list* are

  WRITE (∗,∗) *list*   and   READ (∗,∗) *list*

- Assignment of character expressions to numeric variables (and of numeric expressions to character variables) may be allowed.

- It may be necessary to use a STOP statement (before the END statement) to terminate execution.

4

Control Structures

A journey of a thousand miles begins with a single step.

ANCIENT PROVERB

Then Logic would take you by the throat, and force you to do it!

Achilles in LEWIS CARROLL'S
What the Tortoise Said to Achilles

But what has been said once can always be repeated.

ZENO OF ELEA

In Chapter 2 we described several techniques that assist in designing programs that are easy to understand and whose logical flow is easy to follow. Such programs are more likely to be correct when first written than are poorly structured programs; and if they are not correct, the errors are easier to find and correct. Such programs are also easier to modify, which is especially important, if such modifications must be made by someone other than the original programmer.

In a **structured program,** the logical flow is governed by three basic control structures:

1. Sequential
2. Selection
3. Repetition

Sequential structure, as illustrated in Figure 4.1, simply refers to the sequential execution of the statements in the order in which they appear in the program. The sample programs in Chapter 3 are **straight-line programs** in which the only control used is sequential.

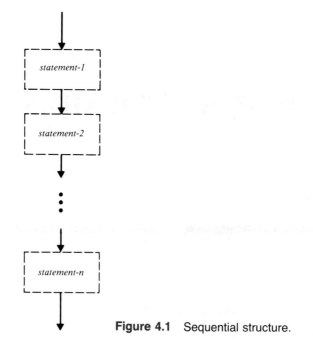

Figure 4.1 Sequential structure.

Selection structures make possible the selection and execution of one of a number of alternative blocks of statements. This enables the programmer to introduce decision points in a program, that is, points at which a decision is made *during program execution* to follow one of several courses of action.

Repetition structures make possible the construction of a **loop,** that is, the controlled repetition of a block of statements. This block may be executed repeatedly a predetermined number of times, or repetition may be controlled by some logical expression.

Because logical expressions are used extensively in selection and repetition structures, we begin this chapter by considering them. We then introduce several control statements that can be used to implement selection and repetition structures in FORTRAN.

4.1 Logical Expressions

In the preceding chapter we discussed numeric expressions in which numeric quantities (integer and real) are combined using arithmetic operations ($+$, $-$, $*$, $/$, $**$) and functions (such as SQRT and MOD) yielding numeric results. It is also possible to construct nonnumeric expressions in which nonnumeric quantities (character and logical) are combined using appropriate operations and functions to give nonnumeric results. In this section we introduce logical expressions and use them in later sections to implement selection and repetition structures. (Chapter 6 describes in more detail the logical data type and the character data type.)

Logical expressions may be either simple or compound. The most common simple logical expressions are **relational expressions** of the form

expression-1 relational-operator expression-2

where *expression-1* and *expression-2* are numeric expressions, and the *relational-operator* may be any of the following:

Symbol	Meaning
.LT.	Is less than
.GT.	Is greater than
.EQ.	Is equal to
.LE.	Is less than or equal to
.GE.	Is greater than or equal to
.NE.	Is not equal to

The periods must appear as parts of these relational symbols, because they serve to distinguish a logical expression such as X.EQ.Y from the variable XEQY.

The following are examples of simple logical expressions:

```
X .LT. 5.2
B ** 2 .GE. 4 * A * C
NUMBER .EQ. 500
```

If X has the value 4.5, the logical expression X .LT. 5.2 is true. If NUMBER has the value 400, the logical expression NUMBER .EQ. 500 is false.

When using the relational operators .EQ. and .NE., it is important to remember that *most real values cannot be stored exactly* (see Section 1.3). *Consequently, logical expressions formed by comparing real quantities with* .EQ. *are often evaluated as false, even though these quantities are algebraically equal.* This is illustrated by the program in Figure 4.3.

Compound logical expressions are formed by combining logical expressions by using the **logical operators**

```
.NOT.
.AND.
.OR.
.EQV.
.NEQV.
```

These operators are defined as follows:

Logical Operator	Logical Expression	Definition
		.NOT. P is true if P is false.
.AND.	P .AND. Q	*Conjunction* of P and Q: P .AND. Q is true if both P and Q are true; it is false otherwise.
.OR.	P .OR. Q	*Disjunction* of P and Q: P .OR. Q is true if P or Q or both are true; it is false otherwise.
.EQV.	P .EQV. Q	*Equivalence* of P and Q: P .EQV. Q is true if both P and Q are true or both are false; it is false otherwise.
.NEQV.	P .NEQV. Q	*Nonequivalence* of P and Q: P .NEQV. Q is the negation of P .EQV. Q; it is true if one of P or Q is true and the other is false; it is false otherwise.

These definitions are summarized by the following **truth tables,** which display all possible values for P and Q and the corresponding values of the logical expression:

P	.NOT. P
T	F
F	T

P	Q	P .AND. Q	P .OR. Q	P .EQV. Q	P .NEQV. Q
T	T	T	T	T	F
T	F	F	T	F	T
F	T	F	T	F	T
F	F	F	F	T	F

Logical expressions may contain more than one operator, either relational or logical. For example, if X has the value 1.5, the logical expression

```
X + 1.1 .GT. 1.0 .AND. .NOT. X .LT. 0.5
```

or with parentheses inserted to improve readability,

```
(X + 1.1 .GT. 1.0) .AND. .NOT. (X .LT. 0.5)
```

is true.

Note that the logical operators .NOT., .AND., .OR., .EQV., and .NEQV. operate only on *logical* expressions. Thus, if NUMBER is an integer variable,

```
NUMBER .EQ. 1 .OR. NUMBER .EQ. 2
```

is valid, whereas

    NUMBER .EQ. 1 .OR. 2

is not, since 2 is not a logical expression.

When a logical expression contains several operators, the order in which they are performed is

1. Relational operators (.GT., .GE., .EQ., .NE., .LT., .LE.)
2. .NOT.
3. .AND.
4. .OR.
5. .EQV. and .NEQV.

Parentheses may be used in the usual way to modify this order. For example, if A, B, and C represent logical expressions, then in the logical expression

    (A .AND. B) .OR. C

the term in parentheses is evaluated first; thus, this expression is true if C is true or both A and B are true. Note that this is equivalent to the expression

    A .AND. B .OR. C

according to the preceding order of priority. In the expression

    A .AND. (B .OR. C)

the parenthesized term is evaluated first; thus, the expression is true if A is true and B or C is true.

Exercises

1. Assuming that M and N are integer variables with the values -5 and 8, respectively, and that X, Y, and Z are real variables with values -3.56, 0, and 44.7, respectively, find the values of the following logical expressions:

   (a) M .LE. N
   (b) 2 * ABS(M) .LE. 8
   (c) X*X .LT. SQRT(Z)
   (d) NINT(Z) .EQ. (6 * N - 3)
   (e) (X .LE. Y) .AND. (Y .LE. Z)
   (f) .NOT. (X .LT. Y)
   (g) .NOT. ((M .LE. N) .AND. (X + Z .GT. Y))
   (h) .NOT. (M .LE. N) .OR. .NOT. (X + Z .GT. Y)
   (i) .NOT. ((M .GT. N) .OR. (X .LT. Z)) .EQV.
          ((M .LE. N) .AND. (X .GE. Z))
   (j) .NOT. ((M .GT. N) .AND. (X .LT. Z)) .NEQV.
          ((M .LE. N) .AND. (X .GE. Z))

2. Assuming that A, B, and C are logical variables, use truth tables to display the values of the following logical expressions for all possible values of A, B, and C:

   (a) A .OR. .NOT. B
   (b) .NOT. (A .AND. B)
   (c) .NOT. A .OR. .NOT. B
   (d) A .AND. .TRUE. .OR. (1 + 2 .EQ. 4)
   (e) A .AND. (B .OR. C)
   (f) (A .AND. B) .OR. (A .AND. C)

3. Write logical expressions to express the following conditions:

   (a) X is greater than 3.
   (b) Y is strictly between 2 and 5.
   (c) R is negative and Z is positive.
   (d) ALPHA and BETA both are positive.
   (e) ALPHA and BETA have the same sign (both are negative or both are positive).
   (f) $-5 < X < 5$.
   (g) A is less than 6 or is greater than 10.
   (h) P = Q = R.
   (i) X is less than 3, or Y is less than 3, but not both.

4. Given the logical variables A, B, and C, write a logical expression that is

   (a) true if and only if A and B are true and C is false.
   (b) true if and only if A is true and at least one of B or C is true.
   (c) true if and only if exactly one of A and B is true.

4.2 Selection Structure: The Logical IF Statement

A **selection structure** makes possible the selection of one of several alternative actions, depending on the value of a logical expression. The simplest selection structure is pictured in Figure 4.2. In this structure, a single statement is executed or bypassed depending on whether the value of a given logical expression is true or false.

Figure 4.2

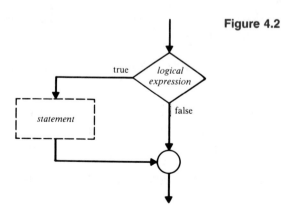

This selection structure is implemented in FORTRAN by using a **logical IF statement** of the form

IF (*logical-expression*) *statement*

If the logical expression is true, the designated statement is executed; otherwise, it is bypassed. The statement must be an executable statement, but it cannot be another logical IF statement, an END statement, a DO statement, or any statement that is part of the block IF structure. (These last two statements are discussed in subsequent sections of this chapter.) It is important to note that *the logical expression in a logical IF statement must be enclosed in parentheses*.

As examples of logical IF statements, consider the following statements where N is an integer variable, DISC and X are real variables:

```
IF (DISC .GE. 0) DISC = SQRT(DISC)
IF (1.5 .LE. X .AND. X .LT. 2.5) PRINT *, X
```

In the first example, the value of DISC is compared with 0 to determine the truth or falsity of the logical expression DISC .GE. 0. If this logical expression is true, the assignment statement DISC = SQRT(DISC) is executed; otherwise, it is bypassed. In the second example, if $1.5 \leq X < 2.5$, the value of X is printed; otherwise, the PRINT statement is bypassed. For each of these logical IF statements, execution continues with the next statement of the program, regardless of whether the logical expression is true or false.

In the preceding section we noted that because most real values cannot be stored exactly, logical expressions formed by comparing two real quantities with the relational operator .EQ. are often evaluated as false, even though the two quantities are algebraically equal. The program in Figure 4.3 demonstrates this by showing that for most real values X, the value of X $*$ (1 / X) is not 1.

```
      PROGRAM APPROX
**********************************************************************
*        Program to show inexact representation of reals.          *
**********************************************************************

      REAL X, Y

      PRINT *, 'ENTER REAL #'
      READ *, X
      Y = X * (1.0 / X)
      PRINT *, 'X = ', X, 'Y = X*(1/X) = ', Y, '1.0 - Y = ', 1.0 - Y
      IF (Y .EQ. 1) PRINT *, '*** YES ***'
      IF (Y .NE. 1) PRINT *, '*** NO ***'
      END
```

Figure 4.3

Figure 4.3   **(continued)**

```
Sample runs:
===========


ENTER REAL #
.1
X =       0.100000     Y = X*(1/X) =        1.00000     1.0 - Y =       1.192093E-07
*** NO ***


ENTER REAL #
.2
X =       0.200000     Y = X*(1/X) =        1.00000     1.0 - Y =       1.192093E-07
*** NO ***


ENTER REAL #
.3
X =       0.300000     Y = X*(1/X) =        1.00000     1.0 - Y =       1.192093E-07
*** NO ***


ENTER REAL #
.4
X =       0.400000     Y = X*(1/X) =        1.00000     1.0 - Y =       1.192093E-07
*** NO ***


ENTER REAL #
.5
X =       0.500000     Y = X*(1/X) =        1.00000     1.0 - Y =       0.000000E+00
*** YES ***


ENTER REAL #
.6
X =       0.600000     Y = X*(1/X) =        1.00000     1.0 - Y =       1.192093E-07
*** NO ***
```

4.3 Selection Structure: The Block IF Statement

The logical IF statement allows the programmer to specify only a single statement to be executed if a given logical expression is true. The **block IF statement** is more powerful because it allows the programmer to specify a *block* of statements to be executed if a logical expression is true. It may even be used to specify one block of statements to be executed if the logical expression is true and a different block to be executed if it is false.

The form of a block IF statement used to specify a set of statements to be executed if a given logical expression is true is

IF (*logical-expression*) THEN
      statement-1
      statement-2
           ⋮   } *block*
      statement-n
END IF

If the logical expression is true, the entire block of statements between THEN and the END IF statement is executed; otherwise, it is bypassed. In either case, execution continues with the next executable statement following the END IF statement, unless some statement within the block transfers control to some other point in the program or halts execution. Thus this statement implements the selection structure pictured in Figure 4.4.

The selection structure in Figure 4.5 specifies one block of statements to be executed when the logical expression is true but a different block when the logical expression is false. The form of the block IF statement that implements

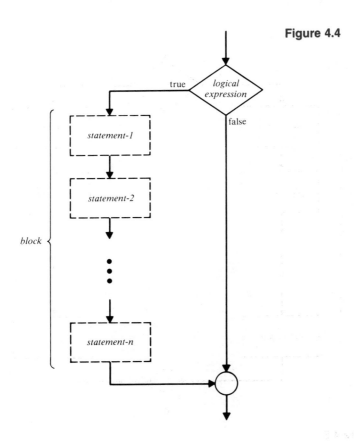

Figure 4.4

this selection structure is

IF (*logical-expression*) THEN
    statement-1 ⎫
    statement-2 ⎬ *block-1*
        ⋮   ⎪
    statement-n ⎭
ELSE
    statement-i   ⎫
    statement-ii ⎬ *block-2*
        ⋮   ⎪
    statement-m ⎭
END IF

If the logical expression is true, the statements in *block-1* are executed, and the statements in *block-2* are bypassed; otherwise, the statements in *block-1* are bypassed, and the statements in *block-2* are executed. In either case, execution continues with the next executable statement following the END IF statement (unless, of course, some statement within one of the blocks transfers control to some other point in the program or stops execution).

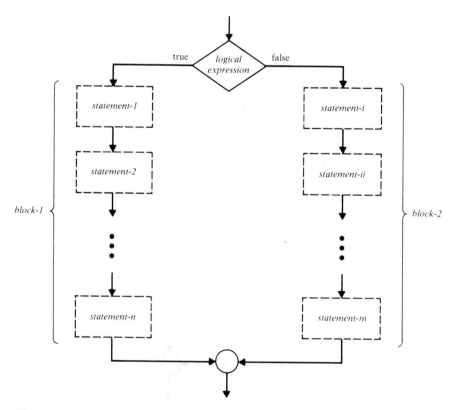

Figure 4.5

As examples of block IF statements, consider the following:

```
IF ((0 .LE. X) .AND. (X .LE. 10.0)) THEN
    Y = SQRT(X)
    PRINT *, X, Y
END IF

IF ((0 .LE. X) .AND. (X .LE. 10.0)) THEN
    Y = SQRT(X)
    PRINT *, X, Y
ELSE
    PRINT *, 'VALUE', X, ' IS OUT OF RANGE'
END IF
```

In the first example, if the value of X is in the range 0 through 10.0, Y is assigned the square root of X, the values of X and Y are displayed, and execution then continues with the next statement of the program. In the second example, an ELSE clause has been attached to specify a course of action in case X is not in this range. As with the first example, if X is in the range 0 through 10.0, its square root is calculated and assigned to Y, the values of X and Y are displayed, the output statement in the ELSE clause bypassed, and execution then continues with the program statement following the END IF. If X is not in the range 0 through 10.0, the assignment statement and the output statement in the IF block are bypassed, the output statement in the ELSE block displays an out-of-range error, and execution then continues with the statement following the END IF.

As another example, consider the problem of calculating the value of the following piecewise continuous function:

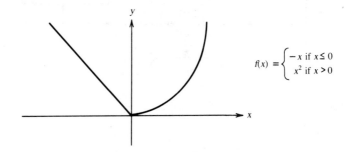

$$f(x) = \begin{cases} -x & \text{if } x \leq 0 \\ x^2 & \text{if } x > 0 \end{cases}$$

A block IF statement makes this very easy to do:

```
IF (X .LE. 0) THEN
    FVAL = -X
ELSE
    FVAL = X ** 2
END IF
```

As another illustration of the block IF statement, consider the problem of solving the quadratic equation

$$Ax^2 + Bx + C = 0$$

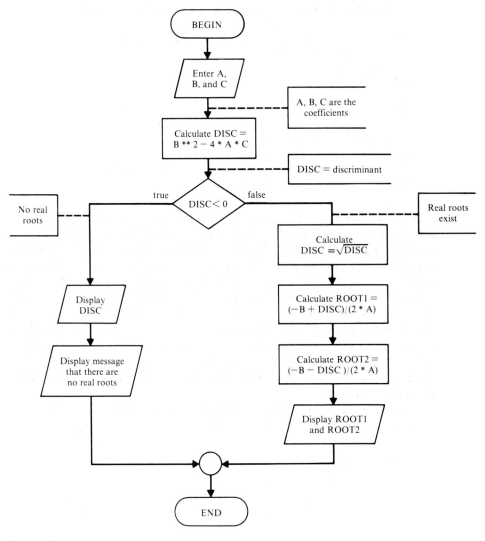

Figure 4.6

by using the quadratic formula to obtain the roots

$$\frac{-B \pm \sqrt{B^2 - 4AC}}{2A}$$

In this problem, the input data are the coefficients A, B, and C of the quadratic equation, and the output is the pair of real roots or a message indicating that there are no real roots (in case $B^2 - 4AC$ is negative). An algorithm for solving a quadratic equation is the following:

ALGORITHM FOR SOLVING QUADRATIC EQUATIONS

```
* This algorithm solves quadratic equations Ax² + Bx + C = 0  *
* using the quadratic formula. The discriminant DISC =        *
* B² − 4AC is checked, and if it is positive, the pair of real roots *
* ROOT1 and ROOT2 is calculated; otherwise, a message is      *
* displayed indicating that there are no real roots.          *
```

1. Enter A, B, and C.
2. Calculate DISC = B ** 2 − 4 * A * C.
3. If DISC < 0 then do the following:
   a. Display DISC.
   b. Display a message that there are no real roots.
   Else do the following:
   a. Calculate DISC = $\sqrt{\text{DISC}}$.
   b. Calculate ROOT1 = (−B + DISC) / (2 * A).
   c. Calculate ROOT2 = (−B − DISC) / (2 * A).
   d. Display ROOT1 and ROOT2.

Figure 4.6 displays this algorithm in flowchart form.

The program in Figure 4.7 implements this algorithm. Note the indentation of the statements within the block IF statement. Although not required, it is good programming style to set off these statements in this manner to emphasize that they constitute a single block.

```
      PROGRAM QUAD1
******************************************************************
* Program to solve a quadratic equation using the quadratic formula.  *
* Variables used are:                                          *
*    A, B, C      : the coefficients of the quadratic equation *
*    DISC         : the discriminant, B ** 2 - 4 * A * C       *
*    ROOT1, ROOT2 : the two roots of the equation              *
******************************************************************

      REAL A, B, C, DISC, ROOT1, ROOT2

      PRINT *, 'ENTER THE COEFFICIENTS OF THE QUADRATIC EQUATION'
      READ *, A, B, C
      DISC = B ** 2 - 4 * A * C
      IF (DISC .LT. 0) THEN
          PRINT *, 'DISCRIMINANT IS', DISC
          PRINT *, 'THERE ARE NO REAL ROOTS'
      ELSE
          DISC = SQRT(DISC)
          ROOT1 = (-B + DISC) / (2 * A)
          ROOT2 = (-B - DISC) / (2 * A)
          PRINT *, 'THE ROOTS ARE', ROOT1, ROOT2
      END IF
      END
```

Figure 4.7

Figure 4.7 (continued)

```
Sample runs:
============


ENTER THE COEFFICIENTS OF THE QUADRATIC EQUATION
1, -5, 6
THE ROOTS ARE      3.00000          2.00000


ENTER THE COEFFICIENTS OF THE QUADRATIC EQUATION
1, 0, -4
THE ROOTS ARE      2.00000         -2.00000


ENTER THE COEFFICIENTS OF THE QUADRATIC EQUATION
1, 0, 4
DISCRIMINANT IS    -16.0000
THERE ARE NO REAL ROOTS


ENTER THE COEFFICIENTS OF THE QUADRATIC EQUATION
3.7, 16.5, 1.7
THE ROOTS ARE    -0.105528         -4.35393
```

The block(s) of statements in a block IF statement may themselves contain other block IF statements. In this case, one block IF statement must be *completely* contained within the block of the other block IF statement and is said to be *nested* within it. For example, suppose the right branch of the earlier piecewise continuous function is modified so that the function becomes constant for $x \geq 1$:

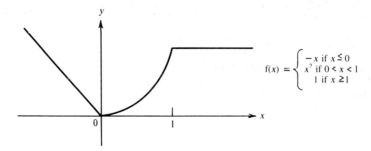

$$f(x) = \begin{cases} -x & \text{if } x \leq 0 \\ x^2 & \text{if } 0 < x < 1 \\ 1 & \text{if } x \geq 1 \end{cases}$$

The earlier block IF statement for evaluating this function can be modified by inserting another block IF within the ELSE block:

```
IF (X .LE. 0) THEN
    FVAL = -X
ELSE
    IF (X .LT. 1) THEN
        FVAL = X ** 2
    ELSE
        FVAL = 1.0
END IF
```

As another illustration of a **nested IF statement,** consider again the quadratic equation problem. If there are real roots of the equation, we wish to determine whether these roots are distinct or repeated. The following algorithm can be used.

REVISED ALGORITHM FOR SOLVING QUADRATIC EQUATIONS

```
*   This algorithm solves quadratic equations Ax² + Bx + C = 0     *
*   using the quadratic formula. The distinct real roots ROOT1 and  *
*   ROOT2 are calculated, if the discriminant DISC = B² - 4AC       *
*   is positive; if it is zero, the repeated real root ROOT1 is     *
*   calculated; if it is negative, a message is displayed indicating that *
*   there are no real roots.                                        *
```

1. Enter A, B, and C.
2. Calculate DISC = B ** 2 - 4 * A * C.
3. If DISC < 0 then do the following:
     a. Display DISC.
     b. Display a message that there are no real roots.
   Else do the following:
   If DISC = 0 then do the following:
     a. Calculate ROOT1 = -B / (2 * A).
     b. Display ROOT1.
   Else do the following:
     a. Calculate DISC = $\sqrt{\text{DISC}}$.
     b. Calculate ROOT1 = (-B + DISC) / (2 * A).
     c. Calculate ROOT2 = (-B - DISC) / (2 * A).
     d. Display ROOT1 and ROOT2.

Figure 4.8 displays this algorithm in flowchart form.

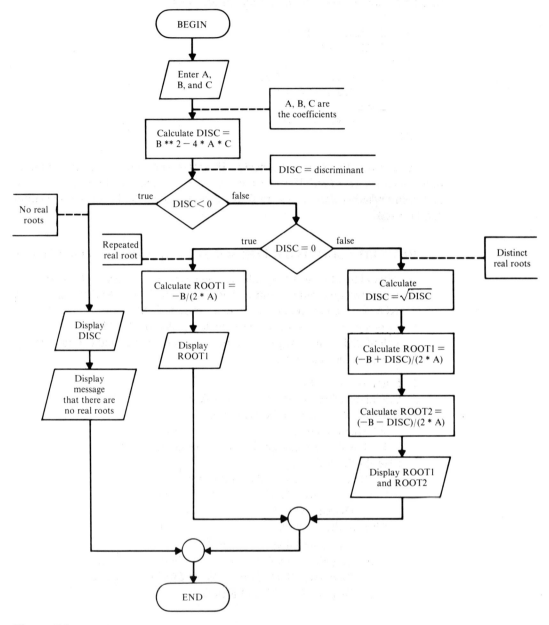

Figure 4.8

The program in Figure 4.9 implements this algorithm. Note again the indentation used to indicate the blocks in the IF statements.

```
        PROGRAM QUAD2
*********************************************************************
* Program to solve a quadratic equation using the quadratic formula. *
* Variables used are:                                               *
*    A, B, C        : the coefficients of the quadratic equation    *
*    DISC           : the discriminant, B ** 2 - 4 * A * C           *
*    ROOT1, ROOT2 : the two roots of the equation                   *
*********************************************************************

        REAL A, B, C, DISC, ROOT1, ROOT2

        PRINT *, 'ENTER THE COEFFICIENTS OF THE QUADRATIC EQUATION'
        READ *, A, B, C
        DISC = B ** 2 - 4 * A * C
        IF (DISC .LT. 0) THEN
            PRINT *, 'DISCRIMINANT IS', DISC
            PRINT *, 'THERE ARE NO REAL ROOTS'
        ELSE
            IF (DISC .EQ. 0) THEN
                ROOT1 = -B / (2 * A)
                PRINT *, 'REPEATED ROOT IS', ROOT1
            ELSE
                DISC = SQRT(DISC)
                ROOT1 = (-B + DISC) / (2 * A)
                ROOT2 = (-B - DISC) / (2 * A)
                PRINT *, 'THE ROOTS ARE', ROOT1, ROOT2
            END IF
        END IF
        END

Sample runs:
===========


ENTER THE COEFFICIENTS OF THE QUADRATIC EQUATION
1, 5, 6
THE ROOTS ARE    -2.00000        -3.00000


ENTER THE COEFFICIENTS OF THE QUADRATIC EQUATION
1, 4, 4
REPEATED ROOT IS    -2.00000


ENTER THE COEFFICIENTS OF THE QUADRATIC EQUATION
4, 1, 2
DISCRIMINANT IS    -31.0000
THERE ARE NO REAL ROOTS
```

Figure 4.9

4.4 Multialternative Selection Structure: The IF–ELSE IF Construct

The selection structures illustrated in the preceding sections involved selecting one of two alternatives. It is also possible to use the block IF statement to design selection structures that contain more than two alternatives. For example, consider again the piecewise continuous function defined by

$$f(x) = \begin{cases} -x & \text{if } x \le 0 \\ x^2 & \text{if } 0 < x < 1 \\ 1 & \text{if } x \ge 1 \end{cases}$$

This definition really consists of three alternatives and was implemented in the preceding section using a nested block IF statement of the form

```
IF (logical-expression-1) THEN
   block-1
ELSE
   IF (logical-expression-2) THEN
      block-2
   ELSE
      block-3
   END IF
END IF
```

But such compound IF statements to implement selection structures with many alternatives can become quite complex, and the correspondence among the IFs, ELSEs, and END IFs may not be clear if indentation is not used properly.

An alternative method of implementing a **multialternative selection structure** is to use an **IF–ELSE IF construct** of the form

```
IF (logical-expression-1) THEN
   block-1
ELSE IF (logical-expression-2) THEN
   block-2
ELSE IF (logical-expression-3) THEN
   block-3
          ⋮
ELSE
   block-n
END IF
```

The logical expressions are evaluated to determine the first true logical expression; the associated block of statements is executed, and execution then continues with the next executable statement following the END IF statement (unless some statement within that block transfers control elsewhere or terminates execution). If none of the logical expressions is true, the block associated with the ELSE statement is executed, and execution then continues with the first executable statement following the END IF statement (unless it is terminated or transferred to some other point by a statement within this block). This block IF statement thus implements an *n*-way selection structure in which exactly one of *block-1, block-2, . . . , block-n* is executed.

The ELSE statement and its corresponding block of statements may be omitted in this structure. In this case, if none of the logical expressions is true, execution continues with the first executable statement following the END IF.

As an example of an IF–ELSE construct, the three-part definition of the preceding function $f(x)$ could be evaluated by

```
IF (X .LE. 0) THEN
   FVAL = −X
ELSE IF (X .LT. 1.0) THEN
   FVAL = X ** 2
ELSE
   FVAL = 1.0
END IF
```

To illustrate further the use of an IF–ELSE IF construct to implement a multialternative selection structure, consider the following alternative description of the algorithm for solving quadratic equations:

ALTERNATIVE ALGORITHM FOR SOLVING QUADRATIC EQUATIONS

```
*   This algorithm solves quadratic equations Ax² + Bx + C = 0    *
*   using the quadratic formula. A multialternative selection structure   *
*   is used to select one of the following actions:                *
*   DISC < 0: Display a message that there are no real roots        *
*   DISC = 0: Calculate repeated real root ROOT1                    *
*   DISC > 0: Calculate distinct real roots ROOT1 and ROOT2         *
*   where DISC is the discriminant B² − 4AC.                        *
```

1. Enter A, B, and C.
2. Calculate DISC = B ** 2 − 4 * A * C.
3. If DISC < 0 then do the following:
   a. Display DISC.
   b. Display a message that there are no real roots.
   Else if DISC = 0 then do the following:
   a. Calculate ROOT1 = −B / (2 * A).
   b. Display ROOT1.
   Else do the following:
   a. Calculate DISC = $\sqrt{\text{DISC}}$.
   b. Calculate ROOT1 = (−B + DISC) / (2 * A).
   c. Calculate ROOT2 = (−B − DISC) / (2 * A).
   d. Display ROOT1 and ROOT2.

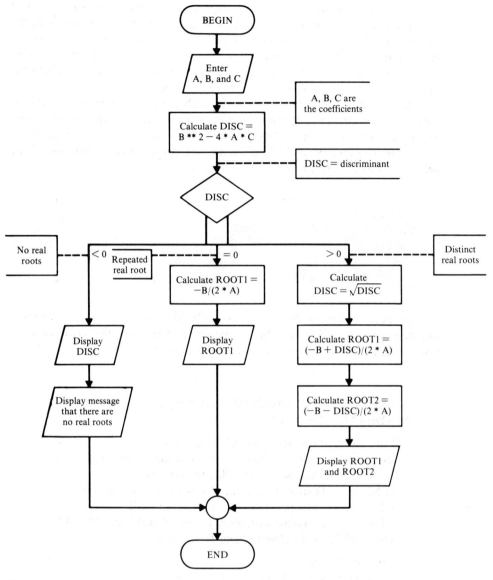

Figure 4.10

The flowchart corresponding to this algorithm in Figure 4.10 clearly shows the three-way selection structure in Step 3. The program in Figure 4.11 uses an IF–ELSE IF construct to implement this three-way selection structure.

```
      PROGRAM QUAD3
***********************************************************************
* Program to solve a quadratic equation using the quadratic formula.  *
* Variables used are:                                                 *
*    A, B, C      : the coefficients of the quadratic equation        *
*    DISC         : the discriminant, B ** 2 - 4 * A * C              *
*    ROOT1, ROOT2 : the two roots of the equation                     *
***********************************************************************

      REAL A, B, C, DISC, ROOT1, ROOT2

      PRINT *, 'ENTER THE COEFFICIENTS OF THE QUADRATIC EQUATION'
      READ *, A, B, C
      DISC = B ** 2 - 4 * A * C
      IF (DISC .LT. 0) THEN
          PRINT *, 'DISCRIMINANT IS', DISC
          PRINT *, 'THERE ARE NO REAL ROOTS'
      ELSE IF (DISC .EQ. 0) THEN
          ROOT1 = -B / (2 * A)
          PRINT *, 'REPEATED ROOT IS', ROOT1
      ELSE
          DISC = SQRT(DISC)
          ROOT1 = (-B + DISC) / (2 * A)
          ROOT2 = (-B - DISC) / (2 * A)
          PRINT *, 'THE ROOTS ARE', ROOT1, ROOT2
      END IF
      END
```

Figure 4.11

There are three additional statements in FORTRAN that may be used to form multialternative selection structures: the arithmetic IF statement, the computed GO TO statement, and the assigned GO TO statement. These statements are less commonly used than are the other control statements and are described in Chapter 13.

Exercises

1. Write FORTRAN program segments for the following:

   (a) If CODE = 1, read X and Y, and calculate and print the sum of X and Y.

   (b) If A is strictly between 0 and 5, set B equal to $1/A^2$; otherwise set B equal to A^2.

   (c) Display the message 'Leap year' if the integer variable YEAR is the number of a leap year. (A leap year is a multiple of 4, and if it is a multiple of 100, it must also be a multiple of 400.)

(d) Assign a value to COST corresponding to the value of DIST given in the following table.

DIST	COST
0 through 100	5.00
More than 100 but not more than 500	8.00
More than 500 but less than 1000	10.00
1000 or more	12.00

2. Write block IF statements to evaluate the following functions:

(a) The output of a simple d-c generator; the shape of the curve is the absolute value of the sine function. (100 V is the maximum voltage.)

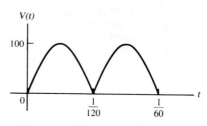

(b) A rectified half-wave; the curve is a sine function for half the cycle and zero for the other half. (Maximum current is 5 amp.)

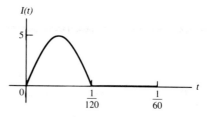

(c) Sawtooth; the graph consists of two straight lines. The maximum voltage of 100 V occurs at the middle of the cycle.

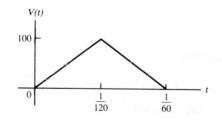

(d) The excess pressure $p(t)$ in a sound wave whose graph is as follows:

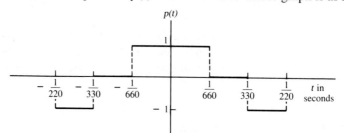

3. A certain city classifies a pollution index of less than 35 as "pleasant" 35 through 60 as "unpleasant," and above 60 as "hazardous." Write a program that accepts a real number representing a pollution index and displays the appropriate classification of it.

4. Write a program to read one of the codes 1 for circle, 2 for square, or 3 for equilateral triangle, and a number representing the radius of the circle, side of the square, or side of the triangle, respectively. Then calculate and display the area and the perimeter of that geometric figure with appropriate labels. (See Exercise 3 on page 86.)

5. Modify the program in Figure 4.11 for solving quadratic equations so that when the discriminant is negative, the complex roots of the equation are displayed. If the discriminant D is negative, these roots are given by

$$\frac{-B \pm \sqrt{-D}i}{2A}$$

(where $i^2 = -1$).

6. Write a program that reads values for the coefficients A, B, C, D, E, and F of the equations

$$Ax + By = C$$

$$Dx + Ey = F$$

of two straight lines. Then determine whether the lines are parallel (slopes are equal) or intersect and, if they intersect, whether the lines are perpendicular (product of slopes = -1).

7. Write a program that reads the coordinates of three points and then determines whether they are collinear.

8. Suppose the following formulas give the safe loading L in pounds per square inch for a column with slimness ratio S:

$$L = \begin{cases} 16500 - .475S^2 & \text{if } S < 100 \\ \dfrac{17900}{2 + (S^2 / 17900)} & \text{if } S \geq 100 \end{cases}$$

Write a program that reads a slimness ratio and then calculates the safe loading.

9. Suppose that charges by a gas company are based on consumption according to the following table:

Gas Used	Rate
First 70 cubic meters	$5.00 minimum cost
Next 100 cubic meters	5.0¢ per cubic meter
Next 230 cubic meters	2.5¢ per cubic meter
Above 400 cubic meters	1.5¢ per cubic meter

Write a program in which the meter reading for the previous month and the current meter reading are entered, each a four-digit number and each representing cubic meters, and which then calculates the amount of the bill. Note: The current reading may be less than the previous one; for example, the previous reading may have been 9897, and the current one is 0103.

4.5　Repetition Structure: The DO and CONTINUE Statements

A **repetition structure** or **loop** makes possible the repeated execution of one or more statements. This repetition must be controlled so that these statements are executed only a finite number of times. There are two basic types of repetition structures, which use different control mechanisms:

1. *Loops controlled by some counter* in which the body of the loop is executed once for each value of some control variable in a specified range of values.
2. *Loops controlled by some logical expression* in which the decision to continue or to terminate repetition is determined by the truth or falsity of some logical expression.

In FORTRAN a repetition of the first type is called a **DO loop** and is implemented using the DO and CONTINUE statements. This structure has one of the forms

DO *n, control-variable* = *initial-value, limit*
　statement-1 ⎫
　　⋮　　　⎬ *body*
　statement-k ⎭
n CONTINUE

DO *n, control-variable* = *initial-value, limit, step-size*
　statement-1 ⎫
　　⋮　　　⎬ *body*
　statement-k ⎭
n CONTINUE

Here *n* is a statement number that is a positive integer of up to five digits; *initial-value, limit,* and *step-size* are integer or real (or double precision) expressions; and *step-size* must be nonzero. The comma following the statement number is optional, and we omit it in our examples of this structure. The first form of a DO loop is equivalent to a DO loop of the second form in which the value of *step-size* is 1.

A DO loop in which the step size is positive implements the repetition structure shown in Figure 4.12(a). As the flowchart shows, when a DO loop is executed, the control variable is assigned the initial value, and the body of the loop is executed unless the initial value is greater than the limit. After the body of the loop has been executed, the control variable is incremented by the

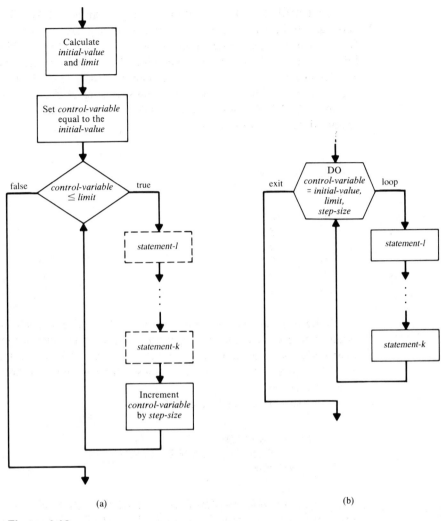

(a)   (b)

Figure 4.12

step size, and if this new value does not exceed the limit, the body of the DO loop is executed again. Execution of the DO loop terminates when the value of the control variable exceeds the limit. Note that if the initial value is greater than the limit, the body of the loop is never executed.

DO loops that appear within larger flowcharts will be represented more compactly, as shown in Figure 4.12(b). The hexagon at the beginning of the loop is intended to include the initialization, testing, and incrementing, which are shown explicitly in Figure 4.12(a).

To illustrate, consider the DO loop

```
    DO 10 NUMBER = 1, 10
        PRINT *, NUMBER, NUMBER ** 2
 10 CONTINUE
```

where NUMBER is of integer type. In this example, NUMBER is the control variable, the initial value is 1, the limit is 10, and the step size is 1. When this DO loop is executed, the initial value 1 is assigned to NUMBER, and the PRINT statement is executed. The value of NUMBER is then increased by 1, and because this new value 2 is less than the limit 10, the PRINT statement is executed again. This repetition continues as long as the value of the control variable NUMBER is less than or equal to the final value 10. Thus, the output produced by this DO loop is

1	1
2	4
3	9
4	16
5	25
6	36
7	49
8	64
9	81
10	100

If the step size in a DO loop is negative, the control variable is decremented rather than incremented, and repetition continues as long as the value of the control variable is greater than or equal to the limit. This is illustrated in Figure 4.13. Note that if the initial value is less than the limit, the body of the loop is never executed.

For example, consider the DO loop

```
    DO 10 NUMBER = 10, 1, −1
        PRINT *, NUMBER, NUMBER ** 2
10 CONTINUE
```

The control variable NUMBER is assigned the initial value 10, and because this value is greater than the limit 1, the PRINT statement is executed. The value of NUMBER is then decreased to 9, and because this new value is greater than the limit, the PRINT statement is executed again. This process continues as long as the value of NUMBER is greater than or equal to the limit 1. Thus, the output produced is

10	100
9	81
8	64
7	49
6	36
5	25
4	16
3	9
2	4
1	1

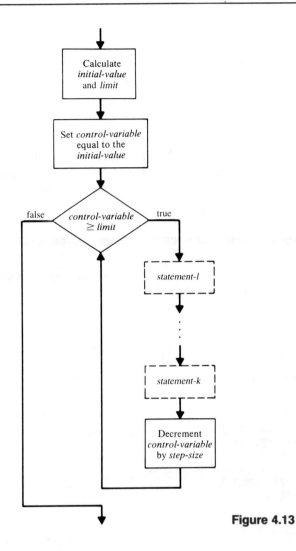

Figure 4.13

The number of times that the statements in a DO loop are executed is determined before repetition begins.[1] Consequently, changing the value of the initial value, limit, and step size within the body of the loop does not affect the number of repetitions. The control variable may be used in the body of the loop, but *it must not be modified*. Upon exit from a DO loop, the control variable retains its value, and so this value may be used later in the program.

The initial value, the limit, and the step size in a DO loop may be variables or expressions. To illustrate, consider the declarations

```
REAL FIRSTX, LASTX, DELTAX, X, Y
```

[1] The number of repetitions is calculated as the larger of the value 0 and the integer part of

$$\frac{limit - initial\text{-}value + step\text{-}size}{step\text{-}size}$$

and the statements

```
READ *, FIRSTX, LASTX, DELTAX
DO 10 X = FIRSTX, LASTX, DELTAX
    Y = EXP(-X) * SIN(X)
    PRINT *, X, Y
10 CONTINUE
```

The values read for FIRSTX, LASTX, and DELTAX are the initial value, limit, and step size, respectively, for the DO loop. The program in Figure 4.14 uses these statements to print a table of points on the damped vibration curve

$$y = e^{-x} \sin x$$

```
      PROGRAM VIBRAT
*********************************************************************
* Program to print a table of points on the curve                 *
*             -x                                                   *
*      y = e  *  sin x                                             *
* Variables used are:                                             *
*   X, Y        : coordinates of the point                         *
*   FIRSTX, LASTX : lower and upper limits on X                    *
*   DELTAX       : step size                                       *
*********************************************************************

      REAL X, Y, FIRSTX, LASTX, DELTAX

      PRINT *, 'ENTER LOWER AND UPPER LIMITS ON X AND STEP SIZE'
      READ *, FIRSTX, LASTX, DELTAX
      PRINT *, '        X                Y'
      PRINT *, '        ===========================
      DO 10 X = FIRSTX, LASTX, DELTAX
          Y = EXP(-X) * SIN(X)
          PRINT *, X, Y
10    CONTINUE
      END


Sample run:
==========


ENTER LOWER AND UPPER LIMITS ON X AND STEP SIZE
1, 3, .25
          X                Y
      ===========================
      1.00000        0.309560
      1.25000        0.271889
      1.50000        0.222571
      1.75000        0.170991
      2.00000        0.123060
      2.25000        8.200830E-02
      2.50000        4.912558E-02
      2.75000        2.439879E-02
      3.00000        7.025976E-03
```

Figure 4.14

The body of a DO loop may contain another DO loop. In this case, the second DO loop is said to be **nested** within the first DO loop. As an example, consider the program in Figure 4.15 that calculates and displays products of the form M * N for M ranging from 1 through LASTM and N ranging from 1 through LASTN for integers M, N, LASTM, LASTN, and PROD. The table of products is generated by the DO loop

```
      DO 20 M = 1, LASTM
         DO 10 N = 1, LASTN
            PROD = M * N
            PRINT *, M, N, PROD
10       CONTINUE
20 CONTINUE
```

In the sample run, LASTM and LASTN both are assigned the value 4. The control variable M is assigned its initial value 1, and the DO loop

```
      DO 10 N = 1, LASTN
         PROD = M * N
         PRINT *, M, N, PROD
10 CONTINUE
```

is executed. This calculates and displays the first four products, 1 * 1, 1 * 2, 1 * 3, and 1 * 4. The value of M is then incremented by 1, and the preceding DO loop is executed again. This calculates and displays the next four products, 2 * 1, 2 * 2, 2 * 3, and 2 * 4. The control variable M is then incremented to 3, producing the next four products, 3 * 1, 3 * 2, 3 * 3, and 3 * 4. Finally, M is incremented to 4, giving the last four products, 4 * 1, 4 * 2, 4 * 3, and 4 * 4.

```
      PROGRAM MULT
*******************************************************************
* Program to calculate and display a list of products of two numbers.  *
* Variables used are:                                             *
*    M, N         : the two numbers being multiplied              *
*    PROD         : their product                                 *
*    LASTM, LASTN : the last values of M and N                    *
*******************************************************************

      INTEGER M, N, LASTM, LASTN, PROD

      PRINT *, 'ENTER THE LAST VALUES OF THE TWO NUMBERS'
      READ *, LASTM, LASTN
      PRINT *, '        M          N          M * N'
      PRINT *, '        =========================='
      DO 20 M = 1, LASTM
         DO 10 N = 1, LASTN
            PROD = M * N
            PRINT *, M, N, PROD
10       CONTINUE
20    CONTINUE
      END
```

Figure 4.15

Figure 4.15 (continued)

```
Sample run:
==========


ENTER THE LAST VALUES OF THE TWO NUMBERS
4, 4
      M             N           M * N
      ===========================
      1             1             1
      1             2             2
      1             3             3
      1             4             4
      2             1             2
      2             2             4
      2             3             6
      2             4             8
      3             1             3
      3             2             6
      3             3             9
      3             4            12
      4             1             4
      4             2             8
      4             3            12
      4             4            16
```

In this example, note that the DO loops have different control variables. *Whenever two or more DO loops are nested, they must have different control variables,* because the value of a control variable cannot be modified within the body of a DO loop. The following diagrams illustrate some correct and incorrect constructions involving DO loops:

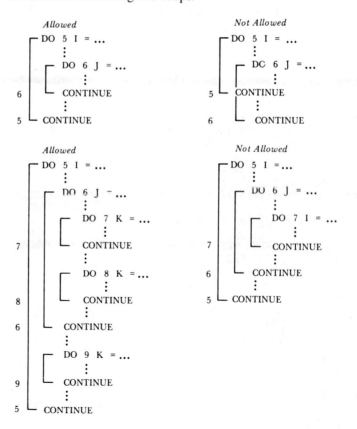

The same CONTINUE statement may be used to "close" nested DO loops. Thus the nested DO loops in the preceding example could also be written

```
      DO 10 M = 1, LASTM
          DO 10 N = 1, LASTN
              PROD = M * N
              PRINT *, M, N, PROD
   10 CONTINUE
```

In fact, the last executable statement within the body of a DO loop may be used to close the loop, as in

```
      DO 10 NUMBER = 1, 10
   10     PRINT *, NUMBER, NUMBER ** 2
```

provided it is not a block IF, ELSE, ELSE IF, END, or another DO statement. (The GO TO, RETURN, arithmetic IF, and assigned GO TO statements, considered later, are also not allowed.) Thus we could also write the nested DO loops as

```
      DO 10 M = 1, LASTM
          DO 10 N = 1, LASTN
              PROD = M * N
   10         PRINT *, M, N, PROD
```

The generally accepted practice, however, is to *use* CONTINUE *statements to close* DO *loops and, in the case of nested* DO *loops, to use different* CONTINUE *statements to close each loop.*

When a block IF statement is used within the body of a DO loop, it must be completely contained within the body of the loop. Similarly, when a DO loop is used in a block IF statement, it must be completely contained within the block in which it begins. Thus program constructions such as the following are not allowed:

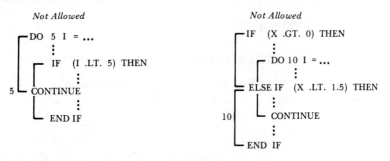

4.6 The While Repetition Structure

A DO loop can be used to implement a repetition structure in which the number of iterations is determined before the loop is executed. In some cases, a repetition structure is required for which the number of iterations is not known in advance but in which repetition continues while some logical expression remains true. Such a repetition structure is called a **while loop** and is pictured in

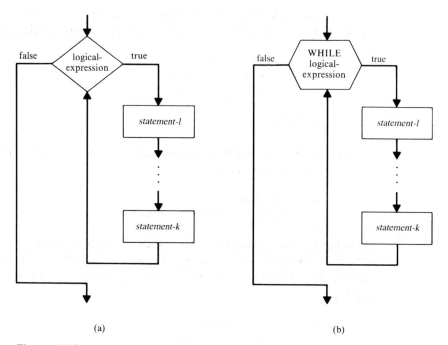

(a)   (b)

Figure 4.16

Figure 4.16(a). It will be represented in flowcharts, as shown in Figure 4.16(b), to emphasize that it is a repetition structure.

To illustrate the use of a while loop, consider the following problem:

For a given value of LIMIT, what is the smallest positive integer NUMBER for which the sum

$$1 + 2 + \cdots + \text{NUMBER}$$

is greater than LIMIT, and what is the value of this sum?

The following algorithm solves this problem:

ALGORITHM FOR SUMMATION PROBLEM

*   Algorithm to find the smallest positive NUMBER for which the   *
*   sum $1 + 2 + \cdots + $ NUMBER is greater than some specified   *
*   value LIMIT.   *

1. Enter LIMIT.
2. Set NUMBER equal to 0.
3. Set SUM equal to 0.
4. While SUM $\leq$ LIMIT, do the following:
   a. Increase NUMBER by 1.
   b. Add NUMBER to SUM.
5. Display NUMBER and SUM.

Figure 4.17 displays this algorithm in flowchart form.

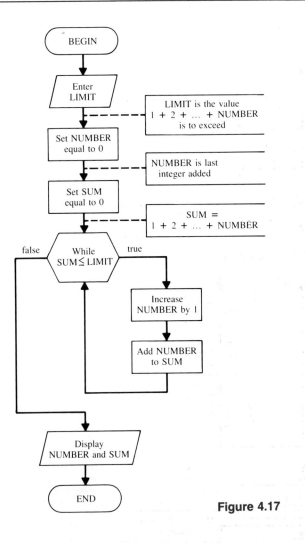

Figure 4.17

As the flowcharts in Figure 4.16 indicate, the logical expression in a while loop is evaluated *before* repetition, and this loop is therefore sometimes called a **pretest loop** or a "test-at-the-top" loop. If the logical expression that controls repetition is false initially, the body of the loop is not executed. Thus, in the preceding summation algorithm, if the value −1 is entered for LIMIT, the body of the while loop is bypassed, and execution continues with the display instruction that follows the while loop; the value 0 will be displayed for both NUMBER and SUM.

As another example that uses a repetition structure in which the number of iterations is not known in advance, we now develop an algorithm to calculate the mean of a set of temperature measurements obtained in some experiment. Because the number of temperature readings is not known in advance, the algorithm must count the data values being averaged.

In this problem, the input is a set of real numbers, one for each temperature measurement. The output is the number of measurements and the mean temperature. The procedure for solving the problem consists of reading a temper-

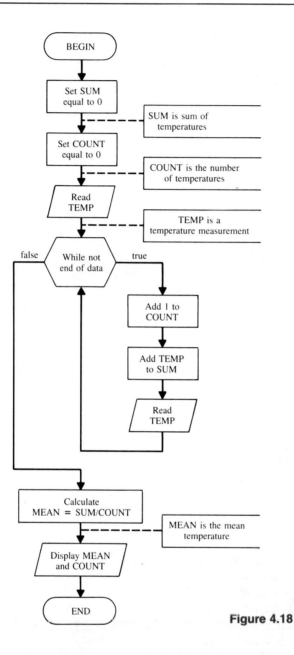

BEGIN

Set SUM
equal to 0

SUM is sum of
temperatures

Set COUNT
equal to 0

COUNT is the number
of temperatures

Read
TEMP

TEMP is a
temperature measurement

false   While not   true
           end of data

Add 1 to
COUNT

Add TEMP
to SUM

Read
TEMP

Calculate
MEAN = SUM/COUNT

MEAN is the mean
temperature

Display MEAN
and COUNT

END

Figure 4.18

ature, counting it, and adding it to the sum of temperatures previously read. This procedure must be repeated for each measurement. In this example, we append to the data an artificial value called a **flag** or **sentinel,** which is distinct from any possible valid data item. As each data item is read, it is checked to determine whether it is this end-of-data flag. When the end of data is reached, the repetition is terminated, the mean is calculated, and the desired information is displayed.

This algorithm is summarized as follows:

ALGORITHM TO CALCULATE MEAN TEMPERATURE
* Algorithm to read a list of temperatures, count them, and find the *
* mean temperature MEAN; TEMP represents the current tempera- *
* ture read, COUNT is the number of temperatures, and SUM is *
* their sum. Values are read until the end-of-data flag is encoun- *
* tered. *

1. Set SUM equal to 0.
2. Set COUNT equal to 0.
3. Read first value of TEMP.
4. While TEMP is not the end-of-data flag, do the following:
   a. Add 1 to COUNT.
   b. Add TEMP to SUM.
   c. Read next value for TEMP.
5. Calculate MEAN = SUM / COUNT.
6. Display MEAN and COUNT.

Figure 4.18 displays this algorithm in flowchart form.

A WHILE statement that implements this important control structure is not included in standard FORTRAN, but it is a common extension that is available in many versions of FORTRAN. In the next section we consider a WHILE statement and show how it can be used in programs that implement the algorithms presented in this section. In Section 4.8 we show how while loops can be implemented in standard FORTRAN and in later programs in this text, all while loops will be implemented in this manner because we wish to conform to the standard. But each while loop in the examples will be clearly marked with a comment to indicate where a WHILE statement could be used.

4.7 The WHILE Statement[2]

The WHILE statement that is provided in many versions of FORTRAN commonly has one of the following forms:

```
WHILE (logical-expression) DO          DO WHILE (logical-expression)
    statement-1                            statement-1
    statement-2                            statement-2
        ⋮                                      ⋮
    statement-n                            statement-n
END WHILE                               END DO
```

use this one for VAX

[2] Both Sections 4.7 and 4.8 discuss implementations of while loops. If your version of FORTRAN provides a WHILE statement, you may wish to study Section 4.7 and omit Section 4.8. It must be noted, however, that using a WHILE statement makes a program less *portable,* as it cannot be compiled correctly by FORTRAN compilers that do not support this extension.

When this statement is executed, the logical expression is evaluated; if it is true, the body of the while loop consisting of *statement-1, statement-2, . . . , statement-n* is executed. The logical expression is then reevaluated, and if it is still true, these statements are executed again. This process of evaluating the logical expression and executing the specified statements is repeated as long as the logical expression is true. When it becomes false, repetition is terminated. This means that execution of the statements within the WHILE statement must eventually cause the logical expression to become false, since otherwise an **infinite loop** would result.

The program in Figure 4.19 implements the summation algorithm of the preceding section for finding the smallest positive integer NUMBER for which the sum $1 + 2 + \cdots + $ NUMBER is greater than some specified value LIMIT. It uses the WHILE statement

```
WHILE (SUM .LE. LIMIT) DO
    NUMBER = NUMBER + 1
    SUM = SUM + NUMBER
END WHILE
```

to implement the while loop

WHILE SUM $\le$ LIMIT, do the following:
    a. Increase NUMBER by 1.
    b. Add NUMBER to SUM.

in this algorithm.

Because the logical expression in a WHILE statement is evaluated before the repetition begins, the statements that comprise the body of the while loop are not executed if this expression is initially false. This is demonstrated in the last sample run, in which the value -1 is entered for LIMIT. The WHILE statement causes an immediate transfer of control to the last PRINT statement which displays the value 0 for both NUMBER and SUM.

```
    PROGRAM ADDER1
******************************************************************
* Program that uses a WHILE statement to find the smallest positive  *
* integer NUMBER for which the sum 1 + 2 + ... + NUMBER is greater   *
* than some specified LIMIT.  Variables used are:                    *
*    NUMBER : the current number being added                         *
*    SUM    : the sum 1 + 2 + ... + NUMBER                           *
*    LIMIT  : the value which SUM is to exceed                       *
******************************************************************

    INTEGER NUMBER, SUM, LIMIT
```

Figure 4.19

Figure 4.19   (continued)

```
* Read LIMIT and initialize NUMBER and SUM

    PRINT *, 'ENTER VALUE 1 + 2 + ... + ? IS TO EXCEED'
    READ *, LIMIT
    NUMBER = 0
    SUM = 0

* While SUM does not exceed LIMIT, increment NUMBER and add to SUM

    WHILE (SUM .LE. LIMIT) DO
        NUMBER = NUMBER + 1
        SUM = SUM + NUMBER
    END WHILE

* Print the results

    PRINT *, 'FOR NUMBER =', NUMBER
    PRINT *, '1 + 2 + ... + NUMBER =', SUM
    END


Sample runs:
===========

ENTER VALUE 1 + 2 + ... + ? IS TO EXCEED
15
FOR NUMBER =             6
1 + 2 + ... + NUMBER =             21


ENTER VALUE 1 + 2 + ... + ? IS TO EXCEED
500
FOR NUMBER =            32
1 + 2 + ... + NUMBER =            528


ENTER VALUE 1 + 2 + ... + ? IS TO EXCEED
-1
FOR NUMBER =             0
1 + 2 + ... + NUMBER =             0
```

The program in Figure 4.20 implements the algorithm given in the preceding section for calculating the mean of a set of temperatures. It uses the statements

```
    PRINT *, 'ENTER TEMPERATURE OF -999 OR LESS TO STOP'
    PRINT *, 'ENTER TEMPERATURE'
    READ *, TEMP

    WHILE (TEMP .GT. -999) DO
        COUNT = COUNT + 1
        SUM = SUM + TEMP
        PRINT *, 'ENTER TEMPERATURE'
        READ *, TEMP
    END WHILE
```

to implement the following instructions in the algorithm:

> 3. Read first value of TEMP.
> 4. While TEMP is not the end-of-data flag, do the following:
>   a. Add 1 to COUNT.
>   b. Add TEMP to SUM.
>   c. Read next value for TEMP.

```
        PROGRAM TEMP1
*************************************************************************
* Program to read a list of temperatures, count them, and find the    *
* mean temperature.  Values are read until an end-of-data flag (any    *
* value less than or equal to -999) is read.  Variables used are:      *
*     TEMP    :   the current temperature read                         *
*     COUNT   :   the number of temperature readings                   *
*     SUM     :   sum of temperatures                                  *
*     MEAN    :   the mean temperature                                 *
*************************************************************************

        INTEGER COUNT
        REAL TEMP, SUM, MEAN

* Initialize SUM and COUNT, and read 1-st temperature

        SUM = 0
        COUNT = 0
        PRINT *, 'ENTER TEMPERATURE OF -999 OR LESS TO STOP'
        PRINT *, 'ENTER TEMPERATURE'
        READ *, TEMP

* While not end-of-data, count, sum, and read temperatures,

        WHILE (TEMP .GT. -999) DO
            COUNT = COUNT + 1
            SUM = SUM + TEMP
            PRINT *, 'ENTER TEMPERATURE'
            READ *, TEMP
        END WHILE

* Calculate and display mean temperature

        MEAN = SUM / COUNT
        PRINT *
        PRINT *, 'NUMBER OF TEMPERATURE READINGS:', COUNT
        PRINT *, 'MEAN TEMPERATURE:', MEAN
        END
```

Figure 4.20

Figure 4.20   (continued)

```
Sample run:
==========


ENTER TEMPERATURE OF -999 OR LESS TO STOP
ENTER TEMPERATURE
78.3
ENTER TEMPERATURE
81.5
ENTER TEMPERATURE
87.7
ENTER TEMPERATURE
90.0
ENTER TEMPERATURE
84.4
ENTER TEMPERATURE
77.4
ENTER TEMPERATURE
-999

NUMBER OF TEMPERATURE READINGS:        6
MEAN TEMPERATURE:     83.2166
```

4.8   Implementing While Loops in Standard FORTRAN

As we noted earlier, standard FORTRAN does not include a WHILE statement. Nevertheless, this important control structure can still be implemented in standard FORTRAN by using a GO TO statement within a block IF statement. The **GO TO statement** is a branching statement and has the form

GO TO *statement-number*

where *statement-number* is the number of an executable statement. The GO TO statement alters the usual sequential execution so that the statement with the specified number is executed next.

A while loop can thus be implemented by a program segment of the form

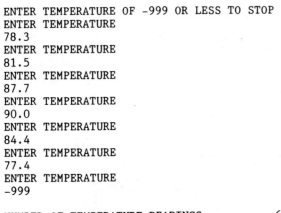

n IF (*logical-expression*) THEN

    statement-1
    statement-2
      ⋮   } *body*
    statement-k
    GO TO *n*
END IF

Repeated execution of the statements in the body of the while loop must eventually cause the logical expression to become false, as an **infinite loop** results otherwise.

The program in Figure 4.21 implements the summation algorithm of the preceding section for finding the smallest positive integer NUMBER for which the sum 1 + 2 + · · · + NUMBER is greater than some specified value LIMIT. It uses the statements

```
10 IF (SUM .LE. LIMIT) THEN
        NUMBER = NUMBER + 1
        SUM = SUM + NUMBER
        GO TO 10
     END IF
```

to implement the while loop

While SUM ≤ LIMIT, do the following:
   a. Increase NUMBER by 1.
   b. Add NUMBER to SUM.

in this algorithm.

Because the logical expression in a while loop is evaluated before the repetition begins, the statements that comprise the body of the while loop are not executed if this expression is initially false. This is demonstrated in the last sample run, where the value − 1 is entered for LIMIT. The while loop causes an immediate transfer of control to the last PRINT statement which displays the value 0 for both NUMBER and SUM.

```
      PROGRAM ADDER2
**********************************************************************
* Program to find the smallest positive integer NUMBER for which the  *
* sum 1 + 2 + ... + NUMBER is greater than some specified value LIMIT. *
* Variables used are:                                                  *
*    NUMBER : the current number being added                           *
*    SUM    : the sum 1 + 2 + ... + NUMBER                             *
*    LIMIT  : the value which SUM is to exceed                         *
**********************************************************************

      INTEGER NUMBER, SUM, LIMIT

* Read LIMIT and initialize NUMBER and SUM

      PRINT *, 'ENTER VALUE 1 + 2 + ... + ? IS TO EXCEED'
      READ *, LIMIT
      NUMBER = 0
      SUM = 0

* While SUM does not exceed LIMIT, increment NUMBER and add to SUM

10    IF (SUM .LE. LIMIT) THEN
          NUMBER = NUMBER + 1
          SUM = SUM + NUMBER
          GO TO 10
      END IF
```

Figure 4.21

Figure 4.21 (continued)

```
* Print the results

      PRINT *, 'FOR NUMBER =', NUMBER
      PRINT *, '1 + 2 + ... + NUMBER =', SUM
      END
```

```
Sample runs:
===========

ENTER VALUE 1 + 2 + ... + ? IS TO EXCEED
15
FOR NUMBER =            6
1 + 2 + ... + NUMBER =           21


ENTER VALUE 1 + 2 + ... + ? IS TO EXCEED
500
FOR NUMBER =           32
1 + 2 + ... + NUMBER =          528


ENTER VALUE 1 + 2 + ... + ? IS TO EXCEED
-1
FOR NUMBER =            0
1 + 2 + ... + NUMBER =            0
```

The program in Figure 4.22 implements the algorithm given in the preceding section for calculating the mean of a set of temperatures. It uses the statements

```
      PRINT *, 'ENTER TEMPERATURE OF -999 OR LESS TO STOP'
      PRINT *, 'ENTER TEMPERATURE'
      READ *, TEMP

   10 IF (TEMP .GT. -999) THEN
         COUNT = COUNT + 1
         SUM = SUM + TEMP
         PRINT *, 'ENTER TEMPERATURE'
         READ *, TEMP
         GO TO 10
      END IF
```

to implement the following instructions in the algorithm:

3. READ first value of TEMP.
4. While TEMP is not the end-of-data flag, do the following:
   a. Add 1 to COUNT.
   b. Add TEMP to SUM.
   c. Read next value for TEMP.

```
      PROGRAM TEMP2
*******************************************************************
* Program to read a list of temperatures, count them, and find the   *
* mean temperature.  Values are read until an end-of-data flag (any   *
* value less than or equal to -999) is read.  Variables used are:     *
*    TEMP    :  the current temperature read                          *
*    COUNT   :  the number of temperature readings                    *
*    SUM     :  sum of temperatures                                   *
*    MEAN    :  the mean temperature                                  *
*******************************************************************

      INTEGER COUNT
      REAL TEMP, SUM, MEAN

* Initialize SUM and COUNT, and read 1-st temperature

      SUM = 0
      COUNT = 0'
      PRINT *, 'ENTER TEMPERATURE OF -999 OR LESS TO STOP'
      PRINT *, 'ENTER TEMPERATURE'
      READ *, TEMP

* While not end-of-data, count, sum, and read temperatures,

10    IF (TEMP .GT. -999) THEN
          COUNT = COUNT + 1
          SUM = SUM + TEMP
          PRINT *, 'ENTER TEMPERATURE'
          READ *, TEMP
          GO TO 10
      END IF

* Calculate and display mean temperature

      MEAN = SUM / COUNT
      PRINT *
      PRINT *, 'NUMBER OF TEMPERATURE READINGS:', COUNT
      PRINT *, 'MEAN TEMPERATURE:', MEAN
      END


Sample run:
==========


ENTER TEMPERATURE OF -999 OR LESS TO STOP
ENTER TEMPERATURE
78.3
ENTER TEMPERATURE
81.5
ENTER TEMPERATURE
87.7
ENTER TEMPERATURE
90.0
ENTER TEMPERATURE
84.4
ENTER TEMPERATURE
77.4
ENTER TEMPERATURE
-999

NUMBER OF TEMPERATURE READINGS:          6
MEAN TEMPERATURE:      83.2166
```

Figure 4.22

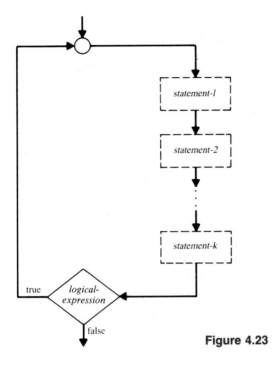

Figure 4.23

*4.9   A Posttest Repetition Structure

A while loop is a **pretest** loop in which the logical expression that controls the repetition is evaluated *before* the body of the loop is executed. Sometimes, however, it is appropriate to use a **posttest** or ''test-at-the-bottom'' loop in which the termination test is made *after* the body of the loop is executed. Such a structure is pictured in the flowchart of Figure 4.23 and can be implemented in FORTRAN with a program segment of the form

$$n \quad statement\text{-}1$$
$$statement\text{-}2$$
$$\vdots$$
$$\text{IF } (logical\text{-}expression) \text{ GO TO } n$$

To illustrate a posttest loop, we reconsider the problem of calculating the mean of a set of temperatures. An alternative to using a ''dummy'' data value to signal the end of data is to repeatedly ask the user if there are more data items. And because there ordinarily will be at least one data item, it seems natural to check the termination condition at the bottom of the loop. Thus the algorithm given earlier can be modifed as follows:

MODIFIED ALGORITHM TO CALCULATE
MEAN TEMPERATURE

* Algorithm to read a list of temperatures, count them, and find the   *
* mean temperature MEAN. TEMP represents the current tempera-   *
* ture read, COUNT is the number of temperatures, and SUM is   *
* their sum. Values are read until the user's RESPONse indicates   *
* that there are no more.   *

1. Set SUM equal to 0.
2. Set COUNT equal to 0.
3. Repeat the following until RESPON = 0:
   a. Read next value for TEMP.
   b. Add 1 to COUNT.
   c. Add TEMP to SUM.
   d. Read RESPON (0 to stop, 1 to continue).
4. Calculate MEAN = SUM / COUNT.
5. Display MEAN and COUNT.

For this algorithm, it is appropriate to implement the posttest loop by the statements

```
10      PRINT *, 'ENTER TEMPERATURE'
        READ *, TEMP
        COUNT = COUNT + 1
        SUM = SUM + TEMP
        PRINT *, 'MORE (0 = NO, 1 = YES)?'
        READ *, RESPON
      IF (RESPON .EQ. 1) GO TO 10
```

as shown in the program of Figure 4.24.

```
      PROGRAM TEMP3
***********************************************************************
* Program to read a list of temperatures, count them, and find the   *
* mean temperature.  The user is asked repeatedly if there are more   *
* data items.  Variables used are:                                    *
*     TEMP    :  the current temperature read                         *
*     COUNT   :  the number of temperature readings                   *
*     SUM     :  sum of temperatures                                  *
*     MEAN    :  the mean temperature                                 *
*     RESPON  :  user response                                        *
***********************************************************************

      INTEGER COUNT, RESPON
      REAL TEMP, SUM, MEAN
```

Figure 4.24

Figure 4.24 **(continued)**

```
* Initialize SUM and COUNT

      SUM = 0
      COUNT = 0

* Read temperatures, count and sum them until there are no more

10        PRINT *, 'ENTER TEMPERATURE'
          READ *, TEMP
          COUNT = COUNT + 1
          SUM = SUM + TEMP
          PRINT *, 'MORE (0 = NO, 1 = YES)'
          READ *, RESPON
      IF (RESPON .EQ. 1) GO TO 10

* Calculate and display mean temperature

      MEAN = SUM / COUNT
      PRINT *
      PRINT *, 'NUMBER OF TEMPERATURE READINGS:', COUNT
      PRINT *, 'MEAN TEMPERATURE:', MEAN
      END


Sample run:
==========


ENTER TEMPERATURE
78.3
MORE (0 = NO, 1 = YES)
1
ENTER TEMPERATURE
81.5
MORE (0 = NO, 1 = YES)
1
ENTER TEMPERATURE
87.7
MORE (0 = NO, 1 = YES)
1
ENTER TEMPERATURE
90.0
MORE (0 = NO, 1 = YES)
1
ENTER TEMPERATURE
84.4
MORE (0 = NO, 1 = YES)
1
ENTER TEMPERATURE
77.4
MORE (0 = NO, 1 = YES)
0

NUMBER OF TEMPERATURE READINGS:        6
MEAN TEMPERATURE:     83.2166
```

It is appropriate to use a posttest loop when we want to ensure that the body of the loop will be executed at least once. In a pretest loop, the body of the loop may never be executed. The exercises explore in more detail the difference between these two repetition structures.

4.10 Program Testing and Debugging Techniques: An Example

In Section 2.5 we noted that there are three types of errors that may occur in developing a program to solve a problem: syntax or compile-time errors, run-time errors, and logical errors. **Syntax errors** such as incorrect punctuation, unbalanced parentheses, and mispelled key words will be detected during the program's compilation, and an appropriate error message will usually be displayed. **Run-time errors** such as division by zero and integer overflow are detected during the program's execution, and again, a suitable error message will often be displayed. These two types of errors are, for the most part, relatively easy to correct, as the system error messages displayed will often indicate the type of error and where it occurred. **Logical errors,** on the other hand, are usually more difficult to detect, as they arise in the design of the algorithm or in coding the algorithm as a program, and in most cases, no error messages are displayed to assist the programmer in identifying such errors.

In this text, the Programming Pointers at the end of each chapter include warnings about some of the more common errors. As programs become increasingly complex, however, the logical errors that occur are more subtle and consequently more difficult to identify and correct. In this section we consider an example of a program that contains logical errors and describe techniques that are useful in detecting them.

Suppose that, as a programming exercise, students were asked to write a program to read a list of positive integers representing noise levels (in decibels) in an automobile under various conditions and to determine the range, that is, the difference between the largest and the smallest values. The following program heading, opening documentation, and variable declarations were given, and the students were asked to write the rest of the program:

```
PROGRAM RANGE

**********************************************************************
*       Program to read a list of noise levels in decibels and      *
*       determine the range of values.  A negative noise level is   *
*       used to signal the end of data.  Variables used are:        *
*       NOISE :   the current noise level being processed           *
*       LARGE :   the largest value read so far                     *
*       SMALL :   "  smallest  "     "   "  "                        *
**********************************************************************

    INTEGER NOISE, LARGE, SMALL
```

One attempted solution was the following (in which the statements have been numbered for easy reference):

```
(1)          PRINT *, 'ENTER NOISE LEVELS IN DECIBELS (INTEGERS).'
(2)          PRINT *, 'ENTER A NEGATIVE VALUE TO STOP.'

      * Initialize largest noise level with a small value
      * and smallest with a very large value

(3)          LARGE = 0
(4)          SMALL = 999

      * Read noise levels until a negative value is entered

(5) 10       PRINT *, 'NOISE LEVEL?'
(6)          READ *, NOISE
(7)          IF (NOISE .GT. LARGE) THEN
(8)             LARGE = NOISE
(9)          ELSE IF (NOISE .LT. SMALL) THEN
(10)            SMALL = NOISE
(11)         END IF
(12)     IF (NOISE .GE. 0) GO TO 10

(13)         PRINT *, 'RANGE OF NOISE LEVELS =', LARGE - SMALL, ' DECIBELS'
(14)         END
```

Execution of the program produced

```
              ENTER NOISE LEVELS IN DECIBELS (INTEGERS).
              ENTER A NEGATIVE VALUE TO STOP.
              NOISE LEVEL?
              94
              NOISE LEVEL?
              102
              NOISE LEVEL?
              88
              NOISE LEVEL?
              -1
              RANGE OF NOISE LEVELS =          103 DECIBELS
```

Although no error messages were displayed, the output clearly indicates that the program is not correct, because the correct range for this set of noise levels is 14.

One common technique used to locate logical errors is to construct manually a **trace table** of the segment of the program that is suspect. This technique is also known as **walking through the code** or **desk checking** and consists of recording in a table, step by step, the values of all or certain key variables in the program segment. In this example, the following trace table for the loop in statements 5–12 might be obtained:

Statements	NOISE	LARGE	SMALL	
	—	0	999	← Initial values
5–6	94	0	999	
7–8, 11–12	94	94	999	First pass through the loop
5–6	102	94	999	
7–8, 11–12	102	102	999	Second pass through the loop
5–6	88	102	88	
7, 9–12	88	102	88	Third pass through the loop
5–6	−1	102	88	
7, 9–12	−1	102	−1	Fourth pass through the loop

The last line in this trace table shows why the range was incorrect: The value of SMALL became −1 on the last pass through the loop, and this occurred because the value −1 used to signal the end of data was read and processed as a noise level.

The execution of a program segment can also be traced automatically by inserting temporary output statements or by using special system-debugging software to display the values of key variables at selected stages of program execution. For example, we might insert the statement

```
PRINT *, 'NOISE LEVEL', NOISE
```

after the READ statement to echo the data values as they are entered, and the statement

```
PRINT *, 'LARGEST', LARGE, ' SMALLEST', SMALL
```

at the bottom of the loop to display the values of these variables at the end of each pass through the loop. The resulting output then is

```
ENTER NOISE LEVELS IN DECIBELS (INTEGERS).
ENTER A NEGATIVE VALUE TO STOP.
NOISE LEVEL?
94
NOISE LEVEL         94
LARGEST         94 SMALLEST         999
NOISE LEVEL?
102
NOISE LEVEL        102
LARGEST        102 SMALLEST         999
NOISE LEVEL?
88
NOISE LEVEL         88
LARGEST        102 SMALLEST          88
NOISE LEVEL?
-1
NOISE LEVEL         -1
LARGEST        102 SMALLEST          -1
RANGE OF NOISE LEVELS =         103 DECIBELS
```

This technique must not be used indiscriminately, however, because an incorrect placement of such temporary debug statements may display output that is not helpful in locating the source of the error. Also, if too many such statements are used, so much output may be produced that it will be difficult to isolate the error.

Either a manual or an automatic tracing of this program reveals that the source of difficulty is that the value -1 used to signal the end of data was processed as an actual noise level. A first reaction might be to fix this error by using a nested IF statement:

```
IF (NOISE .GT. 0) THEN
    IF (NOISE .GT. LARGE) THEN
        LARGE = NOISE
    ELSE IF (NOISE .LT. SMALL) THEN
        SMALL = NOISE
    END IF
END IF
```

Such "quick and dirty patches" are usually not recommended, however, because they often fail to address the real source of the problem and only make the program unnecessarily complicated and messy.

The real source of difficulty in the preceding example is the repetition structure used. The value -1 was read and processed as an actual noise level because the student used a posttest loop in which the termination test is made at the bottom of the loop, *after* the statements in the body of the loop are executed. A better repetition structure would have been a pretest or while loop in which the termination test is made at the beginning of the loop, *before* the loop body is executed.

```
(1)         PRINT *, 'ENTER NOISE LEVELS IN DECIBELS (INTEGERS).'
(2)         PRINT *, 'ENTER A NEGATIVE VALUE TO STOP.'

     * Initialize largest noise level with a small value and smallest
     * with a very large value, and read the first noise level

(3)         LARGE = 0
(4)         SMALL = 999
(5)         PRINT *, 'NOISE LEVEL?'
(6)         READ *, NOISE

     * While noise level is not the end-of-data value do the following:

(7) 10      IF (NOISE .GT. 0) THEN
(8)             IF (NOISE .GT. LARGE) THEN
(9)                 LARGE = NOISE
(10)            ELSE IF (NOISE .LT. SMALL) THEN
(11)                SMALL = NOISE
(12)            END IF
(13)            PRINT *, 'NOISE LEVEL?'
(14)            READ *, NOISE
(15)            GO TO 10
(16)        END IF
(17)        PRINT *, 'RANGE OF NOISE LEVELS =', LARGE - SMALL, ' DECIBELS'
(18)        END
```

A sample run with the same data values now produces the correct output:

```
ENTER NOISE LEVELS IN DECIBELS (INTEGERS).
ENTER A NEGATIVE VALUE TO STOP.
NOISE LEVEL?
94
NOISE LEVEL?
102
NOISE LEVEL?
88
NOISE LEVEL?
-1
RANGE OF NOISE LEVELS =         14 DECIBELS
```

The student may now be tempted to conclude that the program is correct. However, to establish one's confidence in the correctness of a program, it is necessary to test it with several sets of data. For example, the following sample run reveals that the program still contains a logical error:

```
ENTER NOISE LEVELS IN DECIBELS (INTEGERS).
ENTER A NEGATIVE VALUE TO STOP.
NOISE LEVEL?
88
NOISE LEVEL?
94
NOISE LEVEL?
102
NOISE LEVEL?
-1
RANGE OF NOISE LEVELS =         -897 DECIBELS
```

Tracing the execution of the while loop produces the following:

Statements	NOISE	LARGE	SMALL	
	88	0	999	← Initial values
7–9	88	88	999	
12–15	94	88	999	First pass through the loop
7–9	94	94	999	
12–15	102	94	999	Second pass through the loop
7–9	102	102	999	
12–15	-1	102	999	Third pass through the loop

This trace table reveals that the value of SMALL never changes, suggesting that the statement

```
SMALL = NOISE
```

is never executed. This is because the logical expression NOISE .GT. LARGE is true for each data value, because these values are entered in increasing order;

consequently, the ELSE IF statement is never executed. This error can be corrected by using two logical IF statements in place of the IF–ELSE IF construct:

```
IF (NOISE .GT. LARGE) LARGE = NOISE
IF (NOISE .LT. SMALL) SMALL = NOISE
```

The resulting program is then correct but is not as efficient as it could be, because the logical expressions in both of these IF statements must be evaluated on each pass through the loop. A more efficient alternative is described in the exercises.

In summary, logical errors may be very difficult to detect, especially as programs become more complex, and it is very important that test data be carefully selected so that each part of the program is thoroughly tested. The program should be executed with data values entered in several different orders, with large data sets and small data sets, with extreme values, and with "bad" data. For example, entering the noise levels in increasing order revealed the existence of a logical error in the program considered earlier. Also, even though the last version of the program produces correct output if legitmate data values are read, the output

```
RANGE OF NOISE LEVELS = -999 DECIBELS
```

would be produced if a negative value was entered immediately. Although it may not be necessary to guard against invalid data input in student programs, those written for the public domain—especially programs used by computer novices—should be as **robust** as possible and should not "crash" or produce "garbage" results when unexpected data values are read.

When a logical error is detected, a trace table is an effective tool for locating the source of the error. Once it has been found, the program must be corrected and then tested again. It may be necessary to repeat this cycle of testing, tracing, and correcting many times before the program produces correct results for a wide range of test data, allowing us to be reasonably confident of its correctness. It is not possible, however, to check a program with every possible set of data, and thus obscure bugs may still remain. In some applications, this may not be critical, but in others, for example, in programs used to guide a space shuttle, errors cannot be tolerated. Certain formal techniques have been developed for proving that a program is correct and will always executed correctly (assuming no system malfunction), but a study of these techniques is beyond the scope of this introductory text.

4.11 Examples: Numerical Integration, Least Squares Line, Beam Deflection

EXAMPLE 1: Numerical Integration. One problem in which numerical methods are often used is that of approximating the area under the graph of a nonnegative function $y = f(x)$ from $x = a$ to $x = b$, thus obtaining an approximate value for the integral

$$\int_a^b f(x)\ dx$$

One simple method is to divide the interval $[a, b]$ into n subintervals each of length $\Delta x = (b - a)/n$ and then to form rectangles having these subintervals as bases and with altitudes given by the values of the function at the midpoints (or left or right endpoints) $x_1, x_2, \ldots, x_n$ of the subintervals. This is illustrated in Figure 4.25. The sum of the areas of these rectangles

$$f(x_1)\ \Delta x + f(x_2)\ \Delta x + \cdots + f(x_n)\ \Delta x$$

which is the same as

$$[f(x_1) + f(x_2) + \cdots + f(x_n)]\ \Delta x$$

or, written more concisely using Σ (sigma) notation,

$$\left[\sum_{i=1}^n f(x_i) \right] \Delta x$$

is then an approximation to the area under the curve.

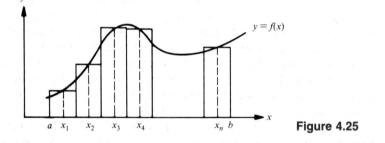

Figure 4.25

Figure 4.25 illustrates this method for a curve lying above the x axis. It may also be used to approximate the integral of a function whose graph falls below the x axis. In this case, the integral does not give the total area between the curve and the axis but, rather, gives the area of the region(s) above the axis minus the area of the region(s) below the axis.

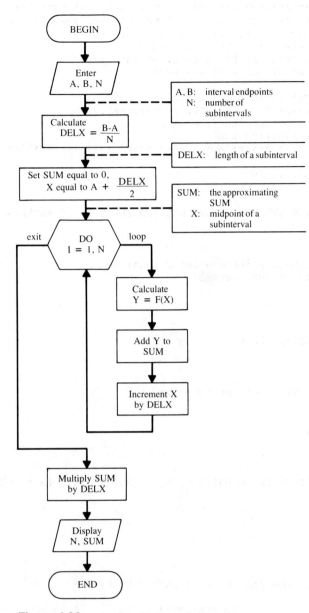

Figure 4.26

The program in Figure 4.27 uses this rectangle method to approximate an integral. The endpoints A and B of the interval of integration and the number N of subintervals are read during execution. It implements the algorithm given by the flowchart in Figure 4.26.

```
      PROGRAM AREA
************************************************************************
* Program to approximate the integral of a function over the interval *
* [A,B] using the rectangle method with altitudes chosen at the       *
* midpoints of the subintervals.  Variables used are:                 *
*     A, B   : the endpoints of the interval of integration           *
*     N      : the number of subintervals used                        *
*     I      : counter                                                 *
*     DELX   : the length of the subintervals                         *
*     X      : the midpoint of one of the subintervals                *
*     Y      : the value of the function at X                         *
*     SUM    : the approximating sum                                  *
************************************************************************

      REAL A, B, X, DELX, Y, SUM
      INTEGER N, I

      PRINT *, 'ENTER THE INTERVAL ENDPOINTS AND THE # OF SUBINTERVALS'
      READ *, A, B, N
      DELX = (B - A) / N

* Initialize the approximating SUM and set X equal to
* the midpoint of the first subinterval

      SUM = 0
      X = A + DELX / 2

* Now calculate and display the sum

      DO 10 I = 1, N

*         Calculate the value of the function at X

         Y = X ** 2 + 1
         SUM = SUM + Y
         X = X + DELX
10    CONTINUE
      SUM = DELX * SUM
      PRINT *, 'APPROXIMATE VALUE USING ', N, ' SUBINTERVALS IS ', SUM
      END


Sample runs:
===========


ENTER THE INTERVAL ENDPOINTS AND THE # OF SUBINTERVALS
0, 1, 10
APPROXIMATE VALUE USING          10 SUBINTERVALS IS      1.33250


ENTER THE INTERVAL ENDPOINTS AND THE # OF SUBINTERVALS
0, 1, 20
APPROXIMATE VALUE USING          20 SUBINTERVALS IS      1.33312


ENTER THE INTERVAL ENDPOINTS AND THE # OF SUBINTERVALS
0, 1, 100
APPROXIMATE VALUE USING          100 SUBINTERVALS IS      1.33332
```

Figure 4.27

EXAMPLE 2: Least Squares Line. Suppose the following data was collected in an experiment to measure the effect of temperature on resistance:

Temperature (°C)	Resistance (ohms)
20.0	761
31.5	817
50.0	874
71.8	917
91.3	1018

The plot of these data in Figure 4.28 indicates that there seems to be a linear relationship between temperature and resistance. We wish to find the equation of the line that "best fits" these data.

In general, whenever the relation between two quantities x and y appears to be roughly linear, that is, when a plot of the points (x, y) indicates that they tend to fall along a straight line, one can ask for the equation

$$y = mx + b$$

of a best-fitting line for these points. Such a **regression equation** can then be used to predict the value of y by evaluating the equation for a given value of x.

A standard method for finding the **regression coefficients** m and b is the **method of least squares,** so named because it produces the line $y = mx + b$, for which the sum of the squares of the deviations of the observed y values

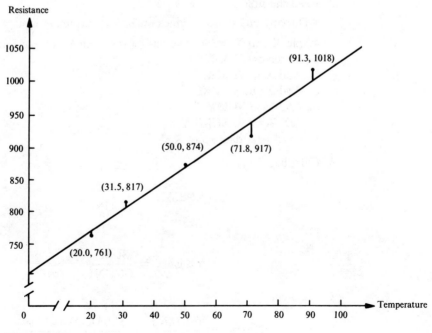

Figure 4.28

from the predicted y values (using the equation) is as small as possible (see Figure 4.28). This least squares line has the equation $y = mx + b$ where

$$\text{slope} = m = \frac{(\Sigma xy) - (\Sigma x)\bar{y}}{(\Sigma x^2) - (\Sigma x)\bar{x}}$$

$$y \text{ intercept} = b = \bar{y} - m\bar{x}$$

where

Σx is the sum of the x values
Σx^2 is the sum of the squares of the x values
Σxy is the sum of the products xy of corresponding x and y values
$\bar{x}$ and $\bar{y}$ are the means of the x and y values, respectively

The program in Figure 4.29 finds the equation of the least squares line for a given set of data points. Note that in this program a while loop controlled by an end-of-data condition is used to read the data values and to calculate the necessary sums. It implements the following algorithm:

ALGORITHM FOR LEAST SQUARES LINE

```
*   Algorithm to find the equation of the least squares line for a set      *
*   of COUNT data points (X, Y). SLOPE is its slope, and YINT is            *
*   its y intercept. SUMX, SUMY, SUMX2, and SUMXY are the                   *
*   sums of the Xs, the Ys, the squares of the Xs, and the products         *
*   X*Y. XMEAN and YMEAN are the means of the Xs and the                    *
*   Ys, respectively.                                                       *
```

1. Initialize COUNT, SUMX, SUMY, SUMX2, and SUMXY all to 0.
2. Read the first data point X, Y.

   * Dummy end-of-data values entered to terminate input *

3. While X and Y are not the end-of-data values, do the following:
   a. Increment COUNT by 1.
   b. Add X to SUMX.
   c. Add X^2 to SUMX2.
   d. Add Y to SUMY.
   e. Add X*Y to SUMXY.
   f. Read next data point X, Y.

4. Calculate

$$\text{XMEAN} = \frac{\text{SUMX}}{\text{COUNT}}$$

and

$$\text{YMEAN} = \frac{\text{SUMY}}{\text{COUNT}}$$

5. Calculate

$$\text{SLOPE} = \frac{(\text{SUMXY} - \text{SUMX}*\text{YMEAN})}{(\text{SUMX2} - \text{SUMX}*\text{XMEAN})}$$

and

$$YINT = YMEAN - SLOPE*XMEAN$$

6. Display SLOPE and YINT.

```
        PROGRAM LSQUAR
*****************************************************************
* Program to find the equation of the least squares line for a set  *
* of data points.  Variables used are:                              *
*     X, Y    : (X,Y) is the observed data point                    *
*     COUNT   : number of data points                               *
*     SUMX    : sum of the X's                                      *
*     SUMX2   : sum of the squares of the X's                       *
*     SUMY    : sum of the Y's                                      *
*     SUMXY   : sum of the products X*Y                             *
*     XMEAN   : mean of the X's                                     *
*     YMEAN   : mean of the Y's                                     *
*     SLOPE   : slope of least squares line                         *
*     YINT    : y-intercept of the line                             *
*****************************************************************

        INTEGER COUNT
        REAL X, Y, SUMX, SUMX2, SUMY, SUMXY, XMEAN, YMEAN, SLOPE, YINT

* Initialize counter and the sums to 0 and read first data point

        COUNT = 0
        SUMX = 0
        SUMX2 = 0
        SUMY = 0
        SUMXY = 0
        PRINT *, 'ENTER POINT (-999, -999 TO STOP)'
        READ *, X, Y

* While there are more data, calculate the necessary sums
* and read the next data point (X, Y)

10      IF ((X .NE. -999.) .AND. (Y .NE. -999.)) THEN
            COUNT = COUNT + 1
            SUMX = SUMX + X
            SUMX2 = SUMX2 + X ** 2
            SUMY = SUMY + Y
            SUMXY = SUMXY + X * Y
            PRINT *, 'ENTER NEXT POINT'
            READ *, X, Y
            GO TO 10
        END IF
```

Figure 4.29

Figure 4.29 **(continued)**

```
* Find equation of least squares line

        XMEAN = SUMX / COUNT
        YMEAN = SUMY / COUNT
        SLOPE = (SUMXY - SUMX * YMEAN) / (SUMX2 - SUMX * XMEAN)
        YINT = YMEAN - SLOPE * XMEAN
        PRINT *
        PRINT *, 'EQUATION OF LEAST SQUARES LINE IS Y = MX + B, WHERE'
        PRINT *, 'SLOPE = M =        ', SLOPE
        PRINT *, 'Y-INTERCEPT = B =', YINT
        END


Sample run:
==========

ENTER POINT (-999, -999 TO STOP)
20.0 761
ENTER NEXT POINT
31.5, 817
ENTER NEXT POINT
50.0, 874
ENTER NEXT POINT
71.8, 917
ENTER NEXT POINT
91.3, 1018
ENTER NEXT POINT
-999, -999

EQUATION OF LEAST SQUARES LINE IS Y = MX + B, WHERE
SLOPE = M =              3.33658
Y-INTERCEPT = B =        700.828
```

EXAMPLE 3: Beam Deflection. The analysis of beams is an important part of the structural analysis carried out before the construction of a building begins. One frequently used type of beam is a *cantilever beam,* which has one end fixed and the other end free. The deflection at the free end of the beam depends on the beam's loading conditions. Three of the many possible loading cases are shown in the following diagrams. In these diagrams, W is the total load, δ is the deflection caused by the load, x is the distance from the free end of the beam, ℓ is the length of the beam, a and b are lengths as shown, and w is the unit load in the uniform loading cases.

1. end load, W

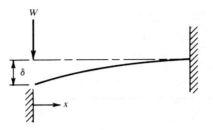

2. intermediate load, W

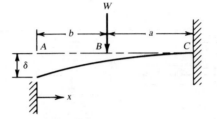

3. uniform load, $W = w\ell$

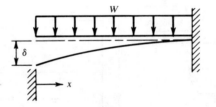

We assume that all forces are coplanar, that the beam is in static equilibrium, and that the mass of the beam may be neglected. With these assumptions, the following equations can be used to calculate the deflections for the three load cases:

1. $\delta = [-W / (6EI)][x^3 - 3\ell^2 x + 2\ell^3]$
2. $\delta = [-W / (6EI)][-a^3 + 3a^2\ell - 3a^2 x]$ from A to B
   $\delta = [-W / (6EI)][(x - b)^3 - 3a^2(x - b) + 2a^3]$ from B to C
3. $\delta = [-W / (24EI\ell)][x^4 - 4\ell^3 x + 3\ell^4]$

Here E is the modulus of elasticity, which depends on the material of which the beam is made, and I is the moment of inertia, which is dependent on the cross section of the beam. In this example we consider an I-beam made of steel where I $= 4.15 \times 10^{-8}$ and E $= 2.05 \times 10^{11}$.

The program in Figure 4.31 reads the beam-loading case and the appropriate parameters for that case. It then calculates the deflections at ten equally

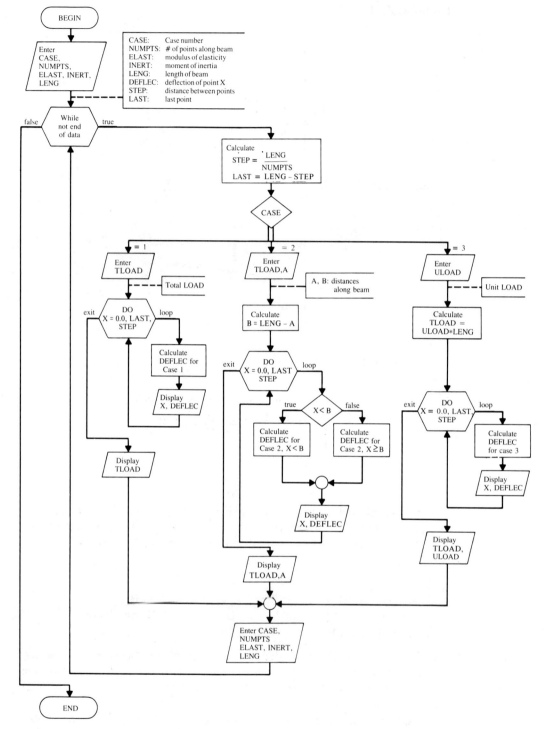

Figure 4.30

spaced points along the beam (including the free end but not the fixed end). It
implements the algorithm given in the flowchart of Figure 4.30.

```
         PROGRAM BEAM
*******************************************************************
*                                                                 *
*     This program calculates deflections in a cantilevered beam  *
*     under a given load. Three different loading conditions are  *
*     analyzed.                                                    *
*                                                                 *
*     Case #1 : a single point load at the free end of the beam   *
*     Case #2 : a single point load at an interior point          *
*     Case #3 : load uniformly distributed along the beam         *
*                                                                 *
*     ELAST  : modulus of elasticity                              *
*     INERT  : moment of inertia                                  *
*     TLOAD  : total load                                         *
*     ULOAD  : unit load when uniformly distributed (Case # 3)    *
*     DEFLEC : deflection at X meters                             *
*     X      : distance from the free end of the beam             *
*     A,B    : distances along the beam (used in Case 2)          *
*     CASE   : number of case in question                         *
*     LENG   : length of the beam                                 *
*     NUMPTS : number of divisions at which deflections are found *
*     STEP   : distance between points                            *
*     LAST   : last point                                         *
*     TEMP   : temporary variable                                 *
*                                                                 *
*******************************************************************

         INTEGER CASE, NUMPTS
         REAL ELAST, INERT, LENG, TLOAD, ULOAD, DEFLEC, X,
     +       A, B, STEP, LAST, TEMP

         PRINT *, 'Enter case #, # points, modulus of elasticity'
         PRINT *, 'moment of inertia, and length of the beam',
     +       ' (all 0''s to stop)'
         READ *, CASE, NUMPTS, ELAST, INERT, LENG

***** While not end of data do the following:

10       IF (CASE .NE. 0) THEN
             STEP = LENG / REAL(NUMPTS)
             LAST = LENG - STEP

         IF (CASE .EQ. 1) THEN
             PRINT *, 'ENTER TOTAL LOAD:'
             READ *, TLOAD

             PRINT *, '     DISTANCE          DEFLECTION'
             DO 20 X = 0.0, LAST, STEP
                 TEMP = X**3 - 3.0*LENG**2*X + 2.0*LENG**3
                 DEFLEC = (-TLOAD / (6.0*ELAST*INERT)) * TEMP
                 PRINT *, X, DEFLEC
```

Figure 4.31

Figure 4.31   (continued)

```
20              CONTINUE
                PRINT *
                PRINT *,
                PRINT *,  'TOTAL LOAD ',TLOAD

         ELSE IF (CASE .EQ. 2) THEN
                PRINT *, 'Enter total load and distance A:'
                READ *, TLOAD, A
                B = LENG - A

                PRINT *, '    DISTANCE            DEFLECTION'
                DO 30 X = 0.0, LAST, STEP
                    IF (X .LT. B) THEN
                        TEMP = -A**3 + 3.0 *A**2*LENG
     +                       - 3.0*A**2*X
                    ELSE
                        TEMP = (X - B)**3 - 3.0* A**2* (X - B)
     +                       + 2.0*A**3
                    ENDIF
                    DEFLEC = (-TLOAD / (6.0*ELAST*INERT)) * TEMP
                    PRINT *, X ,DEFLEC
30              CONTINUE
                PRINT *,
                PRINT *, 'TOTAL LOAD ', TLOAD
                PRINT *, 'DISTANCE A ', A

         ELSE

                PRINT *, 'Enter unit load:'
                READ *, ULOAD
                TLOAD = ULOAD * LENG

                PRINT *, '    DISTANCE            DEFLECTION'
                DO 40 X = 0.0, LAST, STEP
                    TEMP = X**4 - 4.0*LENG**3*X + 3.0*LENG**4
                    DEFLEC = (-TLOAD / (24.0*ELAST*INERT*LENG))*TEMP
                    PRINT *, X, DEFLEC
40              CONTINUE
                PRINT *, ' '
                PRINT *, 'TOTAL LOAD ', TLOAD
                PRINT *, 'UNIT LOAD ', ULOAD
         END IF

         PRINT *,
         PRINT *,
         PRINT *, 'Enter case #, # points, modulus of elasticity'
         PRINT *, 'moment of inertia, and length of the beam',
     +           ' (all 0''s to stop):'
         READ *, CASE, NUMPTS, ELAS, INERT, LENG
         GO TO 10
      END IF
      END
```

Figure 4.31   (continued)

```
Sample run:
==========


Enter case #, # points, modulus of elasticity
moment of inertia, and length of the beam (all 0's to stop)
1  10
2.05E11  4.15E-8  1.0
ENTER TOTAL LOAD:
125.0
        DISTANCE            DEFLECTION
        0.000000E+00       -4.897640E-03
        0.100000          -4.165443E-03
        0.200000          -3.447938E-03
        0.300000          -2.759820E-03
        0.400000          -2.115781E-03
        0.500000          -1.530513E-03
        0.600000          -1.018710E-03
        0.700000          -5.950646E-04
        0.800000          -2.742692E-04
        0.899999          -7.101677E-05


TOTAL LOAD        125.000


Enter case #, # points, modulus of elasticity
moment of inertia, and length of the beam (all 0's to stop):
2  10
2.05E11  4.15E-8  1.0
Enter total load and distance A:
125.0   0.5
        DISTANCE            DEFLECTION
        0.000000E+00       -1.530512E-03
        0.100000          -1.346851E-03
        0.200000          -1.163190E-03
        0.300000          -9.795281E-04
        0.400000          -7.958667E-04
        0.500000          -6.122052E-04
        0.600000          -4.309926E-04
        0.700000          -2.644730E-04
        0.800000          -1.273391E-04
        0.899999          -3.428388E-05

TOTAL LOAD        125.000
DISTANCE A       0.500000


Enter case #, # points, modulus of elasticity
moment of inertia, and length of the beam (all 0's to stop):
3  10
2.05E11  4.15E-8  1.0
```

Figure 4.31 (continued)

```
Enter unit load:
125.0
       DISTANCE            DEFLECTION
       0.000000E+00      -1.836615E-03
       0.100000         -1.591794E-03
       0.200000         -1.347830E-03
       0.300000         -1.106928E-03
       0.400000         -8.727596E-04
       0.500000         -6.504679E-04
       0.600000         -4.466651E-04
       0.700000         -2.694319E-04
       0.800000         -1.283186E-04
       0.899999         -3.434486E-05

TOTAL LOAD      125.000
UNIT LOAD       125.000


Enter case #, # points, modulus of elasticity
moment of inertia, and length of the beam (all 0's to stop):
0 0 0 0 0
```

Exercises

1. Write in pseudocode the algorithm for approximating an integral given by the flowchart of Figure 4.26 in Example 1 of Section 4.11.

2. Display in a flowchart the algorithm for calculating a least squares line given in Example 2 of Section 4.11.

3. Write in pseudocode the algorithm for determining the deflection in a cantilever beam given by the flowchart of Figure 4.30 in Example 3 of Section 4.11.

4. Write FORTRAN program segments to

   (a) Print the first 100 positive integers using a DO loop.
   (b) Branch to statement 50 if the value of X is negative or greater than 10.
   (c) Print the value of X and decrease X by 0.5 as long as X is positive.
   (d) Read values for A, B, and C and print their sum, repeating this procedure while none of A, B, or C is negative.
   (e) Print the square roots of the first 25 odd positive integers.
   (f) Calculate and print the squares of consecutive positive integers until the difference between a square and the preceding one is greater than 50.
   (g) Print a list of points (X, Y) on the graph of the equation $Y = X^3 - 3X + 1$ for X ranging from -2 to 2 steps of .1.

5. Suppose that the pretest loop in the summation algorithm in Section 4.6 were replaced by a posttest loop so that the statements in the programs of Figures 4.19 and 4.21 that implement this algorithm were replaced by

```
        PRINT *, 'ENTER VALUE 1 + 2 + ... + ? IS TO EXCEED'
        READ *, LIMIT
        NUMBER = 0
        SUM = 0

* Increment NUMBER and add it to SUM until SUM exceeds LIMIT

10      NUMBER = NUMBER + 1
        SUM = SUM + NUMBER
        IF (SUM .LE. LIMIT) GO TO 10

* Print the results

        PRINT *, 'FOR NUMBER =', NUMBER
        PRINT *, '1 + 2 + ... + NUMBER =', SUM
        END
```

   Will the resulting program produce the same results as those in Figures 4.19 and 4.21 in all cases?

6. (a) Design an algorithm that uses a posttest loop to count the number of digits in a given integer.
   (b) Write FORTRAN statements to implement the algorithm in part (a).
   (c) Rewrite the algorithm in part (a) so that it uses a pretest loop.
   (d) Write FORTRAN statements to implement the algorithm in part (c).
   (e) Which of these repetition structures seems more natural, and why?

7. The velocity of a falling parachutist might be approximated by the equation

$$V(t) = \frac{gm}{c} (1 - e^{(-c/m)t})$$

   where g is the acceleration due to gravity, c is the drag coefficient, and m is the parachutist's mass. Modify the program in Figure 4.27 to approximate the distance the parachutist falls from time $t = A$ to time $t = B$. (Distance is the integral of the velocity.) Use values of 9.8 (m/sec^2), 12.4 (kg/sec), and 81.7 (kg) for g, c, and m, respectively.

8. Write a program to implement the algorithm displayed in the flowchart of Figure 4.32.

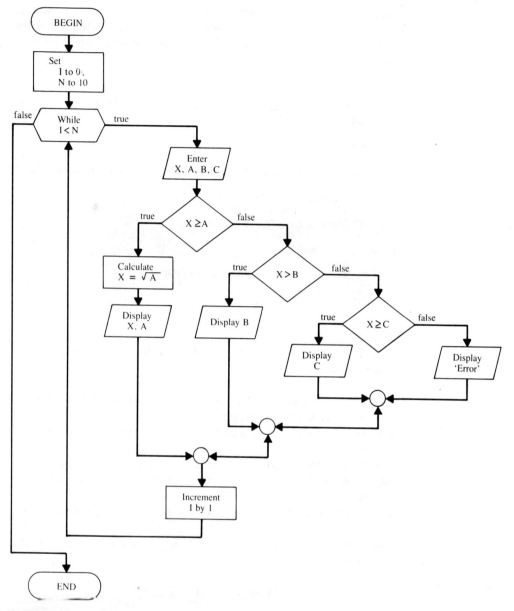

Figure 4.32

9. Write a program to implement the algorithm for approximating the values of the cosine function given in Section 2.3.

10. Write a program for the "divide and average" algorithm for calculating square roots described in Exercise 13 of Chapter 2.

11. Write a program to implement the algorithm for estimating the time required to empty a reservoir described in Exercise 16 of Chapter 2.

12. If a loan of A dollars, which carries a monthly interest rate of I percent, is to be paid off in N months, then the monthly payment P is given by

$$P = A \left[\frac{I(1 + I)^N}{(1 + I)^N - 1} \right]$$

During this time period, some of each monthly payment is used to repay that month's accrued interest, and the rest is used to reduce the balance owed.

Write a program to print an *amortization table* which displays the payment number, the amount of the monthly payment, the interest for that month, the amount of the payment applied to the principal, and the new balance. Use your program to produce an amortization table for a loan of $50,000 to be repaid in 36 months at 1 percent per month.

13. (a) Write a program that solves the noise-level range problem discussed in Section 4.10 but is more efficient than those described in the text. (Hint: Initialize LARGE and SMALL to the first data value.)

   (b) For each of the following data sets, construct a trace table for the repetition structure used in your program and determine the range of noise levels that will be computed by your program:
      (i) 88, 102, 94, −1
      (ii) 88, 94, 102, −1
      (iii) 102, 94, 88, −1
      (iv) 88, −1
      (v) −1

14. Write a program to read a set of numbers, count them, and find and print the largest and smallest numbers in the list and their positions in the list.

15. Write a program to read a set of numbers, count them, and calculate the mean, variance, and standard deviation of the set of numbers. The *mean* and *variance* of numbers $x_1, x_2, \ldots, x_n$ can be calculated using the following formulas:

$$\text{mean} = \frac{1}{n} \sum_{i=1}^{n} x_i, \quad \text{variance} = \frac{1}{n} \sum_{i=1}^{n} x_i^2 - \frac{1}{n^2} \left(\sum_{i=1}^{n} x_i \right)^2$$

The *standard deviation* is the square root of the variance.

16. The following is the initial part of the sequence of *Fibonacci numbers:* 1, 1, 2, 3, 5, 8, 13, 21, . . . , where each number after the first two is the sum of the two preceding numbers. One property of this sequence is that the ratios of consecutive Fibonacci numbers (1/1, 1/2, 2/3, 3/5, . . .) approach the "golden ratio"

$$\frac{\sqrt{5} - 1}{2}$$

Write a program to calculate all the Fibonacci numbers less than 5000 and the decimal values of the ratios of consecutive Fibonacci numbers.

17. Suppose that a ball dropped from a building bounces off the pavement and that on each bounce it returns to a certain constant percentage of its previous height. Write a program to read the height from which the ball was dropped, the percentage rebound, and the number of bounces. Then for the given number of bounces, print the height of the ball at the top of each bounce, the distance traveled during that bounce, and the total distance traveled thus far.

18. Suppose that at a given time, genotypes AA, AB, and BB appear in the proportions x, y, and z, respectively, where $x = .25$, $y = .5$, and $z = .25$. If individuals of type AA cannot reproduce, then the probability that one parent will donate gene A to an offspring is

$$p = \frac{1}{2}\left(\frac{y}{y + z}\right)$$

since $y/(y + z)$ is the probability that the parent is of type AB, and $1/2$ is the probability that such a parent will donate gene A. Then, the proportions x', y', z' of AA, AB, and BB, respectively, in the succeeding generation are given by

$$x' = p^2, \; y' = 2p(1 - p), \; z' = (1 - p)^2$$

and the new probability is given by

$$p' = \frac{1}{2}\left(\frac{y'}{y' + z'}\right)$$

Write a program to calculate and print the generation number and the proportions of AA, AB, and BB under appropriate headings for 30 generations. (Note that the proportions of AA and AB should approach 0, since gene A will gradually disappear.)

19. Suppose that two hallways, one 8 feet wide and another 10 feet wide, meet at a right angle and that a ladder is to be carried around the corner from the narrower hallway into the wider one. Using the similar triangles shown below we see that

$$L = x + \frac{10x}{\sqrt{x^2 - 64}}$$

Write a program that initializes x at 8.1 and then increments it by .1 to find to the nearest .1 foot the length of the longest ladder that can be carried around the corner.

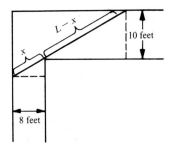

20. Two measures of central tendency other than the (arithmetic) mean (defined in Exercise 15) are the *geometric mean* and the *harmonic mean* defined for a list of numbers $x_1, x_2, \ldots, x_n$ as follows:

$$\text{Geometric mean} = \sqrt[n]{x_1 \cdot x_2 \cdots \cdots x_n}$$

$$= \text{the } n\text{th root of the product of the numbers}$$

$$\text{harmonic mean} = \frac{n}{\dfrac{1}{x_1} + \dfrac{1}{x_2} + \cdots + \dfrac{1}{x_n}}$$

Write a program that reads a list of numbers, counts them, and calculates their arithmetic mean, geometric mean, and harmonic mean. These values should be printed with appropriate labels.

21. The infinite series

$$\sum_{k=0}^{\infty} \frac{1}{k!}$$

converges to the number *e*. (For a positive integer *k*, *k*!, read "*k* factorial," is the product of the integers from 1 through *k*; 0! is defined to be 1.) The *n*th *partial sum* of such a series is the sum of the first *n* terms of the series; for example,

$$\frac{1}{0!} + \frac{1}{1!} + \frac{1}{2!} + \frac{1}{3!}$$

is the fourth partial sum. Write a program to calculate and print the first 10 partial sums of this series.

22. A person's biorhythm index on a given day is the sum of the values of his or her physical, intellectual, and emotional cycles. Each of these cycles begins at birth and forms a sine curve having an amplitude of 1 and periods of 23, 33, and 28 days, respectively. Write a program that accepts the current date, a person's name, and his or her birthdate and then calculates the biorhythm index for that person. (See Exercise 1(c) of Section 4.4 regarding leap years.)

23. In Example 1 of Section 4.11 we considered the numerical approximation of integrals using rectangles. As Figure 4.33 indicates, a better approximation can usually be obtained by using trapezoids rather than rectangles.

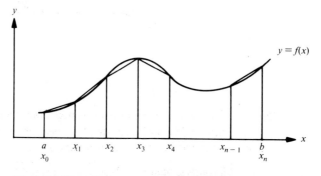

Figure 4.33

The sum of the areas of these trapezoids is given by

$$\sum_{i=1}^{n} [f(x_{i-1}) + f(x_i)] \frac{\Delta x}{2}$$

which can also be written

$$\frac{\Delta x}{2} [f(x_0) + 2f(x_1) + 2f(x_2) + \cdots + 2f(x_{n-1}) + f(x_n)]$$

or

$$\Delta x \left[\frac{f(a) + f(b)}{2} + \sum_{i=1}^{n-1} f(x_i) \right]$$

Write a program to approximate an integral using this *trapezoidal method*.

24. Another method of numerical integration that in general produces better approximations than does the rectangle method described in Example 1 of Section 4.11 or the trapezoidal method described in Exercise 23 is based on the use of parabolas and is known as *Simpson's Rule*. In this method, the interval $[a, b]$ is divided into an even number n of subintervals, each of length Δx, and the sum

$$\frac{\Delta x}{3} [f(x_0) + 4f(x_1) + 2f(x_2) + 4f(x_3)$$
$$+ 2f(x_4) + \cdots + 2f(x_{n-2}) + 4f(x_{n-1}) + f(x_n)]$$

is used to approximate the integral of f over the interval $[a, b]$. Write a program to approximate an integral using Simpson's Rule.

25. In Example 2 of Section 4.11 we considered the problem of fitting a line to a set of data points. In some situations, a better fit is obtained by using an exponential function $y = ae^{bx}$. To determine the constants a and b, one method frequently used is to take logarithms

$$\ln y = \ln a + bx$$

and then use the method of least squares to find values for the constants b and $\ln a$. Write a program that uses this method to fit an exponential curve to a set of data points. Run it for the values in the following table, which gives barometric pressure readings, in millimeters of mercury, at various altitudes.

Altitude (meters) x	Barometric Pressure (millimeters) y
0	760
500	714
1000	673
1500	631
2000	594
2500	563

26. Related to the least squares method (see Example 2 of Section 4.11) is the problem of determining whether there is a linear relationship between two quantities x and y. One statistical measure used in this connection is the *correlation coefficient*. It is equal to 1 if there is a perfect positive linear relationship between x and y, that is, if y increases linearly as x increases. If there is a perfect negative linear relationship between x and y, that is, if y decreases linearly as x increases, then the correlation coefficient has the value -1. A value of zero for the correlation coefficient indicates that there is no linear relationship between x and y, and nonzero values between -1 and 1 indicate a partial linear relationship between the two quantities. The correlation coefficient for a set of n pairs of x and y values is calculated by

$$\frac{n(\Sigma xy) - (\Sigma x)(\Sigma y)}{\sqrt{(n\Sigma x^2 - (\Sigma x)^2)(n\Sigma y^2 - (\Sigma y)^2)}}$$

where

Σx is the sum of all the x values
Σy is the sum of all the y values
Σx^2 is the sum of the squares of the x values
Σy^2 is the sum of the squares of the y values
Σxy is the sum of the products xy of corresponding x and y values

Write a program to calculate the correlation coefficient of a set of data points. Run it for the data points used in the sample run in Figure 4.29 and for several data sets of your own.

Programming Pointers

Program Design

1. *All programs can be written using the three control structures considered in this chapter: sequential, repetition, and selection.*

2. *Multialternative selection structures can be implemented more efficiently with an* IF–ELSE IF–END IF *structure than with a sequence of* IF *statements.* For example, using the statements

```
IF (SCORE .LT. 60) GRADE = 'F'
IF ((SCORE .GE. 60) .AND. (SCORE .LT. 70)) GRADE = 'D'
IF ((SCORE .GE. 70) .AND. (SCORE .LT. 80)) GRADE = 'C'
IF ((SCORE .GE. 80) .AND. (SCORE .LT. 90)) GRADE = 'B'
IF (SCORE .GE. 90) GRADE = 'A'
```

is less efficient than

```
IF (SCORE .LT. 60) THEN
    GRADE = 'F'
ELSE IF (SCORE .LT. 70) THEN
    GRADE = 'D'
ELSE IF (SCORE .LT. 80) THEN
    GRADE = 'C'
ELSE IF (SCORE .LT. 90) THEN
    GRADE = 'B'
ELSE
    GRADE = 'A'
END IF
```

In the first case, all of the IF statements are executed for each score processed, and three of the logical expressions are compound expressions. In the second case, each logical expression is simple, and not all of the expressions are evaluated for each score; for example, for a score of 65, only the logical expressions SCORE .LT. 60 and SCORE .LT. 70 are evaluated.

3. *Use* CONTINUE *statements to close* DO *loops, and for nested* DO *loops, use different* CONTINUE *statements to close each loop.*

4. *The* GO TO *statement should ordinarily be used only in repetition structures. Indiscriminate use of* GO TO *makes the logic of the program difficult to follow and is symptomatic of a poorly designed program.*

Potential Problems

1. *Periods must be used in the relational operators* .LT., .GT., .EQ., .LE., .GE., *and* .NE., *and in the logical operators* .NOT., .AND., .OR., .EQV., *and* .NEQV..

2. *Parentheses must enclose the logical expression in an* IF *statement.*

3. *Real quantities that are algebraically equal may yield a false logical expression when compared with* .EQ. *because most real values are not stored exactly.* For example, even though the two real expressions $X * (1.0 / X)$ and 1.0 are algebraically equal, the logical expression $X * (1.0 / X)$ .EQ. 1.0 is usually false. Thus, if two real values RNUM1 and RNUM2 are subject to the *roundoff error* caused by inexact representation, it is usually not advisable to check whether they are equal. Rather, one should check whether the absolute value of their difference is small:

```
IF (ABS(RNUM1 - RNUM2) .LT. ERRTOL) THEN
       :
       :
```

where ERRTOL is some small positive real value such as 1E-6.

4. *Each block* IF *statement must have an* END IF *following the block.*

5. *The control variable in a* DO *loop may not be modified within the loop. Modifying the initial value, limit, or step size does not affect the number of repetitions.* For example, the statements

```
K = 5
DO 10 I = 1, K
     PRINT *, K
     K = K - 1
10 CONTINUE
```

produce the output

```
5
4
3
2
1
```

Modifying the control variable I, as in the following DO loop

```
DO 10 I = 1, 5
     PRINT *, I
     I = I - 1
10 CONTINUE
```

is an error and produces a message such as

```
A CONTROL VARIABLE MAY NOT BE ALTERED IN A DO LOOP
```

One consequence is that nested DO loops must have different control variables.

6. *The statements within a loop controlled by a logical expression must eventually cause the termination condition to be satisfied, because otherwise an infinite loop results.* For example, if X is a real variable, the statements

```
*      While X is not equal to 1, print its value and
*      increment it
10     IF (X .NE. 1.0) THEN
          PRINT *, X
          X = X + .3
          GO TO 10
       END IF
```

produce an infinite loop.

Output:

```
0.000000
0.300000
0.600000
0.900000
1.200000
1.500000
1.800000
    :
```

Since the value of X is never equal to 1.0, repetition is not terminated. In view of Potential Problem 3, the statements

```
*      While X is not equal to 1, print its value and
*      increment it

10     IF (X .NE. 1.0) THEN
           PRINT *, X
           X = X + .2
           GO TO 10
       END IF
```

may also produce an infinite loop.

Output:

```
0.000000
0.200000
0.400000
0.600000
0.800000
1.000000
1.200000
1.400000
1.600000
    :
    :
```

Since X is initialized to 0 and .2 is added to X five times, X should have the value 1. However, the logical expression X .NE. 1.0 may remain true because most real values are not stored exactly.

7. *It should be assumed that all subexpressions are evaluated in determining the value of a compound logical expression.* Suppose, for example, that we write a statement of the form

```
IF ((X .GE. 0) .AND. (SQRT(X) .LT. 5.0)) THEN
    PRINT *, 'SQUARE ROOT IS LESS THAN 5'
        :
        :
END IF
```

in which the subexpression X .GE. 0 is intended to prevent an attempt to calculate the square root of a negative number when X is negative.

Some FORTRAN compilers may evaluate the subexpression X .GE. 0 and, if it is false, may not evaluate the second subexpression, SQRT(X) .LT. 5.0. Other compilers evaluate both parts, and thus an error results when X is negative. This error can be avoided by rewriting the statement as

```
IF (X .GE. 0) THEN
    IF (SQRT(X) .LT. 5.0) THEN
        PRINT *, 'SQUARE ROOT IS LESS THAN 5'
            :
            :
    END IF
END IF
```

Program Style

In this text, we use the following conventions for formatting the statements considered in this chapter:

1. *The body of a loop should be indented.*

```
************** DO-loops **************
    DO ## variable = init, limit, step
        statement-1

            :
            :

        statement-n
##  CONTINUE

********** WHILE (pretest) loops **********
    WHILE (logical-expression) DO
        statement-1

            :
            :

        statement-n
    END WHILE

##  IF (logical-expression) THEN
        statement-1

            :
            :

        statement-n
        GO TO ##
    END IF

************** Posttest loops **************
##      statement-1

            :
            :

        statement-n
    IF (logical-expression) GO TO ##
```

2. *The block(s) within a block IF statement should be indented.*

```
IF logical-expression
    statement-1
        .
        .
        .
    statement-n
ELSE
    statement-i
        .
        .
        .
    statement-m
END IF
```

3. *Statement labels are arranged in increasing order, usually in increments of ten.* The advantage of using such increments is that if labeled statements must be inserted in later versions of the program, the increasing order can still be maintained.

Variations and Extensions

The standard FORTRAN control structures described in this chapter are provided in nearly every version of FORTRAN. However, some versions have a number of variations and extensions such as the following:

- Comparisons of numeric expressions with character expressions by the relational operators may be allowed.

- There may be an upper limit on the number of iterations specified in a DO loop.

- Other selection and repetition structures may be provided.

See Appendix F for additional details.

5

Input/Output

When I read some of the rules for speaking and writing the English language correctly . . . I think
 Any fool can make a rule
 And every fool will mind it.

H. Thoreau

In Chapter 3 we noted that there are two types of input/output statements in FORTRAN, **list-directed** and **formatted** (or more precisely, user-formatted). In our discussion thus far, we have restricted our attention to list-directed input/ output. This method is particularly easy to use, as the format for the input or output of data is automatically supplied by the compiler. It does not, however, permit the user to control the precise format of the data. For example, using list-directed output, one cannot specify that real values are to be displayed with only two digits to the right of the decimal point, even though this might be appropriate in some applications. The precise form of the output can be specified, however, using the formatted output statement introduced in this chapter.

Sometimes input data has a predetermined form, and the programmer must design the program to read this data. This can be accomplished by using the formatted input statement also introduced in this chapter.

Finally, if the volume of input data is large, a **file** is usually prepared, and during program execution, data is read from it rather than from some input device. In this chapter we introduce some statements for processing files.

List-directed input/output can be viewed as a special case of formatted input/output. Thus, some additional features of list-directed input/output are also considered in this chapter.

5.1 Formatted Output

There are two output statements in FORTRAN, the PRINT statement and the WRITE statement. The **PRINT statement** is the simpler of the two and has the form

> PRINT *format-identifier, output-list*

The *output-list* is a single expression or a list of expressions separated by commas; it may also be empty, in which case the comma preceding the list is omitted. The *format-identifier* specifies the format in which values of the expressions in the output list are to be displayed. A large part of this section is devoted to the design of these format identifiers.

A format identifier may be

1. An asterisk (*).
2. The label of a FORMAT statement (or a variable to which such a label has been assigned by an ASSIGN statement).
3. A character expression or array whose value specifies the format for the output. (This is discussed in Chapter 6.)

As we saw in Chapter 3, an asterisk indicates list-directed output whose format is determined by the types of expressions in the output list. This is adequate when the precise form of the output is not important. However, for reports and other kinds of output in which results must appear in a precise form, list-directed formatting is not adequate, and format identifiers of type 2 or 3 must be used.

In the second type of format identifier, the formatting information is supplied by a **FORMAT statement** whose label is specified. This statement has the form

> FORMAT (*list of format descriptors*)

Each of the format descriptors that appears in the list of either the second or third type of format identifier specifies precisely the format in which to display the items in the output list. For example, some output statements that could be used to display the value 17 of the integer variable NUMBER and the value 10.25 of the real variable TEMP are the following:

```
PRINT *, NUMBER, TEMP
PRINT 20, NUMBER, TEMP
```

where statement 20 is the statement

```
20 FORMAT (1X, I5, F8.2)
```

In the FORMAT statement, 1X, I5, and F8.2 are format descriptors that specify the format in which the values of NUMBER and TEMP are to be displayed. As we know, list-directed output like that in the first statement is compiler dependent but might appear as follows:

```
|_____17_____10.2500
|
```

The output produced by the second form is not compiler dependent and appears as follows:

```
|___17____10.25
|
```

(If control characters are not in effect, there will be one additional space at the beginning of this output line.)

There are many format descriptors that may be used in format identifiers. Table 5.1 gives a complete list of these descriptors. In this section we consider those most commonly used: I, F, E, character strings, T, X, and /, deferring the others to Section 5.6.

Control Characters. In many computer systems, when output is directed to a printer, the first character of each line of output is used to control the vertical spacing. If this character is a **control character,** it is used only to effect the

Table 5.1

Format Descriptor		Use
Iw	Iw.m	Integer data
Fw.d		Real data in decimal notation
Ew.d	Ew.dEe	Real data in scientific notation
Dw.d		Double precision data
Gw.d		F or E input/output, depending on the value of the item
A	Aw	Character data
'x . . . x'	nHx . . . x	Character strings
Lw		Logical data
Tc	TLn	TRn	Tab descriptors
nX		Horizontal spacing
/		Vertical spacing
:		Format scanning control
S	SP	SS	Sign descriptors
kP		Scale factor
BN		BZ	Blank interpretation

w: positive integer constant specifying the field width
m: nonnegative integer constant specifying the minimum number of digits to be displayed
d: nonnegative integer constant specifying the number of digits to the right of the decimal point
e: nonnegative integer constant specifying the number of digits in an exponent
x: character
c: positive integer constant representing a column number
n: positive integer constant specifying the number of columns
k: nonnegative integer constant specifying a scale factor

appropriate printer control and is not printed. The standard control characters with their effects are as follows:

Control Character	Effect
blank	Normal spacing: advance to the next line before printing
0	Double spacing: skip one line before printing
1	Advance to top of next page before printing
+	Overprint the last line printed

Some systems may implement other control characters and may also use such characters to control the output to devices other than the printer. Consequently, if some character other than a standard control character appears in the first position of a line, the resulting output will depend on the computer system being used. The details regarding the use of control characters by your particular system can be obtained from the system manuals, your instructor, or computer center personnel.

In the case of list-directed output, a blank is automatically inserted at the beginning of each output line as a control character. This blank then produces normal spacing and in most systems is not printed.

In the case of formatted output, some attention must be paid to printer control, as otherwise the output may not be what the user intended. To illustrate, suppose that control characters are in effect and consider the following statements:

```
    PRINT 20, N
 20 FORMAT (I3)
```

The format descriptor I3 specifies that the value to be printed is an integer and is to be printed in the first three positions of a line. If the value of N is 15, the three positions are filled with $b15$ (where b denotes a blank). Because the blank appears in the first position, it is interpreted as a control character. This produces normal spacing and displays the value 15 in the first two positions of a new line as follows:

$\underline{15}$

If, however, the value of N is 150, the first three positions are filled with 150. The character 1 in the first position is again interpreted as a control character. It is not printed, but rather the value 50 is printed at the top of a new page:

$\underline{50}$

When control characters are in effect, it is a good practice to use the first print position of each output line to indicate explicitly what printer control is desired. This can be done by making the first descriptor of each format identifier one of the following:

> 1X or   ' '   for normal spacing
>   '0'   for double spacing
>   '1'   for advancing to a new page
>   '+' for overprinting

We follow this practice in the examples in this text.

Integer Output—The I Descriptor   The descriptor used to describe the format in which integer data is to be displayed has the form

> *rIw*   or   *rIw.m*

where

I   denotes integer data.

w   is an integer constant indicating the width of the field in which the data is to be displayed, that is, the number of spaces to be used in displaying it.

r   is an integer constant called a *repetition indicator*, indicating the number of such fields; for example, 4I3 is the same as I3, I3, I3, I3; if there is only one such field, the number 1 need not be given.

m   is the minimum number of digits to be printed.

Integer values are *right justified* in fields of the specified sizes; that is, each value is printed so that its last digit appears in the rightmost position of the field. For example, if the values of the integer variables NUM, L, and KAPPA are

```
NUM = 3
L = 5378
KAPPA = -12345
```

then the statements

```
      PRINT 30, NUM, NUM - 3, L, KAPPA
   30 FORMAT(1X, 2I5, I7, I10)
```

produces the following output:

```
|____3____0____5378____-12345
|_____
```

and the statements

```
      PRINT 31, NUM, NUM - 3, L, KAPPA
      PRINT 32, NUM, NUM - 3, L, KAPPA
   31 FORMAT (1X, 2I5.2, I7, I10.7)
   32 FORMAT (1X, 2I5.0, I7, I10)
```

produce

```
|    0 3    0 0    5 3 7 8   -0 0 1 2 3 4 5
|_____
|    3            5 3 7 8   -1 2 3 4 5
|_____
|
```

If an integer value (including minus sign if the number is negative) requires more spaces than are allowed by the field width specified by a descriptor, the field is filled with asterisks. Thus, the statement

```
    PRINT 40, NUM, NUM - 3, L, KAPPA
40 FORMAT(1X, 4I3)
```

will produce

```
|    3    0 * * * * * *
|_____
|
```

Real Output—The F Descriptor.   One of the descriptors used to describe real (floating point) data has the form

$r\text{F}w.d$

where

F   denotes real (floating point) data.

w is an integer constant indicating the *total width of the field* in which the data is to be displayed.

d is an integer constant indicating the number of digits to the right of the decimal point.

r is the repetition indicator, an integer constant indicating the number of such fields; again, if there is to be only one such field, the number 1 need not be used.

Real values are printed *right justified* in the specified fields. For a descriptor F$w.d$, if the corresponding real value has more than d digits to the right of the decimal point, it is *rounded* to d digits. If it has fewer than d digits, the remaining positions are filled with zeros. In most systems, values less than 1 in magnitude are displayed with a zero to the left of the decimal point (for example, 0.123 rather than .123).

For example, to display the values of the integer variables IN and OUT and the values of the real variables A, B, and C as given by

```
    IN = 625
    OUT = -19
    A = 7.5
    B = .182
    C = 625.327
```

we could use the statements

```
     PRINT 50, IN, OUT, A, B, C
50 FORMAT (1X, 2I4, 2F6.3, F8.3)
```

The resulting output would be

```
 625 -19 7.500 0.182 625.327
```

To provide more space between the numbers and to round each of the real values to two decimal places, we could use

```
50 FORMAT(1X, 2I10, 3F10.2)
```

This would display the numbers right justified in fields containing ten spaces, as follows:

```
       625       -19      7.50      0.18    625.33
```

As with the I descriptor, if the real number being output requires more spaces than are allowed by the field width specified in the descriptor, the entire field is *filled with asterisks*. For example,

```
REAL BETA

BETA = -567.89
PRINT 55, 123.4
PRINT 55, BETA
55 FORMAT(1X, F5.2)
```

produces

```
*****
*****
```

It should be noted that for a descriptor F$w.d$, one should have

$$w \geq d + 3$$

to allow space for the sign of the number, the first digit, and the decimal point.

Real Output—The E Descriptor.   Real data may also be output in scientific notation using a descriptor of the form

*r*E*w.d*   or   *r*E*w.d*E*e*

where

E   indicates that the data is to be output in scientific notation.

w   is an integer constant that indicates the total width of the field in which the data is to be displayed.

d   is an integer constant indicating the number of decimal digits to be displayed.

r   is the repetition indicator, an integer constant indicating the number of such fields; it need not be used if there is only one field.

e   is the number of positions to be used in displaying the exponent.

Although some details of the output are compiler dependent, real values are usually printed in *normalized form*— a minus sign, if necessary, followed by one leading zero, then a decimal point followed by *d* significant digits, and then E with an appropriate exponent in the next four spaces for the first form or *e* spaces for the second form. For example, if values of real variables A, B, C, and D are given by

```
REAL A, B, C, D
A = .12345E8
B = .0237
C = 4.6E-12
D = -76.1684E12
```

the statements

```
   PRINT 60, A, B, C, D
60 FORMAT (1X, 2E15.5, 2E15.4)
```

produces output like the following:

```
    0.12345E+08     0.23700E-01      0.4600E-11    -0.7617E+14
```

As with the F descriptor, a field is *asterisk filled* if it is not large enough for the value to be printed. It should also be noted that for a descriptor E*w*.*d* one should have

$$w \geq d + 7$$

or for the second form,

$$w \geq d + e + 5$$

to allow space for the sign of the number, a leading zero, a decimal point, and E with the exponent.

Character Output   Character constants may be displayed by including them in the list of descriptors of a format identifier. For example, if X and Y have the values .3 and 7.9, respectively, the statements

```
    PRINT 70, X, Y
70 FORMAT (1X, 'X=', F6.2, ' Y =', F6.2)
```

produce as output

```
X = 0.30 Y = 7.90
```

Character data may also be displayed by using an A format descriptor, of the form

rA   or rAw

where

> w (if specified) is an integer constant specifying the field width.
>
> r is the repetition indicator, an integer constant indicating the number of such fields; it may be omitted if there is only one field.

In the first form, the field width is determined by the length of the character value being displayed. In the second form, if the field width exceeds the length of the character value, that value is *right justified* in the field. In contrast with numeric output, however, if the length of the character value exceeds the specified field width, the output consists of the *leftmost w* characters. For example, the preceding output would also be produced if the labels were included in the output list as follows:

```
    PRINT 71, 'X =', X, ' Y =', Y
71 FORMAT (1X, A, F6.2, A, F6.2)
```

This latter method is perhaps preferable to the first, as the format identifier can be used to print other labels and values, as in

```
    PRINT 71, 'MEAN IS', XMEAN,
   +          'WITH STANDARD DEVIATION', STDEV
```

Positional Descriptors—X and T.   There are two format descriptors that can be used to provide spacing in an output line. An X descriptor can be used to insert blanks in an output line. It has the form

nX

where n is a positive integer constant that specifies the number of blanks to be inserted.

The T descriptor has the form

Tc

where c is an integer constant denoting the number of the space on a line at which a field is to begin. This descriptor functions much like a tab key on a typewriter and causes the next output field to begin at the specified position on the current line. One difference is that the value of c may be less than the current position; that is, "tabbing backward" is possible.

As an illustration of these descriptors, suppose that NUMBER is an integer variable and consider the output statement

```
PRINT 75, 'JOHN Q. DOE', 'CPSC', NUMBER
```

together with either of the following FORMAT statements:

```
75 FORMAT (1X, A11, 3X, A4, 2X, I3)
```

or

```
75 FORMAT (1X, A11, T16, A4, 2X, I3)
```

If NUMBER has the value 141, the output produced is

```
JOHN_Q._DOE___CPSC__141
```

Note that the descriptor 2X in either FORMAT statement could be replaced by T22 or that the pair of descriptors 2X, I3 could be replaced by the single descriptor I5. This same output would be produced by the statements

```
    PRINT 75, 'JOHN Q. DOE', NUMBER, 'CPSC'
75 FORMAT (1X, A11, T22, I3, T16, A4)
```

which use the tabbing backward feature possible with the T descriptor.

Repeating Groups of Format Descriptors.   As we have seen, it is possible to repeat some format descriptors by preceding them with a *repetition indicator*. For example,

```
3F10.2
```

is the same as

```
F10.2, F10.2, F10.2
```

It is also possible to repeat a group of descriptors by enclosing the group within parentheses and then preceding the left parenthesis with a repetition indicator. For example, the FORMAT statement

```
80 FORMAT (1X, A, F6.2, A, F6.2)
```

can be written more compactly as

```
80 FORMAT (1X, 2(A, F6.2))
```

Similarly, the format statement

```
81 FORMAT (1X, I10, F10.2, I10, F10.2, I10, F10.2,
   +          E15.8)
```

can be shortened to

```
81 FORMAT (3(I10, F10.2), E15.8)
```

Additional levels of groups are permitted. For example, the format statement

```
82 FORMAT (1X, E18.2, I3, A, I3, A, E18.2, I3, A,
   +          I3, A, F8.4)
```

can be written more compactly as

```
82 FORMAT (1X, 2(E18.2, 2(I3,A)), F8.4)
```

The Slash (/) Descriptor. A single output statement can be used to display values on more than one line, with different formats, by using a slash (/) descriptor. The slash causes the output to begin on a new line. It can also be used repeatedly to skip several lines. It is not necessary to use a comma to separate a slash descriptor from other descriptors. For example, the statements

```
     PRINT *, 'VALUES'
     PRINT *
     PRINT *
     PRINT 85, N, A, M, B
     PRINT 86, C, D
85 FORMAT (1X, 2(I10, F10.2))
86 FORMAT (1X, 2E15.7)
```

could be combined in the pair of statements

```
     PRINT 87, 'VALUES', N, A, M, B, C, D
87 FORMAT (1X, A /// 1X, 2(I10, F10.2) / 1X, 2E15.7)
```

(Note the descriptors 1X following the slashes to indicate the control characters for the new output lines.) If the values of N, A, M, B, C, and D are given by

```
     N = 5173
     A = 617.2
     M = 7623
     B = 29.25
     C = 37.555
     D = 5.2813
```

then in both cases the resulting output is

```
VALUES



       5173      617.20           7623           29.25
    0.3755500E+02   0.5281300E+01
```

Scanning the Format. When a formatted output statement is executed, the corresponding format identifier is scanned from left to right in parallel with the output list to locate the appropriate descriptors for the output items. The type of the descriptors should match the type of the values being displayed; for example, a real value should not be displayed with an I descriptor. If the values of all the items in the output list have been displayed before all the descriptors have been used, scanning of the format identifer continues. Values of character constants are displayed, and the positioning specified by slash, X, and T descriptors continues until one of the following is encountered:

1. The right parenthesis signaling the end of the list of format descriptors.
2. An I, F, E, or A (or L or G or D) descriptor.
3. A colon.

In cases 2 and 3, all remaining descriptors in the format identifier are ignored.

To illustrate, consider the statements

```
      PRINT 100, I, J
100   FORMAT (1X, I5, 3I6)
      PRINT 105, X, Y
105   FORMAT (1X, F5.1, F7.0, F10.5)
      PRINT 110, 'BUMPER', 'HEADLIGHT'
110   FORMAT (1X, 5(' ITEM IS ', A10))
      PRINT 115, 'BUMPER',  'HEADLIGHT'
115   FORMAT (1X, 5(: '  ITEM IS ', A10))
```

If I and J are integer variables with values $I = 1$ and $J = 2$ and X and Y are real variables with values given by $X = 5.6$ and $Y = 7.8$, these statements produce the output

```
     1     2
   5.6     8.
   ITEM IS BUMPER      ITEM IS HEADLIGHT    ITEM IS
   ITEM IS BUMPER      ITEM IS HEADLIGHT
```

Note that like the slash, the colon descriptor need not be separated from other descriptors by a comma.

If the list of descriptors is exhausted before the output list is, a new line of output is begun, and the format identifier or part of it is rescanned. If there are no internal parentheses within the format identifier, the rescanning begins with the first descriptor. For example, the statements

```
INTEGER M1, M2, M3, M4, M5

M1 = 1
M2 = 2
M3 = 3
M4 = 4
M5 = 5
    PRINT 120, M1, M2, M3, M4, M5
120 FORMAT (1X, 2I3)
```

produce the output

```
| _ _1_ _2_ _ _
| _ _3_ _4_ _ _
| _ _5_ _ _ _ _
|
```

If the format identifier does contain internal parentheses, rescanning begins at the left parenthesis that matches the last internal right parenthesis; any repetition counter preceding this format group is in effect. Thus, if integer variables K, L1, L2, and L3 have values

```
K = 3
L1 = 21
L2 = 22
L3 = 23
```

and real variables X, Y1, Y2, and Y3 have values

```
X = 4.0
Y1 = 5.5
Y2 = 6.66
Y3 = 7.77
```

the statements

```
    PRINT 125, K, X, L1, Y1, L2, Y2, L3, Y3
125 FORMAT (1X, I5, F10.3 / (1X, I10, F12.2))
```

produce the output

```
| _ _ _ 3_ _ _ _ 4.000_ _ _ _ _ _
| _ _ _ _ _ _ _ 21_ _ _ _ _ _ 5.50
| _ _ _ _ _ _ _ 22_ _ _ _ _ _ 6.66
| _ _ _ _ _ _ _ 23_ _ _ _ _ _ 7.77
|
```

Thus it is possible to specify a special format for the first output items and a different format for subsequent items by enclosing the last format descriptors in parentheses. In this example, when the right parenthesis of the FORMAT statement is encountered after printing the value of Y1, a new line is begun, and the descriptors following the second left parenthesis are reused to print the values of L2 and Y2 and then again on a new line for L3 and Y3.

5.2 Example: Printing Tables of Computed Values

In some of the sample programs of Chapter 4, the output was displayed in a table format. For example, the output produced in the sample run of the program in Figure 4.14 was

```
            X                 Y
      =============================
      1.00000           0.309560
      1.25000           0.271889
      1.50000           0.222571
      1.75000           0.170991
      2.00000           0.123060
      2.25000           8.200830E-02
      2.50000           4.912558E-02
      2.75000           2.439879E-02
      3.00000           7.025976E-03
```

One unpleasant feature of this table is that the last four values in the second column are printed in scientific notation, whereas all the others are printed in decimal format. Note also that all the values are displayed with five or six digits to the right of the decimal point, even though two or three might be sufficient for our purposes. With list-directed output, however, neither the format of the output nor the number of the decimal places displayed can be controlled by the user.

Positioning headings for the columns of a table above the values in the columns can also be rather difficult, as the user cannot control the format or the spacing of these values. It may be necessary to change the output statements and reexecute the modified program several times before the appearance of the output is satisfactory.

The format descriptors described in this section make it quite easy to control the format of the output and the number of decimal places. Correct placement of items such as table headings is also considerably easier than with list-directed output. The program in Figure 5.1 demonstrates this. It reads a value for an integer LAST and then prints a table of values of N, the square and the cube of N, and its square root for N = 1, 2, . . . , LAST.

```
      PROGRAM TABLE
***********************************************************************
* Program demonstrating use of formatted output to print a table of   *
* values of N, square and cube of N, and the square root of N for      *
* N = 1, 2, ..., LAST where the value of LAST is read during           *
* execution.                                                           *
***********************************************************************

      INTEGER N, LAST

      PRINT *, 'ENTER LAST NUMBER TO BE USED'
      READ *, LAST

*     Print headings

      PRINT 10, 'NUMBER', 'SQUARE', '  CUBE', 'SQ. ROOT'
10    FORMAT(//, 1X, A8, T11, A8, T21, A8, T31, A10 / 1X, 40('='))

*     Print the table

      DO 30 N = 1, LAST
          PRINT 20, N, N**2, N**3, SQRT(REAL(N))
20        FORMAT(1X, I6, 2I10, 2X, F10.4)
30    CONTINUE
      END


Sample run
==========


ENTER LAST NUMBER TO BE USED
10


  NUMBER    SQUARE      CUBE   SQ. ROOT
========================================
       1         1         1    1.0000
       2         4         8    1.4142
       3         9        27    1.7321
       4        16        64    2.0000
       5        25       125    2.2361
       6        36       216    2.4495
       7        49       343    2.6458
       8        64       512    2.8284
       9        81       729    3.0000
      10       100      1000    3.1623
```

Figure 5.1

Exercises

1. Assuming that the following declarations and assignments

```
INTEGER NUMBER
REAL ALPHA

NUMBER = 12345
ALPHA = 87.6543
```

have been made, describe the output that will be produced by the following statements. (Assume that control characters are in effect.)

a.   PRINT *, 'COMPUTER SCIENCE -- EXERCISE 5.3'

b.   PRINT *, NUMBER, NUMBER + 1

c.   PRINT *, 'ALPHA =', ALPHA, ' NUMBER =', NUMBER

d.   PRINT *

e.   PRINT 5, 3 * 2.1 - 1
```
     5 FORMAT (' COMPUTER SCIENCE -- EXERCISE', F4.2)
```

f.   PRINT 10, 'COMPUTER SCIENCE -- EXERCISE 5.3'
```
    10 FORMAT (1X, A)
```

g.   PRINT 15, 'COMPUTER SCIENCE', 5.3
```
    15 FORMAT (1X, A, F4.1)
```

h.   PRINT 20, 'EXERCISE', 5.3
```
    20 FORMAT ('1 COMPUTER SCIENCE --', A10, F6.3).
```

i.   PRINT 25, 'EXERCISE', 5.3
```
    25 FORMAT (' COMPUTER SCIENCE --', A2, F3.1)
```

j.   PRINT 30, NUMBER, NUMBER + 1, ALPHA, ALPHA + 1, ALPHA + 2
```
    30 FORMAT ('0', 2I7, F10.5, F10.3, F10.0)
```

k.   PRINT 35, NUMBER, NUMBER + 1, NUMBER + 2
```
    35 FORMAT (1X, I5, 4X, I4, T20, I6)
```

l.   PRINT 40, NUMBER, ALPHA, NUMBER + 1, ALPHA + 1
```
    40 FORMAT (1X, I5, F7.4 / I5, E12.5)
```

m.   PRINT 45, NUMBER, ALPHA, NUMBER + 1, ALPHA + 1
```
    45 FORMAT (1X, I10, F10.3)
```

n.   PRINT 50, NUMBER, ALPHA, NUMBER + 1, ALPHA + 1
```
    50 FORMAT (1X, I10, F10.2, '---')
```

o.   PRINT 55, NUMBER, ALPHA, NUMBER + 1, ALPHA + 1
```
    55 FORMAT (1X, I10, F10.2 : '---')
```

p.   PRINT 60, 'THE END'
```
    60 FORMAT (1X, 10 ('*'), A, 10 ('*'))
```

2. Write a program that reads two three-digit integers and then calculates and prints their sum and their difference. The output should be formatted to appear as follows:

```
        456              456
    +   123          -   123
        ---              ---
        579              333
```

3. Write a program that reads two three-digit integers and then calculates and prints their product, and the quotient and the remainder that result when the first is divided by the second. The output should be formatted to appear as follows:

```
       739                  61  R    7
                        _ _ _ _ _
   X    12        12  )   739
     _ _ _ _
      8868
```

4. Write a program that reads two three-digit integers and then prints their product in the following format:

```
      749
   X   381
    _ _ _ _ _
      749
    5992
    2247
  _ _ _ _ _ _
  285369
```

   Execute the program with the following values: 749 and 381; -749 and 381; 749 and -381; -749 and -381; 999 and 999.

5. Suppose that a certain culture of bacteria has a constant growth rate r, so that if there are n bacteria present, the next generation will have $n + r \cdot n$ bacteria. Write a program to read the original number of bacteria, the growth rate, and an upper limit on the number of bacteria and then to print a table with appropriate headings that shows the generation number, the increase in the number of bacteria from the previous generation, and the total number of bacteria in that generation, for each generation number from 1 up through the first generation for which the number of bacteria exceeds the specified upper limit.

5.3 Formatted Input

We have seen that input is accomplished in FORTRAN by a **READ statement.** This statement has two forms, the simpler of which is

READ *format-identifier, input-list*

The *input-list* is a single variable or a list of variables separated by commas. The *format-identifier* specifies the format in which the values for the items in the input list are to be entered. As in the case of output, the format identifier may be

1. An asterisk (∗).
2. The label of a FORMAT statement (or a variable to which such a label has been assigned by an ASSIGN statement).
3. A character expression or array whose value specifies the format for the input (as discussed in Chapter 6).

The most commonly used form of the READ statement is that in which the format identifier is an asterisk. As we saw in Chapter 3, this form indicates list-directed input in which the format is determined by the types of variables in the input list. In all situations except those in which the data have a specific predetermined form, list-directed input should be adequate. When the data items are of a predetermined form, it may be necessary to use a format identifier of type 2 or 3 to read these data.

As in the case of output, the format identifier may be the label of a FORMAT statement of the form

FORMAT (*list of format descriptors*)

The format descriptors are essentially the same as those discussed for output in the preceding section. Character constants, however, may not appear in the list of format descriptors, and the colon separator is not relevant to input.

Integer Input.   Integer data can be read using the I descriptor of the form

rIw

where w indicates the width of the field, that is, the number of columns to be read, and r is the repetition indicator specifying the number of such fields. To illustrate, consider the following example:

```
INTEGER I, J, K

READ 5, I, J, K
5 FORMAT (I6, I4, I7)
```

For the values of I, J, and K to be read correctly, the numbers should be entered as follows: the value for I in the first six columns, the value for J in the next four columns, and the value for K in the next seven columns, with each value right justified within its field. Thus, if the values to be read are

I: -123
J: 45
K: 6789

the data may be entered as follows:

```
    -123  45    6789
```

If the format statement were changed to

```
5 FORMAT (I4, I2, I4)
```

the data should be entered as

```
-123456789
```

with no intervening blanks. Here the first four columns are read for I, the next two columns for J, and the next four columns for K.

Blanks within a field read with an I descriptor can be interpreted as zeros or they can be ignored. If they are interpreted as zeros, integer values must be right justified within their fields as in the first example if they are to be read correctly. Had they been entered as

    -123 45 6789

I would have been assigned the value -1230, J the value 4506, and K the value 789000. If blanks are ignored, the location of an integer value within its field is irrelevant. We assume in the examples of this text that *blank columns within numeric fields are ignored* since this agrees with the ANSI standard. (The BZ and BN descriptors described in Section 5.6 can be used to specify which of the two interpretations is to apply.)

Real Input.   One of the descriptors used to input real data is the F descriptor of the form

    *r*F*w.d*

where *w* indicates the width of the field to be read, *d* is the number of digits to the right of the decimal point, and *r* is the repetition counter.

There are two ways that real data may be entered:

1. The numbers may be entered with no decimal points.
2. The decimal point may be entered as part of the input value.

In the first case, the *d* specification in the format descriptor F*w.d* automatically positions the decimal point so that there are *d* digits to its right. For example, if we wish to enter the following values for real variables A, B, C, D, and E

    A: 6.25
    B: -1.9
    C: 75.0
    D: .182
    E: 625.327

we could use the statements

        READ 10, A, B, C, D, E
    10 FORMAT (F3.2, 2F3.1, F3.3, F6.3)

and enter the data in the following form:

    625-19750182625327

Of course, we could use wider fields, for example,

    10 FORMAT (F4.2, 2F4.1, 2F8.3)

and enter the data in the form

```
 625 -19 750        182  625327
```

with the values right justified within their fields.

In the second method for entering real data, the position of the decimal point in the value entered overrides the position determined by the descriptor. Thus, if the number to be read is 9423.68, an appropriate descriptor would be F6.2 if the number is entered without a decimal point and F7.2, or F7.1, or F7.0, and so on, if the number is entered with a decimal point. For example, the preceding values for A, B, C, D, and E could be read using the statements

```
    READ 15, A, B, C, D, E
15 FORMAT (4F5.0, F8.0)
```

with the data entered in the following form:

```
 6.25 -1.9  75.  .182 625.327
```

It should be noted that each field width must be large enough to accommodate the number entered, including the decimal point and the sign.

Real values entered in E notation can also be read using an F descriptor. Thus, for the FORMAT statement

```
15 FORMAT (5F10.0)
```

the data of the preceding example could also have been entered as

```
     .625E1         -1.9        75.0     18.2E-2 6.25327E2
```

In this case, the E need not be entered if the exponent is preceded by a sign. The following would therefore be an alternative method for entering the preceding data:

```
     .625+1         -1.9        75.0     18.2-2 6.25327+2
```

The E descriptor may also be used in a manner similar to that for the F descriptor.

Skipping Columns of Input. The positional descriptors X and T may be used in the format identifier of a READ statement to skip over certain columns of data. For example, if we wish to assign the following values to the integer variables I, J, and K

```
I:   4
J:   56
K:   137
```

by entering data in the form

```
I = 4    J = 56   K = 137
```

the following statements may be used:

```
   READ 20, I, J, K
20 FORMAT (3X, I2, 6X, I3, 5X, I4)
```

or

```
20 FORMAT (T4, I2, T12, I3, T20, I4)
```

Columns of data are also skipped if the end of the input list is encountered before the end of the data line has been reached. To illustrate, if the statements

```
   READ 25, NUM1, X
   READ 25, NUM2, Y
25 FORMAT (I5, F7.0)
```

are used to read values for the integer variables NUM1 and NUM2 and real variables X and Y from the following data lines

```
   17    3.56    34    13.4
  9064 570550 3199 47
```

the values assigned to NUM1 and X are

```
NUM1:  17
   X:  3.56
```

and the values assigned to NUM2 and Y are

```
NUM2:  9064
   Y:  570550.
```

All other information on these two lines is ignored.

Multiple Input Lines. Recall that a new line of data is required each time a READ statement is executed. A new line of data is also required whenever a slash (/) is encountered in the format identifier for the READ statement. This may be used in case one wishes to separate some of the data entries by blank lines, remarks, and the like, which are to be skipped over by the READ statement. For example, the following data

```
AMOUNT TO BE PRODUCED
585.00
REACTION RATE
(THIS ASSUMES CONSTANT TEMPERATURE)
5.75
```

could be read by a single READ statement, and the values 585.00 and 5.75 assigned to AMOUNT and RATE, respectively, in the following manner:

```
REAL AMOUNT, RATE

READ 30, AMOUNT, RATE
30 FORMAT (/ F10.0 /// F5.0)
```

The first slash causes the first line to be skipped, so that the value 585.00 is read for AMOUNT; the three slashes then cause an advance of three lines, so that 5.75 is read for RATE.

A new line of data is also required if all descriptors have been used and there still are variables remaining in the input list for which values must be read. In this case, the format identifier is rescanned, as in the case of output. Thus, the statements

```
INTEGER I, J, K, L, M

READ 35, I, J, K, L, M
35 FORMAT (3I8)
```

require two lines of input, the first containing the values of I, J, and K and the second, the values of L and M.

5.4 The WRITE Statement and the General READ Statement

The PRINT and READ statements used thus far are simple FORTRAN input/output statements. In this section we consider more general input/output statements, the WRITE statement and the general form of the READ statement.

The WRITE Statement. The **WRITE statement** has a more complicated syntax than does the PRINT statement, but it is a more general output statement. It has the form

WRITE (*control-list*) *output-list*

where *output-list* has the same syntax as in the PRINT statement and *control-list* may include items selected from the following:

1. A unit specifier indicating the output device.
2. A format specifier.
3. Other items that are especially useful in file processing. (These are considered in Chapter 12.)

The control list must include a unit specifier and, except for the more advanced applications described in Chapter 12, a format specifier as well. The **unit specifier** is an integer expression whose value designates the output device, or it may be an asterisk, indicating the standard output device (usually a terminal or printer). The unit specifier may be given in the form

> UNIT = *unit-specifier*

or simply

> *unit-specifier*

If the UNIT = clause is not used, the unit specifier must be the first item in the control list.

The **format specifier** has the form

> FMT = *format-identifier*

or simply

> *format-identifier*

where *format-identifier* may be of any of the forms allowed in the PRINT statement. If the format specifier without the FMT = clause is used, then it must be the second item in the control list, and the UNIT = clause must also be omitted for the unit specifier.

To illustrate the WRITE statement, suppose that the values of GRAV and WEIGHT are to be displayed on an output device having unit number 6. The statement

```
WRITE (6, *) GRAV, WEIGHT
```

or any of the following equivalent forms

```
WRITE (6, FMT = *) GRAV, WEIGHT

WRITE (UNIT = 6, FMT = *) GRAV, WEIGHT

WRITE (NOUT, *) GRAV, WEIGHT

WRITE (UNIT = NOUT, FMT = *) GRAV, WEIGHT
```

where NOUT is an integer variable with value 6, produce list-directed output to this device. If this device is the system's standard output device, the unit number 6 may be replaced by an asterisk in any of the preceding statements; for example,

```
WRITE (*, *) GRAV, WEIGHT
```

and each of these is equivalent to the short form

```
PRINT *, GRAV, WEIGHT
```

Formatted output of these values could be produced by statements like the following:

```
        WRITE (6, 30) GRAV, WEIGHT
     30 FORMAT (1X, 2F10.2)

        WRITE (UNIT = 6, FMT = 30) GRAV, WEIGHT
     30 FORMAT (1X, 2F10.2)
```

The program in Figure 5.2 displays tables of numbers together with their squares, cubes, and square roots. It is a modification of the program in Figure 5.1 in which the PRINT statements have been replaced by WRITE statements.

```
      PROGRAM TABLE
***********************************************************************
* Program demonstrating use of formatted output to print a table of  *
* values of N, square and cube of N, and the square root of N for     *
* N = 1, 2, ..., LAST where the value of LAST is read during          *
* execution.                                                          *
***********************************************************************

      INTEGER N, LAST

      WRITE (*, *) 'ENTER LAST NUMBER TO BE USED'
      READ *, LAST

*     Print headings

      WRITE (*, 10) 'NUMBER', 'SQUARE', '  CUBE', 'SQ. ROOT'
   10 FORMAT(//, 1X, A8, T11, A8, T21, A8, T31, A10 / 1X, 40('='))

*     Print the table

      DO 30 N = 1, LAST
          WRITE (*, 20) N, N**2, N**3, SQRT(REAL(N))
   20     FORMAT(1X, I6, 2I10, 2X, F10.4)
   30 CONTINUE
      END


Sample run
==========


ENTER LAST NUMBER TO BE USED
10
```

Figure 5.2

Figure 5.2 **(continued)**

NUMBER	SQUARE	CUBE	SQ. ROOT
1	1	1	1.0000
2	4	8	1.4142
3	9	27	1.7321
4	16	64	2.0000
5	25	125	2.2361
6	36	216	2.4495
7	49	343	2.6458
8	64	512	2.8284
9	81	729	3.0000
10	100	1000	3.1623

The General READ Statement. The general form of the READ statement is

READ (*control-list*) *input-list*

where *control-list* may include items selected from the following:

1. A unit specifier indicating the input device.
2. A format specifier.
3. An END = clause giving the number of a statement to be executed when the end of data occurs, as described in the next section.
4. Other items that are particularly useful in processing files. (These are considered in Chapter 12.)

As an illustration of the general form of the READ statement, suppose that values for CODE, TIME, and RATE are to be read using the input device 5. The statement

```
READ (5, *) CODE, TIME, RATE
```

or any of the following equivalent forms

```
READ (5, FMT = *) CODE, TIME, RATE

READ (UNIT = 5, FMT = *) CODE, TIME, RATE

READ (IN, *) CODE, TIME, RATE

READ (UNIT = IN, FMT = *) CODE, TIME, RATE
```

where IN has the value 5, can be used. If this device is the system's standard input device, an asterisk may be used in place of the device number in any of the preceding unit specifications; for example,

```
READ (*, *) CODE, TIME, RATE
```

Formatted input is also possible with the general READ statement; for example,

```
READ (UNIT = 5, FMT = 10), CODE, TIME, RATE
```

or

```
READ (5, 10) CODE, TIME, RATE
```

where 10 is the number of the following FORMAT statement:

```
10 FORMAT(I6, 2F6.2)
```

5.5 Introduction to File Processing

The programs we have written up to this point have involved relatively small amounts of input/output data. We have assumed that the input data were read from a terminal or cards and that the output was displayed either at the terminal or at a printer. This is adequate if the volume of data involved is not large. However, applications involving large data sets may be processed more conveniently if the data is stored on magnetic tape or a magnetic disk or some other form of external (secondary) memory.

Magnetic tape is a plastic tape coated with a substance that can be magnetized. Such a tape stores information for computer processing in somewhat the same way that an audio tape stores "sound information." Information can be written onto or read from a tape using a device called a **tape drive.** A standard tape drive can record 1600 bytes per inch of tape. Therefore, a 2400-foot reel of tape can store approximately 46 million characters.

A **magnetic disk** is also coated with a substance that can be magnetized. Information is stored on such disks in **tracks** arranged in concentric circles and is written onto or read from a disk using a **disk drive.** This device transfers information by means of a movable read/write head, which is positioned over one of the tracks of the rotating disk. Some **disk packs** consisting of several such disks can store more than a billion characters.

Information stored on such auxiliary devices that is to be processed by a FORTRAN program is usually arranged in structures called **files,** and each line of data in the file is called a **record.** In this section we consider the characteristics of files and some of the FORTRAN statements used in processing them. (Others are described in Chapter 12.)

Each record of a file to be used as an input file must have the entries arranged in a form suitable for reading by a READ statement. These records are read during program execution just as a card of data is read by a card reader or a line of data is read from a terminal. For example, if the variables CODE, TEMP, and PRESS are declared by

```
INTEGER CODE
REAL TEMP, PRESS
```

and the values for these variables are to be read from a file using a list-directed READ statement, this data file might have the following form:

```
37, 77.5, 30.39
22, 85.3, 30.72
1, 100.0, 29.95
78, 99.5, 29.01
        .
        .
```

If the values are to be read using the format statement

```
10 FORMAT (I3, 2F8.0)
```

the file might have the form

```
37      77.5    30.39
22      85.3    30.72
 1     100.0    29.95
78      99.5    29.01
         .
         .
```

whereas the format statement

```
10 FORMAT (I2, F4.1, F4.2)
```

would be appropriate for the file

```
37 7753039
22 8533072
 110002995
78 9952901
    .
    .
```

Opening Files. Before a file can be used for input or output in a FORTRAN program, it must be "opened." This can be accomplished using an **OPEN statement** of the form

OPEN (*open-list*)

where *open-list* includes

1. A unit specifier indicating a unit number connected to the file being opened.

2. A FILE = clause giving the name of the file being opened.
3. A STATUS = clause specifying whether the file is a new or an old file.

(Other items that may be included are described in Chapter 12.)
The unit specifier has the form

UNIT = *integer-expression*

or simply

integer-expression

where the value of *integer-expression* is a nonnegative number that designates the unit number to be connected to this file. Reference to this file by a READ or WRITE statement will be by means of this unit number.
The FILE = clause has the form

FILE = *character-expression*

where the value of *character-expression* (ignoring trailing blanks) is the name of the file to be connected to the specified unit number.
The STATUS = clause has the form

STATUS = *character-expression*

where the value of *character-expression* (ignoring trailing blanks) is

'OLD'

or

'NEW'

OLD means that the file already exists in the system. NEW means that the file does not yet exist and is being created by the program: execution of the OPEN statement creates an empty file with the specified name and changes its status to OLD.

Closing Files.   The **CLOSE statement** has a function opposite to that of the OPEN statement and may be used to disconnect a file from its unit number. This statement is of the form

CLOSE (*close-list*)

where *close-list* must include a unit specifier and may include other items as described in Chapter 12. After a CLOSE statement is executed, the closed file may be reopened by means of an OPEN statement; the same unit number may be connected to it, or a different one may be used. All files that are not explicitly closed by means of a CLOSE statement are automatically closed when a STOP or END statement is executed.

File Input/Output. Once a file has been connected to a unit number, data can be read from or written to that file using the general forms of the READ and WRITE statements in which the unit number appearing in the control list is the same as the unit number connected to the file. For example, to read values for CODE, TEMP, and PRESS from a file named INFO, the statement

```
OPEN (UNIT = 12, FILE = 'INFO', STATUS = 'OLD')
```

opens the file, and the statement

```
READ (12, *) CODE, TEMP, PRESS
```

reads the values.

Similarly, a file named REPORT to which values of CODE, TEMP, and PRESS are to be written could be created by

```
        OPEN (UNIT = 13, FILE = 'REPORT', STATUS = 'NEW')
        WRITE (13, 30), CODE, TEMP, PRESS
30 FORMAT (1X, I3, F7.0, F10.2)
```

Each execution of a READ statement causes an entire record to be read and then positions the file so that the next execution of a READ (WRITE) statement causes values to be read from (written to) the next record of the file. Similarly, execution of a WRITE statement writes an entire record into the file and then positions the file so that the next execution of a WRITE (READ) statement produces output to (input from) the next record of the file.

The END = Clause. In the preceding section, we noted that the control list of a general READ statement may contain an **END = clause** to transfer control automatically when there are no more data values. This clause has the form

> END = *statement-number*

where *statement-number* is the number of an executable statement that is the next statement to be executed when the end of data is encountered. For example, the statement

```
READ (12, *, END = 50) CODE, TEMP, PRESS
```

could be used within a loop to read values for CODE, TEMP, and PRESS from a file. When the end of this file is reached, control transfers to statement 50 which might calculate the mean temperature:

```
50 TMEAN = TSUM / COUNT
```

File-Positioning Statements. There are several FORTRAN statements that may be used to position a file. Two of these statements are

REWIND *unit*

and

BACKSPACE *unit*

where *unit* is the unit number connected to the file.

The **REWIND statement** positions the file at its initial point, that is, at the beginning of the first record of the file. The **BACKSPACE statement** causes the file to be positioned at the beginning of the preceding record. If the file is at its initial point, these statements have no effect.

5.6 Example: Time, Temperature, Pressure, and Volume Readings

Suppose that a device monitoring a process records time, temperature, pressure, and volume and stores this data in a file. Each record in this file contains:

Time in columns 1–4
Temperature in columns 5–8
Pressure in columns 9–12
Volume in columns 13–16

The value for time is an integer representing the time at which the measurements were taken. The values for temperature, pressure, and volume are real numbers but are recorded with no decimal point. Each must be interpreted as a real value having a decimal point between the third and fourth digits.

A program is to be designed to read the values for the temperature and volume, print these values in tabular form, and display the equation of the least squares line (see Section 4.11). Figure 5.3 shows the program along with a listing of the input file and the output produced by the program.

```
      PROGRAM TEMVOL
*****************************************************************
* Program to read temperatures and volumes from a file containing *
* time, temperature, pressure, and volume readings made by some  *
* monitoring device.  The temperature and volume measurements are *
* displayed in tabular form, and the equation of the least squares *
* line y = mx + b (x = temperature, y = volume) is calculated.   *
* Variables used are:                                            *
*      TEMP    : temperature recorded                            *
*      VOLUME  : volume recorded                                 *
*      COUNT   : count of (TEMP, VOLUME) pairs                   *
*      SUMT    : sum of temperatures                             *
*      SUMT2   : sum of squares of temperatures                  *
*      SUMV    : sum of volumes                                  *
*      SUMTV   : sum of the products TEMP * VOLUME               *
*      TMEAN   : mean temperature                                *
*      VMEAN   : mean volume                                     *
*      SLOPE   : slope of the least squares line                 *
*      YINT    : y-intercept of the line                         *
*****************************************************************

      INTEGER COUNT
      REAL TEMP, VOLUME, SUMT, SUMT2, SUMV, SUMTV, TMEAN, VMEAN,
     +     SLOPE, YINT

* Open the file as unit 15, set up the input and output
* formats, print the table heading, and initialize counter
* and the sums to 0.

      OPEN (UNIT = 15, FILE = 'TEMP-VOL-FILE', STATUS = 'OLD')
10    FORMAT (4X, F4.1, T13, F4.1)
20    FORMAT (1X, A11, A10)
21    FORMAT (1X, F8.1, F12.1)
      PRINT 20, 'TEMPERATURE', 'VOLUME'
      PRINT 20, '===========', '======'
      COUNT = 0
      SUMT = 0
      SUMT2 = 0
      SUMV = 0
      SUMTV = 0

* While there are more data, read temperatures and volumes,
* display each in the table, and calculate the necessary sums

30        READ (UNIT = 15, FMT = 10, END = 40) TEMP, VOLUME
          PRINT 21, TEMP, VOLUME
          COUNT = COUNT + 1
          SUMT = SUMT + TEMP
          SUMT2 = SUMT2 + TEMP ** 2
          SUMV = SUMV + VOLUME
          SUMTV = SUMTV + TEMP * VOLUME
          GO TO 30
```

Figure 5.3

Figure 5.3 (continued)

```
* Find equation of least squares line

40      TMEAN = SUMT / COUNT
        VMEAN = SUMV / COUNT
        SLOPE = (SUMTV - SUMT * VMEAN) / (SUMT2 - SUMT * TMEAN)
        YINT = VMEAN - SLOPE * TMEAN
        PRINT 50, SLOPE, YINT
50      FORMAT(//1X, 'EQUATION OF LEAST SQUARES LINE IS'
        +          /1X, '     Y =', F5.1, 'X + ', F5.1,
        +          /1X, 'WHERE X IS TEMPERATURE AND Y IS VOLUME')
        CLOSE (15)
```

Listing of 'TEMP—VOL—FILE':
==========================

```
1200034203221015
1300038803221121
1400044803241425
1500051303201520
1600055503181665
1700061303191865
1800067503232080
1900072103282262
2000076803252564
2100083503272869
2200088903303186
```

Sample run:
==========

TEMPERATURE	VOLUME
===========	======
34.2	101.5
38.8	112.1
44.8	142.5
51.3	152.0
55.5	166.5
61.3	186.5
67.5	208.0
72.1	226.2
76.8	256.4
83.5	286.9
88.9	318.6

```
EQUATION OF LEAST SQUARES LINE IS
     Y =   3.8X + -39.8
WHERE X IS TEMPERATURE AND Y IS VOLUME
```

*5.7   Miscellaneous Input/Output Topics

In this chapter we have described several of the more commonly used format descriptors. These descriptors are used to specify the precise format of output produced by a formatted PRINT or WRITE statement and to specify the format of values to be read by a formatted READ statement. In this section we describe a number of less commonly used format descriptors, as well as some additional features of list-directed input that were not mentioned in Chapter 3.

The G Descriptor.   In addition to the E and F descriptors for the input and output of real data, a G descriptor of the form

$$rGw.d \quad \text{or} \quad rGw.dEe$$

may be used. A real value, that is, output using a G descriptor is displayed using an F or E descriptor, depending on the magnitude (absolute value) of the real number.

Intuitively, the G descriptor functions like an F descriptor for values that are neither very large nor very small, but like an E descriptor otherwise. More precisely, suppose that a real quantity has a value that if expressed in normalized scientific notation would have the form

$$\pm 0.d_1d_2 \cdots d_n \times 10^k$$

and this value is to be displayed using a $Gw.d$ descriptor. If $0 \leq k \leq d$, this value is output in "F form" with a field width of $w - 4$ followed by four blanks. If, however, k is negative or greater than d, it is output using an $Ew.d$ descriptor. In either case, a total of d significant digits are displayed. The following examples illustrate:

Value	G descriptor	Output Produced
0.123456	G12.6	0.123456____
0.123456E1	G11.6	1.23456____
0.123456E5	G11.6	12345.6____
0.123456E6	G11.6	123456.____
0.123456E7	G12.6	0.123456E+07

Although the G descriptor is intended primarily for real output, it may also be used for real input in a manner similar to that of the F descriptor.

Scale Factors.   To permit more general usage of the E, F, G, and D descriptors, they may be preceded by scale factors of the form

$$nP$$

where n is an integer constant. In the case of output, a descriptor of the form

$$nPFw.d$$

causes the displayed value to be multiplied by 10^n. For the E (and D) descriptor,

      nPE$w.d$ or nPE$w.d$Ee

causes the fractional part of the displayed value to be multiplied by 10^n and the exponent decreased by n. For the G descriptor, a scale factor has an effect only if the value being output is in a range that causes it to be displayed in E form, and in this case the effect of the scale factor is as described for the E descriptor.

To illustrate the use of scale factors, suppose that the values of the integer variable N and the real variables X, Y, and Z are given by

```
N:  27
X:  −93.2094
Y:  −0.0076
Z:  55.3612
```

and consider the following statements:

```
      PRINT 1, N, X, Y, Z
      PRINT 2, N, X, Y, Z
      PRINT 3, N, X, Y, Z
    1 FORMAT (1X, I2, 2F11.3, E12.4)
    2 FORMAT (1X, I2, 1P2F11.3, 3PE12.4)
    3 FORMAT (1X, I2, −1P2F11.3, E12.4)
```

The output produced by these statements is

```
27      −93.209       −0.008   0.5536E+02
27     −932.094       −0.076   553.61E−01
27       −9.321       −0.001   0.0554E+03
```

At the last FORMAT statement demonstrates, once a scale factor has been given in a format identifier, it holds for all E, F, G, and D descriptors that follow it in the same format identifier. If a subsequent scale factor of zero is desired in that format identifier, it must be specified by 0P.

In the case of input, scale factors may be used with the descriptors for real data in much the same manner. The only difference is that if a real value is input in E form, the scale factor has no effect. For example, for the statements

```
      REAL A, B, C
      READ 15, A, B, C
   15 FORMAT (2PF6.0, −2PF6.0, F6.0)
```

if the data

```
    1.1    1.1    1.1
```

are read, the following assignments are made:

    A: 110.0
    B: .011
    C: .011

(The scale factor -2 remains in effect for the last descriptor.) If the data were entered in the form

    <u>_1.1E0_____1.1_1.1E0</u>

the assignments would be

    A: 1.1
    B: .011
    C: 1.1

The BN and BZ Descriptors.   As we observed in Section 5.2, blanks within a numeric input field may be interpreted as zeros or they may be ignored. Which interpretation is to be used may be specified by the programmer by including a BN or BZ descriptor in the format identifier. If a BN ("Blank Null") or BZ ("Blank Zero") descriptor is encountered during a scan of the list of descriptors, all blanks in fields determined by subsequent numeric descriptors in that format identifier are ignored or interpreted as zero, respectively. In all cases, a numeric field consisting entirely of blanks is interpreted as the value 0.

    To illustrate, consider the following data line:

    <u>537__6.258E3_</u>

If NUM is an integer variable and ALPHA is a real variable, the statements

```
      READ 40, NUM, ALPHA
   40 FORMAT (BZ, I5, F8.0)
```

assign the following values to NUM and ALPHA:

    NUM: 53700
    ALPHA: 6.258E30

since the BZ descriptor causes the two blank columns in the field corresponding to the I5 descriptor and the single blank column in the field corresponding to the F8.0 descriptor to be interpreted as zeros. On the other hand,

```
      READ 41, NUM, ALPHA
   41 FORMAT (BN, I5, F8.0)
```

assign the values

  NUM: 537
  ALPHA: 6.258E3

since the BN descriptor causes these same blank columns to be ignored. The statements

```
    READ 42, NUM, ALPHA
 42 FORMAT (BZ, I5, BN, F8.0)
```

assigns the values

  NUM: 53700
  ALPHA: 6.258E3

The S, SP, and SS Descriptors. The S, SP, and SS descriptors may be used to control the output of plus (+) signs in a numeric output field. If the SP ("Sign Positive") descriptor appears in a format identifier, all positive numeric values output by the statement are preceded by a + sign. On the other hand, the SS ("Sign Suppress") descriptor suppresses the output of all such + signs. An S descriptor may be used to restore control to the computer system, which has the option of displaying or suppressing a + sign.

The H Descriptor. We have seen that character constants may be displayed by including them in the list of descriptors of a format identifier; for example,

```
(1X, 'FOR', I5, ' SAMPLES, THE AVERAGE IS', F8.2)
```

Strings may also be displayed by using a Hollerith descriptor of the form

  *n*H*string*

where *n* is the number of characters in *string*. Thus, the preceding format identifier could also be written

```
(1X, 3HFOR, I5, 24H SAMPLES, THE AVERAGE IS, F8.2)
```

The TL and TR Descriptors. The TL and TR descriptors are positional descriptors of the form

  TL*n* and TR*n*

where *n* is a positive integer constant. They indicate that input or output of the next data value is to occur *n* positions to the left or right, respectively, of the current position. Thus a descriptor of the form TL*n* causes a backspace of *n* positions. In the case of input, this makes it possible for the same input value to be read several times. For example, for the data line

  <u>123</u>

the statements

```
INTEGER NUM
REAL ALPHA, BETA

READ 50, NUM, ALPHA, BETA
50 FORMAT (I3, TL3, F3.1, TL3, F3.2)
```

assign the integer value 123 to NUM, the real value 12.3 to ALPHA, and the real value 1.23 to BETA:

NUM: 123
ALPHA: 12.3
BETA: 1.23

In the case of output, a descriptor of the form TLn causes the backspace of n positions on the current output line. However, subsequent descriptors may cause characters in these n positions to be replaced rather than overprinted. For both input and output, a descriptor of the form TRn functions in exactly the same manner as does nX.

List-Directed Input.   In a data line, consecutive commas with no intervening characters except blanks represent **null values,** which leave unchanged the corresponding variables in the input list of a list-directed READ statement. If the variables have previously been assigned values, the values are not changed; if they have not been assigned values, the variables remain undefined. A slash in a data line terminates the input and leaves unchanged the values of the remaining variables in the input list.

   If the same value is to be read for r consecutive variables in the input list, this common value may be entered in the corresponding data line in the form

   r∗value

A repeated null value may be indicated by

   r∗

In this case, the corresponding r consecutive items in the input list are unchanged.

   The following examples illustrate these conventions for list-directed input. They are not used in list-directed output except that a given processor has the option of displaying

   r∗value

for successive output items that have the same value.

Statement	Data Entered	Result
READ *, J,K,A,B	1, , ,2.3	J = 1 K and A are unchanged B = 2.3
READ *, J,K,A,B	, , , ,	J,K,A,B all are unchanged
READ *, J,K,A,B	1, 2/	J = 1 K = 2 A and B are unchanged
READ *, J,K,A,B	/	J,K,A,B all are unchanged
READ *, J,K,A,B	2*1, 2*2.3	J = 1 and K = 1 A = 2.3 and B = 2.3
READ *, J,K,A,B	1, 2*, 2.3	J = 1 K and A are unchanged B = 2.3

In the third and fourth examples, any values following the slash would be ignored.

Exercises

1. For each of the following READ statements, show how the data should be entered so tht X, Y, I, and J are assigned the values 123.78, 6.0, 78, and 550, respectively:

   (a)   `READ *, I, J, X, Y`
   (b)   `READ 5, I, J, X, Y`
        `5 FORMAT (2I3, 2F6.0)`
   (c)   `READ 6, I, X, J, Y`
        `6 FORMAT (I3, F7.0, 2X, I5, T20, F5.0)`
   (d)   `READ 7, I, J, X, Y`
        `7 FORMAT (2I3, F5.2, F1.0)`
   (e)   `READ 8, I, X, J, Y`
        `8 FORMAT (I5, F6.0)`
   (f)   `READ 9, I, X, J, Y`
        `9 FORMAT (I2, F5.2 / I3, F2.1)`
   (g)   `READ 10, X, Y, I, J`
        `10 FORMAT (F5.2, 1X, F1.0, T4, I2, T9, I3)`

2. Describe the output that will be produced if the following program is executed with the specified input data:

```
PROGRAM COLUMN

INTEGER N, I
REAL R, DELTAR, R1, S1

READ (5, 100) N, R, DELTAR
PRINT 110
```

```
                    DO 10 I = 1, N
                        R1 = R + DELTAR*(I - 1)
                        IF (R1 .LT. 120.0) THEN
                            S1 = 17000.0 - 0.485*R1**2
                        ELSE
                            S1 = 18000.0 / (1.0 + R1**2/18000.0)
                        END IF

                        IF (MOD(I,2) .EQ. 0) PRINT 120, I, R1, S1
          10    CONTINUE

          100   FORMAT (/, I5, 2F10.4)
          110   FORMAT ('1', T3, 'INDEX', T14, 'S RATIO', T30,
              +           'LOAD')
          120   FORMAT ('0', 2X, I2, 2(5X, F10.3))

                END
```

Input data (The first line is not input data.):

```
          12345678901234567890123456789O:  Column numbers
              4       100.0       100000
```

3. Angles are commonly measured in degrees, minutes ('), and seconds ("). There are 360 degrees in one complete revolution, 60 minutes in one degree, and 60 seconds in one minute. Write a program that reads two angular measurements each in the form

$$dddDmm'ss''$$

where *ddd*, *mm*, and *ss* are the number of degrees, minutes, and seconds, respectively, and then calculates and displays their sum. Use this program to verify each of the following:

```
    74D29'13" + 105D8'16" = 179D37'29"
    7D14'55" + 5D24'55" = 12D39'50"
    20D31'19" + 0D31'30" = 21D2'49"
    122D17'48" + 237D42'12" = 0D0'0"
```

4. A number of students from three different engineering sections, A, B, and C, performed the same experiment to determine the tensile strength of sheets made from two different alloys. Each of these strength measurements is a real number in the range 0 through 10. Write a program to read several lines of data, each consisting of a section code and the tensile strengths of the two types of sheets recorded by a student in that section, and calculate

   (a) For each section, the average of the tensile strengths for each type of alloy.
   (b) The number of persons in a given section who recorded strength measures of 5 or higher.
   (c) The average of the tensile strengths recorded for alloy 2 by students who recorded a tensile strength lower than 3 for alloy 1.

5. Write a program that will read a student's number, his or her old GPA, and old number of course credits, followed by the course credit and grade for each of four courses. Calculate and print the current and cumulative GPAs with appropriate labels. See Exercise 18 at the end of Chapter 3 for details of the calculations.) Design the program so that it will accept data entered in the form

```
SNUMB 34179  GPA 3.25 CREDITS 19.0
CREDITS/GRADES 1.0 3.7 0.5 4.0 1.0 2.7 1.0 3.3
```

6. Write a program that reads the time, temperature, pressure, and volume readings from a data file like that described in the example of Section 5.6, converts the time from military to ordinary time (e.g., 0900 is 9:00 A.M., 1500 is 3:00 P.M.), calculates the average temperature, average pressure, and average volume, and displays a table like the following:

TIME	TEMPERATURE	PRESSURE	VOLUME
12:00 PM	34.2	32.2	101.5
.	.	.	.
.	.	.	.
.	.	.	.
10:00 PM	88.9	33.0	318.6
AVERAGES	?	?	?

(with the ?'s replaced by the appropriate averages).

For the following exercises, see Appendix B for a description of USERS-FILE, STUDENT-FILE, and INVENTORY-FILE.

7. Write a program to search USERS-FILE to find and display the resource limit for a specified user's identification number.

8. Write a program to read STUDENT-FILE and produce a report for all freshmen with GPAs below 2.0. This report should include the student's number and cumulative GPA with appropriate headings.

9. Write a program to search INVENTORY-FILE to find an item with a specified stock number. If a match is found, display the unit price, item name and the number currently in stock; otherwise, display a message indicating that the item was not found.

10. At the end of each month, a report is produced that shows the status of the account of each user in USERS-FILE. Write a program to accept the current date and produce a report of the following form, in which the three asterisks (***) indicate that the user has already used 90

percent or more of the resources available to him or her.

```
        USER ACCOUNTS-12/31/87
              RESOURCE   RESOURCES
   USER-ID      LIMIT       USED
   100101       $750      $380.81
   100102       $650      $598.84***
                  .
                  .
                  .
```

11. Write a program to read STUDENT-FILE and calculate

(a) The average cumulative GPA for all male students.

(b) The average cumulative GPA for all female students.

Programming Pointers

In this chapter we considered formatted input/output and introduced files. Some of the key points to remember when using these features are the following:

1. *When control characters are in effect, the first print position of each output line should be used to indicate explicitly what printer control is desired.* In some computer systems, control characters are always in effect; in others, they are not unless a specific system command or compiler option is used.

2. *Formatted output of a numeric value produces a field filled with asterisks if the output requires more spaces than allowed by the specified field width.* For formatted output of real numbers with a descriptor of the form F$w.d$, one should always have

$$w \geq d + 3$$

and for an E descriptor of the form E$w.d$

$$w \geq d + 7$$

3. *For formatted input, blanks within a numeric field may be interpreted as zeros by some systems and ignored by others.* (The BZ and BN descriptors described in Section 5.7 may be used to specify explicitly which interpretation is to be used.)

Variations and Extensions

There are only a few differences between the input/output capabilities of standard FORTRAN and other common versions, and most of these are not major differences. They include the following:

- A modified form of the print statement such as PRINT, *list* may be used for list-directed output. Similarly, a modified form of READ statement READ, *list* may be used for list-directed input. However, most compilers allow the forms

    READ (∗, ∗) *list*

    WRITE (∗, ∗) *list*

    for list-directed input from or output to the standard input/output devices. Also, input/output statements may not execute exactly as described in the text.

- Additional format descriptors may be allowed, such as a backslash (\) to inhibit the usual advance to a new line after an input/output statement is executed and Z to display integers in hexadecimal form.

- The OPEN and CLOSE statements may not be required.

- In addition to the END = clause, there may be other functions or constructs that can be used to detect the end of file (e.g., the Microsoft EOF function).

See Appendix F for details.

6

Nonnumeric Data Types: Logical and Character

The word *compute* usually suggests arithmetic operations performed on numeric data; thus, computers are often thought to be mere "number crunchers," that is, devices whose only function is to process numeric information. Already in Chapter 1, however, we considered coding schemes used to represent logical and character information in a computer. In most of our example programs, we used character strings to label output and to display messages to prompt the user to enter input data. And in Chapter 4 we explored the use of logical expressions in selection structures and in repetition structures. In this chapter we discuss in more detail how these two nonnumeric data types are processed in FORTRAN and describe some of their applications.

6.1 The LOGICAL Data Type

There are two **logical constants** in FORTRAN,

    .TRUE.

and

    .FALSE.

and logical variables may have only these values. Note the periods that must appear as part of these logical constants. A **logical variable** is declared using a LOGICAL type statement of the form

    LOGICAL *list*

where *list* is a list of variables being typed as logical. Like all type statements, this type statement must appear at the beginning of the program, before all executable statements. For example,

    LOGICAL ENDATA, SORTED, NEG, SATUR

declares that ENDATA, SORTED, NEG, and SATUR are logical variables.

An assignment statement of the form

logical-variable = logical-expression

can be used to assign a value to a logical variable. The logical expression may be either **simple** or **compound.** Simple logical expressions are logical constants or variables or **relational expressions** of the form (see Section 4.1)

expression-1   relational-operator   expression-2

Thus, the logical constant .TRUE. is a simple logical expression, and

```
SATUR = .TRUE.
```

is, therefore, a valid assignment statement; it assigns the value true to SATUR. Likewise,

```
NEG = SATUR
```

is a valid assignment statement and assigns the value of SATUR to the logical variable NEG. The assignment statement

```
ENDATA = (NUMBER .EQ. -999)
```

is also valid and assigns the value true to the logical variable ENDATA if the value of the relational expression (NUMBER .EQ. -999) is true, that is, if NUMBER has the value -999, and assigns the value false otherwise.

Compound logical expressions are formed by combining logical expressions by using the **logical operators**

```
.NOT.
.AND.
.OR.
.EQV.
.NEQV.
```

described in Section 4.1. To illustrate, consider the declarations

```
LOGICAL SORTED, ENDATA, DONE, NEG, INRANG
REAL X
```

The compound logical expression SORTED .OR. ENDATA is a valid expression and may thus be used in an assignment statement such as

```
DONE = SORTED .OR. ENDATA
```

This statement assigns the value true to DONE if and only if one or both of SORTED or ENDATA is true. The assignment statement

```
INRANG = X .LT. 1.5 .AND. .NOT. NEG
```

or with parentheses inserted to improve readability,

```
INRANG = (X .LT. 1.5) .AND. .NOT. NEG
```

assigns the value true to INRANG if and only if the value of the real variable X is less than 1.5 and the value of the logical variable NEG is false.

In Chapter 4 we saw that logical expressions can be used in selection and repetition structures. In particular, logical variables can be used for this purpose. To illustrate, consider the problem of searching the file described in Section 5.6 to find the temperature, pressure, and volume readings at a given time entered by the user. We assume that the last line of the file contains negative values to signal the end of the data. The program in Figure 6.1 uses the following while loop to carry out this searching:

```
*  While the time has not been found and the end of
*  data has not been reached, read another entry from
*  the file.

20     IF (.NOT. FOUND .AND. .NOT. EOF) THEN
          READ (15, 25) TIME, TEMP, PRESS, VOL
25        FORMAT (I4, 2F4.1, F5.1)
          EOF = (TEMP .LT. 0)
          FOUND = (TEMP .EQ. VALUE)
          GO TO 20
       END IF
```

EOF is a logical variable that is initially false and that becomes true if the end of data is reached. FOUND is a logical variable that is initially false and that becomes true if the TIME read from the file matches the VALUE entered by the user.

```
       PROGRAM SEARCH
***********************************************************************
* Program to search a file to find the temperature, pressure, and   *
* volume readings made by some monitoring device at a given time.   *
* Variables used are:                                               *
*      TIME    : time of reading (military time)                    *
*      TEMP    : temperature recorded                               *
*      PRESS   : pressure recorded                                  *
*      VOLUME  : volume recorded                                    *
*      VALUE   : time to be searched form (entered by user)         *
*      FOUND   : true if TIME in file matches VALUE entered by user *
*      EOF     : true if end of data (negative TIME) is reached     *
***********************************************************************

       INTEGER TIME, VALUE
       REAL TEMP, PRESS,VOLUME
       LOGICAL FOUND, EOF

       OPEN (UNIT = 15, FILE = 'TEMP-VOL-FILE', STATUS = 'OLD')
```

Figure 6.1

Figure 6.1   (continued)

```
      PRINT *, 'Enter time to search for (0 to stop)'
      READ *, VALUE

* While there are more values to search for, rewind the
* file and search again.

10    IF (VALUE .NE. 0) THEN
          REWIND(15)
          FOUND = .FALSE.
          EOF = .FALSE.

* While the time has not been found and the end of data has
* not been reached, read another entry from the file

20        IF (.NOT. FOUND .AND. .NOT. EOF) THEN
              READ (15, 25) TIME, TEMP, PRESS, VOLUME
25            FORMAT(I4, 2F4.1, F5.1)
              EOF = (TEMP .LT. 0)
              FOUND = (TIME .EQ. VALUE)
              GO TO 20
          END IF

          IF (FOUND) PRINT 30, TIME, TEMP, PRESS, VOLUME
30        FORMAT (1X,'AT TIME ', I4, / 1X, 'TEMPERATURE = ', F4.1 /
     +            1X, 'PRESSURE = ', F4.1 / 1X, 'VOLUME = ', F5.1)
          PRINT *
          PRINT *, 'Enter time to search for (0 to stop)'
          READ *, VALUE
          GO TO 10
      END IF

      END
```

Listing of TEMP-VOL-FILE:
=========================

```
1200034203221015
1300038803221121
1400044803241425
1500051303201520
1600055503181665
1700061303191865
1800067503232080
1900072103282262
2000076803232364
2100083503272869
2200088903303186
```

Figure 6.1 **(continued)**

```
Sample run:
==========

Enter time to search for (0 to stop)
1900
AT TIME 1900
TEMPERATURE = 72.1
PRESSURE = 32.8
VOLUME = 226.2

Enter time to search for (0 to stop)
1200
AT TIME 1200
TEMPERATURE = 34.2
PRESSURE = 32.2
VOLUME = 101.5

Enter time to search for (0 to stop)
0
```

Logical values can be displayed using either list-directed or formatted output. List-directed output of a logical value consists of only a T or an F, usually preceded by a space. For example, if A, B, and C are logical variables with the values true, false, and false, respectively, the statement

```
PRINT *, A, B, C, .TRUE. .OR. A, A .AND. B
```

produces

```
_T_F_F_T_F
```

as output.

An L descriptor is used for formatted output of logical values. This format descriptor has the form

rLw

where

w is an integer constant specifying the field width

r is the repetition indicator, an integer constant specifying the number of such fields. It may be omitted if there is only one field.

The output field consists of $w - 1$ spaces followed by a T or an F. For example, if A, B, and C are logical variables given by

```
LOGICAL A, B, C

A = .TRUE.
B = .FALSE.
C = .FALSE.
```

the statement

```
      PRINT 30, A, B, C, A .OR. C
   30 FORMAT (1X, L4, L2, 2L5)
```

will produce

```
|    T  F      F       T
|--_-_-_-_-_-_-_-_-_-_-_-
```

Logical values can read using either list-directed or formatted input. For list-directed input, logical values to be read consist of optional blanks followed by an optional period followed by T or F, which may be followed by other characters. The value of true or false is assigned to the corresponding variable according to whether the first letter encountered is T or F. For example, for the statements

```
   LOGICAL A, B, C

   READ *, A, B, C
```

the following data could be entered:

```
   .T., F, .FALSE
```

The values assigned to A, B, and C would be true, false, and false, respectively. This would also be the case if the following data were entered:

```
   T, .FALL, FLASE
```

Logical data can also be read by using an L descriptor of the form

rLw

where r is a repetition indicator and w is the width of the field to be read. This input value consists of optional blanks followed by an optional period followed by a T for true or an F for false; any characters following T or F are ignored. For example, if the line of data

```
   .TRUE   TWO.F FT
```

is read by the statements

```
      LOGICAL A, B, C, D, E

      READ 40, A, B, C, D, E
   40 FORMAT (2L6, 3L2)
```

then A, B, and E are assigned the value true, and C and D the value false.

6.2   Example: Logical Circuits

As an application of logical expressions, consider the following logical circuit called a *binary half-adder:*

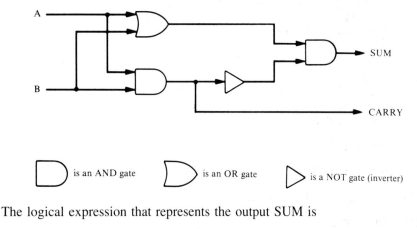

The logical expression that represents the output SUM is

    SUM = (A .OR. B) .AND. .NOT. (A .AND. B)

and the logical expression for the output CARRY is

    CARRY = A .AND. B

The program in Figure 6.2 reads values for the inputs A and B and calculates and displays the values of the two outputs, SUM and CARRY. Note that if we identify the binary digits 0 and 1 with false and true, respectively, the program's output can be interpreted as a demonstration that $1 + 1 = 10$ (SUM = 0, CARRY = 1), $1 + 0 = 01$, $0 + 1 = 01$, and $0 + 0 = 00$. This program, therefore, correctly implements binary addition of one-bit numbers.

```
      PROGRAM HADDER
**********************************************************************
* Program to calculate the outputs from a logical circuit that      *
* represents a binary half-adder.  Variables used are:              *
*    A, B  : the two logical inputs to the circuit                  *
*    SUM, CARRY : the two logical outputs                           *
*    MORE : indicates if more inputs are to be processed            *
**********************************************************************

      LOGICAL A, B, SUM, CARRY, MORE

*     Repeat the following until there are no more inputs

10        PRINT *, 'ENTER LOGICAL INPUTS A AND B:'
          READ *, A, B
          SUM = (A .OR. B) .AND. .NOT. (A .AND. B)
          CARRY = A .AND. B
```

Figure 6.2

Figure 6.2 **(continued)**

```
        PRINT 20, CARRY, SUM
20      FORMAT(1X, 'CARRY, SUM =', 2L2)
        PRINT *
        PRINT *, 'MORE INPUTS (T = YES, F = NO)?'
        READ *, MORE
    IF (MORE) GO TO 10
    END
```

Sample run:
==========

```
ENTER LOGICAL INPUTS A AND B:
T T
CARRY, SUM = T F

MORE INPUTS (T = YES, F = NO)?
T
ENTER LOGICAL INPUTS A AND B:
T F
CARRY, SUM = F T

MORE INPUTS (T = YES, F = NO)?
T
ENTER LOGICAL INPUTS A AND B:
F T
CARRY, SUM = F T

MORE INPUTS (T = YES, F = NO)?
T
ENTER LOGICAL INPUTS A AND B:
F F
CARRY, SUM = F F

MORE INPUTS (T = YES, F = NO)?
F
```

Exercises

1. Write a program that reads triples of real numbers and assigns the appropriate value of true or false to the following logical variables:

TRIANG: true if the three real numbers can represent lengths of the sides of a triangle, and false otherwise. (The sum of any two of the numbers must be greater than the third.)

EQUIL: true if TRIANG is true and the triangle is equilateral (three sides are equal).

ISOS: true if TRIANG is true and the triangle is isosceles (at least two sides are equal).

SCAL: true if TRIANG is true and the triangle is scalene (no two sides are equal).

The output from your program should have a format like the following:

```
FOR A = 2.000, B = 3.000, C = 3.000
TRIANG IS:   T
EQUIL IS:    F
ISOS IS:     T
SCAL IS:     F
```

2. A *binary full-adder* has three inputs: the two bits A and B being added and a "carry-in" bit CIN (representing the carry bit that results from adding the bits to the right of A and B in two binary numbers). It can be constructed from two binary half-adders and an OR gate:

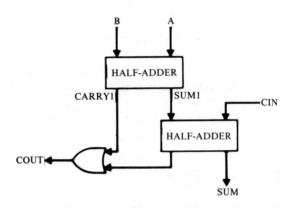

(a) Write logical expressions for
   (i) SUM and CARRY1 in terms of A and B.
   (ii) SUM and COUT in terms of CIN, SUM1, and CARRY1.
(b) Write a program to implement this binary full-adder, and use it to verify the results shown in the following table:

A	B	CIN	SUM	COUT
0	0	0	0	0
0	0	1	1	0
0	1	0	1	0
0	1	1	0	1
1	0	0	1	0
1	0	1	0	1
1	1	0	0	1
1	1	1	1	1

3. An *adder* to calculate binary sums of two-bit numbers

$$\begin{array}{r} A2\ A1 \\ +\ B2\ B1 \\ \hline COUT\ S2\ S1 \end{array}$$

where S1 and S2 are the sum bits and COUT is the carry-out bit can be constructed from a binary half-adder and a binary full-adder:

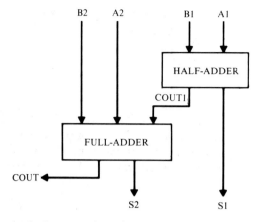

(a) Write logical expressions for
   (i) S1 and COUT1 in terms of A1 and B1.
   (ii) S2 and COUT in terms of A2, B2, and COUT1.
(b) Write a program to implement this adder and use it to demonstrate that $00 + 00 = 000$, $\quad 01 + 00 = 001$, $\quad 01 + 01 = 010$, $10 + 01 = 011$, $\quad 10 + 10 = 100$, $\quad 11 + 10 = 101$, and $11 + 11 = 110$.

6.3 Character Data

Recall that a character constant is a string of characters from the FORTRAN character set enclosed within single quotes (apostrophes) and that the number of characters enclosed is the length of the constant.

The type statement for character variables has the form

CHARACTER*n, *list*

where *list* is a list of variable names typed as character and n is an integer constant specifying the length of character constants to be assigned to the variables in this list. The names in the list must be separated by commas; however, the comma separating the length descriptor *n from the list is optional. In fact, the length descriptor *n itself is optional, and if omitted, the length for the variables in the list is 1. For example, the type statement

```
CHARACTER*10 ALPHA, BETA, IOTA
```

declares ALPHA, BETA, and IOTA to be character variables and specifies that the length of any character constant assigned to any of these variables is 10. The statement

```
CHARACTER INIT, FIRST
```

declares INIT and FIRST to be character variables with values of length 1.

A length descriptor may also be attached to any of the individual variables in the list of a CHARACTER statement. In this case, this length specification for that variable overrides the length specification given for the list. The statement

        CHARACTER*10 FNAME, LNAME*20, INIT*1, STREET, CITY

declares that FNAME, LNAME, INIT, STREET, and CITY are character variables and that the length of values for FNAME, STREET, and CITY is 10, the length of values for LNAME is 20, and values of INIT have length 1.

For character data there is one binary operation that can be used to combine two character values. This operation is **concatenation** and is denoted by //. Thus

        'COM' // 'PUTER'

produces the string 'COMPUTER'; and if MODEL is a variable declared

        CHARACTER*6 MODEL

and is assigned the value 'PRIME ', then

        MODEL // 'COM' // 'PUTER'

yields the string

        'PRIME COMPUTER'

Another operation commonly performed on character strings is the operation of extracting a sequence of consecutive characters from a given string. Such a sequence is called a **substring** of the given string. For example, the substring consisting of the fourth through sixth characters of the character constant

        'COMPUTER'

is the string

        'PUT'

In FORTRAN a substring can be extracted from the value of a character variable by specifying the name of the variable followed by the positions of the first and last characters of the substring, separated by a colon (:) and enclosed within parentheses. If 'COMPUTER' is the value of the character variable ITEM, then

        ITEM(4:6)

has the value

        'PUT'

The initial and final positions of the substring may be specified by any integer constants, variables, or expressions. If the initial position is not specified, it is assumed to be 1, and if the final position is not specified, it is assumed to be the last position in the value of the character variable. To illustrate, consider the following statements:

```
CHARACTER*15 COURSE, NAME*20

COURSE = 'MATHEMATICS'
```

Then

```
COURSE(:5)
```

has the value

```
'MATHE'
```

and the value of

```
COURSE(8:)
```

is

```
'TICS∅∅∅∅'
```

where ∅ denotes a blank. If N has the value 3, then

```
COURSE(N:N + 2)
```

has the value

```
'THE'
```

Care must be taken to ensure that the first position specified for a substring is positive and that the last position is greater than or equal to the first position but not greater than the length of the given string.

Substring names may be used to form character expressions just as character variables are used. For example, they may be concatenated with other character values, as in

```
NAME = 'MR.' // NAME(11:20)
```

As this example illustrates, an assignment statement may be used to assign a value to a character variable. For example, the statements

```
CHARACTER*5 STRA, STRB*14, TRUN, PAD

STRA = 'ALPHA'
STRB = STRA // ' PARTICLE'
```

assign the values 'ALPHA' and 'ALPHA PARTICLE' to the variables STRA and STRB, respectively. In this example, the declared lengths of the variables are equal to the lengths of the corresponding values assigned to these variables. *If, however, the lengths do not match, the values are padded with blanks or truncated as necessary.* If the declared length of the variable is greater than the length of the value being assigned, trailing blanks are added to the value; thus, the statement

```
PAD = 'RAY'
```

assigns the value 'RAY∲∲' to the variable PAD (where ∲ denotes a blank character). If the declared length of the variable is less than the length of the value being assigned, that value is truncated to the size of the variable, and the leftmost characters are assigned; thus, the statement

```
TRUN = 'TEMPERATURE'
```

assigns the value 'TEMPE' to the variable TRUN.

An assignment statement may also be used to modify part of a string by using a substring name to the left of the assignment operator. Only the character positions specified in the substring name are assigned values; the remaining positions are not changed. To illustrate, consider the statements

```
CHARACTER*8 COURSE

COURSE = 'CPSC 141'
```

The assignment statement

```
COURSE(1:4) = 'MATH'
```

or

```
COURSE(:4) = 'MATH'
```

changes the value of COURSE to 'MATH 141'. Positions to which new values are being assigned may not be referenced, however, in the character expression on the right side of such assignment statements. Thus,

```
COURSE(2:4) = COURSE(5:7)
```

is valid, whereas

```
COURSE(2:4) = COURSE(3:5)
```

is not because the substring being modified overlaps the substring being referenced.

Character values may also be compared using the relational operators .LT., .GT., .EQ., .LE., .GE., and .NE. discussed in Section 4.1. These comparisons are carried out using the encoding schemes (such as ASCII and EBCDIC) used to represent character information in a computer, as described in Chapter 1. Each such encoding scheme assigns a unique integer to each character that the machine can process. These characters can then be arranged in an order in which one character precedes another if its numeric code is less than the numeric code of the other. This ordering of characters based on their numeric codes is called the **collating sequence** and varies from one computer to another. The ANSI FORTRAN 77 standard, however, partially specifies this sequence. It requires that uppercase letters be ordered A through Z and the digits from 0 through 9 in the usual way and that the letters and digits not overlap. The blank character must precede both A and 0 in the ordering. It does not specify any particular order for special characters or their relation to other characters.

When characters are compared in a logical expression, this collating sequence is used. Thus,

```
'C' .LT. 'D'
'Z' .GT. 'W'
```

are true logical expressions since C must precede D and Z must follow W in every collating sequence. However, the truth or falsity of the logical expressions

```
'1' .LT. 'A'
'*' .GT. ')'
```

depends on the encoding scheme used in a particular computer. Both logical expressions are true for ASCII but false for EBCDIC.

Two strings are compared character by character using the collating sequence. For example, for a logical expression of the form

string1 .LT. *string2*

if the first character of *string1* is less than the first character of *string2* (that is, precedes it in the collating sequence), then *string1* is less than *string2*. Thus,

```
'CAT' .LT. 'DOG'
```

is true, since 'C' .LT. 'D' is true. If the first characters of *string1* and *string2* are the same, the second characters are compared; if these characters are the same, the third characters are compared, and so on. Thus,

```
'CAT' .LT. 'COW'
```

is true, since A is less than O. Similarly,

```
'JUNE' .GT. 'JULY'
```

is true, since N is greater than L. If the two strings have different lengths, blanks are appended to the shorter string, resulting in two strings of equal length to be compared. For example, the logical expression

```
'CAT' .LT. 'CATTLE'
```

or equivalently

```
'CATøøø' .LT. 'CATTLE'
```

(where ø denotes a blank) is true because a blank character must precede all letters.

Character values can be displayed using either list-directed or formatted output. List-directed output of a character value consists of the string of characters in that value, displayed in a field whose width is equal to the length of that value. For example, if STRA and STRB are declared by

```
CHARACTER*9 STRA, STRB
```

and are assigned values by

```
STRA = 'MIKE'
STRB = 'VANDERLEEST'
```

the statement

```
PRINT *, '***', STRA, '***', STRB, '***'
```

produces the output

```
***MIKE     ***VANDERLEE***
```

Note the five trailing blanks in the value of STRA; these result from the padding that takes place when a string of length 4 is assigned to a character variable of length 9. Note also that the last two characters in the string 'VANDERLEEST' are truncated in the assignment of a value to STRB and are of course, not displayed.

Character expressions may also appear in the output list of a PRINT statement. For example,

```
PRINT *, 'MR. '//STRA(1:4), ' ', STRB(2:4), ' DAVID'
```

produces as output

```
MR. MIKE AND DAVID
```

An A descriptor is used for the formatted output of character values. This descriptor has the form

*r*A   or   *r*A*w*

where

w   (if specified) is an integer constant specifying the field width.

r   is the repetition indicator, an integer constant indicating the number of such fields; it may be omitted if there is only one field.

In the first form, the field width is not specified and is taken to be the length of the character value being displayed. In the second form, if the field width *w* is greater than the length of the character value, then the value is right justified in the field; however, if *w* is less than the length of the value, then only the leftmost *w* characters are displayed.

As an illustration of the output of character data, consider the following program segment:

```
      CHARACTER*15 ITEM, COLOR*5

      ITEM = 'MM CAMERA'
      COLOR = 'BLACK'
      PRINT 5, COLOR, 'RED'
    5 FORMAT (1X, A, A4)
      PRINT 10, COLOR
   10 FORMAT (1X, A1)
      PRINT 15, 'MOVIE-' // ITEM(4:9)
   15 FORMAT (1X, A)
      PRINT 20, 35, ITEM
   20 FORMAT (1X, I2, A)
```

These statements produce the following output:

```
BLACK RED
B
MOVIE-CAMERA
35MM CAMERA
```

Character values can be read using either list-directed or formatted input. For list-directed input, character values must be enclosed within single quotes. Truncation or blank padding is done when necessary, as described earlier for assignment statements. For example, entering the values

```
'MIKE', 'VANDERLEEST'
```

in response to the statement

```
READ *, STRA, STRB
```

assigns the value 'MIKEɃɃɃɃ' to STRA (where Ƀ denotes a blank) and the value 'VANDERLEE' to STRB where STRA and STRB were declared earlier by

```
CHARACTER *9 STRA, STRB
```

Character data can also be read using an A descriptor of the form

$$rA \quad \text{or} \quad rAw$$

where r is a repetition indicator, and in the second form w is the width of the field to be read. In the first form, the width of the field read for a particular variable in the input list is the length specified for that variable in the CHARACTER statement.

When a READ statement whose input list contains a character variable or substring is executed, *all* characters in the field associated with the corresponding A descriptor are read. For example, if the line of data

```
FOURSCORE AND SEVEN YEARS AGO
```

is read by the statements

```
CHARACTER*6 STRA, STRB

READ 20, STRA, STRB
20 FORMAT (2A)
```

the value

```
FOURSC
```

is assigned to STRA and

```
ORE AN
```

to STRB.

Note that six columns were read for each of STRA and STRB, as this is their declared length. If the following line of data

```
AB1''34'AN,APPLE A DAY
```

is entered, the values assigned to STRA and STRB would be

```
AB1''3
```

and

```
4'AN,A
```

respectively.

If the format statement

```
20 FORMAT (2A6)
```

were used, the same values would be assigned to STRA and STRB. If, however, the format statement

```
20 FORMAT (A2, A12)
```

were used, the value assigned to STRA would be

```
ABbbbb
```

and the value assigned to STRB would be

```
AN,APP
```

Note that in the case of STRB, a field of size twelve was read but the *rightmost* six characters were assigned. (See Programming Pointer 6 at the end of this chapter.)

6.4 Examples: Plotting Graphs, Run-Time Formatting

EXAMPLE 1: Plotting Graphs.   Many computer systems include a plotting device and some graphics software that enable the user to generate high-resolution graphs of functions. Output devices such as terminals and printers can also be used for graphic displays (see Figure 6.3), but the quality is not as good as it is for plotters because the resolution is limited to a rather small number of print positions across the page and because the output device can advance in only one direction, from one line to the next. In this example, we consider the problem of producing a rough plot of the graph of a function $y = f(x)$.

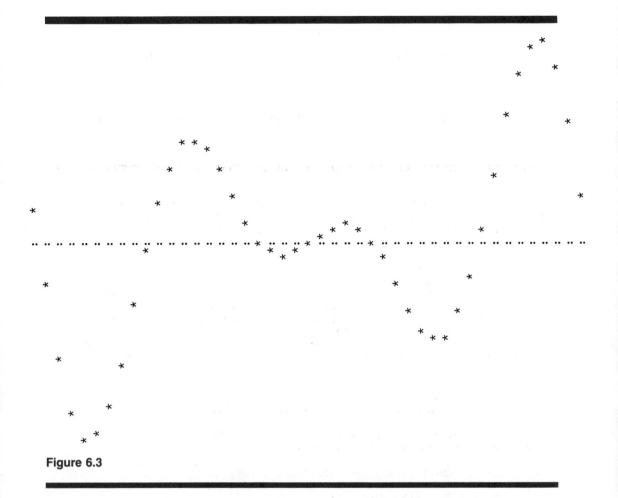

Figure 6.3

The program in Figure 6.4 does such plotting for the function $Y = X * COS(X)$. Values are read for XMIN and XMAX, the minimum and maximum X values, and for YMIN and YMAX, the minimum and maximum Y values. The X axis is represented vertically (directed downward) using 45 vertical print positions, and the Y axis is represented horizontally using 75 horizontal print positions. (The ratio 45/75 corresponds to the ratio 3/5 of character width to height.) The statements

```
DELTAX = (XMAX − XMIN) / 45
DELTAY = (YMAX − YMIN) / 75
```

thus determine the X and Y increments represented by one vertical or horizontal print position, respectively. The character variable LINE represents one line of output. For each X value, it is initialized to blanks, except that the 38th position is set equal to a mark (:) for the X axis. The horizontal print position is determined by rounding the value of Y / DELTAY to the nearest integer and adding this value to 38:

```
     HORIZ = 38 + NINT(Y / DELTAY)
```

and it is this position in LINE that is set equal to the plotting character (∗):

```
     LINE(HORIZ:HORIZ) = '*'
```

LINE is then displayed; X is incremented to its next value; and the process is repeated.

```
      PROGRAM PLOT
***********************************************************************
* Program to plot a graph of a function Y = F(X).  Variables used are: *
*     LINE   : character variable representing one line of output     *
*     X, Y   : coordinates of a point on the graph                    *
*     XMIN   : minimum X value                                        *
*     XMAX   : maximum X value                                        *
*     YMIN   : minimum Y value                                        *
*     YMAX   : maximum Y value                                        *
*     DELTAX : X increment represented by one vertical print position *
*     DELTAY : Y-increment represented by 1 horizontal print position *
*     HORIZ  : counter for horizontal positions                       *
*     VERT   : counter for vertical positions                         *
***********************************************************************

      CHARACTER*75 LINE
      INTEGER HORIZ, VERT
      REAL XMIN, XMAX, X, Y, YMIN, YMAX, DELTAX, DELTAY

* Get initial values and calculate X and Y increments,
* assuming 45 vertical and 75 horizontal print positions

      PRINT *, 'ENTER MINIMUM AND MAXIMUM X VALUES AND'
      PRINT *, 'THE MINIMUM AND MAXIMUM Y-VALUES'
      READ *, XMIN, XMAX, YMIN, YMAX
      DELTAX = (XMAX - XMIN) / 45
      DELTAY = (YMAX - YMIN) / 75

* Produce the plot of the graph

      X = XMIN
      DO 20 VERT = 1, 45

*         Calculate Y value corresponding to current X value

          Y = X * COS(X)

*         Blank out LINE, then set the X axis mark and the
*         position corresponding to this Y value and print LINE

          LINE = ' '
          LINE(38:38) = ':'
          HORIZ = 38 + NINT(Y / DELTAY)
          LINE(HORIZ:HORIZ)='*'
          PRINT *, LINE
          X = X + DELTAX
20    CONTINUE
```

Figure 6.4

Figure 6.4 (continued)

```
* Label the X axis

      LINE = ' '
      LINE(38:38) = 'X'
      PRINT *, LINE
      END
```

Sample run:
==========

```
ENTER MINIMUM AND MAXIMUM X VALUES AND
THE MINIMUM AND MAXIMUM Y-VALUES
-8, 8, -8, 8
                                          :       *
                                       *  :
                                *         :
                           *              :
                     *                    :
                       *                  :
                          *               :
                              *           :
                                  *       :
                                          *:
                                          :       *
                                          :          *
                                          :            *
                                          :            *
                                          :            *
                                          :          *
                                          :       *
                                          *
                                         *:
                                       *  :
                                        *:
                                          *
                                        : *
                                        :  *
                                        :   *
                                        *
                                      * :
                                  *       :
                              *           :
                          *               :
                        *                 :
                        *                 :
                      *                   :
                    *                     :
                  *                       :
                                          : *
                                              *
                                                *
                                                   *
                                                      *
                                                       *
                                                    *
                                                *
                                    *         :
                              *               :
                                          X
```
```
```

EXAMPLE 2: Run-Time Formatting.   In most of our examples of formatted input/output we used a FORMAT statement. As we noted in Chapter 5, however, a format identifier may also be a character expression whose value is the list of format descriptors. For example, if NUM is of type integer and X is of type real, the statement

```
PRINT '(1X, I7, T10, F6.2)', NUM, X
```

is equivalent to the pair of statements

```
    PRINT 20, NUM, X
20 FORMAT (1X, I7, T10, F6.2)
```

A character variable could also be used:

```
CHARACTER*40 FORM
        .
        .
        .
FORM = '(1X, I7, T10, F6.2)'
PRINT FORM, NUM, X
```

Similarly, if X and Y are real variables

```
    PRINT 30, X, Y
30 FORMAT (1X, 'X = ', F6.2, ' Y = ', F6.2)
```

could be written as

```
FORM = '(1X, ''X = '', F6.2, '' Y = '', F6.2)'
PRINT FORM, X, Y
```

Note the two single quotes that must be used to enclose the string constants in the list of format descriptors. Also note that whereas a FORMAT statement may appear anywhere in the program—either before or after a PRINT (or WRITE) statement that uses it—a character variable must be assigned a value *before* it can be used as a format identifier.

A list of format descriptors could also be read at run-time and assigned to a character variable like FORM which is then used as a format identifier. This makes it possible to change the format used for input or output each time a program is run without having to modify the program itself. This is illustrated in the program of Figure 6.5. It reads a file of time, temperature, pressure, and volume measurements and displays a table of temperature and pressure readings.

Two sample runs are shown. The first uses the data file

```
1200034203221015
1300038803221121
1400044803241425
1500051303201520
1600055503181665
1700061303191865
1800067503232080
1900072103282262
2000076803252564
2100083503272869
2200088903303186
```

in which the fifth through eighth digits constitute the temperatures, and the last four digits are the volume. Decimal points must be positioned so there is one digit to its right in both cases. Thus an appropriate format specifier is

```
(4X, F4.1, T13, F4.1)
```

The second data file is .

```
12:00PM
 34.2 32.2 101.5
 1:00PM
 33.8 32.2 112.1
 2:00PM
 44.8 32.4 142.5
 3:00PM
 51.3 32.0 152.0
 4:00PM
 55.5 31.8 166.5
 5:00PM
 61.3 31.9 186.5
 6:00PM
 67.5 32.3 208.0
 7:00PM
 72.1 32.8 226.2
 8:00PM
 76.8 32.5 256.4
 9:00PM
 83.5 32.7 286.9
10:00PM
 88.9 33.0 318.6
```

for which an appropriate format specifier is

```
(/F5.0, 5X, F6.0)
```

When the program is executed, the user enters the name of the file (FNAME) and the appropriate format specifier (FORMI) for that file.

```
      PROGRAM TEMVOL
***********************************************************************
* Program to read temperatures and volumes from a file containing    *
* time, temperature, pressure, and volume readings made by some      *
* monitoring device and display the temperature and volume           *
* measurements in tabular form.  Variables used are:                 *
*      FNAME   :  name of the data file                              *
*      FORMI   :  input format identifier                            *
*      FORMO   :  output format identifier                           *
*      TEMP    :  temperature recorded                               *
*      VOLUME  :  volume recorded                                    *
***********************************************************************

      CHARACTER*50 FORMI, FORMO, FNAME*20
      REAL TEMP, VOLUME

* Open the file as unit 15, set up the input and output
* formats, print the table heading, and initialize counter
* and the sums to 0.

      PRINT *, 'ENTER NAME OF THE DATA FILE'
      READ '(A)', FNAME
      OPEN (UNIT = 15, FILE = FNAME, STATUS = 'OLD')
      PRINT 10, FNAME
10    FORMAT (1X, 'ENTER INPUT FORMAT FOR ', A)
      READ '(A)', FORMI
      FORMO = '(1X, A11, A10)'
      PRINT FORMO, 'TEMPERATURE', 'VOLUME'
      PRINT FORMO, '===========', '======'
      FORMO = '(1X, F8.1, F12.1)'

* While there is more data, read temperatures and
* temperatures, displaying each in the table.

20        READ (UNIT = 15, FMT = FORMI, END = 30) TEMP, VOLUME
          PRINT FORMO, TEMP, VOLUME
          GO TO 20

30    CLOSE (15)
      END
```

Figure 6.5

Figure 6.5   (continued)

```
Sample runs:
============

ENTER NAME OF THE DATA FILE
TEM-VOL-FILE-1
ENTER INPUT FORMAT FOR TEM-VOL-FILE-1
(4X, F4.1, T13, F4.1)
TEMPERATURE     VOLUME
===========     ======
       34.2     101.5
       38.8     112.1
       44.8     142.5
       51.3     152.0
       55.5     166.5
       61.3     186.5
       67.5     208.0
       72.1     226.2
       76.8     256.4
       83.5     286.9
       88.9     318.6


====================================

ENTER NAME OF THE DATA FILE
TEM-VOL-FILE-2
ENTER INPUT FORMAT FOR TEM-VOL-FILE-2
(/F5.0, 5X, F6.0)
TEMPERATURE     VOLUME
===========     ======
       34.2     101.5
       38.8     112.1
       44.8     142.5
       51.3     152.0
       55.5     166.5
       61.3     186.5
       67.5     208.0
       72.1     226.2
       76.8     256.4
       83.5     286.9
       88.9     318.6
```

Exercises

1. For each of the following, write a single type statement to declare the given variable to be of character type whose values have the length indicated.

   (a) STRA, length 10; STRB, length 10; STRC, length 10

   (b) NAME1, length 20; NAME2, length 20; NAME3, length 10

   (c) NAME, length 20; STREET, length 30; CITY, length 15; STATE, length 2

2. Given that the following declarations have been made

```
CHARACTER*10 ALPHA, BETA*5, GAMMA*1, LABEL1*4,
+               LABEL2*3, STR1*3, STR2*4
```

and that STR1 = 'FOR', STR2 = 'TRAN', LABEL1 = 'FOOT', LABEL2 = 'LBS', find the value assigned to the given variable for each of the following, or indicate why the statement is not valid.

(a) GAMMA = 1
(b) GAMMA = '1'
(c) ALPHA = 'ONE' // 'TWO'
(d) ALPHA = '1' // '2'
(e) BETA = 'ABCDEFGHIJKLMNOPQRSTUVWXYZ'
(f) BETA = '123,456,789'
(g) BETA = 'ONE' // 23
(h) ALPHA = STR1 // STR2 // -'77'
(i) BETA = STR1 // STR2 // -'77'
(j) ALPHA = LABEL1 // LABEL2
(k) GAMMA = LABEL1
(l) ALPHA = LABEL1 // '-' // LABEL2
(m) BETA = STR1 // STR2(:1)
(n) ALPHA = STR2(2:3) // 'NDOM'
(o) STR2(2:3) = 'UR'
(p) STR2(:2) = STR2(3:)
(q) STR1(:2) = STR1(2:)

3. Given the following declarations,

```
INTEGER N
REAL A
CHARACTER*40 FORM, S1*10, S2*6
```

show how the data should be entered for each of the following READ statements so that N, A, S1, and S2 are assigned the values 1, 1.1, MODEL-XL11, and CAMERA, respectively.

(a)   READ *, N, A, S1, S2

(b)   READ 10, N, A, S1, S
       10 FORMAT (I2, F4.1, 2A)

(c)   READ '(I1, A, F2.1 A)', N, S1, A, S2

(d)   FORM = '(25X, I3, T1, F5.0, 1X, A, T18, A)'
       READ FORM, N, A, S1, S2

(e)   FORM = '(I5, F5.0, 2A15)'
       READ FORM, N, A, S1, S2

(f)   READ 20, N, A, S1, S2
       20 FORMAT (T9, I1, TL1, F2.1, T1, 2A)

4. Write a program that reads a character string and prints it in reverse order, beginning with the last nonblank character.

5. A character string is said to be a *palindrome* if reversing the order of the characters in the string does not change it. For example,

```
RADAR

MADAM

1467641

ABLE WAS I ERE I SAW ELBA
```

are palindromes. Write a program that reads a character string and determines whether that string, excluding leading and trailing blanks, is a palindrome.

6. Write a program to read STUDENT-FILE and display the name and cumulative GPA of all students with a given major that is entered during execution.

7. A file contains grade records for students in a freshman engineering class. Each record consists of several lines of information. The first line contains the student's name in columns 1 through 30 and the letter T or F in column 31 to indicate whether a letter grade is to be assigned (T) or the course is to be graded on a pass/fail basis (F). The next ten lines contain the test scores for this student, one integer score per line in columns 1 through 3. Write a program to read these records and, for each student, to display his or her name, term average (in the form xxx.x), and final grade on a single line. If the student has selected the pass/fail option, the final grade is 'PASS' for a term average of 70.0 or above and 'FAIL' otherwise. If the student has selected the letter grade option, the final grade is 'A' for a term average of 90.0 or above, 'B' for a term average of 80.0 through 89.9, 'C' for a term average of 70.0 through 79.9, and 'F' otherwise.

8. The following data file contains for each of several objects, its shape (cube or sphere), its critical dimension (edge or radius), its density, and the material from which it is made:

```
sphere    2.0     .00264    aluminum
cube      3.0     .00857       brass
cub       1.5     .0113         lead
sphere    1.85    .0088       nickel
CUBE      13.7    .00035       cedar
SPHERE    2.85    .00075         oak
```

Write a program to read these records and produce a table displaying the following information for each object:

(a) shape
(b) critical dimension
(c) material
(d) volume

(e) mass
(f) whether the object will float when immersed in an oil bath
(g) mass of oil displaced by the object

(An object will float if its density is less than or equal to the density of oil, .00088 kg/cm^3.) Your program should check that each object's shape is one of the strings 'cube', 'CUBE', 'sphere', or 'SPHERE'.

Programming Pointers

In this chapter we described logical and character data. The following are some of the major points to remember when using character type. See the programming pointers at the end of Chapter 4 for special notes concerning logical type.

1. *The first position specified in a substring should be no greater than the last position; also, both positions should be positive and no greater than the length of the string.* For a substring consisting of the leftmost characters of a string, the first position need not be specified. Thus, if STRING is declared by

```
CHARACTER*10 STRING
```

then the substring

```
STRING( :4)
```

is equivalent to

```
STRING(1:4)
```

Similarly, for a substring consisting of the rightmost characters, the last position need not be specified. Thus,

```
STRING(6: )
```

is equivalent to

```
STRING(6:10)
```

2. *In an assignment to a substring, the value being assigned may not be a character expression that references any of the same positions to which values are being assigned.* Thus, for the character variable declared by

```
CHARACTER*10 STRING
```

the following assignment statement is not allowed:

```
STRING(3:7) = STRING(6:10)
```

3. *The collating sequence used to compare characters depends on the encoding system used to store characters.* For example,

```
'123' .LT. 'A23'
```

is true if ASCII coding is used, but it is false for EBCDIC.

4. *Character constants must be enclosed in single quotation marks for list-directed input but not for formatted input.*

5. *In assignment statements and in list-directed input, if the value being assigned or read has a length greater than that specified for the character variable (or substring), the rightmost characters are truncated. If the value has a length less than that of the variable (or substring), blanks are added at the right.* Thus, if STRING is declared by

```
CHARACTER*10 STRING
```

the statement

```
STRING = 'ABCDEFGHIJKLMNO'
```

will assign the string 'ABCDEFGHIJ' to STRING, and

```
STRING = 'ABC'
```

will assign the string 'ABCbbbbbbb' to STRING. An acronym sometimes used to remember this is

- **APT:** For **A**ssignment (and list-directed input), both blank-**P**adding and **T**runcation occur on the right.

6. *For formatted input/output, characters are truncated or blanks are added, depending on whether the field width is too small or too large. For input, truncation occurs on the left, and blank padding on the right; for output, truncation occurs on the right, and blank padding on the left.* The acronymns analogous to that in Programming Pointer 5 are

- **POT:** **P**adding on the left with blanks occurs for formatted **O**utput, or **T**runcation of rightmost characters occurs.
- **TIP:** **T**runcation of leftmost characters occurs for formatted **I**nput, or **P**adding with blanks on the right occurs.

To illustrate, suppose STRING is declared by

```
CHARACTER*10 STRING
```

If STRING = 'ABCDEFGHIJ'

then the output produced by the statements

```
      PRINT 10, STRING
      PRINT 20, STRING
   10 FORMAT(1X, A5)
   20 FORMAT(1X, A15)
```

is

```
ABCDE
bbbbbABCDEFGHIJ
```

For the formatted input statement

```
READ 10, STRING
```

if the value entered is

    ABCDE

(which might be followed by any other characters), the value assigned to STRING is ABCDEØØØØØ. For the statement

    READ 20, STRING

entering the data

    ABCDEFGHIJKLMNO

assigns the value FGHIJKLMNO to STRING.

Variations and Extensions

As noted in the Variations and Extensions section of Chapter 4, there are few differences between the use of the logical data type in standard FOR-TRAN and its use in other common versions. Likewise, there are few differences in the use of character type. Some of the more common ones include the following:

- An upper limit may be imposed on the length of character values.

- Other forms of the LOGICAL and CHARACTER type statements may be allowed.

- Initialization of logical and character variables may be permitted in type statements.

- Comparison of character values and numeric values by relational operators may be allowed.

- Assignment of character values to numeric variables and of numeric values to character variables may be allowed.

See Appendix F for details.

7

One-Dimensional Arrays

With silver bells, and cockle shells,
And pretty maids all in a row.

MOTHER GOOSE

I've got a little list, I've got a little list.

GILBERT AND SULLIVAN, *The Mikado*

There is nothing more difficult to take in hand, more perilous to conduct,
or more uncertain in its success, than to take the lead in the introduction
of a new order of things.

NICCOLO MACHIAVELLI, *The Prince*

The variables we have considered thus far are symbolic addresses of single memory locations that are used to store only one value at a time. Such variables are usually called *simple* variables. In many situations, however, it is necessary to process a collection of values that are related in some way, for example, a list of test scores, a set of measurements resulting from some experiment, or a matrix. Because processing such collections using only simple variables is extremely cumbersome, most high-level languages include special features for structuring such data. In this chapter we consider the **data structure** known as an **array,** and its implementation in FORTRAN.

7.1 Introduction to Arrays and Subscripted Variables

In Chapter 5 we introduced files, which are collections of related data items used in input/output operations. These files are usually stored in secondary memory from which data retrieval is rather slow, and consequently, files are not always practical. For many applications we prefer a **direct access** structure stored in main memory so that data items can be stored in or retrieved from the structure directly by specifying their locations in the structure. One such data structure provided in almost every high-level language is an **array** in which a fixed number of data items, all of the same type, are organized in a sequence and direct access to each item is possible by specifying its position in this sequence.

In FORTRAN we can refer to an entire array using an **array variable** and can access each individual element or **component** of the array by means of a **subscripted** (or **indexed**) **variable** formed by appending a **subscript** (or **index**) enclosed in parentheses to the array variable. Thus if X is an array variable, the subscripted variable X(3) refers to the third element in this array. (This corresponds to the subscript notation X_3 commonly used in mathematics to refer to a specified element in a sequence.)

For example, if 12 pollution readings are to be processed in a program, we might use an array to store these values. The computer must first be instructed to reserve a sequence of 12 memory locations for them. The DIMENSION statement can be used for this purpose. For example, the statements

```
DIMENSION POLLUT(1:12)
INTEGER POLLUT
```

or

```
DIMENSION POLLUT(12)
INTEGER POLLUT
```

instruct the compiler to establish an array with the name POLLUT, consisting of 12 memory locations in which integer values are to be stored, and it associates the subscripted variables

```
POLLUT(1)
POLLUT(2)
      .
      .
      .
POLLUT(12)
```

with these locations.

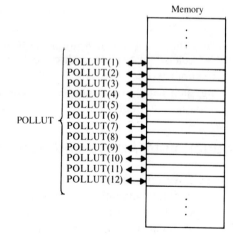

This same array could be declared by including the dimensioning information in the type statement itself,

```
INTEGER POLLUT(1:12)
```

or

```
INTEGER POLLUT(12)
```

Each subscripted variable POLLUT(1), POLLUT(2), . . . , POLLUT(12) names an individual memory location and hence can be used in much the same way as a simple variable can. For example, the assignment statement

```
POLLUT(4) = 57
```

stores the value 57 in the fourth location of the array POLLUT, and the output statement

```
PRINT *, POLLUT(10)
```

displays the value stored in the tenth location of the array POLLUT.

As these examples illustrate, each component of the array POLLUT is directly accessible. This direct access is accomplished by means of **address translation.** The first word in the memory block reserved for an array is used to store the first component. Its address is called the **base address** for the array, and the address of any other component is calculated in terms of this base address. For example, if the base address for the array POLLUT is B and each pollution reading can be stored in a single memory word, then the address of POLLUT(1) is B, the address of POLLUT(2) is $B + 1$, the address of POLLUT(3) is $B + 2$, and in general, the address of POLLUT(I) is $B + I - 1$.

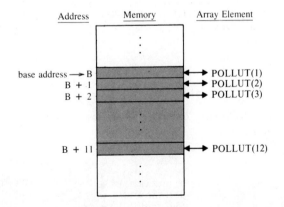

If W memory words are required for each component, then POLLUT(1) would be stored in W consecutive words, beginning at the word located at address B, POLLUT(2) in a block beginning at address $B + W$, and in general, POLLUT(I) in a block of size W beginning at address $B + (I - 1)*W$. Each time an array component is accessed using a subscripted variable, this address translation must be performed by the system software and/or hardware to determine the location of that component in memory.

An important feature of the notation used for arrays is that the subscript attached to the array name may be an integer variable or expression. For example, the statement

```
IF (POLLUT(N) .GT. 90) PRINT *, POLLUT(N), ' HAZARDOUS'
```

retrieves the Nth item of the array POLLUT, compares it with 90, and prints it with the message 'HAZARDOUS' if it exceeds 90. The block IF statement

```
IF (POLLUT(I) .GT. POLLUT(I + 1))THEN
    TEMP = POLLUT(I)
    POLLUT(I) = POLLUT(I + 1)
    POLLUT(I + 1) = TEMP
END IF
```

interchanges the values of POLLUT(I) and POLLUT(I + 1) if the first is greater than the second.

Using an array reference in which the subscript is a variable or an expression within a loop that changes the value of the subscript on each pass through the loop is a convenient way to process each item in the array. Thus,

```
DO 10 I = 1, 12
    IF (POLLUT(I) .GE. 90) PRINT *, POLLUT(I), ' HAZARDOUS'
10 CONTINUE
```

retrieves each item of the array POLLUT in sequence, beginning with POL-LUT(1), compares it with 90, and prints it with the message 'HAZARDOUS' if it is greater than or equal to 90. The effect, therefore, is the same as if we write a sequence of 12 IF statements comparing each element of the array POLLUT with 90:

```
IF (POLLUT(1) .GE. 90) PRINT *, POLLUT(1), ' HAZARDOUS'
IF (POLLUT(2) .GE. 90) PRINT *, POLLUT(2), ' HAZARDOUS'
IF (POLLUT(3) .GE. 90) PRINT *, POLLUT(3), ' HAZARDOUS'
                            .
                            .
                            .
IF (POLLUT(12) .GE. 90) PRINT *, POLLUT(12), ' HAZARDOUS'
```

The following diagram illustrates the output produced for a particular array POLLUT:

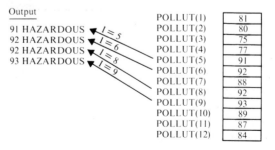

The type of an array may be any of the FORTRAN data types. For example, an array TEXT declared by the statements

```
DIMENSION TEXT(1:60)
CHARACTER*80 TEXT
```

or

```
DIMENSION TEXT(60)
CHARACTER*80 TEXT
```

or simply

```
CHARACTER*80 TEXT(60)
```

consists of 60 character strings, each of which has length 80. Such an array could be used to store the individual lines of a page of text; TEXT(1) would refer to the first line, TEXT(2) to the second line, and in general, TEXT(N) to the Nth line of text on the page. To print the first 40 lines on a page of text, the following statements could be used:

```
    DO 10 I = 1, 40
        PRINT *, TEXT(I)
10 CONTINUE
```

or to print only the first five characters of each line,

```
    DO 10 I = 1, 40
        PRINT *, TEXT(I)(1:5)
10 CONTINUE
```

Arrays such as POLLUT and TEXT involve only a single subscript and are commonly called **one-dimensional arrays.** FORTRAN programs, however, may process arrays of more than one dimension, in which case each element of the array is designated by attaching the appropriate number of subscripts to the array name. In this chapter we consider only one-dimensional arrays; in the next chapter we discuss multidimensional arrays.

The name and the range of subscripts of each one-dimensional array in a program may be declared in a DIMENSION statement of the form

DIMENSION *list*

where *list* is a list of **array declarations** of the form

array-name (l:u)

separated by commas. The pair *l:u* must be a pair of integer constants (or parameters) specifying the range of values for the subscript to be from the lower limit *l* through the upper limit *u*; for example, the pair $-2:5$ declares that a certain subscript may be any of the integers $-2, -1, 0, 1, 2, 3, 4, 5$.

If the minimum value of the subscript for an array is 1, then only the maximum subscript need be specified. Thus, as we noted earlier, the integer array POLLUT that has a subscript ranging from 1 through 12 may be declared by the statements

```
DIMENSION POLLUT(1:12)
INTEGER POLLUT
```

or

```
DIMENSION POLLUT(12)
INTEGER POLLUT
```

Similarly, either

```
DIMENSION POINT(1:20)
REAL POINT
```

or

```
DIMENSION POINT(20)
REAL POINT
```

declares POINT to be a one-dimensional real array with a subscript ranging from 1 through 20. A single DIMENSION statement could be used to declare both arrays:

```
DIMENSION POLLUT(12), POINT(20)
INTEGER POLLUT
REAL POINT
```

As we have noted, the dimension information may also be given in a type statement. Thus,

```
INTEGER POLLUT(1:12)
REAL POINT(1:20)
```

or

```
INTEGER POLLUT(12)
REAL POINT(20)
```

can be used in place of the preceding statements. Similarly,

```
REAL ALPHA(50), BETA(30)
```

is acceptable in place of

```
DIMENSION ALPHA(50), BETA(30)
REAL ALPHA, BETA
```

The subscripts used in our examples of arrays have been positive valued, ranging from 1 through some upper limit. This is probably the most common subscript range, but FORTRAN does allow a subscript to be any integer value, positive, negative, or zero, provided it does not fall outside the range specified in the array declaration. For example, the statements

```
INTEGER GAMMA(-1:3), DELTA(0:5)
REAL KAPPA(4:10)
```

establish three one-dimensional arrays. The integer array GAMMA may have subscripts ranging from -1 through 3; thus, the following subscripted variables may be used: GAMMA(-1), GAMMA(0), GAMMA(1), GAMMA(2), GAMMA(3). The integer array DELTA has subscripts ranging from 0 through 5, and the subscripts of the real array KAPPA may be any of 4, 5, 6, 7, 8, 9, or 10.

DIMENSION *statements are nonexecutable,* as they provide instructions to the compiler to reserve locations in memory for the items in the arrays being declared. *They must be placed at the beginning of the program before all executable statements.*

7.2 Input/Output of Arrays

There are three ways in which the entries of a one-dimensional array can be read or displayed:

1. Use a DO loop containing an input/output statement.
2. Use only the array name in an input/output statement.
3. Use an implied DO loop in an input/output statement.

In this section we describe each of these methods.

Input/Output Using a DO Loop. As we noted in the preceding section, one way to process each item in a one-dimensional array is to use an array reference in which the subscript is a variable within a loop that changes the value of the subscript on each pass through the loop. To read or display the elements of an array, therefore, one might simply place an input or output statement containing an array reference with a variable subscript within a DO loop. For example, if VELOC is a one-dimensional array and we wish to read 10 values into this array, the following statements might be used:

```
REAL VELOC(10)
INTEGER I

DO 10 I = 1, 10
    READ *, VELOC(I)
10 CONTINUE
```

The DO loop containing the READ statement is equivalent to the following sequence of 10 READ statements:

```
READ *, VELOC(1)
READ *, VELOC(2)
READ *, VELOC(3)
READ *, VELOC(4)
READ *, VELOC(5)
READ *, VELOC(6)
READ *, VELOC(7)
READ *, VELOC(8)
READ *, VELOC(9)
READ *, VELOC(10)
```

Recall that each execution of a READ statement requires a new line of input data. Consequently, the 10 values to be read into the array VELOC must be entered on 10 separate lines, one per line.

If we wish to declare a larger array and use only part of it, the statements

```
REAL VELOC(50)
INTEGER NUMVEL, I

PRINT *, 'ENTER NUMBER OF VELOCITIES'
READ *, NUMVEL
DO 10 I = 1, NUMVEL
    READ *, VELOC(I)
10 CONTINUE
```

might be used. The DO loop here has the same effect as the sequence of statements

```
READ *, VELOC(1)
READ *, VELOC(2)
           .
           .
           .
READ *, VELOC(NUMVEL)
```

Arrays can be displayed in a similar manner by using a PRINT statement within a DO loop. Thus, the first 10 elements of the array VELOC can be displayed with the statements

```
DO 20 I = 1, 10
    PRINT *, VELOC(I)
20 CONTINUE
```

This is equivalent to the following sequence of 10 PRINT statements:

```
PRINT *, VELOC(1)
PRINT *, VELOC(2)
PRINT *, VELOC(3)
PRINT *, VELOC(4)
PRINT *, VELOC(5)
PRINT *, VELOC(6)
PRINT *, VELOC(7)
PRINT *, VELOC(8)
PRINT *, VELOC(9)
PRINT *, VELOC(10)
```

Because each execution of a PRINT statement causes output to begin on a new line, the 10 elements of the array VELOC are printed on 10 lines, one value per line.

The program in Figure 7.1 illustrates this method of reading and displaying the elements of a one-dimensional array. The array declaration specifies that VELOC is a real array whose subscripts may range from 1 through 50; thus VELOC may have at most 50 elements. A value is then read for the number NUMVEL of velocities to be processed, and a DO loop is used to read this number of values into the array VELOC. These velocities are then displayed by using a PRINT statement within a DO loop.

In the sample run of the program, the value 10 is entered for NUMVEL. The READ statement in the first DO loop is thus executed 10 times, and as we have noted, this requires that the constants to be read appear on 10 lines, one per line. Similarly, because the PRINT statement in the second DO loop is executed 10 times, the entries of VELOC are displayed on 10 lines, one per line. This requirement that data values must be entered on separate lines and are printed on separate lines is one of the disadvantages of using a DO loop for input/output of lists.

```
      PROGRAM VLIST1
***********************************************************************
* Sample program illustrating the use of DO loops to read and display *
* a list of velocities.  NUMVEL is the number of values read into     *
* the array VELOC.                                                    *
***********************************************************************

      INTEGER NUMVEL, I
      REAL VELOC(50)

* Read the list of velocities

      PRINT *, 'ENTER THE NUMBER OF VELOCITIES:'
      READ *, NUMVEL
      PRINT *, 'ENTER THE VELOCITY VALUES, ONE PER LINE:'
      DO 10 I = 1, NUMVEL
         READ *, VELOC(I)
10    CONTINUE

* Print the list of velocities

      PRINT 20
20    FORMAT (/1X, 'LIST OF VELOCITIES'/1X, 18('='))
      DO 40 I = 1, NUMVEL
         PRINT 30, I, VELOC(I)
30       FORMAT (1X, I3, '  :', F10.1)
40    CONTINUE
      END
```

Figure 7.1

Figure 7.1   (continued)

```
Sample run:
==========


ENTER THE NUMBER OF VELOCITIES:
10
ENTER THE VELOCITY VALUES, ONE PER LINE:
100.0
 98.5
 99.7
120.6
125.8
 88.7
 99.6
115.0
103.4
 98.6

LIST OF VELOCITIES
==================
  1  :      100.0
  2  :       98.5
  3  :       99.7
  4  :      120.6
  5  :      125.8
  6  :       88.7
  7  :       99.6
  8  :      115.0
  9  :      103.4
 10  :       98.6
```

Input/Output Using the Array Name.   An alternative method of reading or displaying an array is to use an input or output statement containing the array name without subscripts. The effect is the same as listing all of the array elements in the input/output statement. For example, if the array VELOC is declared by

```
REAL VELOC(10)
```

the statement

```
READ *, VELOC
```

is equivalent to

```
READ *, VELOC(1), VELOC(2), VELOC(3), VELOC(4), VELOC(5),
+        VELOC(6), VELOC(7), VELOC(8), VELOC(9), VELOC(10)
```

Because the READ statement is executed only once, the entries for VELOC need not be read from separate lines. All of the entries may be on one line, or seven entries may be on the first line with three on the next, or two entries may be on each of five lines, and so on.

This method can also be used with a formatted READ statement. The number of values to be read from each line of input is then determined by the corresponding format identifier. For example, the statements

```
REAL VELOC(10)

READ 20, VELOC
20 FORMAT (5F6.1)
```

read the values for VELOC(1), . . . , VELOC(5) from the first line of data and the values for VELOC(6), . . . , VELOC(10) from a second line.

An array can be displayed in a similar manner. For example, the statements

```
PRINT 30, VELOC
30 FORMAT (1X, 5F10.1)
```

are equivalent to

```
 PRINT 30, VELOC(1), VELOC(2), VELOC(3), VELOC(4), VELOC(5),
+           VELOC(6), VELOC(7), VELOC(8), VELOC(9), VELOC(10)
30 FORMAT (1X, 5F10.1)
```

and display the entries of the array VELOC on two lines, five entries per line, right justified in fields of width 10 with one digit to the right of the decimal point.

The program in Figure 7.2 illustrates this method of reading and displaying the elements of an array. Note that the array declaration

```
REAL VELOC(10)
```

specifies that VELOC is to have 10 elements. One disadvantage of this method of array input/output is that the entire array must be used; that is, the total number of entries specified in the array declaration must be read or displayed. Thus, it is not possible to read or display only part of an array; for example, if the dimension of VELOC is 50, this method cannot be used to read or display values for only VELOC(1), . . . , VELOC(10).

```
      PROGRAM VLIST2
*****************************************************************
* Sample program illustrating input/output of a list of velocities   *
* by using the array name.                                           *
*****************************************************************

      REAL VELOC(10)

* Read the list of velocities

      PRINT *, 'ENTER THE VELOCITY VALUES AS MANY PER LINE AS DESIRED:'
      READ *, VELOC
```

Figure 7.2

Figure 7.2 (continued)

```
* Print the list of velocities

      PRINT 20
20    FORMAT (/1X, 'LIST OF VELOCITIES:'/1X, 19('=')/)
      PRINT 30, VELOC
30    FORMAT (1X, 5F10.1)
      END
```

Sample run:
==========

```
ENTER THE VELOCITY VALUES AS MANY PER LINE AS DESIRED:
100.0  98.5  99.7 120.6 125.8
 88.7  99.6 115.0 103.4  98.6

LIST OF VELOCITIES:
====================

     100.0      98.5      99.7     120.6     125.8
      88.7      99.6     115.0     103.4      98.6
```

Input/Output Using Implied DO Loops. An implied DO loop in an input/ output statement provides the most flexible method for reading or displaying the elements of an array. It allows the programmer to specify that only a portion of the array be transmitted and to specify the arrangement of the values to be read or displayed.

An **implied DO loop** has the form

(*i/o-list, control-variable = initial-value, limit*)

or

(*i/o-list, control-variable = initial-value, limit, step-size*)

The effect of such an implied DO loop is exactly that of a DO loop—as if the left parenthesis were a DO, with indexing information immediately before the matching right parenthesis and the i/o-list constituting the body of the DO loop. The control variable, the initial value, the limit, and the step size are as in a DO statement. The i/o-list may, in general, be a list of variables (subscripted or simple), constants, arithmetic expressions, or other implied DO loops, separated by commas with a comma at the end of the list.

An implied DO loop may be used in a READ, PRINT, or WRITE statement (or in a DATA statement, as described in the next section). For example, if the array VELOC is declared by

```
REAL VELOC(50)
```

and the first 10 entries are to be read, we could use the statement

```
READ *, (VELOC(I), I = 1, 10)
```

which is equivalent to

```
READ *, VELOC(1), VELOC(2), VELOC(3), VELOC(4), VELOC(5)
+        VELOC(6), VELOC(7), VELOC(8), VELOC(9), VELOC(10)
```

or if we also want to read the number NUMVEL of array elements,

```
READ *, NUMVEL, (VELOC(I), I = 1, NUMVEL)
```

which has the same effect as

```
READ *, NUMVEL, VELOC(1), VELOC(2), . . ., VELOC(NUMVEL)
```

In a similar manner, we can display the entries:

```
PRINT *, (VELOC(I), I = 1, NUMVEL)
```

This has the same effect as

```
PRINT *, VELOC(1), VELOC(2), . . ., VELOC(NUMVEL)
```

The program in Figure 7.3 illustrates the use of implied DO loops to read and display the elements of a list.

```
      PROGRAM VLIST3
****************************************************************
* Sample program illustrating the use of an implied DO loop to read  *
* and display a list of velocities.  NUMVEL is the number of values  *
* read into the array VELOC.                                   *
****************************************************************

      INTEGER NUMVEL, I
      REAL VELOC(50)

* Read the list of velocities

      PRINT *, 'ENTER THE NUMBER OF VELOCITIES:'
      READ *, NUMVEL
      PRINT *, 'ENTER THE VELOCITY VALUES AS MANY PER LINE AS DESIRED:'
      READ *, (VELOC(I), I = 1, NUMVEL)

* Print the list of velocities

      PRINT 20, NUMVEL
20    FORMAT (/1X, 'LIST OF', I3, ' VELOCITIES:'/1X, 21('='))
      PRINT 30, (VELOC(I), I = 1, NUMVEL)
30    FORMAT (1X, 5F10.1)
      END
```

Figure 7.3

Figure 7.3   (continued)

```
Sample run:
==========

ENTER THE NUMBER OF VELOCITIES:
10
ENTER THE VELOCITY VALUES AS MANY PER LINE AS DESIRED:
100.0  98.5  99.7 120.6 125.8
 88.7  99.6 115.0 103.4  98.6

LIST OF 10 VELOCITIES:
======================
      100.0       98.5       99.7      120.6      125.8
       88.7       99.6      115.0      103.4       98.6
```

The END = Clause.   In the programs of Figures 7.1 and 7.3, the number NUMVEL of elements in the array VELOC was read before the array elements were read. In some applications, especially when a large number of values are to be processed, it is preferable to design the program to count these values.

In Section 5.5 we saw that the END = clause can be used in programs that count the number of data values entered. Thus it can also be used in programs that must count the number of array elements that are read. When the end of data is encountered, control is automatically transferred to the statement whose number is specified in the END = clause, and processing of the array can continue.

The program in Figure 7.4 uses the END = clause and counts the velocity values as they are read into the array VELOC. It is a modification of the program in Figure 7.3.

```
      PROGRAM VLIST4
*******************************************************************
* Sample program illustrating the use of an implied DO loop and an  *
* END = clause to read, count, and display a list of velocities.    *
* NUMVEL is the number of values read into the array VELOC.          *
*******************************************************************

      INTEGER I, NUMVEL
      REAL VELOC(50)

* Read the list of velocities

      PRINT *, 'ENTER THE VELOCITY VALUES (USING THE END-OF-DATA'
      PRINT *, 'INDICATOR TO SIGNAL THE END OF VALUES):'
      READ (*, *, END = 10) (VELOC(I), I = 1, 50)

* Since the index is one more than the actual count, subtract one

10    NUMVEL = I - 1
```

Figure 7.4

Figure 7.4 **(continued)**

```
* Print the list of velocities

      PRINT 20, NUMVEL
20    FORMAT (/1X, 'LIST OF', I3, ' VELOCITIES:'/1X, 21('='))
      PRINT 30, (VELOC(I), I = 1, NUMVEL)
30    FORMAT (1X, 5F10.1)
      END
```

```
Sample run:
==========


ENTER THE VELOCITY VALUES (USING THE END-OF-DATA
INDICATOR TO SIGNAL THE END OF VALUES):
100.0  98.5  99.7 120.6 125.8
 88.7  99.6 115.0 103.4  98.6
          <---------------------------(end-of-data indicator entered)
LIST OF 10 VELOCITIES:
=====================
     100.0      98.5      99.7     120.6     125.8
      88.7      99.6     115.0     103.4      98.6
```

7.3 Example: Processing a List of Temperatures

Many problems involve processing lists, a list of test scores, a list of temperature readings, a list of employee records, and so on. Such processing includes displaying all the items in the list, inserting new items, deleting items, searching the list for a specified item, and sorting the list so that the items are in a certain order. Because most programming languages do not provide a predefined list type (LISP, an acronym for LISt Processing, is one exception), lists must be processed using some other structure. This is commonly done using an array to store the list, storing the Ith list item in the Ith position of the array.

To illustrate, suppose that a list of temperatures is to be read and counted, and the mean temperature is to be calculated; then a list of those temperatures that are greater than the mean is to be printed.

To solve this problem without using arrays would be quite cumbersome. We might read the temperatures one at a time, counting each as it is read and adding it to a running sum:

```
        COUNT = 0
        SUM = 0
10 READ (*, *, END = 20) ONETEM
        COUNT = COUNT + 1
        SUM = SUM + ONETEM
        GO TO 10
20 TMEAN = SUM / COUNT
```

However, to print a list of those temperatures that are greater than the mean temperature TMEAN, we would be forced to enter each value again, compare it with the mean temperature, and display it if it is greater than the mean:

```
DO 30 I = 1, COUNT
    READ *, ONETEM
    IF (ONETEM .GT. TMEAN) PRINT *, ONETEM
30 CONTINUE
```

But using an array to store the temperatures as they are read makes it unnecessary to reenter the data values. The program in Figure 7.5 does precisely this. It uses an END = clause and an implied DO loop to read a list of up to 25 temperatures, count them, and store then in an array TEMP:

```
    READ (*, *, END = 10) (TEMP(I), I = 1, 25)
10 COUNT = I - 1
```

The mean temperature is then calculated by summming the values that have been stored in the array TEMP:

```
    SUM = 0
    DO 20 I = 1, COUNT
        SUM = SUM + TEMP(I)
20 CONTINUE
    TMEAN = SUM / COUNT
```

A list of temperatures greater than the mean can then be displayed by using another DO loop to examine each element of the array TEMP, compare it with the mean TMEAN, and print it if it is greater than TMEAN:

```
    DO 50 I = 1, COUNT
        IF (TEMP(I) .GT. TMEAN) PRINT *, TEMP(I)
50 CONTINUE
```

```
      PROGRAM TEMPS1
**********************************************************************
* Program to read a list of temperatures, count them, calculate the  *
* mean temperature, and then print a list of temperatures which are  *
* greater than the mean.  Variables used are:                        *
*     TEMP   :  one-dimensional array of temperatures                *
*     I      :  subscript                                            *
*     COUNT  :  # of temperatures                                    *
*     SUM    :  sum of temperatures                                  *
*     TMEAN  :  mean temperature                                     *
**********************************************************************

      INTEGER TEMP(25), I, COUNT
      REAL SUM, TMEAN

      PRINT *, 'ENTER THE TEMPERATURES (USING THE END-OF-DATA'
      PRINT *, 'INDICATOR TO SIGNAL THE END OF VALUES):'
      READ (*, *, END = 10) (TEMP(I), I = 1, 25)
```

Figure 7.5

Figure 7.5 (continued)

```
* Since the index is one more than the actual count, subtract one

10     COUNT = I - 1

* Calculate the mean temperature

       SUM = 0
       DO 20 I = 1, COUNT
           SUM = SUM + TEMP(I)
20     CONTINUE
       TMEAN = SUM / COUNT
       PRINT 30, COUNT, TMEAN
30     FORMAT(//, 1X, I3, ' TEMPERATURES WITH MEAN =', F6.1)

* Print list of temperatures greater than the mean

       PRINT 40
40     FORMAT (// 1X, 'LIST OF TEMPERATURES GREATER THAN THE MEAN:')
       DO 50 I = 1, COUNT
           IF (TEMP(I) .GT. TMEAN) PRINT *, TEMP(I)
50     CONTINUE
       END


Sample run:
==========

ENTER THE TEMPERATURES (USING THE END-OF-DATA
INDICATOR TO SIGNAL THE END OF VALUES):
88, 65, 76, 45, 99 100, 58, 83
75, 74, 89, 99, 96, 65
             <------------------------- (end-of-data indicator entered)


 14 TEMPERATURES WITH MEAN =  79.4


LIST OF TEMPERATURES GREATER THAN THE MEAN:
         88
         99
        100
         83
         89
         99
         96
```

7.4 The PARAMETER and DATA Statements

In the Programming Pointers at the end of Chapter 3 we stressed that "magic numbers" in statements such as

```
CHANGE = (.1758 - .1257) * POPUL
```

should be avoided. Because they appear without explanation, they make the program difficult to understand. They also limit the flexibility of the program, for if the values .1758 and .1257 must be replaced by other values, one must search the program to determine what they represent and locate all the places where they appear. Associating these values with names such as BIRTH and DEATH near the beginning of the program and then using these names in later statements such as

```
CHANGE = (BIRTH - DEATH) * POPUL
```

definitely improves the readability and flexibility of the program.

Other constants are so common that they have been given names; for example, the name "pi" has been given to the constant 3.14159 . . . and "e" to the base 2.71828 . . . of natural logarithms. A statement such as

```
XCOORD = RATE * COS(2.0 * PI * TIME)
```

that uses the name of a constant is preferable to one that uses the specific numeric value,

```
XCOORD = RATE * COS(2.0 * 3.1416 * TIME)
```

as it is more readable and does not require modification if a different value with more or fewer significant digits is required for PI. The PARAMETER and DATA statements introduced in this section make it possible to associate names with values at the beginning of a program; then only these statements need to be changed if other values are required in modifications of the program.

The PARAMETER Statement. The PARAMETER statement is used to define **parameters,** which are *named constants* or *symbolic constants* that are functionally equivalent to ordinary constants; that is, the appearance of a parameter is interpreted as if the constant that it names had appeared instead. Parameters are defined in a **PARAMETER statement** of the form

$$\text{PARAMETER } (p_1 = c_1, \ldots, p_n = c_n)$$

where $p_1, \ldots, p_n$ are the parameter names and $c_1, \ldots, c_n$ are constants or expressions involving only constants and previously defined parameters. *Such PARAMETER statements are nonexecutable and must be placed at the beginning of the program before all executable statements.* They should follow the type statements that declare the types of the parameters. For example, to define the parameter PI to have the value 3.1416, we could use the statements

```
REAL PI
PARAMETER (PI = 3.1416)
```

or to also define an integer parameter LIMIT with the value 25,

```
INTEGER LIMIT
REAL PI
PARAMETER (LIMIT = 25, PI = 3.1416)
```

Parameters may be used anywhere an ordinary constant may be used except that they may not be used in FORMAT statements or as statement numbers (or in complex constants described in Chapter 9). In particular, *parameters may be used to specify dimensions in array declarations*. For example, the program in Figure 7.5 for calculating the mean of a set of temperatures and printing a list of temperatures greater than the mean can be modified as shown in Figure 7.6. This program is more flexible than that in Figure 7.5, as it can be modified to process a list of any other size simply by changing the PARAMETER statement. For example, to process a list of up to 50 numbers, we need only change the PARAMETER statement to

```
PARAMETER (LIMIT = 50)
```

```
      PROGRAM TEMPS2
***********************************************************************
* Program to read a list of temperatures, count them, calculate the  *
* mean temperature, and then print a list of temperatures which are  *
* greater than the mean.  Variables used are:                        *
*     LIMIT   :  limit on # of array elements                        *
*     TEMP    :  one-dimensional array of temperatures               *
*     I       :  subscript                                           *
*     COUNT   :  # of temperatures                                   *
*     SUM     :  sum of temperatures                                 *
*     TMEAN   :  mean temperature                                    *
***********************************************************************

      INTEGER LIMIT
      PARAMETER (LIMIT = 25)
      INTEGER TEMP(LIMIT), I, COUNT

      REAL SUM, TMEAN
      PRINT *, 'ENTER THE TEMPERATURES (USING THE END-OF-DATA'
      PRINT *, 'INDICATOR TO SIGNAL THE END OF VALUES):'
      READ (*, *, END = 10) (TEMP(I), I = 1, LIMIT)

* Since the index is one more than the actual count, subtract one

10    COUNT = I - 1

* Calculate the mean temperature

      SUM = 0
      DO 20 I = 1, COUNT
         SUM = SUM + TEMP(I)
20    CONTINUE
      TMEAN = SUM / COUNT
      PRINT 30, COUNT, TMEAN
30    FORMAT(// 1X, I3, ' TEMPERATURES WITH MEAN =', F6.1)
```

Figure 7.6

Figure 7.6 (continued)

```
* Print list of temperatures greater than the mean

      PRINT 40
40    FORMAT (// ' LIST OF TEMPS GREATER THAN MEAN:')
      DO 50 I = 1, COUNT
         IF (TEMP(I) .GT. TMEAN) PRINT *, TEMP(I)
50    CONTINUE
      END
```

Parameters may also be used to specify the length of values of a character variable. Any length specifier in a CHARACTER statement may be a parameter or an expression formed from integer constants and parameters enclosed within parentheses. Thus the statements

```
INTEGER LENGTH
PARAMETER (LENGTH = 10)
CHARACTER*(LENGTH) ALPHA, BETA*(2*LENGTH)
```

declare ALPHA and BETA to be character variables with lengths 10 and 20, respectively.

If a parameter is of character type, its length need not be explicitly declared. The CHARACTER statement specifying its type may include an *indefinite length specifier* ($*$), where the asterisk replaces the length specifier. In this case, the length of the parameter's value is the length of the string constant that it names. Thus, in the statements

```
INTEGER LIMIT
CHARACTER*(*) TITLE
PARAMETER (LIMIT = 50, TITLE = 'POLLUTION READINGS')
```

the parameter TITLE has length 18.

The DATA Statement. The **DATA statement** may also be used to associate a name with a value, but in contrast to the PARAMETER statement, this name represents a *variable* rather than a named *constant*. This statement has the form

DATA $list_1$/$data_1$/, $list_2$/$data_2$/, . . . , $list_k$/$data_k$/

where each $list_i$ is a list of variable names separated by commas, and each $data_i$ is a list of constants that are to be assigned to the variables in $list_i$. This *initialization of variables is done at the time of compilation.*

For example, to preset the values of variables W, X, Y, and Z to 1.0, 2.5, 7.73, and -2.956, respectively, we could use the statements

```
REAL W, X, Y, Z
DATA W, X, Y, Z / 1.0, 2.5, 7.73, -2.956/
```

The DATA statement could also be written as

```
DATA W /1.0/, X, Y /2.5, 7.73/, Z /-2.956/
```

or in a variety of other forms.

A list of *n* variables all may be assigned the same value by preceding the constant by *n*∗. Here *n* must be an integer constant or parameter. For example, to set ZETA to 1.2; M and N to 3; and each of A, B, C, and D to 3.14, the following statements could be used:

```
REAL ZETA, A, B, C, D
INTEGER M, N
DATA ZETA, M, N, A, B, C, D /1.2, 2*3, 4*3.14/
```

The DATA statement is a *nonexecutable statement*, as it only provides information to the compiler. DATA *statements may appear anywhere in the program after the* PARAMETER, DIMENSION, *and type statements, but it is good practice to place them before all executable statements.*

The DATA statement may also be used to initialize the entries of an array. If all entries of the array are to be assigned values, the array name together with the set of values may appear in the DATA statement. In this case the number of constants must be equal to the size of the array. For example, if ALPHA is a one-dimensional array having 10 entries, the statements

```
REAL ALPHA(10)
DATA ALPHA /5*0.0, 4*1.0, 2.0/
```

initialize ALPHA(1), . . . , ALPHA(5) to have the value 0.0, ALPHA(6), . . . , ALPHA(9) the value 1.0, and ALPHA(10) the value 2.0.

Several variables and arrays may appear in a single DATA statement, as the following example illustrates:

```
INTEGER N
REAL X, ALPHA(10), BETA(25)
DATA N, X, ALPHA, BETA /10, 3.14, 5*1.0, 30*0.0/
```

Here N is assigned the value 10; X is assigned the value 3.14; the value 1.0 is assigned to ALPHA(1), . . . , ALPHA(5); and the value of each of ALPHA(6), . . . , ALPHA(10), BETA(1), . . . , BETA(25) is 0.0.

Implied DO loops may also appear in the list of a DATA statement. For example, to assign 10 to N and 0.0 to the first five entries of the one-dimensional array ALPHA, the following statements could be used:

```
INTEGER N, I
REAL ALPHA(10)
DATA N, (ALPHA(I), I = 1, 5) /10, 5*0.0/
```

Finally, parameters may be used as values and/or repetition indicators in DATA *statements*. The following statements illustrate:

```
INTEGER NUMENT
PARAMETER (NUMENT = 100)
REAL PRESS(NUMENT)
DATA PRESS /NUMENT*0.0/
```

These statements initialize each of the 100 positions of the one-dimensional real array PRESS to 0.0.

7.5 Examples: Averages of Grouped Data, Bar Graphs, Sorting, Searching

EXAMPLE 1: Averages of Grouped Data.   Four kinds of rocket propellants, coded as A, B, C, and D, are being tested. A collection of data pairs consisting of propellant codes and burn rates from test firing the rocket have been recorded. The average burn rate for each of the four kinds of propellants is to be calculated.

In solving this problem, we use three one-dimensional arrays:

COUNT: COUNT(I) is the number of burn rates for propellant I, I = 1, 2, 3, 4,

PROPEL: PROPEL(1) = 'A', PROPEL(2) = 'B', PROPEL(3) = 'C', PROPEL(4) = 'D',

SUM: SUM(I) = sum of the burn rates for all test firings with propellant I, I = 1, 2, 3, 4.

An appropriate algorithm is the following:

ALGORITHM FOR THE BURN RATE PROBLEM

```
*    Algorithm to find the average burn rate for each of four kinds of    *
*    propellants with codes stored in array PROPEL. The arrays            *
*    COUNT and SUM store the number and sum of the burn rates.            *
```

1. Initialize the arrays COUNT and SUM to 0 and the array PROPEL with the propellant codes.
2. While there is more data, do the following:
   a. Read the propellant CODE and BURN rate.
   b. Sct I to 1 and the logical variable FOUND to false.
   c. While I ≤ 4 and not FOUND, do the following:
      If CODE = PROPEL(I) then
         (i)   Add 1 to COUNT(I).
         (ii) Add BURN to SUM(I).
         (iii) Set FOUND to true.
      Else increment I by 1.
   d. If not FOUND, display a data error message.
3. Do the following for I ranging from 1 through 4:
      If COUNT(I) > 0 then
         Display SUM(I) / COUNT(I).
      Else
         Display a message that there was no data
            for this type of propellant.

This algorithm is shown in flowchart form in Figure 7.7.

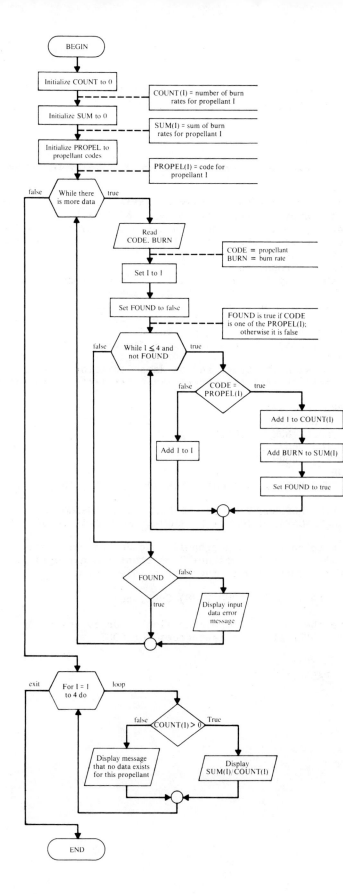

Figure 7.7

The program in Figure 7.8 implements this algorithm. Note the use of PARAMETER and DATA statements to declare and initialize arrays COUNT, SUM, and PROPEL.

```
      PROGRAM ROCKET
*****************************************************************
* Program to find the average burn rate for each of four kinds of  *
* propellants (coded by letters) using data consisting of a propellant *
* code and burn rate observed during test firing of a rocket with that *
* type of propellant.  Variables used are:                         *
*     PROPEL : array of propellant codes                           *
*     NUMPRO : parameter specifying number of kinds of propellants *
*     COUNT  : COUNT(I) = # of burn rates for propellant I         *
*     SUM    : SUM(I) = sum of burn rates for propellant I         *
*     CODE   : current propellant code being processed             *
*     BURN   : current burn rate being processed                   *
*     FOUND  : logical flag to check for legal propellant code     *
*     I      : index                                               *
*  Signal end of data with the usual end-of-data indicator.        *
*****************************************************************

      INTEGER NUMPRO
      PARAMETER (NUMPRO = 4)
      CHARACTER*1 PROPEL(NUMPRO), CODE
      INTEGER COUNT(NUMPRO), I
      REAL SUM(NUMPRO), BURN
      LOGICAL FOUND
      DATA COUNT, SUM, PROPEL /NUMPRO*0, NUMPRO*0.0, 'A', 'B', 'C', 'D'/

      PRINT *, 'ENTER PROPELLANT CODES AND BURN RATES (USING THE'
      PRINT *, 'END-OF-DATA INDICATOR TO SIGNAL THE END OF VALUES):'

* While there are more data, read a propellant code and burn rate,
* determine the number of the propellant, increment the appropriate
* counter, and add the burn rate to the appropriate sum.

10    READ (*, '(A1, F5.0)', END = 30) CODE, BURN

*         Determine the number of the propellant code by searching
*         the list PROPEL of propellant codes for CODE

      I = 1
      FOUND = .FALSE.
```

Figure 7.8

Figure 7.8   (continued)

```
*          While I not greater than NUMPRO and not FOUND:

20         IF ((I .LE. NUMPRO) .AND. .NOT. FOUND) THEN
               IF (CODE .EQ. PROPEL(I)) THEN
                   COUNT(I) = COUNT(I) + 1
                   SUM(I) = SUM(I) + BURN
                   FOUND = .TRUE.
               ELSE
                   I = I + 1
               END IF
               GO TO 20
           END IF
           IF (.NOT. FOUND) PRINT *,
     +          '** ILLEGAL PROPELLANT CODE:  ', CODE
           GO TO 10

* Calculate and print average burn rates

30         PRINT 40
40         FORMAT (//1X, 'FOR PROPELLANT')
           DO 70 I = 1, NUMPRO
               IF (COUNT(I) .GT. 0) THEN
                   PRINT 50, PROPEL(I), SUM(I) / COUNT(I)
50                 FORMAT(1X, A14, ':  AVERAGE BURN RATE IS', F6.2)
               ELSE
                   PRINT 60, PROPEL(I)
60                 FORMAT(1X, A14, ':  THERE WERE NO BURN RATES RECORDED')
               END IF
70         CONTINUE
           END


 Sample run:
 ==========

 ENTER PROPELLANT CODES AND BURN RATES (USING THE
 END-OF-DATA INDICATOR TO SIGNAL THE END OF VALUES):
 A 34.0
 A 32.7
 B 30.1
 E 29.8
  ** ILLEGAL PROPELLANT CODE:   E
 C 29.8
 B 32.8
 A 32.0
 C 28.1
 A 29.4
 B 28.9
 C 27.4


 FOR PROPELLANT
           A:  AVERAGE BURN RATE IS 32.02
           B:  AVERAGE BURN RATE IS 30.60
           C:  AVERAGE BURN RATE IS 28.43
           D:  THERE WERE NO BURN RATES RECORDED
```

EXAMPLE 2: Bar Graphs. A quality control engineer monitors a machine by recording each hour the number of defective parts produced by that machine. This information is to be summarized in a *bar graph* or *histogram* that displays the number of one-hour periods in which there were no defective parts, one defective part, two defective parts, . . . , five or more defective parts, in a format such as

```
DEFECTIVES
        0:******************
        1:***********
        2:***********
        3:******
        4:
        5:***

         ..................
         0  1  2  3  4  5  6
        NUMBER OF HOURS
```

To solve this problem, we use the following arrays:

COUNT: COUNT(I) is the number of one-hour periods during which I defective parts were produced, I = 0, 1, . . . , 5.

BAR: an array of characters used in plotting the bar graph.

An appropriate algorithm is

ALGORITHM TO GENERATE A BAR GRAPH

```
*   Algorithm to read several values for DEFECT, the number of    *
*   defective parts produced by a machine in a given one-hour      *
*   period, and to determine COUNT(I) = the number of periods      *
*   in which there were I defective parts. These counts are then   *
*   to be displayed in a bar graph.                                *
```

1. Initialize array COUNT to all zeros.
2. While there is more data, do the following:
   a. Read DEFECT.
   b. If DEFECT > 5, set DEFECT to 5.
   c. Increase COUNT(DEFECT) by 1.
3. Calculate LARGE = the largest of the counts COUNT(I); this will be used in labeling the horizontal axis.
4. Display the heading for the vertical axis.
5. For I = 0 to 5, do the following:
   a. Fill the character string BAR with blanks.
   b. Set the first 3 * COUNT(I) positions of BAR equal to '*'.
   c. Display I, ':', and BAR.
6. Display the horizontal axis and its label.

The program in Figure 7.9 implements this algorithm. Also shown is a listing of the data file used in the sample run.

```
      PROGRAM BGRAPH
***********************************************************************
* Program to plot a bar graph of the number of 1-hour periods in which *
* there were 0, 1, 2, ... defective parts produced by a machine.  The  *
* data is read from a file.  Variables used are:                       *
*      MAXDEF  :  parameter representing maximum # of defective parts   *
*      LENGTH  :  parameter giving the maximum length of a bar          *
*      COUNT   :  COUNT(I) = # of 1-hour periods with I defective parts *
*      DEFECT  :  # of defective parts read from file                   *
*      FNAME   :  name of data file                                     *
*      LARGE   :  largest of COUNT(1), COUNT(2), ...                    *
*      BAR     :  character variable to print one bar of bar graph      *
*      VLABEL  :  label for vertical axis                               *
*      HLABEL  :  label for horizontal axis                             *
*      I, J    :  indices                                               *
***********************************************************************

      INTEGER MAXDEF, LENGTH
      PARAMETER (MAXDEF = 5, LENGTH = 60)
      CHARACTER*20 FNAME, VLABEL, HLABEL, BAR*(LENGTH)
      INTEGER DEFECT, COUNT(0:MAXDEF), LARGE, I, J
      DATA COUNT, VLABEL, HLABEL /0, MAXDEF*0,
     +      'DEFECTIVES', 'NUMBER OF HOURS'/

* Get file name, open the file as unit 15

      PRINT *, 'ENTER NAME OF DATA FILE'
      READ '(A)', FNAME
      OPEN (UNIT = 15, FILE = FNAME, STATUS = 'OLD')

* While there are more data, read # of defective parts and
* increment appropriate counter

10    READ (15, *, END = 20) DEFECT
      IF (DEFECT .GT. MAXDEF) DEFECT = MAXDEF
      COUNT(DEFECT) = COUNT(DEFECT) + 1
      GO TO 10

* Find largest count

20    LARGE = COUNT(0)
      DO 30 I = 1, MAXDEF
          LARGE = MAX(LARGE, COUNT(I))
30    CONTINUE

* Print the bar graph

      PRINT 40, VLABEL
40    FORMAT (//1X, A)
      DO 70 I = 0, MAXDEF
          BAR = ' '
          DO 50 J = 1, 3*COUNT(I)
              BAR(J:J) = '*'
50        CONTINUE
          PRINT 60, I, ':', BAR
60        FORMAT (1X, I10, 2A)
```

Figure 7.9

Figure 7.9 (continued)

```
70      CONTINUE
        PRINT 80, ('.', I = 0, 3 * LARGE)
        PRINT 81, (I, I = 0, LARGE)
        PRINT 82, HLABEL
80      FORMAT (11X, 80A)
81      FORMAT (9X, 20I3)
82      FORMAT (81X, A)
        CLOSE (15)
        END
```

```
Listing of data file:
=====================

0
1
0
2
2
0
1
6
3
0
3
1
2
0
1
2
0
```

```
Sample run:
==========

ENTER NAME OF DATA FILE
DEFECTS-FILE


DEFECTIVES
        0:******************
        1:************
        2:************
        3:******
        4:
        5:***
        .................
        0  1  2  3  4  5  6
        NUMBER OF HOURS
```

EXAMPLE 3: Sorting.   A common programming problem is **sorting** a list of items, that is, arranging these items so that they are in either ascending or descending order. There are many sorting methods, most of which use arrays to store the list of items to be sorted. In this section we describe the sorting method known as **bubble sort.** Although it is not the most efficient sorting method, it is quite easy to understand; more efficient sorting techniques are described in the exercises at the end of this chapter.

Suppose that the items to be sorted have been read into an array and assigned to X(1), X(2), . . . , X(N). We scan the array, comparing X(1) and X(2) and interchanging them if they are in the wrong order. Then we compare X(2) with X(3), interchanging them if they are in the wrong order. This process of comparing and interchanging continues throughout the entire array. This constitutes one complete pass through the list. For example, suppose that the following list is to be sorted into increasing order:

77
30
89
54
62

We first compare 77 and 30 and interchange them, giving

89
54
62

Now we compare 77 and 89 but do not interchange them, since they are already in the correct order. Next, 89 and 54 are compared and interchanged, giving

30
77

62

Finally, 89 and 62 are compared and interchanged, giving

30
77
54

This completes the first pass through the list.

Note that the largest item in the list "sinks" to the bottom of the list and some of the smaller items have "bubbled up" toward the top. We scan the list again, comparing consecutive items and interchanging them when they are out of order, but this time we leave the last item out of the pass, since it is already in its proper position. For example, this pass produces

30
54
62
77
89

The second largest number sinks to its proper position, and more small numbers bubble up toward the top into their positions.

For this short list, we can easily see that the sorting is now complete, but for a long list, this is not so easy to determine. One method for determining when the sorting is complete is simply to record on each pass through the list whether any interchanges took place during that pass. When we scan the list and find that no interchanges took place, we know that the list is sorted, and we can terminate the procedure.

In general, the algorithm for bubble sort is as follows:

BUBBLE SORT ALGORITHM

*   Algorithm to bubble sort a list of items X(1), . . . , X(N) so   *
*   that they are in ascending order.   *

1. Set PAIRS equal to N − 1; this is the number of pairs that must be examined in the current pass through the list.
2. Set the logical variable DONE to false.
3. While not DONE, do the following:
   a. Set DONE to true. The value of DONE will remain true if a pass through the list is made with no interchanges taking place, thus indicating that the items are in order; it will be set to false if interchanges are made.
   b. For each value of the subscript I from 1 through PAIRS, compare X(I) with X(I + 1). If X(I) > X(I + 1), interchange them and set DONE to false; else proceed to the next pair of items.
   c. Decrease PAIRS by 1. At the end of each pass through the list, the largest item will have sunk into place and thus need not be examined on the next pass.

This algorithm sorts the items into ascending order. To sort them into descending order, one need only change $>$ to $<$ in the comparison of X(I) with X(I + 1) in Step 3b. Figure 7.10 shows a flowchart of this bubble sort algorithm as a module that could be incorporated into a larger algorithm.

One problem that requires sorting is determining the median value of a set of data items. The **median** of a set of numbers $X_1, . . . , X_n$ is the middle value when these numbers have been arranged in ascending order. It should be clear that one half of the numbers are greater than or equal to this median value and one half are smaller and that after the list of numbers has been sorted, the median value is in the position given by the integer quotient $(n + 1)/2$.

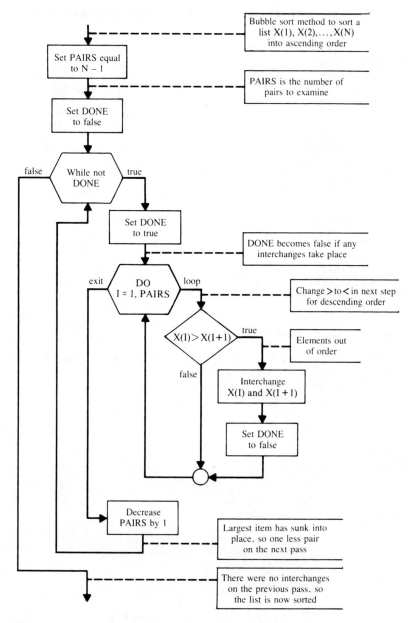

Figure 7.10

To illustrate, suppose that a company is planning to build a new manufacturing facility and that one of the factors in selecting the site is the cost of labor in the various cities under consideration. To analyze this data, it may be helpful to sort the labor costs for these cities so that they can be displayed in order and so that the median cost can be computed. The program in Figure 7.11 reads a list of up to 100 costs, sorts them using the bubble sort algorithm, and then displays the sorted list and the median cost.

```
      PROGRAM SORTER
************************************************************************
* This program first reads and counts a list of labor costs.  It then  *
* sorts them in ascending order and finds the median cost.  For more    *
* costs, change the value of the parameter LIMIT.  Variables used are:  *
*      LIMIT   :  parameter representing maximum # of costs             *
*      COST    :  list of labor costs (in millions).  They are assumed  *
*              :  to be of integer type; if not, declare COST in an     *
*              :  appropriate type statement                            *
*      N       :  number of labor costs                                 *
*      TEMP    :  temporary variable used to interchange two of the     *
*              :  costs  (same type as COST)                            *
*      PAIRS   :  # of pairs to be examined in the current pass         *
*      I       :  subscript                                             *
*      DONE    :  logical flag to record if any interchanges have taken *
*              :  place (DONE = false) during the current scan.         *
************************************************************************

      INTEGER LIMIT
      PARAMETER (LIMIT = 100)
      INTEGER COST(LIMIT), N, TEMP, PAIRS, I
      LOGICAL DONE

* Read the labor costs and count them

      PRINT *, 'ENTER LABOR COSTS IN MILLIONS, AS MANY PER LINE AS'
      PRINT *, 'DESIRED.  ENTER END-OF-DATA INDICATOR TO STOP.'
      READ (*, *, END = 10) (COST(N), N = 1, LIMIT)
10    N = N - 1

* Now sort the list using bubble sort

      PAIRS = N - 1
      DONE = .FALSE.

* While not DONE do the following

20    IF (.NOT. DONE) THEN
          DONE = .TRUE.

*         Scan the list comparing consecutive items

          DO 30 I = 1, PAIRS
             IF (COST(I) .GT. COST(I + 1)) THEN

*                Costs out of order, so interchange them
*                and set DONE to false

                 TEMP = COST(I)
                 COST(I) = COST(I + 1)
                 COST(I + 1) = TEMP
                 DONE = .FALSE.
             END IF
30        CONTINUE
```

Figure 7.11

Figure 7.11   (continued)

```
*          Largest cost has sunk into place so eliminate it on next pass

           PAIRS = PAIRS - 1
           GO TO 20
      END IF

* Sorting is complete, so display the sorted list and the median

      PRINT 40, 'SORTED LIST', '====== ===='
40    FORMAT (2(/, 1X, A))
      DO 60 I = 1, N
           PRINT 50, COST(I)
50         FORMAT (1X, I6)
60    CONTINUE
      PRINT 70, COST((N + 1)/2)
70    FORMAT (/1X, 'MEDIAN = ', I6, ' MILLION DOLLARS')
      END
```

```
Sample run:
==========

ENTER LABOR COSTS IN MILLIONS, AS MANY PER LINE AS
DESIRED.   ENTER END-OF-DATA INDICATOR TO STOP.
870, 778, 655, 640, 956, 538, 1050, 529, 689
                   <----------------------- end-of-data indicator entered
SORTED LIST
====== ====
    529
    538
    640
    655
    689
    778
    870
    956
   1050

MEDIAN =      689 MILLION DOLLARS
```

EXAMPLE 4: Searching.   Another important problem is **searching** a collection of data for a specified item and retrieving some information associated with that item. For example, one searches a telephone directory for a specific name in order to retrieve the phone number listed with that name. In a **linear search,** one begins with the first item in a list and searches sequentially until either the desired item is found or the end of the list is reached. The following algorithm describes this method of searching:

LINEAR SEARCH ALGORITHM

* Algorithm to linear search a list $X(1)$, $X(2)$, . . . , $X(N)$ for a   *
* specified ITEM. The logical variable FOUND is set to true and   *
* LOC to the position of ITEM if the search is successful; other-   *
* wise, FOUND is set to false.   *

1. Initialize LOC to 1 and FOUND to false.
2. While LOC $\leq$ N and not FOUND, do the following:
     If ITEM $=$ X(LOC), then
          Set FOUND to true.
     Else
          Increment LOC by 1.

Although linear search may be an adequate method for small data sets, a more efficient technique is needed for large collections. If the list to be searched has been sorted, the **binary search** algorithm may be used. With this method, we first examine the middle element in the list, and if this is the desired entry, the search is successful. Otherwise, we determine whether the item being sought is in the first half or the second half of the list and then repeat this process, using the middle entry of that list.

To illustrate, suppose the list to be searched is

```
1331
1373
1555
1824
1882
1898
1988
2002
2335
2665
3103
```

and we are looking for 1988. We first examine the middle number 1898 in the sixth position. Because 1988 is greater than 1898, we can disregard the first half of the list and concentrate on the second half,

```
1988
2002
2335
2665
3103
```

The middle number in this sublist is 2335, and the desired item 1988 is less than 2335, so we discard the second half of this sublist and concentrate on the first half.

1988
2002

Because there is no middle number in this sublist, we examine the number immediately preceding the middle position, that is, the number 1988. In this case, we have located the desired entry with three comparisons rather than seven, as required in a linear search.

In general, the algorithm for binary search is as follows:

BINARY SEARCH ALGORITHM

```
*   Algorithm to binary search a list X(1), X(2), . . . , X(N) that    *
*   has been ordered so the elements are in ascending order. The       *
*   logical variable FOUND is set to true and LOC to the position      *
*   of the ITEM being sought if the search is successful; other-       *
*   wise, FOUND is set to false.                                       *
```

1. Initialize FIRST to 1 and LAST to N. These values represent the positions of the first and last items of the list or sublist being searched.
2. Initialize the logical variable FOUND to false.
3. While FIRST $\leq$ LAST and not FOUND, do the following:
   a. Find the middle position in the sublist by setting MIDDLE equal to the integer quotient (FIRST + LAST)/2.
   b. Compare the ITEM being searched for with X(MIDDLE). There are three possibilities:
      (i) ITEM < X(MIDDLE): ITEM is in the first half of the sublist; set LAST equal to MIDDLE − 1.
      (ii) ITEM > X(MIDDLE): ITEM is in the second half of the sublist; set FIRST equal to MIDDLE + 1.
      (iii) ITEM = X(MIDDLE): ITEM has been found; set LOC equal to MIDDLE and FOUND to true.

Figure 7.12 shows a flowchart of this binary search procedure as a module that could be incorporated into a larger algorithm. The program in Figure 7.13 uses this binary search algorithm to search a file in which each record contains the chemical formula and name of an inorganic compound and its specific heat (the ratio of the amount of heat required to raise the temperature of a body 1°C to that required to raise an equal mass of water 1°C). The file is assumed to be sorted so that the chemical formulas are in alphabetical order. A formula is entered during program execution; the list is searched using a binary search; and if the formula is found, the name and specific heat are displayed.

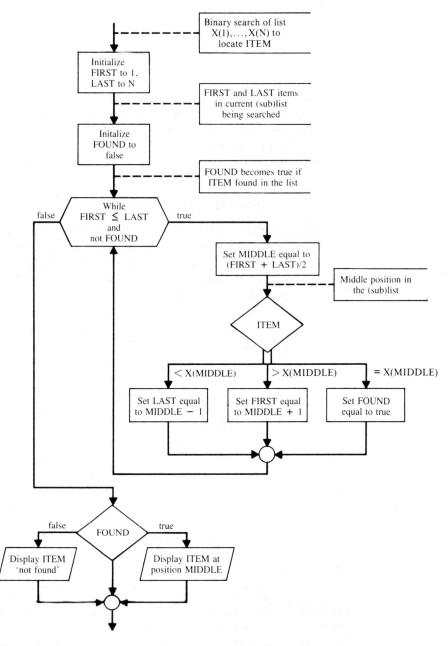

Figure 7.12

```
      PROGRAM SEARCH
***********************************************************************
* Program to read a file containing the chemical formula, name, and  *
* specific heat for various inorganic compounds and store these in   *
* parallel arrays.  File is sorted so that the formulas are in       *
* alphabetical order.  The user enters a formula, the list of formulas *
* is searched using the binary search algorithm, and if the formula is *
* found, its name and specific heat are displayed.   Variables used  *
* are:                                                               *
*     FNAME   :  name of data file                                   *
*     LIMIT   :  parameter specifying maximum # of array elements    *
*     LENGTH  :  parameter specifying length of character strings     *
*     FORMUL  :  array of formulas                                   *
*     NAME    :  array of names                                      *
*     SPHEAT  :  array of specific heats                             *
*     N       :  number of records in the file                       *
*     ITEM    :  item to be searched for                             *
*     FIRST   :  first item in (sub)list being searched              *
*     LAST    :  last    "    "     "      "       "                 *
*     MIDDLE  :  middle  "    "     "      "       "                 *
*     FOUND   :  logical variable indicating if formula found         *
***********************************************************************
      INTEGER LIMIT, LENGTH, N, FIRST, LAST, MIDDLE
      PARAMETER (LIMIT = 100, LENGTH = 10)
      CHARACTER*(LENGTH) FORMUL(LIMIT), ITEM, FNAME*(2*LENGTH),
     +    NAME(LIMIT)*(2*LENGTH)
      REAL SPHEAT(LIMIT)
      LOGICAL FOUND

* Open the file, then read, count, and store the items

      PRINT *, 'ENTER NAME OF FILE'
      READ 10, FNAME
10    FORMAT (A)
      PRINT *
      OPEN (UNIT = 15, FILE = FNAME, STATUS = 'OLD')
      READ (15, 20, END = 30)
     +    (FORMUL(N), NAME(N), SPHEAT(N), N = 1, LIMIT)
20    FORMAT (2A, F5.0)
30    N = N - 1

* Search the list FORMUL for ITEM entered by user
* User enters  QUIT  to stop searching

      PRINT *, 'ENTER FORMULA TO SEARCH FOR, (QUIT TO STOP)'
      READ '(A)', ITEM

* While ITEM not equal to QUIT do

40    IF (ITEM .NE. 'QUIT') THEN
          FIRST = 1
          LAST = N
          FOUND = .FALSE.
```

Figure 7.13

Figure 7.13 (continued)

```
*           Perform binary search of array FORMUL for ITEM
*           While FIRST not greater than LAST and FOUND is false do

50          IF ((FIRST .LE. LAST) .AND. .NOT. FOUND) THEN
                MIDDLE = (FIRST + LAST) / 2
                IF (ITEM .EQ. FORMUL(MIDDLE)) THEN
                    FOUND = .TRUE.
                ELSE IF (ITEM .LT. FORMUL(MIDDLE)) THEN
                    LAST = MIDDLE - 1
                ELSE
                    FIRST = MIDDLE + 1
                END IF
                GO TO 50
            END IF

*           Display information

            IF (FOUND) THEN
                PRINT 60, 'HAS SPECIFIC HEAT', SPHEAT(MIDDLE)
60              FORMAT(6X, A, F7.4)
            ELSE
                PRINT 60, '*** NOT FOUND ***'
            END IF
            PRINT *
            PRINT *, 'ENTER FORMULA'
            READ 10, ITEM
            GO TO 40
        END IF
        CLOSE (15)
        END
```

```
Listing of data file:
=====================

AGCL      SILVER CHLORIDE      .0804
ALCL3     ALUMINUM CHLORIDE    .188
AUI       GOLD IODIDE          .0404
BACO3     BARIUM CARBONATE     .0999
CACL2     CALCIUM CHLORIDE     .164
CACO3     CALCIUM CARBONATE    .203
FE2O3     FERRIC OXIDE         .182
H2O2      HYDROGEN PEROXIDE    .471
KCL       POTASSIUM CHLORIDE   .162
LIF       LITHIUM FLOURIDE     .373
NABR      SODIUM BROMIDE       .118
NACL      SODIUM CHLORIDE      .204
PBBR2     LEAD BROMIDE         .0502
SIC       SILICON CARBIDE      .143
SNCL2     STANNOUS CHLORIDE    .162
ZNSO4     ZINC SULFATE         .174
```

```
Sample run:
==========

ENTER NAME OF FILE
SPECHEAT-FILE
```

Figure 7.13 (continued)

```
 ENTER FORMULA TO SEARCH FOR, (QUIT TO STOP)
AGCL
      HAS SPECIFIC HEAT 0.0804

 ENTER FORMULA
NACL
      HAS SPECIFIC HEAT 0.2040

 ENTER FORMULA
FECO3
      *** NOT FOUND ***

 ENTER FORMULA
FE2O3
      HAS SPECIFIC HEAT 0.1820

 ENTER FORMULA
ZNSO4
      HAS SPECIFIC HEAT 0.1740

 ENTER FORMULA
QUIT
```

Exercises

1. Assume that the following declarations have been made:

```
INTEGER NUMBER(10), I
REAL POINT(-5:5)
CHARACTER*1 SYMBOL(5)
```

Assume also that the following format statements are given,

```
100 FORMAT (5(A1, A2))
110 FORMAT (10(1X, I1))
120 FORMAT (5A1)
```

and that the following data are entered:

```
A1B2C3D4E5F6G7H8I9J0
```

For each of the following, tell what value (if any) will be assigned to each array element, or explain why an error occurs.

(a)
```
    DO 10 I = 1, 10
         NUMBER(I) = I / 2
 10 CONTINUE
```

(b)
```
    DO 10 I = 1, 6
         NUMBER(I) = I * I
 10 CONTINUE
    DO 20 I = 7, 10
         NUMBER(I) = NUMBER(I - 5)
 20 CONTINUE
```

(c)
```
     I = 0
  10 IF (I .NE. 10) THEN
         IF (MOD(I,3) .EQ. 0) THEN
             NUMBER(I) = 0
         ELSE
             NUMBER(I) = I
         END IF
         I = I + 1
         GO TO 10
      END IF
```

(d)
```
     NUMBER(1) = 1
     I = 2
  10    NUMBER(I) = NUMBER(I - 1)
         I = I + 1
     IF (I .LT. 10) GO TO 10
```

(e)
```
     DO 10 I = 1, 10
         READ 110, NUMBER(I)
  10 CONTINUE
```

(f)
```
     READ 110, NUMBER
```

(g)
```
     READ 110, (NUMBER(I), I = 1, 10)
```

(h)
```
     READ 110, (POINT(I), I = -5, 5)
```

(i)
```
     READ 100, (SYMBOL(I), I = 1, 5)
```

(j)
```
     READ 120, SYMBOL
     DO 10 I = 1, 5
         IF (('A' .LE. SYMBOL(I)) .AND.
     +      (SYMBOL(I) .LE. 'Z')) THEN
             POINT(I - 4) = -1.1 * I
             POINT(I) = 1.1 * I
         ELSE
             POINT(I - 4) = 0
             POINT(I) = 0
         END IF
  10 CONTINUE
```

2. For each of the following, write appropriate declarations and state-ments to create the specified array:

   (a) An array whose subscripts are the integers from 0 through 5 and in which each element is the same as the subscript.

   (b) An array whose subscripts are the integers from -5 through 5 and in which the elements are the subscripts in reverse order.

   (c) An array whose subscripts are the integers from 1 through 20 and in which an array element has the value true if the corresponding subscript is even, and false otherwise.

   (d) An array whose subscripts are the integers from 0 through 359 and whose elements are the values of the sine function at the angles $0°, 1°, \ldots, 359°$.

3. Assuming that integer and logical values are stored in one memory word, that real values require two memory words, and that character values are packed two per word, indicate with a diagram like that in Section 7.1, where each component of an array A declared as follows would be stored if the base address of A is B. Also, give the general address translation formula for A(I).

   (a) INTEGER A(5)
   (b) REAL A(5)
   (c) CHARACTER*8 A(5)
   (d) INTEGER A(-5:5)
   (e) REAL A(5:15)
   (f) CHARACTER A(0:9)

4. Assuming a list of N real numbers representing noise levels has been read and stored in an array NOISE, write a program segment to implement the linear search algorithm to find a given real number NVALUE in this list or to determine that it is not in the list.

5. In general, one need not search an entire list to determine that it does not contain a given item if the list has been previously sorted so the elements are in ascending order. Write a modified linear search algorithm for such an ordered list.

6. The following data was collected by a company and represents discrete values of a function for which an explicit formula is not known:

x	f(x)
1.123400	167.5600
2.246800	137.6441
3.370200	110.2523
4.493600	85.38444
5.617000	63.04068
6.740400	43.22099
7.863800	25.92535
8.987200	11.15376
10.11060	-1.093781
11.23400	-10.81726
12.35740	-18.01665
13.48080	-22.69202
14.60420	-24.84334
15.72760	-24.47060
16.85100	-21.57379
17.97440	-16.15295
19.09780	-8.208008
20.22120	2.260895
21.34460	15.25394
22.46800	30.77100
23.59140	48.81213
24.71480	69.37738
25.83820	92.46655
26.96160	118.0799
28.08500	146.2172

One can, however, use *linear interpolation* to approximate the $f(x)$ value for any given x value between the smallest and largest x values. First find the two x values x_i and x_{i+1} in the list that bracket the given x value, using a modified linear search procedure similar to that in Exercise 5, and then interpolate to find the corresponding $f(x)$ value:

$$f(x) = f(x_i) + \frac{f(x_{i+1}) - f(x_i)}{x_{i+1} - x_i}(x - x_i)$$

(If the x value is out of range, print a message.) Test your program with the following x values: -7.8, 1.1234, 13.65, 22.5, 23.5914, 25, 25.085, 33.8.

7. If **a** and **b** are *n-dimensional vectors* given by

$$\mathbf{a} = (a_1, a_2, \ldots, a_n)$$

$$\mathbf{b} = (b_1, b_2, \ldots, b_n)$$

then

$$|\mathbf{a}| = \sqrt{a_1^2 + a_2^2 + \cdots + a_n^2}$$

is the *norm* (or *length* or *magnitude*) of **a,** and

$$\frac{1}{|\mathbf{a}|}\mathbf{a} = \left(\frac{a_1}{|\mathbf{a}|}, \frac{a_2}{|\mathbf{a}|}, \ldots, \frac{a_n}{|\mathbf{a}|}\right)$$

is a *unit vector* in the same direction as **a.** The *sum* and *difference* of **a** and **b** are defined by

$$\mathbf{a} + \mathbf{b} = (a_1 + b_1, a_2 + b_2, \cdots, a_n + b_n)$$

$$\mathbf{a} - \mathbf{b} = (a_1 - b_1, a_2 - b_2, \cdots, a_n - b_n)$$

and the *dot* (or *scalar*) *product* of **a** and **b** is defined by

$$\mathbf{a} \cdot \mathbf{b} = \sum_{i=1}^{n} a_i b_i = a_1 b_1 + a_2 b_2 + \cdots + a_n b_n$$

Write a program to read two n-dimensional vectors and then calculate

(a) the norm of each vector.
(b) unit vectors having the same direction as the vectors.
(c) the sum, difference, and dot product of the vectors.
(d) the cosine of the angle between the vectors calculated using

$$\cos \theta = \frac{\mathbf{a} \cdot \mathbf{b}}{|\mathbf{a}| \, |\mathbf{b}|}$$

8. The Cawker City Candy Company records the number of cases of candy produced each day over a four-week period. Write a program that reads these production numbers and stores them in an array. The program should then accept from the user a week number and a day

number and should display the production level for that day. Assume that each week consists of five workdays.

9. The Cawker City Candy Company manufactures different kinds of candy, each identified by a product number. Write a program that reads two arrays, NUMBER and PRICE, in which NUMBER(1) and PRICE(1) are the product number and the unit price for the first item, NUMBER(2) and PRICE(2) are the product number and the unit price for the second item, and so on. The program should then allow the user to select one of the following options:

   1. Retrieve and display the price of a product whose number is entered by the user. (Use the linear search procedure developed in Exercise 5 to determine the location in the array NUMBER of the specified item.)
   2. Print a table displaying the product number and the price of each item.

10. The Cawker City Candy Company maintains two warehouses, one in Chicago and one in Detroit, each of which stocks at most 25 different items. Write a program that first reads the product numbers of the items stored in the Chicago warehouse and stores them in an array, and then repeats this for the items stored in the Detroit warehouse, storing these product numbers in another array. The program should then find and display the *intersection* of these two lists of numbers, that is, the collection of product numbers common to both lists. The lists should not be assumed to have the same number of elements.

11. Repeat Exercise 10, but find and display the *union* of the two lists, that is, the collection of product numbers that are elements of at least one of the lists.

12. A hardware store sells lawn sprinklers. Past experience has indicated that the selling season is only six months long, lasting from April 1 through September 30. The sales division has forecast the following sales for next year:

Month	Demand
April	40
May	20
June	30
July	40
August	30
September	20

All sprinklers are purchased from an outside source at a cost of $8.00 per sprinkler. However, the supplier will sell them only in lots of 10, 20, 30, 40, or 50; monthly orders for fewer than 10 sprinklers or more than 50 are not accepted. Discounts based on the size of the lot ordered are as follows:

Lot Size	Discount (percent)
10	5
20	5
30	10
40	20
50	25

For each order placed, the store is charged a fixed cost of $15.00 to cover shipping costs, insurance, packaging, and so on, regardless of the number ordered (except that there is no charge for a month when none are ordered). Assume that orders are placed on the first of the month and are received immediately. The store also incurs a carrying charge of $1.80 for each sprinkler remaining in stock at the end of any one month.

Write a program to calculate the total seasonal cost, the price that must be charged per sprinkler in order for the hardware store to break even, and the price that must be charged to realize a profit of 30 percent. Run your program with each of the following six ordering policies and determine which is the best:

Policy Number	Number Ordered/Month					
	April	May	June	July	August	September
1	40	20	30	40	30	20
2	50	50	50	30	0	0
3	40	50	0	40	50	0
4	50	50	40	40	0	0
5	50	10	50	20	50	0
6	50	50	0	50	30	0

13. Write a program that reads two lists of integers that have been sorted so that they are in ascending order and then *merges* these lists into a third list in which the integers are also in ascending order. Run the program for at least the following lists:

    (a) List-1: 1, 3, 5, 7, 9
        List-2: 2, 4, 6, 8, 10

    (b) List-1: 1, 4, 5, 6, 9, 10
        List-2: 2, 3, 7, 8

    (c) List-1: 1, 2, 3, 4, 5, 6, 7
        List-2: 8, 9, 10

    (d) List-1: 10
        List-2: 1, 2, 3, 4, 5, 6, 7, 8, 9

14. Write a program that reads a list of numbers, counts them, and then calculates their mean, variance, and standard deviation. Print how many numbers there are and their mean, variance, and standard deviation with appropriate labels. If $\bar{x}$ denotes the mean of the numbers $x_1, \ldots, x_n$, then the *variance* is the average of the squares of the deviations of the numbers from the mean:

$$\text{variance} = \frac{1}{n} \sum_{i=1}^{n} (x_i - \bar{x})^2$$

and the *standard deviation* is the square root of the variance.

15. Letter grades are sometimes assigned to numeric scores by using the grading scheme commonly called *grading on the curve*. In this scheme, a letter grade is assigned to a numeric score, according to the following table:

x = numeric score	Letter grade
$x < m - \frac{3}{2}\sigma$	F
$m - \frac{3}{2}\sigma \le x < m - \frac{1}{2}\sigma$	D
$m - \frac{1}{2}\sigma \le x < m + \frac{1}{2}\sigma$	C
$m + \frac{1}{2}\sigma \le x < m + \frac{3}{2}\sigma$	B
$m + \frac{3}{2}\sigma \le x$	A

where m is the mean score and σ is the standard deviation. Extend the program of Exercise 14 to read a list of real numbers representing numeric scores, and then calculate their mean and standard deviation, and find and display the letter grade corresponding to each numeric score.

16. One problem with bubble sort is that although larger values move toward their proper positions rapidly, smaller values move slowly in the other direction. *Shell sort* (named after Donald Shell) attempts to improve this. A series of compare–interchange scans is made, but consecutive items are not compared on each scan. Instead, there is a fixed ''gap'' between the items that are compared. When no more interchanges can be made for a given gap, the gap is cut in half, and the compare–interchange scans continue. The initial gap is commonly taken to be $n/2$, for a list of n items. For example, for the list 6, 1, 5, 2, 3, 4, 0, the following sequence of gaps and scans would be used:

Scan #	Gap	Rearranged List	Interchanges
1	3	2, 1, 4, 0, 3, 5, 6	(6,2), (5,4), (6,0)
2	3	0, 1, 4, 2, 3, 5, 6	(2,0)
3	3	0, 1, 4, 2, 3, 5, 6	none
4	1	0, 1, 2, 3, 4, 5, 6	(4,2), (4,3)
5	1	0, 1, 2, 3, 4, 5, 6	none

Write a program to sort a list of items using the Shell sort method.

17. *Insertion sort* is an efficient sorting method for small data sets. It consists of beginning with the first item $x(1)$, then inserting $x(2)$ into this one-item list in the correct position to form a sorted two-element list, then inserting $x(3)$ into this two-element list in the correct position, and so on. For example, to sort the list 7, 1, 5, 2, 3, 4, 6, 0, the steps are as follows (the element being inserted is underlined):

List

7

1, 7   (shift 7 to the right one position)

1, 5, 7   (shift 7 right again)

1, 2, 5, 7   (shift 5 and 7 to the right)

1, 2, 3, 5, 7   (shift 5 and 7 to the right)

1, 2, 3, 4, 5, 7   (shift 5 and 7 to the right)

1, 2, 3 4, 5, 6, 7   (shift 7 to the right)

0, 1, 2, 3, 4, 5, 6, 7   (shift all of 1 through 7 to the right)

Write a program to sort a list of items using this insertion sort method.

18. The investment firm of Shyster and Shyster has been recording the trading price of a particular stock over a 15-day period. Write a program that reads these prices and sorts them into increasing order, using the insertion sort scheme described in the preceding exercise. The program should display the trading range, that is, the lowest and highest prices recorded, and also the median price.

19. A *prime number* is an integer greater than 1 whose only positive divisors are 1 and the integer itself. One method for finding all the prime numbers in the range from 2 through n is known as the *Sieve of Eratosthenes*. Consider the list of numbers from 2 through n. Here 2 is the first prime number, but the multiples of 2 (4, 6, 8, . . .) are not, so they are "crossed out" in the list. The first number after 2 that was not crossed out is 3, the next prime. We then cross out all higher multiples of 3 (6, 9, 12, . . .) from the list. The next number not crossed out is 5, the next prime; we cross out all higher multiples of 5 (10, 15, 20, . . .). We repeat this procedure until we reach the first number in the list that has not been crossed out and whose square is greater than n. Then all the numbers that remain in the list are the primes from 2 through n. Write a program that uses this sieve method to find all the prime numbers from 2 through n. Run it for $n = 50$ and for $n = 500$.

20. Write a program to add two large integers of any length, say up to 300 digits. A suggested approach is as follows: Treat each number as a list, each of whose elements is a block of digits of the number. For example, the integer 179,534,672,198 might be stored with $N(1) = 198$, $N(2) = 672$, $N(3) = 534$, $N(4) = 179$. Then add the two integers (lists) element by element, carrying from one element to the next when necessary.

21. Proceeding as in Exercise 20, write a program to multiply two large integers, say of length up to 300 digits.

22. Peter the postman became bored one night, and to break the monotony of the night shift, he carried out the following experiment with a row of mailboxes in the post office. These mailboxes were numbered 1 through 150, and beginning with mailbox 2, he opened the doors of all the even-numbered mailboxes. Next, beginning with mailbox 3, he went to every third mail box, opening its door if it was closed and closing it if it was open. Then he repeated this procedure with every fourth mailbox, then every fifth mailbox, and so on. When he finished, he was surprised at the distribution of open mailboxes. Write a program to determine which mailboxes these were.

23. Write a program to read the files STUDENT-FILE and STUDENT-UPDATE (see Appendix B) and produce an updated grade report. This grade report should show

(a) The current date.
(b) The student's name and student number.
(c) A list of the names, grades, and credits for each of the current courses under the headings COURSE, GRADE, and CREDITS.
(d) Current GPA (multiply the credits by the numeric grade— $A = 4.0$, $A- = 3.7$, $B+ = 3.3$, $B = 3.0$, . . . , $D- = 0.7$, $F = 0.0$—for each course to find honor points earned for that course; sum these to find the total new honor points; then divide the total new honor points by the total new credits to give the current GPA, rounded to two decimal places).
(e) Total credits earned (old credits from STUDENT-FILE plus total new credits).

(f) New cumulative GPA (first, calculate old honor points = old credits times old cumulative GPA, then new cumulative GPA = sum of old honor points and new honor points divided by updated total credits).

Programming Pointers

In this chapter we discussed arrays. It is quite common for beginning programmers to have some difficulty when using arrays. The following are some of the major points to remember.

1. *All arrays in a FORTRAN program must be dimensioned.* If, for example, ALPHA has been declared by

```
REAL ALPHA
```

but has not been dimensioned, the compiler may interpret a reference to an element of ALPHA, as in

```
X = ALPHA(1)
```

as a reference to a function named ALPHA, which is an error.

2. *Arrays must be declared using constants or parameters to specify the dimensions.* Memory locations must be reserved for array elements at compile time, which requires specifying the number of array elements within the program. One cannot, for example, use a variable as in

```
DIMENSION ALPHA(N)
```

and then read a value for N during execution.

3. *Subscripts must be integer valued and must stay within the range specified in the array declarations.* Related to this requirement are two kinds of errors that can easily arise when using arrays. The first error results from forgetting to declare a subscript to be of integer type. For example, consider the program segment

```
      INTEGER ALPHA(10)

      DO 10 ELM = 1, 10
          ALPHA(ELM) = 0
   10 CONTINUE
          .
          .
          .
```

Because the type of ELM has not been declared, the FORTRAN naming convention implies that it is of real type. Consequently, an error results when the array ALPHA is referenced by the statement

```
ALPHA(ELM) = 0
```

because the subscript is not of integer type.

Another error results from allowing a subscript to get "out of bounds," that is, to have a value less than the lower bound or greater than the upper bound specified in the array declaration. The result of an out-of-range subscript is compiler dependent. If a compiler does range checking, an error results, and execution is usually terminated. For some compilers, however, no such range checking is done, and the memory location that is accessed is determined by simply counting forward or backward from the memory location associated with the first array element. This is illustrated by the program in Figure 7.14. Here A, B, and C are arrays declared by

```
INTEGER A(4), B(4), C(4)
```

and the illegal array references $B(-2)$ and $B(7)$ access the memory locations associated with $A(2)$ and $C(3)$:

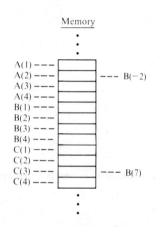

Thus, modifying $B(-2)$ and $B(7)$ changes $A(2)$ and $C(3)$, respectively. This change is obviously undesirable. An array reference such as $B(500)$ that is very much out of range may even cause a program instruction to be modified! Consequently, *it is important to ensure that subscripts do not get out of range.*

```
      PROGRAM ARRAYS
*******************************************************************
* Program to demonstrate what may result when subscripts get out of   *
* bounds.  Variables used are                                         *
*     A, B, C : one-dimensional arrays of integers                    *
*******************************************************************

      INTEGER A(4), B(4), C(4)
      DATA A /1,2,3,4/, B /5,6,7,8/, C /9,10,11,12/
```

Figure 7.14

Figure 7.14   (continued)

```
* Display the original arrays

        PRINT *, 'A =', A
        PRINT *, 'B =', B
        PRINT *, 'C =', C

* Reference array B with a subscript that is out of bounds

        B(-2) = -999
        B(7) = 999

* Print each of the arrays again

        PRINT *
        PRINT *, 'A =', A
        PRINT *, 'B =', B
        PRINT *, 'C =', C
        END


Sample run:
==========

A =         1           2           3           4
B =         5           6           7           8
C =         9          10          11          12

A =         1        -999           3           4
B =         5           6           7           8
C =         9          10         999          12
```

4. *DATA statements are nonexecutable statements that initialize variables at compile time, not during execution.* To illustrate, consider the following program:

```
            INTEGER NUMBER, SUM
            DATA SUM /0/

      ******While there is more data do the following:

      10    READ (*, *, END = 30) NUMBER

      ******While NUMBER is not -999 do the following:

      20        IF (NUMBER .NE. -999) THEN
                    SUM = SUM + NUMBER
                    READ *, NUMBER
                    GO TO 20
                END IF
                PRINT *, 'SUM = ', SUM
                GO TO 10
      30    END
```

If the following data are entered

```
10
20
30
-999
0
15
25
-999
```

the output produced will be

```
SUM  =              60
SUM  =              100
```

When the second set of numbers is processed, SUM is not reset to 0, because the DATA statement does this at compile time, not during execution. This problem cannot be solved by simply attaching a label to the DATA statement and then branching to it, because DATA statements are not executable. The obvious solution is to insert the statement

```
SUM  =  0
```

after statement 10 and delete the DATA statement.

Variations and Extensions

There are only a few variations from or extensions to the array-processing features of standard FORTRAN in other versions of FORTRAN. Two of these are (see Appendix F for additional details):

●Real subscripts may be allowed. In this case, the fractional part is truncated, and the remaining integer part is used for the subscript.

●Compile-time initialization may be done using type statements. For example,

```
INTEGER A, B/100/, C(3)/3*0/
```

may be equivalent to

```
INTEGER A, B, C(3)
DATA B, C/100, 3*0/
```

8

Multidimensional Arrays

Yea, from the table of my memory
I'll wipe away all trivial fond records.

WILLIAM SHAKESPEARE, *Hamlet*

In the preceding chapter, we considered one-dimensional arrays and used them to process lists of data. We also observed that FORTRAN allows arrays of more than one dimension and that two-dimensional arrays are useful when the data being processed can be arranged in rows and columns. Similarly, a three-dimensional array is appropriate when the data can be arranged in rows, columns, and ranks. When there are several characteristics associated with the data, still higher dimensions may be appropriate, with each dimension corresponding to one of these characteristics. In this chapter we consider how such multidimensional arrays are processed in FORTRAN programs.

8.1 Introduction to Multidimensional Arrays and Multiply Subscripted Variables

There are many problems in which the data being processed can be naturally organized as a table. For example, suppose that water temperatures are recorded four times each day at each of three locations near the discharge outlet of the cooling system of a nuclear power plant. These temperature readings can be arranged in a table having four rows and three columns:

Time	Location 1	Location 2	Location 3
1	65.5	68.7	62.0
2	68.8	68.9	64.5
3	70.4	69.4	66.3
4	68.5	69.1	65.8

In this table, the three temperature readings at time 1 are in the first row, the three temperatures at time 2 are in the second row, and so on.

These 12 data items can be conveniently stored in a two-dimensional array. The array declaration

```
DIMENSION TEMTAB(1:4, 1:3)
REAL TEMTAB
```

or

```
DIMENSION TEMTAB(4,3)
REAL TEMTAB
```

reserves 12 memory locations for these data items. The dimensioning information can also be included in the type statement:

```
REAL TEMTAB(1:4, 1:3)
```

or

```
REAL TEMTAB(4,3)
```

The doubly subscripted variable

```
TEMTAB(2,3)
```

then refers to the entry in the second row and third column of the table, that is, to the temperature 64.5 recorded at time 2 at location 3. In general

```
TEMTAB(I,J)
```

refers to the entry in the Ith row and Jth column, that is, to the temperature recorded at time I at location J.

To illustrate the use of an array with more than two dimensions, suppose that the temperature readings are made for one week so that seven such tables are collected:

Time	Location 1	2	3	
1	66.5	69.4	68.4	
2	68.4	71.2	69.3	Day 7
3	70.1	71.9	70.2	
4	69.5	70.0	69.4	

Time	Location 1	2	3	
1	63.7	66.2	64.3	
2	64.0	66.8	64.9	Day 2
			66.3	
			65.8	

Time	Location 1	2	3	
1	65.5	68.7	62.0	
2	68.8	68.9	64.5	Day 1
3	70.4	69.4	66.3	
4	68.5	69.1	65.8	

A three-dimensional array TEMP declared by

```
DIMENSION TEMP(1:4, 1:3, 1:7)
REAL TEMP
```

or

```
DIMENSION TEMP(4,3,7)
REAL TEMP
```

or

```
REAL TEMP(1:4, 1:3, 1:7)
```

or

```
REAL TEMP(4,3,7)
```

can be used to store these 84 temperature readings. The value of the triply subscripted variable

```
TEMP(1,3,2)
```

is the temperature recorded at time 1 at location 3 on day 2, that is, the value 64.3 in the first row, third column, second rank. In general

```
TEMP(TIME,LOC,DAY)
```

is the temperature recorded at time TIME at location LOC on day DAY.

The general form of an **array declaration** is

$$array\text{-}name(l_1{:}u_1, \ l_2{:}u_2, \ \ldots \ , \ l_k{:}u_k)$$

where the number k of dimensions is at most seven, and each pair $l_i{:}u_i$ must be a pair of integer constants or parameters specifying the range of values for the ith subscript to be from l_i through u_i. There must be one such array declaration for each array used in a program, and these declarations may appear in DIMENSION or type statements. For example, the statements

```
DIMENSION GAMMA(1:2, -1:3), KAPPA(5:12),
+        BETA(0:2, 0:3, 1:2)
REAL GAMMA, BETA
INTEGER KAPPA
```

or

```
REAL GAMMA(1:2, -1:3), BETA(0:2, 0:3, 1:2)
INTEGER KAPPA(5:12)
```

establish three arrays. The array GAMMA is a two-dimensional 2×5 real array, with the first subscript either 1 or 2 and the second subscript ranging from -1 through 3; thus, the doubly subscripted variables GAMMA$(1,-1)$, GAMMA(1,0), GAMMA(1,1), GAMMA(1,2), GAMMA(1,3), GAMMA$(2,-1)$, GAMMA(2,0), GAMMA(2,1), GAMMA(2,2), and GAMMA(2,3) may be used. The three-dimensional $3 \times 4 \times 2$ real array BETA has the first subscript equal to 0, 1, or 2; the second subscript ranging from 0 through 3; and the third subscript equal to 1 or 2. The one-dimensional integer array KAPPA has subscripts ranging from 5 through 12.

8.2 Processing Multidimensional Arrays

In the preceding section we gave several examples of multidimensional arrays and showed how such arrays are declared in a FORTRAN program. We also noted that each element of the array can be accessed directly by using a multiply subscripted variable consisting of the array name followed by the subscripts that specify the location of that element in the array. In this section we consider the processing of multidimensional arrays, including the input and output of arrays or parts of arrays.

As we observed in the preceding chapter, the most natural order for processing the elements of a one-dimensional array is the usual sequential order, from first item to last. For multidimensional arrays, however, there are several orders in which the subscripts may be varied when processing the array elements.

Two-dimensional arrays are often used when the data can be organized as a table consisting of rows and columns. This leads to two natural orders for processing the entries of a two-dimensional array, **rowwise** and **columnwise.** Rowwise processing means that the array elements in the first row are processed first, then those in the second row, and so on, as shown in Figure 8.1a for the 3×4 array A, which has three rows and four columns. In columnwise processing, the entries in the first column are processed first, then those in the second

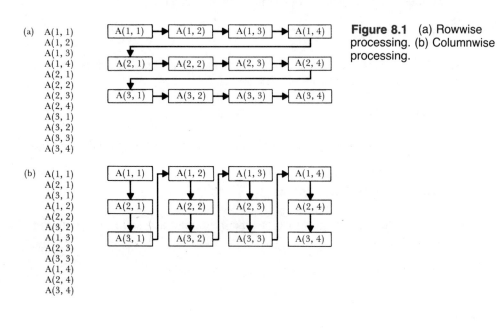

Figure 8.1 (a) Rowwise processing. (b) Columnwise processing.

column, and so on, as illustrated in Figure 8.1b. In most cases, the user can select one of these orderings by controlling the manner in which the subscripts vary. *If this is not done, the FORTRAN convention is that two-dimensional arrays will be processed columnwise.*

To illustrate these two ways to process a two-dimensional array, we reconsider the table of temperature readings described in the preceding section:

Time	Location 1	Location 2	3
1	65.5	68.7	62.0
2	68.8	68.9	64.5
3	70.4	69.4	66.3
4	68.5	69.1	65.8

Suppose that these 12 temperatures are to be read and stored in the two-dimensional 4×3 real array TEMTAB declared by

```
REAL TEMTAB(4,3)
```

so that TEMTAB has the value

$$\begin{bmatrix} 65.5 & 68.7 & 62.0 \\ 68.8 & 68.9 & 64.5 \\ 70.4 & 69.4 & 66.3 \\ 68.5 & 69.1 & 65.8 \end{bmatrix}$$

If these 12 temperatures are to be entered in the order 65.5, 68.7, 62.0, 68.8, 68.9, 64.5, 70.4, 69.4, 66.3, 68.5, 69.1, 65.8, then rowwise processing is required. We must first read the three temperatures recorded at time 1; that is, we must read the values for the first row of TEMTAB:

Row 1 of TEMTAB: 65.5 68.7 62.0

After these values are read, the three temperatures at time 2 must be entered and stored in the second row of TEMTAB:

Row 2 of TEMTAB: 68.8 68.9 64.5

We then enter the three temperatures recorded at time 3 and store them in the third row of TEMTAB

Row 3 of TEMTAB: 70.4 69.4 66.3

Finally, the three values recorded at time 4 are read and stored in the fourth row of TEMTAB:

Row 4 of TEMTAB: 68.5 69.1 65.8

On the other hand, if the 12 temperature readings are to be entered in the order 65.5, 68.8, 70.4, 68.5, 68.7, 68.9, 69.4, 69.1, 62.0, 64.5, 66.3, 65.8, then columnwise processing is required. The four temperatures recorded at location 1 must be read and stored in the first column of TEMTAB:

Column 1 of TEMTAB:

```
65.5
68.8
70.4
68.5
```

After these four values have been read, the four temperatures at location 2 must be read and stored in the second column of TEMTAB:

Column 2 of TEMTAB:

```
68.7
68.9
69.4
69.1
```

Finally, the four temperatures recorded at location 3 are read and stored in the third column of TEMTAB:

Column 3 of TEMTAB:

```
62.0
64.5
66.3
65.8
```

In the list of array elements shown in Figure 8.1a, we observe that in rowwise processing of a two-dimensional array, it is the second subscript that varies first and the first subscript second; that is, the second subscript must vary over its entire range of values before the first subscript changes. It is just the opposite for columnwise processing, as we see from Figure 8.1b; the first subscript varies first and the second subscript second; that is, the first subscript must vary over its entire range before the second subscript changes.

For arrays of three or more dimensions, there are many ways that the elements can be processed. One of the more common ways is the analog of columnwise processing for the two-dimensional case; that is, the first subscript varies first, followed by the second subscript, then by the third, and so on. This method is illustrated in Figure 8.2 for the $2 \times 4 \times 3$ array B, which has two rows, four columns, and three ranks.

In Section 7.2 we considered three ways in which data could be input or output for one-dimensional arrays:

1. Use an input/output statement within a DO loop.

B(1, 1, 1)
B(2, 1, 1)
B(1, 2, 1)
B(2, 2, 1)
B(1, 3, 1)
B(2, 3, 1)
B(1, 4, 1)
B(2, 4, 1)
B(1, 1, 2)
B(2, 1, 2)
B(1, 2, 2)
B(2, 2, 2)
B(1, 3, 2)
B(2, 3, 2)
B(1, 4, 2)
B(2, 4, 2)
B(1, 1, 3)
B(2, 1, 3)
B(1, 2, 3)
B(2, 2, 3)
B(1, 3, 3)
B(2, 3, 3)
B(1, 4, 3)
B(2, 4, 3)

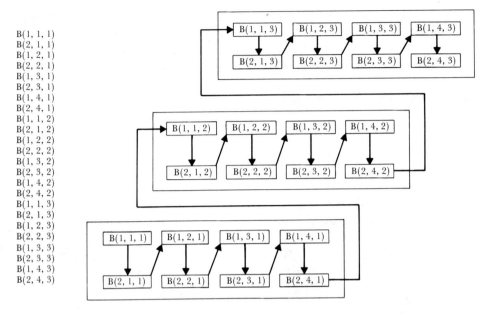

Figure 8.2

2. Use the array name in an input/output statement.
3. Use an implied DO loop in an input/output statement.

Each of these three techniques can also be used for the input and output of multidimensional arrays, and we consider each in turn, paying particular attention to the order in which the values are processed.

Input/Output Using a DO Loop. In this method of reading or displaying an array, the input/output statement is placed within a set of nested DO loops, each of whose indices controls one of the subscripts of the array. For example, reconsider the problem of reading temperature values into the 4×3 real array TEMTAB declared by

    REAL TEMTAB(4,3)

so that it has the value

$$\begin{bmatrix} 65.5 & 68.7 & 62.0 \\ 68.8 & 68.9 & 64.5 \\ 70.4 & 69.4 & 66.3 \\ 68.5 & 69.1 & 65.8 \end{bmatrix}$$

Suppose we use the following statements:

```
     DO 20 TIME = 1, 4
         DO 10 LOC = 1, 3
             READ *, TEMTAB(TIME,LOC)
10       CONTINUE
20 CONTINUE
```

Here the outer DO loop sets the value of the index TIME to 1, and the inner DO loop is then executed using 1 as the value for TIME; the effect, therefore, is the same as executing

```
      DO 10 LOC = 1, 3
            READ *, TEMTAB(1,LOC)
   10 CONTINUE
```

which is equivalent to the following three READ statements:

```
   READ *, TEMTAB(1,1)
   READ *, TEMTAB(1,2)
   READ *, TEMTAB(1,3)
```

The first pass through the outer DO loop thus reads values for the first row of TEMTAB, so the first three values entered must be

```
   65.5
   68.7
   62.0
```

Note that they must be entered on separate lines, one per line, because the READ statement is executed three times and each execution requires a new line of input.

Now the outer DO loop sets the value of the index TIME to 2, and the inner DO loop is executed again,

```
      DO 10 LOC = 1, 3
            READ *, TEMTAB(2,LOC)
   10 CONTINUE
```

which is equivalent to the three READ statements

```
   READ *, TEMTAB(2,1)
   READ *, TEMTAB(2,2)
   READ *, TEMTAB(2,3)
```

so the next three values entered must be

```
   68.8
   68.9
   64.5
```

again on separate lines. The outer DO loop then causes the inner DO loop to be executed again, with TIME set equal to 3

```
      DO 10 LOC = 1, 3
            READ *, TEMTAB(3,LOC)
   10 CONTINUE
```

which is equivalent to

```
READ *, TEMTAB(3,1)
READ *, TEMTAB(3,2)
READ *, TEMTAB(3,3)
```

so the values for the third row of TEMTAB must be entered on separate lines:

```
70.4
69.4
66.3
```

Finally, the value of TIME is set to 4, and the inner DO loop is executed again

```
DO 10 LOC = 1, 3
     READ *, TEMTAB(4,LOC)
10 CONTINUE
```

which has the same effect as

```
READ *, TEMTAB(4,1)
READ *, TEMTAB(4,2)
READ *, TEMTAB(4,3)
```

for which the values for the fourth row of TEMTAB must be entered:

```
68.5
69.1
65.8
```

Columnwise input is also possible; we need only reverse the order of the two DO loops:

```
DO 20 LOC = 1, 3
     DO 10 TIME = 1, 4
         READ *, TEMTAB(TIME,LOC)
10     CONTINUE
20 CONTINUE
```

These statements are equivalent to the following sequence of 12 READ statements:

```
READ *, TEMTAB(1,1)
READ *, TEMTAB(2,1)
READ *, TEMTAB(3,1)
READ *, TEMTAB(4,1)
READ *, TEMTAB(1,2)
READ *, TEMTAB(2,2)
READ *, TEMTAB(3,2)
READ *, TEMTAB(4,2)
READ *, TEMTAB(1,3)
READ *, TEMTAB(2,3)
READ *, TEMTAB(3,3)
READ *, TEMTAB(4,3)
```

Because the READ statement is encountered 12 times, the data values must be entered on 12 separate lines, one per line:

```
65.5
68.8
70.4
68.5
68.7
68.9
69.4
69.1
62.0
64.5
66.3
65.8
```

Because the data values must appear on separate lines, one value per line, this method of input is cumbersome for large arrays. A similar problem also occurs with output, since each execution of a PRINT or WRITE statement within nested DO loops such as

```
      DO 20 TIME = 1, 4
          DO 10 LOC = 1, 3
              PRINT *, TEMTAB(TIME,LOC)
10        CONTINUE
20 CONTINUE
```

causes output to begin on a new line. Thus, the entries of the array are displayed on separate lines, one entry per line. It is therefore not possible to display the array in tabular form using this output method.

Input/Output Using the Array Name. In this method of reading or displaying an array, the array name without subscripts appears in the input/output statement. As we observed for one-dimensional arrays, this is equivalent to listing a *complete* set of array elements in the input/output list. Thus, the total number of entries as specified in the array declaration must be read or displayed. Therefore, it is not possible to read or display only part of an array using this method.

Another disadvantage of this method is the order in which multidimensional arrays are read or displayed. Because the order in which the subscripts vary is not specified by the programmer, the standard columnwise order (or its analog for arrays of more than two dimensions) is used. For example, the statements

```
INTEGER MAT(3,4)

READ *, MAT
```

cause values to be read into the array MAT columnwise. Thus, for the input data

```
77, 56, 32, 25, 99, 10
100, 46, 48, 89, 77, 33
```

the value assigned to MAT is

$$
\begin{bmatrix}
77 & 25 & 100 & 89 \\
56 & 99 & 46 & 77 \\
32 & 10 & 48 & 33
\end{bmatrix}
$$

The output statement

```
PRINT '(1X, 4I5/)', MAT
```

displays the elements in columnwise order and so produces the output

```
    77    56    32    25

    99    10   100    46

    48    89    77    33
```

We note that in contrast with the first method for input/output of arrays, the form in which the data is prepared for input or displayed by output may be specified. The number of items on each line of input or output is determined by the programmer.

Input/Output Using Implied DO Loops. An implied DO loop, introduced in Section 7.2, has the form

(*i/o-list, control-variable* = *initial-value, limit*)

or

(*i/o-list, control-variable* = *initial-value, limit, step-size*)

The fact that the input/output list may contain other implied DO loops makes it possible to use implied DO loops to read or display multidimensional arrays. For example, the statement

```
READ *, ((MAT(ROW,COL), COL = 1, 4), ROW = 1, 3)
```

is equivalent to the statement

```
READ *, (MAT(ROW,1), MAT(ROW,2),
+        MAT(ROW,3), MAT(ROW,4)), ROW = 1, 3)
```

which has the same effect as

```
READ *, MAT(1,1), MAT(1,2), MAT(1,3), MAT(1,4),
+        MAT(2,1), MAT(2,2), MAT(2,3), MAT(2,4),
+        MAT(3,1), MAT(3,2), MAT(3,3), MAT(3,4)
```

and thus reads the entries of the array MAT in rowwise order. Note that because the READ statement is encountered only once, the data values to be read can be entered all on the same line, or with four values on each of three lines, or with seven values on one line, four on the next, and one on another line, and so on.

By interchanging the indexing information in the nested implied DO loops, columnwise input is possible. Thus, the statement

```
READ *, ((MAT(ROW,COL), ROW = 1, 3), COL = 1, 4)
```

which is equivalent to

```
READ *, (MAT(1,COL), MAT(2,COL), MAT(3,COL), COL = 1, 4)
```

or

```
READ *, MAT(1,1), MAT(2,1), MAT(3,1),
+        MAT(1,2), MAT(2,2), MAT(3,2),
+        MAT(1,3), MAT(2,3), MAT(3,3),
+        MAT(1,4), MAT(2,4), MAT(3,4)
```

may be used if the entries of MAT are to be entered in columnwise order. Similarly, the statement

```
READ *, (((B(I,J,K), I = 1, 2), J = 1, 4), K = 1, 3)
```

reads values into the three-dimensional array B in the standard order indicated in Figure 8.2.

Note the use of parentheses and commas in these statements. They should be used exactly as indicated, or an error message may result. Each implied DO loop must be enclosed within parentheses, and a comma must separate the list from the indexing information in the implied DO loop.

In contrast with the two preceding methods of array input/output, using an implied DO loop in an input/output list permits the programmer to determine the form of the input/output data and to read or display only part of an array. For example, if ALPHA is a 3×10 real array, the statements

```
PRINT 50, ((ALPHA(K,L), L = 4, 10, 3), K = 1, 3, 2)
50 FORMAT (1X, 3F12.4)
```

will display the values of ALPHA(1,4), ALPHA(1,7), ALPHA(1,10), AL-PHA(3,4), ALPHA(3,7), and ALPHA(3,10) in this order, with three numbers per line.

The program in Figure 8.3 illustrates this flexibility of implied DO loops. It reads the number NTIMES of times at which temperatures are recorded and the number NLOCS of locations at which these readings are made, and then uses implied DO loops to read NTIMES * NLOCS values into the two-dimensional array TEMTAB declared by

```
REAL TEMTAB(MAXTIM,MAXLOC)
```

where MAXTIM and MAXLOC are integer parameters with values 24 and 10, respectively, and to display these temperatures in tabular format.

```
      PROGRAM TEMPS
***********************************************************************
* Program illustrating use of nested implied DO loops to read and     *
* print the elements of a two-dimensional array.  Variables used are: *
*      TEMTAB : two-dimensional array of temperatures                 *
*      MAXTIM : parameter specifying maximum # of times               *
*      MAXLOC : parameter specifying maximum # of locations           *
*      NTIMES : # of times temperatures are recorded                  *
*      NLOCS  : # of locations at which temperatures are recorded     *
*      TIME   : row subscript for the table                           *
*      LOC    : column subscript for the table                        *
***********************************************************************

      INTEGER MAXTIM, MAXLOC, NTIMES, NLOCS, TIME, LOC
      PARAMETER (MAXTIM = 24, MAXLOC = 10)
      REAL TEMTAB(MAXTIM,MAXLOC)

      PRINT *, 'ENTER # OF TIMES TEMPERATURES ARE RECORDED'
      PRINT *, 'AND # OF LOCATIONS WHERE RECORDED:'
      READ *, NTIMES, NLOCS
      PRINT *, 'ENTER THE TEMPERATURES AT THE FIRST LOCATION,'
      PRINT *, 'THEN THOSE AT THE SECOND LOCATION, AND SO ON:'
      READ *, ((TEMTAB(TIME,LOC), LOC = 1, NLOCS), TIME = 1, NTIMES)
      PRINT *
      PRINT 10, (LOC, LOC = 1, NLOCS)
10    FORMAT (1X, '         LOCATION' / 1X, 'TIME', 10I6)
      DO 30 TIME = 1, NTIMES
         PRINT 20, TIME, (TEMTAB(TIME,LOC), LOC = 1, NLOCS)
20       FORMAT (/1X, I3, 2X, 10F6.1/)
30    CONTINUE
      END
```

Figure 8.3

Figure 8.3   (continued)

```
Sample run:
==========

ENTER # OF TIMES TEMPERATURES ARE RECORDED
AND # OF LOCATIONS WHERE RECORDED:
4, 3
ENTER THE TEMPERATURES AT THE FIRST LOCATION,
THEN THOSE AT THE SECOND LOCATION, AND SO ON:
65.5, 68.7, 62.0
68.8, 68.9, 64.5
70.4, 69.4, 66.3
68.5, 69.1, 65.8

          LOCATION
TIME    1     2     3

  1    65.5  68.7  62.0

  2    68.8  68.9  64.5

  3    70.4  69.4  66.3

  4    68.5  69.1  65.8
```

The following examples exhibit some of the additional flexibility available with implied DO loops. In these examples the integer variable NTOT has the value 152; NUM is the one-dimensional integer array containing the four numbers 16, 37, 76, and 23; and RATE is a 3 × 4 real array having the value

$$\begin{bmatrix} 16.1 & 7.3 & 18.4 & 6.5 \\ 0.0 & 1.0 & 1.0 & 3.5 \\ 18.2 & 16.9 & 0.0 & 0.0 \end{bmatrix}$$

Input/output statement:

```
READ *, N, (NUM(I), I = 1, N), M, ((RATE(I,J), J = 1, N), I = 1, M)
```

Possible lines of input data:

```
4
16, 37, 76, 23
3
16.1,   7.3, 18.4, 6.5
0.0,    1.0,  1.0, 3.5
18.2, 16.9,  0.0, 0.0
```

Input/output statement:

```
PRINT 5, ('ROW', I, (RATE(I,J), J = 1, 4), I = 1, 3)
5 FORMAT(1X, A, I2, '--', 4F6.1/)
```

Output produced:

```
ROW 1--    16.1    7.3   18.4    6.5

ROW 2--     0.0    1.0    1.0    3.5

ROW 3--    18.2   16.9    0.0    0.0
```

Input/output statement:

```
 PRINT 6, (J, (RATE(I,J), I = 1,3), NUM(J), J = 1,4), 'TOTAL',NTOT
6 FORMAT (4(1X, I4, 5X, 3F6.1, I10/), 1X, A, T35, I3)
```

Output produced:

```
    1         16.1   0.0   18.2           16
    2          7.3   1.0   16.9           37
    3         18.4   1.0    0.0           76
    4          6.5   3.5    0.0           23
TOTAL                                    152
```

8.3   Examples: Pollution Table, Oceanographic Data Analysis

EXAMPLE 1. Pollution Table.   Suppose that in a certain city, the pollution level is measured at two-hour intervals, beginning at midnight. These measurements were recorded for a one-week period and stored in the file POLLUTION-FILE, the first line of which contains the pollution levels for day 1, the second line for day 2, and so on. For example, suppose the pollution file for a certain week contains the following data

```
30 30 31 32 35 40 43 44 47 45 40 38
33 32 30 34 40 48 46 49 53 49 45 40
38 35 34 37 44 50 51 54 60 58 51 49
49 48 47 53 60 70 73 75 80 75 73 60
55 54 53 65 70 80 90 93 95 94 88 62
73 70 65 66 71 78 74 78 83 75 66 58
50 47 43 35 30 33 37 43 45 52 39 31
```

A program is to be written to produce a weekly report displaying the pollution levels in a table of the form

```
                                      TIME
DAY:    1     2     3     4     5     6     7     8     9     10    11    12
─────────────────────────────────────────────────────────────────────────
  1 :   30    30    31    32    35    40    43    44    47    45    40    38
  2 :   33    32    30    34    40    48    46    49    53    49    45    40
  3 :   38    35    34    37    44    50    51    54    60    58    51    49
  4 :   49    48    47    53    60    70    73    75    80    75    73    60
  5 :   55    54    53    65    70    80    90    93    95    94    88    62
  6 :   73    70    65    66    71    78    74    78    83    75    66    58
  7 :   50    47    43    35    30    33    37    43    45    52    39    31
```

and which also displays the average pollution level for each day and the average pollution level for each sampling time.

The input to the program is to be a file of pollution levels, as previously described, and the output is to be a report of the indicated form. The required algorithm is as follows:

ALGORITHM FOR POLLUTION REPORT

```
*   Algorithm to read a two-dimensional array POLTAB from a file    *
*   containing pollution levels measured at selected times for several  *
*   days. These measurements are displayed in tabular form. The      *
*   average pollution level for each day and the average pollution    *
*   level for each sampling time are then calculated.            *
```

1. Read the contents of the pollution file into the 7 × 12 array POL-TAB so that each of the 7 rows contains the pollution measurements for a given day and each of the 12 columns contains the pollution measurements for a given time.
2. Print the array POLTAB with appropriate headings.
3. Calculate the average pollution level for each day, that is, the average of each of the rows, as follows:
   a. For DAY ranging from 1 through the number NDAYS of days, do the following:
      (i) Set SUM equal to 0.
      (ii) For TIME ranging from 1 through the number NTIMES of sampling times, add POLTAB(DAY, TIME) to SUM.
   b. Display SUM / NTIMES.
4. Calculate the average pollution level for each sampling time, that is, the average of each of the columns, as follows:
   a. For TIME ranging from 1 through NTIMES, do the following:
      (i) Set SUM equal to 0.
      (ii) For DAY ranging from 1 through NDAYS, add POLTAB(DAY,TIME) to SUM.
   b. Display SUM / NDAYS.

Figure 8.4 displays this algorithm in flowchart form.

The program in Figure 8.5 implements this algorithm and uses the data file described previously.

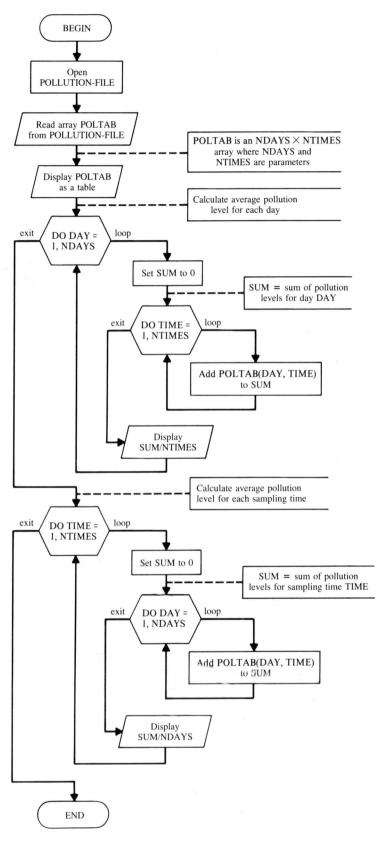

Figure 8.4

```
      PROGRAM POLLUT
***********************************************************************
* This program reads the entries of the two-dimensional array  POLTAB  *
* from the file  POLLUTION-FILE  and produces a report showing a table *
* of pollution levels, the average pollution level for each day, and   *
* the average pollution level for each sampling time.  Variables used  *
* are:                                                                 *
*      NDAYS   : parameter giving the number of rows (days)            *
*      NTIMES  : parameter giving the number of columns (times)        *
*      POLTAB  : an NDAYS X NTIMES array of pollution levels           *
*      DAY,TIME: row, column subscripts                                *
*      SUM     : variable used in accumulating row & column sums       *
***********************************************************************

      INTEGER NDAYS, NTIMES
      PARAMETER (NDAYS = 7, NTIMES = 12)
      INTEGER POLTAB(NDAYS,NTIMES), DAY, TIME
      REAL SUM

* Read in the pollution levels and display them in a table
* of the required form.

      OPEN (UNIT = 15, FILE = 'POLLUTION-FILE', STATUS = 'OLD')
      READ (15,*) ((POLTAB(DAY,TIME), TIME = 1, NTIMES), DAY = 1, NDAYS)
      PRINT 10, (TIME, TIME = 1, NTIMES)
10    FORMAT(T30, 'TIME' / 1X, 'DAY:', 12I4 / 1X, 53('-'))
      PRINT 20,
     +   (DAY, (POLTAB(DAY,TIME), TIME = 1, NTIMES), DAY = 1, NDAYS)
20    FORMAT(1X, I2, ' :', 12I4)

* Calculate average pollution level for each day (row averages)

      PRINT *
      DO 50 DAY = 1, NDAYS
          SUM = 0
          DO 30 TIME = 1, NTIMES
              SUM = SUM + POLTAB(DAY,TIME)
30        CONTINUE
          PRINT 40, 'FOR DAY', DAY, SUM / NTIMES
40        FORMAT('AVERAGE POLLUTION LEVEL ', A7, I3, ':', F6.1)
50    CONTINUE

* Calculate average pollution level for each time (column averages)

      PRINT *
      DO 70 TIME = 1, NTIMES
          SUM = 0
          DO 60 DAY = 1, NDAYS
              SUM = SUM + POLTAB(DAY,TIME)
60        CONTINUE
          PRINT 40, 'AT TIME', TIME, SUM / NDAYS
70    CONTINUE
      CLOSE (15)
      END
```

Figure 8.5

Figure 8.5 (continued)

```
Listing of data file:
=====================

30 30 31 32 35 40 43 44 47 45 40 38
33 32 30 34 40 48 46 49 53 49 45 40
38 35 34 37 44 50 51 54 60 58 51 49
49 48 47 53 60 70 73 75 80 75 73 60
55 54 53 65 70 80 90 93 95 94 88 62
73 70 65 66 71 78 74 78 83 75 66 58
50 47 43 35 30 33 37 43 45 52 39 31


Sample run:
==========

                               TIME
DAY:    1    2    3    4    5    6    7    8    9   10   11   12
--------------------------------------------------------------
  1 :  30   30   31   32   35   40   43   44   47   45   40   38
  2 :  33   32   30   34   40   48   46   49   53   49   45   40
  3 :  38   35   34   37   44   50   51   54   60   58   51   49
  4 :  49   48   47   53   60   70   73   75   80   75   73   60
  5 :  55   54   53   65   70   80   90   93   95   94   88   62
  6 :  73   70   65   66   71   78   74   78   83   75   66   58
  7 :  50   47   43   35   30   33   37   43   45   52   39   31

AVERAGE POLLUTION LEVEL FOR DAY   1:   37.9
AVERAGE POLLUTION LEVEL FOR DAY   2:   41.6
AVERAGE POLLUTION LEVEL FOR DAY   3:   46.7
AVERAGE POLLUTION LEVEL FOR DAY   4:   63.6
AVERAGE POLLUTION LEVEL FOR DAY   5:   74.9
AVERAGE POLLUTION LEVEL FOR DAY   6:   71.4
AVERAGE POLLUTION LEVEL FOR DAY   7:   40.4

AVERAGE POLLUTION LEVEL AT TIME   1:   46.9
AVERAGE POLLUTION LEVEL AT TIME   2:   45.1
AVERAGE POLLUTION LEVEL AT TIME   3:   43.3
AVERAGE POLLUTION LEVEL AT TIME   4:   46.0
AVERAGE POLLUTION LEVEL AT TIME   5:   50.0
AVERAGE POLLUTION LEVEL AT TIME   6:   57.0
AVERAGE POLLUTION LEVEL AT TIME   7:   59.1
AVERAGE POLLUTION LEVEL AT TIME   8:   62.3
AVERAGE POLLUTION LEVEL AT TIME   9:   66.1
AVERAGE POLLUTION LEVEL AT TIME  10:   64.0
AVERAGE POLLUTION LEVEL AT TIME  11:   57.4
AVERAGE POLLUTION LEVEL AT TIME  12:   48.3
```

EXAMPLE 2: Oceanographic Data Analysis. A petroleum exploration company has collected some depth readings for a square section of the ocean. The diagonal of this square is parallel to the equator. The company has divided the square into a grid with each intersection point (node) of the grid separated by 5 miles. The entire square is 50 miles on each side. Two separate crews did exploratory drilling in this area, one in the northern half (above the diagonal) and the other in the southern half. A program is to be written to find the approximate average ocean depth for each crew and the overall average for the entire square. The depth data (in feet) collected by the crews was

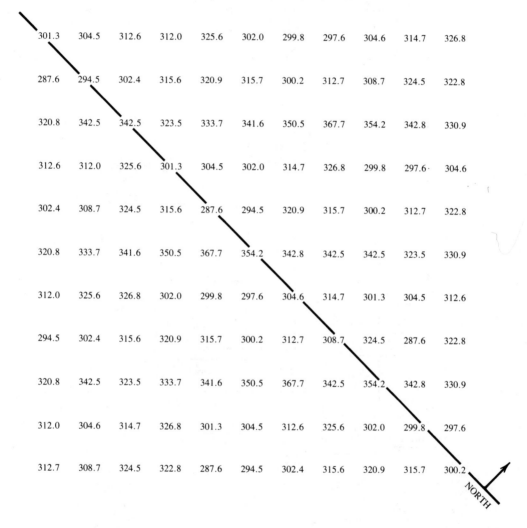

301.3	304.5	312.6	312.0	325.6	302.0	299.8	297.6	304.6	314.7	326.8
287.6	294.5	302.4	315.6	320.9	315.7	300.2	312.7	308.7	324.5	322.8
320.8	342.5	342.5	323.5	333.7	341.6	350.5	367.7	354.2	342.8	330.9
312.6	312.0	325.6	301.3	304.5	302.0	314.7	326.8	299.8	297.6	304.6
302.4	308.7	324.5	315.6	287.6	294.5	320.9	315.7	300.2	312.7	322.8
320.8	333.7	341.6	350.5	367.7	354.2	342.8	342.5	342.5	323.5	330.9
312.0	325.6	326.8	302.0	299.8	297.6	304.6	314.7	301.3	304.5	312.6
294.5	302.4	315.6	320.9	315.7	300.2	312.7	308.7	324.5	287.6	322.8
320.8	342.5	323.5	333.7	341.6	350.5	367.7	342.5	354.2	342.8	330.9
312.0	304.6	314.7	326.8	301.3	304.5	312.6	325.6	302.0	299.8	297.6
312.7	308.7	324.5	322.8	287.6	294.5	302.4	315.6	320.9	315.7	300.2

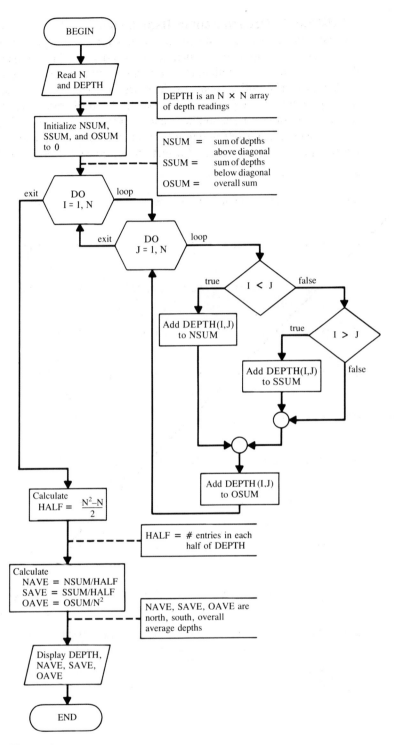

Figure 8.6

The following algorithm calculates the desired averages. It uses a two-dimensional array DEPTH to store the depth readings.

ALGORITHM FOR OCEANOGRAPHIC DATA ANALYSIS

```
*   Algorithm to find the average ocean depth in each half (separated    *
*   by the diagonal) of a square section of the ocean and the overall    *
*   average. The depth readings are stored in the N × N two-             *
*   dimensional array DEPTH.                                              *
```

1. Read N and the array DEPTH.
2. Initialize the north, south, and overall sums NSUM, SSUM, and OSUM to 0.
3. Do the following for I ranging from 1 to N:

   Do the following for J ranging from 1 to N:

   a. If I < J then
      Add DEPTH(I,J) to NSUM
      Else if I > J then
      Add DEPTH(I,J) to SSUM.

   b. Add DEPTH(I,J) to OSUM.

4. Set HALF equal to $(N^2 - N)/2$; this is the number of entries in each half.
5. Calculate the north, south, and overall average depths by
   NAVE = NSUM / HALF, SAVE = SSUM / HALF, and
   OAVE = OSUM / N^2.
6. Display DEPTH, NAVE, SAVE, and OAVE.

Figure 8.6 shows this algorithm in flowchart form, and the program in Figure 8.7 implements the algorithm.

```
     PROGRAM RANGE

*****************************************************************************
* Program to find the average ocean depth in each half (separated by    *
* the diagonal) of a square section of the ocean.  Variables used are:  *
*     DEPTH   : a two-dimensional array of depth readings               *
*     FNAME   : name of file containing depth readings                  *
*     LIMIT   : limit on size of DEPTH (parameter)                      *
*     N       : the number of rows (or columns)                         *
*     NSUM    : the sum of the northern depths                          *
*     NAVE    : the average of the northern depths                      *
*     SSUM    : the sum of the southern depths                          *
*     SAVE    : the average of the southern depths                      *
*     OSUM    : the overall sum                                         *
*     OAVE    : the overall average                                     *
*     HALF    : number of elements in each half                        *
* Note : it is assumed that the elements on the diagonal are            *
*        included in the overall average but not in either half         *
*****************************************************************************
```

Figure 8.7

Figure 8.7(continued)

```
      INTEGER LIMIT
      PARAMETER (LIMIT = 11)
      CHARACTER*20 FNAME
      INTEGER HALF
      REAL DEPTH(LIMIT,LIMIT), NSUM, NAVE, SSUM, SAVE, OSUM, OAVE
      DATA NSUM, SSUM, OSUM /3*0.0/

      PRINT *, 'ENTER NAME OF DATA FILE:'
      READ 10, FNAME
10    FORMAT(A)
      OPEN (UNIT = 10, FILE = FNAME, STATUS = 'OLD')
      READ (10,*) N, ((DEPTH(I,J), J = 1, N), I = 1, N)

      DO 30 I = 1,N
         DO 20 J = 1, N

            IF (I .LT. J) THEN
               NSUM = NSUM + DEPTH(I,J)
            ELSE IF (I .GT. J) THEN
               SSUM = SSUM + DEPTH(I,J)
            END IF

            OSUM = OSUM + DEPTH(I,J)

20       CONTINUE
30    CONTINUE

      HALF = (N**2 - N) / 2
      NAVE = NSUM / REAL(HALF)
      SAVE = SSUM / REAL(HALF)
      OAVE = OSUM / REAL(N**2)

      PRINT 40
      PRINT 50, ((DEPTH(I,J), J = 1, N), I = 1, N)
40    FORMAT (1X, T29, 'OCEAN DEPTHS')
50    FORMAT (/1X, 11F6.1)

      PRINT 60, NAVE, SAVE, OAVE
60    FORMAT(//,1X,'NORTHERN HALF AVERAGE DEPTH',T30,F6.2,' FEET',
     +       //,1X,'SOUTHERN HALF AVERAGE DEPTH',T30,F6.2,' FEET',
     +       //,1X,'OVERALL AVERAGE DEPTH',T30,F6.2,' FEET')
      END
```

Sample run:
==========

ENTER NAME OF DATA FILE:
OCEAN

Figure 8.7 (continued)

OCEAN DEPTHS

```
301.3 304.5 312.6 312.0 325.6 302.0 299.8 297.6 304.6 314.7 326.8

287.6 294.5 302.4 315.6 320.9 315.7 300.2 312.7 308.7 324.5 322.8

320.8 342.5 342.5 323.5 333.7 341.6 350.5 367.7 354.2 342.8 330.9

312.6 312.0 325.6 301.3 304.5 302.0 314.7 326.8 299.8 297.6 304.6

302.4 308.7 324.5 315.6 287.6 294.5 320.9 315.7 300.2 312.7 322.8

320.8 333.7 341.6 350.5 367.7 354.2 342.8 342.5 342.5 323.5 330.9

312.0 325.6 326.8 302.0 299.8 297.6 304.6 314.7 301.3 304.5 312.6

294.5 302.4 315.6 320.9 315.7 300.2 312.7 308.7 324.5 287.6 322.8

320.8 342.5 323.5 333.7 341.6 350.5 367.7 342.5 354.2 342.8 330.9

312.0 304.6 314.7 326.8 301.3 304.5 312.6 325.6 302.0 299.8 297.6

312.7 308.7 324.5 322.8 287.6 294.5 302.4 315.6 320.9 315.7 300.2
```

NORTHERN HALF AVERAGE DEPTH 318.31 FEET

SOUTHERN HALF AVERAGE DEPTH 318.63 FEET

OVERALL AVERAGE DEPTH   318.02 FEET

8.4 Matrix Applications: Matrix Multiplication, *Solving Linear Systems, *Least Squares Curve Fitting

A two-dimensional array with numeric entries having m rows and n columns is called an $m \times n$ **matrix**. Matrices arise naturally in many problems in engineering and applied mathematics, and in this section we consider three examples.

EXAMPLE 1: Matrix Multiplication. One important operation of matrix algebra is matrix multiplication, defined as follows. Suppose that MAT1 is an L $\times$ M matrix and MAT2 is an M $\times$ N matrix. Note that the number of columns (M) in MAT1 is equal to the number of rows in MAT2; this must be the case for the product of MAT1 with MAT2 to be defined. The product PROD of MAT1 with MAT2 is an L $\times$ N matrix with the entry PROD(I,J) which appears in the Ith row and Jth column given by

PROD(I,J) = The sum of the products of the entries in row I of
MAT1 with the entries of column J of MAT2

= MAT1(I,1) * MAT2(1,J) + MAT1(I,2) * MAT2(2,J)
+ · · · + MAT1(I,M) * MAT2(M,J).

For example, suppose that MAT1 is the 2 × 3 matrix

$$\begin{bmatrix} 1 & 0 & 2 \\ 3 & 0 & 4 \end{bmatrix}$$

and MAT2 is the 3 × 4 matrix

$$\begin{bmatrix} 4 & 2 & 5 & 3 \\ 6 & 4 & 1 & 8 \\ 9 & 0 & 0 & 2 \end{bmatrix}$$

Because the number of columns (3) in MAT1 equals the number of rows in MAT2, the product matrix PROD is defined. The entry in the first row and the first column, PROD(1,1) is

$$1 * 4 + 0 * 6 + 2 * 9 = 22$$

Similarly, the entry PROD(1,2) in the first row and second column is

$$1 * 2 + 0 * 4 + 2 * 0 = 2$$

The complete product matrix PROD is the 2 × 4 matrix given by

$$\begin{bmatrix} 22 & 2 & 5 & 7 \\ 48 & 6 & 15 & 17 \end{bmatrix}$$

In general, the algorithm for multiplying matrices is as follows:

MATRIX MULTIPLICATION ALGORITHM

```
*   Algorithm to calculate the matrix product PROD of the          *
*   ROWS1 × COLS1 matrix MAT1 with the ROWS2 × COLS2               *
*   matrix MAT2. COLS1 must equal ROWS2 for the product to be       *
*   defined.                                                        *
```

1. If COLS1 does not equal ROWS2, the number of columns in MAT1 is not equal to the number of rows in MAT2, and the product PROD = MAT1 * MAT2 is not defined; terminate the algorithm. Otherwise, proceed with the following steps:
2. For an index I ranging from 1 to the number of rows ROWS1 of MAT1, do the following:
     For an index J ranging from 1 to the number of columns COLS2 of MAT2, do the following:
      (i) Set SUM equal to 0.
     (ii) For an index K ranging from 1 to the number of columns COLS1 of MAT1 (which is equal to the number of rows ROWS2 of MAT2):
            Add MAT1(I,K) * MAT2(K,J) to SUM.
    (iii) Set PROD(I,J) equal to SUM.

Figure 8.8 displays this algorithm as a flowchart.

The program in Figure 8.9 reads two matrices and uses this algorithm to calculate and display their product. Note that part of the output format identifier FORM used to display the product matrix is initialized in a DATA statement but that a repetition indicator is supplied at execution time. This repetition indicator is the number of columns in MAT2 and is obtained by reading the second dimension of MAT2 a second time as two characters and assigning them to the substring FORM(6:7).

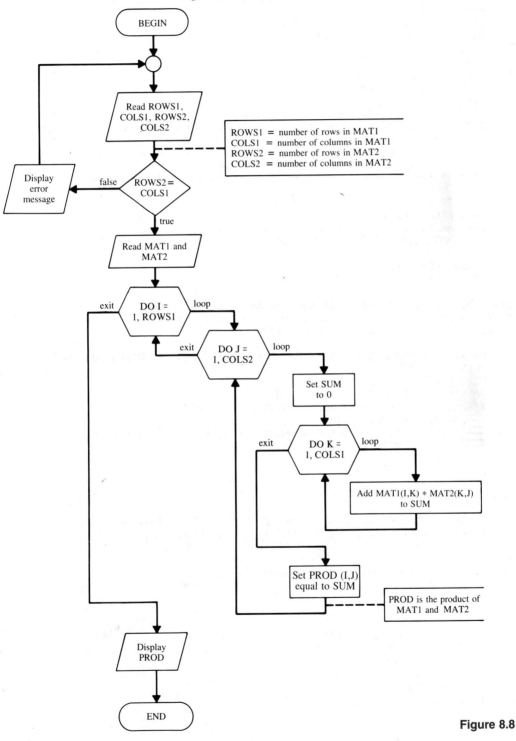

Figure 8.8

```
          PROGRAM MATMUL
**************************************************************************
* This program calculates the product of a ROWS1 X COLS1 matrix with   *
* a ROWS2 X COLS2 matrix (where COLS1 must equal ROWS2) producing a    *
* ROWS1 X COLS2 matrix.  Variables used are:                           *
*     LIMIT  : parameter specifying maximum dimensions of matrices     *
*     ROWS1  : # of rows in 1-st matrix                                *
*     COLS1  : # of columns in 1-st matrix                             *
*     ROWS2  : # of rows in 2-nd matrix                                *
*     COLS2  : # of columns in 2-nd matrix                             *
*     I,J,K  : subscripts                                              *
*     MAT1   : the first matrix                                        *
*     MAT2   : the second matrix                                       *
*     SUM    : sum of products of entries                             *
*     PROD   : the product of MAT1 and MAT2                            *
*     FORM   : character variable used to output PROD.  It is          *
*            : initialized as   '(1X, ##F8.2)'   and the repetition    *
*            : indicator  ##  will be replaced by the value of ROWS2   *
*            : entered during program execution.                      *
**************************************************************************

          INTEGER LIMIT
          PARAMETER (LIMIT = 10)
          INTEGER ROWS1, COLS1, ROWS2, COLS2, I, J, K
          REAL MAT1(LIMIT,LIMIT), MAT2(LIMIT,LIMIT), PROD(LIMIT,LIMIT),
     +        SUM
          CHARACTER*12 FORM
          DATA FORM /'(1X, ##F8.2)'/

* Read the actual dimensions of the two matrices MAT1 and
* MAT2 and set up the output format for the product matrix PROD.
* Repeat the following until COLS1 = ROWS2

10        PRINT *,'ENTER RIGHT-JUSTIFIED IN 2 SPACE ZONES THE DIMENSIONS OF'
          PRINT *, 'MATRIX 1:'
          READ '(2I2)', ROWS1, COLS1
          PRINT *, 'MATRIX 2:'
          READ '(2I2, TL2, A2)', ROWS2, COLS2, FORM(6:7)
          IF (COLS1 .NE. ROWS2) THEN
              PRINT *, '# OF COLUMNS OF MATRIX 1 MUST = # OF ROWS IN ',
     +                 'MATRIX 2'
              GO TO 10
          END IF

* Read in MAT1 and MAT2 (rowwise)

          PRINT *, 'ENTER THE ELEMENTS OF THE TWO MATRICES ROWWISE'
          READ *, ((MAT1(I,J), J = 1, COLS1), I = 1, ROWS1),
     +            ((MAT2(I,J), J = 1, COLS2), I = 1, ROWS2)

* Now calculate the product of MAT1 and MAT2

          DO 40 I = 1, ROWS1
              DO 30 J = 1, COLS2
                  SUM = 0
                  DO 20 K = 1, COLS1
                      SUM = SUM + MAT1(I,K) * MAT2(K,J)
20                CONTINUE
                  PROD(I,J) = SUM
30            CONTINUE
40        CONTINUE
```

Figure 8.9

322

Figure 8.9 **(continued)**

```
* Now print the matrix PROD

      PRINT *
      PRINT *, 'PRODUCT MATRIX IS:'
      DO 50 I = 1, ROWS1
          PRINT FORM, (PROD(I,J), J = 1, COLS2)
50    CONTINUE
      END
```

```
 Sample run:
 ==========

 ENTER RIGHT-JUSTIFIED IN 2 SPACE ZONES THE DIMENSIONS OF
 MATRIX 1:
 0203
 MATRIX 2:
 0405
 # OF COLUMNS OF MATRIX 1 MUST = # OF ROWS IN MATRIX 2
 ENTER RIGHT-JUSTIFIED IN 2 SPACE ZONES THE DIMENSIONS OF
 MATRIX 1:
 0203
 MATRIX 2:
 0304
 ENTER THE ELEMENTS OF THE TWO MATRICES ROWWISE
 1 0 2
 3 0 4

 4 2 5 3
 6 4 1 8
 9 0 0 2

 PRODUCT MATRIX IS:
    22.00    2.00    5.00    7.00
    48.00    6.00   15.00   17.00
```

EXAMPLE 2: Solving Linear Systems—Electrical Networks.   Consider the following electrical network containing six resistors and a battery:

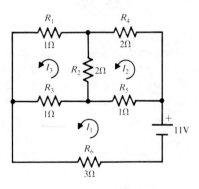

If the currents in the three loops are denoted by I_1, I_2, and I_3 (where current is considered positive when the flow is in the direction indicated by the arrows), then the current through resistor R_1 is I_3, the current through resistor R_2 is $2(I_2 - I_3)$, and so on. The voltage drop across a resistor is $R * I$, where R is the resistance in ohms and I is the current in amperes. One of Kirchhoff's laws states that the algebraic sum of the voltage drops around any loop is equal to the applied voltage. This law gives rise to the following **system of linear equations** for the loop currents I_1, I_2, and I_3:

$$3I_1 + 1(I_1 - I_2) + 1(I_1 - I_3) = 11$$

$$2I_2 + 2(I_2 - I_3) + 1(I_2 - I_1) = 0$$

$$1I_3 + 1(I_3 - I_1) + 2(I_3 - I_2) = 0$$

Collecting terms gives the simplified linear system

$$5I_1 - 1I_2 - 1I_3 = 11$$

$$-1I_1 + 5I_2 - 2I_3 = 0$$

$$-1I_1 - 2I_2 + 4I_3 = 0$$

This linear system can be written as the vector equation

$$Ax = b$$

where A is the **coefficient matrix**

$$A = \begin{bmatrix} 5 & -1 & -1 \\ -1 & 5 & -2 \\ -1 & -2 & 4 \end{bmatrix}$$

b is the **constant vector**

$$\mathbf{b} = \begin{bmatrix} 11 \\ 0 \\ 0 \end{bmatrix}$$

and **x** is the **vector of unknowns**

$$\mathbf{x} = \begin{bmatrix} I_1 \\ I_2 \\ I_3 \end{bmatrix}$$

To find the loop currents, we must solve this linear system; that is, we must find the values for I_1, I_2, and I_3 that satisfy these equations simultaneously.

One method for solving the linear system is called **Gaussian elimination.** To use this method, we first form the **augmented matrix** by adjoining the constant vector to the coefficient matrix. The augmented matrix for this example is

$$\begin{bmatrix} 5 & -1 & -1 & 11 \\ -1 & 5 & -2 & 0 \\ -1 & -2 & 4 & 0 \end{bmatrix}$$

We first eliminate I_1 from the second and third equations by multiplying the first row of the augmented matrix by 1/5 and adding this row to the second and third row:

$$\begin{bmatrix} 5.000 & -1.000 & -1.000 & 11.000 \\ 0 & 4.800 & -2.200 & 2.200 \\ 0 & -2.200 & 3.800 & 2.200 \end{bmatrix}$$

We then eliminate I_2 from the third equation by adding 2.200/4.800 times the second row of this matrix to the third row:

$$\begin{bmatrix} 5.000 & -1.000 & -1.000 & 11.000 \\ 0 & 4.800 & -2.200 & 2.200 \\ 0 & 0 & 2.792 & 3.208 \end{bmatrix}$$

This matrix corresponds to the following linear system:

$$5.000I_1 - 1.000I_2 - 1.000I_3 = 11.000$$

$$4.800I_2 - 2.200I_3 = 2.200$$

$$2.792I_3 = 3.208$$

It is clear from the last equation that the value of I_3 is 3.208/2.792 = 1.149. Substituting this value for I_3 in the second equation and solving for I_2 gives $I_2 = 0.985$, and substituting these values for I_2 and I_3 in the first equation gives $I_1 = 2.627$.

In general, the method of Gaussian elimination to solve a linear system is as follows:

GAUSSIAN ELIMINATION ALGORITHM

* Algorithm to solve the linear system AX = B, using Gaussian *
* elimination. A is the N × N coefficient matrix, B is the *
* N × 1 constant vector, and X is the N × 1 vector of unknowns. *

1. Form the N × (N + 1) augmented matrix AUG by adjoining B to A:
$$AUG = [A \mid B]$$
2. For I ranging from 1 to N, do the following:
   a. If AUG(I,I) = 0, interchange the Ith row of AUG with any row below it for which the coefficient of X(I) is nonzero. (If there is no such row, matrix A is said to be *singular*, and the system does not have a unique solution.)
   b. For J ranging from I + 1 to N, do the following:
      Add −AUG(J,I) / AUG(I,I) times the Ith row of AUG to the Jth row of AUG to eliminate X(I) from the Jth equation.
3. Set X(N) equal to AUG(N, N + 1) / AUG(N,N).
4. For J ranging from N − 1 to 1 in steps of −1, do the following:
   Substitute the values of X(J + 1), . . . , X(N) in the Jth equation and solve for X(J).

The program in Figure 8.10 implements this algorithm for Gaussian elimination.

```
      PROGRAM LINSYS
***********************************************************************
* Program to solve a linear system  using Gaussian elimination.     *
* Variables used are:                                               *
*     LIMIT  : parameter giving maximum dimensions of matrix        *
*     LIMAUG : parameter (LIMIT + 1) for maximum # columns in AUG   *
*     N      : number of equations and unknowns                     *
*     AUG    : augmented matrix for the linear system               *
*     X      : solution vector                                      *
*     I,J,K  : indices                                              *
*     MULT   : multiplier used to eliminate an unknown              *
*     PIVOT  : used to find nonzero diagonal entry                  *
***********************************************************************

      INTEGER LIMIT,LIMAUG
      PARAMETER (LIMIT = 10, LIMAUG = LIMIT + 1)
      REAL AUG(LIMIT,LIMAUG), X(LIMIT), MULT
      INTEGER I, J, K, PIVOT

* Read coefficient matrix and constant vector

      PRINT *, 'ENTER NUMBER OF EQUATIONS'
      READ *, N
      PRINT *, 'ENTER COEFFICIENT MATRIX ROWWISE'
      READ *, ((AUG(I,J), J = 1, N), I = 1, N)
      PRINT *, 'ENTER CONSTANT VECTOR'
      READ *, (AUG(I, N + 1), I = 1, N)

* Gaussian elimination

      DO 70 I = 1, N

*         Locate nonzero diagonal entry

          IF (AUG(I,I) .EQ. 0) THEN
              PIVOT = 0
              J = I + 1
30            IF ((PIVOT .EQ. 0) .AND. (J .LE. N)) THEN
                  IF (AUG(J,I) .NE. 0) PIVOT = J
                  J = J + 1
                  GO TO 30
              END IF
              IF (PIVOT .EQ. 0) THEN
                  STOP 'MATRIX IS SINGULAR'
              ELSE

*                 Interchange rows I and PIVOT

                  DO 40 J = 1, N + 1
                      TEMP = AUG(I,J)
                      AUG(I,J) = AUG(PIVOT,J)
                      AUG(PIVOT,J) = TEMP
40                CONTINUE
              END IF
          END IF
```

Figure 8.10

Figure 8.10 (continued)

```
*           Eliminate Ith unknown from equations I + 1, ..., N

            DO 60 J = I + 1, N
                MULT = -AUG(J,I) / AUG(I,I)
                DO 50 K = I, N + 1
                    AUG(J,K) = AUG(J,K) +  MULT * AUG(I,K)
50              CONTINUE
60          CONTINUE
70      CONTINUE

* Find the solutions

        X(N) = AUG(N, N + 1) / AUG(N,N)
        DO 90 J = N - 1, 1, -1
            X(J) = AUG(J, N + 1)
            DO 80 K = J + 1, N
                X(J) = X(J) - AUG(J,K) * X(K)
80          CONTINUE
            X(J) = X(J) / AUG(J,J)
90      CONTINUE
        PRINT *
        PRINT *, 'SOLUTION VECTOR IS'
        DO 110 I = 1, N
            PRINT 100, I, X(I)
100         FORMAT (1X, 'X(', I2, ') =', F6.3)
110     CONTINUE
        END


  Sample runs:
  ===========

  ENTER NUMBER OF EQUATIONS
  3
  ENTER COEFFICIENT MATRIX ROWWISE
   5 -1 -1
  -1  5 -2
  -1 -2  4
  ENTER CONSTANT VECTOR
  11  0  0

  SOLUTION VECTOR IS
  X( 1) = 2.627
  X( 2) = 0.985
  X( 3) = 1.149


  ENTER NUMBER OF EQUATIONS
  3
  ENTER COEFFICIENT MATRIX ROWWISE
  1 2 3
  1 2 4
  1 2 4
  ENTER CONSTANT VECTOR
  0 0 0
  **** STOP MATRIX IS SINGULAR
```

*EXAMPLE 3: Least Squares Curve Fitting. In Example 2 of Section 4.11, we described the method of least squares for finding the equation of a line that best fits a set of data points. This method can also be used to find best-fitting curves of higher degree. For example, to find the equation of the parabola

$$y = A + Bx + Cx^2$$

that best fits a set of n data points, the values of A, B, and C must be determined for which the sum of the squares of the deviations of the observed y values from the predicted y values (using the equation) is as small as possible. These values are found by solving the linear system

$$nA + (\Sigma x)B + (\Sigma x^2)C = \Sigma y$$

$$(\Sigma x)A + (\Sigma x^2)B + (\Sigma x^3)C = \Sigma xy$$

$$(\Sigma x^2)A + (\Sigma x^3)B + (\Sigma x^4)C = \Sigma x^2 y$$

This system can be solved using the program in Example 2.

Similar linear systems must be solved to find least squares curves of higher degree. For example, for a least squares cubic

$$y = A + Bx + Cx^2 + Dx^3$$

the coefficients A, B, C, and D can be found by solving the system of equations

$$nA + (\Sigma x)B + (\Sigma x^2)C + (\Sigma x^3)D = \Sigma y$$

$$(\Sigma x)A + (\Sigma x^2)B + (\Sigma x^3)C + (\Sigma x^4)D = \Sigma xy$$

$$(\Sigma x^2)A + (\Sigma x^3)B + (\Sigma x^4)C + (\Sigma x^5)D = \Sigma x^2 y$$

$$(\Sigma x^3)A + (\Sigma x^4)B + (\Sigma x^5)C + (\Sigma x^6)D = \Sigma x^3 y$$

Exercises

1. Assume that the following declarations have been made

```
INTEGER MAT(3,3), NUM(6), I, J
```

and that the following data are entered for those of the following statements that involve input:

```
1, 2, 3, 4, 5, 6, 7, 8, 9
```

For each of the following, tell what value (if any) is assigned to each array element, or explain why an error results:

(a)
```
      DO 20 I = 1, 3
         DO 10 J = 1, 3
            MAT(I,J) = I + J
10       CONTINUE
20 CONTINUE
```

(b)   DO 20 I = 1, 3
                    DO 10 J = 3, 1, -1
                          IF (I .EQ. J) THEN
                                MAT(I,J) = 0
                          ELSE
                                MAT(I,J) = 1
                          END IF
          10   CONTINUE
          20 CONTINUE

(c)   DO 20 I = 1, 3
                    DO 10 J = 1, 3
                          IF (I .LT. J) THEN
                                MAT(I,J) = -1
                          ELSE IF (I .EQ. J) THEN
                                MAT(I,J) = 0
                          ELSE
                                MAT(I,J) = 1
                          END IF
          10   CONTINUE
          20 CONTINUE

(d)   DO 30 I = 1, 3
                    DO 10 J = 1, I
                          MAT(I,J) = 0
          10   CONTINUE
                    DO 20 J = I + 1, J
                          MAT(I,J) = 2
          20   CONTINUE
          30 CONTINUE

(e)   DO 20 I = 1, 3
                    DO 10 J = 1, 3
                          READ *, MAT(I,J)
          10   CONTINUE
          20 CONTINUE

(f)   READ *, MAT

(g)   READ *, ((MAT(I,J), J = 1, 3), I = 1, 3)

(h)   READ *, ((MAT(J,I), I = 1, 3), J = 1, 3)

(i)   READ *, ((MAT(I,J), I = 1, 3), J = 1, 3)

(j)   DO 10 I = 1, 3
                    READ *, (MAT(I,J), J = 1, 3)
          10 CONTINUE

(k)   READ *, NUM
             DO 20 I = 1, 3
                    DO 10 J = 1, 3
                          MAT(I,J) = NUM(I) + NUM(J)
          10   CONTINUE
          20 CONTINUE

(l)
```
      READ *, NUM, (MAT(1,J), J = 1, 3)
      DO 20 I = 1, 2
          DO 10 J = 1, 3
              MAT(NUM(I + 1), NUM(J)) = NUM(I + J)
   10     CONTINUE
   20 CONTINUE
```

2. Write a program to add two $m \times n$ matrices (m rows and n columns). If A_{ij} and B_{ij} are the entries in the ith row and jth column of $m \times n$ matrices A and B, respectively, then $A_{ij} + B_{ij}$ is the entry in the ith row and jth column of the *sum*, which will also be an $m \times n$ matrix.

3. Modify the following program so that when the square array A is displayed, it has been changed into its transpose. The *transpose* of an $m \times n$ matrix A is the $n \times m$ matrix whose rows are the columns of A.

```
      PROGRAM MAT3
************************************************
* Program to read matrix A, change it to its   *
* transpose, and display it.                    *
************************************************
      INTEGER N
      REAL A(10,10)

      PRINT *, 'ENTER THE # OF ROWS (= # OF COLUMNS)'
      READ *, N

      READ 100, ((A(I,J), J = 1, N), I = 1, N)
  100 FORMAT(10F10.3)
*
*   Place your statements to replace A by its transpose here
*
      PRINT 110
  110 FORMAT(///,T30,'THE TRANSPOSE OF A',//)
      PRINT 120, ((A(I,J), J = 1, N), I = 1, N)
  120 FORMAT (1X, 10F10.3)
      END
```

4. Given the following program:

   a. Write declarations for all the arrays and other variables used in the program.
   b. Calculate (by hand) the values stored in arrays A, B, and C.
   c. Add statements to create array D = A * B + C (see Exercise 2 for the definition of matrix addition).
   d. Add statements to create array E, the transpose of array D (see the preceding exercise).

```
        PROGRAM MAT4
**********************************************
* Program to do various matrix calculations *
**********************************************

*
* Place your declaration statements here
*
        DO 20 I = 1, 3
            DO 10 J = 1, 3
                A(J,I) = I + J
                B(I,J) = I - J
10          CONTINUE
20      CONTINUE
        DO 40 I = 1, 3
            DO 30 J = 1, 3
                C(I,J) = 5
30          CONTINUE
40      CONTINUE
*
* Place your statements to calculate D here
*
        DO 50 I = 1, 3
            PRINT 60, (D(I, J), J = 1, 3)
60          FORMAT (1X, 3I7)
50      CONTINUE
*
* Place your statements to find E here
*
        PRINT *
        DO 70 I = 1, 3
            PRINT 60, (E(I,J),J=1,3)
70      CONTINUE
        END
```

5. A certain company manufactures four electronic devices using five different components that cost $10.95, $6.30, $14.75, $11.25, and $5.00, respectively. The number of components used in each device is given in the following table:

Device Number	Component Number				
	1	2	3	4	5
1	10	4	5	6	7
2	7	0	12	1	3
3	4	9	5	0	8
4	3	2	1	5	6

Write a program to:

(a) Calculate the total cost of each device.
(b) If the estimated labor cost for each device is 10 percent of the cost in part (a), calculate the total cost of producing each device.

6. A car manufacturer has collected some data on the noise level (measured in decibels) produced at 7 different speeds by 6 different

models of cars that it produces. This data is summarized in the following table:

Car	Speed (MPH)						
	20	30	40	50	60	70	80
1	88	90	94	102	111	122	134
2	75	77	80	86	94	103	113
3	80	83	85	94	100	111	121
4	68	71	76	85	96	110	125
5	77	84	91	98	105	112	119
6	81	85	90	96	102	109	120

Write a program that will display this table in a nice format, and calculate and display the average noise level for each car model, the average noise level at each speed, and the overall average noise level.

7. Write a program to calculate and print the first 10 rows of *Pascal's triangle*. The first part of the triangle has the form

```
          1
        1   1
      1   2   1
    1   3   3   1
  1   4   6   4   1
```

in which each row begins and ends with 1s and each other entry in a row is the sum of the two entries just above it. If the preceding form for the printout seems too challenging, you might have the printout appear as follows:

```
1
1 1
1 2 1
1 3 3 1
1 4 6 4 1
```

8. A *magic square* is an $n \times n$ matrix in which each of the integers 1, 2, 3, . . . , n^2 appears exactly once, and all column sums, row sums, and diagonal sums are equal. For example, the following is a 5 × 5 magic square in which all rows, columns, and diagonals sum to 65:

The following is a procedure for constructing an $n \times n$ magic square for any odd integer n. Place 1 in the middle of the top row. Then, after integer k has been placed, move up one row and to the right one column to place the next integer $k + 1$, unless one of the following occurs:

(a) If a move takes you above the top row in the jth column, move to the bottom of the jth column and place the integer there.

(b) If a move takes you outside to the right of the square in the ith row, place the integer in the ith row at the left side.

(c) If a move takes you to an already filled square, or if you move out of the square at the upper right-hand corner, place $k + 1$ immediately below k.

Write a program to construct a magic square for any odd value of n.

9. Suppose that each of the four edges of a thin square metal plate is maintained at a constant temperature and that we wish to determine the steady-state temperature at each interior point of the plate. To do this, we divide the plate into squares (the corners of which are called *nodes*) and find the temperature at each interior node by averaging the four neighboring temperatures; that is, if T_{ij} denotes the old temperature at the node in row i and column j, then

$$\frac{T_{i-1,j} + T_{i,j-1} + T_{i,j+1} + T_{i+1,j}}{4}$$

will be the new temperature.

To model the plate, we can use a two-dimensional array, with each array element representing the temperature at one of the nodes. Write a program that first reads the four constant temperatures (possibly different) along the edges of the plate, and some guess of the temperature at the interior points, and uses these values to initialize the elements of the array. Then determine the steady-state temperature at each interior node by repeatedly averaging the temperatures at its four neighbors, as just described. Repeat this procedure until the new temperature at each interior node differs from the old temperature by no more than some specified small amount. Then print the array and the number of iterations used to produce the final result. (It may also be of interest to print the array at each stage of the iteration.)

10. Write a program similar to that in Exercise 9 to find steady-state temperatures in a fireplace, a diagram of which follows. The north, west, and east wall temperatures are held constant, and the south wall is insulated. The steady-state temperatures at each interior node are to be calculated using the averaging process described in Exercise 9, but those for the nodes along the south wall are to be calculated using the formula

$$\frac{2T_{i-1,j} + T_{i,j-1} + T_{i,j+1}}{4}$$

Your program should read the constant north, west, and east temperatures and a constant fire wall temperature (e.g., 10, 50, 40, 1500), the number of row and columns in the grid (e.g., 4, 7), the numbers of the first and last rows of the fire and the first and last columns of the fire (e.g., 3, 4 and 3, 6), a small value to be used as a termination criterion (e.g., .0001), and an initial guess for the interior temperatures (e.g., 500).

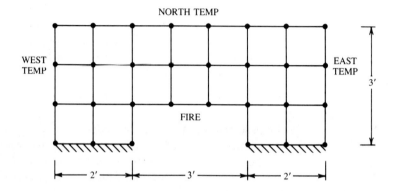

11. The game of *Life*, invented by the mathematician John H. Conway, is intended to model life in a society of organisms. Consider a rectangular array of cells, each of which may contain an organism. If the array is considered to extend indefinitely in both directions, each cell will have eight neighbors, the eight cells surrounding it. Births and deaths occur according to the following rules:

    (a) An organism is born in any empty cell that has exactly three neighbors.
    (b) An organism dies from isolation if it has fewer than two neighbors.
    (c) An organism dies from overcrowding if it has more than three neighbors.

    To illustrate, the following display shows the first five generations of a particular configuration of organisms:

    Write a program to play the game of Life and investigate the patterns produced by various initial configurations. Some configurations die off rather rapidly; others repeat after a certain number of generations; others change shape and size and may move across the array; and still others may produce "gliders" that detach themselves from the society and sail off into space.

12. A *Markov chain* is a system that moves through a discrete set of states in such a way that when the system is in state i there is probability P_{ij} that it will next move to state j. These probabilities are given by

a *transition matrix P*, whose (i,j) entry is P_{ij}. It is easy to show that the (i,j) entry of P^n then gives the probability of starting in state i and ending in state j after n steps.

One model of gas diffusion is known as the *Ehrenfest urn model*. In this model there are two urns A and B containing a given number of balls (molecules). At each instant, a ball is chosen at random and transferred to the other urn. This is a Markov chain if we take as a state the number of balls in urn A and let P_{ij} be the probability that a ball is transferred from A to B if there are i balls in urn A. For example, for four balls, the transition matrix P is given by

$$\begin{bmatrix} 0 & 1 & 0 & 0 & 0 \\ \frac{1}{4} & 0 & \frac{3}{4} & 0 & 0 \\ 0 & \frac{1}{2} & 0 & \frac{1}{2} & 0 \\ 0 & 0 & \frac{3}{4} & 0 & \frac{1}{4} \\ 0 & 0 & 0 & 1 & 0 \end{bmatrix}$$

Write a program that reads a transition matrix P for such a Markov chain and calculates and displays the value of n and P^n for several values of n. (See Example 1 of Section 8.4 for a description of matrix multiplication.)

13. A *directed graph,* or *digraph,* consists of a set of *vertices* and a set of *directed arcs* joining certain of these vertices. For example, the following diagram pictures a directed graph having five vertices numbered 1, 2, 3, 4, and 5, and seven directed arcs joining vertices 1 to 2, 1 to 4, 1 to 5, 3 to 1, 3 to itself, 4 to 3, and 5 to 1:

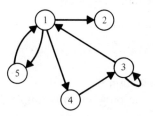

A directed graph having n vertices can be represented by its *adjacency matrix*, which is an $n \times n$ matrix, with the entry in the ith row and jth column a 1 if vertex i is joined to vertex j, 0 otherwise. The adjacency matrix for this graph is

$$\begin{bmatrix} 0 & 1 & 0 & 1 & 1 \\ 0 & 0 & 0 & 0 & 0 \\ 1 & 0 & 1 & 0 & 0 \\ 0 & 0 & 1 & 0 & 0 \\ 1 & 0 & 0 & 0 & 0 \end{bmatrix}$$

If A is the adjacency matrix for a directed graph, the entry in the ith row and jth column of A^k gives the number of ways that vertex j can be reached from vertex i by following k edges. Write a program to read the number of vertices in a directed graph and a collection of ordered pairs of vertices representing directed arcs, to construct the adjacency matrix, and then to find the number of ways that each vertex can be reached from every other vertex by following k edges for some value of k.

*14. Consider the following material balance problem: A solution that is 80 percent oil, 15 percent usable by-products, and 5 percent impurities enters a refinery. One output is 92 percent oil and 6 percent usable by-products. The other output is 60 percent oil and flows at the rate of 1000 L/h.

X L/h

	Assume	0.92X L/h OIL
Y L/h	no oil	0.06X L/h UBP
0.8Y L/h OIL	accumulates	0.02X L/h IMP
0.15Y L/h UBP		1000 L/h
0.05Y L/h IMP		

600 L/h OIL
1000V L/h UBP
1000W L/h IMP
$V + W = 0.4$

We thus have the following material balance equations:

Total:	$Y =\quad X + 1000$
Oil:	$0.8Y = 0.92X + 600$
Usable by-products:	$0.15Y = 0.06X + 1000V$
Impurities:	$0.05Y = 0.02X + 1000W$
Also:	$V + W = 0.4$

Substituting $W = 0.4 - V$ and using three of the first four equations, use the program in Example 2 of Section 8.4 to find a solution.

*15. Write a program to find the equation of the least squares parabola (see Example 3 of Section 8.4) for the following set of data points:

x	y
0.05	0.957
0.12	0.851
0.15	0.832
0.30	0.720
0.45	0.583
0.70	0.378
0.84	0.295
1.05	0.156

*16. Write a program to find the equation of the least squares cubic (see Example 3 of Section 8.4) for the set of data points in Exercise 15.

*17. The *inverse* of an $n \times n$ matrix A is a matrix A^{-1} for which the products $A * A^{-1}$ and $A^{-1} * A$ both are equal to the *identity matrix* having 1s on the diagonal from the upper left to the lower right and 0s elsewhere. An approximate inverse for matrix A can be calculated by solving the linear systems $A\mathbf{x} = \mathbf{b}$ for each of the following constant vectors $\mathbf{b}$:

$$\begin{bmatrix} 1 \\ 0 \\ 0 \\ \cdot \\ \cdot \\ \cdot \\ 0 \end{bmatrix} \begin{bmatrix} 0 \\ 1 \\ 0 \\ \cdot \\ \cdot \\ \cdot \\ 0 \end{bmatrix} \begin{bmatrix} 0 \\ 0 \\ 1 \\ \cdot \\ \cdot \\ \cdot \\ 0 \end{bmatrix} \cdots \begin{bmatrix} 0 \\ 0 \\ 0 \\ \cdot \\ \cdot \\ \cdot \\ 1 \end{bmatrix}$$

These solutions give the first, second, third, . . . , nth column of A^{-1}. Write a program that uses Gaussian elimination (see Example 2 of Section 8.4) to solve these linear systems and thus calculate the inverse of a matrix.

Programming Pointers

The difficulties encountered when using multidimensional arrays are similar to those for one-dimensional arrays, considered in the preceding chapter. The first three programming pointers that follow are simply restatements of some of the programming pointers in Chapter 7, and the reader should refer to those pointers for an expanded discussion.

1. *All arrays in a FORTRAN program must be dimensioned.*

2. *Arrays must be declared using constants or parameters to specify the dimensions.*

3. *Subscripts must be integer-valued and must stay within the range specified in the array declarations.*

4. *Unless some other order is specified, two-dimensional arrays are processed columnwise.* In general, the FORTRAN convention for processing multidimensional arrays is to vary each subscript over its entire range before varying the subscript that follows it. Any other processing order must be established by the programmer.

To illustrate, suppose that the two-dimensional array TABLE is declared by

```
INTEGER TABLE(3,4)
```

and the following data is to be read into the array:

```
11, 22, 27, 35, 39, 40, 48, 51, 57, 66, 67, 92
```

If these values are to be read and assigned in a rowwise manner so that the value of TABLE is the matrix

$$\begin{bmatrix} 11 & 22 & 27 & 35 \\ 39 & 40 & 48 & 51 \\ 57 & 66 & 67 & 92 \end{bmatrix}$$

then the following READ statement is appropriate:

```
READ *, ((TABLE(I,J), J = 1, 4), I = 1, 3)
```

If the values are to be read and assigned in a columnwise manner so that the value of TABLE is the matrix

$$\begin{bmatrix} 11 & 35 & 48 & 66 \\ 22 & 39 & 51 & 67 \\ 27 & 40 & 57 & 92 \end{bmatrix}$$

then the statements should be

```
READ * ((TABLE(I,J), I = 1, 3), J = 1,4)
```

or

```
READ *, TABLE
```

Variations and Extensions

As in the case of one-dimensional arrays, other versions of FORTRAN allow only a few variations from or extensions to the array-processing features of standard FORTRAN. Two that we noted at the end of Chapter 7 were:

- Real subscripts may be allowed. In this case, the fractional part is truncated, and the remaining integer part is used for the subscript.

- Compile-time initialization may be done using type statements.

  See Appendix F for additional details.

9 Functions and Subroutines

Great things can be reduced to small things, and small things can be reduced to nothing.

CHINESE PROVERB

The problems we have considered thus far have been simple enough that algorithms for their complete solution are quite straightforward. As we noted in Chapter 2, more complex problems are best solved using a **top-down** approach that uses a **divide-and-conquer** strategy to divide a problem into a number of simpler subproblems. Each of these subproblems is then considered individually, and in some cases it may be necessary to divide them further until the resulting subproblems are simple enough that algorithms for their solution can be easily designed. The complete algorithm for the original problem is then described in terms of these subalgorithms. **Subprograms** or **modules** can be written to implement each of these subalgorithms, and these subprograms combined to give a complete program that solves the original problem. In FORTRAN these subprograms are **functions** and **subprograms** whose execution is controlled by some other program unit, either the main program or some other subprogram.

Because the program units in this modular style of programming are independent of one another, the programmer can write each module and test it without worrying about the details of the other modules. This makes it considerably easier to locate an error when it arises, because it often occurs in the module most recently written and added to the program and the effects of these modules are easily isolated. Programs developed in this manner are also usually easier to understand because the structure of each program unit can be studied independently of that of the other program units.

9.1 Library Functions and Statement Functions

The FORTRAN language provides many **intrinsic,** or **library functions.** These library functions include not only the numeric functions introduced in Chapter 3 but also a number of other numeric functions, as well as character and logical functions. Table 9.1 gives a complete list of the standard FORTRAN library functions.

Table 9.1 Standard FORTRAN library functions.

FORTRAN Function	Description	Type of Arguments*	Type of Value
ABS(x)	Absolute value of x	I, R, DP C	Same as argument R
ACOS(x)	Arccosine (in radians) of x	R, DP	Same as argument
AIMAG(z)	Imaginary part of z (Section 10.2)	C	R
AINT(x)	Value resulting from truncation of fractional part of x	R, DP	Same as argument
ANINT(x)	x rounded to the nearest integer INT(x + .5) if $x \geq 0$ INT(x − .5) if $x < 0$	R, DP	Same as argument
ASIN(x)	Arcsine (in radians) of x	R, DP	Same as argument
ATAN(x)	Arctangent (in radians) of x	R, DP	Same as argument
ATAN2(x,y)	Arctangent (in radians) of x / y	R, DP	Same as argument
CHAR(i)	Character in ith position of the collating sequence (Section 11.3)	I	Character
CMPLX(x,y)	The complex number (x,y) (Section 10.2)	I, R, DP	C
CMPLX(x)	The complex number $(x,0)$ if x is type I, R, or DP; the complex number x if x is type C (Section 10.2)	I, R, DP, C	C
CONJG(z)	Conjugate of z (Section 10.2)	C	C
COS(x)	Cosine of x (in radians)	R, DP, C	Same as argument
COSH(x)	Hyperbolic cosine of x	R, DP	Same as argument
DBLE(x)	Conversion of x to double precision (Section 10.1)	I, R, DP, C	DP
DIM(x,y)	$x − y$ if $x \geq y$ 0 if $x < y$	I, R, DP	Same as argument
DPROD(x,y)	Double precision product of x and y (Section 10.1)	R	DP
EXP(x)	Exponential function e^x	R, DP, C	Same as argument
ICHAR(c)	Position of c in the collating sequence (Section 11.3)	Character	I
INDEX(c_1,c_2)	Location of substring c_2 in string c_1 (Section 11.2)	Character	I

Table 9.1 Standard FORTRAN library functions (cont.).

FORTRAN Function	Description	Type of Arguments*	Type of Value
INT(x)	Conversion of x to integer type; sign of x or real part of x times the greatest integer $\leq$ ABS(x)	I, R, DP, C	I
LEN(c)	Length of character string c (Section 11.2)	Character	I
LGE(c_1,c_2) LGT(c_1,c_2) LLE(c_1,c_2) LLT(c_1,c_2)	Value of true if, and only if, c_1 is lexically greater than or equal to c_2, greater than c_2, less than or equal to c_2, less than c_2, respectively (Section 11.3)	Character	Logical
LOG(x)	Natural logarithm of x	R, DP, C	Same as argument
LOG10(x)	Common (base 10) logarithm of x	R, DP	Same as argument
MAX($x_1, \ldots, x_n$)	Maximum of $x_1, \ldots, x_n$	I, R, DP	Same as arguments
MIN($x_1, \ldots, x_n$)	Minimum of $x_1, \ldots, x_n$	I, R, DP	Same as arguments
MOD(x,y)	$x(\bmod y)$; $x - \text{INT}(x / y) * y$	I, R, DP	Same as arguments
NINT(x)	x rounded to the nearest integer [See ANINT(x)]	R, DP	I
REAL(x)	Conversion of x to real type (Sections 10.1 and 10.2)	I, R, DP, C	R
SIGN(x,y)	Transfer of sign: ABS(x) if $y \geq 0$ $-$ABS(x) if $y < 0$	I, R, DP	Same as arguments
SIN(x)	Sine of x (in radians)	R, DP, C	Same as argument
SINH(x)	Hyperbolic sine of x	R, DP	Same as argument
SQRT(x)	Square root of x	R, DP, C	Same as argument
TAN(x)	Tangent of x (in radians)	R, DP	Same as argument
TANH(x)	Hyperbolic tangent of x	R, DP	Same as argument

*I = integer, R = real, DP = double precision, C = complex. Types of arguments in a given function reference must be the same.

As we have seen, any of these functions may be used to calculate some value in an expression by giving its name followed by the actual arguments to which it is to be applied, enclosed in parentheses. For example, if ALPHA, NUM1, NUM2, SMALL, BETA, and X are decared by

```
INTEGER ALPHA, NUM1, NUM2, SMALL
REAL BETA, X
```

then the statements

```
PRINT *, ABS(X)
ALPHA = NINT(100.0 * BETA) / 100
SMALL = MIN(0, NUM1, NUM2)
```

display the absolute value of X, assign to ALPHA the value of BETA rounded to the nearest hundredth, and assign to SMALL the smallest of the three integers 0, NUM1, and NUM2.

In some programs it may be convenient for the user to define additional functions. Such **user-defined functions** are possible in FORTRAN, and once defined, they are used in the same way as are the library functions. In this section we define **statement functions**, which are the simplest user-defined functions, and in the next section we consider **function subprograms.**

A statement function must be defined by a single statement of the form

> *name(argument-list)* $=$ *expression*

where *argument-list* is a list (possibly empty) of variables separated by commas. The *expression* may contain constants, variables, formulas, or references to library functions, to previously defined statement functions, or to functions defined by subprograms, but not references to the function being defined. *Such statements must appear in the program unit in which the functions are referenced, and they must be placed after the specification statements and before all executable statements.*

In a statement defining a function, the function *name* may be any legal FORTRAN name. It must differ from other function and variable names in the same program unit. The type of the value of the function is determined by the type of its name. The variables in the argument list are called **formal arguments** and indicate the number, order, and type of arguments of the function. For example,

```
REAL A, B, HYPO
HYPO(A, B) = SQRT(A ** 2 + B ** 2)
```

define a real-valued function of two real arguments.

The arguments in a function reference are called **actual arguments.** When a function is referenced, the values of these actual arguments become the values of the corresponding formal arguments and are used in computing the value of the function. For example, if X, Y, and Z have been declared to be real variables and the values of X and Y are 3.0 and 4.0, respectively, then in the statement

```
Z = HYPO(X, Y)
```

the values of the actual arguments X and Y become the values of the formal arguments A and B, respectively. The value of the function

$$\sqrt{3.0^2 + 4.0^2} = 5.0$$

is then computed and assigned to Z.

Because of this association between actual arguments and formal arguments, *the number and type of the actual arguments must agree with the number and type of the formal arguments.* To illustrate, consider the statements

```
INTEGER M, N, NUMBER, K, L, J1, J2
REAL X, BETA
NUMBER(M, N, X) = M * INT(X) + N
```

which define an integer-valued function of three variables, the first two of integer type and the third of real type. The function reference

```
PRINT *, NUMBER(K, 2, BETA)
```

is legal, but

```
J1 = NUMBER(L, 2)
J2 = NUMBER(L, 2.5, BETA)
```

are not, because the first function reference has an incorrect number of arguments, and in the second the argument 2.5 is not the correct type.

The variable names used for formal arguments may also be used for some other purpose elsewhere in the program. For example, if the function POLY is defined by the statements

```
REAL X, Y, POLY, A, B
INTEGER K, M
POLY(X, Y, K) = X ** K + 3.5 * Y ** K
```

then the statements

```
X = POLY(A, B, 3) - A ** 4
Y = .5 * POLY(1.0, X + 4, M - 3)
```

can be used in the program, provided, of course, that A, B, and M are assigned values before they are used in these statements.

The expression used to define a function may also contain variables that do not appear in the argument list. For example, if the function F is defined by

```
REAL X, A, F, BETA
F(X) = X ** 2 + A
```

then the following statements assign the value 19.5 to BETA:

```
A = 3.5
BETA = F(4.0)
```

It is also possible to define functions whose arguments and/or values are of logical or character type. For example, the statements

```
CHARACTER*10 STRA, STRB, JOIN*21
LOGICAL XOR, P, Q
JOIN(STRA, STRB) = STRA // ' ' // STRB
XOR(P, Q) = (P .OR. Q) .AND. .NOT. (P .AND. Q)
```

define a function JOIN of character type whose values are strings of length 21 and whose arguments are of character type with length 10, and a logical-valued function XOR, whose arguments are of logical type.

To illustrate the use of statement functions, we consider once again the problem of approximating the definite integral of a function. In Example 1 of Section 4.11 we approximated the integral

$$\int_a^b (x^2 + 1)\, dx$$

using the rectangle method. In the program in Figure 4.27, we used the expression X**2 + 1 to calculate the function values within the loop that accumulated the areas of the approximating rectangles.

Although this program correctly calculated the approximate value of the integral, it is preferable to separate the definition of the function from the part of the program that calculates the approximation of the integral. This approach indicates clearly what function is being integrated and thus what part of the program must be changed in order to integrate some other function. The program in Figure 9.1 is a modification of the program in Figure 4.27 that uses a statement function to define the function to be integrated.

```
      PROGRAM AREA
*************************************************************************
* Program to approximate the integral of a function over the interval  *
* [A,B] using the rectangle method with altitudes chosen at the        *
* midpoints of the subintervals.  Variables used are:                  *
*     A, B   : the endpoints of the interval of integration            *
*     N      : the number of subintervals used                         *
*     I      : counter                                                  *
*     DELX   : the length of the subintervals                          *
*     X      : the midpoint of one of the subintervals                 *
*     F      : the function being integrated                           *
*     SUM    : the approximating sum                                    *
*************************************************************************

      REAL F, A, B, X, DELX, SUM
      INTEGER N, I

      F(X) = X ** 2 + 1

      PRINT *, 'ENTER THE INTERVAL ENDPOINTS AND THE # OF SUBINTERVALS'
      READ *, A, B, N
      DELX = (B - A) / N

* Initialize the approximating SUM and set X equal to
* the midpoint of the first subinterval

      SUM = 0
      X = A + DELX / 2
```

Figure 9.1

Figure 9.1 **(continued)**

```
* Now calculate and display the sum

      DO 10 I = 1, N
         SUM = SUM + F(X)
         X = X + DELX
10    CONTINUE
      SUM = DELX * SUM
      PRINT *, 'APPROXIMATE VALUE USING ', N, ' SUBINTERVALS IS ', SUM
      END
```

```
Sample runs:
===========

ENTER THE INTERVAL ENDPOINTS AND THE # OF SUBINTERVALS
0, 1, 10
APPROXIMATE VALUE USING          10 SUBINTERVALS IS      1.33250


ENTER THE INTERVAL ENDPOINTS AND THE # OF SUBINTERVALS
0, 1, 20
APPROXIMATE VALUE USING          20 SUBINTERVALS IS      1.33312


ENTER THE INTERVAL ENDPOINTS AND THE # OF SUBINTERVALS
0, 1, 100
APPROXIMATE VALUE USING         100 SUBINTERVALS IS      1.33332
```

9.2 Function Subprograms

A statement function consists of a single statement and thus can be used only to define a function whose definition can be given by a single formula. Also, a statement function must be defined within the program unit in which it is referenced. In contrast, a **function subprogram** consists of several statements and thus makes possible the definition of a function whose value cannot be specified by a single expression. Moreover, subprograms are separate program units. Consequently, once a subprogram has been prepared and saved in a user's library, it may be used in any program, by simply attaching it to that program.

The syntax of a function subprogram is similar to that of a FORTRAN (main) program:

> FUNCTION statement
> Declaration part
> Subprogram statements
> END

The first statement must be a **FUNCTION statement** of the form

> FUNCTION *name(argument-list)*

Here *name* is the name of the function and must follow the usual naming rules, with the type of the function name determining the type of the value of this function; *argument-list* is a list (possibly empty) of variables separated by commas. These variables are **formal arguments** and indicate the number, order, and types of the arguments of the function.

Like the main program, a subprogram should also include opening documentation to describe briefly what the subprogram does, what its arguments and other variables represent, and other information that explains the subprogram. These opening comments and the rest of the subprogram must conform to the usual rules governing FORTRAN programs. For example, DIMENSION, type, and DATA statements must precede all of the executable statements in the subprogram.

At least one of the executable statements should assign a value to the function. Normally, this is done with an assignment statement of the form

name = expression

The *expression* may be any expression involving constants, the formal arguments of the function, other variables already assigned values in this subprogram, as well as references to other functions.

The last statement of the subprogram must be

END

The value of the function is returned to the program unit that references the function when the END statement or a **RETURN statement** of the form

RETURN

is executed.[1]

Functions defined by subprograms are referenced in the same manner as are other functions we have considered. Care must be taken to ensure that the actual arguments have the same types as do the formal arguments listed in the FUNCTION statement. In the case of character arguments, the length of the actual argument must be at least as great as the length of the corresponding formal argument.

---

[1] Some versions of FORTRAN require that every subprogram include a RETURN statement to return control to the program unit that referenced the subprogram. In these versions, the END statement is a nonexecutable statement that serves only to mark the physical end of the subprogram.

As an example, suppose we wish to use the function

$$f(x,y) = \begin{cases} x + 1 & \text{if } x < y \\ x^n + y^n & \text{if } x \geq y \end{cases}$$

The following function subprogram defines this function:

```
FUNCTION F(X, Y, N)
REAL F, X, Y
INTEGER N

IF (X .LT. Y) THEN
    F = X + 1
ELSE
    F = X ** N + Y ** N
END IF
END
```

This function F can then be referenced by such statements as

```
W = F(A, B + 3.0, 2)
Z = F(TOP(I), SIN(A), K)
IF (F(1.1, BETA, 2) .LT. EPS) DONE = .TRUE.
```

provided the types of the actual arguments used in these statements match those of the formal arguments X, Y, and N.

As another example, we consider again the problem of approximating the definite integral of a function. In the preceding section, we used a statement function to define the function being integrated. However, a statement function could not be used to define the integrand

$$f(x) = \begin{cases} 1 & \text{if } x < 0 \\ 1 - x^2 & \text{if } 0 \leq x \leq 1 \\ \ln x & \text{if } x > 1 \end{cases}$$

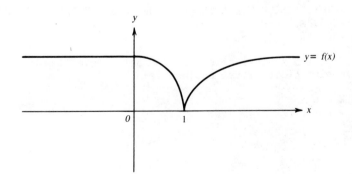

In this case, this function can easily be defined using a function subprogram:

```
**F(X)*********************************************
* Function subprogram that defines the integrand  *
***************************************************

      FUNCTION F(X)

      REAL X, F

      IF (X .LT. 0) THEN
          F = 1
      ELSE IF (X .LE. 1.0) THEN
          F = 1 - X ** 2
      ELSE
          F = LOG(X)
      END IF
      END
```

This subprogram is used in the program in Figure 9.2, which approximates the definite integral of a function.

```
      PROGRAM AREA
**********************************************************************
* Program to approximate the integral of a function over the interval  *
* [A,B] using the rectangle method with altitudes chosen at the        *
* midpoints of the subintervals.  Variables used are:                  *
*      A, B   : the endpoints of the interval of integration           *
*      N      : the number of subintervals used                        *
*      I      : counter                                                 *
*      DELX   : the length of the subintervals                         *
*      X      : the midpoint of one of the subintervals                *
*      F      : the function being integrated                          *
*      SUM    : the approximating sum                                   *
**********************************************************************

      REAL F, A, B, X, DELX, SUM
      INTEGER N, I

      PRINT *, 'ENTER THE INTERVAL ENDPOINTS AND THE # OF SUBINTERVALS'
      READ *, A, B, N
      DELX = (B - A) / N

* Initialize the approximating SUM and set X equal to
* the midpoint of the first subinterval

      SUM = 0
      X = A + DELX / 2
```

Figure 9.2

Figure 9.2 (continued)

```
* Now calculate and display the sum

      DO 10 I = 1, N
         SUM = SUM + F(X)
         X = X + DELX
10    CONTINUE
      SUM = DELX * SUM
      PRINT *, 'APPROXIMATE VALUE USING ', N, ' SUBINTERVALS IS ', SUM
      END

**F(X)*****************************************
* Function subprogram that defines the integrand *
**********************************************

      FUNCTION F(X)

      REAL X, F

      IF (X .LT. 0) THEN
         F = 1
      ELSE IF (X .LE. 1.0) THEN
         F = 1 - X ** 2
      ELSE
         F = LOG(X)
      END IF
      END


Sample runs:
===========

ENTER THE INTERVAL ENDPOINTS AND THE # OF SUBINTERVALS
-1, 0, 1
APPROXIMATE VALUE USING            1 SUBINTERVALS IS      1.00000


ENTER THE INTERVAL ENDPOINTS AND THE # OF SUBINTERVALS
-2, 2, 50
APPROXIMATE VALUE USING           50 SUBINTERVALS IS      3.05122


ENTER THE INTERVAL ENDPOINTS AND THE # OF SUBINTERVALS
-2, 2, 100
APPROXIMATE VALUE USING          100 SUBINTERVALS IS      3.05311
```

Another function that cannot be defined by a statement function is the **factorial function.** The factorial of a nonnegative integer n is denoted by $n!$ and is defined by

$$n! = \begin{cases} 1 \text{ if } n = 0 \\ 1 \cdot 2 \cdot 3 \cdot \ \cdots \ \cdot n \text{ if } n > 0 \end{cases}$$

This function can be defined by the following function subprogram:

```
**FACTOR****************************************************
* Function to calculate the factorial N! of N which *
* is 1 if N = 0, 1 * 2 * · · · * N if N > 0. It     *
* uses I as a counter.                               *
************************************************************


      FUNCTION FACTOR (N)

      INTEGER FACTOR, N, I

      FACTOR = 1
      IF (N .GT. 0) THEN
          DO 10 I = 2, N
              FACTOR = FACTOR * I
10        CONTINUE
      END IF
      END
```

The program in Figure 9.4 uses this subprogram in calculating values of the **Poisson probability function**, which is the probability function of a random variable such as the number of radioactive particles striking a given target in a given period of time, the number of flaws in a given length of magnetic tape, or the number of failures in an electronic device during a given time period. This function is defined by

$$P(n) = \frac{\lambda^n \cdot e^{-\lambda}}{n!}$$

where

λ = the average number of of occurrences of the phenomenon per time period
n = the number of occurrences in that time period

For example, if the average number of particles passing through a counter during 1 millisecond in a laboratory experiment is 3 ($\lambda = 3$), then the probability that exactly five particles enter the counter ($n = 5$) in a given millisecond will be

$$P(5) = \frac{3^5 \cdot e^{-3}}{5!} = 0.1008$$

The program in Figure 9.4 reads values for N and LAMBDA, references the function subprogram POISS, which calculates the Poisson probability, and displays this probability. The value of N! is obtained by the function POISS from the function subprogram FACTOR. This program implements the algorithm shown in flowchart form in Figure 9.3. Note the use of double-lined rectangles to indicate references to subprograms.

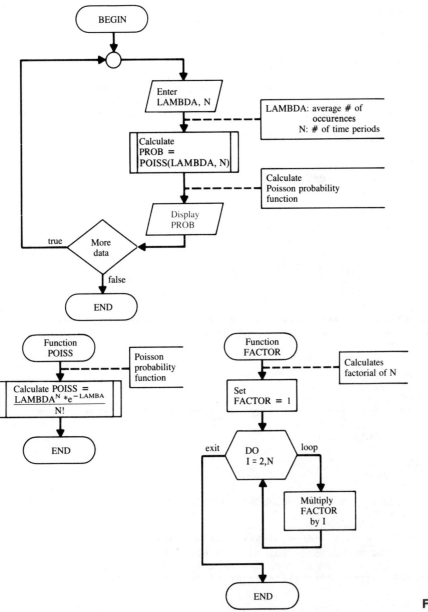

Figure 9.3

```
      PROGRAM PROB
***********************************************************************
* Program to calculate the Poisson probability function using the     *
* function subprogram POISS.  Variables used are:                     *
*     LAMBDA : average # of occurrences of phenomenon per time period *
*     N      : number of occurrences in a time period                 *
*     PROB   : Poisson probability                                    *
*     RESPON : user response                                          *
***********************************************************************
```

Figure 9.4

Figure 9.4   (continued)

```
      REAL LAMBDA, POISS, PROB
      INTEGER N
      CHARACTER*3 RESPON

      PRINT *, 'THIS PROGRAM CALCULATES THE POISSON PROBABILITY FOR'
      PRINT *, 'LAMBDA = AVERAGE # OF OCCURRENCES PER TIME PERIOD'
      PRINT *, 'N = # OF OCCURRENCES FOR WHICH PROBABILITY TO BE FOUND'

* Repeat the following until user response = NO

10          PRINT *
            PRINT *, 'ENTER LAMBDA AND N'
            READ *, LAMBDA, N
            PROB = POISS(LAMBDA, N)
            PRINT 20, PROB
20          FORMAT (1X, 'POISSON PROBABILITY = ', F6.4)
            PRINT *, 'MORE (YES OR NO)'
            READ '(A)', RESPON
      IF (RESPON .NE. 'NO') GO TO 10

      END


**POISS***********************************************************************
* Function to calculate the Poisson probability                            *
*                          N    -LAMBDA                                     *
*                    LAMBDA * e                                             *
*         POISS(N) = -------------------                                    *
*                          N!                                               *
* Function FACTOR is called to calculate N!                                *
*****************************************************************************

      FUNCTION POISS(LAMBDA, N)

      INTEGER N, FACTOR
      REAL POISS, LAMBDA

      POISS = (LAMBDA ** N * EXP(-LAMBDA)) / FACTOR(N)
      END


**FACTOR**********************************************************************
* Function to calculate the factorial N! of N which is 1 if N = 0,         *
* 1 * 2 * ... * N for N > 0.  It uses variable I as a  counter.            *
*****************************************************************************

      FUNCTION FACTOR(N)

      INTEGER FACTOR, N, I

      FACTOR = 1
      IF (N .GT. 0) THEN
          DO 10 I = 1, N
              FACTOR = FACTOR * I
10          CONTINUE
      END IF
      END
```

Figure 9.4 (continued)

```
Sample run:
==========

THIS PROGRAM CALCULATES THE POISSON PROBABILITY FOR
LAMBDA = AVERAGE # OF OCCURRENCES PER TIME PERIOD
N = # OF OCCURRENCES FOR WHICH PROBABILITY TO BE FOUND

ENTER LAMBDA AND N
3, 5
POISSON PROBABILITY = 0.1008
MORE (YES OR NO)
YES

ENTER LAMBDA AND N
4, 6
POISSON PROBABILITY = 0.1042
MORE (YES OR NO)
NO
```

The order in which subprograms are arranged following the main program is irrelevant. Thus, in Figure 9.4, the subprogram FACTOR could just as well precede the subprogram POISS. Notice that there is no conflict between statement numbers in different program units; for example, both the main program and the subprogram FACTOR have a statement numbered 10. Similarly, variables that are not arguments and that appear in separate program units may have the same name. No conflict results, because these are independent program units connected only via the function name and the arguments. The relationship between variables in different program units is considered in detail in Sections 9.6 and 9.8.

Normally when control returns from a subprogram, all variables in the subprogram that are not arguments become undefined. (Exceptions include variables initialized by a DATA statement within that subprogram that are not redefined and variables in common blocks, as described in Section 9.8.) In particular, this means that the values of such variables are not available in subsequent references to the subprogram. If it is necessary to save their values from one execution of the subprogram to the next, this can be accomplished by listing their names in a **SAVE statement** of the form

> SAVE *list*

If *list* is omitted, all such variables in the subprogram will be saved. The program in Figure 9.10 of the next section illustrates the use of the SAVE statement.

As another example of function subprograms, consider the following:

```
CHARACTER*20 STR, SUBSTR*10
INTEGER NUM, LOCATE, LOC
     :
     :
LOC = LOCATE(STR, SUBSTR, NUM)
     :
     :
END
```

```
**LOCATE*********************************************
* Function to search STRA for the substring     *
* consisting of the first N characters of STRB  *
****************************************************

      FUNCTION LOCATE(STRA, STRB, N)

      CHARACTER*20 STRA, STRB*10
      INTEGER LOCATE, N

      LOCATE = INDEX(STRA, STRB(1:N))
      END
```

We could also specify the type and lengths of the formal arguments STRA and STRB using the **assumed length specifier** (∗) in the statement

```
CHARACTER*(*) STRA, STRB
```

In this case, the lengths of STRA and STRB are taken to be the same as the lengths of the corresponding actual arguments STR and SUBSTR, respectively. Thus, STRA is assumed to be of length 20 and STRB of length 10.

As illustrated in the examples, *the type of a function must be declared both in the subprogram defining the function and in each program unit that references the function.* The declaration in the subprogram can be done in two ways. The first method is to list the function name in a type statement in the subprogram, as we have done in our examples thus far and as illustrated in the following:

```
FUNCTION PHI(X, Y)
INTEGER PHI
REAL X, Y
     :
     :
END
```

```
FUNCTION TRUN(STRING, N)
CHARACTER*15 STRING, TRUN*10
INTEGER N
     :
     :
END
```

In the last example, we could specify the type and length of the function TRUN and/or the formal arguments STRING using the assumed length specifier (*) as follows:

```
FUNCTION TRUN(STRING, N)
CHARACTER*(*) STRING, TRUN
INTEGER N
```

In this case, the length of TRUN is the length specified in the program unit referencing the function, and the length of STRING is the length of the corresponding actual argument.

The second method of declaring the type of a function is to use a modified form of the FUNCTION statement in which the type of the function is placed before the word FUNCTION. Thus, the preceding examples could also be written

```
INTEGER FUNCTION PHI(X, Y)
REAL X, Y

CHARACTER*10 FUNCTION TRUN(STRING, N)
CHARACTER*15 STRING
INTEGER N
```

or using the assumed length specifier in the last example,

```
CHARACTER*(*) FUNCTION TRUN(STRING, N)
CHARACTER*(*) STRING
INTEGER N
```

Exercises

1. Write a statement function RANGE that calculates the range between two integers, that is, the larger integer minus the smaller one.

2. Write a real-valued statement function ROUND that has a real argument AMOUNT and an integer argument N, and returns the value of AMOUNT rounded to N places. For example, the function references ROUND(10.536, 0), ROUND(10.536, 1), and ROUND(10.536, 2) should give the values 11.0, 10.5, and 10.54, respectively.

3. Write a program to accept a temperature and the letter C or F, indicating that it is Celsius or Fahrenheit, respectively, and that then uses an appropriate function to convert the temperature to the other scale. (One of the conversion formulas is $F = \frac{9}{5}C + 32$.)

4. The number of bacteria in a culture can be estimated by

$$N \cdot e^{kt}$$

where N is the initial population, k is a rate constant, and t is time. Write a statement function to calculate the number of bacteria present at time t for given values of k and N; use it in a program that reads values for the initial population, the rate constant, and the time (e.g., 1000, 0.15, 100), and displays the number of bacteria at that time.

5. Using statement functions to define the logical functions

$$\sim p \wedge \sim q \qquad (\text{not } p \text{ and not } q)$$

and

$$\sim(p \vee q) \qquad (\text{not}(p \text{ or } q))$$

write a program to calculate and print truth tables for these logical expressions.

6. Write a logical-valued function that determines whether a character is one of the digits 0 through 9. Use it in a program that reads several characters and checks to see whether each is a digit.

7. Write a statement function that defines the logical-valued function HASUM with two logical arguments, A and B, and with a value that represents the sum output of a binary half-adder with inputs A and B. Write another statement function to give the carry output for this half-adder. Then use these functions in a program that implements a binary full-adder, as described in Exercise 2 of Section 6.2.

8. If an amount of A dollars is borrowed at an interest rate r (expressed as a decimal) for y years and n is the number of payments to be made per year, then the amount of each monthly payment is given by

$$\frac{r \cdot A/n}{1 - \left(1 + \dfrac{r}{n}\right)^{-n \cdot y}}$$

Define a statement function to calculate these payments. Use it in a program that reads several values for the amount borrowed, the interest rate, the number of years, and the number of payments per year and, for each set of values, displays the corresponding monthly payment.

9. (a) Write a real-valued function NGRADE that accepts a letter grade and returns the corresponding numeric value (A = 4.0, B = 3.0, C = 2.0, D = 1.0, F = 0.0).
  (b) Write a character-valued function LGRADE that assigns a letter grade to an integer score using the following grading scale:

    90–100: A
    80–89: B
    70–79: C
    60–69: D
  Below 60: F

(c) Use these functions in a program that reads several scores and, for each, displays the corresponding letter grades and numeric value.

10. Write a program to calculate *binomial coefficients*

$$\binom{n}{k} = \frac{n!}{k!(n - k)!}$$

using a function subprogram to calculate factorials. Let n run from 1 through 10, and for each such n, let k run from 0 through n.

11. Suppose that in an experiment the probability that a certain outcome will occur is p; then $1 - p$ is the probability that it will not occur. The probability that out of n trials the desired outcome will occur exactly k times is given by

$$\binom{n}{k} p^k (1 - p)^{n-k}$$

Write a program to calculate this probability for several values of n and k, using a subprogram to calculate factorials.

12. The *power series*

$$1 + x + \frac{x^2}{2!} + \frac{x^3}{3!} + \cdots = \sum_{n=0}^{\infty} \frac{x^n}{n!}$$

converges to e^x for all values of x. Write a function subprogram that uses this series to calculate values for e^x to five-place accuracy (that is, using terms up to the first one that is less than 10^{-5} in absolute value) and that uses a subprogram to calculate factorials. Use these subprograms in a main program to calculate and print a table of values for the function

$$\cosh(x) = \frac{e^x + e^{-x}}{2}$$

and also the corresponding values of the library function COSH for $x = -1$ to 1 in increments of .1.

13. A more efficient procedure for evaluating the power series in Exercise 12 is to observe that if $a_n = x^n/n!$ and $a_{n+1} = x^{n+1}/(n + 1)!$ are two consecutive terms of the series, then

$$a_{n+1} = \frac{x}{n + 1} a_n$$

Write a function subprogram to calculate e^x using the series of Exercise 12 and using this relationship between consecutive terms. Then use this in a main program to print a table of values for the function

$$\sinh(x) = \frac{e^x - e^{-x}}{2}$$

and also the corresponding values of the library function SINH for $x = -2$ to 2 in increments of .1.

14. The *greatest common divisor* of two integers a and b, not both of which are zero, is the largest positive integer that divides both a and b. The *Euclidean algorithm* for finding this greatest common divisor of a and b, GCD(a,b), is as follows: Divide a by b to obtain quotient q and remainder r, so $a = bq + r$. (If $b = 0$, GCD(a,b) is a.) Then GCD(a,b) = GCD(b,r). Replace a by b and b by r and repeat this procedure. Because the remainders are decreasing, eventually a remainder of 0 will result. The last nonzero remainder is then GCD(a,b). For example:

$$
\begin{array}{ll}
1260 = 198{\cdot}6 + 72 & \text{GCD}(1260,\ 198) = \text{GCD}(198,\ 72) \\
198 = 72{\cdot}2 + 54 & \hspace{2.3cm} = \text{GCD}(72,\ 54) \\
72 = 54{\cdot}1 + 18 & \hspace{2.3cm} = \text{GCD}(54,\ 18) \\
54 = 18{\cdot}3 + 0 & \hspace{2.3cm} = 18
\end{array}
$$

Note: If either a or b is negative, we replace it by its absolute value.

Write a function subprogram to calculate the GCD of two integers. Then use it in a program that will calculate the GCD of any finite set of integers using the following:

$$
\text{If } d = \text{GCD}(a_1, \ldots, a_n), \text{ then}
$$
$$
\text{GCD}(a_1, \ldots, a_n, a_{n+1}) = \text{GCD}(d, a_{n+1})
$$

For example:

$$
\begin{array}{l}
\text{GCD}(1260,\ 198) = 18 \\
\text{GCD}(1260,\ 198,\ 585) = \text{GCD}(18,\ 585) = 9 \\
\text{GCD}(1260,\ 198,\ 585,\ 138) = \text{GCD}(9,\ 138) = 3
\end{array}
$$

15. A *prime number* is an integer $n > 1$ whose only positive divisors are 1 and n itself. Write a logical-valued function that determines whether n is a prime number. Use it in a program that reads several integers, uses the function to determine whether each is a prime, and displays each number with the appropriate label 'IS PRIME' or 'IS NOT PRIME'.

16. Write a program to approximate $f'(a)$, the value of the derivative of f at a, for f defined by a statement function, and a given number a. The *derivative of f at a* is given by

$$
f'(a) = \lim_{h \to 0} \frac{f(a + h) - f(a)}{h}
$$

Calculate values of this *difference quotient* for various values of h approaching 0, say first for $h = 1/2^n$, then for $h = -1/2^n$, as n runs from 0 to 15.

17. Write a program to plot the graph of a function f defined by a statement function. (See Example 1 of Section 6.4.) For a flexible program, you should enter the domain of x values and the number of points to be plotted, and then scale the y axis after calculating the approximate maximum and minimum values of $f(x)$ to obtain the range of y values to be plotted. For example, if you use 75 print positions across the page for the y values and the range of $f(x)$ values is 100, then each unit on the y axis represents 100/75 units.

9.3 Examples: Root Finding, Numerical Solutions of Differential Equations, Simulation

EXAMPLE 1: Root Finding. In many applications, it is necessary to find a **zero** or **root** of a function f, that is, a number c for which

$$f(c) = 0$$

For some functions f, it may be very difficult or even impossible to find this value c exactly. Examples include the function

$$f(v) = 50 \cdot 10^{-9}(e^{40v} - 1) + v - 20$$

which may arise in a problem of determining the dc operating point in an electronic circuit, or the function

$$f(x) = x \tan x - a$$

for which a zero must be found in some heat conduction problems.

For such functions, an iterative numerical method is used to find an approximate zero. One method that is often used for differentiable functions is **Newton's method.** This method consists of taking an initial approximation x_1 to the zero and constructing the tangent line to the graph of f at point $P_1(x_1, f(x_1))$. The point x_2 at which this tangent line crosses the x axis is the second approximation to the zero. Another tangent line may be constructed at point $P_2(x_2, f(x_2))$, and the point x_3, where this tangent line crosses the x axis, is the third approximation. For many functions, this sequence of approximations $x_1, x_2, x_3, \ldots$ converges to the zero, provided that the first approximation is sufficiently close to the zero. Figure 9.5 illustrates Newton's method.

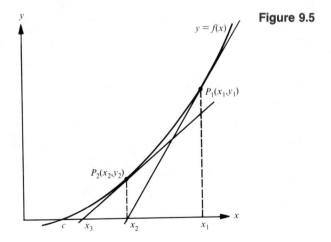

Figure 9.5

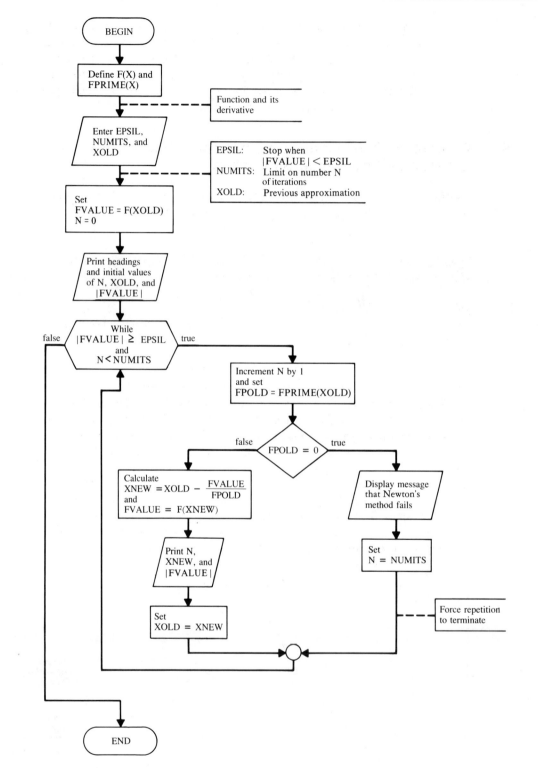

Figure 9.6

If x_n is an approximation to the zero of f, then the formula for obtaining the next approximation x_{n+1} by Newton's method is

$$x_{n+1} = x_n - \frac{f(x_n)}{f'(x_n)}$$

where f' is the derivative of f. Note that Newton's method fails if $f'(x_n)$ is 0 at some approximation x_n.

Figure 9.6 shows a flowchart for Newton's method and the program in Figure 9.7 uses it to find an approximate zero of the function

$$f(x) = x - \cos x$$

Statement functions are used to define this function and its derivative

$$f'(x) = 1 + \sin x$$

The program reads an initial approximation to a zero of f and generates and displays successive approximations using Newton's method as long as

$$|f(x)| \geq \epsilon$$

for some small positive number ϵ (denoted in the program by EPSIL). If the number of iterations exceeds an upper limit NUMITS (in case of divergence), execution is terminated.

```
      PROGRAM NEWTON
*************************************************************************
* Program to find an approximate zero of a function F using Newton's   *
* method.  Variables used are:                                         *
*     XOLD    : previous approximation (initially the first one)       *
*     FPOLD   : value of the derivative of F at XOLD                   *
*     XNEW    : the new approximation                                  *
*     FVALUE  : value of F at an approximation                         *
*     EPSIL   : repetition stops when ABS(FVALUE) is less than EPSIL   *
*     NUMITS  : limit on number of iterations                          *
*     N       : number of iterations                                   *
*************************************************************************

      INTEGER NUMITS, N
      REAL XOLD, FPOLD, XNEW, EPSIL,  F, X, FPRIME, FVALUE

* Define the function F and its derivative F'

      F(X) = X - COS(X)
      FPRIME(X) = 1 + SIN(X)
```

Figure 9.7

Figure 9.7 (continued)

```
* Get termination values EPSIL & NUMITS and initial approximation

      PRINT *, 'ENTER EPSILON, LIMIT ON # OF ITERATIONS, AND'
      PRINT *, 'THE INITIAL APPROXIMATION'
      READ *, EPSIL, NUMITS, XOLD
      FVALUE = F(XOLD)
      N = 0
      PRINT *, '  N        X(N)      ABS(F(X(N))'
      PRINT *, '============================='
      PRINT 10, 0, XOLD, ABS(FVALUE)
10    FORMAT(1X, I3, F10.5, E15.6)

* Iterate using Newton's method while ABS(FVALUE) is greater
* than or equal to EPSIL and N does not exceed NUMITS.
* Terminate if the derivative is 0 at some approximation.

20    IF ((ABS(FVALUE) .GE. EPSIL) .AND. (N .LT. NUMITS)) THEN
         N = N + 1
         FPOLD = FPRIME(XOLD)
         IF (FPOLD .EQ. 0) THEN
             PRINT *, 'NEWTON''S METHOD FAILS -- DERIVATIVE = 0'
*            Force repetition to terminate
             N = NUMITS
         ELSE
             XNEW = XOLD - (FVALUE / FPOLD)
             FVALUE = F(XNEW)
             PRINT 10, N, XNEW, ABS(FVALUE)
             XOLD = XNEW
         END IF
         GO TO 20
      END IF
      END


Sample run:
==========

ENTER EPSILON, LIMIT ON # OF ITERATIONS, AND
THE INITIAL APPROXIMATION
1E-5, 20, 1.0
  N        X(N)      ABS(F(X(N))
=============================
  0     1.00000    0.459698E+00
  1     0.75036    0.189229E-01
  2     0.73911    0.462532E-04
  3     0.73909    0.000000E+00
```

EXAMPLE 2: Numerical Solutions of Differential Equations. Equations that involve derivatives or differentials are called **differential equations**. These equations arise in a large number of problems in science and engineering. For many differential equations, it is very difficult or even impossible to find the exact solution, but it may be possible to find an approximate solution using a numerical method. There are many such methods, and in this example we describe two of the simpler ones.

Suppose we wish to approximate the solution of the **first-order differential equation**

$$y' = f(x, y)$$

satisfying the **initial condition**

$$y(x_0) = y_0$$

The **Euler method** for obtaining an approximation solution over some interval $[a, b]$ where $a = x_0$ is as follows:

EULER'S METHOD

1. Select an x increment Δx.
2. For $n = 0, 1, 2, \ldots$, do the following:
   a. Set $x_{n+1} = x_n + \Delta x$.
   b. Find the point $P_{n+1}(x_{n+1}, y_{n+1})$ on the line through $P_n(x_n, y_n)$ with slope $f(x_n, y_n)$.
   c. Display y_{n+1}, which is the approximate value of y at x_{n+1}.

Figure 9.8 illustrates Euler's method.

The program in Figure 9.9 uses Euler's method to obtain an approximate solution for

$$y' = 2xy$$
$$y(0) = 1$$

The program displays the approximate y values, the exact y values as given by the solution $y = e^{x^2}$ of the differential equation, and their difference. Sample runs with $a = 0$, $b = .5$, $\Delta x = .1$, and $a = 0$, $b = .5$, $\Delta x = .05$ are shown. Note the improved accuracy when the smaller x increment is used.

Figure 9.8

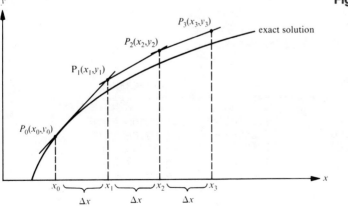

```
      PROGRAM EULER
***********************************************************************
* Program that uses Euler's method to obtain an approximate solution  *
* to a first order differential equation.  Variables used are:        *
*     X0, Y0 : Y(X0) = Y0 is the initial condition                    *
*     B      : [X0,B] is the interval over which solution is obtained  *
*     X      : the current X-value                                    *
*     XNEXT  : the next X-value (X + DELTAX)                          *
*     Y      : the approximate Y-value corresponding to X             *
*     YEXACT : the exact Y-value corresponding to X                   *
*     DELTAX : the X-increment used                                  *
***********************************************************************

      REAL X0, Y0, B, XNEXT, Y, YEXACT, DELTAX, F

* Define the function F

      F(X,Y) = 2 * X * Y

* Get given information, initialize variables, and print headings

      PRINT *, 'ENTER INITIAL X AND Y, RIGHT ENDPOINT OF INTERVAL,'
      PRINT *, 'AND THE X-INCREMENT TO USE'
      READ *, X0, Y0, B, DELTAX
      X = X0
      Y = Y0
      PRINT *, '           X          Y-APPROX          Y-EXACT',
     +         '           DIFFERENCE'
      PRINT *, '=============================================',
     +         '==================='
      PRINT *, X, Y, Y, 0

* Iterate with Euler's method

      DO 10 XNEXT = X0 + DELTAX, B, DELTAX
         Y = Y + F(X,Y) * (XNEXT - X)
         X = XNEXT
         YEXACT = EXP(X ** 2)
         PRINT *, X, Y, YEXACT, Y - YEXACT
10    CONTINUE
      END


Sample runs:
===========

ENTER INITIAL X AND Y, RIGHT ENDPOINT OF INTERVAL,
AND THE X-INCREMENT TO USE
0, 1, .5, .1
```

X	Y-APPROX	Y-EXACT	DIFFERENCE
0.000000E+00	1.00000	1.00000	0
0.100000	1.00000	1.01005	-1.005006E-02
0.200000	1.02000	1.04081	-2.081060E-02
0.300000	1.06080	1.09417	-3.337431E-02
0.400000	1.12445	1.17351	-4.906297E-02
0.500000	1.21440	1.28403	-6.962204E-02

Figure 9.9

Figure 9.9 **(continued)**

```
ENTER INITIAL X AND Y, RIGHT ENDPOINT OF INTERVAL,
AND THE X-INCREMENT TO USE
0, 1, .5, .05
         X          Y-APPROX        Y-EXACT        DIFFERENCE
=================================================================
   0.000000E+00     1.00000         1.00000             0
   5.000000E-02     1.00000         1.00250       -2.502918E-03
   0.100000         1.00500         1.01005       -5.050182E-03
   0.150000         1.01505         1.02275       -7.705212E-03
   0.200000         1.03028         1.04081       -1.053524E-02
   0.250000         1.05088         1.06449       -1.361370E-02
   0.300000         1.07715         1.09417       -1.702166E-02
   0.350000         1.10947         1.13032       -2.085209E-02
   0.400000         1.14830         1.17351       -2.521253E-02
   0.450000         1.19423         1.22446       -3.022981E-02
   0.500000         1.24797         1.28402       -3.605485E-02
```

One of the most popular and most accurate numerical methods for solving a first-order differential equation is the following **Runge–Kutta method**:

RUNGE–KUTTA METHOD

1. Select an x increment Δx.
2. The approximate solution y_{n+1} at $x_{n+1} = x_0 + (n + 1) \Delta x$ for $n = 0, 1, 2, \ldots$, is given by

$$y_{n+1} = y_n + \tfrac{1}{6}(K_1 + 2K_2 + 2K_3 + K_4)$$

where

$$K_1 = \Delta x \cdot f(x_n, y_n)$$

$$K_2 = \Delta x \cdot f\left(x_n + \frac{\Delta x}{2}, y_n + \frac{K_1}{2}\right)$$

$$K_3 = \Delta x \cdot f\left(x_n + \frac{\Delta x}{2}, y_n + \frac{K_2}{2}\right)$$

$$K_4 = \Delta x \cdot f(x_n + \Delta x, y_n + K_3)$$

A program implementing the Runge–Kutta method is left as an exercise.

EXAMPLE 3: Simulation. The term **simulation** refers to modeling a dynamic process and using this model to study the behavior of the process. This model may consist of an equation or a set of equations that describe the process. For example, an equation of the form $A(t) = A_0(.5)^{t/h}$ was used in Section 2.1 to model the radioactive decay of polonium, and linear systems were used in Example 2 of Section 8.4 to model an electrical network. In many problems, the process being studied involves **randomness**, for example, Brownian motion, arrival of airplanes at an airport, number of defective parts manufactured by a machine, and so on. Computer programs that simulate such processes use a **random number generator**, which is a subprogram that produces a number selected "at random" from some fixed range in such a way that a sequence of these numbers tends to be uniformly distributed over the given range. Although it is not possible to develop an algorithm that produces truly random numbers, there are some .methods that produce sequences of **pseudorandom numbers** that are adequate for most purposes.

Many computer systems provide a random number generator that produces random real numbers uniformly distributed over the range 0 to 1. The numbers produced by such a generator can be used to generate random real numbers in other ranges or to generate random integers. To demonstrate how this is done, suppose that the random number generator is implemented as a function RAND having one integer argument. The expression

```
A + (B - A) * RAND(N)
```

can be used to generate random real numbers in the range A to B, and the expression

```
M + INT(K * RAND(N))
```

can be used to generate random integers in the range M through M + K − 1.

As an illustration, suppose that a slab of material is used to shield people from a nuclear reactor and that a particle entering the shield follows a random path by moving forward, backward, left, or right with equal likelihood, in jumps of one unit. A change of direction is interpreted as a collision with an atom in this shield. After 10 such collisions, suppose that the particle's energy is dissipated and that it dies within the shield, provided that it has not already passed back inside the reactor or outside through the shield. A program is to be written to simulate particles entering this shield and to determine what percentage of them gets through it.

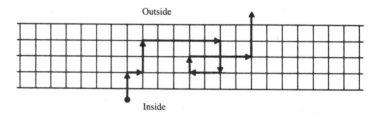

An algorithm for this simulation is

ALGORITHM TO SIMULATE SHIELDING OF NUCLEAR REACTOR

```
*   Algorithm to simulate particles entering a shield and to determine    *
*   how many reach the outside. The particles are assumed to move         *
*   forward, backward, left, and right with equal likelihood and to       *
*   die within the shield if a certain number of collisions (changes of   *
*   direction) have occurred. A random number generator is assumed.       *
```

1. Read the thickness (THICK) of the shield, the limit on the number of collisions (LIMCOL), and the number (N) of particles to simulate.
2. Read a SEED for the random number generator.
3. Initialize COUNT to 0 (number of particles reaching the outside).
4. Do the following for I = 1 to N:
   a. Initialize FORW to 1 (net units forward), OLDDIR to 0 (previous direction of particle), and COLLIS to 0 (number of collisions).
   b. Repeat the following until particle reaches the outside of the shield (FORW ≥ THICK), returns inside the reactor (FORW ≤ 0) or dies within the shield (COLLIS ≥ LIMCOL):
      i. Generate a random integer 1, 2, 3, or 4 for the direction DIR.
      ii. If DIR ≠ OLDDIR, increment COLLIS by 1.
      iii. If DIR = 1, increment FORW by 1.
         Else if DIR = 2, decrement FORW by 1.
      iv. Set OLDDIR equal to DIR.
   c. If FORW = THICK, increment COUNT by 1.
5. Display 100 * COUNT/N.

The program in Figure 9.10 implements this algorithm. It uses the function subprogram RAND to generate random real numbers in the range 0 to 1, which are then transformed into random integers 1, 2, 3, or 4, corresponding to the four directions forward, backward, left, and right, respectively. For best results, the initial argument for this function RAND should be an odd integer.[2]

---

[2] For details of the *congruential method* of generating random numbers and other techniques, see Donald Knuth, *The Art of Computer Programming, Seminumerical Algorithms,* vol. 2 (Reading, Mass.: Addison-Wesley, 1981).

```
      PROGRAM SHIELD
**********************************************************************
* This program uses the random number generator  RAND  to simulate  *
* particles entering a shield and to determine what percentage reach *
* the outside.  The particles are assumed to move forward, backward, *
* left, right with equal likelihood, and to die within the shield if *
* a certain number of collisions (changes of direction) have occurred. *
* Variables used are:                                               *
*     THICK  : thickness of shield                                  *
*     LIMCOL : limit on # of collisions (before energy dissipated)  *
*     DIR    : a random integer 1, 2, 3, or 4 representing direction *
*     OLDDIR : previous direction of particle                       *
*     COLLIS : # of collisions (changes of direction)               *
*     FORW   : net units forward traveled                           *
*     N      : # of particles simulated                             *
*     COUNT  : # of particles reaching outside of shield            *
*     SEED   : a seed for RAND                                      *
*     I      : index variable                                       *
**********************************************************************
```

Figure 9.10

Figure 9.10   (continued)

```
      INTEGER THICK, LIMCOL, DIR, OLDDIR, COLLIS, FORW, N, COUNT,
     +       SEED, I
      REAL RAND

      PRINT *, 'ENTER THICKNESS OF SHIELD, LIMIT ON # OF COLLISIONS,'
      PRINT *, 'AND THE NUMBER OF PARTICLES TO SIMULATE'
      READ *, THICK, LIMCOL, N
      PRINT *, 'SEED FOR RANDOM NUMBER GENERATOR'
      READ *, SEED
      COUNT = 0

* Begin the simulation

      DO 20 I = 1, N
         FORW = 1
         OLDDIR = 0
         COLLIS = 0

*        Repeat the following until particle reaches outside of
*        shield, returns inside reactor, or dies within shield

10          DIR = 1 + 4 * RAND(SEED)
            IF (DIR .NE. OLDDIR) COLLIS = COLLIS + 1
            IF (DIR .EQ. 1) THEN
               FORW = FORW + 1
            ELSE IF (DIR .EQ. 2) THEN
               FORW = FORW - 1
            END IF
            OLDDIR = DIR
            IF ((FORW .LT. THICK) .AND. (FORW .GT. 0) .AND.
     +         (COLLIS .LT. LIMCOL)) GO TO 10

         IF (FORW .EQ. THICK) COUNT = COUNT + 1
20    CONTINUE
      PRINT 30, 100 * COUNT / REAL(N)
30    FORMAT(1X, F6.2, '% OF THE PARTICLES ESCAPED')
      END
```

```
**RAND*********************************************************************
* This function generates a random real number in the interval from    *
* 0 to 1.  The variable M is initially the seed supplied by the        *
* user;  thereafter, it is the random integer generated on the pre-    *
* ceding call to the function and saved using the SAVE statement.      *
* NOTE:  The constants 2147483647 and .4656613E-9 used in this sub-    *
* program are appropriate when it is executed on a machine having      *
* 32-bit memory words.  For a machine having M-bit words, these two    *
* constants should be replaced by the values of  2**M - 1  and         *
* 1/(2**M - 1) , respectively.                                         *
*************************************************************************
```

Figure 9.10 **(continued)**

```
FUNCTION RAND(K)

INTEGER K, M, CONST1
REAL RAND, CONST2
PARAMETER (CONST1 = 2147483647, CONST2 = .4656613E-9)
SAVE
DATA M /0/

IF (M .EQ. 0) M = K
M = M * 65539
IF (M .LT. 0) M = (M + 1) + CONST1
RAND = M * CONST2
END
```

```
Sample runs:
============

ENTER THICKNESS OF SHIELD, LIMIT ON # OF COLLISIONS,
AND THE NUMBER OF PARTICLES TO SIMULATE
4, 5, 100
SEED FOR RANDOM NUMBER GENERATOR
5773
 11.00% OF THE PARTICLES ESCAPED




ENTER THICKNESS OF SHIELD, LIMIT ON # OF COLLISIONS,
AND THE NUMBER OF PARTICLES TO SIMULATE
8, 10, 500
SEED FOR RANDOM NUMBER GENERATOR
5773
  0.60% OF THE PARTICLES ESCAPED
```

Most random number generators generate random numbers having a **uniform distribution**, but they can also be used to generate random numbers having other distributions. An especially important distribution is the **normal distribution** because many physical processes can be modeled by it, for example, heights and weights of people, the lifetime of light bulbs, the tensile strength of steel produced by a machine, and, in general, variations in parts produced in almost any manufacturing process. The normal distribution has the familiar bell-shaped curve shown in Figure 9.11, where μ is the mean of the distribution, σ is the standard deviation, and approximately two thirds of the area under the curve lies between $\mu - \sigma$ and $\mu + \sigma$.

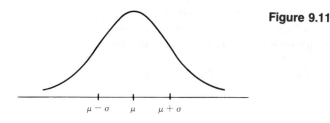

Figure 9.11

A normal distribution having $\mu = 0$ and $\sigma = 1$ is called a **standard normal distribution**, and random numbers having approximately this distribution can be generated quite easily from a uniform distribution with the following algorithm:

ALGORITHM FOR THE STANDARD NORMAL DISTRIBUTION

* Algorithm to generate random numbers having an approximate   *
* standard normal distribution from a uniform distribution.   *

1. Set SUM equal to 0.
2. Do the following 12 times:
   a. Generate a random number X from a uniform distribution.
   b. Add X to SUM.
3. Calculate Z = (SUM − 6).

The numbers Z generated by this algorithm have an approximate standard normal distribution. To generate random numbers having a normal distribution with mean μ and standard deviation σ, we simply add the following step to the algorithm:

4. Calculate Y = μ + σ * Z.

Implementing this algorithm as a program is left as an exercise.

Exercises

1. Another method for finding an approximate zero of a function is the *bisection method*. If f is a continuous function between $x = a$ and $x = b$—that is, if there is no break in the graph of $y = f(x)$ between these two values—and if $f(a)$ and $f(b)$ are of opposite signs, then f must have at least one zero between $x = a$ and $x = b$. To locate such a zero, or at least an approximation to it, we first bisect the interval $[a, b]$ and determine in which half f changes sign; then f must have a zero in that half of the interval. Now bisect this subinterval and determine in which half f changes sign. Repeating this process gives a sequence of smaller and smaller subintervals, each of which contains a zero of the function (see Figure 9.12). The process can be terminated when a small subinterval, say of length less than 0.0001, is obtained or f has the value 0 at one of the endpoints.

   Define a function to compute $x - \cos x$, and then write a program to find a zero of this function in the interval

$$\left[0, \frac{\pi}{2}\right]$$

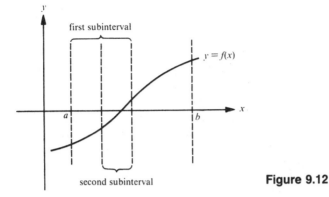

Figure 9.12

2. Cawker City Cookie Company can purchase a new microcomputer for $4,440 or by paying $141.19 per month for the next 36 months. You are to determine what annual interest rate is being charged in the monthly payment plan.

   The equation that governs this calculation is the *annuity formula*

$$A = P\left(\frac{(1 + I)^N - 1}{I(1 + I)^N}\right)$$

   where A is the amount borrowed, P is the monthly payment, I is the monthly interest rate (annual rate/12), and N is the number of payments. In this problem, this equation is to be solved for I. Write a program that uses Newton's method or the bisection method (see Exercise 1) to find an approximate solution by finding an approximate zero of the function

$$F(x) = A - P\left(\frac{(1 + x)^N - 1}{x(1 + x)^N}\right)$$

3. In level flight, the total drag on the Cawker City Cookie Company jet is equal to the sum of parasite drag (D_P) and drag due to lift (D_L) which are given by

$$D_P = \frac{\sigma f V^2}{391} \qquad \text{and} \qquad D_L = \frac{1245}{\sigma e}\left(\frac{W}{b}\right)^2 \frac{1}{V^2}$$

   where V is velocity (mph), W is weight (15,000 lbs), b is the span (40 ft), e is the wing efficiency rating (0.80), f = parasite drag area (4 ft^2), and σ = (air density at altitude)/(air density at seal level) = 0.533 at 20,000 ft (for standard atmosphere). Write a program that uses Newton's method or the bisection method (see Exercise 1) to find the constant velocity V needed to fly at minimum drag (level flight), which occurs when $D_P = D_L$. (*Hint:* Consider the function $F(V) = D_P(V) - D_L(V)$.)

4. Write a program to implement the Runge–Kutta method for solving differential equations as described in Example 2 of Section 9.3. Run

the program using the differential equation given in Example 2 and print tables like that in Figure 9.9.

5. Suppose that an object at a certain temperature T_0 is dropped into a liquid at a lower temperature T_s. If the amount of liquid is quite large and is stirred, we can assume that the object's heat will spread quickly enough through the liquid so that the temperature of the liquid will not change appreciably. We can then assume that the object loses heat at a rate proportional to the difference between its temperature and the temperature of the liquid. Thus, the differential equation that models this problem is

$$T' = k(T - T_s)$$

where $T(t)$ is the temperature of the object at time t, k is the constant of proportionality, and

$$T(0) = T_0$$

is the initial condition. The exact solution of this differential equation can be shown to be

$$T = T_s + (T_0 - T_s)e^{-kt}$$

Write a program that uses the Runge–Kutta method (see Example 2 of Section 9.3) to obtain an approximate solution. Run the program with $T_s = 70$, $T_0 = 300$, and $k = .19$ for $t = 0$ to $t = 20$ with various t increments. Print a table of approximate T values, exact T values, and the differences between them similar to those in Figure 9.9.

Simulation Exercises

6. Write a program to investigate the *birthday problem:* If there are n persons in a room, what is the probability that two or more of them have the same birthday? You might consider values of n, say from 10 through 40, and for each value of n, generate n random birthdays, and then scan the list to see whether two of them are the same. To obtain some approximate probabilities, you might do this 100 times for each value of n.

7. The tensile strength of a certain metal component has an approximate normal distribution with a mean of 10,000 pounds per square inch and a standard deviation of 100 pounds per square inch. Specifications require that all components have a tensile strength greater than 9800; all others must be scrapped. Write a program that uses the algorithm in Example 3 of Section 9.3 to generate 1000 normally distributed random numbers representing the tensile strength of these components, and determine how many must be rejected.

8. Extend the program in Exercise 7 to print a bar graph (see Example 2 in Section 7.5) that displays the number of tensile strengths in each of the intervals 9700–9749, 9750–9799, . . . , 10250–10299.

9. Modify the shield program in Example 3 of Section 9.3 to allow the particle to travel in any direction rather than simply left, right, forward, or backward. Choose a direction (angle) at random and let the particle travel a fixed (or perhaps random) distance in that direction.

10. Write a program to simulate the random path of a particle in a box. A direction (angle) is chosen at random, and the particle travels a fixed (or random) distance in that direction. This procedure is repeated until the particle either passes out through the top of the box or collides with one of the sides or the bottom and stops. Calculate the average number of times the particle escapes from the box and the average number of jumps needed for it to get out.

    Some possible modifications are as follows: Use a two-dimensional box if a three-dimensional one seems too challenging. Let the particle bounce off the sides or the bottom of the box at the same angle with which it hits, rather than stop when it collides with these boundaries.

11. The classic *drunkard's walk problem:* Over an eight-block line, the home of an intoxicated chap is at block eight, and a pub is at block one. Our poor friend starts at block n, $1 < n < 8$, and wanders at random, one block at a time, either toward or away from home. At any intersection, he moves toward the pub with a certain probability, say 2/3, and toward home with a certain probability, say 1/3. Having gotten either home or to the pub, he remains there. Write a program to simulate 500 trips in which he starts at block two, another 500 in which he starts at block three, and so forth up to block seven. For each starting point, calculate and print the percentage of the time he ends up at home and the average number of blocks he walked on each trip.

12. The famous *Buffon Needle problem* is as follows: A board is ruled with equidistant parallel lines, and a needle whose length is equal to the distance between these lines is dropped at random on the board. What is the probability that it crosses one of these lines? The answer to this problem is $2/\pi$. Write a program to simulate this experiment and obtain an estimate for π.

13. An unusual method for approximating the area under a curve is the following *Monte Carlo technique.* As illustrated in the following figure, consider a rectangle that has base $[a, b]$ and height m, where $m \geq f(x)$ for all x in $[a,b]$. Imagine throwing q darts at rectangle $ABCD$ and counting the total number p that hit the shaded region. For

a large number of throws, we would expect

$$\frac{p}{q} \simeq \frac{\text{area of shaded region}}{\text{area of rectangle } ABCD}$$

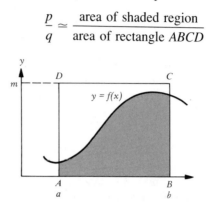

Write a program to calculate areas using this Monte Carlo method. To simulate throwing the darts, generate two random numbers, X from $[a,b]$ and Y from $[0,m]$, and consider point (X,Y) as being where the dart hits.

14. A problem from the area of *artificial intelligence:* The game of *Nim* is played by two players. There are three piles of objects, and each player is allowed to take any number (at least one) of objects from any one pile on his or her turn. The player taking the last object wins. Write a program in which the computer ''learns'' to play Nim. One way to ''teach'' the computer is to have the program assign a value to every possible move based on experience gained from playing games. The value of each possible move is stored in some array, and each value is initially set to 0. The program then keeps track of each move the computer makes as it plays the game. At the end of each game that the computer wins, the value of each move the computer made in that game is increased by 1. At the end of any game lost by the computer, 1 is subtracted from the value of each move made. The computer plays by selecting, from all legal moves, the one that has the largest value. When there are several possible moves having this same largest value, some strategy must be chosen. (One possibility is to have it select a move randomly.)

9.4 Subroutine Subprograms

Subroutine subprograms, like function subprograms, are program units designed to perform a particular task. They differ from function subprograms, however, in the following respects:

1. Functions are designed to return a single value to the program unit that references them. Subroutines often return more than one value, or they may return no value at all but simply perform some task such as displaying a list of instructions to the user.

2. Functions return values via function names; subroutines return values via arguments.
3. A function is referenced by using its name in an expression, whereas a subroutine is referenced by a CALL statement.

The syntax of subroutine subprograms is similar to that of function subprograms and thus to that of FORTRAN (main) programs:

> SUBROUTINE statement
> Declaration part
> Subprogram statements
> END

Subroutine subprograms must begin with a **SUBROUTINE statement** of the form

> SUBROUTINE *name*(*argument-list*)

Here *name* represents the name given to the subroutine and may be any legal FORTRAN name, but no type is associated with the name of a subroutine; *argument-list* is a list (possibly empty) of variables separated by commas. These variables are the **formal arguments** and indicate the number, order, and type of values transferred to and returned from the subroutine. If there are no formal arguments, the parentheses in the SUBROUTINE statement may be omitted.

A subroutine is referenced by a **CALL statement** of the form

> CALL *name*(*argument-list*)

Here *name* is the name of the subroutine being called, and *argument-list* contains the variables, constants, or expressions that are the **actual arguments.** The number of actual arguments must equal the number of formal arguments, and each actual argument must agree in type with the corresponding formal argument. If there are no actual arguments, the parentheses in the CALL statement may be omitted.

As a simple illustration, suppose we wish to develop a subroutine that accepts from the main program a month number, a day number, and a year number, and displays them in the form

> *mm*/*dd*/*yy*

For example, the values 8, 14, 1941 are to be displayed as

> 08/14/41

and the values 9, 3, 1905 as

> 09/03/05

This subroutine must have three formal arguments, each of integer type, representing the number of the month, day, and year, respectively. Thus, an appropriate SUBROUTINE statement is

```
SUBROUTINE DATE(MONTH, DAY, YEAR)
```

where MONTH, DAY, and YEAR must be declared of type INTEGER in the declaration part of this subroutine.

Only the last two digits of the year are to be displayed, and these can be obtained using the statement

```
YEAR = MOD(YEAR, 100)
```

For example, if the value passed to YEAR is 1941, this statement assigns the value 41 to YEAR, which can then be displayed. If the value passed to YEAR is 1905, this statement assigns the value 5 to YEAR, which we wish to display as 05. Similarly, when the month and day numbers are single digits, we wish to display them with a leading zero. Formatting the output using a format descriptor I2.2 achieves the desired result:

```
   PRINT 10, MONTH, DAY, YEAR
10 FORMAT (1X, 2(I2.2, '/'), I2.2)
```

Using these statements, we obtain the following complete subroutine subprogram:

```
**DATE*****************************************
* Subroutine to display a date in the form *
* mm/dd/yy. The MONTH, DAY, and YEAR       *
* number are passed as arguments.          *
**********************************************

      SUBROUTINE DATE(MONTH, DAY, YEAR)

      INTEGER MONTH, DAY, YEAR

      YEAR = MOD(YEAR, 100)
      PRINT 10, MONTH, DAY, YEAR
10    FORMAT (1X, 2(I2.2, '/'), I2.2)
      END
```

This subprogram is referenced in the program in Figure 9.13 by the CALL statement

```
CALL DATE(BMONTH, BDAY, BYEAR)
```

This statement causes the values of the actual arguments BMONTH, BDAY, and BYEAR to be passed to the formal parameters MONTH, DAY, and YEAR, respectively, and initiates execution of the subroutine. When the end of the subroutine is reached, execution resumes with the statement following this CALL statement in the main program.

```
      PROGRAM DATES
***********************************************************************
* Program demonstrating use of a subroutine subprogram DATE to display *
* a given date in the form      mm/dd/yy                               *
* Variables used are:                                                  *
*     BMONTH : birth month                                             *
*     BDAY   : birth day                                               *
*     BYEAR  : birth year                                              *
***********************************************************************

      INTEGER BMONTH, BDAY, BYEAR

      PRINT *, 'ENTER BIRTH MONTH, DAY, AND YEAR (ALL 0''S TO STOP)'
      READ *, BMONTH, BDAY, BYEAR

* While there is more data do the following:

10    IF (BMONTH .GT. 0) THEN
          CALL DATE(BMONTH, BDAY, BYEAR)
          PRINT *
          PRINT *, 'ENTER BIRTH MONTH, DAY, AND YEAR (ALL 0''S TO STOP)'
          READ *, BMONTH, BDAY, BYEAR
          GO TO 10
      END IF

      END

**DATE****************************************************************
* Subroutine to display a data in the form mm/dd/yy.  The MONTH, DAY, *
* and YEAR number are passed as arguments.                           *
***********************************************************************

      SUBROUTINE DATE(MONTH, DAY, YEAR)

      INTEGER MONTH, DAY, YEAR

      YEAR = MOD(YEAR, 100)
      PRINT 10, MONTH, DAY, YEAR
10    FORMAT (1X, 2(I2.2, '/'), I2.2)
      END


Sample run:
==========

ENTER BIRTH MONTH, DAY, AND YEAR (ALL 0'S TO STOP)
8 14 1941
08/14/41

ENTER BIRTH MONTH, DAY, AND YEAR (ALL 0'S TO STOP)
9 3 1905
09/03/05

ENTER BIRTH MONTH, DAY, AND YEAR (ALL 0'S TO STOP)
1 1 1901
01/01/01

ENTER BIRTH MONTH, DAY, AND YEAR (ALL 0'S TO STOP)
0 0 0
```

Figure 9.13

In this example, the subroutine DATE does not calculate and return new values to the main program; it only displays the information passed to it. As an illustration of a subroutine that does return values, consider the problem of converting polar coordinates (r, θ) of a point P to rectangular coordinates (x, y). The first polar coordinate r is the distance from the origin to P, and the second polar coordinate θ is the angle from the positive x axis to the ray joining the origin with P.

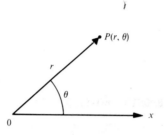

The formulas that relate the polar coordinates to the rectangular coordinates for a point are

$$x = r \cos \theta$$

$$y = r \sin \theta$$

Because the subprogram that performs this conversion must return *two* values, it is natural to use a subroutine subprogram like the following to accomplish this:

```
**CONVER********************************************************
* Subroutine to convert polar coordinates (R,THETA) *
* to rectangular coordinates (X, Y)                  *
********************************************************

      SUBROUTINE CONVER(R, THETA, X, Y)

      REAL R, THETA, X, Y

      X = R * COS(THETA)
      Y = R * SIN(THETA)
      END
```

This subroutine can be referenced by the CALL statement

```
CALL CONVER(RCOORD, TCOORD, XCOORD, YCOORD)
```

where RCOORD, TCOORD, XCOORD, and YCOORD are real variables. When this CALL statement is executed, the actual arguments RCOORD, TCOORD, XCOORD, and YCOORD are associated with the formal arguments

R, THETA, X, and Y, respectively, so that corresponding arguments have the same values:

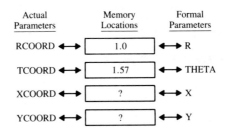

These values are used to calculate the rectangular coordinates X and Y, and these values are then the values of the corresponding actual arguments XCOORD and YCOORD.

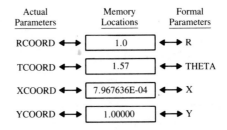

The program in Figure 9.14 reads values for RCOORD and TCOORD, calls the subroutine CONVER to calculate the corresponding rectangular coordinates, and then displays these coordinates.

```
      PROGRAM POLAR
***********************************************************************
* This program accepts the polar coordinates of a point & displays   *
* the corresponding rectangular coordinates.  The subroutine CONVER is *
* used to effect the conversion.  Variables used are:                 *
*     RCOORD, TCOORD : polar coordinates of a point                   *
*     XCOORD, YCOORD : rectangular coordinates of a point             *
***********************************************************************

      REAL RCOORD, TCOORD, XCOORD, YCOORD

* While there is more data do the following

10    PRINT *, 'ENTER POLAR COORDINATES (IN RADIANS)'
      READ (*, *, END = 20) RCOORD, TCOORD
      CALL CONVER(RCOORD, TCOORD, XCOORD, YCOORD)
      PRINT *, 'RECTANGULAR COORDINATES:'
      PRINT *, XCOORD, YCOORD
      PRINT *
      GO TO 10
20    END
```

Figure 9.14

Figure 9.14 (continued)

```
**CONVER*****************************************************************
* Subroutine to convert polar coordinates (R,THETA) to rectangular     *
* coordinates (X,Y).                                                   *
***********************************************************************

        SUBROUTINE CONVER(R, THETA, X, Y)

        REAL R, THETA, X, Y

        X = R * COS(THETA)
        Y = R * SIN(THETA)
        END


Sample run:
==========

ENTER POLAR COORDINATES (IN RADIANS)
1.0, 0
RECTANGULAR COORDINATES:
    1.00000          0.000000E+00

ENTER POLAR COORDINATES (IN RADIANS)
0, 1.0
RECTANGULAR COORDINATES:
    0.000000E+00     0.000000E+00

ENTER POLAR COORDINATES (IN RADIANS)
1.0, 1.57
RECTANGULAR COORDINATES:
    7.967636E-04     1.00000

ENTER POLAR COORDINATES (IN RADIANS)
4.0, 3.14159
RECTANGULAR COORDINATES:
    -4.00000         1.498028E-05

ENTER POLAR COORDINATES (IN RADIANS)
                    <----------------------(end of data signaled)
```

Exercises

1. Write a subroutine subprogram that displays the name of a month whose number is passed to it.

2. Write a subroutine subprogram SWITCH that interchanges the values of two integer variables. For example, if A has the value 3 and B has the value 4, then the statement CALL SWITCH(A, B) causes A to have the value 4 and B the value 3.

3. Write a program that reads the diameters and heights of several right circular cylinders and displays the circumference, total surface area (including the ends), and the volume of each. The circumference should be calculated by a statement function, the surface area by a function subprogram, and the volume in a subroutine subprogram.

4. Consider a simply supported beam to which a single concentrated load is applied:

For $a \geq b$, the maximum deflection is given by

$$\text{MAX} = \frac{-Pb(L^2 - b^2)^{3/2}}{9\sqrt{3}\ EIL}$$

the deflection at the load by

$$\text{LDEF} = \frac{-Pa^2b^2}{3EIL}$$

and the deflection at the center of the beam by

$$\text{CEN} = \frac{-Pb(3L^2 - 4b^2)}{48EI}$$

where P is the load, E is the modulus of elasticity, and I is the moment of inertia. For $a \leq b$, simply replace b with a and a with b in the preceding equations.

Write a program that produces a table of values for MAX, LDEF, and CEN as the load position is moved along the beam in 6-in increments. Run your program with the following values: $L = 360$ inches, $P = 24,000$ pounds, $E = 30 \times 10^6$ psi, and $I = 795.5$ in^4.

5. The *greatest common divisor* GCD(A, B) of two integers A and B, not both of which are zero, can be calculated by the Euclidean Algorithm described in Exercise 14 of Section 9.2. The *least common multiple* of A and B, LCM(A, B), is the smallest nonnegative integer that is a multiple of both A and B and can be calculated using

$$\text{LCM(A,B)} = \frac{|A * B|}{\text{GCD(A,B)}}$$

Write a program that reads two integers, calls a subroutine that calculates and returns their greatest common divisor and least common multiple and then displays these two values.

6. Write a program that reads a positive integer and then calls a subprogram that displays its prime factorization, that is, a subprogram that expresses a positive integer as a product of primes or indicates that it is a prime (see Exercise 15 of Section 9.2 for the definition of a prime number).

7. Write a program that reads two positive integers *n* and *b* and calls a subprogram to calculate and display the base-*b* representation of *n*. Assume that *b* is not greater than 10 (see Exercise 12 of Chapter 1 for one method for converting from base 10 to another base).

8. Write a program that reads a positive integer *n* and then calls a subprogram to display the hexadecimal (base-16) representation of *n*. The symbols A, B, C, D, E, and F should be used for 10, 11, 12, 13, 14, and 15, respectively (see Section 1.3 and the preceding exercise).

9. One simple method of calculating depreciation is the *straight-line* method. If the value of the asset being depreciated is AMOUNT dollars and is to be depreciated over NYEARS years, then AMOUNT/ NYEARS dollars is depreciated in each year. Write a program that reads the current year and values for AMOUNT and NYEARS, calls a subprogram to calculate the annual depreciation, and then displays this value.

10. Another method of calculating depreciation is the *sum-of-the-years-digits* method. To illustrate, suppose that $30,000 is to be depreciated over a five-year period. We first calculate the sum $1 + 2 + 3 + 4 + 5 = 15$. Then 5/15 of $30,000 ($10,000) is depreciated the first year, 4/15 of $30,000 ($8,000) is depreciated the second year, 3/15 the third year, and so on. Write a program that reads the current year, an amount to be depreciated, and the number of years over which it is to be depreciated. It should then call a subroutine that displays a depreciation table with suitable headings that shows each year number and the amount to be depreciated for that year for the specified number of years, beginning with the current year.
   A possible addition to your program: To find how much is saved in taxes, assume a fixed tax rate over these years, and assume that the amounts saved in taxes by claiming the depreciation as a deduction are invested and earn interest at some fixed annual rate.

11. Another method of calculating depreciation is the *double-declining balance* method. For an asset with value AMOUNT dollars that is to be depreciated over NYEARS years, 2/NYEARS times the undepreciated balance is depreciated annually. Because in each year only a fraction of the remaining balance is depreciated, the entire amount would never be depreciated. Consequently, it is permissible to switch to the straight-line method (Exercise 9) at any time. Write a program that reads values for AMOUNT, NYEARS, and the year in which to switch to the straight-line method and that calls a subroutine to print a table showing the year number and the amount to be depreciated.
   A possible addition to your program: Calculate the tax savings as described in the preceding exercise.

12. Proceed as in Exercise 11, but print one table giving the amount to be depreciated each year, assuming that we switch in year 1 (use

straight-line method for all NYEARS years), and another table giving the amount to be depreciated each year, assuming that we switch in year 2, and so on.

13. Write a subroutine that calculates the amount of city income tax and the amount of federal income tax to be withheld from an employee's pay for one pay period. Assume that the city income tax withheld is computed by taking 1.15 percent of gross pay on the first $15,000 earned per year and that the federal income tax withheld is computed by taking the gross pay less $15 for each dependent claimed and multiplying by 20 percent.

Use this subroutine in a program that for each of several employees reads his or her employee number, number of dependents, hourly pay rate, city income tax withheld to date, federal income tax withheld to date, and hours worked for this pay period and that then calculates and prints the employee number, gross pay and net pay for this pay period, the amount of city income tax and the amount of federal income tax withheld for this pay period, and the total amounts withheld through this pay period.

14. Write a menu-driven program that allows the user to convert measurements from either miles to kilometers (1 mile = 1.60935 kilometers) or feet to meters (1 foot = 0.3048 meter), or from degrees Fahrenheit to degrees Celsius ($C = \frac{5}{9}(F - 32)$). Use subroutines to implement the various options. A sample run of the program should proceed somewhat as follows:

```
Available options are:
0. Display this menu.
1. Convert miles to kilometers.
2. Convert feet to meters.
3. Convert degrees Fahrenheit to degrees Celsius.
4. Quit.

Enter an option (0 to see menu): 3
Enter degrees Fahrenheit; 212
This is equivalent to 100.0 degrees Celsius.

Enter an option (0 to see menu): 5
***5 is not a valid option***

Enter an option (0 to see menu): 0
Available options are:
0. Display menu.
1. Convert miles to kilometers.
2. Convert feet to meters.
3. Convert degrees Fahrenheit to degrees Celsius.
4. Quit.

Enter an option (0 to see menu): 1
Enter miles: 10
This is equivalent to 16.0935 kilometers.
```

```
Enter an option (0 to see menu): 2
Enter number of feet: 1
This is equivalent to 0.3048 meters.

Enter an option (0 to see menu): 4
```

15. Write a menu-driven program that allows the user to select one of the following methods of depreciation:

1. Straight-line (see Exercise 9).
2. Sum-of-the-years-digits (see Exercise 10).
3. Double-declining balance (see Exercise 11).

Design the program to be modular, using subprograms to implement the various options.

9.5 Arguments: Variables, Expressions, Arrays

When program units are combined to form a complete program, certain items of information must be shared among these program units. In this section we consider one of the techniques for linking together the various program units, which make possible this sharing of information.

Recall that in the case of subprograms, information is transmitted between program units by means of the argument lists (and by the function name in the case of a function subprogram). This is accomplished by making available to the subprogram the *addresses* of the memory locations in which the values of the actual arguments are stored. For a formal argument in a subprogram, the address of the corresponding actual argument is used to obtain the value of the formal argument. If a value is assigned to a formal argument in the subprogram, this value replaces the contents of the memory location associated with this formal argument and so also changes the value of the corresponding actual argument. This method of linking the actual and formal arguments, appropriately named **call by address,** is described in this section.

Simple Variables As Formal Arguments. If a simple variable appears in the argument list of a subprogram and the corresponding actual argument is also a simple variable, then the call-by-address technique causes both of these variables to refer to the same memory location. Consequently, assigning a value to the formal argument in the subprogram has the effect of changing the value of both arguments, because both refer to the same memory location.

For example, consider the program

```
REAL A, B
INTEGER K, L

A = 6.0
B = 2.0
K = 2
L = 3
CALL CHANGE(A, B, K, L)
PRINT *, A, B, K, L
END
```

and the subroutine subprogram

```
SUBROUTINE CHANGE(X, Y, M, N)

REAL X, Y
INTEGER M, N

X = X / 2
M = M + 1
END
```

In the main program, the type statements

```
REAL A, B
INTEGER K, L
```

associate memory locations with the four variables A, B, K, and L:

A ⟷ [6.0]

B ⟷ [2.0]

K ⟷ [2]

L ⟷ [3]

When the statement

```
CALL CHANGE(A, B, K, L)
```

is executed, the formal parameters X, Y, M, and N are associated with the existing memory locations of the corresponding actual arguments A, B, K, and L, respectively:

A ⟷ [6.0] ⟷ X

B ⟷ [2.0] ⟷ Y

K ⟷ [2] ⟷ M

L ⟷ [3] ⟷ N

Because *corresponding pairs of actual and formal arguments are associated with the same memory locations,* changing the value of the formal argument in the subprogram also changes the value of the corresponding actual argument. Thus, when the subprogram CHANGE is executed, new values are determined for X and M, and because X and M are associated with the same memory locations as A and K, respectively, these values are also the values of A and K.

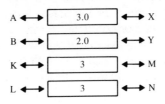

A ⟷ [3.0] ⟷ X

B ⟷ [2.0] ⟷ Y

K ⟷ [3] ⟷ M

L ⟷ [3] ⟷ N

Thus, the statement

```
PRINT *, A, B, K, L
```

displays the values

```
3.00000  2.00000  3  3
```

If the actual argument is an array element or a substring name, the processing of that argument is similar to the processing of a simple variable. If the actual argument is an expression, its value is placed in a temporary memory location by the processor, and the address of this location is made available to the subprogram. The values of the variables and constants that comprise the expression are not changed by any processing that takes place in the subprogram, even though the value of the formal argument corresponding to the expression may change. Thus, execution of the statements

```
K = 1
CHANGE(6.0, 2.0, K + 1, 3)
PRINT *, 6.0, 2.0, K + 1, 3
```

produces as output

```
6.00000  2.00000  2  3
```

Even though the values of the formal arguments X and M corresponding to the expressions 6.0 and K + 1 are changed in the subprogram CHANGE, the values of the constant 6.0 and the variable K are not changed. *If a variable is enclosed within parentheses in the actual argument, it is treated as an expression, and its value is not changed by a subprogram.*

The association of arguments for function subprograms is the same as for subroutine subprograms. Ordinarily, however, we do not use arguments of a function to return values to another program unit but, rather, use the function name. Nevertheless, it is important to remember that changing the value of a formal argument does, in fact, change the value of the corresponding actual argument.

Arrays As Arguments.   The arguments that appear in the argument list of a subprogram reference may be arrays. In this case, a formal argument corresponding to an actual array argument must also be an array and must be dimensioned in the subprogram. When the subprogram is referenced, the address of the first element of the actual array argument is associated with the first element of the corresponding formal array argument. Successive actual array elements are then associated with the corresponding formal array elements.

The program in Figure 9.15 illustrates the use of array arguments. It reads a list of numbers and then calls a function to calculate the mean of the numbers.

```
      PROGRAM AVE
***********************************************************************
* Program to read a list of numbers ITEM(1), ITEM(2), ... , ITEM(NUM) *
* and calculate their mean using the function subprogram MEAN.        *
* Variables used are:                                                 *
*     ITEM    : one-dimensional array of numbers                      *
*     I       : subscript                                             *
*     NUM     : number of items                                      *
***********************************************************************

      REAL ITEM(50), MEAN
      INTEGER NUM, I

      PRINT *, 'ENTER NUMBER OF ITEMS AND THE ITEMS'
      READ *, NUM, (ITEM(I), I = 1, NUM)
      PRINT 10, NUM, MEAN(ITEM, NUM)
10    FORMAT(1X, 'MEAN OF THE ', I3, ' NUMBERS IS ', F6.2)
      END

**MEAN****************************************************************
* Function to find the mean of X(1), X(2), ... , X(N).  Variables used:*
*     SUM     : sum of the numbers                                    *
*     I       : subscript                                             *
***********************************************************************

      FUNCTION MEAN(X, N)

      REAL MEAN, X(50), SUM
      INTEGER N, I

      SUM = 0
      DO 10 I = 1, N
          SUM = SUM + X(I)
10    CONTINUE
      MEAN = SUM / N
      END


Sample run:
==========

ENTER NUMBER OF ITEMS AND THE ITEMS
10
55, 88.5, 90, 71.5, 100, 66.5, 70.3, 81.2, 93.7, 42
MEAN OF THE  10 NUMBERS IS  75.87
```

Figure 9.15

Execution of this program associates the actual array ITEM with the formal array X so that corresponding pairs of array elements refer to the same memory locations:

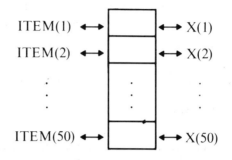

Thus, if any of the array elements X(1), . . . , X(50) are assigned a value in the subprogram, the corresponding elements of the array ITEM are also changed.

If the array X in the subprogram is dimensioned by

```
REAL X(-5:44)
```

then the first element ITEM(1) of the actual array ITEM and the first element X(−5) of the formal array X are associated; that is, they refer to the same memory location. The successive elements of the array ITEM are then associated in order with the elements in the array X:

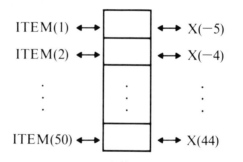

When higher-dimensional arrays are used as arguments, the elements are associated in the standard columnwise order described in Section 8.2. Suppose, for example, that the array ALPHA declared by

```
REAL ALPHA(3,4)
```

is used as the actual argument and the corresponding formal argument is declared in the subprogram by

```
REAL TABLE(3,4)
```

Then the first elements of the arrays ALPHA and TABLE are associated and successive elements are associated in columnwise order as follows:

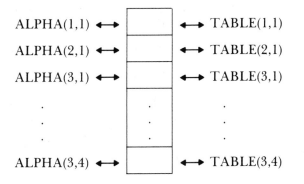

The same method of establishing the correspondence between elements of two arrays is used even if they are of different dimensions. For example, if the array ALPHA is associated with the array T declared by

```
REAL T(2,6)
```

then the array elements are associated as follows:

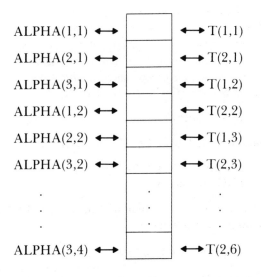

If ALPHA is associated with a one-dimensional array Y declared by

```
REAL Y(12)
```

then the association of array elements is the following:

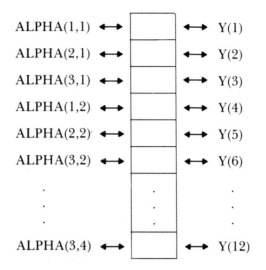

Each element of an array used as a formal argument in a subprogram should be associated with an element of the corresponding actual array. *Consequently, the number of elements in the formal array should be less than or equal to the number of elements in the actual array. In the case of character arrays, the total number of characters specified for the formal array should be less than or equal to the total number of characters specified for the actual array.*

Normally, when two arrays are associated as arguments, the first element of the actual array is associated with the first element of the formal array. It is possible, however, to specify that some other element of the actual array be matched with the first element of the formal array. This is accomplished by using that array element name as the actual argument. To illustrate, consider the actual array GAMMA declared by

```
REAL GAMMA(4,5)
```

and the formal array CONST declared by

```
SUBROUTINE EXTRAC(CONST)
REAL CONST(4)
```

To associate the last column of the array GAMMA with the array CONST, we could use the statement

```
CALL EXTRAC(GAMMA(1,5))
```

The association of array elements is as follows:

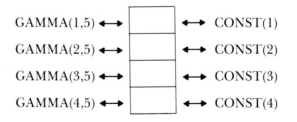

Although dimensions of arrays in a main program must be specified by an integer constant or parameter, *dimensions in a subprogram may be given by integer variables.* Such an array is said to have **adjustable dimensions.** In this case, the integer variables used to specify the dimensions of the formal array must also be formal arguments. For example, the program in Figure 9.15 that used the function subprogram MEAN to calculate the mean of a list of numbers could be rewritten as shown in Figure 9.16.

```
      PROGRAM AVE
*********************************************************************
* Program to read a list of numbers ITEM(1), ITEM(2), ... , ITEM(NUM)  *
* and calculate their mean using the function subprogram MEAN.     *
* Variables used are:                                              *
*      ITEM    : one-dimensional array of numbers                  *
*      I       : subscript                                         *
*      NUM     : number of items                                   *
*********************************************************************

      REAL ITEM(50), MEAN
      INTEGER NUM, I

      PRINT *, 'ENTER NUMBER OF ITEMS AND THE ITEMS'
      READ *, NUM, (ITEM(I), I = 1, NUM)
      PRINT 10, NUM, MEAN(ITEM, NUM)
10    FORMAT(1X, 'MEAN OF THE ', I3, ' NUMBERS IS ', F6.2)
      END


**MEAN***********************************************************
* Function to find the mean of X(1), X(2), ... , X(N).  Variables used:*
*      SUM     : sum of the numbers                                *
*      I       : subscript                                         *
*********************************************************************

      FUNCTION MEAN(X, N)

      INTEGER N, I
      REAL MEAN, X(N), SUM

      SUM = 0
      DO 10 I = 1, N
         SUM = SUM + X(I)
10    CONTINUE
      MEAN = SUM / N
      END
```

Figure 9.16

To illustrate the processing of higher-dimensional arrays by subprograms, we reconsider the problem of reading two matrices and, if they have appropriate dimensions, calculating and displaying their product. The program in Figure 9.17 performs the input/output processing in the main program and the matrix multiplication in the subroutine MATMUL. Note how easily the matrix multiplication algorithm of Example 1 in Section 8.4 is implemented as a subroutine.

In this program, the parameter SIZE is used to dimension the arrays A, B, and C in the main program. It is also used as an actual argument corresponding to the formal argument LIMIT used to dimension the arrays MAT1, MAT2, and PROD in the subroutine. The subroutine MATMUL is, therefore, a general subprogram that can be used with arrays of other dimensions.

```
      PROGRAM MATRIX
***********************************************************************
* This program reads in a ROWS1 X COLS1 matrix and a ROWS2 X COLS2   *
* matrix, calls the subroutine MATMUL to multiply them, and displays *
* the product.  Variables used are:                                  *
*     SIZE    :  parameter giving maximum dimensions of matrices      *
*     ROWS1   :  # of rows in 1-st matrix                             *
*     COLS1   :  # of columns in 1-st matrix                          *
*     ROWS2   :  # of rows in 2-nd matrix                             *
*     COLS2   :  # of columns in 2-nd matrix                          *
*     A, B    :  the two matrices being multiplied                    *
*     C       :  the product of A and B                               *
*     I, J    :  indices                                              *
*     FORM    :  character variable used to output C.  It is          *
*             :  initialized as   '(1X, ##F8.2)'   and the repetition *
*             :  indicator  ##  will be replaced by  the value of     *
*             :  COLS2 entered during program execution.              *
*     MATCH   :  true if product defined (COLS1 = ROWS2) else false   *
***********************************************************************

      INTEGER SIZE, ROWS1, COLS1, ROWS2, COLS2, I, J
      PARAMETER (SIZE = 10)
      REAL A(SIZE,SIZE), B(SIZE,SIZE), C(SIZE,SIZE)
      CHARACTER*15 FORM
      LOGICAL MATCH
      DATA FORM /'(1X, ##F8.2)'/

* Read the actual dimensions of the two matrices A and
* B and set up the output format for the product matrix C

      PRINT *,'ENTER RIGHT-JUSTIFIED IN 2 SPACE ZONES THE DIMENSIONS OF'
      PRINT *, 'MATRIX 1:'
      READ '(2I2)', ROWS1, COLS1
      PRINT *, 'MATRIX 2:'
      READ '(2I2,TL2,A2)', ROWS2, COLS2, FORM(6:7)

* Read in A and B (rowwise)

      PRINT *, 'ENTER THE ELEMENTS OF THE TWO MATRICES ROWWISE'
      READ *, ((A(I,J), J = 1, COLS1), I = 1, ROWS1),
     +        ((B(I,J), J = 1, COLS2), I = 1, ROWS2)
```

Figure 9.17

Figure 9.17 (continued)

```
* Calculate C = A * B and display C

      CALL MATMUL(A, B, C, SIZE, ROWS1, COLS1, ROWS2, COLS2, MATCH)
      IF (MATCH) THEN
          PRINT *, 'PRODUCT MATRIX IS:'
          DO 10 I = 1, ROWS1
              PRINT FORM, (C(I,J), J = 1, COLS2)
10        CONTINUE
      ELSE
          PRINT *, 'PRODUCT NOT DEFINED -- # OF COLUMNS IN FIRST'
          PRINT *, 'MATRIX IS NOT EQUAL TO # OF ROWS IN SECOND'
      END IF
      END

**MATMUL********************************************************
* Subroutine to calculate the product of an M X N matrix with a P X Q *
* matrix.  N must equal P for the product to be defined (MATCH =      *
* .TRUE.), and the product PROD is then an M X Q matrix.  Variables   *
* used are:                                                           *
*     LIMIT   :  limit on dimensions of the matrices                  *
*     M       :  # of rows in 1-st matrix                             *
*     N       :  # of columns in 1-st matrix                          *
*     P       :  # of rows in 2-nd matrix                             *
*     Q       :  # of columns in 2-nd matrix                          *
*     MAT1    :  the first matrix                                     *
*     MAT2    :  the second matrix                                    *
*     PROD    :  the product of MAT1 and MAT2                         *
*     I, J, K :  indices                                              *
*     SUM     :  used to calculate the product matrix                 *
*****************************************************************

      SUBROUTINE MATMUL(MAT1, MAT2, PROD, LIMIT, M, N, P, Q, MATCH)

      INTEGER M, N, P, Q, LIMIT, I, J, K
      REAL MAT1(LIMIT, LIMIT), MAT2(LIMIT, LIMIT), PROD(LIMIT, LIMIT),
     +     SUM
      LOGICAL MATCH

      IF (N .EQ. P) THEN
          MATCH = .TRUE.
          DO 30 I = 1, M
              DO 20 J = 1, Q
                  SUM = 0
                  DO 10 K = 1, N
                      SUM = SUM + MAT1(I,K) * MAT2(K,J)
10                CONTINUE
                  PROD(I,J) = SUM
20            CONTINUE
30        CONTINUE
      ELSE
          MATCH = .FALSE.
      END IF
      END
```

Figure 9.17 **(continued)**

```
Sample run:
==========


 ENTER RIGHT-JUSTIFIED IN 2 SPACE ZONES THE DIMENSIONS OF
 MATRIX 1:
0202
 MATRIX 2:
0203
 ENTER THE ELEMENTS OF THE TWO MATRICES ROWWISE
 2 0
 0 2

 1 2 3
 4 5 6
 PRODUCT MATRIX IS:
      2.00    4.00    6.00
      8.00   10.00   12.00
```

Some care must be exercised in using variables to declare higher-dimensional arrays in subprograms in order to ensure that the formal arrays have dimensions that match those of the corresponding actual arrays. If, for example, we use the formal arguments M, N, P, and Q to declare MAT1, MAT2, and PROD by

```
REAL MAT1(M,N), MAT2(P,Q), PROD(M,Q)
```

and the values of M, N, P, and Q are 2, 2, 2, and 3, respectively, then the association between the elements of the actual arrays and the formal arrays is the following:

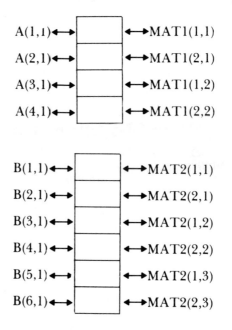

$$
\begin{array}{lcl}
C(1,1) \longleftrightarrow & \boxed{} & \longleftrightarrow PROD(1,1) \\
C(2,1) \longleftrightarrow & & \longleftrightarrow PROD(2,1) \\
C(3,1) \longleftrightarrow & & \longleftrightarrow PROD(1,2) \\
C(4,1) \longleftrightarrow & & \longleftrightarrow PROD(2,2) \\
C(5,1) \longleftrightarrow & & \longleftrightarrow PROD(1,3) \\
C(6,1) \longleftrightarrow & & \longleftrightarrow PROD(2,3)
\end{array}
$$

This association obviously does not produce the desired results. The desired correspondence is established, however, if the dimensions of the actual arrays, A, B, and C are 2 × 2, 2 × 3, and 2 × 3, respectively, so that the dimensions of the actual and formal arrays correspond exactly.

In a subprogram, it is possible to specify that a one-dimensional formal array is to have the size of the corresponding actual array. This is done by using an asterisk (*) to specify the dimension. In this case, it is not permissible to use the array name in any statement that requires information about the array size. Thus, one would not be allowed to give only the array name in an input/output statement. For higher-dimensional arrays, only the upper bound of the last dimension may be specified by an asterisk.

9.6 An Example: Top-Down Design and Modular Programming

The solution to a complex problem may require so many steps in the final algorithm that they cannot all be anticipated at the outset. To attack such problems, a **top-down** approach is commonly used. We begin by identifying the major tasks to be performed to solve the problem and arranging them in the order in which they are to be carried out. This step-by-step outline serves as a first description of the algorithm and provides an overview of the main sequence of activities to be performed. Usually, most of the steps in this first outline are incomplete and must be refined. Thus, we expand the outline, adding more details to these steps, and so we obtain a second outline of the algorithm. Some of the steps of this second outline may still require additional refinement, which then leads to a third description of the algorithm. For complex problems, several levels of refinement may be needed before a clear, precise, and complete algorithm can be obtained.

Subprograms enable the programmer to develop programs for complex problems using this top-down approach. Individual subprograms can be designed to carry out particular tasks and can be invoked by a sequence of function references and/or CALL statements. To illustrate this style of program development, we consider the important problem of updating a master file with the contents of a transaction file. For example, the master file may be an inventory file that is to be updated with a transaction file containing the day's sales; or the master file might be a file of students' records and the transaction file a file containing the students' grades for the semester just concluded.

In this section, we consider the problem of updating a master file containing information regarding the users of a university's computing system. Suppose that the records of this file contain the following information about each system user: identification number, name, password, limit on resources, and resources used to date. (For the details of this file, see the description of USERS-FILE in Appendix B.) A daily log of the system's activity is also maintained. Among other items of information, this log contains a list of user identification numbers and resources used for each job entered into the system. This list is maintained in the transaction file USER-UPDATE (also described in Appendix B). At the end of each day, the master file USERS-FILE must be updated with the contents of USER-UPDATE incorporating the activities of that day, and a report must be generated that lists the name, identification number, and resources used for all users whose resources used to date exceed some specified upper limit. This information should be displayed in the order of decreasing resources used to date.

In analyzing this problem, we identify two main procedures required to solve it: an initialization routine and a processing routine. In the initialization routine two tasks must be accomplished. First, the master user file and the user update file must be opened; second, the user update file must be sorted in order of increasing user identification number so that it is arranged in the same order as the master user file.

In the processing routine, we can also identify two main tasks to be performed. The first task is to update the master user file, and the second is to generate the required report.

Each of these procedures and routines can be implemented with a subprogram. The relationship between these subprograms is indicated in the **structure diagram** of Figure 9.18, in which each name has been selected to suggest the purpose of the subprogram.

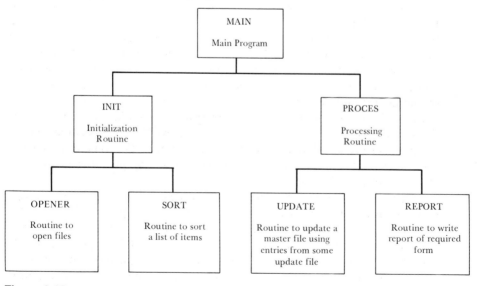

Figure 9.18

It is not necessary to develop the details of all of these subprograms before a program can be written to test the main logic of the algorithm for solving the problem. One need only insert a **program stub** for each undeveloped subprogram to signal its execution. This technique allows one to concentrate on the main logic of a program and verify its correctness without being overly concerned with the details of individual routines. The FORTRAN program in Figure 9.19 reflects the structure indicated in Figure 9.18. The main program and the subprograms INIT and PROCES are complete, whereas OPENER, SORT, UPDATE, and REPORT are program stubs.

```
      PROGRAM USERS
**MAIN******************************************************************
* This program reads records from a users file (ordered according to  *
* identification number), updates them with entries from a users update*
* file (which must first be sorted according to id-number).  Another   *
* (updated) user file is produced.  A report showing information about *
* users whose resources used to date exceed some upper bound is also   *
* produced. (These are to be listed in order of decreasing amounts of  *
* resources.)  Variables used are:                                     *
*     FNAME1, FNAME2  :  names of user master and update files, resp.  *
*     UNIT1, UNIT2    :  Unit numbers for these two files              *
**********************************************************************

      CHARACTER*20 FNAME1, FNAME2
      INTEGER UNIT1, UNIT2

      CALL INIT(FNAME1, FNAME2, UNIT1, UNIT2)
      CALL PROCES(UNIT1, UNIT2)
      END

**INIT******************************************************************
* Subroutine for initialization.  It gets names of user master and     *
* update files, and opens them.  It also sorts the user update file.   *
* Variables:  FNAME1, FNAME2, UNIT1, UNIT2 as in MAIN.                 *
**********************************************************************

      SUBROUTINE INIT(FNAME1, FNAME2, UNIT1, UNIT2)

      CHARACTER*20 FNAME1, FNAME2
      INTEGER UNIT1, UNIT2

      PRINT *, 'ENTER NAME OF MASTER FILE'
      READ *, FNAME1
      CALL OPENER(FNAME1, UNIT1, 'OLD')
      PRINT *, 'ENTER NAME OF UPDATE FILE'
      READ *, FNAME2
      CALL OPENER(FNAME2, UNIT2, 'OLD')
      CALL SORT(UNIT2)
      END
```

Figure 9.19

Figure 9.19   **(continued)**

```
**PROCES*************************************************************
* Subroutine to carry out the updating and reporting.  Variables used  *
* are UNIT1, UNIT2  as in MAIN;  UNIT3 is unit number of new master    *
* file; UNIT4 is unit number of file used to generate report.          *
********************************************************************

      SUBROUTINE PROCES(UNIT1, UNIT2)

      INTEGER UNIT1, UNIT2, UNIT3, UNIT4

      CALL UPDATE(UNIT1, UNIT2, UNIT3, UNIT4)
      CALL REPORT(UNIT4)
      END


**OPENER*************************************************************
* Subroutine to open a file and assign it a unit number.  Successive   *
* calls to this subroutine will assign unit numbers 10, 11, 12, ...    *
* Variables used:                                                      *
*     FNAME  :  Name of file to be opened                              *
*     NUNIT  :  Unit number to be connected to file (integer)          *
*     STAT   :  Status of file ('OLD' or 'NEW', 'SCRATCH', etc.)       *
********************************************************************

      SUBROUTINE OPENER(FNAME, NUNIT, STAT)

      CHARACTER*(*) FNAME, STAT
      INTEGER NUNIT

      PRINT *, FNAME, ' IS OPEN'
      END


**SORT***************************************************************
* This subroutine reads records from a file and sorts them.            *
* Variables used:                                                      *
*     NUNIT :  Unit number of file                                     *
********************************************************************

      SUBROUTINE SORT(NUNIT)

      INTEGER NUNIT

      PRINT *, 'FILE IS SORTED'
      END


**UPDATE*************************************************************
* Subroutine to update user master file with user update file producing*
* a new (updated) master file.  It also generates a report file of     *
* information re users whose (updated) resources used to date exceed    *
* some upper bound supplied by the user.  Variables used:              *
*     UNIT1, UNIT2   :  Unit # of master file, update file, resp.      *
*     UNIT3, UNIT4   :  Unit # of new master file, report file, resp.  *
********************************************************************

      SUBROUTINE UPDATE(UNIT1, UNIT2, UNIT3, UNIT4)

      INTEGER UNIT1, UNIT2, UNIT3, UNIT4

      PRINT *, 'UPDATING'
      END
```

Figure 9.19 (continued)

```
**REPORT****************************************************************
* Subroutine to sort a report file containing records for users whose  *
* resources used to date exceed a given upper bound so that amounts of *
* resources used will be in decreasing order.  It then prints a report *
* from this file. Variable used:   NUNIT = unit # of report file.      *
**********************************************************************

        SUBROUTINE REPORT(NUNIT)

        INTEGER NUNIT

        PRINT *, 'REPORT PRINTED'
        END


Sample run:
==========

ENTER NAME OF MASTER FILE
'TEST-USERS'
TEST-USERS              IS OPEN
ENTER NAME OF UPDATE FILE
'TEST-UPDATE'
TEST-UPDATE             IS OPEN
FILE IS SORTED
UPDATING
REPORT PRINTED
```

Execution of this program (see the sample run in Figure 9.19) indicates that the main logic of the program is correct. We may, therefore, now turn to developing the subprograms OPENER, SORT, UPDATE, and REPORT. Further examination of the type of report required leads us to identify two *subtasks,* one to sort a work file containing the contents of the report so that the resources used to date are in decreasing order, and the other to actually write the report. Having previously developed a program for sorting a list (see Example 3 of Section 7.5), we can easily modify it for use here. Our structure diagram at this stage is shown in Figure 9.20. (The shaded corner in the SORT box indicates that this subprogram is shared by two or more procedures.) The program that results from supplying the details of OPENER, SORT, and REPORT and adding a new program stub GENREP is shown in Figure 9.21.

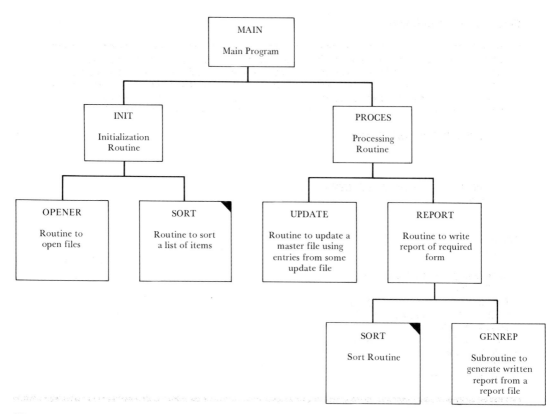

Figure 9.20

```
      PROGRAM USERS
**MAIN*******************************************************************
* This program reads records from a users file (ordered according to   *
* identification number), updates them with entries from a users update*
* file (which must first be sorted according to id-number).  Another    *
* (updated) user file is produced.  A report showing information about  *
* users whose resources used to date exceed some upper bound is also    *
* produced. (These are to be listed in order of decreasing amounts of   *
* resources.)  Variables used are:                                      *
*    FNAME1, FNAME2  :  names of user master and update files, resp.    *
*    UNIT1, UNIT2    :  Unit numbers for these two files                *
************************************************************************

      CHARACTER*20 FNAME1, FNAME2
      INTEGER UNIT1, UNIT2

      CALL INIT(FNAME1, FNAME2, UNIT1, UNIT2)
      CALL PROCES(UNIT1, UNIT2)
      END
```

Figure 9.21

Figure 9.21 (continued)

```
**INIT***********************************************************
* Subroutine for initialization.  It gets names of user master and   *
* update files, and opens them.  It also sorts the user update file.  *
* Variables:  FNAME1, FNAME2, UNIT1, UNIT2 as in MAIN.                *
*****************************************************************

        SUBROUTINE INIT(FNAME1, FNAME2, UNIT1, UNIT2)

        CHARACTER*20 FNAME1, FNAME2
        INTEGER UNIT1, UNIT2

        PRINT *, 'ENTER NAME OF MASTER FILE'
        READ *, FNAME1
        CALL OPENER(FNAME1, UNIT1, 'OLD')
        PRINT *, 'ENTER NAME OF UPDATE FILE'
        READ *, FNAME2
        CALL OPENER(FNAME2, UNIT2, 'OLD')
        CALL SORT(UNIT2)
        END


**PROCES*********************************************************
* Subroutine to carry out the updating and reporting.  Variables used  *
* are UNIT1, UNIT2  as in MAIN;  UNIT3 is unit number of new master   *
* file; UNIT4 is unit number of file used to generate report.         *
*****************************************************************

        SUBROUTINE PROCES(UNIT1, UNIT2)

        INTEGER UNIT1, UNIT2, UNIT3, UNIT4

        CALL UPDATE(UNIT1, UNIT2, UNIT3, UNIT4)
        CALL REPORT(UNIT4)
        END


**OPENER*********************************************************
* Subroutine to open a file and assign it a unit number.  Successive  *
* calls to this subroutine will assign unit numbers 10, 11, 12, ...   *
* Variables used:                                                     *
*      FNAME  :  Name of file to be opened                            *
*      NUNIT  :  Unit number to be connected to file (integer)        *
*      N      :  Unit number generated (increased by 1 with each call) *
*      STAT   :  Status of file ('OLD', 'NEW', 'SCRATCH', etc.)       *
*****************************************************************

        SUBROUTINE OPENER(FNAME, NUNIT, STAT)

        CHARACTER*20 FNAME, STAT*(*)
        INTEGER NUNIT, N
        SAVE N
        DATA N / 9 /

        N = N + 1
        OPEN (UNIT = N, FILE = FNAME, STATUS = STAT, ERR = 10)
        NUNIT = N
        RETURN
10      PRINT *, FNAME, ' CANNOT BE OPENED'
        STOP
        END
```

Figure 9.21 (continued)

```
**SORT************************************************************
* This subroutine reads records from a file, stores them in a character*
* array  ITEM, and sorts them in ascending alphabetic order.  For       *
* more than 1000 items, change the value of the parameter LIMIT.        *
* Variables used:                                                       *
*      ITEM  :  List of character strings to be sorted.  Each string is *
*            :  one line of the file.                                   *
*      NUNIT :  Unit number of file                                     *
*      N     :  Number of items                                         *
*      I     :  index                                                   *
*      TEMP  :  Temporary variable used to interchange two of the items *
*      PAIRS :  # of pairs to be examined in bubble sort scan           *
*      DONE  :  Logical flag to record interchanges on bubble sort scan *
******************************************************************
        SUBROUTINE SORT(NUNIT)

        PARAMETER (LIMIT = 1000)
        INTEGER NUNIT, N, PAIRS, I
        LOGICAL DONE
        CHARACTER*80 ITEM(LIMIT), TEMP

* Read the items from a file and count them

        READ (NUNIT, '(A)', END = 10) (ITEM(N), N = 1, LIMIT)
10      N = N - 1

* Now sort the list using bubble sort

        PAIRS = N - 1

* Repeat until DONE is true

20      DONE = .TRUE.

*       Scan the list comparing consecutive items

        DO 30 I = 1, PAIRS
            IF (ITEM(I) .GT. ITEM(I + 1)) THEN

*           Items out of order, so interchange them
*           and set DONE to false

                TEMP = ITEM(I)
                ITEM(I) = ITEM(I + 1)
                ITEM(I + 1) = TEMP
                DONE = .FALSE.
            END IF
30      CONTINUE

*       Largest item has sunk into place so eliminate it on next pass

        PAIRS = PAIRS - 1
        IF (.NOT. DONE) GO TO 20
```

Figure 9.21   (continued)

```
* Now write the sorted items back to the file

      REWIND NUNIT
      DO 40 I = 1, N
          WRITE (NUNIT, '(A)') ITEM(I)
40    CONTINUE
      REWIND NUNIT
      END


**UPDATE********************************************************
* Subroutine to update user master file with user update file producing*
* a new (updated) master file.  It also generates a report file of    *
* information re users whose (updated) resources used to date exceed   *
* some upper bound supplied by the user.  Variables used:             *
*     UNIT1, UNIT2 :  Unit # of master file, update file, resp.       *
*     UNIT3, UNIT4 :  Unit # of new master file, report file, resp.   *
***************************************************************

      SUBROUTINE UPDATE(UNIT1, UNIT2, UNIT3, UNIT4)

      INTEGER UNIT1, UNIT2, UNIT3, UNIT4

      PRINT *, 'UPDATING'
      END


**REPORT********************************************************
* Subroutine to sort a report file containing records for users whose *
* resources used to date exceed a given upper bound so that amounts of *
* resources used will be in decreasing order.  It then prints a report *
* from this file.   Variable used:  NUNIT = unit # of report file.    *
***************************************************************

      SUBROUTINE REPORT(NUNIT)

      INTEGER NUNIT

      PRINT *, 'SORTING THE WORK FILE'
      CALL GENREP(NUNIT)
      END


**GENREP********************************************************
* Subroutine to actually generate the report from the report file.    *
* Variables used:                                                     *
*     NUNIT  :  Unit number of file                                   *
***************************************************************

      SUBROUTINE GENREP(NUNIT)

      INTEGER NUNIT

      PRINT *, 'REPORT GENERATED'
      END
```

Figure 9.21   (continued)

```
Original file TEST-UPDATE used in sample run:
=============================================

200113    234
100110   2245
200113    150
100111   1025
100110    732


Sample run:
==========

 ENTER NAME OF MASTER FILE
 'TEST-USERS'
 ENTER NAME OF UPDATE FILE
 'TEST-UPDATE'
 UPDATING
 SORTING THE WORK FILE
 REPORT GENERATED


Sorted file TEST-UPDATE produced by sample run:
===============================================

100110    732
100110   2245
100111   1025
200113    150
200113    234
```

Once again we observe that the logic of the program appears to be correct. The listings of the test file TEST-UPDATE before and after execution indicate that the subroutine SORT is indeed functioning correctly. Consequently, we may proceed to develop the remaining subprograms UPDATE and GENREP. The details of GENREP are straightforward, but the subroutine UPDATE is somewhat more complicated. An algorithm for performing the file update is as follows:

ALGORITHM FOR UPDATING A FILE

* Algorithm to update a master USERS-FILE with the update file   *
* USER-UPDATE to produce a new master file and a report file   *
* for all users whose resources used to date exceed RBOUND.   *

1. Open a new master file and a report file.
2. Read the resource bound RBOUND.
3. Read the first record from the master file USERS-FILE.
4. Read the first record from the update file USER-UPDATE.
5. Set a logical variable EOU (denoting end-of-update) to false.

6. While not EOU, do the following:

Compare the identification numbers in the master record with those in the update record. If they match, do the following:

a. Update the master record by adding the resources used from the update record to the resources used to date in the master record.

b. If there is more data in the update file, read the next record from this update file; otherwise, set EOU to true.

If the identification numbers do not match, do the following:

a. Write the record to the new master file.

b. If the resources used to date exceed RBOUND, write the record to the report file.

c. Read a new record from the master file.

7. Because the last updated user record has not been written, write it to the new master file.

8. Copy any remaining records in the master file to the new master file, checking each to see if the resources used to date exceed RBOUND and writing the record to the report file if this is the case.

The final version of the program is shown in Figure 9.22. Also shown are listings of test master and update files used in the sample run and listings of the new master file and the report file produced.

```
      PROGRAM USERS
**MAIN*********************************************************************
* This program reads records from a users file (ordered according to   *
* identification number), updates them with entries from a users update*
* file (which must first be sorted according to id-number). Another     *
* (updated) user file is produced.  A report showing information about  *
* users whose resources used to date exceed some upper bound is also    *
* produced. (These are to be listed in order of decreasing amounts of   *
* resources.)  Variables used are:                                      *
*     FNAME1, FNAME2  :  names of user master and update files, resp.   *
*     UNIT1, UNIT2    :  Unit numbers for these two files               *
*************************************************************************

      CHARACTER*20 FNAME1, FNAME2
      INTEGER UNIT1, UNIT2

      CALL INIT(FNAME1, FNAME2, UNIT1, UNIT2)
      CALL PROCES(UNIT1, UNIT2)
      END
```

Figure 9.22

Figure 9.22 (continued)

```
**INIT***************************************************************
* Subroutine for initialization.  It gets names of user master and  *
* update files, and opens them.  It also sorts the user update file. *
* Variables: FNAME1, FNAME2, UNIT1, UNIT2 as in MAIN.               *
********************************************************************

      SUBROUTINE INIT(FNAME1, FNAME2, UNIT1, UNIT2)

      CHARACTER*20 FNAME1, FNAME2
      INTEGER UNIT1, UNIT2

      PRINT *, 'ENTER NAME OF MASTER FILE'
      READ *, FNAME1
      CALL OPENER(FNAME1, UNIT1, 'OLD')
      PRINT *, 'ENTER NAME OF UPDATE FILE'
      READ *, FNAME2
      CALL OPENER(FNAME2, UNIT2, 'OLD')
      CALL SORT(UNIT2)
      END


**PROCES*************************************************************
* Subroutine to carry out the updating and reporting.  Variables used *
* are UNIT1, UNIT2  as in MAIN;  UNIT3 is unit number of new master *
* file; UNIT4 is unit number of file used to generate report.       *
********************************************************************

      SUBROUTINE PROCES(UNIT1, UNIT2)

      INTEGER UNIT1, UNIT2, UNIT3, UNIT4

      CALL UPDATE(UNIT1, UNIT2, UNIT3, UNIT4)
      CALL REPORT(UNIT4)
      END


**OPENER*************************************************************
* Subroutine to open a file and assign it a unit number.  Successive *
* calls to this subroutine will assign unit numbers 10, 11, 12, ... *
* Variables used:                                                   *
*     FNAME  :  Name of file to be opened                           *
*     NUNIT  :  Unit number to be connected to file (integer)       *
*     N      :  Unit number generated (increased by 1 with each call) *
*     STAT   :  Status of file ('OLD', 'NEW', 'SCRATCH', etc.)      *
********************************************************************

      SUBROUTINE OPENER(FNAME, NUNIT, STAT)

      CHARACTER*20 FNAME, STAT*(*)
      INTEGER NUNIT, N
      SAVE N
      DATA N / 9 /

      N = N + 1
      OPEN (UNIT = N, FILE = FNAME, STATUS = STAT, ERR = 10)
      NUNIT = N
      RETURN
10    PRINT *, FNAME, ' CANNOT BE OPENED'
      STOP
      END
```

Figure 9.22 (continued)

```
**SORT*********************************************************
* This subroutine reads records from a file, stores them in a character*
* array  ITEM, and sorts them in ascending alphabetic order.  For      *
* more than 1000 items, change the value of the parameter LIMIT.       *
* Variables used:                                                      *
*     ITEM  :  List of character strings to be sorted.  Each string is *
*           :  one line of the file.                                   *
*     NUNIT :  Unit number of file                                     *
*     N     :  Number of items                                         *
*     I     :  index                                                   *
*     TEMP  :  Temporary variable used to interchange two of the items *
*     PAIRS :  # of pairs to be examined in bubble sort scan           *
*     DONE  :  Logical flag to record interchanges on bubble sort scan *
***********************************************************************

      SUBROUTINE SORT(NUNIT)

      PARAMETER (LIMIT = 1000)
      INTEGER NUNIT, N, PAIRS, I
      LOGICAL DONE
      CHARACTER*80 ITEM(LIMIT), TEMP

* Read the items from a file and count them

      READ (NUNIT, '(A)', END = 10) (ITEM(N), N = 1, LIMIT)
10    N = N - 1

* Now sort the list using bubble sort

      PAIRS = N - 1

* Repeat until DONE is true

20    DONE = .TRUE.

*     Scan the list comparing consecutive items

      DO 30 I = 1, PAIRS
         IF (ITEM(I) .GT. ITEM(I + 1)) THEN

*         Items out of order, so interchange them
*         and set DONE to false

            TEMP = ITEM(I)
            ITEM(I) = ITEM(I + 1)
            ITEM(I + 1) = TEMP
            DONE = .FALSE.
         END IF
30    CONTINUE
```

Figure 9.22 (continued)

```
*      Largest item has sunk into place so eliminate it on next pass

       PAIRS = PAIRS - 1
       IF (.NOT. DONE) GO TO 20

* Now write the sorted items back to the file

       REWIND NUNIT
       DO 40 I = 1, N
          WRITE (NUNIT, '(A)') ITEM(I)
40     CONTINUE
       REWIND NUNIT
       END

**UPDATE*********************************************************
* Subroutine to update user master file with user update file producing*
* a new (updated) master file.  It also generates a report file of    *
* information re users whose (updated) resources used to date exceed   *
* some upper bound supplied by the user.  Variables used:             *
*      UNIT1, UNIT2  :  Unit # of master file, update file, resp.     *
*      UNIT3, UNIT4  :  Unit # of new master file, report file, resp. *
*      NEWMAS        :  Name of new master file                        *
*      RBOUND        :  Upper bound for resources used to date         *
*      NAME          :  Name of user                                   *
*      IDENTM, IDENTU:  Users identification number in master file,    *
*                    :  update file, respectively                      *
*      PASSWD        :  User's password                                *
*      LIMIT         :  User's resource limit                          *
*      RTODAT        :  User's resources used to date                  *
*      RUSED         :  Current resources used  (in update file)       *
*      EOU           :  logical variable signaling end-of-update       *
*********************************************************************

       SUBROUTINE UPDATE(UNIT1, UNIT2, UNIT3, UNIT4)

       CHARACTER NAME*30, PASSWD*5, NEWMAS*20
       INTEGER UNIT1, UNIT2, UNIT3, UNIT4, LIMIT, IDENTM, IDENTU,
     +       RTODAT, RUSED
       REAL RBOUND
       LOGICAL EOU

* Get name for and open new master file, get resource bound
* for report, and open a report file

       PRINT *, 'ENTER NAME FOR NEW MASTER FILE'
       READ *, NEWMAS
       CALL OPENER(NEWMAS, UNIT3, 'NEW')
       PRINT *, 'ENTER RESOURCE BOUND FOR REPORT FILE'
       READ *, RBOUND
       CALL OPENER('REPORT-FILE', UNIT4, 'NEW')

* Read first records from master and update files

       READ (UNIT1, 10) NAME, IDENTM, PASSWD, LIMIT, RTODAT
10     FORMAT(A30, I6, A5, I4, I6)
       READ (UNIT2, '(I6, 1X, I5)') IDENTU, RUSED
       EOU = .FALSE.
```

Figure 9.22 (continued)

```
* While EOU is false, do the following updating:

20    IF (.NOT. EOU) THEN
          IF (IDENTM .EQ. IDENTU) THEN
              RTODAT = RTODAT + RUSED
              READ (UNIT2, '(I6, 1X, I5)', END = 30) IDENTU, RUSED
              GO TO 20
30            EOU = .TRUE.
              GO TO 20
          ELSE
              WRITE (UNIT3, 10) NAME, IDENTM, PASSWD, LIMIT, RTODAT

*             Check if user should be reported

              IF (RTODAT / 100. .GE. RBOUND)
     +            WRITE (UNIT4, '(F6.2, 1X, I6, 1X, A)')
     +                RTODAT / 100., IDENTM, NAME
              READ (UNIT1, 10) NAME, IDENTM, PASSWD, LIMIT, RTODAT
          ENDIF
          GO TO 20
      END IF

* No more updates, so write last updated record
* and copy rest of master file

40    WRITE (UNIT3, 10) NAME, IDENTM, PASSWD, LIMIT, RTODAT
      IF (RTODAT / 100. .GE. RBOUND)
     +    WRITE (UNIT4, '(F6.2, 1X, I6, 1X, A)')
     +        RTODAT / 100., IDENTM, NAME
      READ (UNIT1, 10, END = 50) NAME, IDENTM, PASSWD, LIMIT, RTODAT
      GO TO 40
50    END

**REPORT************************************************************
* Subroutine to sort a report file containing records for users whose  *
* resources used to date exceed a given upper bound so that amounts of *
* resources used will be in decreasing order.  It then prints a report *
* from this file.  Variable used:   NUNIT = unit # of report file.     *
********************************************************************

      SUBROUTINE REPORT(NUNIT)

      INTEGER NUNIT

      REWIND NUNIT
      CALL SORT(NUNIT)
      CALL GENREP(NUNIT)
      END
```

Figure 9.22 (continued)

```
**GENREP*********************************************************
* Subroutine to actually generate the report from the report file.  *
* Variables used:                                                    *
*     NUNIT   :   Unit number of file                                *
*     RES     :   Resources used to date                             *
*     ID      :   User's id-number                                   *
*     NAME    :   User's name                                        *
*********************************************************************

        SUBROUTINE GENREP(NUNIT)

        CHARACTER*30 NAME
        INTEGER NUNIT, ID
        REAL RES


* Rewind the file and print headings

        REWIND NUNIT
        PRINT *, 'USER-ID          NAME                  RESOURCES USED'
        PRINT *, '=======          ====                  =============='
        PRINT *

* While there is more data do the following:

10      READ (NUNIT, '(F6.2, I6, 1X, A)', END = 20) RES, ID, NAME
        PRINT '(1X, I7, 2X, A, ''$'', F6.2)', ID, NAME, RES
        GO TO 10
20      END


Original TEST-USERS file used in sample run:
=============================================

SMITH          JOHN           100110HELLO 200 12345
DOE            MARY           100111AAAAA 200  2233
BROWN          BOB            200113BROWN 300 23456
GREEN          HUGH           200167SEVEN 500 44444


Original TEST-UPDATE file used in sample run:
=============================================

200113    234
100110   2245
100110    732
```

Figure 9.22   (continued)

```
Sample run:
==========

ENTER NAME OF MASTER FILE
'TEST-USERS'
ENTER NAME OF UPDATE FILE
'TEST-UPDATE'
ENTER NAME FOR NEW MASTER FILE
'NEW-MASTER-FILE'
ENTER RESOURCE BOUND FOR REPORT FILE
100
USER-ID          NAME                RESOURCES USED
=======          ====                ==============

  10011    SMITH       JOHN          $153.22
  20011    BROWN       BOB           $236.90
  20016    GREEN       HUGH          $444.44


Listing of updated userfile NEW-MASTER-FILE produced:
======================================================

SMITH           JOHN        100110HELLO 200 15322
DOE             MARY        100111AAAAA 200  2233
BROWN           BOB         200113BROWN 300 23690
GREEN           HUGH        200167SEVEN 500 44444


Listing of REPORT-FILE generated and used to print report:
==========================================================

153.22 100110 SMITH         JOHN
236.90 200113 BROWN         BOB
444.44 200167 GREEN         HUGH
```

*9.7   Arguments: Functions and Subroutines

FORTRAN permits the use of a function name or a subroutine name as an argument in a subprogram reference. In this case, the name of the subprogram being used as an argument must be listed in an EXTERNAL or INTRINSIC statement in the program unit in which it is used as an actual argument.

The EXTERNAL Statement.   The **EXTERNAL statement** has the form

EXTERNAL *name1, name2, . . .*

where *name1, name2, . . .* are the names of *user-written* subprograms to be used as arguments. *The EXTERNAL statement is nonexecutable and must precede all executable statements in the program unit.*

The INTRINSIC Statement. In our discussion of the FORTRAN intrinsic functions, we have in most cases used the *generic* names of these functions. These generic names simplify references to the functions, as the same function may be used with more than one type of argument. Intrinsic functions may, however, also be referenced by *specific* names, as indicated in the table of Appendix D. These specific names—but not the generic names—of the FORTRAN intrinsic functions may be used as arguments in a subprogram reference, provided they have been listed in an **INTRINSIC statement** in the same program unit as the subprogram reference. This statement has the form

INTRINSIC *fun1, fun2, . . .*

where *fun1, fun2, . . .* are specific names of intrinsic library functions to be used as actual arguments in a subprogram reference. Of the functions listed in Appendix D, LGE, LGT, LLE, LLT, INT, REAL, DBLE, CMPLX, ICHAR, CHAR, MAX, and MIN may not be used as actual arguments to a subprogram. *Like the EXTERNAL statement, the INTRINSIC statement is nonexecutable and must precede all executable statements in the program unit.*

To illustrate, consider a function subprogram DEFINT that approximates an integral

$$\int_a^b f(x) \; dx$$

using the rectangle method in Example 1 of Section 4.11 (see also Figures 9.1 and 9.2). We wish to use this subprogram in another program to calculate the integral of the function POLY, defined by $POLY(x) = x^2 + 3x + 2$, for $0 \le x \le 4$. We indicate that POLY is to be an argument by using an EXTERNAL statement and define POLY in a function subprogram (*not* as a statement function), as shown in Figure 9.23.

```
      PROGRAM APPROX
*****************************************************************
* Program to approximate the integral of a function over the interval  *
* [A,B] using the rectangle method.  This approximation is calculated   *
* by the function subprogram DEFINT; the integrand, the interval of     *
* integration, and the # of subintervals are passed as arguments to     *
* DEFINT.  Variables used are:                                          *
*     A, B  : the endpoints of the interval of integration              *
*     SUBS  : the number of subintervals used                           *
*****************************************************************

      REAL A, B, DEFINT, POLY
      INTEGER SUBS
      EXTERNAL POLY

      PRINT *, 'ENTER THE INTERVAL ENDPOINTS AND THE # OF SUBINTERVALS'
      READ *, A, B, SUBS
      PRINT 10, SUBS, DEFINT(POLY, A, B, SUBS)
10    FORMAT(1X, 'RECTANGLE APPROXIMATION WITH ',I3,
     +       ' SUBINTERVALS IS ', F10.4)
      END
```

Figure 9.23

Figure 9.23 (continued)

```
**DEFINT*****************************************************************
* Function to calculate the rectangle approximation of the integral   *
* of the function F over the interval [A,B] using N subintervals.     *
* Altitudes of rectangles are chosen at the midpoints of the          *
* subintervals.  Variables used are:                                  *
*     N      : the number of subintervals used                        *
*     I      : counter                                                *
*     DELX   : the length of the subintervals                         *
*     X      : midpoint of one of the subintervals                    *
***********************************************************************

      FUNCTION DEFINT(F, A, B, N)

      INTEGER N, I
      REAL DELX, X, DEFINT, F, A, B

      DELX = (B - A) / N
      DEFINT = 0
      X = A + DELX / 2
      DO 10 I = 1, N
          DEFINT = DEFINT + F(X)
          X = X + DELX
10    CONTINUE
      DEFINT = DEFINT * DELX
      END

**POLY*******************************************************************
*                         The integrand                               *
***********************************************************************

      FUNCTION POLY(X)

      REAL X, POLY
      POLY = X ** 2 + 3 * X + 2
      END


Sample run:
==========

ENTER THE INTERVAL ENDPOINTS AND THE # OF SUBINTERVALS
 0, 4, 50
RECTANGLE APPROXIMATION WITH  50 SUBINTERVALS IS     53.3310
```

To approximate the integral of the sine function from 0 to .5, we could simply change the definition of POLY to

```
POLY = SIN(X)
```

or we could delete the function subprogram POLY and pass the library function SIN as an argument to DEFINT, provided we indicate that it is to be an argument by using an INTRINSIC statement, as shown in the program of Figure 9.24.

```
      PROGRAM APPROX
***********************************************************************
* Program to approximate the integral of a function over the interval *
* [A,B] using the rectangle method.  This approximation is calculated  *
* by the function subprogram DEFINT; the integrand, the interval of    *
* integration, and the # of subintervals are passed as arguments to    *
* DEFINT.  Variables used are:                                         *
*     A, B   : the endpoints of the interval of integration            *
*     SUBS   : the number of subintervals used                         *
***********************************************************************

      REAL A, B, DEFINT
      INTEGER SUBS
      INTRINSIC SIN

      PRINT *, 'ENTER THE INTERVAL ENDPOINTS AND THE # OF SUBINTERVALS'
      READ *, A, B, SUBS
      PRINT 10, SUBS, DEFINT(SIN, A, B, SUBS)
10    FORMAT(1X, 'RECTANGLE APPROXIMATION WITH ',I3,
     +       ' SUBINTERVALS IS ', F10.4)
      END


**DEFINT*************************************************************
* Function to calculate the rectangle approximation of the integral *
* of the function F over the interval [A,B] using N subintervals.    *
* Altitudes of rectangles are chosen at the midpoints of the         *
* subintervals.  Variables used are:                                 *
*     N      : the number of subintervals used                       *
*     I      : counter                                               *
*     DELX   : the length of the subintervals                        *
*     X      : midpoint of one of the subintervals                   *
***********************************************************************

      FUNCTION DEFINT(F, A, B, N)

      INTEGER N, I
      REAL DELX, X, DEFINT, F, A, B

      DELX = (B - A) / N
      DEFINT = 0
      X = A + DELX / 2
      DO 10 I = 1, N
          DEFINT = DEFINT + F(X)
          X = X + DELX
10    CONTINUE
      DEFINT = DEFINT * DELX
      END


Sample run:
==========



ENTER THE INTERVAL ENDPOINTS AND THE # OF SUBINTERVALS
0, .5, 20
RECTANGLE APPROXIMATION WITH  20 SUBINTERVALS IS     0.1224
```

Figure 9.24

Just as the names of user-written function subprograms must be listed in an EXTERNAL statement if they are to be used as actual arguments for a subprogram, so also must the names of user-written subroutine subprograms be listed in an EXTERNAL statement if they are to be used as actual arguments.

*9.8 The COMMON Statement

As illustrated in Section 9.6, large programming projects are usually developed as a collection of program units, each of which is designed to perform a particular part of the total processing required. Usually each of these program units must access a common set of data. Although *sharing this information via argument lists is preferred* (as we have done in the preceding sections), it is also possible to establish certain common memory areas in which this data can be stored and accessed *directly* by each of the program units. These common regions are established using the COMMON statement introduced in this section. Additional details regarding the COMMON statement are found in Chapter 13.

It must be emphasized, however, that although common regions can be used to share data among program units, it is usually unwise to do so, because this practice destroys the independence of these program units and thus makes modular programming more difficult. If several program units share a common area and one of these program units changes the value of a variable that has been allocated memory in this common region, the value of that variable is changed in all of the other program units. Consequently, it is difficult to determine the value of that variable at any particular point in the program.

Blank Common.   One form of the **COMMON statement** establishes a common region to which no name is assigned. This region is thus called **blank** or **unnamed common.** The form of the COMMON statement for this is

COMMON *list*

where *list* is a list of variables or arrays separated by commas. The variables and elements of the arrays specified in the COMMON statement are allocated memory locations in blank common in the order in which they are listed, with array elements allocated in the standard order. The COMMON statement is nonexecutable and must precede all executable statements in the program unit.

When COMMON statements are used in different program units, the first item in each list is allocated the first memory location in blank common. These items are thus associated, because they refer to the same memory location. Successive items in the lists are similarly associated because they are allocated the successive memory locations in the common region.

The following restrictions apply to items that are allocated memory locations in blank common:

1. Associated items must be of the same type.
2. If they are of character type, they should be of the same length.
3. They may not be initialized in DATA statements (A BLOCK DATA subprogram, as described in Section 13.4, can be used for this purpose.)

4. They may not be used as formal arguments in the subprogram in which the COMMON statement appears.
5. Numeric and character variables or arrays may not both be allocated memory locations from blank common.

To illustrate, suppose that one program unit contains the statements

```
REAL A, B
INTEGER M, N
COMMON A, B, M, N
```

where each of A, B, M, and N is a simple variable. These four variables are allocated memory locations in the common region in the following order:

Variable	Blank Common Location
A	#1
B	#2
M	#3
N	#4

If another program unit contains the statements

```
REAL W, X
INTEGER I, J
COMMON W, X, I, J
```

where the variables are simple variables, then W, X, I, and J are also allocated the first four memory locations in the common region:

Variable	Blank Common Location
W	#1
X	#2
I	#3
J	#4

It follows that these eight variables are then associated in the following manner:

Variable	Blank Common Location	Variable
A	#1	W
B	#2	X
M	#3	I
N	#4	J

As a simple illustration of the use of COMMON, the program in Figure 9.14 can be rewritten as shown in Figure 9.25. Notice that no arguments are listed in the CALL statement or in the SUBROUTINE statement. The COMMON statements associate the variables RCOORD, TCOORD, XCOORD, and YCOORD in the main program with the variables R, THETA, X, and Y, respectively, in the subprogram CONVER.

```
      PROGRAM POLAR
*****************************************************************
* This program accepts the polar coordinates of a point & displays *
* the corresponding rectangular coordinates.  The subroutine CONVER is *
* used to effect the conversion; a COMMON statement is used to  *
* associate variables in the main program with variables in CONVER.  *
* Variables used are:                                          *
*     RCOORD, TCOORD : polar coordinates of a point            *
*     XCOORD, YCOORD : rectangular coordinates of a point      *
*****************************************************************

      REAL RCOORD, TCOORD, XCOORD, YCOORD
      COMMON RCOORD, TCOORD, XCOORD, YCOORD

* While there are more data do the following

10    PRINT *, 'ENTER POLAR COORDINATES (IN RADIANS)'
      READ (*, *, END = 20) RCOORD, TCOORD
      CALL CONVER
      PRINT *, 'RECTANGULAR COORDINATES:'
      PRINT *, XCOORD, YCOORD
      PRINT *
      GO TO 10
20    END

**CONVER********************************************************
* This subroutine converts polar coordinates (R,THETA) to rectangular *
* coordinates (X,Y).                                           *
*****************************************************************

      SUBROUTINE CONVER

      REAL R, THETA, X, Y
      COMMON R, THETA, X, Y

      X = R * COS(THETA)
      Y = R * SIN(THETA)
      END
```

Figure 9.25

To illustrate the use of arrays in COMMON statements, suppose that the statements

```
      REAL A(3,3)
      COMMON A
```

appear in one program unit and that the statements

```
REAL ALPHA(3,3)
COMMON ALPHA
```

appear in another program unit. These COMMON statements will allocate the first nine memory locations of blank common to both of the arrays A and ALPHA in columnwise order so that the array elements are associated in the following manner:

Array Element	Blank Common Location	Array Element
A(1,1)	#1	ALPHA(1,1)
A(2,1)	#2	ALPHA(2,1)
A(3,1)	#3	ALPHA(3,1)
A(1,2)	#4	ALPHA(1,2)
A(2,2)	#5	ALPHA(2,2)
A(3,2)	#6	ALPHA(3,2)
A(1,3)	#7	ALPHA(1,3)
A(2,3)	#8	ALPHA(2,3)
A(3,3)	#9	ALPHA(3,3)

In the preceding examples we used different names for the same common locations. Although this is legal, the association between elements in different program units is much clearer if the same names are used in each program unit. This is especially important if there are a large number of program units and/ or a large number of shared variables.

Named Common.   In some situations it may be preferable to share one set of variables among some program units and to share another set among other program units. But this sharing is not possible using the form of COMMON statement considered thus far, as it establishes a single common region. It is possible, however, using a form of the COMMON statement that establishes common regions that are **named.** This form is

COMMON /*name1*/ *list1* /*name2*/ *list2* . . .

where each of *name1, name2,* . . . is the name of a list of items (namely, those in *list1, list2,* . . . , respectively) that are to be associated with the items in a block having the same name in another program unit. This association must be complete; that is, there must be a one-to-one correspondence between the items in associated blocks.

For example, suppose that the variables A, B, L, and M are to be shared by a program and a subroutine GAMMA, and the variables A, B, N1, N2, N3 shared by the main program and the subroutine BETA. The following program scheme would be appropriate:

```
      REAL A, B
      INTEGER L, M, N1, N2, N3
      COMMON /FIRST/ A, B /SECOND/ L, M /THIRD/ N1, N2, N3
            .
            .
      END

      SUBROUTINE GAMMA
      REAL A, B
      INTEGER L, M
      COMMON /FIRST/ A, B /SECOND/ L, M
            .
            .
      END

      SUBROUTINE BETA
      REAL A, B
      INTEGER N1, N2, N3
      COMMON /FIRST/ A, B, /THIRD/ N1, N2, N3
            .
            .
      END
```

It is possible to use a single COMMON statement to establish both named and unnamed common regions. In this case, the unnamed region is "named" by a blank (or no space at all) between the slashes (thus the name "blank" COMMON). In the preceding example, therefore, we could also have used

```
      REAL A, B
      INTEGER L, M, N1, N2, N3
      COMMON // A,B /SECOND/ L,M /THIRD/ N1, N2, N3
            .
            .
      END

      SUBROUTINE GAMMA
      REAL A, B
      INTEGER L, M
      COMMON // A,B /SECOND/ L,M
            .
            .
      END

      SUBROUTINE BETA
      REAL A, B
      INTEGER N1, N2, N3
      COMMON // A,B /THIRD/ N1, N2, N3
            .
            .
      END
```

Exercises

1. The *norm* of a vector, *unit vector*, and the *sum*, the *difference*, and the *dot product* of two vectors were defined in Exercise 7 of Section 7.5.

(a) Write a function subprogram that accepts a value for n and an n-dimensional vector and that calculates the norm of that vector.

(b) Write a subroutine subprogram that accepts a value for n and an n-dimensional vector and that returns a unit vector in the same direction as that vector.

(c) Write a subroutine subprogram that accepts a value for n and two n-dimensional vectors and that returns the sum, the difference, and the dot product of the vectors.

Use these subprograms in a main program that reads several pairs of n-dimensional vectors for various values of n and displays their norms, unit vectors in the same direction as the vectors, the sum, the difference, and the dot product of each pair of vectors.

2. Write a subprogram that, for values of m, n, and an $m \times n$ matrix A supplied to it, will calculate the *transpose* of A (the $n \times m$ matrix obtained by writing the rows as columns). Use this subprogram in a main program that reads a matrix and prints out both the matrix and its transpose.

3. Write a subprogram that calculates the sum of two matrices whose dimensions and entries are supplied to it. (See Exercise 2 at the end of Chapter 8.) Use this subprogram in a main program that reads two matrices and then prints them and their sum.

4. Write a subprogram to accept a list of numbers and to calculate and return the mean and standard deviation of the numbers in this list. Then write a program to read and count a list of test scores, call this subprogram to calculate their mean and standard deviation, and then assign letter grades to each of their scores using "grading on the curve" (see Exercises 14 and 15 at the end of Chapter 7).

5. Write a subprogram to evaluate a polynomial $a_0 + a_1x + a_2x + \cdots + a_nx^n$ for any degree n, coefficients $a_0, a_1, \ldots, a_n$, and value of x that are supplied to it as arguments. Then write a program that reads a value of n, the coefficients, and various values of x and then uses this subprogram to evaluate the polynomial at x.

6. Proceed as in Exercise 5, but use *nested multiplication* (also known as *Horner's method*) to evaluate the polynomial; that is, use the fact that

$$a_0 + a_1x + \cdots + a_nx^n =$$
$$a_0 + (a_1 + (a_2 + \cdots + (a_{n-1} + a_nx)x) \cdots x)x$$

For example:

$$7 + 6x + 5x^2 + 4x^3 + 3x^4 = 7 + (6 + (5 + (4 + 3x)x)x)x$$

7. An electronics firm manufactures four types of radios. The number of capacitors, resistors, and transistors (denoted by C, R, and T) in each of these is given in the following table:

Radio Type	C	R	T
1	2	6	3
2	6	11	5
3	13	29	10
4	8	14	7

Each capacitor costs 35¢, a resistor costs 20¢, and a transistor costs $1.40. Write a program that uses the subroutine MATMUL in Section 9.5 to find the total cost of the components for each of the types of radios.

8. A company produces three different products. The products are processed through four different departments, A, B, C, and D, and the following table gives the number of hours each department spends on each product:

Product	A	B	C	D
1	20	10	15	13
2	18	11	11	10
3	28	0	16	17

The cost per hour of operation in each of the departments is as follows:

Department	A	B	C	D
Cost per hour	$140	$295	$225	$95

Write a program that uses the subroutine MATMUL in Section 9.5 to find the total cost charged to each of the products.

9. The vector-matrix equation

$$
\begin{bmatrix} N \\ E \\ D \end{bmatrix} =
\begin{bmatrix} \cos\alpha & -\sin\alpha & 0 \\ \sin\alpha & \cos\alpha & 0 \\ 0 & 0 & 1 \end{bmatrix}
\begin{bmatrix} \cos\beta & 0 & \sin\beta \\ 0 & 1 & 0 \\ -\sin\beta & 0 & \cos\beta \end{bmatrix}
\begin{bmatrix} 1 & 0 & 0 \\ 0 & \cos\gamma & -\sin\gamma \\ 0 & \sin\gamma & \cos\gamma \end{bmatrix}
\begin{bmatrix} I \\ J \\ K \end{bmatrix}
$$

is used to transform local coordinates (I, J, K) for a space vehicle to inertial coordinates (N, E, D). Write a program that reads values for α, β, and γ and a set of local coordinates (I, J, K) and then uses the subroutine MATMUL in Section 9.5 to determine the corresponding inertial coordinates.

10. A data structure that is sometimes implemented using an array is a *stack*. A stack is a list in which elements may be inserted or deleted at only one end of the list, called the *top* of the stack. Because the last element added to a stack will be the first one removed, a stack is called a *Last-In-First-Out (LIFO)* structure. A stack can be implemented as an array STACK, with STACK(1) representing the bottom of the stack and STACK(TOP) the top, where TOP is the position of the top element of the stack. Write subprograms PUSH and POP to implement insertion and deletion operations for a stack. Use these subprograms in a program that reads a command I (Insert) or D (Delete); for I, an integer is then read and inserted into ("pushed onto") the stack; for D, an integer is deleted ("popped") from the stack and displayed.

11. Another data structure that can be implemented as an array is a *queue*. A queue is a list in which elements may be inserted at one end, called the *rear,* and removed at the other end, called the *front*. Because the first element added is the first to be removed, a queue is called a *First-In-First-Out (FIFO)* structure. Write subprograms to implement insertion and deletion operations for a queue. Use these subprograms in a program like that in Exercise 10 to insert integers into or delete integers from a queue. (*Note:* The most efficient representation of a queue as an array is obtained by thinking of the array as being circular, with the first array element immediately following the last array element.)

*12. In Example 2 and Exercise 25 of Section 4.11, and in Example 3 of Section 8.4, we considered the problem of *least squares curve fitting* for a set of data points. A general three-term equation for fitting a curve is

$$y = A + Bf(x) + Cg(x)$$

where f and g can be any functions of x. The least squares curve of this type can then be found by solving the linear system

$$nA + (\Sigma f(x))B + (\Sigma g(x))C = \Sigma y$$
$$(\Sigma f(x))A + (\Sigma f(x)^2)A + (\Sigma f(x)g(x))C = \Sigma f(x)y$$
$$(\Sigma g(x))A + (\Sigma f(x)g(x))B + (\Sigma g(x)^2)C = \Sigma g(x)y$$

for A, B, and C. Write a subprogram whose arguments are the functions f and g and a set of data points, and that finds the coefficients A, B, and C, for this least squares curve.

13. Write a program to update INVENTORY-FILE using INVENTORY-UPDATE to produce a new inventory file (see Appendix B). Each

record in INVENTORY-FILE for which there is no record in INVEN-TORY-UPDATE with a matching item number should remain unchanged. Each record with one or more corresponding records in IN-VENTORY-UPDATE should be updated with the entries in the update file. For transaction code R, the number of items returned should be added to the number in stock. For transaction code S, the number of items sold should be subtracted from the number in stock. If more items are sold than are in stock, display a message showing the order number, stock number, item name, and the number that should be back-ordered (that is, the difference between the number ordered and the number in stock), and set the number currently in stock to zero.

*14. Design a subprogram whose arguments are a function f and the endpoints of an interval known to contain a zero of the function, and that uses the bisection method described in Exercise 1 of Section 9.3 to find an approximation to this zero. Use this subprogram in a program to find a zero of the function $f(x) = x - \cos x$ in the interval $[0, \pi/2]$.

*15. Proceed as in Exercise 14, but use *Newton's method* (see Example 1 of Section 9.3) instead of the bisection method. Both the function and its derivative should be passed as arguments to the root-finding subprogram.

16. Many everyday situations involve *queues* (waiting lines): at supermarket checkout lanes, at ticket counters, at bank windows, and so on. Consider the following example: An airport has one runway. Each airplane takes three minutes to land and two minutes to take off. On the average, in one hour, eight planes land and eight take off. Assume that the planes arrive at random instants of time. (Delays make the assumption of randomness quite reasonable.) There are two types of queues: airplanes waiting to land and airplanes waiting to take off. Because it is more expensive to keep a plane airborne than to have one waiting on the ground, we assume that an airplane waiting to land has priority over one waiting to take off.

  Write a computer simulation of this airport's operation. To simulate landing arrivals, generate a random number corresponding to a one-minute interval; if it is less than 8/60, then a "landing arrival" occurs and joins the queue of planes waiting to land. Generate another random number to determine whether a "takeoff" arrival occurs; if so, it joins the takeoff queue. Next, check to determine whether the runway is free. If so, first check the landing queue, and if planes are waiting, allow the first airplane in the landing queue to land; otherwise, consider the queue of planes waiting to take off. Have the program calculate the average queue lengths and the average time an airplane spends in a queue. For this exercise, you might simulate a 24-hour day. You might also investigate the effect of varying arrival and departure rates to simulate prime and slack times of the day, or what happens if the amount of time it takes to land or take off is increased or decreased.

17. The spread of a contagious disease and the propagation of a rumor have a great deal in common. Write a program to simulate the spread of a disease or a rumor. You might proceed as follows: Establish a population of N individuals, and assign to each individual four parameters (perhaps different numbers to various individuals):

(a) A "resistance" parameter: the probability that the individual will be infected by the disease (rumor) upon transmission from a carrier.

(b) A "recovery" (or "forgetting") parameter: the probability that the infected individual will recover from the disease (forget the rumor) before transmitting it to others in the population.

(c) An "activity" parameter: the number of persons that the individual is likely to contact.

(d) A "transmission" parameter: the probability that the individual will in fact transmit the disease (rumor) to another person he or she contacts.

A person who comes in contact with an infected person either becomes infected or not; comparison of a random number with his or her resistance parameter can be used to determine the result.

Once a person is infected, that is, becomes a carrier, another random number compared with his or her recovery (forgetting) parameter can be used to determine whether or not he or she recovers from the disease (forgets the rumor) before contacting other persons.

The activity parameter of a person who does not recover from the disease (forget the rumor) before contacting other persons determines how many persons he or she will contact, and the transmission parameter determines the actual number of these persons to whom the disease (rumor) will be transmitted. The specific individuals can then be selected at random from the population and the disease (rumor) transmitted to them.

Select one individual to initiate the process. You might keep track of the number of persons infected in each stage; the "degrees of exposure (credibility)," that is, the number of persons exposed once, twice, and so on; the effect of building in certain percentages to indicate the decreased chances of reinfection; and so on.

Programming Pointers

Program Design

1. *Programs for solving complex problems should be designed in a modular fashion.* The problem should be divided into simpler subproblems so that a subprogram can be written to solve each of them.

2. *Information should be shared among program units by using argument lists rather than common regions.* The use of common regions destroys the independence of program units and thus hinders modular design.

Potential Problems

1. *When a subprogram is referenced, the number of actual arguments must be the same as the number of formal arguments, and the type of each actual argument must agree with the type of the corresponding formal argument.* For example, consider the declarations

   ```
   INTEGER NUM1, NUM2, PYTHAG, K, L, M ,
   PYTHAG(NUM1, NUM2) = NUM1 ** 2 + NUM2 ** 2
   ```

   The function references

   ```
   PYTHAG(K, L, M)
   ```

   and

   ```
   PYTHAG(K, 3.5)
   ```

   are then incorrect. In the first case, the number of actual arguments does not agree with the number of formal arguments, and in the second, the real value 3.5 cannot be associated with the integer argument NUM2.

2. *Information is shared among different program units only via the arguments and the function name for function subprograms (or via common regions).* Thus, if the value of a variable in one program unit is needed by another program unit, it must be passed as an argument (or by using a common region), as this variable is not otherwise accessible to the other program unit. One consequence is that *local variables*— those not used as arguments or listed in COMMON statements—as well as statement labels in one program unit may be used in another program unit without conflict.

3. *When control returns from a subprogram, all local variables in that subprogram become undefined unless a SAVE statement is used.*

4. *The type of a function must be declared both in the function subprogram and in the program unit that references the function.*

5. *The types of variables and arrays must be declared both in a subprogram and in a program unit that references that subprogram.*

6. *Corresponding actual arguments and formal arguments are associated with the same memory locations.* Therefore, if the value of one of the formal arguments is changed in a subprogram, the value of the corresponding actual argument also changes. For example, if the function F is defined by the function subprogram

   ```
   FUNCTION F(X, Y)
   REAL F, X, Y

   F = X ** 2 - 2.5 * Y + 3.7 * Y ** 2
   X = 0
   END
   ```

then when the function is referenced in the main program by a statement such as

```
ALPHA = F(BETA, GAMMA)
```

where ALPHA, BETA, and GAMMA are real variables, the value of the function is assigned to ALPHA, but BETA is also set equal to zero, since it corresponds to the formal argument X, whose value is changed in the subprogram. The value of a constant cannot be changed in this manner, however. For example, the function reference

```
F(2.0, GAMMA)
```

does not change the value of the constant 2.0 to zero. Values of constants and expressions that are used as actual arguments in a subprogram reference are placed in temporary memory locations, and it is the contents of these memory locations that are changed. If a variable name is enclosed within parentheses in the actual argument list, then this argument is treated as an expression, and thus the value of that variable cannot be changed by a subprogram reference. For example, the function reference

```
F((BETA), GAMMA)
```

does not change the value of BETA.

7. *The dimension of a formal array should be less than or equal to the dimension of the corresponding actual array, and for character arrays, the total number of characters specified for the formal array should be less than or equal to the total number of characters specified for the actual array.* It is usually best to use formal arrays and actual arrays with matching dimensions, especially in the case of higher-dimensional arrays, since, as illustrated in Section 9.5, the correspondence between array elements may not be what was intended. Two FORTRAN features that are useful in this connection are

   - Arrays in subprograms may be dimensioned by integer variables, provided these variables are formal arguments of the subprogram.
   - An assumed length specifier as in the statement

   CHARACTER*(*) STRING

   may be used in a subprogram to declare the length of a formal argument of character type.

8. *User-defined functions used as actual arguments in a subprogram reference must be defined by function subprograms, not statement functions, and must be listed in an EXTERNAL statement in the program unit that contains that reference.*

9. *Specific names, but not generic names, of library functions may be used as actual arguments in a subprogram reference, provided they are listed in an INTRINSIC statement in the program unit that contains that reference.*

10. *Variables and arrays that are allocated memory locations in a common region are subject to the following restrictions:*

- Associated items must be of the same type.
- Associated items of character type should have the same length.
- Numeric items and character items cannot be allocated memory locations in the same common region.
- They may not be initialized in DATA statements.
- They may not be used as formal arguments in the subprogram in which the COMMON statement appears.

Program Style

1. *Subprograms should be documented in the same manner as the main program.* The documentation should include a brief description of the processing carried out by the subprogram, the values passed to it, the values returned by it, and what the arguments and local variables represent.

2. *Subprograms are separate program units, and the program format should reflect this fact.* In this text, we

- Insert a blank comment line before and after each subprogram to set it off from other program units.
- Follow the stylistic standards described in earlier chapters when writing subprograms.

3. *In the formal argument list of a subroutine, it is usually considered good practice to list arguments whose values are passed to the subroutine (input arguments) before arguments whose values are returned by the subroutine (output arguments).*

Variations and Extensions

There are only a few variations from and extensions to standard FORTRAN in the processing of functions and subroutines. They include:

- An assortment of additional library functions and subroutines is usually provided. These typically include additional arithmetic functions, random number generators, special input/output routines, and special graphics subprograms.

- The SAVE statement may not be provided or may be unnecessary because all variables in a subprogram are saved from one reference to the next.

See Appendix F for additional details.

10

Double Precision and Complex Data Types

Ten decimals are sufficient to give the circumference of the earth to the fraction of an inch.

S. NEWCOMB

All such expressions as $\sqrt{-1}$, $\sqrt{-2}$ . . . are neither nothing, nor greater than nothing, nor less than nothing, which necessarily constitutes them imaginary or impossible.

L. EULER

There are two types of numeric data that we have not yet explored: double precision and complex. These are the focus of this chapter.

Real data are commonly called **single precision** data, because each real constant is usually stored in a single memory location. In a machine that has 32-bit words, for example, this provides approximately seven significant digits for each real value. In many computations, particularly those involving iteration or long sequences of calculations, single precision is not adequate to express the precision required. To overcome this limitation, FORTRAN allows the use of **double precision** data. Each double precision value is usually stored in two consecutive memory locations, thus providing approximately twice as many significant digits as does single precision.[1]

The second data type considered in this chapter is the complex type. A **complex number** is a number of the form

$$a + bi$$

---

[1] In machines with a smaller word length, single precision values may be stored in two or more memory words. For example, in a 16-bit machine, each real value will be stored in two consecutive memory words; double precision values are then stored in four consecutive words.

where *a* and *b* are real numbers and

$$i^2 = -1$$

The first real number, *a*, is called the **real part of the complex number**, and the second real number, *b*, is called the **imaginary part**. In FORTRAN a complex number is represented as a pair of real numbers, and thus each complex datum is usually stored in a pair of memory locations.

10.1 Double Precision Type

In Chapter 1 we considered the internal representation of data and noted that because of the finite length of memory words, most real (floating point) numbers cannot be stored exactly. Even such "nice" decimal fractions as .1 do not have terminating binary representations and thus cannot be represented exactly in the computer's memory. In this connection, we observed in Sections 4.1 and 4.2 that because of this approximate representation, logical expressions formed by comparing two real quantities with .EQ. will often be evaluated as false, even though the quantities are algebraically equal. In particular, we observed in Figure 4.3 that even though

```
X * (1.0 / X)
```

is algebraically equal to 1 for all nonzero values of X, the logical expression

```
X * (1.0 / X) .EQ. 1
```

is false for most real values of X. Many other familiar algebraic equalities fail to hold for real data values; for example, values of the real variables A, B, and C can be found for which the values of the following real expressions are not equal:

(A + B) + C	and	A + (B + C)
(A * B) * C	and	A * (B * C)
A * (B + C)	and	(A * B) + (A * C)

As another example of the effect of approximate representation, consider the following short program:

```
REAL A, B, C

READ *, A, B
C = ((A + B) ** 2 - 2 * A * B - B ** 2) / A ** 2
PRINT *, C
END
```

The following table shows the output produced by one computer system for various values of A and B:

A	B	C
.5	888.	1.00000
.1	888.	−12.5000
.05	888.	−50.0000
.003	888.	−13888.9
.001	888.	−125000.

These results are rather startling, as the algebraic expression

$$\frac{(A + B)^2 - 2AB - B^2}{A^2}$$

can be written as

$$\frac{A^2 + 2AB + B^2 - 2AB - B^2}{A^2}$$

which simplifies to

$$\frac{A^2}{A^2}$$

and thus is identically 1 (provided $A \neq 0$).

For computations in which more precision is needed than is available using the real data type, FORTRAN provides the double precision data type. When the preceding program with A, B, and C declared to be double precision was executed with the given values for A and B, the value displayed for C in each case differed from 1 by less than .017.

The names of variables, arrays, or functions that are double precision may be any legal FORTRAN names, but their types must be declared using the **DOUBLE PRECISION type statement.** For example, the statement

```
DOUBLE PRECISION Z, BETA(5,5)
```

declares the variable Z and the 5 × 5 array BETA to be double precision. The statements

```
DOUBLE PRECISION FUNCTION F(X, Y)
DOUBLE PRECISION X, Y
```

or

```
FUNCTION F(X, Y)
DOUBLE PRECISION F, X, Y
```

declare F to be a double precision valued function of two double precision arguments X and Y.

Double precision constants are written in scientific notation with a D used to indicate the exponent. Thus.

```
3.1415926535898D0
1D-3
.2345678D+05
```

are double precision constants.

All variables, arrays, and functions that are to have double precision values must be declared double precision. If X is a double precision variable and A has not been declared to be double precision, the computation in the statement

```
A = 3.1415926535898D0 * X ** 2
```

is carried out in double precision, but the resulting value is then assigned to the single precision variable A, thus losing approximately half of the significant digits.

Similarly, double precision values should be assigned to double precision variables. For example, consider the following program:

```
PROGRAM DEMO

REAL X
DOUBLE PRECISION A, B

X = .1
B = .1D0
A = X
PRINT *, A
A = B
PRINT *, A
END
```

On some systems the values displayed for A by the two PRINT statements resemble the following:

```
0.99999994039536D-01
0.10000000000000D+00
```

Here the value .1 of the single precision variable X is stored in only one memory location (actually, a binary approximation of .1 is stored), but the value .1D0 of the double precision variable B is stored with more precision in two memory locations. This accounts for the discrepancy between the two printed values of A.

Although mixed-mode expressions involving double precision, real, and integer constants and variables are permitted and are evaluated to produce double precision values, accuracy may be lost because of the use of single precision constants or variables. For example, consider the following statements:

```
DOUBLE PRECISION X, A
      :
      :
A = (X + 3.7) ** 2
```

Because of the presence of the single precision constant 3.7, the value for A is limited to single precision accuracy. To ensure double precision accuracy for the value of A, the assignment statement

```
A = (X + 3.7D0) ** 2
```

should be used.

Double precision variables and arrays may be assigned initial values in a DATA statement. In this case, a double precision form for the constants being assigned must be used.

Formatted input and output of double precision data can be accomplished with a D descriptor of the form

rDw.d

where

D   indicates that the data is to be input or output in D form.

w   is an integer constant indicating the total width of the field from which the data is to be read in the case of input or displayed in the case of output.

d   is an integer constant indicating the number of digits to the right of the decimal point.

r   is an integer constant indicating the number of times the field is to be repeated.

For example, the statements

```
DOUBLE PRECISION A, B, C

    READ 10, A, B, C
10 FORMAT (2D15.0, D7.0)
```

can be used to read values from the input data line

```
1.6693250617200   -.7325379D-02   1.1D0
```

When double precision values are displayed using a D descriptor, they usually appear in a *normalized form:* a negative sign, if necessary, followed by one leading zero; then the decimal point followed by the specified number of digits to the right of the decimal point; and then D with the appropriate exponent displayed in the next four spaces. The F, G, and E descriptors may also be used for the input and output of double precision values. For example, for the variables A, B, and C assigned values by the preceding READ statement, the statements

```
      PRINT 20, A, B, C
      PRINT 30, A, B, C
      PRINT 40, A, B, C
   20 FORMAT (1X, D20.12, 2D20.6)
   30 FORMAT (1X, F20.12, 2F20.6)
   40 FORMAT (1X, E20.12, 2E20.6)
```

produce output resembling the following:

```
 0.166932506172D+01          -0.732538D-02            0.110000D+01
      1.669325061720          -0.007325                1.100000
 0.166932506172E+01          -0.732538E-02            0.110000E+01
```

Three library functions (see Table 9.1) are especially useful for processing double precision data:

DBLE(x)	Transforms the value of the integer or real argument x or the real part of the complex argument x to double precision form.
DPROD(x_1, x_2)	Calculates the double precision product of the real arguments x_1, x_2.
REAL(x)	Converts the double precision argument x to a single precision number.

One problem in which double precision arithmetic is required is in solving certain systems of linear equations. For example, consider the linear system

(I)
$$2x + 6y = 8$$
$$2x + 5.999999y = 8.000002$$

for which the solution is

$$x = 10$$
$$y = -2$$

This linear system is an example of an *ill-conditioned system*. One characteristic of such systems is that they are very sensitive to perturbations of the coefficients and constant terms. Small changes in one or more of these coefficients or constants may produce large changes in the solution. For example, if this linear system is changed to

(II)
$$2x + 6y = 8$$
$$2x + 6.000001y = 8.000001$$

the solution becomes

$$x = 1$$
$$y = 1$$

When these systems were solved using the program in Figure 8.10 for solving linear systems with Gaussian elimination, the results produced were

$$x = 7.000$$
$$y = -1.000$$

for system (I) and

$$x = 4.000$$
$$y = 0.000$$

for system (II).

The program in Figure 10.1 uses double precision arithmetic to carry out the computations involved in Gaussian elimination. Note that in the sample runs, the correct solutions to these linear systems are obtained.

```
      PROGRAM DGAUSS
*********************************************************************
* Program to solve a linear system  using Gaussian elimination with  *
* double precision arithmetic.  Variables used are:                  *
*     LIMIT   : parameter giving maximum dimensions of matrix        *
*     LIMAUG  : parameter (LIMIT + 1) for maximum # columns in AUG    *
*     N       : number of equations and unknowns                     *
*     AUG     : augmented matrix for the linear system               *
*     X       : solution vector                                      *
*     I,J,K   : indices                                              *
*     MULT    : multiplier used to eliminate an unknown              *
*     PIVOT   : used to find nonzero diagonal entry                  *
*********************************************************************

      INTEGER LIMIT, LIMAUG
      PARAMETER (LIMIT = 10, LIMAUG = LIMIT + 1)
      DOUBLE PRECISION AUG(LIMIT,LIMAUG), X(LIMIT), MULT
      INTEGER I, J, K, PIVOT

* Read coefficient matrix and constant vector

      PRINT *, 'ENTER NUMBER OF EQUATIONS'
      READ *, N
      PRINT *, 'ENTER COEFFICIENT MATRIX ROWWISE'
      READ *, ((AUG(I,J), J = 1, N), I = 1, N)
      PRINT *, 'ENTER CONSTANT VECTOR'
      READ *, (AUG(I, N + 1), I = 1, N)

* Gaussian elimination

      DO 70 I = 1, N
```

Figure 10.1

Figure 10.1   **(continued)**

```
*          Locate nonzero diagonal entry

           IF (AUG(I,I) .EQ. 0) THEN
               PIVOT = 0
               J = I + 1
30             IF ((PIVOT .EQ. 0) .AND. (J .LE. N)) THEN
                   IF (AUG(J,I) .NE. 0) PIVOT = J
                   J = J + 1
                   GO TO 30
               END IF
               IF (PIVOT .EQ. 0) THEN
                   STOP 'MATRIX IS SINGULAR'
               ELSE

*                  Interchange rows I and PIVOT

                   DO 40 J = 1, N + 1
                       TEMP = AUG(I,J)
                       AUG(I,J) = AUG(PIVOT,J)
                       AUG(PIVOT,J) = TEMP
40                 CONTINUE
               END IF
           END IF

*          Eliminate Ith unknown from equations I + 1, ..., N

           DO 60 J = I + 1, N
               MULT = -AUG(J,I) / AUG(I,I)
               DO 50 K = I, N + 1
                   AUG(J,K) = AUG(J,K) +  MULT * AUG(I,K)
50             CONTINUE
60         CONTINUE
70     CONTINUE

* Find the solutions

       X(N) = AUG(N, N + 1) / AUG(N,N)
       DO 90 J = N - 1, 1, -1
           X(J) = AUG(J, N + 1)
           DO 80 K = J + 1, N
               X(J) = X(J) - AUG(J,K) * X(K)
80         CONTINUE
           X(J) = X(J) / AUG(J,J)
90     CONTINUE
       PRINT *
       PRINT *, 'SOLUTION VECTOR IS'
       DO 110 I = 1, N
           PRINT 100, I, X(I)
100        FORMAT (1X, 'X(', I2, ') = ', F6.3)
110    CONTINUE
       END
```

Figure 10.1 **(continued)**

```
Sample run:
==========

ENTER NUMBER OF EQUATIONS
2
ENTER COEFFICIENT MATRIX ROWWISE
2 6
2 5.999999
ENTER CONSTANT VECTOR
8 8.000002

SOLUTION VECTOR IS
X( 1) = 10.000
X( 2) = -2.000


ENTER NUMBER OF EQUATIONS
2
ENTER COEFFICIENT MATRIX ROWWISE
2 6
2 6.000001
ENTER CONSTANT VECTOR
8 8.000001

SOLUTION VECTOR IS
X( 1) =  1.000
X( 2) =  1.000
```

It should be noted, however, that although double precision reduces the effects of limited precision, it is not a panacea. Simply declaring everything in the program to be double precision does not avoid all of the problems caused by single precision, because double precision representations of most real numbers are still only approximate.

10.2 Complex Type

Complex numbers arise in many problems in science and engineering, especially in physics and in electrical engineering. As noted in the introduction to this chapter, a complex number has the form

$$a + bi$$

where a and b are real numbers called the **real part** and the **imaginary part**, respectively, and

$$i^2 = -1$$

Complex numbers can be plotted in the plane by taking the horizontal axis to be the real axis and the vertical axis to be the imaginary axis, so that the complex number $a + bi$ is represented as the point $P(a,b)$:

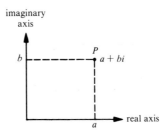

An alternative geometric representation is to associated the complex number $z = a + bi$ with the vector $\overrightarrow{OP}$ from the origin to the point $P(a,b)$:

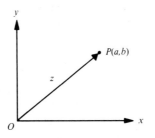

In FORTRAN, a complex constant is also represented as a pair of real constants

$$(a,b)$$

where a and b are single precision constants representing the real part and the imaginary part of the complex number, respectively. For example,

```
(1.0,1.0)
(-6.0,7.2)
(-5.432,-1.4142)
```

are complex constants equivalent to

$$1.0 + 1.0i$$
$$-6.0 + 7.2i$$
$$-5.432 - 1.4142i$$

respectively.

The names of variables, arrays, or functions that are complex may be any legal FORTRAN names, but their types must be declared using the **COMPLEX type statement.** For example, the statement

```
COMPLEX A, RHO(10,10)
```

declares the variable A and the 10×10 array RHO to be complex. The statements

```
COMPLEX FUNCTION GAMMA(Z, W)
COMPLEX Z, W
```

or

```
FUNCTION GAMMA(Z, W)
COMPLEX GAMMA, Z, W
```

declare GAMMA to be a complex-valued function of two complex arguments Z and W.

The **sum** of two complex numbers $z = a + bi$ and $w = c + di$ is

$$z + w = (a + c) + (b + d)i$$

If the vector representation is used for complex numbers, this corresponds to the usual sum of vectors; that is, the vector representing $z + w$ is the sum of the vectors representing z and w:

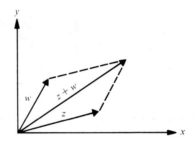

Similarly, the **difference** of z and w defined by

$$z - w = (a - c) + (b - d)i$$

corresponds to vector subtraction.

The **product** of two complex numbers $z = a + bi$ and $w = c + di$ is

$$z \cdot w = (ac - bd) + (ad + bc)i$$

This complex number is represented by a vector whose magnitude is the product of the magnitudes of the vectors representing z and w and whose angle of inclination is the sum $\theta_1 + \theta_2$ of the angles of inclination of the vectors:

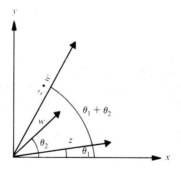

The **quotient** of z and w is

$$\frac{z}{w} = \frac{ac + bd}{c^2 + d^2} + \frac{bc - ad}{c^2 + d^2} i \quad \text{(provided } c^2 + d^2 \neq 0\text{)}$$

This quotient corresponds to a vector whose magnitude is the quotient of the magnitudes of the vectors representing z and w and whose angle of inclination is the difference $\theta_1 - \theta_2$ of the angles of inclination of the vectors.

These four basic arithmetic operations for complex numbers are denoted in FORTRAN by the usual operators $+$, $-$, $*$, and $/$. The exponentiation operation $**$ is defined for a complex number only when the exponent is an integer.

Mixed-mode expressions and assignments involving integer, real, and complex values are allowed, but *double precision values may not be combined with complex values; nor may a double precision value be assigned to a complex variable or a complex value to a double precision variable.* For example, suppose that C and Z are complex variables with the value of C given by

```
C = (6.2,2.4)
```

Then the assignment statement

```
Z = 4.0 * C / 2
```

assigns the complex value (12.4, 4.8) to Z. If this same expression is assigned to the real variable X

```
X = 4.0 * C / 2
```

only the real part of the expression's value is assigned to X; thus, X has the value 12.4. Similarly, if N is an integer variable, the statement

```
N = 4.0 * C / 2
```

will assign the integer part of this value to N, so that N has the value 12.

The only relational operators that may be used with complex values are .EQ. and .NE. . Two complex values are **equal** if, and only if, their real parts are equal and their imaginary parts are equal.

Some of the mathematical functions commonly used with complex numbers are the absolute value, conjugate, and complex exponential functions. For the complex number $z = a + bi$, these functions are defined as follows:

Absolute value: $|z| = \sqrt{a^2 + b^2}$

Conjugate: $\bar{z} = a - bi$

Complex exponential: $e^z = e^a(\cos b + i \sin b)$

If the vector representation is used for complex numbers, $|z|$ is the magnitude of the vector representing z; $\bar{z}$ is represented by the vector obtained by reflecting the vector representing z in the x axis; and the complex exponential e^z is associated with the polar representation of z (see Exercise 11).

These three functions are implemented in FORTRAN by the library functions ABS, CONJG, and EXP, respectively. Several of the other library functions listed in Table 9.1 such as SIN, COS, and LOG may also be used with complex arguments. Three library functions that are useful in converting from real type to complex type, and vice versa, are

AIMAG(z)	Gives the imaginary part of the complex argument z as a single precision real number.
CMPLX(x,y) or CMPLX(x)	Converts the two integer, real, or double precision arguments x and y into a complex number. The first argument x becomes the real part of the complex number; the second argument y becomes the imaginary part. The second form is equivalent to CMPLX(x,0).
REAL(z)	Gives the real part of the complex argument z.

Complex values may be read using a list-directed READ statement, with the complex numbers entered as pairs of real numbers enclosed within parentheses. They may also be read using a formatted READ statement. In this case, a pair of F, E, or G descriptors must be used for each complex value to be read, and the parentheses are not used to enclose the parts of the complex number when it is entered. Complex values displayed using a list-directed output statement are displayed as a pair of real values separated by a comma and enclosed within parentheses. For formatted output of complex values, a pair of F, E, or G descriptors is used for each complex value.

The following program illustrates the input and output of complex numbers and complex arithmetic:

```
      PROGRAM DEMO
      COMPLEX X, Y, W, Z, A
      READ *, X, Y
      READ 5, W
    5 FORMAT (2F2.0)
      PRINT *, X, Y, W
      PRINT 10, X, Y, W
   10 FORMAT (1X, F6.2, ' +' F8.2, 'I')
      Z = (X + Y) / (1.0,2.2)
      A = X * Y
      PRINT 10, Z, A
      END
```

If the following data are entered,

```
(3,4), (.75,-2.23)
 5 7
```

the output produced is

```
(3.00000,4.00000)    (0.750000,-2.23000)    (5.00000,7.00000)
   3.00 +    4.00I
   0.75 +   -2.23I
   5.00 +    7.00I
   1.31 +   -1.11I
  11.17 +   -3.69I
```

In Section 4.4 we considered the problem of solving quadratic equations

$$Ax^2 + Bx + C = 0$$

and noted that if the discriminant $B^2 - 4AC$ is negative, there are no real roots. In this case, the quadratic equation has two complex solutions, which can be found by using the quadratic formula. For example, for the equation

$$x^2 + 2x + 5 = 0$$

the discriminant is

$$2^2 - 4 \cdot 1 \cdot 5 = -16$$

so the roots are complex. The quadratic formula gives the roots

$$\frac{-2 \pm \sqrt{-16}}{2} = \frac{-2 \pm 4i}{2} = -1 \pm 2i$$

The program in Figure 10.2 reads the complex coefficients A, B, and C of a quadratic equation, uses the quadratic formula to calculate the roots, and displays them as complex numbers.

```
      PROGRAM CQUAD
*********************************************************************
* Program to solve a quadratic equation having complex coefficients *
* using the quadratic formula.  Variables used are:                 *
*    A, B, C    : the coefficients of the quadratic equation        *
*    DISC       : the discriminant, B ** 2 - 4 * A * C              *
*    ROOT1, ROOT2 : the two roots of the equation                   *
*********************************************************************

      COMPLEX A, B, C, DISC, ROOT1, ROOT2

      PRINT *, 'ENTER THE COEFFICIENTS OF THE QUADRATIC EQUATION'
      READ *, A, B, C
      DISC = SQRT(B ** 2 - 4 * A * C)
      ROOT1 = (-B + DISC) / (2 * A)
      ROOT2 = (-B - DISC) / (2 * A)
      PRINT *, 'THE ROOTS ARE:'
      PRINT 10, ROOT1, ROOT2
10    FORMAT(5X, F7.3, ' +', F7.3, 'I')
      END
```

Figure 10.2

Figure 10.2 **(continued)**

```
Sample runs:
===========

ENTER THE COEFFICIENTS OF THE QUADRATIC EQUATION
(1,0), (-5,0), (6,0)
THE ROOTS ARE:
        3.000 +  0.000I
        2.000 +  0.000I


ENTER THE COEFFICIENTS OF THE QUADRATIC EQUATION
(1,0), (2,0), (5,0)
THE ROOTS ARE:
       -1.000 +  2.000I
       -1.000 + -2.000I


ENTER THE COEFFICIENTS OF THE QUADRATIC EQUATION
(1,0), (0,0), (1,0)
THE ROOTS ARE:
        0.000 +  1.000I
        0.000 + -1.000I
```

In Example 2 of Section 8.4, we considered the problem of determining the loop currents in a dc circuit and found these currents by solving a system of linear equations. Whereas the current, voltage, and resistance of a dc circuit can be represented by real numbers, these same quantities are represented by complex numbers for ac circuits. Consequently, the equations in a linear system for finding loop currents in an ac circuit have coefficients that are complex numbers. Such a system can be solved using Gaussian elimination (or other methods used for solving linear systems) if the real operations are replaced by complex operations.

Exercises

1. Assuming that all values are represented with three significant digits (rounded when necessary), find values for A, B, and C for which

   (a) (A + B) + C does not have the same value as A + (B + C).
   (b) (A ∗ B) ∗ C does not have the same value as A ∗ (B ∗ C).
   (c) A ∗ (B + C) does not have the same value as (A ∗ B) + (A ∗ C).

2. For $z = 1 + 2i$ and $w = 3 - 4i$, calculate

   (a) $z + w$ (b) $z - w$ (c) $z \cdot w$ (d) $\dfrac{z}{w}$

(e) z^2 | **(f)** $\bar{z}$ | **(g)** $\overline{w}$ | **(h)** $\dfrac{z + \bar{z}}{2}$

(i) $\dfrac{z - \bar{z}}{2i}$ | **(j)** $z \cdot \bar{z}$ | **(k)** $\dfrac{1}{z}$ | **(l)** $\dfrac{z + w}{z - w}$

3. Repeat Exercise 2 for $z = 6 - 5i$ and $w = 5 + 12i$.

4. Assuming the declarations

```
INTEGER N1, N2
REAL R1, R2
DOUBLE PRECISION D1, D2
COMPLEX C1, C2
```

and the assignment statements

```
N1 = 2
R1 = 0.5
D1 = .1D0
C1 = (6.0,8.0)
```

find the value assigned to the specified variable in each of the following assignment statements or indicate why there is an error:

(a) `R2 = D1`
(b) `N2 = D1`
(c) `R2 = C1`
(d) `N2 = C1`
(e) `D2 = C1`
(f) `D2 = N1`
(g) `R2 = REAL(C1)`
(h) `R2 = AIMAG(C1)`
(i) `C2 = C1 * (0,1)`
(j) `C2 = 1 / C1`
(k) `R2 = ABS(C1)`
(l) `N2 = CONJG(C1)`
(m) `C2 = C1 ** N1`
(n) `C2 = C1 ** R1`
(o) `C2 = CMPLX(N1, R1)`
(p) `C2 = N1 + R1 * D1 + C1`
(q) `C2 = REAL(C1) + AIMAG(C1)`
(r) `C2 = EXP((0,0))`

5. For the sequence of numbers $a_0, a_1, a_2, \ldots$ defined by

$$a_0 = e^1 - 1$$

and

$$a_{n+1} = (n + 1)a_n - 1 \qquad \text{for} \qquad n = 0, 1, 2, \ldots$$

it can be shown that for each n,

$$a_n = n! \left[e^1 - \left(1 + 1 + \frac{1}{2!} + \cdots + \frac{1}{n!} \right) \right]$$

so that this sequence converges to 0. Write a program that prints a table of values of a_n for $n = 0, 1, 2, \ldots, 15$, calculated first in single precision and then in double precision.

6. Write a program to find a double precision approximation to the zero of a function using Newton's method (see Example 1 of Section 9.3).

7. Write a program to find a double precision approximation to an integral using the trapezoidal method or Simpson's rule (see Exercises 23 and 24 at the end of Chapter 4).

8. Repeat Exercise 13 of Section 9.2 for calculating values of the hyperbolic sine function sinh by using a subprogram to calculate e^x, but perform all calculations in double precision. In particular, use the series to calculate values for e^x using double precision arithmetic to achieve 10-place accuracy.

9. Write a program that reads three complex numbers P, Q, and R and that then determines whether the triangle whose vertices are the points corresponding to P, Q, and R in the complex plane is a right triangle.

10. The exponentiation operator $**$ is defined for complex values only when the exponent is an integer. To calculate z^a when z is complex and a is real or complex, we can use

$$z^a = e^{a \log z}$$

Write a function that calculates z^a. Use the function in a program that reads values for z and a and then calls the function to calculate the value of z^a.

11. In Section 10.2 we noted that a complex number $z = a + bi$ can be represented geometrically by the vector $\overrightarrow{OP}$ from the origin to the point P having rectangular coordinates (a, b). Using polar coordinates for P gives the following *polar representation* for z:

$$z = r(\cos \theta + i \sin \theta)$$

which can be equivalently written as

$$z = re^{i\theta}$$

where r is the length of $\overrightarrow{OP}$ and θ is the angle from the positive x axis to $\overrightarrow{OP}$. Write a subroutine that converts a complex number from its usual representation to its polar representation. Use the subroutine in a program that reads a complex number z and a positive integer n and

finds the *nth roots of z* as given by

$$z^{1/n} = r^{1/n}\left[\cos\left(\frac{\theta + 2k\pi}{n}\right) + i\sin\left(\frac{\theta + 2k\pi}{n}\right)\right]$$

$$k = 0, 1, \ldots, n - 1$$

12. Suppose that an ac circuit contains a capacitor, an inductor, and a resistor in series:

The impedance Z_R for the resistor is simply the resistance R, but for inductors and capacitors, it is a function of the frequency. The impedance Z_L of the inductor is the complex value given by

$$Z_L = \omega L i$$

where ω is the frequency (in radians per second) of the ac source and L is the self-inductance (in henries). For the capacitor, the impedance is

$$Z_C = \frac{-i}{\omega C}$$

where C is the capacitance (in farads). Write a program that reads values for R, L, and C, then reads several pairs of values for the frequency ω (a real number) and instantaneous voltage V (a complex number), and calculates for each pair the total impedance

$$Z = Z_R + Z_L + Z_C$$

and the instantaneous current I and its magnitude where

$$I = \frac{V}{Z}$$

13. Repeat Exercise 6 at the end of Chapter 9 for polynomial evaluation using nested multiplication, but allow the coefficients of the polynomial and the value of x to be complex numbers.

Programming Pointers

In this chapter we considered the two numeric data types, double precision and complex. The main points to remember when using these data types are the following:

1. *Precision may be lost in double precision expressions and assignments because of the presence of single precision constants and/or variables.*

To illustrate, consider the declarations

```
REAL X
DOUBLE PRECISION A, B
```

In the assignment statement

```
B = 0.1 * A ** 2
```

precision may be lost because of the single precision constant 0.1. This statement should be written

```
B = 0.1D0 * A ** 2
```

Similarly, in the assignment statement

```
X = (A + B) * (A - B)
```

the expression on the right side is evaluated in double precision, but the resulting value is then assigned to the single precision variable X. Remember, however, that simply declaring everything to be double precision does not solve all of the problems arising from limited precision. For example, the logical expression

```
A * (1.0D0 / A) .EQ. 1.0D0
```

is still false for most double precision values of A.

2. *Double precision and complex values may not both be used in an expression, nor is assignment of a double precision (complex) value to a complex (double precision) variable allowed.*

3. *A pair of real constants representing a complex data value is enclosed within parentheses for list-directed input but not for formatted input.*

4. *Formatted output of complex values requires two real descriptors.*

5. *Complex values may be compared only with the relational operators .EQ. and .NE. .* Remember, however, the danger of comparing real numbers with these relational operators (see Sections 4.1 and 4.2).

Variations and Extensions

There are only a few variations from or extensions to the standard features regarding double precision and complex data in other versions of FORTRAN. Two of these are

● Modified forms of the type statements for double precision and/or complex data may be allowed or required.

● Complex values with double precision real and imaginary parts and mixed-mode expressions containing both double precision and complex values may be allowed.

See Appendix F for additional details regarding these variations and extensions.

11

Advanced Character Data

Everyone knows how laborious the usual Method is of attaining to Arts and Sciences; whereas by his Contrivance, the most ignorant Person at a reasonable Charge, and with a little bodily Labour, may write Books in Philosophy, Poetry, Politicks, Law, Mathematicks, and Theology, without the least Assistance from Genius or Study. He then led me to the Frame, about the sides whereof all his Pupils stood in Ranks. It was Twenty Foot square . . . linked by slender Wires. These Bits . . . were covered on every Square with Paper pasted upon them; and on These Papers were written all the Words of their Language. . . .

The Professor then desired me to observe, for he was going to set his Engine at work. The Pupils at this Command took each of them hold of an Iron Handle, whereof there were Forty fixed round the Edges of the Frame; and giving them a sudden Turn, the whole Disposition of the Words was entirely changed. . . .

JONATHAN SWIFT, *Gulliver's Travels*

The word *compute* usually suggests arithmetic operations performed on numeric data; thus, computers are sometimes thought to be mere "number crunchers," devices whose only function is to process numeric information. In Chapter 1, however, we considered coding schemes used to represent character information in a computer, and in subsequent chapters we introduced some of the character-processing capabilities of FORTRAN. We have discussed character constants, character variables and their declarations, the character operations of concatenation and substring extraction, assignment of values to character variables, input and output of character data, and comparison of character values in a logical expression. In this chapter we continue our study of character data.

447

11.1 Review of Character Data and Operations

Recall that a character constant is a string of characters from the FORTRAN character set enclosed in apostrophes (single quotes) and that the number of characters enclosed is the length of the constant.

As we have seen, character variables may be declared using a type statement of the form

CHARACTER*n, *list*

where *list* is a list of variables being typed as character and n is the length of their values. The comma preceding the list may be omitted; also, the length specification n may be omitted, in which case it is assumed to be 1.

The statement

```
CHARACTER*10 CITY, STATE, COUNTRY
```

declares CITY, STATE, and COUNTRY to be of character type with string values of length 10. The length specification of any variable in the list may be overridden by appending a length descriptor of the form *m to its name; thus

```
CHARACTER*10 CITY*20, STATE, COUNTRY
```

declares CITY to have values of length 20.

In Section 6.3 we considered the character operation of **concatenation.** This operation is denoted by // and can be used to combine two or more character constants or variables. Another operation we described is the extraction of a sequence of consecutive characters, called a **substring,** from a given string. This is done by attaching to a character variable the positions of the first and last characters of the substring, separated by a colon (:) and enclosed in parentheses. Thus if UNITS is declared by

```
CHARACTER*20 UNITS
```

and assigned the value

```
UNITS = 'FEET PER SECOND'
```

then UNITS(6:8) has the value 'PER'. The first position specified for a substring should be positive; the last position must be greater than or equal to the first position and less than or equal to the length of the given string. If the initial position of the substring is not specified, it is assumed to be 1; if the final position is not specified, it is assumed to be the last position in the value of the character variable. Thus, UNITS(:4) has the value 'FEET', and UNITS(10:) has the value 'SECONDｂｂｂｂｂ', where ｂ denotes a blank.

We have also seen that a substring name may appear to the left of the assignment operator in an assignment statement or in the input list of a READ statement. In either case, the character positions specified in the substring name are assigned values, but the remaining positions are not changed. For example, the assignment statement

```
UNITS(10:16) = 'MINUTE'
```

changes the value of UNITS to 'FEET PER MINUTEⱠⱠⱠⱠ'. In such assignment statements, however, those positions to which new values are being assigned may not be referenced in the character expression on the right side. Thus,

```
UNITS(6:8) = UNITS(10:12)
```

is valid, whereas

```
UNITS(6:8) = UNITS(7:9)
```

is not because the substring being modified overlaps the substring being referenced.

11.2 The INDEX and LEN Functions

In extracting or modifying substrings, it is often convenient to locate a given pattern within a string. For example, we might wish to search the string

```
'ATOMIC WEIGHT OF KRYPTON'
```

to find the location of the substring

```
'WEIGHT'
```

This can be done using the FORTRAN library function INDEX of the form

INDEX(*string1, string2*)

where *string1* and *string2* are any expressions of character type. The first argument is the string being searched, and the second is the substring whose location is to be determined. The value of the function is the integer value corresponding to the character position at which the first occurrence of that substring begins, or 0 if the substring does not appear in the given string. Thus, the value of

```
INDEX('ATOMIC WEIGHT OF KRYPTON', 'WEIGHT')
```

is 8, whereas the value of

```
INDEX('ATOMIC WEIGHT OF KRYPTON', 'NUMBER')
```

is 0.

The following table gives more examples of the index function. In these examples, UNITS and DIST are assumed to be declared by

```
CHARACTER UNITS*15, DIST*6
```

and to have the values

```
UNITS = 'FEET PER SECOND'
DIST = 'METERS'
```

Expression	Value
INDEX(UNITS, DIST)	0
INDEX(UNITS, 'PER')	6
INDEX(UNITS, DIST(4:5))	7
INDEX(UNITS, 'E')	2
UNITS(INDEX(UNITS, 'S'):)	'SECOND'
DIST(3:INDEX(UNITS, ' '))	'TER'
DIST // UNITS(INDEX(UNITS, ' '):)	'METERS PER SECOND'

Another FORTRAN library function that may be used with character data is the LEN function of the form

```
LEN(string)
```

where *string* is any character expression. The value of this function is the length of the specified string.

Suppose that NAME has been declared to be of character type by the statement

```
CHARACTER*20 NAME
```

and consider the assignment statement

```
NAME = 'JOHN DOE'
```

The following table shows the results of several uses of the LEN function:

Function Reference	Result
PRINT *, LEN('JOHN DOE')	8 is displayed
PRINT *, LEN(NAME)	20 is displayed
N = LEN('MR. '//NAME)	24 is assigned to N
PRINT *, LEN(NAME(9:))	12 is displayed
DO 10 I = 1, LEN(NAME)	Loop is repeated 20 times

As the preceding examples show, for a character constant, the value of the LEN function is simply the number of characters in that constant; for a character variable, it is the declared length of that variable. Consequently, this function is of rather limited use. However, a statement such as

```
DO 10 I = 1, LEN(NAME)
```

is preferred over

```
DO 10 I = 1, 20
```

because it does not have to be changed if the program is modified by changing the declared length of NAME. The LEN function is also useful in subprograms in which an indefinite length specifier is used to declare arguments of character type.

The preparation of textual material such as research papers, books, and computer programs often involves the insertion, deletion, and replacement of parts of the text. The software of most computer systems includes an **editing** package that makes it easy to carry out these operations. As an example showing the text-processing capabilities of FORTRAN, we consider the editing problem of replacing a specified substring in a given line of text with another string. A solution to this problem is given in the program in Figure 11.1. The sample run shows that in addition to string replacements, the program can be used to make insertions and deletions. For example, changing the substring

```
A N
```

in the line of text

```
A NATION CONCEIVED IN LIBERTY AND AND DEDICATED
```

to

```
A NEW N
```

yields the edited line

```
A NEW NATION CONCEIVED IN LIBERTY AND AND DEDICATED
```

Entering the edit change

```
AND //
```

changes the substring

```
ANDb
```

(where b denotes a blank) in the line of text to an *empty* or *null* string containing no characters, and so the edited result is

```
A NEW NATION CONCEIVED IN LIBERTY AND DEDICATED
```

```
      PROGRAM EDITOR
************************************************************************
* Program to perform some basic text-editing functions on lines of   *
* text.  The basic operation is that of replacing a substring of     *
* the text by another string.  This replacement is accomplished      *
* by a command of the form                                           *
*                      oldstring/newstring/                          *
* where oldstring specifies the substring in the text to be replaced *
* with newstring; newstring may be an empty string which then causes *
* oldstring (if found) to be deleted.  The text lines are read from a *
* file, and after editing, the edited lines are written to another   *
* file.  Variables used are:                                         *
*     OLDFIL  : name of the input file                               *
*     NEWFIL  : name of the output file                              *
*     TEXT    : a character string representing a line of text       *
*     CHANGE  : a character string specifying the edit operation.    *
*               Value is of the form:                                *
*                      'oldstring/newstring/'                        *
*     TEMP    : intermediate edited version of TEXT                  *
*     IND1    : end position of old string in CHANGE                 *
*     IND2    : end position of new string in CHANGE                 *
*     LNEW    : number of characters in new string                   *
*     LOC     : index of old string in TEXT                          *
*     RESPON  : user response (Y or N)                               *
*     DONE    : logical variable to indicate when editing is done    *
************************************************************************

      CHARACTER*80 TEXT, CHANGE, TEMP, OLDFIL*20, NEWFIL*20, RESPON*1
      INTEGER IND1, IND2, LOC, LNEW
      LOGICAL DONE

      PRINT *, 'ENTER THE NAME OF THE INPUT FILE'
      READ '(A)', OLDFIL
      PRINT *, 'ENTER THE NAME OF THE OUTPUT FILE'
      READ '(A)', NEWFIL
      OPEN (UNIT = 15, FILE = OLDFIL, STATUS = 'OLD')
      OPEN (UNIT = 16, FILE = NEWFIL, STATUS = 'NEW')

* While there are more data do the following:

10    READ (15, '(A)', END = 30) TEXT
      PRINT *, TEXT
      PRINT *, 'EDIT THIS LINE (Y OR N)?'
      READ '(A)', RESPON
      DONE = (RESPON .EQ. 'N')

* While not DONE (there is more editing) do the following:

20    IF (.NOT. DONE) THEN
          PRINT *, 'ENTER EDIT CHANGE'
          READ '(A)', CHANGE
```

Figure 11.1

Figure 11.1 (continued)

```
*           Replace first occurrence of oldstring by newstring

            IND1 = INDEX(CHANGE, '/') - 1
            IND2 = IND1 + INDEX(CHANGE(2 + IND1: ), '/')
            IF (IND1 .LT. 0 .OR. IND2 .EQ. IND1) THEN
                PRINT *, 'MISSING SLASH'
            ELSE
                LOC = INDEX(TEXT, CHANGE( :IND1))
                IF (LOC .GT. 0) THEN
                    TEMP = CHANGE(2 + IND1 : IND2)
   +                       // TEXT(LOC + IND1: )
                    IF (LOC .EQ. 1) THEN
                        TEXT = TEMP
                    ELSE
                        TEXT = TEXT( :LOC - 1) // TEMP
                    END IF
                END IF
            END IF

*           Display edited line and see if more editing is desired

            PRINT *, TEXT
            PRINT *, 'MORE EDITING (Y OR N)'
            READ '(A)', RESPON
            DONE = (RESPON .EQ. 'N')
            GO TO 20
        ELSE
            WRITE (16, '(A)') TEXT
            PRINT *
            GO TO 10
        END IF
30      CLOSE(15)
        CLOSE(16)
        END
```

```
Listing of TEXT-FILE used in sample run:
=========================================

FOURSCORE AND FIVE YEARS AGO, OUR MOTHERS
BROUGHT FORTH ON CONTINENT
A NATION CONCEIVED IN LIBERTY AND AND DEDICATED
TO THE PREPOSITION THAT ALL MEN
ARE CREATED EQUAL.


Listing of NEW-TEXT-FILE produced by sample run:
================================================

FOURSCORE AND SEVEN YEARS AGO, OUR FATHERS
BROUGHT FORTH ON THIS CONTINENT
A NEW NATION CONCEIVED IN LIBERTY AND DEDICATED
TO THE PROPOSITION THAT ALL MEN
ARE CREATED EQUAL.
```

Figure 11.1   (continued)

```
Sample run:
==========

 ENTER THE NAME OF THE INPUT FILE
TEXT-FILE
 ENTER THE NAME OF THE OUTPUT FILE
NEW-TEXT-FILE
 FOURSCORE AND FIVE YEARS AGO, OUR MOTHERS
 EDIT THIS LINE (Y OR N)?
Y
 ENTER EDIT CHANGE
FIVE/SEVEN/
 FOURSCORE AND SEVEN YEARS AGO, OUR MOTHERS
 MORE EDITING (Y OR N)
Y
 ENTER EDIT CHANGE
MOTHERS/FATHERS/
 FOURSCORE AND SEVEN YEARS AGO, OUR FATHERS
 MORE EDITING (Y OR N)
N

 BROUGHT FORTH ON CONTINENT
 EDIT THIS LINE (Y OR N)?
Y
 ENTER EDIT CHANGE
ON C/ON THIS C/
 BROUGHT FORTH ON THIS CONTINENT
 MORE EDITING (Y OR N)
N

 A NATION CONCEIVED IN LIBERTY AND AND DEDICATED
 EDIT THIS LINE (Y OR N)?
Y
 ENTER EDIT CHANGE
N/NEW N/
 A NEW NATION CONCEIVED IN LIBERTY AND AND DEDICATED
 MORE EDITING (Y OR N)
Y
 ENTER EDIT CHANGE
AND //
 A NEW NATION CONCEIVED IN LIBERTY AND DEDICATED
 MORE EDITING (Y OR N)
N

 TO THE PREPOSITION THAT ALL MEN
 EDIT THIS LINE (Y OR N)?
Y
 ENTER EDIT CHANGE
PRE/PRO/
 TO THE PROPOSITION THAT ALL MEN
 MORE EDITING (Y OR N)
N

 ARE CREATED EQUAL.
 EDIT THIS LINE (Y OR N)?
N
```

11.3   Character Comparison

In Section 6.3 we described the **collating sequence** which defines the ordering of characters: one character precedes another if its numeric code (as determined by an encoding scheme such as ASCII or EBCDIC) is less than the numeric code of the other. We observed, however, that the ANSI FORTRAN 77 standard only partially specifies the collating sequence: uppercase letters are ordered A through Z; digits are ordered 0 through 9; letters and digits may not overlap; and the blank character must precede all letters and digits. No particular order is specified for special characters or for their relation to other characters.

For example,

```
'C' .LT. 'H'
```

is a true logical expression, since C must precede H in every collating sequence. Similarly, the logical expressions

```
'HCL' .LT. 'NACL'
'CO2' .GT. 'C'
```

are true, since strings are compared character by character using the collating sequence and in the first case, H must precede N, and in the second case, O must follow a blank character. (Recall that with strings of different lengths, the shorter string is blank padded so that two strings of equal length are compared.) However, the truth or falsity of such logical expressions as

```
'3' .LT. 'B'
'PDQ+123' .GT. 'PDQ*123'
```

depends on the collating sequence used in a particular computer.

The variation in collating sequences may cause the same program to execute differently on one machine than it does on another. This difficulty can be circumvented by using the special functions LLT, LLE, LGT, and LGE. The LLT function has the form

LLT(*string1, string2*)

where *string1* and *string2* are character expressions. The value of this function is true if *string1* precedes *string2* using the collating sequence *determined by ASCII encoding* and is false otherwise. Thus,

```
LLT('1','A')
```

is true, *regardless* of which collating sequence is in effect.

Similarly,

LLE(*string1, string2*)

is true if *string1* precedes or is equal to *string2* using the ASCII collating sequence;

    LGT(*string1, string2*)

is true if *string1* follows *string2*, and

    LGE(*string1, string2*)

is true if *string1* follows or is equal to *string2* using the ASCII collating sequence.

The position of a character in the collating sequence can be obtained by using the ICHAR function of the form

    ICHAR(*char*)

where *char* is an expression whose value is a single character. The value of this function is the integer that corresponds to the character's position in the computer's collating sequence.

The inverse function CHAR has the form

    CHAR(*integer*)

and produces a single character whose position in the collating sequence is the specified integer, provided, of course, that this integer is in the appropriate range. Thus, if X has a single character as its value,

```
CHAR(ICHAR(X))
```

is equal to X, and if K is an integer variable,

```
ICHAR(CHAR(K))
```

is equal to K. The program in Figure 11.2 uses these character functions to implement a simple cryptographic scheme, that is, a scheme for coding a message as a scrambled sequence of characters, known as a *cryptogram*. It encodes a message by converting each character to its numeric representation (ASCII or EBCDIC) using the function ICHAR and then adding a key value. Because this sum may be outside the range of legal numeric codes (usually 0–255), the MOD function is used to obtain a legal value, which is then converted to a character using the CHAR function.

```
        PROGRAM CODER
***********************************************************************
* This program scrambles a message by converting each character of the *
* message to its numeric code, adding an integer to this code, and    *
* then converting the resulting number back to a character.  Variables *
* used are the following:                                             *
*       MESS    :  the message to be scrambled                        *
*       KEY     :  the integer to be added in scrambling the message  *
*       SYMBOL  :  an individual character of the message             *
*       CODE    :  numeric code for SYMBOL                            *
*       I       :  counter                                            *
***********************************************************************

        CHARACTER*80 MESS, SYMBOL*1
        INTEGER KEY, I, CODE

        PRINT *, 'ENTER MESSAGE (END WITH #):'
        READ '(A)', MESS
        PRINT *, 'ENTER KEY:'
        READ *, KEY
        I = 1
        SYMBOL = MESS(1:1)

* While not end of string do

10      IF (I .LT. LEN(MESS) .AND. SYMBOL .NE. '#') THEN
           CODE = MOD(ICHAR(SYMBOL) + KEY, 256)
           MESS(I:I) = CHAR(CODE)
           I = I + 1
           SYMBOL = MESS(I:I)
           GO TO 10
        END IF

        PRINT *, 'CODED MESSAGE:  ', MESS
        END


Sample run (assuming ASCII):
============================

 ENTER MESSAGE (END WITH #):
THE REDCOATS ARE COMING#
 ENTER KEY:
5
 CODED MESSAGE:   YMJ%WJIHTFYX%FWJ%HTRNSL#
```

Figure 11.2

11.4   Examples: Plotting Surfaces, Plotting Level Curves, Lexical Analysis, Reverse Polish Notation

EXAMPLE 1: Plotting Surfaces.   As noted in Example 1 of Section 6.4, many computer systems include a plotting device and some graphics software that may be used to produce high-resolution graphs of functions. We also noted that a terminal or printer can also be used for graphic displays, but with poorer

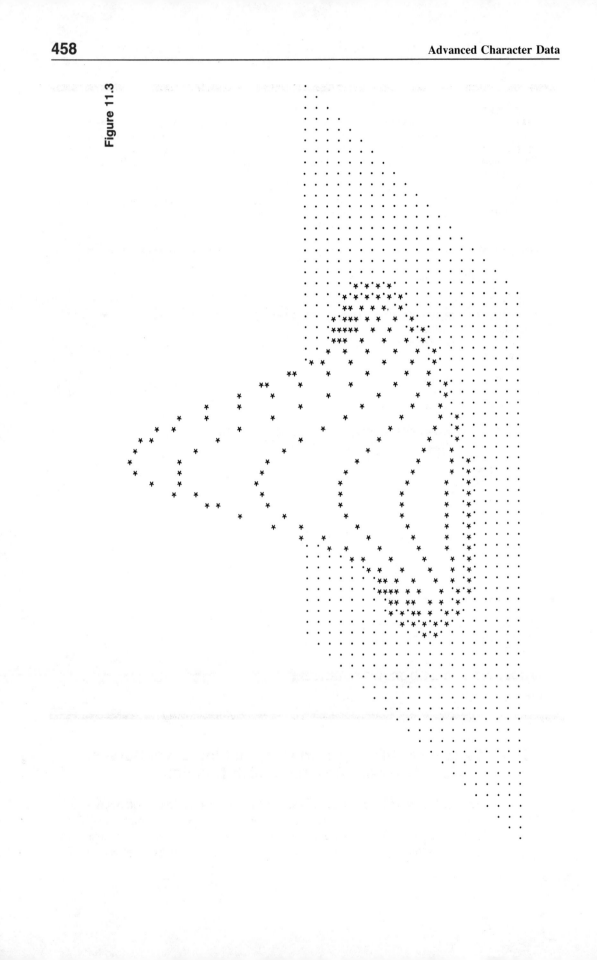

Figure 11.3

quality owing to the limited resolution caused by the small number of print positions across the page and the ability of such output devices to advance in only one direction, from one line to the next. This is, however, adequate for bar graphs (see Example 2 of Section 7.5), and it is adequate for approximate graphs of functions $y = f(x)$ (see Example 1 of Section 6.4).

Plotters are especially useful for displaying surfaces that represent the graph of a function of two variables, $z = f(x,y)$. But a rough sketch of certain surfaces is also possible using a terminal or printer (see Figure 11.3), and in this example we consider the problem of producing such plots.

To display the surface $z = f(x,y)$, it is convenient to let the x axis be vertical (directed downward), with the y axis at a $45°$ angle to the x axis and the z axis horizontal.

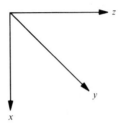

A scaling problem arises because the width and height of characters displayed by a terminal or printer are not the same. In this example, we assume that the ratio of width to height is $3/5 = .6$. Another problem that occurs in graphing surfaces is that certain portions of the surface cannot be seen because they are hidden by other portions.

The program in Figure 11.4 plots the graph of the function defined by the function subprogram F. The parameter HPOS is the number of horizontal print positions and is thus used to specify the length of LINE, which represents one line of output. The parameter VPOS is the number of vertical print positions.

The plot is generated by displaying periods (.) for points in the base xy plane and asterisks (∗) for points on cross sections of the surface cut by planes parallel to the xz plane. The number of cross sections SLICES is entered during program execution. This number is used to determine the horizontal increment between slices

```
ZINC = NINT(HPOS / (2.0 * SLICES))
```

and the corresponding X and Y increments

```
XINC = NINT(.6 * ZINC)
YINC = SQRT(XINC ** 2 + YINC ** 2)
```

The DO loop controlled by

```
DO 10 N = 0, VPOS + SLICES * XINC
```

displays the points on the base plane and on each of the cross sections corresponding to the Nth line of output. This line of output LINE is initially blank, and the substring operation is used to insert characters (. or *) in the appropriate positions. The logical expressions

```
NSLICE .GT. NINT(N / XINC)
```

and

```
NSLICE .GE. NINT((N - VPOS) / XINC)
```

are used to prevent the output of points outside the region used to display the *xy* plane.

The two IF statements

```
IF (HORIZ .GT. MAXZ) THEN
    LINE(HORIZ - 1 : HORIZ - 1) = '.'
    MAXZ = HORIZ
END IF
```

and

```
IF (HORIZ .GT. MAXZ) THEN
    LINE(HORIZ - 1 : HORIZ - 1) = '*'
    MAXZ = HORIZ
END IF
```

solve the hidden line problem by keeping track of the rightmost print position MAXZ for this output line. Any horizontal position less than MAXZ represents a hidden point and is not plotted.

```
      PROGRAM PLOT
**********************************************************************
* Program to plot the graph of a surface Z = F(X,Y).  Variables used *
* are:                                                              *
*     HPOS   : parameter giving # of horizontal print positions     *
*     VPOS   : parameter giving # of vertical print positions       *
*     ZINC   : horizontal increment between slices                  *
*     XINC   : corresponding X increment                            *
*     YINC   : corresponding Y increment                            *
*     X, Y, Z: coordinates of a point                               *
*     SLICES : number of cross sections                             *
*     NSLICE : number of a cross section                            *
*     HORIZ  : number of a horizontal print position                *
*     LINE   : a line of output                                     *
*     MAXZ   : rightmost print position used in LINE                *
*     N      : count of output lines                                *
*     FILLED : logical variable indicating when LINE is filled      *
**********************************************************************
      INTEGER HPOS, VPOS, SLICES, N, MAXZ, NSLICE, HORIZ
      REAL XINC, YINC, ZINC, X, Y, Z, F
      PARAMETER (HPOS = 72, VPOS = 50)
      CHARACTER*(HPOS) LINE
      LOGICAL FILLED

      PRINT *, 'ENTER # SLICES'
      READ *, SLICES
```

Figure 11.4

Figure 11.4 **(continued)**

```
*       Set increments for the axes

        ZINC = NINT(HPOS/(2. * SLICES))
        XINC = NINT(.6 * ZINC)
        YINC = SQRT(XINC ** 2 + ZINC ** 2)

*       Plot the surface by displaying a line of output showing
*       the points (.) in the base plane and the points (*) on
*       the cross sections corresponding to the Nth output line

        DO 20 N = 0, VPOS + SLICES * XINC

            LINE = ' '
            MAXZ = 0
            NSLICE = 0
            FILLED = .FALSE.

*           While there are more points in the output line to be found
*           do the following:

10          IF ((NSLICE .LE. SLICES) .AND. .NOT. FILLED) THEN
                IF (NSLICE .GT. NINT(N / XINC)) THEN
                    FILLED = .TRUE.
                ELSE IF (NSLICE .GE. NINT((N - VPOS) / XINC)) THEN
                    HORIZ = NINT(NSLICE * ZINC)

*                   Check for hidden point

                    IF (HORIZ .GT. MAXZ) THEN
                        LINE (HORIZ - 1 : HORIZ - 1) = '.'
                        MAXZ = HORIZ
                    END IF

*                   Determine where to plot a point

                    X = N - NSLICE * XINC
                    Y = NSLICE * YINC
                    Z = F(X,Y)
                    HORIZ = NINT(Z + NSLICE * ZINC)

*                   Check for hidden point again

                    IF (HORIZ .GT. MAXZ) THEN
                        LINE(HORIZ - 1 : HORIZ - 1) = '*'
                        MAXZ = HORIZ
                    END IF
                END IF

*               Move to next cross section

                NSLICE = NSLICE + 1
                GO TO 10
            END IF
            PRINT *, LINE
20      CONTINUE
        END

        FUNCTION F(X,Y)
        REAL F, X, Y
        F = 50 * EXP(-.02 * ((X - 25) **2 + (Y - 25) **2))
        END
```

Figure 11.4 (continued)

```
Sample run:
==========

ENTER # SLICES
20
```

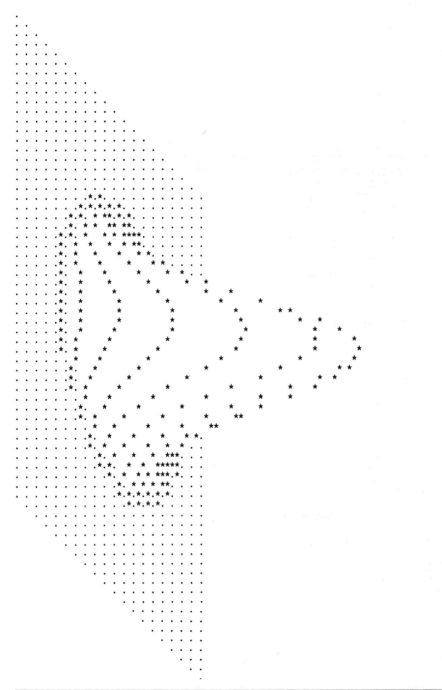

EXAMPLE 2: Plotting Level Curves. Another representation of a three-dimensional surface $z = f(x,y)$ in two dimensions is obtained by displaying its **level curves** or **contour maps.** A level curve consists of all points (x,y) where the function has a particular constant value. For example, if $f(x,y)$ represents temperature at point (x,y), the level curve $f(x,y) = 30$ is an iso-thermal curve consisting of all points where the temperature is 30.

The program in Figure 11.5 plots the level curves for a function F. It uses the character variable LINE to display points on the various level curves for a given Y value. It uses 10 different characters to represent 10 levels on the surface corresponding to function values in the intervals [ZMIN, ZMIN + DELZ], [ZMIN + DELZ, ZMIN + 2 ∗ DELZ], . . . , [ZMIN + 9 ∗ DELZ, ZMAX] where ZMIN and ZMAX are entered during execution. The sample run shows the output produced for the function

```
F(X,Y) = 50 * EXP(-.02 * ((X - 25) ** 2) + (Y - 25) ** 2)
```

with ZMIN = 0 and ZMAX = 50 using the characters '0', '1', . . . , '9' to represent the various levels.

```
      PROGRAM LEVELS
***********************************************************************
* Program to plot level curves F(X,Y) = constant for a function F.   *
* Variables used are:                                                *
*     HORIZ      : parameter = number of horizontal print positions  *
*     I, J       : indices used to find intervals and level curves   *
*     VERT       : parameter = number of vertical print positions    *
*     NSYM       : parameter = the number of different characters     *
*     SYMBOL     : array of NSYM characters used to plot level curves *
*     LINE       : a line of output                                  *
*     XMIN,XMAX  : minimum, maximum value of X                       *
*     YMIN,YMAX  :    "          "        "    of Y                  *
*     ZMIN,ZMAX  :    "          "        "    of Z                  *
*     DELTAX     : X-increment                                       *
*     DELTAY     : Y-increment                                       *
*     DELTAZ     : Z-increment                                       *
*     X,Y,Z      : coordinates of a point on the surface Z = F(X,Y)  *
*     H, V       : count horizontal, vertical, print positions       *
***********************************************************************

      INTEGER HORIZ, VERT, NSYM, H, V, I, J
      PARAMETER (HORIZ = 75, VERT = 45, NSYM = 10)
      CHARACTER SYMBOL(NSYM), LINE*(HORIZ)
      REAL XMIN, XMAX, YMIN, YMAX, ZMIN, ZMAX, DELTAX, DELTAY, DELTAZ,
     +     X, Y, Z, F
```

Figure 11.5

Figure 11.5 (continued)

```
*    Initialize array of characters to indicate level curves

     DATA SYMBOL /'0','1','2','3','4','5','6','7','8','9'/

     PRINT *, 'ENTER MINIMUM AND MAXIMUM X-VALUES, THEN Y-VALUES'
     READ *, XMIN, XMAX, YMIN, YMAX
     PRINT *, 'ENTER MINIMUM AND MAXIMUM VALUES OF FUNCTION'
     READ *, ZMIN, ZMAX
     DELTAX = (XMAX - XMIN) / HORIZ
     DELTAY = (YMAX - YMIN) / VERT
     DELTAZ = (ZMAX - ZMIN) / NSYM
     Y = YMAX
     DO 20 V = 1, VERT
         X = XMIN
         DO 10 H = 1, HORIZ

*        Generate a line of output for this Y value

             LINE(H:H) = SYMBOL(1)
             Z = F(X,Y)

*            Find interval in which Z lies to find level curve

             J = 0
             IF (Z .GE. ZMAX) THEN
                 LINE(H:H) = SYMBOL(NSYM)
             ELSE

*                Repeatedly subtract DELTAZ until Z < ZMIN

30               Z = Z - DELTAZ
                 J = J + 1
                 IF (Z .GT. ZMIN) GO TO 30

*                Set character for (Jth) level curve

                 LINE(H:H) = SYMBOL(J)
             END IF
             X = X + DELTAX
10       CONTINUE
         Y = Y - DELTAY
         PRINT *, LINE
20   CONTINUE

* Print the intervals represented by the level curves

     PRINT *
     Z = ZMIN
     DO 50 I = 1, NSYM - 1
         PRINT 40, SYMBOL(I), Z, ' TO ', Z + DELTAZ
40       FORMAT(1X, 'LEVEL CURVE ', A, ' -- ', F6.2, A, F6.2)
         Z = Z + DELTAZ
50   CONTINUE
     PRINT 40, SYMBOL(NSYM), ZMAX, ' AND ABOVE'
     END

     FUNCTION F(X,Y)
     REAL X, Y, F
     F = 50 * EXP(-.02 * ((X - 25) **2 + (Y - 25) **2))
     END
```

...st be broken down into the following units:

ALPHA – – – – – – variable
=   – – – – – – assignment operator
200   – – – – – – integer constant
*   – – – – – – operator
BETA   – – – – – – variable
+   – – – – – – operator
5   – – – – – – integer constant

These units are called **tokens,** and the section of the compiler that recognizes these tokens is called the **lexical analyzer.**

An algorithm to carry out this lexical analysis is as follows:

ALGORITHM FOR LEXICAL ANALYZER

```
* Algorithm to implement a simple lexical analyzer that processes    *
* FORTRAN assignment statements involving only variables,            *
* integer constants, arithmetic operators +, −, *, /, and ** and a   *
* special end-of-statement mark.                                     *
```

1. Read the statement STAT to be processed.
2. Set I equal to 1.
3. While the Ith character in STAT is not the end-of-statement mark, do the following:
   a. Skip over blanks by increasing I by 1 so long as the Ith character in STAT is a blank.
   b. Now there are five possible cases for the Ith character in STAT Determine which one holds and call an appropriate subalgorithm to take the action specified:

   (i)   letter: Call VAR to process a variable name.
   (ii) digit: Call CONST to process an integer constant.
   (iii) +, −, *, or /:   Call OPER to process an arithmetic operator.
   (iv) =:   Call ASSIGN to process an assignment operator.
   (v)   other symbol: Call ILLEG to process an illegal symbol unless the character is the end-of-statement mark.

Subalgorithms to process the various tokens must also be designed. The subalgorithm VAR for variable names is

SUBALGORITHM VAR

```
* Subalgorithm to process a variable name in statement STAT    *
* beginning at position I.                                     *
```

1. Initialize NAME to blanks and J to 1.
2. While the Ith character of STAT is a letter or a digit, do the following:

Figure 11.5 (continued)

```
Sample run:
==========

ENTER MINIMUM AND MAXIMUM X-VALUES, THEN Y-VALUES
10, 40, 10, 40
ENTER MINIMUM AND MAXIMUM VALUES OF FUNCTION
0, 50
0000000000000000000000000000000000000000000000000000000000000000000000000000
0000000000000000000000000000000000000000000000000000000000000000000000000000
0000000000000000000000000000000000000000000000000000000000000000000000000000
0000000000000000000000000000000000000000000000000000000000000000000000000000
0000000000000000000000000000000000000000000000000000000000000000000000000000
0000000000000000000000000000000000000000000000000000000000000000000000000000
0000000000000000000000000000000000000000000000000000000000000000000000000000
000000000000000000000000000001111111111111110000000000000000000000000000000
000000000000000000000000001111111111111111111111110000000000000000000000000
000000000000000000000000111111111111111111111111111110000000000000000000000
00000000000000000000011111111222222222222222211111111100000000000000000000
00000000000000000001111111122222222233333322222222211111111100000000000000
00000000000000000111111222222333333333333333322222211111100000000000000000
00000000000000001111112222233333444444444444433333222211111100000000000000
0000000000000011111122223333344444555555544444333322221111110000000000000
0000000000000111112222333344455555566665555544443333222211111000000000000
00000000000001111122223333444555566666666666655554444333322211111000000000
000000000000111112223334455566667777777776666555443332221111100000000000
00000000000011111222333445556667778888888877766655544333222111110000000000
0000000000011111222333445556667778888999999988877766555443322211110000000000
000000000001111122233344555667788889999999998887766555443322211110000000000
0000000000111112223334455667778889999999999998877766655443322211110000000000
000000000011111222333445556677788999999999999988877766554433222111110000000000
00000000001111122233344555667778889999999999998887766555443322211110000000000
0000000000111112223334455667778889999999998887766555443322211110000000000
00000000001111122233344555667778888888888887776665554433222111110000000000
0000000000011111222333445556666777788888887776665554433222111110000000000
000000000001111122233344555666677777777766665554433322211110000000000
00000000000011111222233344455666666666666665554443332221111100000000000
0000000000000111112222333444555666665555554444433332221111100000000000
00000000000000111111222222333333333333333332222211111100000000000000
0000000000000000011111112222222222333333222222222211111110000000000000
00000000000000000011111111222222222222222211111111000000000000000000
0000000000000000000001111111111111111111111100000000000000000000000
0000000000000000000000011111111111111111111110000000000000000000000
000000000000000000000000001111111111111110000000000000000000000000
0000000000000000000000000000000000000000000000000000000000000000000000000000
0000000000000000000000000000000000000000000000000000000000000000000000000000
0000000000000000000000000000000000000000000000000000000000000000000000000000
0000000000000000000000000000000000000000000000000000000000000000000000000000
0000000000000000000000000000000000000000000000000000000000000000000000000000
0000000000000000000000000000000000000000000000000000000000000000000000000000
0000000000000000000000000000000000000000000000000000000000000000000000000000
```

Figure 11.5 (continued)

```
LEVEL CURVE 0 --     0.00 TO    5.00
LEVEL CURVE 1 --     5.00 TO   10.00
LEVEL CURVE 2 --    10.00 TO   15.00
LEVEL CURVE 3 --    15.00 TO   20.00
LEVEL CURVE 4 --    20.00 TO   25.00
LEVEL CURVE 5 --    25.00 TO   30.00
LEVEL CURVE 6 --    30.00 TO   35.00
LEVEL CURVE 7 --    35.00 TO   40.00
LEVEL CURVE 8 --    40.00 TO   45.00
LEVEL CURVE 9 --    50.00 AND ABOVE
```

Characters other than '0', '1', . . . , '9' can be used simply by changing the DATA statement in this program. For example, we could use the characters

```
. - : = + % & $ @ #
```

to represent various levels, with more dense characters corresponding to higher levels. Figure 11.6 shows the output produced when the DATA statement in the program of Figure 11.5 is changed to

```
DATA SYMBOL /'.', '-', ':', '=', '+', '%', '&', '$', '@', '#'/
```

The ideas in this example can be modified to display an image that is represented in digitized form and to enhance this image. This digitized representation might be a table of light intensities transmitted from a remote sensor such as a television camera in a satellite. This problem of visual image processing and enhancement is described in the exercises.

EXAMPLE 3: Lexical Analysis. In our discussion of system software in Chapter 1, we mentioned **compilers,** which are programs whose function is to translate a source program written in a high-level language, such as FORTRAN, into an object program in machine code. This object program is then executed by the computer.

The input to a compiler is a stream of characters that comprises the source program. Before the translation can actually be carried out, this stream of characters must be broken up into meaningful groups, such as variable names, reserved words, constants, and operators. For example, the assignment statement

```
ALPHA = 200 * BETA + 5
```

is input as the string of characters

```
ALPHAb=b200*BETAb+b5
```

```
ENTER MINIMUM AND MAXIMUM X-VALUES, THEN Y-V
10, 40, 10, 40
ENTER MINIMUM AND MAXIMUM VALUES OF FUNCTI
0, 50
```

Figure 11.6

```
LEVEL CURVE . --     0.00 TO    5.00
LEVEL CURVE - --     5.00 TO   10.00
LEVEL CURVE : --    10.00 TO   15.00
LEVEL CURVE = --    15.00 TO   20.00
LEVEL CURVE + --    20.00 TO   25.00
LEVEL CURVE % --    25.00 TO   30.00
LEVEL CURVE & --    30.00 TO   35.00
LEVEL CURVE $ --    35.00 TO   40.00
LEVEL CURVE @ --    40.00 TO   45.00
LEVEL CURVE # --    50.00 AND ABOVE
```

      a. Set the Jth character of NAME equal to the Ith character of STAT.

      b. Increment I and J by 1.

  3. Display NAME and a message indicating that a variable has been recognized.

The subalgorithm CONST for integer constants is similar:

SUBALGORITHM CONST

  * Subalgorithm to process an integer constant in statement STAT   *
  * beginning at position I.   *

  1. Initialize NUMBER to blanks and J to 1.

  2. While the Ith character of STAT is a digit, do the following:

      a. Set the Jth character of NUMBER equal to the Ith character of STAT.

      b. Increment I and J by 1.

  3. Display NUMBER and a message indicating that an integer constant has been recognized.

The other algorithms OPER, ASSIGN, and ILLEG are somewhat simpler:

SUBALGORITHM OPER

  * Subalgorithm to recognize an arithmetic operator in statement   *
  * STAT beginning at position I.   *

  1. If the Ith and (I + 1)st characters of STAT are both *'s, then do the following:

      a. Display '**' and a message indicating that an arithmetic operator has been recognized.

      b. Increment I by 2.

  2. Otherwise do the following:

      a. Display the Ith character of STAT and a message indicating that an arithmetic operator has been recognized.

      b. Increment I by 1.

SUBALGORITHM ASSIGN

  * Subalgorithm to recognize an assignment operator in statement   *
  * STAT at position I.   *

  1. Display ' = ' and a message indicating that an assignment operator has been recognized.

  2. Increment I by 1.

SUBALGORITHM ILLEG

* Subalgorithm to process an illegal character in statement STAT at   *
* position I.   *

1. Display the Ith character of STAT and a message indicating that an illegal character has been found.
2. Increment I by 1.

In the program in Figure 11.7, the main program implements the main algorithm for lexical analysis. The five subalgorithms are implemented by the subroutines VAR, CONST, OPER, ASSIGN, and ILLEG.

```
      PROGRAM LEX
**MAIN******************************************************************
* This program implements a simple lexical analyzer for FORTRAN       *
* assignment statements involving only variables, integer constants,  *
* arithmetic operators, and an end-of-statement mark.  Variables      *
* used are:                                                           *
*     MARK   : end-of-statement mark                                  *
*     STAT   : assignment statement being processed                   *
*     SYMBOL : one of the symbols in STAT                             *
*     I      : index                                                  *
***********************************************************************

      INTEGER I
      CHARACTER*1, MARK, SYMBOL, STAT*80
      DATA MARK /';'/

      PRINT *, 'ENTER ASSIGNMENT STATEMENT (END WITH ', MARK, ')'
      READ '(A)', STAT
      I = 1

* While Ith symbol in STAT is not the end-of-statement mark do

10    IF (STAT(I:I) .NE. MARK) THEN

*         While Ith symbol is blank do (skip blanks):

20        IF (STAT(I:I) .EQ. ' ') THEN
             I = I + 1
             GO TO 20
          END IF
          SYMBOL = STAT(I:I)

*         Process a variable name

          IF (('A' .LE. SYMBOL) .AND. (SYMBOL .LE. 'Z'))THEN
             CALL VAR(STAT, I)

*         Process an integer constant

          ELSE IF (('0' .LE. SYMBOL) .AND. (SYMBOL .LE. '9')) THEN
             CALL CONST(STAT, I)
```

Figure 11.7

Figure 11.7 (continued)

```
*          Process an arithmetic operator

           ELSE IF ((SYMBOL .EQ. '+') .OR. (SYMBOL .EQ. '-')
     +          .OR. (SYMBOL .EQ. '*') .OR. (SYMBOL .EQ. '/')) THEN
              CALL OPER(STAT, I)

*          Process an assignment operator

           ELSE IF (SYMBOL .EQ. '=') THEN
              CALL ASSIGN(STAT, I)

*          Illegal character if not end-of-statement mark

           ELSE IF (SYMBOL .NE. MARK) THEN
              CALL ILLEG(STAT, I)
           END IF
           GO TO 10
        END IF
        END


**VAR*****************************************************************
* Subroutine to process a variable name; Ith character of STAT is the  *
* first letter in the name.  Variables used are:                       *
*      NAME    : name of the variable                                  *
*      SYMBOL : a symbol in statement STAT                             *
*      J       : index                                                 *
********************************************************************

        SUBROUTINE VAR(STAT, I)
        CHARACTER*6 NAME, SYMBOL*1, STAT*(*)

        INTEGER I, J

        SYMBOL = STAT(I:I)
        J = 1
        NAME = ' '

* While Ith symbol is a letter or digit do:

10      IF ((('A' .LE. SYMBOL) .AND. (SYMBOL .LE. 'Z')) .OR.
     +      (('0' .LE. SYMBOL) .AND. (SYMBOL .LE. '9'))) THEN
           IF (J .LE. LEN(NAME)) THEN
              NAME(J:J) = SYMBOL
              J = J + 1
           END IF
           I = I + 1
           SYMBOL = STAT(I:I)
           GO TO 10
        END IF
        PRINT 20, NAME
20      FORMAT(1X, A, T12, '<VARIABLE>')
        END
```

Figure 11.7   **(continued)**

```
**CONST****************************************************************
* Subroutine to process an integer constant; Ith character of STAT is  *
* first digit of the constant.  Variables used are:                    *
*      NUMBER : string of digits in the integer constant               *
*      SYMBOL : a symbol in statement STAT                             *
*      J      : index                                                  *
***********************************************************************

       SUBROUTINE CONST(STAT, I)

       CHARACTER*10 NUMBER, SYMBOL*1, STAT*(*)
       INTEGER I, J

       SYMBOL = STAT(I:I)
       NUMBER = ' '
       J = 1

* While Ith symbol in statement STAT is a digit do:

10     IF (('0' .LE. SYMBOL) .AND. (SYMBOL .LE. '9')) THEN
           IF (J .LE. LEN(NUMBER)) THEN
               NUMBER(J:J) = SYMBOL
               J = J + 1
           END IF
           I = I + 1
           SYMBOL = STAT(I:I)
           GO TO 10
       END IF
       PRINT 20, NUMBER
20     FORMAT(1X, A, T12, '<INTEGER CONSTANT>')
       END

**OPER*****************************************************************
* Subroutine to process Ith character of STAT as an arithmetic         *
* operator.                                                            *
***********************************************************************

       SUBROUTINE OPER(STAT, I)

       CHARACTER*(*) STAT
       INTEGER I

       IF (STAT(I : I + 1) .EQ. '**') THEN
           PRINT 10, '**'
10         FORMAT(1X, A, T12, '<OPERATOR>')
           I = I + 2
       ELSE
           PRINT 10, STAT(I:I)
           I = I + 1
       END IF
       END

**ASSIGN**************************************************************
* Subroutine to process Ith character of STAT as an assignment         *
* operator.                                                            *
***********************************************************************
```

Figure 11.7 (continued)

```
      SUBROUTINE ASSIGN(STAT, I)

      CHARACTER*(*) STAT
      INTEGER I

      PRINT 10, '='
10    FORMAT(1X, A, T12, '<ASSIGNMENT OPERATOR>')
      I = I + 1
      END

**ILLEG***********************************************************
* Subroutine to handle processing when Ith symbol in statement STAT  *
* is not a legal character.                                          *
******************************************************************

      SUBROUTINE ILLEG(STAT, I)

      CHARACTER*(*) STAT
      INTEGER I

      PRINT 10, STAT(I:I)
10    FORMAT(1X, A, T12, '<ILLEGAL CHARACTER>')
      I = I + 1
      END
```

Sample runs:
===========

```
ENTER ASSIGNMENT STATEMENT (END WITH ;)
ALPHA = 37*BETA - GAMMA/DELTA      -3;
ALPHA      <VARIABLE>
=          <ASSIGNMENT OPERATOR>
37         <INTEGER CONSTANT>
*          <OPERATOR>
BETA       <VARIABLE>
-          <OPERATOR>
GAMMA      <VARIABLE>
/          <OPERATOR>
DELTA      <VARIABLE>
-          <OPERATOR>
3          <INTEGER CONSTANT>


ENTER ASSIGNMENT STATEMENT (END WITH ;)
X123  =    Z456* 456% ZETA - 12345 # 6**N;
X123       <VARIABLE>
=          <ASSIGNMENT OPERATOR>
Z456       <VARIABLE>
*          <OPERATOR>
456        <INTEGER CONSTANT>
%          <ILLEGAL CHARACTER>
ZETA       <VARIABLE>
-          <OPERATOR>
12345      <INTEGER CONSTANT>
#          <ILLEGAL CHARACTER>
6          <INTEGER CONSTANT>
**         <OPERATOR>
N          <VARIABLE>
```

EXAMPLE 4: Reverse Polish Notation. The task of a compiler is to generate the machine language instructions required to carry out the instructions of the source program written in a high-level language (see Section 1.3). One part of this task is to generate the machine instructions for evaluating arithmetic expressions like that in the assignment statement

```
X = A * B + C
```

The compiler must generate machine instructions to

1. Retrieve the value of A from the memory location where it is stored and load it into the accumulating register.
2. Retrieve the value of B and multiply it by the value in the accumulating register.
3. Retrieve the value of C and add it to the value in the accumulating register.
4. Store the value in the accumulating register in the memory location associated with X.

Arithmetic expressions are ordinarily written using *infix* notation like the preceding, in which the symbol for each binary operation is placed between the operands. In many compilers, the first step in evaluating such infix expressions is to transform them into *postfix* notation in which the operation symbol follows the operands; machine instructions are then generated to evaluate this postfix expression. Likewise, calculators commonly evaluate arithmetic expressions using postfix notation. The reason for this is that conversion from infix to postfix is straightforward and postfix expressions are in general easier to evaluate mechanically than are infix expressions.

When infix notation is used for arithmetic expressions, parentheses are often needed to indicate the order in which the operations are to be carried out. For example, parentheses are placed in the expression $2 * (3 + 4)$ to indicate that the addition is to be performed before the multiplication. If the parentheses were omitted, giving $2 * 3 + 4$, the standard priority rules would dictate that the multiplication is to be performed before the addition.

In the early 1950s, the Polish logician Jan Lukasiewicz observed that parentheses are not necessary in postfix notation, also called **Reverse Polish Notation (RPN).** For example, the infix expression

$$2 * (3 + 4)$$

can be written in RPN as

$$2\ 3\ 4\ +\ *$$

To illustrate how such RPN expressions are evaluated, consider

$$1\ 5\ +\ 8\ 4\ 1\ -\ -\ *$$

which corresponds to the infix expression $(1 + 5) * (8 - (4 - 1))$. This expression is scanned from left to right until an operator is found. At that point, the last two preceding operands are combined, using this operator. For our example, the first operator encountered is $+$, and its operands are 1 and 5, as indicated by the underline in the following:

$$\underline{1\ 5\ +}\ 8\ 4\ 1\ -\ -\ *$$

Replacing this subexpression with its value 6 yields the reduced RPN expression

$$6\ 8\ 4\ 1\ -\ -\ *$$

Resuming the left-to-right scan, we next encounter the operator $-$ and determine its two operands:

$$6\ 8\ \underline{4\ 1\ -}\ -\ *$$

Applying this operator then yields

$$6\ 8\ 3\ -\ *$$

The next operator encountered is another $-$ and its two operands are 8 and 3:

$$6\ \underline{8\ 3\ -}\ *$$

Evaluating this difference gives

$$6\ 5\ *$$

The final operator is $*$,

$$\underline{6\ 5\ *}$$

and the value 30 is obtained for this expression.

This method of evaluating an RPN expression requires that the operands be stored until an operator is encountered in the left-to-right scan. At this point, the last two operands must be retrieved and combined using this operation. Thus, a **Last-In-First-Out** (**LIFO**) data structure, that is, a *stack,* should be used to store the operands.

A **stack** (or **push-down stack**) is a list in which elements may be inserted or deleted at only one end of the list, called the **top** of the stack. This structure is so named because it functions in the same manner as a spring-loaded stack of plates or trays used in a cafeteria. Plates are added to the stack by pushing them onto the top of the stack. When a plate is removed from the top of the stack, the spring causes the next plate to pop up. For this reason, the insertion and deletion operations for a stack are commonly called *push* and *pop,* respectively.

The following algorithm for evaluating an RPN expression uses a stack to store the operands in the expression. When an operator is encountered, the top two values are popped from the stack, the operator is applied to them, and the result is pushed back onto the stack.

ALGORITHM TO EVALUATE RPN EXPRESSIONS

```
*   Algorithm to evaluate an expression given in RPN. A stack          *
*   is used to store operands.                                         *
```

1. Initialize an empty stack.
2. Repeat the following until the end of the expression is encountered:
   a. Get the next token (constant, variable, arithmetic operator) in the RPN expression.
   b. If the token is an operand, push it onto the stack. If it is an operator, then do the following:

(i) Pop the top two values from the stack. (If the stack does not contain two items, an error due to a malformed RPN expression has occurred, and evaluation is terminated.)

(ii) Apply the operator to these two values.

(iii) Push the resulting value back onto the stack.

3. When the end of the expression is encountered, its value is on top of the stack (and in fact must be the only value in the stack).

Figure 11.8 illustrates the application of this algorithm to the RPN expression

$$2\ 4 * 9\ 5 + -$$

The up-arrow (↑) indicates the current token.

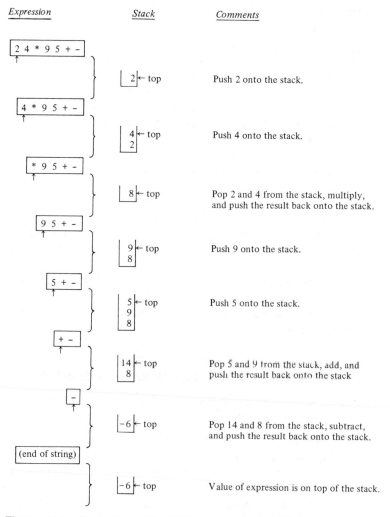

Expression   *Stack*   *Comments*

Push 2 onto the stack.

Push 4 onto the stack.

Pop 2 and 4 from the stack, multiply, and push the result back onto the stack.

Push 9 onto the stack.

Push 5 onto the stack.

Pop 5 and 9 from the stack, add, and push the result back onto the stack

Pop 14 and 8 from the stack, subtract, and push the result back onto the stack.

Value of expression is on top of the stack.

Figure 11.8   Evaluation of the RPN expression 2 4 * 9 5 + − .

To illustrate how a stack is also used in the conversion from infix to RPN, consider the infix expression

$$7 + 2 * 3$$

In a left-to-right scan of this expression, 7 is encountered and may be immediately displayed. Next, the operator $+$ is encountered, but since its right operand has not yet been displayed, it must be stored and thus is pushed onto a stack of operators:

Next, the operand 2 is encountered and displayed. At this point, it must be determined whether 2 is the right operand for the preceding operator $+$ or the left operand for the next operator. This is determined by comparing the operator $+$ on the top of the stack with the next operator $*$. Because $*$ has higher priority than $+$, the preceding operand 2 that was displayed is the left operand for $*$; thus we push $*$ onto the stack and search for its right operand:

The operand 3 is encountered next and displayed. Because the end of the expression has now been reached, the right operand for the operator $*$ on the top of the stack has been found, so $*$ can now be popped and displayed:

The end of the expression also signals that the right operand for the remaining operator $+$ in the stack has been found, so it too can be popped and displayed, yielding the RPN expression

$$7 \quad 2 \quad 3 \quad * \quad +$$

Parentheses within infix expressions present no real difficulties. A left parenthesis indicates the beginning of a subexpression, and when encountered, it is pushed onto the stack. When a right parenthesis is encountered, operators are popped from the stack until the matching left parenthesis rises to the top. At this point, the subexpression originally enclosed by the parentheses has been converted to RPN, so the parentheses may be discarded and conversion continues. All of this is contained in the following algorithm:

ALGORITHM TO CONVERT INFIX EXPRESSION TO RPN

```
*    Algorithm to convert an infix expression to RPN. A stack is used    *
*    to store operators.                                                  *
```

1. Initialize an empty stack.

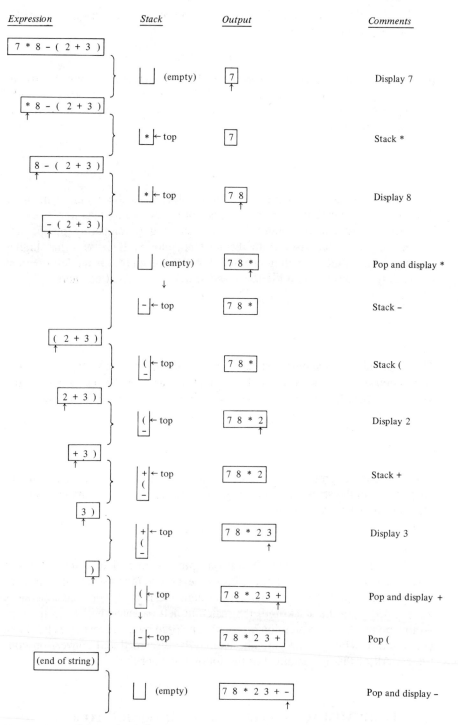

Figure 11.9   Converting infix expression 7 * 8 − (2 + 3) to RPN.

2. Repeat the following until the end of the infix expression is reached.
   a. Get the next input token (constant, variable, arithmetic operator, left parenthesis, right parenthesis) in the infix expression.
   b. If this token is
      (i) a left parenthesis: Push it onto the stack.
      (ii) an operand: Display it.
      (iii) an operator: If the stack is empty or the operator has a higher priority than the top stack element, push the operator onto the stack.

      Otherwise, pop an operator from the stack and display it; then repeat the comparison of the current token with the new top stack item.

      Note: A left parenthesis in the stack is assumed to have a lower priority than that of operators.

      (iv) a right parenthesis: Pop and display stack elements until a left parenthesis is on top of the stack. Pop it also, but do not display it.

3. When the end of the infix expression is reached, pop and display stack items until the stack is empty.

Figure 11.9 illustrates this algorithm for the infix expression

$$7 * 8 - (2 + 3)$$

An up-arrow (↑) has been used to indicate the current input symbol and the symbol displayed by the algorithm. The program in Figure 11.10 implements this algorithm.

```
      PROGRAM RPNCON
**MAIN*****************************************************************
* Program to convert an infix expression to Reverse Polish Notation.  *
* Variables used are:                                                 *
*     RESPON : user response                                          *
*     STKLIM : parameter = limit on stack size                        *
*     STACK  : character array used as a stack                        *
*     TOP    : pointer to top of stack                                *
*     EXPR   : infix expression                                       *
*     RPN    : Reverse Polish expression                              *
*     SYMBOL : a symbol in expression EXPR                            *
*     TEMP   : temporary symbol                                       *
*     MARK   : end-of-statement marker                                *
*     I      : index for infix expression EXPR                        *
*     R      : index for RPN                                          *
**********************************************************************
```

Figure 11.10

Figure 11.10   (continued)

```
      INTEGER STKLIM, I, R
      PARAMETER (STKLIM = 80)
      CHARACTER*2, STACK(1:STKLIM), SYMBOL, TEMP, EXPR*80, RPN*80,
     +           MARK*1, RESPON*1
      INTEGER TOP, PRIOR
      LOGICAL ISOPER
      DATA MARK /';'/

* Repeat the following until RESPON = 'N'

10    PRINT *, 'ENTER INFIX EXPRESSION'
      READ '(A)', EXPR

* Initialize empty stack, indices, and RPN

      TOP = 0
      I = 1
      R = 1
      RPN = ' '
      SYMBOL = EXPR(1:1)

* While not end of expression do:

20    IF (SYMBOL .NE. MARK) THEN

*         If symbol is a blank, put it in RPN only if preceding
*         symbol was not a blank

      IF (SYMBOL .EQ. ' ') THEN
          IF (RPN(R:R) .NE. ' ') THEN
              R = R + 1
              RPN (R:R) = SYMBOL
          END IF
      ELSE

*             If symbol is a left parenthesis, push it onto stack

          IF (SYMBOL .EQ. '(') THEN
              CALL PUSH(STACK, TOP, STKLIM, SYMBOL)

*             If symbol is a right parenthesis, pop stack symbols until
*             a left parenthesis is on the top of the stack, and
*             then pop it also.

          ELSE IF (SYMBOL .EQ. ')') THEN
30            IF (STACK(TOP) .NE. '(') THEN
                  CALL POP(STACK, TOP, STKLIM, SYMBOL)
                  R = R + 1
                  RPN(R : R+1) = ' ' // SYMBOL
                  R = R + 1
                  GO TO 30
              END IF
              CALL POP(STACK, TOP, STKLIM, SYMBOL)
```

Figure 11.10 (continued)

```
*              If symbol is part of an operand, place it in RPN and
*              go on to next symbol

               ELSE IF ((('A' .LE. SYMBOL) .AND. (SYMBOL .LE.'Z')) .OR.
     +                 (('0' .LE. SYMBOL) .AND. (SYMBOL .LE. '9'))) THEN
                  R = R + 1
                  RPN(R:R) = SYMBOL

*              If symbol is an operator, check priorities and
*              then push or pop as necessary

               ELSE IF (ISOPER(SYMBOL)) THEN
                  R = R + 1
                  RPN(R:R) = ' '

*                 Check for exponentiation operator

                  IF ((SYMBOL .EQ. '*') .AND.
     +                (EXPR(I+1 : I+1) .EQ. '*')) THEN
                     SYMBOL = '**'
                     I = I + 1
                  END IF

*                 While stack is not empty and symbol's priority
*                 is less than or equal to priority of top of stack,
*                 pop elements; then push symbol onto stack

40                IF ((TOP .GT. 0) .AND.
     +                (PRIOR(SYMBOL) .LE. PRIOR(STACK(TOP)))) THEN
                     CALL POP(STACK, TOP, STKLIM, TEMP)
                     R = R + 1
                     IF (TEMP .EQ. '**') THEN
                        RPN(R : R + 3) = ' ' // TEMP // ' '
                        R = R + 3
                     ELSE
                        RPN(R : R + 2) = ' ' // TEMP
                        R = R + 2
                     END IF
                     GO TO 40
                  END IF
                  CALL PUSH(STACK, TOP, STKLIM, SYMBOL)

*              Else symbol is an illegal character; indicate this,
*              and set symbol = MARK to terminate processing

               ELSE
                  PRINT *, SYMBOL, ' IS ILLEGAL CHARACTER -- IGNORED'
                  SYMBOL = MARK
               END IF
            END IF
            I = I + 1
            SYMBOL = EXPR(I:I)
            GO TO 20
         END IF
```

Figure 11.10   (continued)

```
* While stack not empty, pop symbols into RPN

50      IF (TOP .GT. 0) THEN
            CALL POP(STACK, TOP, STKLIM, SYMBOL)
            R = R + 1
            IF (SYMBOL .EQ. '**') THEN
                RPN(R : R + 3) = ' ' // SYMBOL //' '
                R = R + 3
            ELSE
                RPN(R : R + 1) = ' ' // SYMBOL
                R = R + 1
            END IF
            GO TO 50
        END IF

* Display RPN expression

        PRINT *, RPN
        PRINT *,
        PRINT *, 'MORE (Y OR N)'
        READ '(A)', RESPON
        IF (RESPON .EQ. 'Y') GO TO 10
        END

**PUSH*********************************************************************
*       Subroutine to push character symbol onto top of stack           *
*************************************************************************

        SUBROUTINE PUSH(STACK, TOP, STKLIM, SYMBOL)

        INTEGER TOP, STKLIM
        CHARACTER*(*) STACK(STKLIM), SYMBOL

        IF (TOP .EQ. STKLIM) THEN
            STOP '*** STACK OVERFLOW ***'
        ELSE
            TOP = TOP + 1
            STACK(TOP) = SYMBOL
        END IF
        END

**POP**********************************************************************
* Subroutine to pop top symbol from stack                               *
*************************************************************************

        SUBROUTINE POP(STACK, TOP, STKLIM, SYMBOL)

        INTEGER TOP, STKLIM
        CHARACTER*(*) STACK(STKLIM), SYMBOL

        IF (TOP .EQ. 0) THEN
            PRINT *, '*** EMPTY STACK ***'
        ELSE
            SYMBOL = STACK(TOP)
            TOP = TOP - 1
        END IF
        END
```

Figure 11.10 (continued)

```
**PRIOR*******************************************************************
* Function to calculate the priority of operator OPER                   *
*************************************************************************

        FUNCTION PRIOR(OPER)

        INTEGER PRIOR
        CHARACTER*2 OPER

        IF (OPER .EQ. '(') THEN
            PRIOR = 0
        ELSE IF ((OPER .EQ. '+ ') .OR. (OPER .EQ. '- ')) THEN
            PRIOR = 1
        ELSE IF ((OPER .EQ. '* ') .OR. (OPER .EQ. '/ ')) THEN
            PRIOR = 2
        ELSE IF (OPER .EQ. '**') THEN
            PRIOR = 3
        ELSE
            PRIOR = -1
        END IF
        END


**ISOPER******************************************************************
* Logical-valued function that determines if SYMBOL is an operator      *
*************************************************************************

        FUNCTION ISOPER(SYMBOL)

        LOGICAL ISOPER
        CHARACTER*(*) SYMBOL, OPER(5)*2
        INTEGER OP
        DATA OPER / '+ ', '- ','* ','/ ', '**'/

        ISOPER = .FALSE.
        DO 10 OP = 1, 5
            IF (SYMBOL .EQ. OPER(OP)) ISOPER = .TRUE.
10      CONTINUE
        END


  Sample run:
  ==========

  ENTER INFIX EXPRESSION
  A + B;
   A  B +

  MORE (Y OR N)
 Y
  ENTER INFIX EXPRESSION
 A - B - C;
   A  B   - C -

  MORE (Y OR N)
 Y
  ENTER INFIX EXPRESSION
 A - (B - C);
   A  B  C - -
```

Figure 11.10   (continued)

```
 MORE (Y OR N)
Y
 ENTER INFIX EXPRESSION
((A + 525)/BETA - 2)*GAMMA;
  A  525 + BETA   / 2 - GAMMA *

 MORE (Y OR N)
Y
 ENTER INFIX EXPRESSION
(B**2 - 4*A*C)/ %PER;
 %  IS ILLEGAL CHARACTER -- IGNORED
  B 2   ** 4 A  * C * - PER /

 MORE (Y OR N)
N
```

Exercises

1. Write a program to determine whether a specified string occurs in a given string, and if so, print an asterisk (*) under the first position of each occurrence.

2. Write a program to count the occurrences of a specified character in several lines of text.

3. Write a program to count the occurrences of a specified string in several lines of text.

4. Write a program that permits the input of a name consisting of a first name, a middle name or initial, and a last name, in that order, and then prints the last name followed by a comma and then the first and middle initials, each followed by a period. For example, the input JOHN HENRY DOE should produce DOE, J. H..

5. The encoding scheme used to produce a cryptogram in the program of Figure 11.2 consists simply in adding a specified integer to the code of each character of the message. This is a special case of the technique known as *keyword* encoding, in which a sequence of integers corresponding to the characters of a specified keyword is added in order to the codes of the message characters. To illustrate, if the keyword is 'ABC' and the message is 'MEETATNOON', the codes for 'A', 'B', and 'C' are added to the codes for 'M', 'E', and 'E', respectively, then added to the codes for 'T', 'A', and 'T', respectively, and so on, producing the cryptogram 'NGHUCWOQRO' (assuming an ASCII machine). Write a program to implement this keyword method of encoding.

6. The Morse code is a standard encoding scheme that uses substitutions similar to the scheme described in Exercise 5. The substitutions used in this case are

A · –	M – –	Y – · – –
B – · · ·	N – ·	Z – – · ·
C – · – ·	O – – –	1 · – – – –
D – · ·	P · – – ·	2 · · – – –
E ·	Q – – · –	3 · · · – –
F · · – ·	R · – ·	4 · · · · –
G – – ·	S · · ·	5 · · · · ·
H · · · ·	T –	6 – · · · ·
I · ·	U · · –	7 – – · · ·
J · – – –	V · · · –	8 – – – · ·
K – · –	W · – –	9 – – – – ·
L · – · ·	X – · · –	0 – – – – –

Write a program to accept as input a message in plain text or in Morse code and then encode or decode the message, respectively. (For a terminal with a bell or "beep" you might try to output Morse code as sound.)

7. The Rev. Mr. Zeller developed a formula for computing the day of the week on which a given date fell or will fall. Suppose that we let a, b, c, and d be integers defined as follows:

a = the month of the year, with March = 1, April = 2, and so on, with January and February being counted as months 11 and 12 of the preceding year.
b = the day of the month.
c = the year of the century.
d = the century.

For example, July 31, 1929, gives $a = 5$, $b = 31$, $c = 29$, $d = 19$; January 3, 1988, gives $a = 11$, $b = 3$, $c = 87$, $d = 19$. Now calculate the following integer quantities:

w = the integer quotient $(13a - 1)/5$.
x = the integer quotient $c/4$.
y = the integer quotient $d/4$.
$z = w + x + y + b + c - 2d$.
r = z reduced modulo 7; that is, r is the remainder of z divided by 7; $r = 0$ represents Sunday, $r = 1$ represents Monday, and so on.

Write a program to accept a date as input and then calculate on what day of the week that date fell or will fall.

(a) Verify that December 12, 1960, fell on a Monday and that January 1, 1981, fell on a Thursday.
(b) On what day of the week did January 25, 1963, fall?
(c) On what day of the week did June 2, 1964, fall?

(d) On what day of the week did July 4, 1776, fall?

(e) On what day of the week were you born?

8. Write a program that will convert ordinary Hindu-Arabic numerals into Roman numerals and/or vice versa. (I = 1, V = 5, X = 10, L = 50, C = 100, D = 500, and M = 1000. Roman numeration also uses a subtraction principle: IV = 5 − 1 = 4, IX = 10 − 1 = 9, XL = 50 − 10 = 40, XC = 100 − 10 = 90, CD = 500 − 100 = 400, CM = 1000 − 100 = 900, but no other cases of a smaller number preceding a larger are allowed.)

9. A string is said to be a *palindrome* if it does not change when the order of the characters in the string is reversed. For example,

```
MADAM
463364
ABLE WAS I ERE I SAW ELBA
```

are palindromes. Write a program to read a string and then determine whether it is a palindrome.

10. Write a simple *text-formatting* program that reads a file of text and produces another file in which no lines are longer than some given length. Put as many words as possible on the same line. You will have to break some lines of the given file, but do not break any words or put punctuation marks at the beginning of a new line.

11. Extend the text-formatting program of Exercise 10 to right-justify each line in the new file by adding evenly distributed blanks in lines where necessary. Also, preserve all indentations of lines in the given file that begin a new paragraph.

12. In Example 2 of Section 11.4, we noted that the ideas in that example can be modified to carry out *visual image processing and enhancement*. Make a file that represents light intensities of an image in digitized form, say, with intensities from 0 through 9. Write a program that reads these intensities from the file and then reconstructs and displays them using a different character for each intensity. This image might then be enhanced to sharpen the contrast. For example, "gray" areas might be removed by replacing all intensities in the range 0 through some value by 0 (light) and intensities greater than this value by 9 (dark). Design your program to accept a threshold value that distinguishes light from dark and then enhances the image in the manner described.

13. An alternative method for enhancing an image (see Exercise 12) is to accept three successive images of the same object and, if two or more of the intensities agree, to use that value; otherwise, the average of the three values is used. Modify the program of Exercise 12 to use this technique for enhancement.

14. A real number in FORTRAN has one of the forms $m.n$, $+m.n$, or $-m.n$, where m and n are nonnegative integers; or it may be expressed in scientific form $x\mathrm{E}e$, $x\mathrm{E}+e$, or $x\mathrm{E}-e$ where x is an integer or a real number not in scientific form and e is a nonnegative integer. Write a program that reads a string of characters and then checks to see if it represents a valid real constant.

15. A *rational number* is of the form a/b where a and b are integers with $b \neq 0$. Write a program to do rational number arithmetic. The program should read and display each rational number in the format a/b, or simply a if the denominator is 1. The following examples illustrate the menu of commands that the user should be allowed to enter:

Input	Output	Comments
3/8 + 1/6	13/24	$a/b + c/d = (ad + bc)/bd$ reduced to lowest terms.
3/8 − 1/6	5/24	$a/b - c/d = (ad - bc)/bd$ reduced to lowest terms.
3/8 * 1/6	1/16	$a/b * c/d = ac/bd$ reduced to lowest terms.
3/8 / 1/6	9/4	$a/b / c/d = ad/bc$ reduced to lowest terms.
3/8 I	8/3	Invert a/b
8/3 M	2 + 2/3	Write a/b as a mixed fraction
6/8 R	3/4	Reduce a/b to lowest terms.
6/8 G	2	Greatest common divisor of numerator and denominator.
1/6 L 3/8	24	Lowest common denominator of a/b and c/d.
1/6 < 3/8	true	$a/b < c/d$?
1/6 <= 3/8	true	$a/b \leq c/d$?
1/6 > 3/8	false	$a/b > c/d$?
1/6 >= 3/8	false	$a/b \leq c/d$?
3/8 = 9/24	true	$a/b = c/d$?
2/3 X + 2 = 4/5	X = −9/5	Solution of linear equation $(a/b)X + c/d = e/f$.

16. Write a program for a lexical analyzer to recognize assignment statements of the form

variable = *string-constant*

17. Extend the program of Exercise 16 to allow substrings and the concatenation operator.

18. Write a program for a lexical analyzer to process assignment statements of the form

logical-variable = *logical-value*

Have it recognize the following tokens: variable, logical constant, assignment operator, and logical operator (.NOT., .AND., .OR.).

19. Suppose that $A = 7.0, B = 4.0, C = 3.0, D = -2.0$. Evaluate the following RPN expressions:

   (a) $A\ B\ +\ C\ /\ D*$ **(b)** $A\ B\ C\ +\ /\ D\ *$
   (c) $A\ B\ C\ D\ +\ /\ *$ **(d)** $A\ B\ +\ C\ +\ D\ +$
   (e) $A\ B\ +\ C\ D\ +\ +$ **(f)** $A\ B\ C\ +\ +\ D\ +$
   (g) $A\ B\ C\ D\ +\ +\ +$ **(h)** $A\ B\ -\ C\ -\ D\ -$
   (i) $A\ B\ -\ C\ D\ -\ -$ **(j)** $A\ B\ C\ -\ -\ D\ -$
   (k) $A\ B\ C\ D\ -\ -\ -$

20. Convert the following infix expressions to RPN:

   (a) $A\ *\ B\ +\ C\ -\ D$ **(b)** $A\ +\ B\ /\ C\ +\ D$
   (c) $(A\ +\ B)\ /\ C\ +\ D$ **(d)** $A\ +\ B\ /\ (C\ +\ D)$
   (e) $(A\ +\ B)\ /\ (C\ +\ D)$ **(f)** $(A\ -\ B)\ *\ (C\ -\ (D\ +\ E))$
   (g) $(((A\ -\ B)\ -\ C)\ -\ D)\ -\ E$ **(h)** $A\ -\ (B\ -\ (C\ -\ (D\ -\ E)))$

21. Convert the following RPN expressions to infix notation:

   (a) $A\ B\ C\ +\ -\ D\ *$ **(b)** $A\ B\ +\ C\ D\ -\ *$
   (c) $A\ B\ C\ D\ +\ -\ *$ **(d)** $A\ B\ +\ C\ -\ D\ E\ *\ /$
   (e) $A\ B\ /\ C\ /\ D\ /$ **(f)** $A\ B\ /\ C\ D\ /\ /$
   (g) $A\ B\ C\ /\ D\ /\ /$ **(h)** $A\ B\ C\ D\ /\ /\ /$

22. An alternative to postfix notation is *prefix* notation, in which the symbol for each operation precedes the operands. For example, the infix expression $2\ *\ 3\ +\ 4$ would be written in prefix notation as $+\ *\ 2\ 3\ 4$ and $2\ *\ (3\ +\ 4)$ would be written as $*\ 2\ +\ 3\ 4$. Convert each of the infix expressions in Exercise 20 to prefix notation.

23. Suppose that $A = 7.0, B = 4.0, C = 3.0,$ and $D = -2.0$. Evaluate the following prefix expressions:

   (a) $*\ A\ /\ +\ B\ C\ D$ **(b)** $*\ /\ +\ A\ B\ C\ D$
   (c) $-\ A\ -\ B\ -\ C\ D$ **(d)** $-\ -\ A\ B\ -\ C\ D$
   (e) $-\ A\ -\ -\ B\ C\ D$ **(f)** $-\ -\ -\ -\ A\ B\ C\ D$
   (g) $+\ A\ B\ *\ -\ C\ D$ **(h)** $+\ *\ A\ B\ -\ C\ D$
   (i) $+\ *\ -\ A\ B\ C\ D$

24. Convert the following prefix expressions to infix notation:

   (a) $+\ A\ B\ *\ -\ C\ D$ **(b)** $+\ *\ A\ B\ -\ C\ D$
   (c) $-\ -\ A\ B\ -\ C\ D$ **(d)** $-\ -\ A\ -\ B\ C\ D$
   (e) $-\ -\ -\ A\ B\ C\ D$ **(f)** $/\ +\ *\ A\ B\ -\ C\ D\ E$
   (g) $/\ +\ *\ A\ B\ C\ -\ D\ E$ **(h)** $/\ +\ A\ *\ B\ C\ -\ D\ E$

25. The symbol $-$ cannot be used for the unary minus operation in prefix or postfix notation. For example, 5 3 $-$ $-$ could be interpreted as either $5 - (-3) = 8$ or $-(5 - 3) = -2$. Suppose that $\sim$ is used for unary minus.

(a) Evaluate the following RPN expressions if $A = 7$, $B = 5$, $C = 3$:

(i) $A \sim B\ C\ +\ -$ **(ii)** $A\ B \sim C\ +\ -$

(iii) $A\ B\ C \sim\ +\ -$ **(iv)** $A\ B\ C\ +\ \sim\ -$

(v) $A\ B\ C\ +\ -\ \sim$ **(vi)** $A\ B\ C\ -\ -\ \sim\ \sim\ \sim$

(b) Convert the following infix expressions to RPN:

(i) $A * (B + \sim C)$ **(ii)** $\sim(A + B\ /\ (C - D))$

(iii) $(\sim A) * (\sim B)$ **(iv)** $\sim(A - (\sim B * (C + \sim D)))$

(c) Convert the infix expressions in (b) to prefix notation.

26. Convert the following logical expressions to RPN:

(a) `A .AND. B .OR. C`
(b) `A .AND. (B .OR. .NOT. C)`
(c) `.NOT. (A .AND. B)`
(d) `(A .OR. B) .AND. (C .OR. (D .AND. .NOT. E))`
(e) `(A .EQ. B) .OR. (C .EQ. D)`
(f) `((A .LT. 3) .AND. (A .GT. 9))`
    `.OR. .NOT. (A .GT. 0)`
(g) `((B * B - 4 * A * C) .GE. 0)`
    `.AND. ((A .GT. 0) .OR. (A .LT. 0))`

27. Convert each of the logical expressions in Exercise 26 to prefix notation.

28. Write a program to implement the algorithm in Example 4 of Section 11.4 for evaluating RPN expressions that involve only one-digit integers and the binary operators $+$, $-$, $*$, and $/$.

29. Write a program that converts infix expressions to prefix.

30. Write a program to evaluate prefix expressions containing only one-digit integers and the binary operators $+$, $-$, $*$, and $/$.

31. The program in Figure 11.10 does not check that the infix expression is well formed (parentheses match, each binary operation has two operands, and so on) and thus may not generate a well-formed RPN expression. Write a program that reads an RPN expression and determines whether it is well formed, that is, whether each binary operator has two operands and the unary operator $\sim$ has one. (See Exercise 25.)

Programming Pointers

The character data type was introduced in Chapter 6 and has been described in detail in this chapter. The following programming pointers are the summaries of the programming pointers in Chapter 6, and the reader should refer to those for an expanded discussion.

1. *The first position specified in a substring should be no greater than the last position; also, both positions should be positive and no greater than the length of the string.*

2. *In an assignment to a substring, the value being assigned may not be a character expression that references any of the same positions to which values are being assigned.*

3. *The collating sequence used to compare characters depends on the encoding system used to store characters.*

4. *Character constants must be enclosed in single quotation marks for list-directed input but not for formatted input.*

5. *In assignment statements and in list-directed input, if the value being assigned or read has a length greater than that specified for the character variable (or substring), the rightmost characters are truncated. If the value has a length less than that of the variable (or substring), blanks are added at the right.* An acronym sometimes used to remember this is

   ●**APT**: For **A**ssignment (and list-directed input), blank-**P**adding and **T**runcation both occur on the right.

6. *For formatted input/output, characters are truncated or blanks are added according to whether the field width is too small or too large. For input, truncation occurs on the left and blank padding on the right; for output, truncation occurs on the right and blank padding on the left.* The acronyms analogous to that in Programming Pointer 5 are

   ●**POT**: **P**adding on the left with blanks occurs for formatted **O**utput, or **T**runcation of rightmost characters occurs.
   ●**TIP**: **T**runcation of leftmost characters occurs for formatted **I**nput, or **P**adding with blanks on the right occurs.

Variations and Extensions

As noted in the Variations and Extensions section of Chapter 6, there are not many differences between the use of the character data type in standard FORTRAN and its use in other common versions. Some of the common ones are:

- An upper limit may be imposed on the length of character values.
- Other forms of the LOGICAL and CHARACTER type statements may be allowed.
- Initialization of logical and character variables may be allowed in type statements.
- Comparison of character values and numeric values with relational operators may be allowed.
- Assignment of character values to numeric variables and of numeric values to character variables may be allowed.

See Appendix F for details.

12

File Processing

. . . it became increasingly apparent to me that, over the years, Federal agencies have amassed vast amounts of information about virtually every American citizen. This fact, coupled with technological advances in data-collecting and dissemination, raised the possibility that information about individuals conceivably could be used for other than legitimate purposes and without the prior knowledge or consent of the individuals involved.

PRESIDENT GERALD R. FORD

The right of the people to be secure in their persons, houses, papers, and effects against unreasonable searches and seizures, shall not be violated. . . .

FOURTH AMENDMENT OF THE U.S. CONSTITUTION

We have more useless information than ignorance of what is useful.

VAUVENARGUES

In Chapter 5 we introduced file processing for those applications involving large data sets that can be processed more conveniently if stored on magnetic tape or disk or some other external media. We considered simple forms of several FORTRAN statements that are used to process files. In this chapter we review these statements, give their complete forms, and introduce some additional file concepts.

The files we have considered thus far are called **sequential files.** These are files in which the lines of data or **records** are written in sequence and must be read in that same order. This means that to read a particular record in a sequential file, all of the preceding records must first be read. In contrast, **direct-access files** are files in which each record may be accessed directly, usually by referring to a record number. This means that a particular record may be accessed without reading (or writing) those records that precede it. Records in a direct-access file must all have the same fixed length, whereas records in a sequential file may be of varying lengths.

Another distinction between files is that they may be **formatted** or **unformatted.** The files we have considered thus far all have been formatted, which means that they consist of records in which information is represented in external character form. In contrast, unformatted files are those in which the information is represented in internal binary form. Thus, the precise form of the records in an unformatted file is machine dependent, as it depends on the manner in which values are stored internally in a particular system. For this reason, unformatted files are discussed only briefly in this chapter, and we focus our attention on formatted files.

12.1 The OPEN, CLOSE, and INQUIRE Statements

A file must be connected to a unit number using the OPEN statement introduced in Section 5.5 before input from or output to that file can take place. When such input/output is completed, the file should be disconnected from its unit number using the CLOSE statement, also introduced in Section 5.5. In some situations, it may also be convenient to inquire about certain properties of a file. The INQUIRE statement may be used for this purpose.

Opening Files. The **OPEN statement** has the general form

OPEN (*open-list*)

where *open-list* must include

1. A unit specifier indicating a unit number to be connected to the file being opened.

In most cases, it also includes

2. A FILE = clause giving the name of the file being opened.
3. A STATUS = clause specifying whether the file is new, old, scratch, or has an unknown status.

It may also include other specifiers selected from the following list:

4. An IOSTAT = clause indicating whether the file has been successfully opened.
5. An ERR = clause specifying a statement to be executed if an error occurs while attempting to open the file.
6. An ACCESS = clause specifying the type of access as sequential or direct.
7. A FORM = clause specifying whether the file is formatted or unformatted.
8. A RECL = clause specifying the record length for a direct-access file.
9. A BLANK = clause specifying whether blank columns in a numeric field are to be interpreted as zeros or are to be ignored.

The unit specifier has the form

UNIT = *integer-expression*

or simply

    integer-expression

where the value of *integer-expression* is a nonnegative integer that designates the unit number to be connected to this file. Reference to this file by subsequent READ or WRITE statements is by means of this unit number. If the second form of the unit specifier is used, it must be the first item in the open list.

    The FILE = clause has the form

    FILE = *character-expression*

where the value of *character-expression* (ignoring trailing blanks) is the name of the file to be connected to the specified unit number.

    The STATUS = clause has the form

    STATUS = *character-expression*

where the value of *character-expression* (ignoring trailing blanks) is one of the following:

```
OLD
NEW
SCRATCH
UNKNOWN
```

If the value is OLD or NEW, the name of the file must have been given in the FILE = clause. OLD means that the file already exists in the system. NEW means that the file does not yet exist and is being created by the program; the OPEN statement creates an empty file with the specified name and changes its status to OLD. If the status is SCRATCH, the file must not be named in a FILE = clause; the OPEN statement creates a work file that is used during execution of this program but that is deleted by a CLOSE statement or by normal termination of the program. A status of UNKNOWN means that none of the preceding apply. In this case, the status of the file depends on the particular system being used. If the STATUS = clause is omitted, the file is assumed to have an UNKNOWN status.

    The IOSTAT = clause is of the form

    IOSTAT = *status-variable*

where *status-variable* is an integer variable to which a value of 0 is assigned if the file is opened successfully, and a positive value is assigned otherwise. A positive value usually represents the number of an appropriate error message in a list found in system manuals.

    The ERR = clause has the form

    ERR = *n*

where *n* is the label of an executable statement that is the next statement executed if an error occurs in attempting to open the file.

The ACCESS = clause is of the form

ACCESS = *access-method*

where *access-method* is a character expression whose value (ignoring trailing blanks) is

SEQUENTIAL   or   DIRECT

If this clause is omitted, the file is assumed to be sequential.

The FORM = clause is of the form

FORM = *form-specifier*

where *form-specifier* is a character expression whose value (ignoring trailing blanks) is either

FORMATTED   or   UNFORMATTED

If this clause is omitted, the file being opened is assumed to be formatted if it is a sequential file or unformatted if it is a direct-access file.

The RECL = clause has the form

RECL = *record-length*

where *record-length* is an integer expression whose value must be positive. This clause is used only for direct-access files and specifies the length of the records in the file. For a formatted file, the record length is the number of characters in each record of that file. For an unformatted file, it is a processor-dependent measure of the record length.

The BLANK = clause has the form

BLANK = *blank-specifier*

where *blank-specifier* is a character expression whose value (ignoring trailing blanks) is either

ZERO   or   NULL

The first specification causes blanks within numeric fields of records in the file being opened to be interpreted as zeros, whereas the NULL specifier causes such blanks to be ignored. In all cases, however, a numeric field consisting only of blanks is interpreted as zero.

As an illustration, suppose that a file has been previously created and saved under the name 'INFO1', and data values are to be read from this file. A unit number such as 10 must first be connected to this file by an OPEN statement such as

```
OPEN (UNIT = 10, FILE = 'INFO1', STATUS = 'OLD')
```

Alternatively, the name of the file can be read during execution:

```
CHARACTER*10 INFILE
PRINT *, 'ENTER NAME OF INPUT FILE'
READ *, INFILE
OPEN (UNIT = 10, FILE = INFILE, STATUS = 'OLD')
```

Because the ACCESS = and FORM = clauses are not used, the file is assumed to be sequential and formatted. If we wish to specify this explicitly, we can use

```
 OPEN (UNIT = 10, FILE = INFILE, STATUS = 'OLD'),
+       FORM = 'FORMATTED', ACCESS = 'SEQUENTIAL')
```

The statement

```
OPEN (UNIT = 10, FILE = INFILE, STATUS = 'OLD', ERR = 50)
```

serves the same purpose, but if an error occurs during the opening of the file, the ERR = clause causes execution to continue with the statement labeled 50.

If the program is to create a new file named 'INFO2', we might attach the unit number 11 to it with the statement

```
OPEN (UNIT = 11, FILE = 'INFO2', STATUS = 'NEW')
```

Execution of this statement changes the status of this file to OLD, so that it will exist after execution of the program is completed. On the other hand, if a temporary work file is needed only during execution, we might use a statement such as

```
OPEN (UNIT = 12, STATUS = 'SCRATCH')
```

This temporary file will then be deleted if it is closed by a CLOSE statement or when execution terminates.

Closing Files. The **CLOSE statement** is used to disconnect a file from its unit number. This statement is of the form

CLOSE (*close-list*)

where *close-list* must include

1. A unit specifier.

It may also include items selected from the following:

2. An IOSTAT = clause.
3. An ERR = clause.
4. A STATUS = clause specifying whether the file is to be kept or deleted.

The IOSTAT = and ERR = clauses are used to detect errors that occur in attempting to close the file and have the same form as the corresponding clauses in the OPEN statement. The STATUS = clause has the form

STATUS = *character-expression*

where the value of *character-expression* (ignoring trailing blanks) is

KEEP   or   DELETE

depending on whether the file is to continue to exist or not exist after the CLOSE statement is executed. KEEP may not be used for a SCRATCH file. If the STATUS = clause is omitted, scratch files are deleted, but all other types are kept. Thus, to close the file INFO2 with unit number 11 referred to earlier so that it is saved after execution, we could use any of the following statements:

```
CLOSE (11)
CLOSE (UNIT = 11)
CLOSE (UNIT = 11, STATUS = 'KEEP')
```

A file that has been closed by a CLOSE statement may be reopened by an OPEN statement; the same unit number may be connected to it, or a different one may be used. All files that are not explicitly closed with a CLOSE statement are automatically closed when execution of the program is terminated (except when termination is caused by an error).

The INQUIRE Statement. The **INQUIRE statement** may be used to ascertain the properties of a file or of its connection to a unit number. It has the form

INQUIRE (*inquiry-list*)

where *inquiry-list* must include a unit specifier or a file specifier, but not both, and may include an IOSTAT = clause and/or an ERR = clause. The inquiry list may also contain a number of other clauses, each of which serves as a question concerning some property of the file. When the INQUIRE statement is executed, a value is assigned to the variable in each clause that provides an answer to the question. A complete list of the clauses and their meanings is given in Table 12.1.

TABLE 12.1 Clauses Allowed in an INQUIRE Statement

Clause	Variable Type	Values and Their Meanings
IOSTAT = variable	Integer	Zero if no error condition exists; positive if an error exists.
EXIST = variable	Logical	True if the file with the specified name or unit number exists; false otherwise.
OPENED = variable	Logical	True if the specified file or unit number has been connected to a unit number or file, respectively; false otherwise.
NUMBER = variable	Integer	The file's unit number or undefined.
NAMED = variable	Logical	True if the file has a name; false otherwise.
NAME = variable	Character	Name of the file; undefined if file has no name.
ACCESS = variable	Character	SEQUENTIAL if file is open for sequential access; DIRECT if it is open for direct access; undefined otherwise.
SEQUENTIAL = variable	Character	YES if file can be connected for sequential access; NO if it cannot; UNKNOWN if suitability of file for sequential access cannot be determined.
DIRECT = variable	Character	YES if file can be connected for direct access; NO if it cannot; UNKNOWN if suitability of file for direct access cannot be determined.
FORM = variable	Character	FORMATTED if file open for formatted data transfer; UNFORMATTED if file open for unformatted data transfer; undefined if file not open.
FORMATTED = variable	Character	YES if file is formatted; NO if file is unformatted; UNKNOWN if record type cannot be determined.
UNFORMATTED = variable	Character	YES if file is unformatted; NO if file is formatted; UNKNOWN if record type cannot be determined.
RECL = variable	Integer	Record length for a direct-access file; undefined if file not connected for direct access.
NEXTREC = variable	Integer	1 plus the number of the last record read from or written to a direct-access file; undefined if file not connected for direct access or record number cannot be determined.
BLANK = variable	Character	ZERO if blanks in numeric fields are to be interpreted as zeros; NULL if they are to be ignored; undefined if file not connected.

12.2 File Input/Output and Positioning

File input/output is accomplished using the general READ and WRITE statements introduced in Chapter 5. The complete forms of these statements are considered in this section. Some file positioning is also carried out by these statements. Other positioning statements that may be used for sequential files are the REWIND, BACKSPACE, and ENDFILE statements.

File Input. Data can be read from a file using a **READ statement** of the general form

READ (*control-list*) *input-list*

The *input-list* is a list of variable names, substring names, array names, or implied DO loops, separated by commas. The *control-list* must include

1. A unit specifier indicating the unit number connected to the file.

It may also include one or more of the following:

2. A format specifier describing the format of the information to be read.
3. An END = clause specifying a statement to be executed when the end of a sequential file is reached.
4. An ERR = clause specifying a statement to be executed if an input error occurs.
5. An IOSTAT = clause to check the status of the input operation.
6. A REC = clause indicating the number of the record to be read for a direct-access file.

The forms of the unit specifier, format specifier, and the END = clause were described in detail in Chapter 5.

The ERR = clause has the form

ERR = *n*

where *n* is the label of a statement to be executed if an input error occurs. For example, suppose that NUMBER and NAME are declared by

```
INTEGER NUMBER
CHARACTER*20 NAME
```

For the READ statement

```
      READ (15, 10, ERR = 20) NUMBER, NAME
10 FORMAT (I5, A20)
```

if the following data is read from the file with unit number 15

```
   123 JOHN HENRY DOE
```

an input data error occurs because the character J in the fifth column is read as part of the value for the integer variable NUMBER. The ERR = clause then causes execution to continue with the statement numbered 20, which might be a statement to print an error message such as

```
20 PRINT *, 'INPUT DATA ERROR'
```

The IOSTAT = clause has the form

IOSTAT = *status-variable*

where *status-variable* is an integer variable. When the READ statement is executed, this variable is assigned

1. A positive value if an input error occurs.
2. A negative value if the end of data is encountered but no input error occurs.
3. Zero if neither an input error nor the end of data occurs.

In the first case, the value is usually the number of an error message in a list found in the system manuals.

The REC = clause has the form

REC = *integer-expression*

where the value of the *integer-expression* is positive and indicates the number of the record to be read from a direct-access file. The clause must be used if input is to be from a file connected for direct access. The control list may not contain both a REC = clause and an END = clause.

All the files used in example programs in the text have thus far been sequential files. The program in Figure 12.1 uses a direct-access file to retrieve information in a parts inventory file. The name FNAME of the file is read during execution and is then opened with the statement

```
OPEN (UNIT = 10, FILE = FNAME, STATUS = 'OLD',
+      ACCESS = 'DIRECT', FORM = 'FORMATTED',
+      RECL = RECLEN)
```

The user then enters a part number, which is used to access a record of the file:

```
READ (10, '(A)', REC = PARTNO, IOSTAT = BADNUM), INFO
```

The information in this record INFO is then displayed to the user.

```
     PROGRAM INVEN
*********************************************************************
* Program to read a part number during execution, access a record in  *
* a direct access parts inventory file, and display this record.       *
* Variables used are:                                                  *
*     RECLEN : a parameter specifying record length                    *
*     PARTNO : part number                                             *
*     FNAME  : name of the file                                        *
*     INFO   : a record in the file                                    *
*     BADNUM : 0 if valid part number, otherwise nonzero               *
*********************************************************************
```

Figure 12.1

Figure 12.1   (continued)

```
        INTEGER PARTNO, RECLEN, BADNUM
        PARAMETER (RECLEN = 30)
        CHARACTER*20 FNAME, INFO*(RECLEN)

* Get the name of the file and open it for direct access

        PRINT *, 'ENTER NAME OF FILE'
        READ '(A)', FNAME
        OPEN (UNIT = 10, FILE = FNAME, STATUS = 'OLD',
     +        ACCESS = 'DIRECT', FORM = 'FORMATTED', RECL = RECLEN)

        PRINT *, 'ENTER PART NUMBER (0 TO STOP)'
        READ *, PARTNO

* While there are more part numbers to process do the following

10      IF (PARTNO .NE. 0) THEN
            READ (10, '(A)', REC = PARTNO, IOSTAT = BADNUM) INFO
            IF (BADNUM .EQ. 0) THEN
                PRINT '(1X, ''PART'', I3, '': '', A)', PARTNO, INFO
            ELSE
                PRINT '(1X, ''INVALID PART NUMBER: '', I3)', PARTNO
            END IF
            PRINT *
            PRINT *, 'PART NUMBER?'
            READ *, PARTNO
            GO TO 10
        END IF
        CLOSE(10)
        END
```

Listing of test file used in sample run:
==

```
CHROME-BUMPER...$152.95.....15
SPARK-PLUG........$1.25....125
DISTRIBUTOR-CAP..$39.95.....57
FAN-BELT..........$5.80.....32
DOOR-HANDLE......$18.85.....84
```

  Sample run:
  ==========

  ENTER NAME OF FILE
PARTSFILE
  ENTER PART NUMBER (0 TO STOP)
4
  PART 4: FAN-BELT..........$5.80.....32

  PART NUMBER?
2
  PART 2: SPARK-PLUG........$1.25....125

  PART NUMBER?
10
  INVALID PART NUMBER: 10

  PART NUMBER?
0

File-Positioning Statements. There are three FORTRAN statements that may be used to position a file. Each of these statements has two possible forms:

REWIND *unit*	or	REWIND (*position-list*)
BACKSPACE *unit*	or	BACKSPACE (*position-list*)
ENDFILE *unit*	or	ENDFILE (*position-list*)

In the first form, *unit* is the unit number connected to the file. In the second form, *position-list* must contain

1. A unit specifier of the form *unit* or UNIT = *unit*.

It may also contain

2. An ERR = clause specifying the number of a statement to be executed if an error occurs in positioning the file.
3. An IOSTAT = clause specifying a status variable that is assigned 0 if the file is successfully positioned or a positive value if some error occurs.

The **REWIND statement** positions the file at its initial point, that is, at the beginning of the first record of the file. The **BACKSPACE statement** positions the file at the beginning of the preceding record. If the file is at its initial point, these statements have no effect.

The **ENDFILE statement** writes a special record called an **end-of-file record** into the file. When this record is encountered by a READ statement containing an END = clause, the statement specified in the END = clause is executed next. After the execution of an ENDFILE statement, no further data transfer to or from this file can take place until the file is repositioned at some record preceding the end-of-file record.

File Output. Data are written to a file using a **WRITE statement** of the general form

    WRITE (*control-list*) *output-list*

The *output-list* is a list of expressions, array names, or implied DO loops separated by commas. The *control-list* must include

1. A unit specifier indicating the unit number connected to the file.

It may also include one or more of the following:

2. A format specifier describing the form of the information being output.
3. An ERR = clause specifying a statement to be executed if an output error occurs.
4. An IOSTAT = clause to check the status of the output operation.
5. A REC = clause indicating the number of the record to which the information is to be output for a direct-access file.

The form of each of these items is the same as for a READ statement.

The format of the output to a direct-access file must be supplied by the user. Also, the REC = clause may not appear when the output is list directed (indicated by an asterisk for the format specifier).

EXAMPLE 1. Merging Files. An important problem in file processing is merging two files that have been previously sorted so that the resulting file is also sorted. To illustrate, suppose that FILE1 and FILE2 have been sorted and contain the following integers

FILE1: 2 4 5 7 9 15 16 20   FILE2: 1 6 8 10 12

To merge these files to produce FILE3, we read one element from each file, say, X from FILE1 and Y from FILE2:

FILE1: $\boxed{2}$4 5 7 9 15 16 20   FILE2: $\boxed{1}$6 8 10 12
  ↑   ↑
  X   Y

We write the smaller of these values, in this case Y, into FILE3:

FILE3: 1

and then read another value for Y from FILE2:

FILE1: $\boxed{2}$4 5 7 9 15 16 20   FILE2: 1 $\boxed{6}$8 10 12
  ↑   ↑
  X   Y

Now X is smaller than Y, and so it is written to FILE3, and a new value for X is read from FILE1:

FILE1: 2 $\boxed{4}$5 7 9 15 16 20   FILE2: 1 $\boxed{6}$8 10 12
  ↑   ↑
  X   Y
FILE3: 1 2

Again X is less than Y, and so X is written to FILE3 and a new X value is read from FILE1:

FILE1: 2 4 $\boxed{5}$7 9 15 16 20   FILE2: 1 $\boxed{6}$8 10 12
   ↑   ↑
   X   Y
FILE3: 1 2 4

Continuing in this manner, we eventually reach the value 15 for X and the value 12 for Y:

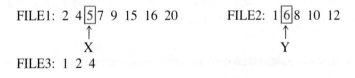

FILE1: 2 4 5 7 9 $\boxed{15}$16 20   FILE2: 1 6 8 10$\boxed{12}$
    ↑   ↑
    X   Y
FILE3: 1 2 4 5 6 7 8 9 10

Because Y is smaller than X, we write Y to FILE3:

FILE3: 1 2 4 5 6 7 8 9 10 12

Because the end of FILE2 has been reached, we simply copy the remaining values in FILE1 to FILE3 to obtain the final sorted file FILE3:

FILE3: 1 2 4 5 6 7 8 9 10 12 15 16 20

The general algorithm to merge two sorted files is as follows:

ALGORITHM TO MERGE FILES

* Algorithm to merge sorted files FILE1 and FILE2 to produce the   *
* sorted file FILE3.   *

1. Open FILE1, FILE2, and FILE3.
2. Read the first element X from FILE1 and the first element Y from FILE2.
3. While the end of neither FILE1 nor FILE2 has been reached, do the following:
   If X ≤ Y then
       (1) Write X to FILE3.
       (2) Read a new X value from FILE1.
   Else do the following:
       (1) Write Y to FILE3.
       (2) Read a new Y value from FILE2.
4. If the end of FILE1 has not been reached, copy the rest of FILE1 into FILE3. If the end of FILE2 has not been reached, copy the rest of FILE2 into FILE3.

In this algorithm, we assumed that the file components are numbers, strings, and so on that can be compared. If the files contain records that are sorted on the basis of some key field in the records, then the key field of X is compared with the key field of Y in step 3. The program in Figure 12.2 implements this modified merge algorithm. It merges two files whose records consist of a student number, student name, and cumulative GPA, and have been sorted so that the student numbers are in ascending order.

```
      PROGRAM MERGE
*********************************************************************
* Program to read two files of records containing a student number, a  *
* student name, and a cumulative GPA, where the files are sorted so    *
* that student numbers are in ascending order, and merge these two     *
* files to produce another which is also sorted.  Variables used are:  *
*      FNAME1, FNAME2   : names of files to be merged                  *
*      FNAME3           : name of file produced                        *
*      SNAME1, SNAME2   : name of student in FILE1, FILE2              *
*      SNUMB1, SNUMB2   : number of student in FILE1, FILE2            *
*      GPA1, GPA2       : cumulative GPA of student in FILE1, FILE2    *
*      EOF1, EOF2       : indicator of end of FILE1, FILE2            *
*********************************************************************
```

Figure 12.2

Figure 12.2 (continued)

```
      CHARACTER *20, FNAME1, FNAME2, FNAME3, SNAME1, SNAME2
      INTEGER SNUMB1, SNUMB2, EOF1, EOF2
      REAL GPA1, GPA2

* Get the names of the files and open them.

      PRINT *, 'ENTER THE NAMES OF THE FILES TO BE MERGED AND THE NAME'
      PRINT *, 'OF THE FILE TO BE PRODUCED. (ENCLOSE NAMES IN QUOTES.)'
      READ *, FNAME1, FNAME2, FNAME3
      OPEN (UNIT = 10, FILE = FNAME1, STATUS = 'OLD',
     +      ACCESS = 'SEQUENTIAL')
      OPEN (UNIT = 20, FILE = FNAME2, STATUS = 'OLD',
     +      ACCESS = 'SEQUENTIAL')
      OPEN (UNIT = 30, FILE = FNAME3, STATUS = 'NEW',
     +      ACCESS = 'SEQUENTIAL')

* Read the first two records from each file

      READ (10, 10, IOSTAT = EOF1) SNUMB1, SNAME1, GPA1
      READ (20, 10, IOSTAT = EOF2) SNUMB2,SNAME2, GPA2
10    FORMAT (I5, 1X, A, F4.2)

* While neither the end of FILE1 or FILE2 has been reached,
* do the following:

20    IF (EOF1 .EQ. 0 .AND. EOF2 .EQ. 0) THEN
          IF (SNUMB1 .LE. SNUMB2) THEN
              WRITE (30, 10) SNUMB1, SNAME1, GPA1
              READ (10, 10, IOSTAT = EOF1) SNUMB1, SNAME1, GPA1
          ELSE
              WRITE (30,10) SNUMB2, SNAME2, GPA2
              READ (20, 10, IOSTAT = EOF2) SNUMB2, SNAME2, GPA2
          END IF
          GO TO 20
      END IF

* If more records remain in FILE1 copy them to FILE3

30    IF (EOF1 .EQ. 0) THEN
          WRITE (30,10) SNUMB1, SNAME1, GPA1
          READ (10, 10, IOSTAT = EOF1) SNUMB1, SNAME1, GPA1
          GO TO 30
      END IF

* If more records remain in FILE2 copy them to FILE3

40    IF (EOF2 .EQ. 0) THEN
          WRITE (30,10) SNUMB2, SNAME2, GPA2
          READ (20, 10, IOSTAT = EOF2) SNUMB2, SNAME2, GPA2
          GO TO 40
      END IF
      PRINT *
      PRINT *, 'FILE MERGING IS COMPLETE'
      END
```

Figure 12.2 (continued)

Sample run:
==========

ENTER THE NAMES OF THE FILES TO BE MERGED AND THE NAME
OF THE FILE TO BE PRODUCED. (ENCLOSE NAMES IN QUOTES.)
'FILE1', 'FILE2', 'FILE3'

FILE MERGING IS COMPLETE

Data files used in sample run:
==============================

FILE1:
=====

```
12320 JOHN HENRY DOE      3.50
12346 FRED SAMUEL DOE     3.48
13331 MARY JANE SMITH     3.85
13345 PETER VANDER VAN    2.99
14400 ALFRED E. NEWMAN    1.00
15555 HENRY SMITHSMA      2.05
```

FILE2:
=====

```
12360 ALICE M. VAN DOE    2.15
12365 JANE E. JONES       1.89
13400 JESSE JAMES         1.66
14001 RICHARD VAN VAN     4.00
```

FILE3 produced by the sample run:
=================================

```
12320 JOHN HENRY DOE      3.50
12346 FRED SAMUEL DOE     3.48
12360 ALICE M. VAN DOE    2.15
12365 JANE E. JONES       1.89
13331 MARY JANE SMITH     3.85
13345 PETER VANDER VAN    2.99
13400 JESSE JAMES         1.66
14001 RICHARD VAN VAN     4.00
14400 ALFRED E. NEWMAN    1.00
15555 HENRY SMITHSMA      2.05
```

EXAMPLE 2. External Sorting: Mergesort. The sorting algorithms we considered in Chapter 7 are *internal* sorting schemes; that is, the entire collection of items to be sorted must be stored in main memory. In many sorting problems, however, the data sets are too large to store in main memory and must be stored in external memory. To sort such collections of data, an *external* sorting algorithm is required. One popular and efficient external sorting method is the **mergesort** technique, a variation of which, called **natural mergesort,** is examined here.

As the name *mergesort* suggests, the basic operation in this sorting scheme is merging data files. To see how the merge operation can be used in sorting a file, consider the following file F containing fifteen integers:

F: 75 55 15 20 80 30 35 10 70 40 50 25 45 60 65

Notice that several segments of F contain elements that are already in order:

F: | 75 | 55 | 15 20 80 | 30 35 | 10 70 | 40 50 | 25 45 60 65 |

These segments, enclosed by the vertical bars, are called *subfiles* or *runs* in F and subdivide F in a natural way.

We begin by reading these subfiles of F and alternately writing them to two other files, F1 and F2

F1: | 75 | 15 20 80 | 10 70 | 25 45 60 65 |
F2: | 55 | 30 35 | 40 50 |

and then identifying the sorted subfiles in F1 and F2.

F1: | 75 | 15 20 80 | 10 70 | 25 45 60 65 |
F2: | 55 | 30 35 40 50 |

Note that although the subfiles of F1 are the same as those copied from F, two of the original subfiles written into F2 have combined to form a larger subfile.

We now merge the first subfile of F1 with the first subfile of F2, storing the elements back in F.

F: | 55 75 |

Next the second subfile of F1 is merged with the second subfile of F2 and written to F.

F: | 55 75 | 15 20 30 35 40 50 80 |

This merging of corresponding subfiles continues until the end of either or both of the files F1 and F2 is reached. If either file still contains subfiles, these are simply copied into F. Thus, in our example, because the end of F2 has been reached, the remaining subfiles of F1 are copied back into F.

F: | 55 75 | 15 20 30 35 40 50 80 | 10 70 | 25 45 60 65 |

Now file F is again split into files F1 and F2 by copying its subfiles alternately into F1 and F2.

F1: | 55 75 | 10 70 |
F2: | 15 20 30 35 40 50 80 | 25 45 60 65 |

Identifying the sorted subfiles in each of these files, we see that for this splitting, none of the original subfiles written into either F1 or F2 combine to form larger ones. Once again we merge corresponding subfiles of F1 and F2 back into F.

F: | 15 20 30 35 40 50 55 75 80 | 10 25 45 60 65 70 |

When we now split F into F1 and F2, each of the files F1 and F2 contains a single sorted subfile, and each is, therefore, completely sorted.

F1: | 15 20 30 35 40 50 55 75 80 |
F2: | 10 25 45 60 65 70 |

Thus, when we merge F1 and F2 back into F, F will also contain only one sorted subfile and hence will be sorted.

F: | 10 15 20 25 30 35 40 45 50 55 60 65 70 75 80 |

This example shows that the mergesort method has two steps: (1) splitting file F into two other files, F1 and F2, and (2) merging corresponding subfiles in these two files. These steps are repeated until each of the smaller files contains a single sorted subfile; when these are merged, the resulting file is completely sorted. Designing an algorithm to split the file and a program to implement the mergesort scheme is left as an exercise.

Unformatted Files. Information is stored in a formatted file using a standard coding scheme such as ASCII or EBCDIC, and when such a file is listed, these codes are automatically converted to the corresponding characters by the terminal, printer, or other output device. In contrast, information is stored in an **unformatted file** using the internal representation scheme for the particular computer being used. This representation usually cannot be correctly displayed in character form by the output device, nor can it be used easily with another computer system.

There are, however, some advantages in using unformatted files. When information in a formatted file is read by a FORTRAN program, two separate processes are involved: (1) the transfer of the information from the file and (2) the conversion of this information to internal form. Similarly, the output of information to a formatted file involves two steps: (1) conversion to external form and (2) the actual transfer of this information to the file. Because such conversion is time-consuming, it may be desirable to eliminate it, especially when a file is to be read and processed only by a computer and not displayed to the user. Another advantage in using unformatted files is that data are usually stored more compactly using their internal representation rather than their external representation in one of the standard coding schemes.

Unformatted file input/output is accomplished by using a READ or WRITE statement in which the format specification is omitted. For example, the statement

```
WRITE (UNIT = 10, ERR = 100) NUM, RATE, TIME
```

writes values of NUM, RATE, and TIME to the unformatted file having unit number 10.

The variables in the input list of a READ statement used to read information from an unformatted file should match in number and type the variables in the output lists of the WRITE statements that produced that file. Also, one may not use both formatted and unformatted input/output statements with the same file.

Internal Files.   An **internal file** is a sequence of memory locations containing information stored in character form and named by a character variable, a character array or array element, or a character substring. Such internal files are useful in converting information from character form to numeric form.

For example, suppose the character variable DATE is assigned the value

```
DATE = 'JULY 4, 1776'
```

and we wish to extract the year 1776 from this character string and convert it to a numeric form suitable for computations. The extraction is easily done using the substring operation

```
YEAR = DATE(9:12)
```

The value of the character variable YEAR is the character string '1776', and thus YEAR can be viewed as an internal file. The information

```
1776
```

stored in this file can be read and assigned to a numeric variable NYEAR by using a READ statement in which the name YEAR of this internal file is used as the unit specifier:

```
READ (UNIT = YEAR, FMT = '(I4)') NYEAR
```

or simply

```
READ (YEAR, '(I4)') NYEAR
```

The integer 1776 could also be read and assigned to NYEAR by using the character substring name DATE (9:12) as the name of the internal file:

```
READ (DATE(9:12), '(I4)') NYEAR
```

or by considering DATE as the name of the internal file and using the appropriate positioning descriptors in the format identifier:

```
READ (DATE, '(8X, I4)') NYEAR
```

In no case, however, would list-directed input be allowed.

Conversely, a numeric constant can be converted to the corresponding character string and assigned to a character variable by considering that character variable to be an internal file and writing to it. For example, suppose the integer variable N has been assigned the value

```
N = 1776
```

and we wish to concatenate the corresponding character string '1776' to the character constant 'JULY 4,'. To accomplish this, we first convert the value of N to character form and assign the resulting string to the character variable REVOL by the statement

```
WRITE (UNIT = REVOL, FMT = '(I4)') N
```

or simply

```
WRITE (REVOL, '(I4)') N
```

in which REVOL is viewed as an internal file. The value of REVOL can then be concatenated with 'JULY 4,' and assigned to the character variable DATE by

```
DATE = 'JULY 4, ' // REVOL
```

When a character array is viewed as an internal file, the number of records in that file is equal to the number of elements in the array, and the length of each record is equal to the declared length of the array elements. Each READ and WRITE statement using this array as an internal file begins data transfer with the first array element.

List-directed input/output is not allowed for internal files nor may the auxiliary input/output statements

```
OPEN
CLOSE
INQUIRE
BACKSPACE
ENDFILE
REWIND
```

be used for such files.

12.3 Example: Inventory Update

To illustrate some of the file concepts discussed in this chapter, we consider the problem of maintaining an inventory file. A program must be written that accepts as input an order number followed by a list of item numbers and order quantities for several items. For each of these items, the appropriate record in the inventory file must be read to determine whether there is sufficient stock of this item to fill the order. If there is, the quantity ordered is subtracted from the number in stock and a message is displayed indicating this fact. If the number remaining in stock is less than the reorder point for that item, an appropriate message must be displayed. If there are not enough items to fill the order, a message indicating how much of the order can be filled at this time must be displayed.

Because an inventory file typically contains a large number of records and because a large number of transactions is processed using this file, sequential access to such a file is inefficient. Consequently, the inventory file will be organized as a direct-access file, which allows one to access a specific record directly rather than to search sequentially through all the records preceding it. In order to access a specific record in a direct-access file, it is necessary to know its record number. Thus, a correspondence must be established between the item number and the number of the record in the inventory file that contains the information relevant to this item. This is accomplished by constructing an array INDEX, consisting of a list of item numbers arranged in the same order as in the file. Thus, the position of a given item number in this array is the same as the number of the corresponding record in the file. When the program is executed, the elements of the array INDEX are read from a file that contains the item numbers. This file is unformatted, because it is read only by the program and is not intended for display to the user.

There are two major tasks that the program must carry out. The first is the initialization task, which consists of opening the necessary files and constructing the array INDEX. The second task is the transaction processing, which consists of accepting the order information from the user, searching the index file to determine the appropriate record number, and carrying out the necessary processing using the order information and the information found in this record. The structure diagram in Figure 12.3 displays these tasks and subtasks and the relationship between them.

The program and sample run in Figure 12.4 represent an early stage in the development of the program to solve this problem. The main program calls the subroutine INIT and then repeatedly calls the subroutine TRANS until the user

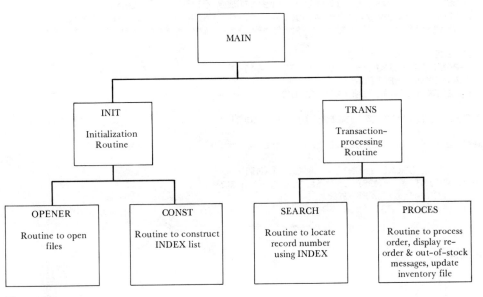

Figure 12.3

indicates that there are no more transactions to process. INIT opens the inventory file and the index file by calling the subroutine OPENER, which is designed to generate a unit number and to attach it to a specified file whose name is passed to it as an argument; the appropriate character strings to be used in the FORM = , STATUS = , and ACCESS = clauses of the OPEN statement are also to be passed as parameters. In this early version of the program, the subroutine OPENER is a program stub that merely displays some of the information passed to it.

The subroutine INIT also calls CONST to construct the array INDEX of items numbers. In Figure 12.4 this is also a program stub that displays a message that the subroutine has been called.

After the files are opened and the array INDEX is constructed, the transaction processing begins. Subroutine TRANS accepts an order for a certain item and calls subroutine SEARCH to search the array INDEX in order to find the position of this item in the inventory file. If the item is found, subroutine PROCES then processes the order. In the program in Figure 12.4, these two subroutines are also implemented as program stubs.

```
      PROGRAM INVEN
**MAIN*******************************************************************
* This program accepts an order from the terminal, searches an inven- *
* tory file to see if the item ordered is in stock, updates the file, *
* displays an out-of-stock message and reorder message at the terminal *
* when necessary.  The search of the inventory file makes use of an   *
* index of stock numbers.  This index is read into main memory from an *
* unformatted file.  Variables used are:                              *
*     LIMIT   :  Upper limit on the number of items in inventory file *
*     LREC    :  Length of records in inventory file                  *
*     INUNIT  :  Unit number of INFILE                                *
*     INDEX   :  Array of item numbers (INDEX(0) = # of items)        *
*     RESPON  :  Response from user (Y or N) re more orders to process *
************************************************************************

      INTEGER LREC, LIMIT
      PARAMETER (LIMIT = 1000, LREC = 44)
      CHARACTER*1 RESPON
      INTEGER INUNIT, INDEX(0:LIMIT)

      CALL INIT(INUNIT, INDEX, LIMIT, LREC)

* Repeat the following until there are no more transactions

10    CALL TRANS(INUNIT, INDEX, LIMIT)
      PRINT *, 'MORE TRANSACTIONS (Y OR N)?'
      READ '(A)', RESPON
      IF (RESPON .EQ. 'Y') GO TO 10

      END
```

Figure 12.4

Figure 12.4 (continued)

```
**INIT*********************************************************************
* This subroutine opens the inventory file and the index file and con- *
* structs the array INDEX of item numbers.  Variables used:            *
*     INUNIT, INDEX, LIMIT, LREC as in MAIN                            *
*     INFILE          :  Name of inventory file                        *
*     IXFILE, IXUNIT  :  Name and unit number of index file            *
***************************************************************************

       SUBROUTINE INIT( INUNIT, INDEX, LIMIT, LREC)

       CHARACTER*20 INFILE, IXFILE
       INTEGER INUNIT, INDEX( 0:LIMIT), LIMIT, IXUNIT, LREC

       PRINT *, 'ENTER NAME OF INVENTORY FILE:'
       READ '(A)', INFILE
       CALL OPENER( INFILE, INUNIT, 'FORMATTED', 'OLD', 'DA', LREC)
       PRINT *, 'ENTER NAME OF INDEX FILE:'
       READ '(A)', IXFILE
       CALL OPENER( IXFILE, IXUNIT, 'UNFORMATTED', 'OLD', 'SE', 0)
       CALL CONST( IXUNIT, INDEX, LIMIT)
       END


**OPENER******************************************************************
* Subroutine to open a file and assign it a unit number.  Successive   *
* calls to this subroutine will assign unit numbers 10, 11, 12, ...    *
* A call to OPENER with TYPE = 'SE' will open a sequential file, while  *
* a call with TYPE = 'DA' will open a direct access file.  Variables   *
* used are:                                                            *
*     FNAME  :  Name of file to be opened                              *
*     NUNIT  :  Unit number to be connected to file (integer)          *
*     FORMSP :  'FORMATTED' or 'UNFORMATTED' according as file is      *
*            :  formatted or unformatted.                              *
*     STAT   :  Status of file ('OLD', 'NEW', 'SCRATCH', etc.)         *
*     TYPE   :  Indicates if file is sequential or direct access       *
*     LREC   :  Length of records for direct access files              *
***************************************************************************

       SUBROUTINE OPENER( FNAME, NUNIT, FORMSP, STAT, TYPE, LREC)

       CHARACTER*(*) FNAME, FORMSP, STAT, TYPE
       INTEGER LREC, NUNIT

       IF (TYPE .EQ. 'SE') THEN
           PRINT *, FNAME, ' IS OPENED FOR SEQUENTIAL ACCESS'
       ELSE
           PRINT *, FNAME, ' IS OPENED FOR DIRECT ACCESS'
       END IF
       END


**CONST*******************************************************************
* This subroutine constructs the array INDEX of item numbers from the  *
* (unformatted) file IXFILE.  IXFILE, IXUNIT, INDEX, and               *
* LIMIT are as in MAIN.                                                *
***************************************************************************

       SUBROUTINE CONST( IXUNIT, INDEX, LIMIT)

       INTEGER LIMIT, INDEX( 0:LIMIT), IXUNIT

       PRINT *, 'INDEX CONSTRUCTED'
       END
```

513

Figure 12.4 (continued)

```
**TRANS************************************************************
* This subroutine processes a transaction by accepting an order for  *
* a certain item from the terminal, searching the array INDEX to find *
* the number of the record in the inventory file describing this item, *
* and then updating this record (displaying out-of-stock and/or reorder*
* messages at the terminal when necessary).  Variables used:          *
*     INUNIT, INDEX, LIMIT as in MAIN and INIT                        *
*     NUMORD  :  Order number                                         *
*     INDEX   :  Item number                                          *
*     QUANT   :  Number of items ordered                              *
*     NUMREC  :  Number of record containing information re INDEX     *
*             :  (VALUE 0 indicates item not found)                   *
*****************************************************************

      SUBROUTINE TRANS(INUNIT, INDEX, LIMIT)

      INTEGER INDEX (0:LIMIT), LIMIT, INUNIT, NUMORD, ITNUM, QUANT,
     +        NUMREC

      CALL SEARCH(INDEX, ITNUM, LIMIT, NUMREC)
      CALL PROCES(NUMREC, QUANT, NUMORD, INUNIT)
      END


**SEARCH***********************************************************
* This subroutine searches the array INDEX of item numbers to locate *
* the number NUMREC of the record in the inventory file containing    *
* information re the item with item number INDEX.  LIMIT is as in MAIN.*
*****************************************************************

      SUBROUTINE SEARCH(INDEX, ITNUM, LIMIT, NUMREC)

      INTEGER INDEX(0:LIMIT), LIMIT, ITNUM, NUMREC

      PRINT *, 'SEARCHING INDEX'
      END


**PROCES***********************************************************
* This subroutine processes an order (order # NUMORD) for QUANT items. *
* The NUMREC-th record of the inventory file (unit number INUNIT) is  *
* examined to determine if the number in stock is sufficient to fill   *
* the order.  If not, an out-of-stock message will be displayed at the *
* terminal.  In either case, this record will be updated.  Also, if    *
* the new number in stock is below the reorder point, a reorder message*
* will be displayed at the terminal.                                  *
*****************************************************************

      SUBROUTINE PROCES(NUMREC, QUANT, NUMORD, INUNIT)

      INTEGER NUMREC, QUANT, NUMORD, INUNIT

      PRINT *, 'PROCESSING ORDER'
      END
```

Figure 12.4   (continued)

```
Sample run:
==========


ENTER NAME OF INVENTORY FILE:
TEST-FILE
   TEST-FILE               IS OPENED FOR DIRECT ACCESS
   ENTER NAME OF INDEX FILE:
INDEX-FILE
   INDEX-FILE              IS OPENED FOR SEQUENTIAL ACCESS
   INDEX CONSTRUCTED
   SEARCHING INDEX
   PROCESSING ORDER
   MORE TRANSACTIONS (Y OR N)?
N
```

Figure 12.5 shows the final program in which the subroutines OPENER, CONST, SEARCH, and PROCES have been developed. Also shown is a small test file used in a sample run and a listing of the updated test file produced by this run.

```
      PROGRAM INVEN
**MAIN*****************************************************************
* This program accepts an order from the terminal, searches an inven- *
* tory file to see if the item ordered is in stock, updates the file,  *
* displays an out-of-stock message and reorder message at the terminal *
* when necessary.  The search of the inventory file makes use of an    *
* index of stock numbers.  This index is read into main memory from an *
* unformatted file.  Variables used are:                               *
*     LIMIT   :  Upper limit on the number of items in inventory file  *
*     LREC    :  Length of records in inventory file                   *
*     INUNIT  :  Unit number of INFILE                                 *
*     INDEX   :  Array of item numbers (INDEX(0) = # of items)         *
*     RESPON  :  Response from user (Y or N) re more orders to process *
**********************************************************************

      INTEGER LREC, LIMIT
      PARAMETER (LIMIT = 1000, LREC = 44)
      CHARACTER*1 RESPON
      INTEGER INUNIT, INDEX(0:LIMIT)

      CALL INIT (INUNIT, INDEX, LIMIT, LREC)

* Repeat the following until there are no more transactions

10    CALL TRANS(INUNIT, INDEX, LIMIT)
      PRINT *, 'MORE TRANSACTIONS (Y OR N)'
      READ '(A)', RESPON
      IF (RESPON .EQ. 'Y') GO TO 10

      END
```

Figure 12.5

Figure 12.5 (continued)

```
**INIT***************************************************************
* This subroutine opens the inventory file and the index file and con- *
* structs the array INDEX of item numbers.  Variables used:           *
*     INUNIT, INDEX, LIMIT, LREC as in MAIN                           *
*     INFILE           :  Name of inventory file                     *
*     IXFILE, IXUNIT  :  Name and unit number of index file          *
*********************************************************************

      SUBROUTINE INIT(INUNIT, INDEX, LIMIT, LREC)

      CHARACTER*20 INFILE, IXFILE
      INTEGER INUNIT LIMIT, INDEX(0:LIMIT), IXUNIT, LREC

      PRINT *, 'ENTER NAME OF INVENTORY FILE:'
      READ '(A)', INFILE
      CALL OPENER(INFILE, INUNIT, 'FORMATTED', 'OLD', 'DA', LREC)
      PRINT *, 'ENTER NAME OF INDEX FILE:'
      READ '(A)', IXFILE
      CALL OPENER(IXFILE, IXUNIT, 'UNFORMATTED', 'OLD', 'SE', 0)
      CALL CONST(IXUNIT, INDEX, LIMIT)
      END


**OPENER*************************************************************
* Subroutine to open a file and assign it a unit number.  Successive  *
* calls to this subroutine will assign unit numbers 10, 11, 12, ...   *
* A call to OPENER with TYPE = 'SE' will open a sequential file, while *
* a call with TYPE = 'DA' will open a direct access file.  Variables  *
* used are:                                                           *
*     FNAME  :  Name of file to be opened                            *
*     NUNIT  :  Unit number to be connected to file (integer)        *
*     N      :  Last unit number assigned by subroutine              *
*     FORMSP :  'FORMATTED' or 'UNFORMATTED' according as file is    *
*            :  formatted or unformatted.                            *
*     STAT   :  Status of file ('OLD', 'NEW', 'SCRATCH', etc.)       *
*     TYPE   :  Indicates if file is sequential or direct access     *
*     LREC   :  Length of records for direct access files           *
*********************************************************************

      SUBROUTINE OPENER(FNAME, NUNIT, FORMSP, STAT, TYPE, LREC)

      CHARACTER*(*) FNAME, FORMSP, STAT, TYPE
      INTEGER LREC, NUNIT, N
      SAVE N
      DATA N/10/

      IF(TYPE .EQ. 'SE') THEN
          OPEN(UNIT = N, FILE = FNAME, FORM = FORMSP, STATUS = STAT,
     +         ERR = 10)
      ELSE
          OPEN(UNIT = N, FILE = FNAME, FORM = FORMSP, STATUS = STAT,
     +         ACCESS = 'DIRECT', RECL = LREC, ERR = 10)
      END IF
      NUNIT = N
      N = N + 1
      RETURN
10    PRINT *, FNAME, ' CANNOT BE OPENED'
      STOP
      END
```

Figure 12.5 (continued)

```
**CONST***********************************************************************
* This subroutine constructs the array INDEX of item numbers from the   *
*(unformatted) file IXFILE.  IXFILE, IXUNIT, INDEX, and LIMIT are as     *
* in MAIN.  Other variables used are:                                    *
*      I       :  Count of records in inventory file (stored in          *
*              :  INDEX(0) before return)                                 *
*      ITNUM   :  Item number                                            *
******************************************************************************

        SUBROUTINE CONST(IXUNIT, INDEX, LIMIT)

        INTEGER INDEX(0:LIMIT), IXUNIT, LIMIT, I, ITNUM

        I = 0

* While there is more data, do the following:

10      READ (IXUNIT, END = 20) ITNUM
        I = I+1
        INDEX(I) = ITNUM
        GO TO 10

* Store the count in INDEX(0)

20      INDEX(0) = I
        END


**TRANS***********************************************************************
* This subroutine processes a transaction by accepting an order for      *
* a certain item from the terminal, searching the array INDEX to find    *
* the number of the record in the inventory file describing this item,   *
* and then updating this record (displaying out-of-stock and/or reorder* 
* messages at the terminal when necessary).  Variables used:             *
*      INUNIT, INDEX, LIMIT as in MAIN and INIT                          *
*      NUMORD  :  Order number                                           *
*      ITNUM   :  Item number                                            *
*      QUANT   :  Number of items ordered                                *
*      NUMREC  :  Number of record containing information re ITNUM        *
*              :  (VALUE 0 indicates item not found)                     *
******************************************************************************

        SUBROUTINE TRANS(INUNIT, INDEX, LIMIT)

        INTEGER LIMIT, INDEX (0:LIMIT), INUNIT, NUMORD, ITNUM, QUANT,
     +          NUMREC
        PRINT *, 'ENTER ORDER #'
        READ *, NUMORD
        PRINT *, '(ENTER 0/ FOR ITEM # TO TERMINATE ORDER)'
        PRINT *, 'ITEM #, QUANTITY'
        READ *, ITNUM, QUANT

* While ITNUM not equal to 0 do the following:

10      IF (ITNUM .NE. 0) THEN
            CALL SEARCH(ITNUM, INDEX, LIMIT, NUMREC)
            IF (NUMREC .NE. 0)
     +          CALL PROCES(NUMREC, QUANT, NUMORD, INUNIT)
            PRINT *, 'ITEM #, QUANTITY'
            READ *, ITNUM, QUANT
            GO TO 10
        END IF
        END
```

Figure 12.5 **(continued)**

```
**SEARCH***************************************************************
* This subroutine searches the array INDEX of item numbers to locate  *
* the number NUMREC of the record in the inventory file containing     *
* information re the item with item number ITNUM.  LIMIT is as in MAIN *
* and FOUND is a boolean indicating if the item is found.              *
**********************************************************************

        SUBROUTINE SEARCH(ITNUM, INDEX, LIMIT, NUMREC)

        INTEGER INDEX(0:LIMIT), LIMIT, ITNUM, NUMREC, I
        LOGICAL FOUND

        I = 1
        FOUND = .FALSE.

* While FOUND is false and I is less than or equal to the
* number of items in the array INDEX do the following:

10      IF ((.NOT. FOUND) .AND. (I .LE. INDEX(0))) THEN
            IF (ITNUM .EQ. INDEX(I)) THEN
                NUMREC = I
                FOUND = .TRUE.
            ELSE
                I = I + 1
            END IF
            GO TO 10
        END IF
        IF (.NOT. FOUND) THEN
            PRINT *, 'BAD ITEM NUMBER'
            NUMREC = 0
        END IF
        END


**PROCES**************************************************************
* This subroutine processes an order (order # NUMORD) for QUANT items. *
* The NUMREC-th record of the inventory file (unit number INUNIT) is   *
* examined to determine if the number in stock is sufficient to fill   *
* the order.  If not, an out-of-stock message will be displayed at the *
* terminal.  In either case, this record will be updated.  Also, if    *
* the new number in stock is below the reorder point, a reorder message*
* will be displayed at the terminal.  New variables used are:          *
*       INFO   :  Unused information in a record                       *
*       REORD  :  Reorder point                                        *
*       INSTOK :  Number of items in stock                             *
*       INLEV  :  Desired inventory level                              *
*       STOCK  :  INSTOK - QUANT (# remaining in stock)                *
*       FORM   :  An i/o format                                        *
**********************************************************************

        SUBROUTINE PROCES(NUMREC, QUANT, NUMORD, INUNIT)

        CHARACTER*29 INFO, FORM
        INTEGER NUMREC, QUANT, NUMORD, INUNIT, REORD, INSTOK, INLEV, STOCK
        SAVE FORM
        DATA FORM / '(I6, A29, 3I3)'/
```

Figure 12.5   (continued)

```
      READ (INUNIT, FORM, REC=NUMREC) ITNUM, INFO, REORD, INSTOK,
     +     INLEV
      STOCK = INSTOK - QUANT
      IF (STOCK .LT. 0) THEN
          PRINT 10, 'OUT OF STOCK ON ITEM #', ITNUM
10        FORMAT(1X, 3(A, I7))
          PRINT 10, 'BACK ORDER', -1*STOCK, ' FOR ORDER #', NUMORD
          PRINT 10, 'ONLY', INSTOK,' UNITS CAN BE SHIPPED AT THIS TIME'
          PRINT 10, 'THE DESIRED INVENTORY LEVEL IS', INLEV
          INSTOK = 0
      ELSE
          INSTOK = STOCK
          PRINT 10, 'DONE'
      END IF
      WRITE (INUNIT, FORM, REC = NUMREC) ITNUM, INFO, REORD, INSTOK,
     +     INLEV
      IF ((STOCK .GE. 0) .AND. (STOCK .LE. REORD)) THEN
          PRINT 10, 'ONLY',INSTOK,' UNITS OF',ITNUM,' REMAIN IN STOCK'
          PRINT 10, 'REORDER POINT IS', REORD
          PRINT 10, 'DESIRED INVENTORY LEVEL IS', INLEV
      END IF
      END


 Sample run:
 ==========

 ENTER NAME OF INVENTORY FILE:
TEST-FILE
 ENTER NAME OF INDEX FILE:
INDEX-FILE
 ENTER ORDER #
11111
 (ENTER 0/ FOR ITEM # TO TERMINATE ORDER)
 ITEM #, QUANTITY
102003, 2
 DONE
 ITEM #, QUANTITY
102003, 5
 DONE
 ITEM #, QUANTITY
102003, 8
 DONE
 ONLY      0 UNITS OF 102003 REMAIN IN STOCK
 REORDER POINT IS      5
 DESIRED INVENTORY LEVEL IS      15
 ITEM #, QUANTITY
101001, 12
 DONE
 ONLY      8 UNITS OF 101001 REMAIN IN STOCK
 REORDER POINT IS      15
 DESIRED INVENTORY LEVEL IS      25
 ITEM #, QUANTITY
101001, 10
 OUT OF STOCK ON ITEM # 101001
 BACK ORDER      2 FOR ORDER #  11111
 ONLY      8 UNITS CAN BE SHIPPED AT THIS TIME
 THE DESIRED INVENTORY LEVEL IS      25
```

Figure 12.5   (continued)

```
 ITEM #, QUANTITY
0/
 MORE TRANSACTIONS (Y OR N)
Y
 ENTER ORDER #
22222
 (ENTER 0/ FOR ITEM # TO TERMINATE ORDER)
 ITEM #, QUANTITY
101002, 15
 OUT OF STOCK ON ITEM # 101002
 BACK ORDER       3 FOR ORDER #   22222
 ONLY       12 UNITS CAN BE SHIPPED AT THIS TIME
 THE DESIRED INVENTORY LEVEL IS       20
 ITEM #, QUANTITY
0/
 MORE TRANSACTIONS (Y OR N)
N
```

```
Listing of original file TEST-FILE used in sample run:
=========================================================

101001TELEPHOTO POCKET CAMERA  5495 15 20 25
101002MINI POCKET CAMERA       2495 15 12 20
102001POL. ONE-STEP CAMERA     4995 10 20 20
102002SONAR 1-STEP CAMERA     18995 12 13 15
102003PRONTO CAMERA            7495  5 15 15
1030018MM ZOOM MOVIE CAMERA   27999 10  9 15
```

```
Listing of updated TEST-FILE produced by sample run:
=========================================================

101001TELEPHOTO POCKET CAMERA  5495 15  0 25
101002MINI POCKET CAMERA       2495 15  0 20
102001POL. ONE-STEP CAMERA     4995 10 20 20
102002SONAR 1-STEP CAMERA     18995 12 13 15
102003PRONTO CAMERA            7495  5  0 15
1030018MM ZOOM MOVIE CAMERA   27999 10  9 15
```

Exercises

1. Write a program to concatenate two files, that is, to append one file to the end of the other.

2. Following the example of the text, show the various splitting-merging stages of mergesort for the following lists of numbers:

   (a) 1, 5, 3, 8, 7, 2, 6, 4
   (b) 1, 8, 2, 7, 3, 6, 5, 4
   (c) 1, 2, 3, 4, 5, 6, 7, 8
   (d) 8, 7, 6, 5, 4, 3, 2, 1

3. **(a)** Design an algorithm to perform the file splitting required by mergesort.

   (b) Write a program to read records from USERSFILE (described in Appendix B) and sort them using mergesort so that the resources used to date are in increasing order.

4. Information about computer terminals in a computer network is maintained in a direct-access file. The terminals are numbered 1 through 100, and information about the nth terminal is stored in the nth record of the file. This information consists of a terminal type (string), the building in which it is located (string), the transmission rate (integer), an access code (character), and the date of last service (month, day, year). Write a program to read a terminal number, retrieve and display the information about that terminal, and modify the date of last service for that terminal.

5. Most system text formatters allow command lines to be placed within the file of unformatted text. These command lines might have forms such as the following:

   .P m n Insert m blank lines before each paragraph and indent each paragraph n spaces.

   .W n Page width (line length) is n.

   .L n Page length (number of lines per page) is n

   .I n Indent all lines following this command line n spaces.

   .U   Undent all following lines and reset to the previous left margin.

   Write a program to read a file containing lines of text and some of these command lines throughout, and produce a new file in which these formatting commands have been implemented.

6. Modify and extend the *text-editor* program of Section 11.2 so that other editing operations can be performed. Include commands of the following forms in the menu of options:

   F n Find and display the nth line of the file.

   P n Print n consecutive lines beginning with the current line.

   M n Move ahead n lines from the current line.

   T   Move to the top line of the file.

   C/*string1*/*string2*/ Change the current line by replacing *string1* with *string2*.

   L *string*   Search the file starting from the current line to find a line containing *string*.

   D n Delete n consecutive lines beginning with the current line.

   I *line*   Insert the given *line* after the current line.

7. A *pretty printer* is a special kind of text formatter that reads a file containing a source program and then prints it in a "pretty" format. For example, a pretty printer for FORTRAN might insert blank lines between subprograms, indent and align statements within other statements such as block IF statements and DO loops, and so on, to produce a format similar to that used in the sample programs in this text. Write a pretty print program for FORTRAN programs to indent and align statements in a pleasing format.

8. Write a menu-driven program that uses STUDENT-FILE and STUDENT-UPDATE (see Appendix B) and allows (some of) the following options. For each option, write a separate subprogram so that options and corresponding subprograms can be easily added or removed.

(1) Locate a student's permanent record when given his or her student number and print it in a nicer format than that in which it is stored.

(2) Same as option 1, but locate the record when given his or her name.

(3) Print a list of all student names and numbers in a given class (1, 2, 3, 4, 5).

(4) Same as option (3) but for a given major.

(5) Same as option (3) but for a given range of cumulative GPAs.

(6) Find the average cumulative GPAs for (a) all females, (b) all males, (c) all students with a specified major, and (d) all students.

(7) Produce updated grade reports with the following format:

```
        GRADE REPORT - SEMESTER 1    12/18/87

                    DISPATCH UNIVERSITY

    10103     JAMES L. JOHNSON


                            GRADE                        CREDITS
                            =====                        =======
        ENGL 176              C                             4
        EDUC 268              B                             4
        EDUC 330              B+                            3
        P E 281               C                             3
        ENGR 317              D                             4

        CUMULATIVE CREDITS:      28
        CURRENT GPA:           1.61
        CUMULATIVE GPA:        2.64
```

Here, letter grades are assigned according to the following scheme: A = 4.0, A − = 3.7, B+ = 3.3, B = 3.0, B− = 2.7, C+ = 2.3, C = 2.0, C− = 1.7, D+ = 1.3,

D $=$ 1.0, D$-$ $=$ 0.7, and F $=$ 0.0. (See Exercise 23 at the end of Chapter 7 for details on the calculation of GPAs.)

(8) Same as option (7), but instead of producing grade reports, produce a new file containing the updated total credits and new cumulative GPAs.

(9) Produce an updated file when a student (a) drops or (b) adds a course.

(10) Produce an updated file when a student (1) transfers into or (2) withdraws from the university.

Variations and Extensions

The Variations and Extensions section in Chapter 5 dealt with input and output and thus is also pertinent to the discussion of files in this chapter. The major variations from and extensions to the file-processing features of standard FORTRAN that may be provided in other versions include the following, and additional details can be found in Appendix F.

● The OPEN and CLOSE statements may not be required.

● In addition to the END $=$ clause, there may be other functions or constructs that can be used to detect the end of file (e.g., the Microsoft EOF function).

● Some unit numbers may be preset (e.g., 5 $=$ the keyboard, 6 $=$ the screen).

● Other clauses may be allowed in the OPEN and INQUIRE statements.

13

Miscellany

I can only assume that a "Do Not File" document is filed in a "Do Not File" file.

SENATOR FRANK CHURCH

There are a number of FORTRAN features that we have not yet discussed, as they are not commonly used and in some cases are not consistent with the principles of structured programming. But because they are part of the standard FORTRAN language, we examine these miscellaneous topics in this chapter.

13.1 The PAUSE Statement

The STOP and END statements described in Section 3.6 serve to terminate execution of a program. In some cases, it may be desirable to interrupt the program execution and then either terminate it or continue after examining some of the results produced. A **PAUSE statement** may be used for this purpose. This statement has the form

PAUSE

or

PAUSE *constant*

where *constant* is an integer constant with five or fewer digits or a character constant that is usually displayed when execution is interrupted; the exact message (if any) depends on the compiler.

When the PAUSE statement is encountered, execution of the program is interrupted, but it may be resumed by means of an appropriate command. Execution will resume with the first executable statement following the PAUSE statement that caused execution to be suspended. The action required to resume execution will depend on the system.

13.2 The IMPLICIT Statement

The usual FORTRAN naming convention is that unless otherwise specified all variable names beginning with I, J, K, L, M, *or* N *are integer and all other variables are real.* The programmer can override this naming convention with an **IMPLICIT statement.** This statement has the form

IMPLICIT *type1* $(a_1, a_2, \ldots)$, *type2* $(b_1, b_2, \ldots)$, . . .

where each a_i, b_i, . . . is a letter or a pair of letters separated by a hyphen (-), and each *typei* is one of the following:

INTEGER
REAL
CHARACTER*n
LOGICAL
DOUBLE PRECISION
COMPLEX

The effect of this statement is to declare that all variables whose names begin with one of the letters a_1, a_2, . . . are *type1* variables, all whose names begin with one of the letters b_1, b_2, . . . are *type2* variables, and so on. For example, the statement

```
IMPLICIT INTEGER (A-F, Z), CHARACTER*10 (L,X,Y)
```

declares that all variables whose names begin with A, B, C, D, E, F, or Z are of integer type and that those whose names begin with L, X, or Y are character variables of length 10.

The IMPLICIT statement and all type statements (as well as other declaration statements considered in earlier chapters) must precede all executable statements in a program, and among these, the IMPLICIT statement must precede all others. All variables whose names begin with letters other than those listed in the IMPLICIT statement have types determined by the naming convention or by subsequent type declarations. Thus, in the following set of statements

```
IMPLICIT CHARACTER*10 (A, L-N, Z), CHARACTER*5 (D-G)
INTEGER NUMBER, ZIP
CHARACTER*20 ADDRESS, LNAME, FNAME*12
REAL ALPHA, LAMBDA
```

the last three type statements override the types specified for the indicated variables by the naming convention established by the IMPLICIT statement or by the default FORTRAN naming convention.

As we have noted, however, it is a good programming practice to declare explicitly the type of each variable, because this encourages the programmer to think carefully about what each variable represents and how it is to be used. It is important that variables of a given type be used in a manner that is consistent with that data type, as the program may not execute correctly otherwise. Consequently, the programmer should not rely on the IMPLICIT statement or the default FORTRAN naming convention to determine the types of variables.

13.3 Other Control Statements: Arithmetic IF, Computed GO TO, Assigned GO TO

In our discussion in Chapter 4 of the three basic control structures—sequential structure, selection structure, and repetition structure—the selection structure was implemented using the logical IF statement and the block IF statement. There are three additional statements in FORTRAN that may be used to implement selection structures, but they are less commonly used than are the logical and block IF statements. They are the arithmetic IF statement, the computed GO TO statement, and the assigned GO TO statement.

The Arithmetic IF Statement.   The **arithmetic IF statement** has the form

IF (*expression*) n_1, n_2, n_3

where the expression enclosed in parentheses is an arithmetic expression and n_1, n_2, and n_3 are labels of executable statements, not necessarily distinct. When this statement is executed, the value of the expression is calculated, and execution will continue with statement n_1 if this value is negative, with statement n_2 if it is zero, and with statement n_3 if it is positive. For example, consider the arithmetic IF statement

```
IF (X ** 2 - 10.5) 10, 15, 20
```

If X has the value 3.1, statement 10 will be executed next.

The program in Figure 13.1 is a modification of the program in Figure 4.7 to solve quadratic equations

$$Ax^2 + Bx + C = 0$$

An arithmetic IF statement is used in place of a block IF statement to select the appropriate statements for execution, depending on whether the value of the discriminant $B^2 - 4AC$ is negative, zero, or positive.

```
      PROGRAM QUAD4
**********************************************************************
* Program to solve a quadratic equation using the quadratic formula. *
* It uses an arithmetic IF statement to select the appropriate action *
* depending on whether the discriminant DISC is negative, zero, or   *
* positive.  Variables used are:                                     *
*    A, B, C      : the coefficients of the quadratic equation        *
*    DISC         : the discriminant, B ** 2 - 4 * A * C              *
*    ROOT1, ROOT2 : the two roots of the equation                    *
**********************************************************************

      REAL A, B, C, DISC, ROOT1, ROOT2

      PRINT *, 'ENTER THE COEFFICIENTS OF THE QUADRATIC EQUATION'
      READ *, A, B, C
      DISC = B ** 2 - 4 * A * C
      IF (DISC) 10, 20, 30

* No real roots

10    PRINT *, 'DISCRIMINANT IS', DISC
      PRINT *, 'THERE ARE NO REAL ROOTS'
      STOP

* Repeated real root

20    ROOT1 = -B / (2 * A)
      PRINT *, 'REPEATED ROOT IS', ROOT1
      STOP

* Distinct real roots

30    DISC = SQRT(DISC)
      ROOT1 = (-B + DISC) / (2 * A)
      ROOT2 = (-B - DISC) / (2 * A)
      PRINT *, 'THE ROOTS ARE', ROOT1, ROOT2
      END
```

Figure 13.1

The Computed GO TO Statement.   The **computed GO TO statement** has the form

GO TO $(n_1, n_2, \ldots, n_k)$, *integer-expression*

where $n_1, n_2, \ldots, n_k$ are labels of executable statements, not necessarily distinct. The comma preceding the integer expression is optional. When this statement is executed, the value of the expression is computed. If this value is the integer i, execution will continue with the statement whose label is n_i. The computed GO TO statement can thus be used to implement a multialternative selection structure. For example, if J and K are integer variables, the statement

```
GO TO (50, 10, 5, 50, 80, 100), J - K
```

selects one of the statements 5, 10, 50, 80, 100 for execution, depending on the value of the expression J − K. If J − K has the value 5, statement 80 is executed next.

The Assigned GO TO Statement. The **assigned GO TO statement** uses an integer variable to select the statement to be executed next. It has the form

GO TO *integer-variable*

or

GO TO *integer-variable*, $(n_1, \ldots, n_k)$

where $n_1, \ldots, n_k$ are labels of executable statements. The comma following the integer variable in the second form is optional.

Before execution of this statement, a statement label must be assigned to the integer variable by an **ASSIGN statement** of the form

ASSIGN *statement-label* TO *integer-variable*

The assigned GO TO statement then causes execution to continue with the statement whose label has been assigned to the specified integer variable.

In the second form of the assigned GO TO statement, at the time of execution a check is made to determine whether the statement label assigned to the integer variable is in the list $n_1, \ldots, n_k$. If it is not, an error message results. In the first form of the assigned GO TO statement, no such validation of the value of the integer variable takes place; if it is out of range, execution continues with the next executable statement in the program.

13.4 More About COMMON and Block Data Subprograms

Other COMMON Features. In Section 9.8 we used the COMMON statement to establish common regions for simple variables and for arrays with the same dimensions. It is also possible to use the COMMON statement to establish common regions for arrays of different dimensions. For example, the statements

```
INTEGER B(3,4)
COMMON B
```

in one program unit and the statements

```
INTEGER BETA(2,6)
COMMON BETA
```

in another allocate the first twelve memory locations of the blank common region to both B and BETA, resulting in the following associations:

Array Element	Blank Common Location	Array Element
B(1,1)	#1	BETA(1,1)
B(2,1)	#2	BETA(2,1)
B(3,1)	#3	BETA(1,2)
B(1,2)	#4	BETA(2,2)
B(2,2)	#5	BETA(1,3)
B(3,2)	#6	BETA(2,3)
B(1,3)	#7	BETA(1,4)
B(2,3)	#8	BETA(2,4)
B(3,3)	#9	BETA(1,5)
B(1,4)	#10	BETA(2,5)
B(2,4)	#11	BETA(1,6)
B(3,4)	#12	BETA(2,6)

A COMMON statement may be used to associate two or more arrays with a single array. If the statements

```
REAL A(3,3), CONS(3)
COMMON A, CONS
```

appear in one program unit and

```
REAL AUG(3,4)
COMMON AUG
```

appear in another, the following associations will be established:

Array Element	Blank Common Location	Array Element
A(1,1)	#1	AUG(1,1)
A(2,1)	#2	AUG(2,1)
A(3,1)	#3	AUG(3,1)
A(1,2)	#4	AUG(1,2)
A(2,2)	#5	AUG(2,2)
A(3,2)	#6	AUG(3,2)
A(1,3)	#7	AUG(1,3)
A(2,3)	#8	AUG(2,3)
A(3,3)	#9	AUG(3,3)
CONS(1)	#10	AUG(1,4)
CONS(2)	#11	AUG(2,4)
CONS(3)	#12	AUG(3,4)

It is also possible to mix both simple variables and arrays in COMMON statements. For example, if the statements

```
REAL COEFF(2,2), C, D
COMMON COEFF, C, D
```

appear in one program unit and the statements

```
REAL GAUSS(2,3)
COMMON GAUSS
```

appear in another, these variables and array elements are associated as follows:

Variable or Array Element	Blank Common Location	Array Element
COEFF(1,1)	#1	GAUSS(1,1)
COEFF(2,1)	#2	GAUSS(2,1)
COEFF(1,2)	#3	GAUSS(1,2)
COEFF(2,2)	#4	GAUSS(2,2)
C	#5	GAUSS(1,3)
D	#6	GAUSS(2,3)

When arrays are listed in a COMMON statement, it is possible to dimension the arrays in the COMMON statement itself. For example, the preceding two pairs of statements could be written as

```
REAL COEFF, C, D
COMMON COEFF(2,2), C, D
```

and

```
REAL GAUSS
COMMON GAUSS(2,3)
```

In our examples thus far, the association established between items has been complete; that is, there is a one-to-one correspondence between the items. It is also possible to establish a partial correspondence, in which some of the items listed in one of the COMMON statements are not associated with items in the other COMMON statement. For example, the statements

```
REAL A, X(3)
COMMON A, X
```

in one program unit and

```
REAL B(6)
COMMON B
```

in another program unit establish a partial association as follows:

$$A \leftrightarrow B(1)$$
$$X(1) \leftrightarrow B(2)$$
$$X(2) \leftrightarrow B(3)$$
$$X(3) \leftrightarrow B(4)$$
$$B(5)$$
$$B(6)$$

Numeric and character type variables may not be allocated memory locations from the same common region. Named common regions, however, are separate regions. Consequently, numeric variables may be allocated to one named region and character variables to another, with both regions established in the same COMMON statement. Thus, the statements

```
REAL X, Y
INTEGER M, N
CHARACTER*10 A, B, C
COMMON /NUMER/ X, Y, M, N /CHARAC/ A, B, C
```

may appear in one program unit and the statements

```
REAL X, Z
INTEGER I, J
CHARACTER*10 ALPHA, BETA, GAMMA
COMMON /NUMER/ X, Z, I, J /CHARAC/ ALPHA, BETA, GAMMA
```

in another.

Block Data Subprograms.   We noted in Section 9.8 that items that are allocated memory locations in blank common may not be initialized in DATA statements. However, items allocated memory locations from a named common region may be initialized in a DATA statement, provided this initialization is done in a special kind of subprogram called a **block data subprogram.**
  The first statement of a block data subprogram is

BLOCK DATA

or

BLOCK DATA *name*

A program may contain more than one block data subprogram, but at most, one of these may be unnamed. A *block data subprogram contains no executable statements*. Only comments and the following statements may appear in block data subprograms:

IMPLICIT
PARAMETER
DIMENSION
COMMON
SAVE
EQUIVALENCE
DATA
END
Type statements

The last statement of the subprogram must, of course, be an END statement.

A block data subprogram initializes items in named common regions by listing these items in COMMON statements and specifying their values in DATA statements. Suppose, for example, that variables A and B and the array LIST are allocated memory locations in common region BLOCK1 and that the character variable CODE and character array NAME are allocated locations in common region BLOCK2. The following block data subprogram could be used to initialize A, B, LIST(1), . . . , LIST(5), CODE, and the entire array NAME:

```
BLOCK DATA
INTEGER M, N
PARAMETER (M = 20, N = 50)
REAL A, B
INTEGER LIST(M)
CHARACTER*10 CODE, NAME(N)
COMMON /BLOCK1/ A,B,LIST /BLOCK2/ CODE,NAME
DATA A, B, (LIST(I), I = 1,5) /2.5, 3.5, 5*0/
DATA CODE, NAME /'&', N*' '/
END
```

13.5 The EQUIVALENCE Statement

The **EQUIVALENCE statement** makes it possible to associate variables and arrays in the *same* program unit so that they refer to the same memory locations. This statement is of the form

EQUIVALENCE (*list1*), (*list2*), . . .

where each of *list1, list2,* . . . is a list of variables, arrays, array elements, or substring names separated by commas, which are to be allocated the same memory locations. Each of the sets of items that constitute one of the lists in parentheses is said to be an **equivalence class.** *The EQUIVALENCE statement is nonexecutable and must appear at the beginning of the program before all executable statements.*

As an illustration, consider the statements

```
INTEGER M1, M2, NUM
REAL X, Y, ALPHA(5), BETA(5)
EQUIVALENCE (X,Y), (M1, M2, NUM), (ALPHA, BETA)
```

The variables and elements of the arrays that appear in the EQUIVALENCE statement are associated in the following manner:

$$X \leftrightarrow Y$$
$$M1 \leftrightarrow M2 \leftrightarrow NUM$$
$$ALPHA(1) \leftrightarrow BETA(1)$$
$$ALPHA(2) \leftrightarrow BETA(2)$$
$$ALPHA(3) \leftrightarrow BETA(3)$$
$$ALPHA(4) \leftrightarrow BETA(4)$$
$$ALPHA(5) \leftrightarrow BETA(5)$$

Because associated variables refer to the same memory locations, changing the value of one of these variables also changes the value of all variables in the same equivalence class.

The following rules govern the use of EQUIVALENCE statements:

1. Two (or more) items may not be equivalenced if they *both* appear in a COMMON statement(s) in the same program unit.
2. Formal arguments may not be equivalenced.
3. Items of character type may be equivalenced only with other items of character type. Numeric items of different types may be equivalenced, but extreme care must be exercised because of the different internal representations used for different numeric types.

The EQUIVALENCE statement is most often used to make efficient use of memory by associating the elements in large arrays. Suppose, for example, a program processes a 100 × 100 array BIG and a 40 × 250 array TABLE. If the array BIG is no longer needed when the processing of TABLE begins, the two arrays could be equivalenced by the statement

```
EQUIVALENCE (BIG, TABLE)
```

In the preceding examples, arrays have been equivalenced by specifying the array names in the same equivalence class. This has the effect of associating the first elements in these arrays and successive elements. For example, the statements

```
REAL A(5), B(5)
EQUIVALENCE (A, B)
```

associate the elements of the arrays A and B in the following manner:

$$A(1) \quad A(2) \quad A(3) \quad A(4) \quad A(5)$$
$$\updownarrow \qquad \updownarrow \qquad \updownarrow \qquad \updownarrow \qquad \updownarrow$$
$$B(1) \quad B(2) \quad B(3) \quad B(4) \quad B(5)$$

The name of an array element may also be used in specifying the items of an equivalence class. The statement

```
EQUIVALENCE (A(1), B(1))
```

establishes the same associations as in the preceding example. This same association could also be established with the statement

```
EQUIVALENCE (A(3), B(3))
```

or

```
EQUIVALENCE (A(4), B(4))
```

and so on. The array elements listed in an equivalence class indicate the elements at which the association is to begin, with the remaining elements in the arrays associated in the natural way. Thus, the statement

```
EQUIVALENCE (A(2), B(3))
```

establishes the following associations:

	A(1)	A(2)	A(3)	A(4)	A(5)
		↕	↕	↕	↕
	B(1)	B(2)	B(3)	B(4)	B(5)

Similarly, the statements

```
REAL P, X(3), Y(5), Z(7)
EQUIVALENCE (P, X, Y(3), Z(4))
```

establish the following associations:

				P			
				↕			
			X(1)	X(2)	X(3)		
			↕	↕	↕		
	Y(1)	Y(2)	Y(3)	Y(4)	Y(5)		
	↕	↕	↕	↕	↕		
Z(1)	Z(2)	Z(3)	Z(4)	Z(5)	Z(6)	Z(7)	

If variables of character type are equivalenced, association begins with the first character position of each variable and continues with successive positions. If substrings are equivalenced, association begins with the first positions of the specified substrings with the remaining character positions associated in the natural way. For example, the statements

```
CHARACTER*5, F, G, H, I, J*7, K*8
EQUIVALENCE (F, G), (H, J), (I(2: ), K(4: ))
```

establish the following associations:

When character arrays are equivalenced using the array names, association begins with the first character position of the first elements of each array and region. For example, the statements

```
REAL X, Y, Z, A(5)
COMMON X, Y, Z
EQUIVALENCE (Y, A(2))
```

establish the following associations:

Variable	Blank Common Location	Array Element
X	#1	A(1)
Y	#2	A(2)
Z	#3	A(3)
	#4	A(4)
	#5	A(5)

with the implied extension of blank common by the addition of memory locations #4 and #5. Such an extension "in the direction of increasing locations" is allowed, but an extension to locations preceding the first one is not. Thus, replacement of the preceding EQUIVALENCE statement by

```
EQUIVALENCE (Y, A(3))
```

is not allowed, since this statement would require the following extension:

Variable	Blank Common Location	Array Element
		A(1)
X	#1	A(2)
Y	#2	A(3)
Z	#3	A(4)
	#4	A(5)

13.6 Alternate Entries and Returns

The ENTRY Statement.   The normal entry point of a subprogram is the first executable statement following the FUNCTION or SUBROUTINE statement. In some cases, some other entry may be convenient. For example, it may be necessary to assign values to certain variables the first time a subprogram is referenced but not on subsequent references.

Multiple entry points in subprograms are introduced by using **ENTRY statements** of the form

ENTRY *name(argument-list)*

continues with successive character positions of successive array elements
example, the statements

```
CHARACTER*4 A(3), B(6)*2
EQUIVALENCE (A, B)
```

establish the following associations:

$$A(1) \quad\quad A(2) \quad\quad A(3)$$

$$B(1)\ B(2)\ B(3)\ B(4)\ B(5)\ B(6)$$

Specifying an array element or a substring of an array element in
equivalence class is also possible. In this case, association begins with the
character position of the array element or substring indicated and continue
the manner described for arrays and substrings.

It is possible for a variable or an array to appear in both an EQUI
LENCE statement and a COMMON statement. To illustrate, suppose one
gram unit contains the statements

```
REAL BIG(100, 100), LARGE(40, 250)
EQUIVALENCE (BIG, LARGE)
COMMON BIG
```

and another program unit contains the statements

```
REAL X(10000)
COMMON X
```

Each of the following triples of array elements then refers to the same mem
location:

BIG(1,1)	LARGE(1,1),	X(1)
BIG(2,1)	LARGE(2,1),	X(2)
⋮	⋮	⋮
BIG(100,1),	LARGE(20,3),	X(100)
BIG(1,2),	LARGE(21,3),	X(101)
⋮	⋮	⋮
BIG(100,100),	LARGE(40,250),	X(10000)

Some care must be exercised, however, when such a combination
EQUIVALENCE and COMMON statements is used. When an array appe
in an EQUIVALENCE statement, it may imply an extension of a comm

where *name* is the name of the entry point and *argument-list* is similar to the argument list in a FUNCTION or SUBROUTINE statement.

ENTRY statements are *nonexecutable* and thus have no effect on the normal execution sequence in the subprogram. Entry into the subprogram can be directed to the first executable statement following an ENTRY statement.

Suppose we wish to prepare a function subprogram to evaluate $Ax^2 + Bx + C$ for various values of x. In this case, we could use the following function subprogram:

```
FUNCTION QUAD(X)
REAL QUAD, X, A, B, C, POLY

READ *, A, B, C

ENTRY POLY(X)
QUAD = A * X ** 2 + B * X + C
SAVE A, B, C
END
```

The first reference to this function in the main program would be with a statement such as

```
VAL = QUAD(Z)
```

which would cause values for A, B, and C in the subprogram to be read and the function evaluated at Z. Subsequent references to the function might be by statements such as

```
Y = POLY(Z)
```

In such cases, entry into the subprogram would be at the first statement following the ENTRY statement; thus, the function would be evaluated at Z using the values for A, B, and C read previously.

Different entry points in a subprogram may have different argument lists. In this case, care must be taken to ensure that the actual argument list in a reference agrees with the formal argument list in the corresponding ENTRY statement.

Normally, all entry names in a function subprogram are the same type as the type of the function name. In this case, any of these names may be used to assign the function value to be returned. Thus, the statement

```
POLY = A * X ** 2 + B * X + C
```

could be used in place of the statement

```
QUAD = A * X ** 2 + B * X + C
```

in the function subprogram QUAD.

If any entry name is of character type, then all entry names, including the function name, must be of character type, and all must have the same lengths. For numeric-valued functions, entry names may be of different types, but for each reference to some entry name, there must be at least one statement that assigns a value to an entry name having the same type as the name being referenced.

Alternate Returns.   In certain situations, it may be convenient to return from a subroutine at some point other than the normal return point (the first executable statement following the CALL statement). This can be accomplished as follows:

1. In the CALL statement, specify the alternate points of return by using arguments of the form

    n

    where *n* denotes a statement label indicating the statement to be executed upon return from the subprogram.
2. Use asterisks (*) as the corresponding formal arguments in the SUB-ROUTINE statement.
3. Use a statement in the subroutine of the form

    RETURN *k*

    where *k* is an integer expression whose value indicates which of the alternate returns is to be used.

The following example illustrates:

Main Program:

```
       :
       :
    CALL SUBR (A, B, C, *30, *40)
 20 D = A * B
       :
       :
 30 D = A + B
       :
       :
 40 D = A − B
       :
       :
    END

    SUBROUTINE SUBR (X, Y, TERM, *, *)
       :
       :
    IF (TERM .LT. 0) RETURN 1
    IF (TERM .GT. 0) RETURN 2
    END
```

The return to the main program from the subroutine SUBR is to statement 30 if the value of TERM is less than zero, to statement 40 if it is greater than zero, and to statement 20 (normal return) if it is equal to zero.

"Where shall I begin, please Your Majesty?" he asked. "Begin at the beginning," the King said, gravely, "and go on till you come to the end; then stop."

LEWIS CARROLL, *Alice's Adventures in Wonderland*

A

ASCII and EBCDIC

Decimal	Binary	Octal	Hexa-decimal	ASCII	EBCDIC
0	00000000	0	0	NUL	NUL
.	.	.	.	.	.
.	.	.	.	.	.
.	.	.	.	.	.
32	00100000	40	20	space	
33	00100001	41	21	!	
34	00100010	42	22	''	
35	00100011	43	23	#	
36	00100100	44	24	$	
37	00100101	45	25	%	
38	00100110	46	26	&	
39	00100111	47	27	'	
40	00101000	50	28	(	
41	00101001	51	29	)	
42	00101010	52	2A	*	
43	00101011	53	2B	+	
44	00101100	54	2C	,	
45	00101101	55	2D	−	
46	00101110	56	2E	.	
47	00101111	57	2F	/	
48	00110000	60	30	0	
49	00110001	61	31	1	
50	00110010	62	32	2	
51	00110011	63	33	3	
52	00110100	64	34	4	
53	00110101	65	35	5	
54	00110110	66	36	6	
55	00110111	67	37	7	
56	00111000	70	38	8	
57	00111001	71	39	9	
58	00111010	72	3A	:	
59	00111011	73	3B	;	
60	00111100	74	3C	<	
61	00111101	75	3D	=	
62	00111110	76	3E	>	
63	00111111	77	3F	?	
64	01000000	100	40	@	blank

Decimal	Binary	Octal	Hexa-decimal	ASCII	EBCDIC
65	01000001	101	41	A	
66	01000010	102	42	B	
67	01000011	103	43	C	
68	01000100	104	44	D	
69	01000101	105	45	E	
70	01000110	106	46	F	
71	01000111	107	47	G	
72	01001000	110	48	H	
73	01001001	111	49	I	
74	01001010	112	4A	J	¢
75	01001011	113	4B	K	.
76	01001100	114	4C	L	<
77	01001101	115	4D	M	(
78	01001110	116	4E	N	+
79	01001111	117	4F	O	|
80	01010000	120	50	P	&
81	01010001	121	51	Q	
82	01010010	122	52	R	
83	01010011	123	53	S	
84	01010100	124	54	T	
85	01010101	125	55	U	
86	01010110	126	56	V	
87	01010111	127	57	W	
88	01011000	130	58	X	
89	01011001	131	59	Y	
90	01011010	132	5A	Z	!
91	01011011	133	5B	[	$
92	01011100	134	5C	\	*
93	01011101	135	5D	]	)
94	01011110	136	5E	$\wedge$ (or $\uparrow$)	;
95	01011111	137	5F	_ (or $\leftarrow$)	¬
96	01100000	140	60	`	_
97	01100001	141	61	a	/
98	01100010	142	62	b	
99	01100011	143	63	c	
100	01100100	144	64	d	
101	01100101	145	65	e	
102	01100110	146	66	f	
103	01100111	147	67	g	
104	01101000	150	68	h	
105	01101001	151	69	i	
106	01101010	152	6A	j	
107	01101011	153	6B	k	,
108	01101100	154	6C	l	%
109	01101101	155	6D	m	_
110	01101110	156	6E	n	>
111	01101111	157	6F	o	?
112	01110000	160	70	p	
113	01110001	161	71	q	
114	01110010	162	72	r	
115	01110011	163	73	s	
116	01110100	164	74	t	
117	01110101	165	75	u	
118	01110110	166	76	v	
119	01110111	167	77	w	

Decimal	Binary	Octal	Hexa-decimal	ASCII	EBCDIC
120	01111000	170	78	x	
121	01111001	171	79	y	
122	01111010	172	7A	z	:
123	01111011	173	7B	{	#
124	01111100	174	7C	|	@
125	01111101	175	7D	}	'
126	01111110	176	7E	~	=
127	01111111	177	7F	DEL	''
128	10000000	200	80		
129	10000001	201	81		a
130	10000010	202	82		b
131	10000011	203	83		c
132	10000100	204	84		d
133	10000101	205	85		e
134	10000110	206	86		f
135	10000111	207	87		g
136	10001000	210	88		j
137	10001001	211	89		i
.	.	.	.		.
.	.	.	.		.
.	.	.	.		.
145	10010001	221	91		j
146	10010010	222	92		k
147	10010011	223	93		l
148	10010100	224	94		m
149	10010101	225	95		n
150	10010110	226	96		o
151	10010111	227	97		p
152	10011000	230	98		q
153	10011001	231	99		r
.	.	.	.		.
.	.	.	.		.
.	.	.	.		.
162	10100010	242	A2		s
163	10100011	243	A3		t
164	10100100	244	A4		u
165	10100101	245	A5		v
166	10100110	246	A6		w
167	10100111	247	A7		x
168	10101000	250	A8		y
169	10101001	251	A9		z
.	.	.	.		.
.	.	.	.		.
.	.	.	.		.
192	11000000	300	C0		}
193	11000001	301	C1		A
194	11000010	302	C2		B
195	11000011	303	C3		C
196	11000100	304	C4		D
197	11000101	305	C5		E
198	11000110	306	C6		F
199	11000111	307	C7		G
200	11001000	310	C8		H
201	11001001	311	C9		I

Decimal	Binary	Octal	Hexa-decimal	ASCII	EBCDIC
.	.	.	.		.
.	.	.	.		.
.	.	.	.		.
208	11010000	320	D0		}
209	11010001	321	D1		J
210	11010010	322	D2		K
211	11010011	323	D3		L
212	11010100	324	D4		M
213	11010101	325	D5		N
214	11010110	326	D6		O
215	11010111	327	D7		P
216	11011000	330	D8		Q
217	11011001	331	D9		R
.	.	.	.		.
.	.	.	.		.
224	11100000	340	E0		\
225	11100001	341	E1		
226	11100010	342	E2		S
227	11100011	343	E3		T
228	11100100	344	E4		U
229	11100101	345	E5		V
230	11100110	346	E6		W
231	11100111	347	E7		X
232	11101000	350	E8		Y
233	11101001	351	E9		Z
.	.	.	.		.
.	.	.	.		.
.	.	.	.		.
240	11110000	360	F0		0
241	11110001	361	F1		1
242	11110010	362	F2		2
243	11110011	363	F3		3
244	11110100	364	F4		4
245	11110101	365	F5		5
246	11110110	366	F6		6
247	11110111	367	F7		7
248	11111000	370	F8		8
249	11111001	371	F9		9
.	.	.	.		.
.	.	.	.		.
.	.	.	.		.
255	11111111	377	FF		

Note: Entries for which there is no character shown indicate that these codes have not been assigned or are used for control.

Sample Files

Several exercises in the text use the files INVENTORY-FILE, STUDENT-FILE, USERS-FILE, INVENTORY-UPDATE, STUDENT-UPDATE, and USER-UPDATE. This appendix describes the contents of the records in these files and gives a sample listing for each.

INVENTORY-FILE

Columns	Contents
1–6	Item number
7–30	Item name
31–35	Unit price (no decimal point, but three digits before and two after the decimal point are assumed)
36–38	Reorder point
39–41	Number currently in stock
42–44	Desired Inventory level

The file is sorted so that the item numbers of the records are in increasing order.

```
INVENTORY-FILE
==============


101001TELEPHOTO POCKET CAMERA   5495 15 20 25
101002MINI POCKET CAMERA        2495 15 12 20
102001POL. ONE-STEP CAMERA      4995 10 20 20
102002SONAR 1-STEP CAMERA      18995 12 13 15
102003PRONTO CAMERA             7495  5 15 15
1030018MM ZOOM MOVIE CAMERA    27999 10  9 15
103002SOUND/ZOOM 8MM CAMERA    31055 10 15 15
```

```
10400135MM SLR XG-7 MINO. CAM.38900 12 10 20
10400235MM SLR AE-1 PENT. CAM.34995 12 11 20
10400335MM SLR ME CAN. CAM.  31990 12 20 20
10410135MM HI-MATIC CAMERA   11995 12 13 20
10410235MM COMPACT CAMERA     8999 12 20 20
151001ZOOM MOVIE PROJECTOR   12995  5  7 10
151002ZOOM-SOUND PROJECTOR   23999  5  9 15
152001AUTO CAROUSEL PROJECTOR 21999 5 10 10
152002CAR. SLIDE PROJECTOR   11495  5  4 10
201001POCKET STROBE           1495  5  4 15
201002STROBE SX-10            4855 10 12 20
201003ELEC.FLASH SX-10        2899 15 10 20
301001TELE CONVERTER          3299 15 13 30
30100228MM WIDE-ANGLE LENS    9799 15 14 25
301003135MM TELEPHOTO LENS    8795 15 13 25
30100435-105 MM ZOOM LENS    26795  5  8 10
30100580-200 MM ZOOM LENS    25795  5  7 10
311001HEAVY-DUTY TRIPOD       6750  5  4 10
311002LIGHTWEIGHT TRIPOD      1995  5 10 10
35100135MM ENLARGER KIT      15999  5 10 10
40100140X40 DELUXE SCREEN     3598  5  4 15
40100250X50 DELUXE SCREEN     4498  5 10 10
501001120-SLIDE TRAY          429 25 17 40
501002100-SLIDE TRAY          295 25 33 40
502001SLIDE VIEWER            625 15 12 25
503001MOVIE EDITOR           5595 10 12 20
601001CONDENSER MICROPHONE   5995  5 10 10
611001AA ALKALINE BATTERY      89100 80200
701001GADGET BAG             1979 20 19 35
801001135-24 COLOR FILM       149 50 45100
802001110-12 COLOR FILM        99 50 60100
802002110-24 COLOR FILM       145 50 42100
802003110-12 B/W FILM          59 25 37 75
802004110-24 B/W FILM          95 25 43 75
803001126-12 COLOR FILM        89 50 44100
803002126-12 B/W FILM          59 25 27 50
8040018MM FILM CASSETTE       689 50 39100
```

STUDENT-FILE

Columns	Contents
1–6	Student number
7–21	Student's last name
22–36	Student's first name
37	Student's middle initial
38–60	Address
61–67	Phone number
68	Sex (M or F)
69	Class level (1, 2, 3, 4, or 5 for special)
70–73	Major (four-letter abbreviation)
74–77	Total credits earned to date (no decimal point, but three digits before and one after the decimal point are assumed)
78–80	Cumulative GPA (no decimal point, but one digit before and two after the decimal point are assumed)

The file is sorted so that the student numbers are in increasing order.

STUDENT-FILE
============

```
010103JOHNSON         JAMES       LWAUPUN, WISCONSIN         7345229M1ENGR0150315
010104ANDREWS         PETER       JGRAND RAPIDS, MICHIGAN    9493301M2CPSC0425278
010110PETERSON        SAMUEL      LLYNDEN, WASHINGTON        3239550M5ART 0630205
010113VANDEN KLOP     MARILYN     KFREMONT, MICHIGAN         5509237F4HIST1105374
010126BROOKS          SUSAN       RCHINO, CALIFORNIA         3330861F3PHILO785310
010144LUCKETT         FREDERICK   MGRANDVILLE, MICHIGAN      7745424M5HISTO660229
010179DE VRIES        NANCY       LKALAMAZOO, MICHIGAN       6290017F1MATHO155383
010191NAKAMURA        BENJAMIN    CCHICAGO, ILLINOIS         4249665M1SOCIO125195
010226MORRIS          REBECCA     JLYNDEN, WASHINGTON        8340115F1PSYCO150185
010272JEFFERSON       GREGORY     WGRAND RAPIDS, MICHIGAN    2410744M5ENGL1025295
010274JACKOWSKI       MICHELLE    MBYRON CENTER, MICHIGAN    8845115F3MUSCO790275
010284ORANGE          WILLIAM     BZEELAND, MICHIGAN         3141660M2ENGRO420298
010297KING            RODNEY      LDENVER, COLORADO          4470338M4HIST1175325
010298BLAINE          DAWN        JDE MOTTE, INDIANA         5384609F4PSYC1200299
010301ELDER           KENNETH     LGALLUP, NEW MEXICO        6632997M1EDUCO145195
010302PATRICK         ELIZABETH   ASHEBOYGAN, WISCONSIN      5154997F2CHEMO400385
0103040LSON           KATHLEEN    ESPARTA, MICHIGAN          8861201F5GERMO145305
010307ANDREWS         STEVEN      JGRAND RAPIDS, MICHIGAN    2410744M3MUSCO765287
010310ISMOND          SIDNEY      OLAKEWOOD, CALIFORNIA      7172339M2CPSCO465383
010319HOPKINS         GREGORY     LYORKTOWN, PENNSYLVANIA    3385494M2MATHO410300
010323HOLMES          JILL        DMUSKEGON, MICHIGAN        6763991F3MATHO775275
010330JACOBSON        MARSHA      ASILVER SPRINGS, MD        4847932F5HISTO255298
010339NOOYER          ROCHELLE    JSALT LAKE CITY, UTAH      6841129F2EDUCO410383
010348BRINK           ALBERT      JHUDSONVILLE, MICHIGAN     6634401M4CPSC1155325
010355ZYLSTRA         CATHERINE   EHOLLAND, MICHIGAN         7514008F1ENGLO160195
010377WORKMAN         RONALD      KCOLUMBUS, OHIO            4841771M2SOCIO440278
010389YOUNG           GLORIA      LKALAMAZOO, MICHIGAN       7712399F4EDUC1155299
010395MENDELSON       DOUGLAS     MWHITINSVILLE, MA          9294401M3ENGRO805310
010406KRAMER          CHERYL      LSEATTLE, WASHINGTON       5582911F1CPSCO150299
010415ANDERSON        DANIEL      RGRANDVILLE, MICHIGAN      5325912M2ENGRO435279
010422BROUWER         DAVID       JWHEATON, ILLINOIS         6631212M2PSYCO425248
010431VAN DER PLOEG   THOMAS      KCAWKER CITY, KANSAS       6349971M1CPSCO150400
010448SMITTER         DEBORAH     SSIOUX CENTER, IOWA        2408113F1ART 0775220
010458LOTTERMAN       ALICE       HREDLANDS, CALIFORNIA      9193001F1POLSO155315
010467HUITING         THEODORE    AHAWTHORNE, NEW JERSEY     5513915M3ECONO780275
010470PARKS           SANDRA      LTROY, MICHIGAN            8134001F4MUSC1185325
010482NYENBERG        WILLIAM     KROCHESTER, NEW YORK       7175118M1ENGLO155315
010490CHAPMAN         ROBERT      JCHINO, CALIFORNIA         3132446M2P E 0435278
010501COOPER          REBECCA     JWINDOW ROCK, ARIZONA      4245170F1BIOLO160310
010509HOUSEMAN        JANICE      ABOZEMAN, MONTANA          8183226F3SPEEO775340
010511RIDDERING       ELIZABETH   LNEW ERA, MICHIGAN         6461125F4E SC1140337
010515ALLENHOUSE      GERALD      TBOISE, IDAHO              5132771M5EDUCO875199
010523VOS             ROGER       DKENTWOOD, MICHIGAN        9421753M1BIOLO135177
010530VERMEER         SHARLENE    MOKLAHOMA CITY, OK         3714377F5ENGLO950266
010538ROSSMAN         STEVEN      GST LOUIS, MISSOURI        8354112M3ENGRO745275
010547PATTERSON       SHIRLEY     APETOSKEY, MICHIGAN        4543116F5CPSCO555295
010553SMITH           GERRIT      CBURKE, VIRGINIA           2351881M1HISTO150177
010560VELDERMAN       MARILYN     KFT LAUDERDALE, FLORIDA    4421885F1SOCIO130195
010582JEMISON         JONATHAN    BRUDYARD, MICHIGAN         3451220M3MATHO760299
010590STRONG          ELLEN       MLANSING, ILLINOIS         6142449F1CPSCO140188
010597QUIST           MICHAEL     JPORTLAND, OREGON          4631744M4P E 1165198
010610BLACK           CALVIN      RGRAND RAPIDS, MICHIGAN    9491221M5E SC1350295
```

```
010623ENGELSMA       CAROL        JCINCINATTI, OHIO       3701228F4GREE1190325
010629COOPER         FREDERICK    ABOULDER, COLORADO      5140228M1MATH0135195
010633BROWN          CAROLYN      JRIPON, CALIFORNIA      4341883F5GEOG0895229
010648PETERSON       PAMELA       JCHEYENNE, WYOMING      7145513F1EDUC0140175
010652JACKSON        FREDERICK    RRAPID CITY, SD         3335910M3LATI0775287
010657WILSON         STEVEN       LDETROIT, MICHIGAN      4841962M4PHIL1150299
010663LONG           ALIDA        CLINCOLN, NEBRASKA      7120111F5EDUC1005270
010668FREDRICKSON    ALBERT       MBURKE, VIRGINIA        3710225M2ENGR0415278
010675GREGORY        ROBERT       LNASHVILLE, TENNESSEE   4921107M4MATH1155325
010682HEERES         STEPHANIE    MAUSTIN, TEXAS          5132201F4ART 1170374
010688STONE          DANIEL       EBROOKLYN, NEW YORK     7412993M1CPSC0155198
```

USERS-FILE

Columns	Contents
1–15	User's last name
16–30	User's first name
31–36	Identification number
37–41	Password
42–45	Resource limit (in dollars)
46–50	Resources used to date (no decimal point, but three digits before and two after the decimal point are assumed)

The file is sorted so that the identification numbers of the records are in increasing order.

```
USERS-FILE
==========


MILTGEN          JOSEPH         100101MOE   75038081
SMALL            ISAAC          100102LARGE 65059884
SNYDER           LAWRENCE       100103R2-D2 25019374
EDMUNDSEN        RONALD         100104ABCDE 25017793
BRAUNSCHNEIDER   CHRISTOPHER    100105BROWN 85019191
PIZZULA          NORMA          100106PIZZA 35022395
VANDERPOL        HENRY          100107VAN   75016859
VANZWALENBERG    FLORENCE       100108VANZ  450 7661
ALEXANDER        ALVIN          100109AL    65040504
COSTEMAN         MICHAEL        100110MICKY  50 4257
WYZOREK          GEORGE         100111ZIGGY 350 7350
NAWSADIS         BARBARA        100112HAPPY 850 3328
SINKE            LAUREL         100113SWIM  75032753
VELTEMA          DONALD         100114DONV  55038203
KENIEWSKI        KEN            100115KEKEN 550 2882
BEECHEM          WILLIAM        100116BOAT  95025618
DOYLE            YVONNE         100117CONAN 45033701
ZWIER            ALEXANDER      100118GREAT 35024948
JESTER           MICHELLE       100119JOKER 45028116
MCCONNEL         STEPHEN        100120STEVE 250 3500
```

```
WITCZAK       ROGER         100121WITTY 650 3836
VRIESMAN      BENJAMIN      100122DUTCH 850 3732
JAGER         JEFFREY       100123TIGER 25024673
TRAVIS        DANIEL        100124XXXXX 15010019
BRYANT        MARY          100125CUTIE 250    3
BRINK         MARILEE       100126LEE   750 6735
ARMSTRONG     KENNETH       100127JACK  55039200
ENGELS        BARBARA       100128HOUSE 150 1639
KONYNDYK      KRISTINE      100129KK    950 8957
FELTON        GEORGE        100130JAWGE 85046695
ZEILSTRA      LAWRENCE      100131LARRY 75033212
SMITH         ALEXANDER     100132RADIO 85033743
VITO          ANTHONY       200101TONY   50 3281
VENEMA        VERNON        200102VEVE  25010934
GRIGGS        LINDA         200103LAUGH 35026993
KUIPERS       JESSAMINE     200104JESSE 95018393
BROWN         CALVIN        200105GREEN 35012869
RHODES        LAWRENCE      200106HIWAY 15010031
NYHOFF        MICHELLE      200107MICKY 350 6363
LEESTMA       JAMES         200108SANDY 85020224
MULLER        CHRISTOPHER   200109KRIS  55016849
JOHNSON       JANET         200110JJ    55033347
STEVENS       JEFFREY       200111CONNY 950 3702
BOONSTRA      ALFRED        200112BOON  75033774
HARRISON      BENJAMIN      200113BEN   55026297
JAMES         JESSE         200114GUNS  250 5881
SCOTT         FRANCINE      200115FLAG  35016811
PHILLIPS      JAMES         200116GAS66 65032222
BROOKS        ANN-MARIE     200117WATER 350 2634
SANDERS       PETER         200118BEACH 350 2286
LEWIS         GEORGE        200119LULU  95046030
NEWMANN       ALFRED        200120MAD   45011600
VAN TOL       GEORGE        200121VAN   55048605
PETERSON      STEVEN        200122PETE  250 3531
JANSMA        BENJAMIN      200124SMOKE 15012770
```

INVENTORY-UPDATE

Columns	Contents
1–7	Order number (three letters followed by four digits)
8–13	Item number (same as those used in INVENTORY FILE)
14	Transaction code (S = sold, R = returned)
15–17	Number of items sold or returned

The file is sorted so that item numbers are in increasing order. (Some items in INVENTORY-FILE may not have update records; others may have more than one.)

```
INVENTORY-UPDATE
================


CCI7543101002S    2
LTB3429101002S    7
DJS6762102001S    9
NQT1850102002S    1
WYP6425102003S    4
YOK2210102003R    2
QGM3144102003S    1
NPQ8685103001S    5
MAP8102103001S   13
JRJ6335103001S    1
UWR9386103002S    3
TJY1913103002S   11
YHA9464104001S    5
SYT7493104001S    3
FHJ1657104002S    7
OJQ2215104003S    8
UOX7714104003S    2
ERZ2147104003S    7
MYW2540104101S    1
UKS3587104102S    2
AAN3759104102S    2
WZT4171104102S   12
TYR9475151001S    1
FRQ4184151001S    1
TAV3604151002S    2
DCW9363152002S    1
EXN3964152002R    1
OIN5524152002S    1
EOJ8218152002S    1
YFK0683201001S    2
PPX4743201002S    4
DBR1709201003S    4
JOM5408201003S    3
PKN0671201003S    1
LBD8391301001S    9
DNL6326301002S    9
BTP5396301003S    1
GFL4913301003S    8
EHQ7510301003S    7
QQL6472301003S    5
SVC6511301004S    4
XJQ9391301004S    4
ONO5251311001S    3
CXC7780311001S    1
VGT8169311002S    8
IMK5861351001S    2
QHR1944351001S    1
ZPK6211401001S    2
VDZ2970401002S    6
BOJ9069501001S    6
MNL7029501001S    9
MRG8703502001S   10
DEM9289502001S    1
BXL1651503001S    2
```

```
VAF8733611001S 65
UYI0368701001S  2
VIZ6879801001S 16
GXX9093801001S 19
HHO5605802001S 41
BOL2324802001S 49
PAG9289802003S 15
MDF5557802003S 17
IQK3388802004S 12
OTB1341802004S 28
SVF5674803001S 24
ZDP9484803001S 15
OSY8177803002S 15
GJQ0185803002S  8
VHW0189804001S 20
WEU9225804001S  6
YJO3755804001S  8
```

STUDENT-UPDATE

Columns	Contents
1–6	Student number (same as those used in STUDENT-FILE)
7–13	Name of course #1 (e.g., CPSC141)
14–15	Letter grade received for course #1 (e.g., A −, B +, C◊)
16	Credits received for course #1
17–23	Name of course #2
24–25	Letter grade received for course #2
26	Credits received for course #2
27–33	Name of course #3
34–35	Letter grade received for course #3
36	Credits received for course #3
37–43	Name of course #4
44–45	Letter grade received for course #4
46	Credits received for course #4
47–53	Name of course #5
54–55	Letter grade received for course #5
56	Credits received for course #5

The file is sorted so that the student numbers are in increasing order. There is one update record for each student in STUDENT-FILE.

```
STUDENT-UPDATE
==============


010103ENGL176C 4EDUC268B 4EDUC330B+3P E 281C 3ENGR317D 4
010104CPSC271D+4E SC208D-3PHIL340B+2CPSC146D+4ENGL432D+4
010110ART 520D 3E SC259F 1ENGL151D+4MUSC257B 4PSYC486C 4
010113HIST498F 3P E 317C+4MUSC139B-3PHIL165D 3GEOG222C 3
010126PHIL367C-4EDUC420C-3EDUC473C 3EDUC224D-3GERM257F 4
010144HIST559C+3MATH357D 3CPSC323C-2P E 246D-4MUSC379D+4
```

```
010179MATH169C-4CHEM163C+4MUSC436A-3MATH366D-2BIOL213A-4
010191SOCI177F 4POLS106A 4EDUC495A-3ENGR418B+2ENGR355A 4
010226PSYC116B 3GERM323B-4ART 350A 4HIST269B+4EDUC214C+3
010272ENGL558A-4EDUC169D+3PSYC483B+4ENGR335B+2BIOL228B 4
010274MUSC351B 4PSYC209C-4ENGR400F 1E SC392A 4SOCI394B-3
010284ENGR292D 4PSYC172C 4EDUC140B 4MATH274F 4MUSC101C+4
010297HIST464F 1HIST205F 1ENGR444F 1MATH269F 1EDUC163F 1
010298PSYC452B 3MATH170C+4EDUC344C-2GREE138C-2SPEE303A-3
010301EDUC197A 4P E 372B 3ENGR218D 4MATH309C 4E SC405C-4
010302CHEM283F 1P E 440A 2MATH399A-3HIST455C-4MATH387C-3
010304GERM526C-2CHEM243C 4POLS331B-4EDUC398A 3ENGR479D+4
010307MUSC323B+3MATH485C 4HIST232B+4EDUC180A 3ENGL130B+4
010310CPSC264B 2POLS227D+3ENGR467D-3MATH494D-4ART 420C+4
010319MATH276B 2E SC434A 3HIST197B-4GERM489B-2ART 137C-3
010323MATH377D-4EDUC210D 4MATH385D-4ENGR433C 2HIST338A-4
010330HIST546C+3E SC440B+3GREE472C+3BIOL186B 4GEOG434C+2
010339EDUC283B 3CPSC150B 3ENGR120D 4CPSC122F 4ART 216B 4
010348CPSC411C-3HIST480C+4PSYC459B 4BIOL299B+4ECON276B+3
010355ENGL130C-3CPSC282C+4CPSC181A-4CPSC146C-4SOCI113F 1
010377SOCI213D+3PSYC158D 4MUSC188C 3PSYC281D-4ENGR339B+4
010389EDUC414B+4PSYC115C+2PSYC152C-4ART 366A-3ENGR366B+4
010395ENGR396B 4HIST102F 3ENGL111A 4PSYC210D-2GREE128A 4
010406CPSC160C+4CPSC233C 1LATI494C+3ENGL115C-3MATH181A 3
010415ENGR287C 4EDUC166B-4EDUC106A-3P E 190F 3MATH171B-3
010422PSYC275A-4MATH497A 4EDUC340F 1GERM403C-4MATH245D+4
010431CPSC187D-4CPSC426F 4ENGR476B-4BIOL148B+3CPSC220F 3
010448ART 171D+3CPSC239C-3SOCI499B-4HIST113D+3PSYC116C 4
010458POLS171F 1CPSC187C+4CHEM150B 2PHIL438D-4PHIL254D 4
010467ECON335D-3E SC471B+4MATH457C+3MATH207C 2BIOL429D 4
010470MUSC415C+3POLS177C 3CPSC480A 4PSYC437B 3SOCI276D 4
010482ENGL158D-4EDUC475B 3HIST172B-2P E 316F 4ENGR294A-3
010490P E 239F 4ENGL348F 3LATI246F 4CPSC350F 4MATH114F 1
010501BIOL125F 4CPSC412F 3E SC279F 4ENGR153F 2ART 293F 1
010509SPEE386B+4HIST479C 4PSYC249B-2GREE204B-4P E 421A 1
010511E SC416B 3MATH316D-4MATH287C 2MATH499A-4E SC288D 3
010515EDUC563D+3PHIL373D-3ART 318B 4HIST451F 1ART 476C+3
010523BIOL183D-2HIST296D+4HIST380B+4ENGR216C 4MATH412B-2
010530ENGL559F 1EDUC457D+4CPSC306A 3ENGR171B+1CPSC380A 4
010538ENGR328A-4EDUC336C 3EDUC418D+3PHIL437B+4CPSC475D 4
010547CPSC537A-4ART 386D 4HIST292D-4ENGR467A-4P E 464B+4
010553HIST170A-4SOCI496D-3PHIL136B+4CPSC371D-4CPSC160A-1
010560SOCI153D+3MATH438D+4CPSC378C 4BIOL266F 3EDUC278D+3
010582MATH388A-3P E 311B 3ECON143D 4MATH304C+3P E 428C+4
010590CPSC134B-3E SC114B+3CPSC492C 4ENGL121C 4ENGR403A-4
010597P E 423A-3BIOL189D+3PHIL122D-4ENGL194C-4SOCI113D+3
010610E SC594C-3PHIL344F 4CPSC189B+2ENGR411D-3MATH241A 4
010623GREE412B-4ENGL415D-3ENGL234D-4MATH275F 1SOCI124B+3
010629MATH137D 2MATH481F 3E SC445F 1MATH339D 4ART 219B+4
010633GEOG573B 4ENGL149C+4EDUC113B+4ENGR458C-2HIST446D+4
010648EDUC132D+4MUSC103D-4ENGL263C 4ENGL134B+4E SC392A 3
010652LATI363F 3BIOL425F 1CPSC267C 4EDUC127C+3MATH338B 4
010657PHIL429F 1ART 412D-4MUSC473B-4SOCI447C-4MATH237D+2
010663EDUC580B-4ENGR351B+4SOCI283D 4ART 340C 4PSYC133D+3
010668ENGR274B+4SOCI438C 1P E 327C 4BIOL158A 4EDUC457A-4
010675MATH457A 4ENGR114C 4CPSC218C 3E SC433C-3PSYC243C+1
010682ART 483D+3GERM432C 3ENGL103B+4MUSC169C-3SOCI381C-2
010688CPSC182F 1HIST371C+4PSYC408F 1MUSC214B+4MATH151C 3
```

USER-UPDATE

Columns	Contents
1–6	Account number
7	Blank
8–11	Resources used (no decimal point, but three digits before and two after the decimal point are assumed)

The file is sorted so that the account numbers are in increasing order.

```
USER-UPDATE
===========


100101   732
100101  2133
101003  3502
100105   555
100105   329
100105    89
100105  1053
100109  8934
100116  1234
100116   583
100116  1563
100117  5023
100117  9823
100118  4523
100118   234
100118  8993
100120  2331
100122   345
100122   679
100122    78
100122  3402
100122   222
100122   328
100123  3409
100130    45
100130    89
100130   328
100132  4412
100132  1210
200101  1122
200101   534
200101  1001
200101   634
200111  1164
200111   154
200111  3226
200111  9923
200121  5545
200121  6423
200121  3328
```

C

Program Composition

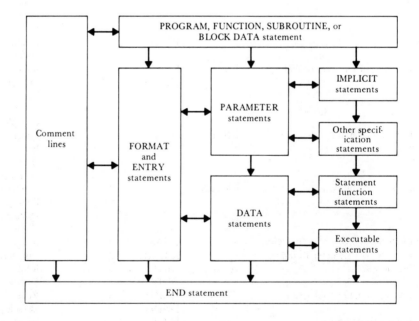

This diagram indicates the correct placement of the various types of FORTRAN statements in a program unit. The arrows indicate the order in which the statements may be used. For example, the arrow from the PARAMETER statements block to the DATA statements block indicates that all PARAMETER statements must precede all DATA statements in a program unit. The horizontal two-headed arrows indicate that these types of statements may be interspersed. For example, comment lines may appear anywhere in a program unit before the END statement.

D

Generic and Specific Names of Functions

Function Description	Generic Name	Specific Name	Number of Arguments	Type of Arguments	Type of Function
Conversion of numeric to integer	INT	—	1	Integer	Integer
		INT		Real	Integer
		IFIX		Real	Integer
		IDINT		Double	Integer
		—		Complex	Integer
Conversion of numeric to real	REAL	REAL	1	Integer	Real
		FLOAT		Integer	Real
		—		Real	Real
		SNGL		Double	Real
		—		Complex	Real
Conversion of numeric to double precision	DBLE	—	1	Integer	Double
		—		Real	Double
		—		Double	Double
		—		Complex	Double
Conversion of numeric to complex	CMPLX	—	1	Integer	Complex
		—		Real	Complex
		—		Double	Complex
		—		Complex	Complex
Conversion of integer to character	—	CHAR	1	Integer	Character
Conversion of character to integer	—	ICHAR	1	Character	Integer
Truncation	AINT	AINT	1	Real	Real
		DINT		Double	Double
Rounding to nearest integer	ANINT	ANINT	1	Real	Real
		DNINT		Double	Double
Rounding to nearest integer	NINT	NINT	1	Real	Integer
		IDNINT	1	Double	Integer
Absolute value	ABS	IABS	1	Integer	Integer
		ABS		Real	Real
		DABS		Double	Double
		CABS		Complex	Real
Remaindering	MOD	MOD	2	Integer	Integer
		AMOD		Real	Real
		DMOD		Double	Double
Transfer of sign	SIGN	ISIGN	2	Integer	Integer
		SIGN		Real	Real
		DSIGN		Double	Double

Function Description	Generic Name	Specific Name	Number of Arguments	Type of Arguments	Type of Function
Positive difference	DIM	IDIM	2	Integer	Integer
		DIM		Real	Real
		DDIM		Double	Double
Double precision product		DPROD	2	Real	Double
Maximum value	MAX	MAX0	≥2	Integer	Integer
		AMAX1		Real	Real
		DMAX1		Double	Double
	—	AMAX0		Integer	Real
	—	MAX1		Real	Integer
Minimum value	MIN	MIN0	≥2	Integer	Integer
		AMIN1		Real	Real
		DMIN1		Double	Double
	—	AMIN0		Integer	Real
	—	MIN1		Real	Integer
Length of character item	—	LEN	1	Character	Integer
Index of a substring	—	INDEX	2	Character	Integer
Imaginary part of a complex value	—	AIMAG	1	Complex	Real
Conjugate of a complex value	—	CONJG	1	Complex	Complex
Square root	SQRT	SQRT	1	Real	Real
		DSQRT		Double	Double
		CSQRT		Complex	Complex
Exponential	EXP	EXP	1	Real	Real
		DEXP		Double	Double
		CEXP		Complex	Complex
Natural logarithm	LOG	ALOG	1	Real	Real
		DLOG		Double	Double
		CLOG		Complex	Complex
Common logarithm	LOG10	ALOG10	1	Real	Real
		DLOG10		Double	Double
Sine	SIN	SIN	1	Real	Real
		DSIN		Double	Double
		CSIN		Complex	Complex
Cosine	COS	COS	1	Real	Real
		DCOS		Double	Double
		CCOS		Complex	Complex
Tangent	TAN	TAN	1	Real	Real
		DTAN		Double	Double
Arcsine	ASIN	ASIN	1	Real	Real
		DASIN		Double	Double
Arccosine	ACOS	ACOS	1	Real	Real
		DACOS		Double	Double
Arctangent	ATAN	ATAN	1	Real	Real
		DATAN		Double	Double
	ATAN2	ATAN2	2	Real	Real
		DATAN2		Double	Double
Hyperbolic sine	SINH	SINH	1	Real	Real
		DSINH		Double	Double
Hyperbolic cosine	COSH	COSH	1	Real	Real
		DCOSH		Double	Double
Hyperbolic tangent	TANH	TANH	1	Real	Real
		DTANH		Double	Double
Lexically greater than or equal to	—	LGE	2	Character	Logical
Lexically greater than	—	LGT	2	Character	Logical
Lexically less than or equal to	—	LLE	2	Character	Logical
Lexically less than	—	LLT	2	Character	Logical

Answers to Selected Exercises

Section 1.3 (p. 22)

5.	**(a)** 9	**(c)** 64	**(e)** 1.5
6.	**(a)** 83	**(c)** 4096	**(e)** 7.25
7.	**(a)** 18	**(c)** 2748	**(e)** 8.75
8.	**(a)** 1010011	**(c)** 1000000000000	**(e)** 111.01
9.	**(a)** 10010	**(c)** 101010111100	**(e)** 1000.11
10.	**(a)** 11	**(c)** 100	**(e)** 1.4
11.	**(a)** 9	**(c)** 40	**(e)** 1.8

12. **(a)** **(i)** 11011_2 **(ii)** 33_8 **(iii)** $1B_{16}$
    (c) **(i)** 100111010_2 **(ii)** 472_8 **(iii)** $13A_{16}$

13. **(a)** **(i)** 0.1_2 **(ii)** 0.4_8 **(iii)** 0.8_{16}
    (d) **(i)** 10000.0001_2 **(ii)** 20.04_8 **(iii)** 10.1_{16}

14. **(a)** **(i)** $0.0\overline{1001}_2$ **(ii)** $0.2\overline{3146}_8$ **(iii)** $0.4\overline{C}_{16}$
    (c) **(i)** $0.00\overline{0011}_2$ **(ii)** $0.0\overline{3146}_8$ **(iii)** $0.0\overline{C}_{16}$

15. **(a)** 64   **(c)** -65 **(e)** -256

16. **(a)** 0000000011111111
    (c) 1111111100000001
    (e) 1100011010001001

18. **(a)** **(i)** 0110000000010001 **(ii)** Same as (i)
    (c) **(i)** 0101000000010001 **(ii)** Same as (i)
    (e) **(i)** 0110011001111101 **(ii)** Same as (i)

19. **(a)** **(i)**

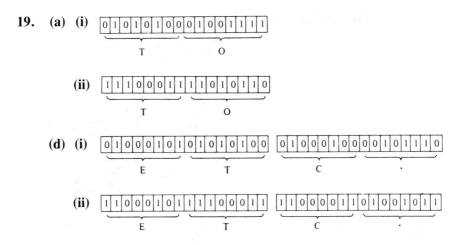

The algorithm for solving the problem is now straightforward:

Section 2.6 (p. 51)

6. Given information: Two temperature scales. Celsius and Fahrenheit, with 0° Celsius corresponding to 32° Fahrenheit, 100° Celsius corresponding to 212° Fahrenheit, and that a linear relationship of the form $F = aC + b$ holds in general. Also given some temperature C on the Celsius scale.

To find: The corresponding number F of degrees on the Fahrenheit scale.

We first must find the specific linear relationship between the two scales. In general, $C°$ Celsius corresponds to $F°$ Fahrenheit, where $F = aC + b$ for some constants a and b. Because 0° Celsius corresponds to 32° Fahrenheit, we must have

$$32 = a \cdot 0 + b$$

so that $b = 32$. This means, then, that

$$F = aC + 32$$

Because 100° Celsius corresponds to 212° Fahrenheit, we must have

$$212 = a \cdot 100 + 32$$

which gives $a = 9/5$, so that our equation becomes

$$F = \frac{9}{5}C + 32$$

The algorithm for solving the problem is now straightforward:

* This algorithm converts a temperature of C degrees on the Cel-   *
* sius scale to the sorresponding F degrees on the Fahrenheit scale.   *

1. Enter C.
2. Calculate

$$F = \frac{9}{5}C + 32$$

3. Display F.

Expressed in flowchart form, the algorithm is:

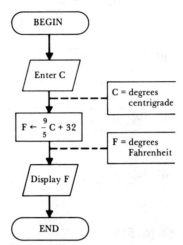

9. Input—Pollution index: INDEX
Output—Air quality description: Pleasant, Unpleasant, or Hazardous.

ALGORITHM

```
*   Algorithm for air quality based on pollution index. Indices are    *
*   classified until a negative value for INDEX is entered.            *
```

1. Enter INDEX.
2. While INDEX ≥ 0 do the following:
     a. If INDEX < 35 then display 'Pleasant'
        else if INDEX ≥ 60 display 'Unpleasant'
        else display 'Hazardous'.
     b. Enter INDEX.

22.
```
        PROGRAM TEMPS
  *************************************************
  * Program to convert a temperature of C degrees *
  * on the Celsius scale to the corresponding     *
  * temperature F on the Fahrenheit scale.        *
  *************************************************

        REAL C, F

        PRINT *, 'ENTER TEMPERATURE IN DEGREES CELSIUS:'
        READ *, C
        F = (9.0/5.0) * C + 32.0
        PRINT *, 'FAHRENHEIT TEMPERATURE IS', F
        END
```

Section 3.2 (p. 63)

2. (a) 12 is integer.
    (b) 12. is real.
    (c) '12' is neither.
    (d) 8 + 4 is neither.

3. (a) 'X' is legal.
    (b) RATE' is not legal.

(c)   '$1.98' is legal.

4.   (a) REAL TEMP, PRESS, VOLUME
     (b) INTEGER ZETA

5.   (a) GAUSS is of real type.
     (b) FORTRAN is not a legal variable
          (name too long).
     (c) H is of real type.
     (d) I is of integer type.

Section 3.3 (p. 68)

1.   (a) 1   (c) .5   (e) 25
     (g) 729   (i) 6561   (k) −9
     (m) 5   (o) 1   (q) 3.0

2.   (a) 11.0   (c) 10.5625   (e) 4.0
     (g) 3.0

3.   (a) $10 + 5 * B - 4 * A * C$
     (c) SQRT(A + 3 * B ** 2)

Section 3.4 (p. 73)

1.   (a) Valid
     (c) Valid
     (e) Valid

2.   (a) 125.0   (c) 6.1   (e) 0.0
     (g) 10   (i) 1

3.   (a) DIST = RATE * TIME
     (d) VALUE = P * (1 + R) ** N
     (g) RANGE = 2 * V ** 2 * SIN(A) * COS(A) / G

4.   (a) I = 3, J = 4, K = 6

Section 3.7 (p. 86)

3.
```
      PROGRAM TRIANG
*****************************************************
* Program to read three sides of a triangle and then *
* calculate its perimeter and area.  Variables used: *
*    A, B, C : 3 sides of a triangle                 *
*    S       : One-half the perimeter                *
*    AREA    : Area of triangle                      *
*****************************************************

      REAL A, B, C, S, AREA

      PRINT *, 'ENTER THREE SIDES OF TRIANGLE:
      READ *, A, B, C
      S = (A + B + C) / 2
      AREA = SQRT(S * (S - A) * (S - B) * (S - C))
      PRINT *, 'PERIMETER =', 2 * S
      PRINT *, 'AREA = ', AREA
      END
```

Section 4.1 (p. 101)

1. **(a)** .TRUE.
    (d) .TRUE.
    (g) .FALSE.
    (j) .TRUE.

2. **(a)**

A	B	A .OR. .NOT. B
T	T	T
T	F	T
F	T	F
F	F	T

    (c)

A	B	.NOT. A .OR. .NOT. B
T	T	F
T	F	T
F	T	T
F	F	T

    (e)

A	B	C	A .AND. (B .OR. C)
T	T	T	T
T	T	F	T
T	F	T	T
T	F	F	F
F	T	T	F
F	T	F	F
F	F	T	F
F	F	F	F

3. **(a)** X GT. 3
    (d) (ALPHA .GT. 0) .AND. (BETA .GT. 0)
    (g) (A .LT. 6) .OR. (A .GT. 10)

4. **(a)** A .AND. B .AND. .NOT. C

Section 4.4 (p. 117)

1. **(a)** IF (CODE .EQ. 1) THEN
             READ *, X, Y
             PRINT *, 'SUM = ', X + Y
          END IF

2. IF (0 .LE. T .AND. T .LE. 1.0/60.0) THEN
         V = 100 * ABS(SIN(120 * 3.1416 * T))
      END IF

Section 4.11 (p. 160)

4. **(a)**   DO 10 I = 1, 100
         100   PRINT *, I
          10 CONTINUE
    (b)   IF (X .LT. 0 .OR. X .GT. 10) GO TO 50

6. **(a)** 1. Initialize COUNT to 0.
          2. Read NUMBER.

3. Repeat the following until NUMBER = 0:
   a. Increment COUNT by 1.
   b. Set NUMBER = NUMBER / 10 (integer division).

Section 5.2 (p. 188)

1. **(a)** <u>COMPUTER SCIENCE -- EXERCISE 5.3</u>

   (d) blank line

   (g) <u>COMPUTER SCIENCE 5.3</u>

   (j) <u>_____</u>
   <u>_____</u>
   <u>__12345__12346__87.65430____88.654_____87.</u>

   (m) <u>_____12345____87.654</u>
   <u>_____12346____88.654</u>

   (p) <u>**********THE END**********</u>

Section 5.7 (p. 210)

1. **(a)** 78, 550, 123.78, 6.0
   (c) b̸78b̸123.78b̸b̸b̸b̸550b̸b̸b̸b̸6.0   (b̸ denotes a blank)
   (e) b̸b̸b̸78123.78
   b̸b̸550b̸b̸b̸6.0
   (g) 12378b̸6b̸550

Section 6.2 (p. 222)

2. **(a)** **(i)** SUM1 = (A .OR. B) .AND. .NOT. (A .AND. B)
   CARRY1 = A .AND. B
   (ii) SUM = (SUM1 .OR. CIN) .AND.
   .NOT. (SUM1 .AND. CIN)
   CARRY = CARRY1 .OR. (SUM1 .AND. CIN)

Section 6.4 (p. 239)

1. **(a)** CHARACTER*10 STRA, STRB, STRC

2. **(a)** Not valid — 1 is not of character type
   (d) '12'
   (g) Not valid — 23 is not of character type
   (j) 'FOOTLBS'
   (m) 'FORT'
   (p) 'ANAN'

3. **(a)** 1, 1.1, 'MODEL-XL11', 'CAMERA'
   (c) 1MODEL-XL1111CAMERA
   (e) b̸b̸b̸b̸1b̸b̸1.1MODEL-XL11b̸b̸b̸b̸b̸CAMERAb̸b̸b̸b̸

Section 7.5 (p. 283)

1. (a) NUMBER(1) = 0
       NUMBER(2) = 1
       NUMBER(3) = 1
       NUMBER(4) = 2
       NUMBER(5) = 2
       NUMBER(6) = 3
       NUMBER(7) = 3
       NUMBER(8) = 4
       NUMBER(9) = 4
       NUMBER(10) = 5

   (d) NUMBER(1), . . . , NUMBER(9) are all equal to 1, but
       NUMBER(10) is not assigned a value.

   (g) NUMBER(1) = 1
       NUMBER(2) = 2
       NUMBER(3) = 3
       NUMBER(4) = 4
       NUMBER(5) = 5
       NUMBER(6) = 6
       NUMBER(7) = 7
       NUMBER(8) = 8
       NUMBER(9) = 9
       NUMBER(10) = 0

2. (a)
```
      INTEGER X(0:5), I,
      DO 10 I = 0, 5
         X(I) = I
10    CONTINUE
```

   (c)
```
      LOGICAL L(20)
      INTEGER I
      DO 10 I  = 1, 20
         L(I) = (MOD(I,2) .EQ. 0)
10    CONTINUE
```

3. (a)

$$A(I) \rightarrow B + (I - 1)$$

(d)

 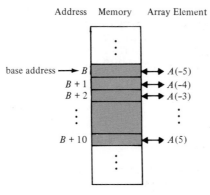

$$A(I) \rightarrow B + (I + 5)$$

Section 8.4 (p. 328)

1. **(a)**
$$\begin{bmatrix} 2 & 3 & 4 \\ 3 & 4 & 5 \\ 4 & 5 & 6 \end{bmatrix}$$

(d)
$$\begin{bmatrix} 0 & 2 & 2 \\ 0 & 0 & 2 \\ 0 & 0 & 0 \end{bmatrix}$$

(g)
$$\begin{bmatrix} 1 & 2 & 3 \\ 4 & 5 & 6 \\ 7 & 8 & 9 \end{bmatrix}$$

(j) First row of MAT is 1 2 3, but all other entries are undefined.

4. **(a)**
```
INTEGER I, J, A(3,3), B(3,3), C(3,3)
+           D(3,3), E(3,3)
```

(b) $A = \begin{bmatrix} 2 & 3 & 4 \\ 3 & 4 & 5 \\ 4 & 5 & 6 \end{bmatrix}$, $C = \begin{bmatrix} 5 & 5 & 5 \\ 5 & 5 & 5 \\ 5 & 5 & 5 \end{bmatrix}$

Section 9.2 (p. 355)

1. `RANGE(NUM1, NUM2) = ABS(NUM1 - NUM2)`

9. **(a)**
```
      FUNCTION NGRADE(LETTER)
**************************************
* Function returns the numeric grade *
* corresponding to a LETTER grade.   *
**************************************

      REAL NGRADE
      CHARACTER*1 LETTER

      IF (LETTER .EQ. 'A') THEN
         NGRADE = 4.0
      ELSE IF (LETTER .EQ. 'B') THEN
```

```
            NGRADE = 3.0
      ELSE IF (LETTER .EQ. 'C') THEN
            NGRADE = 2.0
      ELSE IF (LETTER .EQ. 'D') THEN
            NGRADE = 1.0
      ELSE
            NGRADE = 0
      END IF
      END
```

Section 9.4 (p. 380)

2.
```
            SUBROUTINE SWITCH(A,B)
      *********************************
      * Subroutine to interchange the *
      * values of integers A and B    *
      *********************************

            INTEGER A, B, TEMP

            TEMP = A
            A = B
            B = TEMP
            END
```

Section 9.8 (p. 420)

1. (a)
```
            FUNCTION NORM(V, N)
      ******************************************
      * Function returns the norm of the      *
      * N-dimensional vector V.  SUM is the    *
      * sum of the squares of the components   *
      * and I is an index.                     *
      ******************************************

            INTEGER I, N
            REAL NORM, SUM, V(N)

            SUM = 0
            DO 10 I = 1, N
                SUM = SUM + V(I) ** 2
      10    CONTINUE
            NORM = SQRT(SUM)
            END
```

Section 10.2 (p. 442)

1. (a) $A = 12.3, B = .045, C = .045$

2. (a) $4 - 2i$ **(c)** $11 + 2i$
  (e) $-3 + 4i$ **(g)** $3 + 4i$
  (i) 2 **(h)** $\dfrac{1}{5} - \dfrac{2}{5} i$

4. (a) $.1$
  (c) 6.0
  (e) Not valid. Complex value may not be assigned to a double precision variable.

(g) 6.0
(i) (-8.0, 6.0)
(k) 10.0
(m) (-28.0, 96.0)
(o) (2.0, 0.5)
(q) (14.0, 0.0)

Section 11.4 (p. 484)

19. **(a)** $-7.\overline{3}$ **(d)** 12.0   **(g)** 12.0   **(j)** 8.0

20. **(a)** $A\ B * C + D -$ **(d)** $A\ B\ C\ D + / +$
   (g) $A\ B - C - D - E -$

21. **(a)** $(A - (B + C)) * D$ **(d)** $((A + B) - C) / (D * E)$
   (g) $A / ((B / C) / D)$

22. **(a)** $- + * A\ B\ C\ D$ **(d)** $+ A / B + C\ D$
   (g) $- - - - A\ B\ C\ D\ E$

23. **(a)** -24.5 **(d)** -2.0 **(g)** 55.0

24. **(a)** $(A + B) * (C - D)$ **(d)** $A - (B - C) - D$
   (g) $(A * B + C) / (D - E)$

25. **(a)** **(i)** $- 15$ **(iv)** 15
   (b) **(i)** $A\ B\ C \sim + *$ **(iii)** $A \sim B \sim *$
   (c) **(i)** $* A + B \sim C$ **(iii)** $* \sim A \sim B$

26. **(a)** A B .AND. C .OR.   **(e)** A B .EQ. C D .EQ. .OR.

27. **(a)** .OR. .AND. A B C   **(e)** .OR. .EQ. A B .EQ. C D

Section 12.3 (p. 520)

2. **(a)** F: $|\ 1\quad 5\ |\ 3\quad 8\ |\ 7\ |\ 2\quad 6\ |\ 4\ |$
   F1: $|\ 1\quad 5\quad 7\ |\ 4\ |$
   F2: $|\ 3\quad 8\ |\ 2\quad 6\ |$
   F: $|\ 1\quad 3\quad 5\quad 7\quad 8\ |\ 2\quad 4\quad 6\ |$
   F1: $|\ 1\quad 3\quad 5\quad 7\quad 8\ |$
   F2: $|\ 2\quad 4\quad 6\ |$
   F: $|\ 1\quad 2\quad 3\quad 4\quad 5\quad 6\quad 7\quad 8\ |$

F

Other Versions of FORTRAN

As we have noted, there are several versions of FORTRAN 77 that vary somewhat from the ANSI standard version described in this text. In this appendix, we summarize the major variations and extensions in two popular versions of FORTRAN for personal computers.

IBM Personal Computer Professional FORTRAN

The IBM Professional FORTRAN compiler is written specifically for personal computers that contain a math coprocessor. The following is a summary of the major variations from and extensions to standard FORTRAN 77 in version 1.30 of Professional FORTRAN. They are organized by chapters for easy reference.

Chapter 3

- *Continuation lines.* There is no limit on the number of continuation lines.
- *Conditionally compiled statements.* The letter D or d in column 1 of a line specifies a statement that will be compiled only if the /D compiler option is used; otherwise, such lines are treated as comment lines. This makes it possible to include output statements (with a D in column 1) to help with debugging a program and then to exclude them in the final object program.
- *Lowercase letters are allowed.* No distinction is made between uppercase and lowercase letters except in character constants.
- *$ is considered to be an alphabetic character.* This means that it may be used as the first letter of a FORTRAN identifier.
- *Length of character constants.* The length of a character constant is limited to 255.

- *Hexadecimal constants.* Hexadecimal constants have the form Z'*hh*. . .', where each *h* is one of the hexadecimal digits 0, 1, 2, 3, 4, 5, 6, 7, 8, 9, A, B, C, D, E, F. They may be used wherever integer constants are used (and in DATA statements to specify character constants).

- *Lengths of identifiers.* The program name (and other global names such as subprogram names and names of common blocks) may consist of from 1 through 8 characters. Names of variables (and other local names like constants, arrays, and statement functions) may have up to 31 characters. The first letter may be a dollar sign ($) since it is considered to be an alphabetic character.

- *Alternative forms of type statements.* Alternative forms of the INTEGER type identifier are allowed:

INTEGER*2 and INTEGER*4

These are used to specify 2-byte and 4-byte integers for which the range of values is -2^{15} through $2^{15} - 1$ (-32768 through 32767) and -2^{31} through $2^{31} - 1$ (-2147483648 through 214748647), respectively. Type INTEGER is equivalent to INTEGER*4 unless the /I compiler option is used.

The REAL type identifier can also be written

REAL*4

to declare real (single-precision) variables that use 4 bytes of storage.

Chapter 4

The control statements provided in IBM Professional FORTRAN are the same as those provided in standard FORTRAN 77. No WHILE statement is provided.

Chapter 5

- *Z format descriptor.* In addition to the format descriptors provided in standard FORTRAN, IBM Professional FORTRAN also provides a Z descriptor of the form

Z*w*

for input/output of hexadecimal values (where *w* is as usual the field width). In the case of output, this descriptor causes the internal data value to be processed four bits at a time using base sixteen and a string of hexadecimal digits is output. For input, the input value is assumed to be a string of hexadecimal digits.

Chapter 6

- *Alternative forms of type statements.* Alternative forms of the LOGICAL type identifier are allowed:

LOGICAL*1 and LOGICAL*4

The second form is equivalent to LOGICAL type and specifies that logical values are to be stored in four bytes. The first form specifies a 1-byte logical value and is used to provide compatibility with FORTRAN 66 in which 1-byte logical variables could be used to store characters.

- *Length of character constants*. The length of character constants is limited to 255.

Chapters 7 and 8

- *Hexadecimal Constants in DATA Statements*. Hexadecimal constants can be used in DATA statements to initialize any type of variable or array. For character variables, each pair of consecutive hexadecimal digits represents one character; the length of the hexadecimal string must therefore be even. The character value is truncated or blank-padded on the right if necessary.
- *Lengths of parameter names*. Names of parameters (and other local names like variables, arrays, and statement functions) may have up to 31 characters. The first letter may be a dollar sign ($) because it is considered to be an alphabetic character.

Chapter 9

- *Lengths of global names*. Subprogram names and names of common blocks (as well as program names) may consist of from 1 through 8 characters. The first letter may be a dollar sign ($) since it is considered to be an alphabetic character.
- *SAVE statement*. The SAVE statement is not necessary since all storage is static; that is, values of local variables in subprograms are saved from one subprogram reference to the next.

Chapter 10

- *Alternative forms of type statements*. The type identifier

REAL*8

can be used to specify double-precision real variables, arrays, and functions that use 8 bytes of storage. The COMPLEX type may also be written as

COMPLEX*8

Chapter 11

- *Length of character constants*. The length of a character constant is limited to 255.

Chapter 12

The file-processing features provided in IBM Professional FORTRAN are the same as those described in the text for standard FORTRAN.

Chapter 13

- *INCLUDE statement.* The INCLUDE statement is a compiler directive of the form

  INCLUDE *pathname*

  It instructs the compiler to insert the file with the specified path name into the program at this point. This statement may not be continued from one line to the next. Also, the included file may itself not contain any INCLUDE statements.

Microsoft FORTRAN

The Microsoft FORTRAN compiler is a popular FORTRAN compiler for personal computers. The following is a summary of the major variations from an extensions to standard FORTRAN 77 in version 4.0 of this compiler. They are organized by chapters for easy reference.

Chapter 3

- *Continuation lines.* There is no limit on the number of continuation lines (unless the $STRICT metacommand is set).
- *Metacommands.* Metacommand lines have a dollar sign ($) in column 1. They are compiler directives and include the following: $DEBUG, $DECLARE, $FREEFORM, $INCLUDE: *'filename'*, $NOTRUN-CATE, and $STRICT. The $FREEFORM metacommand allows free-form source code in which:

  - A double quote mark (*''*) in column 1 indicates a comment line.
  - Lines may start in any column.
  - If the last character of a line is a minus sign ($-$), it is discarded and the next line is a continuation line.

- Any letter other than 'C', 'c', '*', or '$' in column 1 of a line specifies a statement that will be compiled only if the /D compiler option is used; otherwise, such lines are treated as comment lines. This makes it possible to include output statements (with a letter other than 'C', 'c', '*', or '$' in column 1) to help with debugging a program and then to exclude them in the final object program.
- *Lowercase letters are allowed.* They are converted to uppercase except in character constants.
- *$ is considered to be an alphabetic character.* This means that it may be used as the first letter of a FORTRAN identifier. It follows 'Z' in the collating sequence.
- *Nondecimal representation of integers.* Integer constants may be given in the form

  sign base #constant

  where *base* is any integer from 2 through 36; *constant* is the representation of the integer in this base using digits 0, 1, . . . , 9, A, B, . . . , Z, and *sign* is an optional algebraic sign; for example, 2#1000001 is the base-two representation of 65. If *base* but not # is omitted, base 16 is assumed.

- *Lengths of identifiers.* Only the first six characters in a name are significant and the rest are ignored, unless the $NOTRUNCATE metacommand has been set, in which case the limit is 31 characters. The first character may be a dollar sign ($), because it is considered to be an alphabetic character. All names beginning with two underscores (_ _) or ending with QQ as well as the name _main are reserved by the compiler.

- *Alternative forms of type statements.* Alternative forms of the INTEGER type identifiers are allowed:

INTEGER*1, INTEGER*2, and INTEGER*4

These are used to specify 1-byte, 2-byte, and 4-byte integers for which the range of values is $-(2^7 - 1)$ through $2^7 - 1$ (-127 through 127), $-(2^{15} - 1)$ through $2^{15} - 1$ (-32767 through 32767), and $-(2^{31} - 1)$ through $2^{31} - 1$ (-21474836487 through 2147483647), respectively. Type INTEGER is equivalent to INTEGER*4 (unless the $STORAGE metacommand has been set). A length specifier 1, 2, or 4 can also be attached to any name in the type statement to override the byte specifier; for example,

INTEGER*4 A, B, C*2, D*1

The REAL type identifier can also be written

REAL*4

to specify real (single-precision) values that occupy 4 bytes of storage.

- *Initialization in type statements.* A list of constants and repeated constants, separated by commas and enclosed within slashes can be attached to variable names in type statements (in the same manner as for DATA statements) to initialize variables; for example,

INTEGER A,B,C,D, /2*0, 1, 2/

or

INTEGER A,B /2*0/, C/1/, D/2/

- *Mixed mode assignment.* Character expressions may be assigned to non-character variables (unless the metacommand $STRICT is in effect).

Chapter 4

The control statements provided in Microsoft FORTRAN are the same as those in standard FORTRAN 77. No WHILE statement is provided.

Chapter 5

- *Z format descriptor.* In addition to the format descriptors provided in standard FORTRAN, Microsoft FORTRAN also provides a Z descriptor for hexadecimal editing. (See the notes on Chapter 5 for IBM Professional FORTRAN.)

- \ *format decriptor*. In addition to the format descriptors provided in standard FORTRAN, IBM Professional FORTRAN also provides a backslash (\) descriptor for formatted output. If the last format descriptor encountered in scanning a format specifier is a backslash, no advance to a new line occurs. This is convenient for issuing prompts to the screen and then reading a response from the same line; for example:

```
PRINT '(A\)', 'Enter the tolerance: '
READ *, TOLER
```

- *Terminating input fields*. A comma may be used to terminate input fields for I, Z, F, E, G, D, and L descriptors. (However, one cannot then rely on positional descriptors such as X and T.)
- *EOF function*. The EOF function is a logical-valued function that may be used in a reference of the form

$$EOF(\textit{unit-number})$$

It returns the value .TRUE. if the file is positioned at or past the end-of-file record; otherwise, it returns the value .FALSE.
- *Preset unit numbers*. Unit numbers * and 0 are preset to the keyboard and screen, 5 to the keyboard, and 6 to the screen. Unit numbers 0, 5, and 6 can be attached to any file, however, by using the OPEN statement; closing these units automatically reconnects them to the keyboard and screen, keyboard, or screen, respectively.

Chapter 6

- *Alternative forms of LOGICAL type statement*. Alternative forms of the LOGICAL type identifier are allowed:

$$\text{LOGICAL}*1, \text{LOGICAL}*2, \text{ and LOGICAL}*4$$

Values of these types occupy 1, 2, or 4 bytes, respectively. The third form is equivalent to LOGICAL type and specifies that logical values are to be stored in 4 bytes. A length specifier 1, 2, or 4 can also be attached to any name in the type statement to override the byte specifier; for example,

$$\text{LOGICAL}*4 \text{ A, B, C}*2, \text{ D}*1$$

- *Length of character constants*. The length of a character constant is limited to 32767.
- *Substring specifiers*. Position specifiers in substrings may be any arithmetic expressions (unless the $STRICT metacommand is in effect). Noninteger specifiers will be truncated to integers.
- *Mixed mode comparisons*. Relational operators can be used to compare arithmetic expressions and character expressions (unless the $STRICT metacommand is in effect). Arithmetic expressions are treated as character expressions in such mixed mode comparisons.
- *Mixed mode assignment*. Character expressions may be assigned to noncharacter variables and a noncharacter variable or array element (but not an expression) can be assigned to a character variable (unless $STRICT is in effect).

- *Initialization in type statements.* A list of constants and repeated constants, separated by commas and enclosed within slashes can be attached to variable names in type statements (in the same manner as for DATA statements) to initialize variables; for example,

```
LOGICAL P,Q,R /2*.TRUE., .FALSE./
CHARACTER*10 NAME/'SAM Q. DOE'/
```

Chapters 7 and 8

- *Number of dimensions.* Arrays may have any number of dimensions (unless the $STRICT metacommand is in effect, in which case the limit is 7).
- *Subscripts.* Array subscripts and dimension declarators may be any arithmetic expressions (unless the $STRICT metacommand is in effect). Noninteger subscripts will be truncated to integers.
- *Initialization of arrays in type statements.* Arrays may be initialized in type statements in the same manner as described for variables in the notes for Chapter 3; for example,

$$\text{INTEGER MAT(3,3) /9*0/}$$

- *Lengths of parameter names.* Only the first six characters in a name are significant and the rest are ignored, unless the $NOTRUNCATE metacommand has been set, in which case the limit is 31 characters. The first character may be a dollar sign ($), because it is considered to be an alphabetic character. All names beginning with two underscores (_ _) or ending with QQ as well as the name _main are reserved by the compiler.
- *Data statement.* Character values may be used to initialize variables and arrays of any type (unless the $STRICT metacommand is in effect).

Chapter 9

- *Lengths of subprogram names.* Only the first six characters in a name are significant and the rest are ignored, unless the $NOTRUNCATE metacommand has been set in which case the limit is 31 characters. The first character may be a dollar sign ($) because it is considered to be an alphabetic character. All names beginning with two underscores (_ _) or ending with QQ as well as the name _main are reserved by the compiler.
- *Additional instrinsic functions.* Several additional library functions are provided. These include type conversion functions, double-precision complex functions, the end-of-file function EOF (see notes on Chapter 5), address functions, and bit-manipulation functions.
- *SAVE statement.* The SAVE statement is not necessary, since values of local variables in subprograms are saved from one subprogram reference to the next.

Chapter 10

- *Alternative forms of type statments.* The type identifier

  REAL*8

  can be used to declare double-precision real variables, arrays, and functions that use 8 bytes of storage. The COMPLEX type can also be written equivalently as

  COMPLEX*8

- *Complex values.* Complex numbers may be signed; for example,

  $$-(7, 3.2)$$

  is equivalent to $(-7, -3.2)$.

- *Double-precision complex type.* Complex values whose real and imaginary parts are double-precision real numbers can be processed using the type

  COMPLEX*16

  which specifies that variables of this type are to be stored using 16 bytes of memory.

- *Mixed mode expressions.* In mixed mode expressions, COMPLEX*16 has the highest rank. If double-precision values and complex(*8) values are combined, the result is COMPLEX*16.

- *Initialization in type statements.* A list of constants and repeated constants, separated by commas and enclosed within slashes can be attached to variable names and array names in type statements (in the same manner as for DATA statements) to initialize variables; for example,

```
DOUBLE PRECISION X,Y /2*0.1D0/
COMPLEX U,V,Z /2*(0,0), (-1.1, 2.4)/
COMPLEX*16 W / (0, 0.1D0)/
```

Chapter 11

- *Length of character constants.* The length of a character constant is limited to 32767.

- *Substring specifiers.* Position specifiers in substrings may be any arithmetic expressions (unless the $STRICT metacommand is in effect). Noninteger specifiers will be truncated to integers.

- *Mixed mode comparisons.* Relational operators can be used to compare arithmetic expressions and character expressions (unless the $STRICT metacommand is in effect). Arithmetic expressions are treated as character expressions in such mixed mode comparisons.

- *Mixed mode assignment.* Character expressions may be assigned to noncharacter variables and a noncharacter variable or array element (but not an expression) can be assigned to a character variable (unless $STRICT is in effect).

- *Initialization in type statements.* A list of constants and repeated constants, separated by commas and enclosed within slashes can be attached to variable names in type statements (in the same manner as for DATA statements) to initialize variables and arrays.

Chapter 12

- *EOF function.* The EOF function is a logical-valued function that may be used in a reference of the form

  EOF(*unit-number*)

  It returns the value .TRUE. if the file is positioned at or past the end-of-file record; otherwise, it returns the value .FALSE.
- *Preset unit numbers.* Unit numbers ∗ and 0 are preset to the keyboard and screen, 5 to the keyboard, and 6 to the screen. Unit numbers 0, 5, and 6 can be attached to any file, however, by using the OPEN statement; closing these units automatically reconnects them to the keyboard and screen, keyboard, or screen, respectively.
- *Sequential processing of direct access files.* Sequential operations on files opened for direct access are allowed. Each such operation is applied to the next record in the file.
- *OPEN statement.* If a blank filename is specified in the FILE = clause, then the name of the file to be opened is read from a list of names supplied on the command line used to execute the program, or if none is supplied, the user is prompted for the file name.

  If no OPEN statement is used and the first operation using a file is READ, an implicit OPEN statement is executed as if a blank file name were specified, access is sequential, status is old. Whether the file is formatted or unformatted is determined by the READ statement. For a WRITE operation, the status of the file is unknown.

  Other options are also allowed in the OPEN statement. These include a BLOCKSIZE = clause to specify the size of an internal buffer, a MODE = clause to specify read/write access to the file ('READ', 'WRITE', or 'READWRITE'), and a SHARE = clause to control sharing of files ('COMPAT', 'DENYRW', 'DENYWR', 'DENYRD', or 'DENYNONE').
- *Closing files.* Closing units 0, 5, and 6 automatically reconnects these unit numbers to the keyboard and screen, keyboard, or screen, respectively.
- *The FORM = clause.* The FORM = clause can also specify that a file is BINARY, that is, a sequence of bytes with no internal structure.
- *The INQUIRE statement.* Additional clauses are permitted in the INQUIRE statement:

BINARY = *binary*	Assigns 'YES' to *binary* if the file has been formatted as binary, 'NO', or 'UNKNOWN' otherwise.
BLOCKSIZE = *blocksize*	Assigns the I/O buffer size to *blocksize*.

MODE $=$ *mode*   Assigns to *mode* the value 'READ',
                        'WRITE', or 'READWRITE' as
                        specified in the MODE $=$ clause of
                        the OPEN statement.

SHARE $=$ *share*   Assigns to *share* the value 'COM-
                        PAT', 'DENYRW', 'DENYWR,
                        'DENYRD', or 'DENYNONE' as
                        specified in the SHARE $=$ clause of
                        the OPEN statement.

- *The LOCKING statement.* A LOCKING statement is provided to lock direct-access files and records to prevent access by other users in a network environment.

Chapter 13

The miscellaneous features provided in Microsoft FORTRAN are the same as those provided in standard FORTRAN 77.

Index of Programming Exercises

Chapter 9

INDEX

581

Examples and Sample Programs

Chapter 2

Radioactive decay (pp. 27, 29–31, 40–46)
Pollution index classification (pp. 27, 32–33)
Summation of integers (pp. 28, 33–36)
Approximation using infinite series (pp. 36–38)

Chapter 3

Velocity of a projectile (pp. 74–80)
Acid dilution (pp. 82–86)

Chapter 4

Effect of roundoff error (pp. 103–104)
Quadratic equations (pp. 107–117)
Damped vibration curve (pp. 124)
List of products of two numbers (pp. 125)
Summation of integers (pp. 127–129, 132–133, 136–137)
Mean temperature (pp. 131, 134–135, 138, 140–141)
Range of noise levels (in decibels) (pp. 142–47)
Numerical integration (pp. 147–150)
Least squares line (pp. 151–154)
Beam deflection (pp. 154–160)

Chapter 5

Table of squares, cubes, and square roots (pp. 186–87, 196–197)
Time, temperature, pressure, and volume readings (pp. 202–204)

Chapter 6

Searching a file of time, temperature, pressure and volume readings (pp. 217–219)
Logical circuits (pp. 221–222)
Plotting graphs (pp. 232–235) .
Runtime formatting (pp. 236–239)

Chapter 7

I/O of a list of velocities (pp. 253–259)
Processing a list of temperatures (pp. 259–261, 263–264)
Average burn rates of rocket propellants (pp. 266–269)
Bar graphs in quality control (pp. 270–272)
Sorting a list of labor costs (pp. 272–277)
Searching a file of chemical formulas and specific heats (pp. 277–283)

Chapter 8

I/O of water temperature tables (pp. 299–309)
Processing pollution tables (pp. 310–314)